Islamic Civilization

History, Contributions, and Influence: A Compendium of Literature

S.M. Ghazanfar

The Scarecrow Press, Inc.
Lanham, Maryland • Toronto • Oxford
2006

SCARECROW PRESS, INC.

Published in the United States of America
by Scarecrow Press, Inc.
A wholly owned subsidary of
The Rowman & Littlefield Publishing Group, Inc.
4501 Forbes Boulevard, Suite 200, Lanham, Maryland 20706
www.scarecrowpress.com

PO Box 317
Oxford
OX2 9RU, UK

British Library Cataloguing in Publication Information Available

Library of Congress Cataloging-in-Publication Data

Ghazanfar, Shaikh M.
  Islamic civilization : history, contributions, and influence : a compendium of
literature / Shaikh Mohammed Ghazanfar.
    p. cm.
  Includes bibliographical references and index.
  ISBN-13: 978-0-8108-5264-8 (hardcover : alk. paper)
  ISBN-10: 0-8108-5264-0
  1. Civilization, Islamic. I. Title.
  DS36.85.G49 2006
  909′.09767—dc22

                                                              2005019150

To my father,
who gave me so much
in so little time

and

To the anchors of my life:
my wife and children—
and some close friends

Contents

Preface

In order to convey a general sense of the present undertaking, a quotation from one of the most eminent 20th-century European scholars of Islamic civilization seems appropriate: "For our cultural indebtedness to Islam, we Europeans have a 'blind spot.' We sometimes belittle the extent and importance of Islamic influence in our heritage, and sometimes overlook it altogether. For the sake of good relations with Arabs and Muslims, we must acknowledge our indebtedness to the full. To try to cover it over and deny it is a mark of false pride" (Watt, 1972, p.2). One can multiply such observations from numerous other scholars.

Islamic Civilization: History, Contributions, and Influence, however, is not a narrative of what this quotation suggests. The purpose here is more modest: to provide a readily accessible compendium of literature on Islamic civilization, with a particular focus. Specifically, the book represents a window to some of the literature pertaining to Islamic history, contributions to knowledge, and the influence of that reservoir once it was assimilated in medieval Europe. Over a period of several centuries, indeed, that knowledge "laid the foundations for a quite unprecedented revival of learning in Europe" and stimulated "the Renaissance in the thirteenth century, the Protestant Reformation in the sixteenth century, and eventually the rise of modern science in the seventeenth century" (Nebelsick, p.9). The book is uniquely different in that it presents more than mere annotations; it is a compendium of "literature briefs," that is, it provides a more detailed and focused description of each of the more than 600 books and articles covered. Nonetheless, it must be hastily confessed that the coverage is by no means exhaustive, nor all-inclusive; that would be an impossible task for any such venture.

In the post-9/11 environment, there has been almost an explosion of interest about things Islamic, as evident by a plethora of recent publications—what some have called the emergence of an "Islamic industry." While some of the new literature is refreshingly positive, some seems to reflect a revival of the centuries-old, well-embedded misconceptions about the Islamic world. This book is a complement to that interest, and we hope it serves a positive purpose. The coverage relates primarily to the literature that the author accumulated over the last 15–20 years in connection with other research endeavors pertaining to the early Islamic social thought. Thus, most references tend to have a social-science/humanities orientation.

The book is intended to serve as an exploratory research tool and a reference document for a variety of potential users: students at all levels (public and private schools, colleges and universities, graduate and undergraduate); research scholars and other professionals who may find some initial, "start-up," information here and then may wish to explore further; those seeking an addition to resources available in various academic programs and departments (especially those with interdisciplinary/area studies emphasis) as well as university/college and local libraries; and the interested educated, curious readers, especially those who are globally minded, with historical, cross-cultural propensities. Readers may find the briefs as useful sources and stimulus for further reading. Indeed, given the wealth of material covered and the somewhat "encyclopedic" nature of the contents, the book can be a handy reference tool for general information about the Islamic civilization in any environment where open-minded curiosity flourishes. For all such users, however, the briefs will serve chiefly as an important beginning, not an exhaustive resource.

As indicated, these briefs are more than mere annotations. The detail and focus provided for each reference usually cover about a page for books and a few paragraphs for articles, depending upon the content and comprehensiveness of the particular reference. In all cases, despite the possibility that some readers may dispute some of the contents, the briefs attempt to highlight the main purpose of this volume, that is, a glimpse into Islamic civilization and its history, contributions, and influence. Moreover, for books particularly, titles of parts, sections, and/or chapters have typically been provided; this should assist readers who may wish to explore some specific sections or articles in the book. For larger references, however, selected chapter listings are generally provided. For each book briefed, other details are also noted; for example, whether bibliographies and indexes are available. Obviously, bibliographies and references provided in books and articles are sources of additional research possibilities.

It is also to be noted that in many cases, while the title of a referenced book or article may not signify much relevance to the objective of this compendium, closer scrutiny would reveal considerable coverage of Islamic civilization's history, contributions, and/or influence. Where a book or article title does not sufficiently reflect this objective, the briefs provide appropriate quotations that may help to convey that sense, and those quotations may prompt further curiosity and exploration. Parenthetically, it may be noted that some word spellings in the quotations have been retained from the original source.

Given the nature of this venture, organization of these briefs provided a special challenge. After considering various options, it was decided to divide the presentations separately in two parts: Books and Articles. All references and briefs for each part are then grouped into three main classifications: (A) Sciences/Humanities; (B) Islam–West Linkages; (C) General. Both for book-briefs and article-briefs, most references are in the first classification, that is, Sciences/Humanities-oriented. And both for books and articles, classifications (A) and (C) are further divided into broad subject groups. For classification (A), there are two main groups: (i) Social Sciences/Humanities, further divided into seven subgroups— (a) History, (b) Economics/Commerce, (c) Philosophy, (d) Education/Learning, (e) Geography, (f) Humanities, and (g) Social Sciences, General; *and* (ii) Sciences. Classification (B), Islam–West Linkages stands alone, but classification (C) is divided into three groups: (i) Spain/Al-Andalus, (ii) Crusades, (iii) Miscellaneous. The guiding principle for these classifications and subdivisions is to enable ease of accessibility to readers. There is some arbitrariness, however, as to where a particular reference has been placed. There are references that could easily fit in one or another classification or its subdivision. For example, the book entitled *Europe and Islam*, by Hichem Djait, is placed in classification (B), Islam–West Linkages, but, given its considerable historical content, it could as well belong in classification (A), under (a) History. Similarly, *Medieval Technology and Cultural Change*, by Lynn White, is included in classification (A), under (g) Social Sciences, but could as well be placed under the (ii) Sciences subgroup of that classification. And *Europe: A History*, by Norman Davies, is included in classification (A), under (a) History, but given its considerable emphasis on linkages it could as well belong in classification (B), Islam–West Linkages. The same goes for the articles. What this means is that any consultant of this compendium looking for a reference in a particular classification or its subdivision may also want to explore elsewhere in the book for additional leads.

While the book provides a fairly large coverage of literature on Islamic civilization, there are several similar sources; some are simply listings of references, others provide some annotations. Several of these are enumerated below:

1. F. Adamson and R. Taylor (editors), *The Cambridge Companion to Arabic Philosophy*, Cambridge University Press, Cambridge, UK, 2005.

2. Therese-Anne Druart, *Brief Bibliographical Guide in Medieval Philosophy and Theology, 1998–2002*, Catholic University of America, Washington, DC, 2003.

3. Hans Daiber, *A Bibliography of Islamic Philosophy*, 2 volumes, E.J. Brill, Leiden, Netherlands, 1999.

4. David Ede, *Guide to Islam*, G.K. Hall and Company, Boston, MA, 1983.

5. Seyyed Hossein Nasr (with the collaboration of William C. Chittick), *An Annotated Bibliography of Islamic Science*, 3 volumes (6,173 references, covering about 1,200 pages), Cultural Studies and Research Institute, Tehran, Iran, 1975–1991.

6. J.D. Pearson (with assistance of Julia F. Ashton), *Index Islamicus, 1906–*

1955: A Catalogue of Articles on Islamic Subjects in Periodicals and Other Collective Publications, W. Heffer and Sons Limited, Cambridge, UK, 1958.

7. Michelle Raccagni, *The Modern Arab Woman: A Bibliography*, Scarecrow Press, Metuchen, NJ, and London, 1978.

8. Jean Sauvaget (as recast by Claude Cahen), *Introduction to the History of the Muslim East: A Bibliographical Guide*, University of California Press, Berkeley and Los Angeles, 1965.

9. Helaine Selin, *Science Across Cultures: An Annotated Bibliography of Books on Non-Western Science, Technology, and Medicine*, Garland Publishing, Inc., New York and London, 1992 (there is a large section on Islamic Science and the Middle East).

In addition, a current Internet website <http://www.muslimphilosophy.com/ip/is-biblio.htm> includes, among other things, a rather comprehensive bibliography (126 pages, over 1,700 book titles) on Islamic Studies, classified in 12 categories: (1) General, (2) Muhammad, (3) The Qur'an, (4) Shi'i Islam, (5) Sufism, (6) Theology and Philosophy, (7) Jurisprudence, (8) The Arts, (9) History, (10) Geographic-Regions and Nation-States, (11) Culture, Economics, and Politics, (12) Miscellany. It was assembled in 2004 by Patrick S. O'Donnell, Department of Philosophy, Santa Barbara City College, Santa Barbara, California.

A final note on acknowledgments. I extend my deep appreciation to the editors of Scarecrow Press, in particular my most recent connections: Dr. Martin Dillon, whose prompt suggestions during the writing phase were very helpful, and to Sally Craley in the production department—thanks. Also, acknowledged herewith is the assistance of the University of Idaho's Interlibrary Loan staff— Jennifer McLaughlin, Hannah Etherton, and Carl Westberg; their cooperation enabled me to expeditiously access numerous books and articles. And thanks to the College of Business and Economics, University of Idaho, for extending me some research assistance over the years, enabling me to undertake explorations that brought to light quite a bit of the literature covered here.

And, most importantly, I extend my deepest love and gratitude to my family— first and foremost my wife, Rukhsana, our daughter Farah and her family, our sons Asif and Kashif, and to my brother-in-law, Dr. M. Ameen Farooq, and his family, for they are "family." Their enduring love and care have always been the fodder for my strength and sustenance.

S.M. Ghazanfar
Professor/Chair (Emeritus, 2002)
Department of Economics
University of Idaho
Moscow, Idaho 83843 (USA)
December 2005

I
BOOKS

(A) Sciences/Humanities

(I) SOCIAL SCIENCES/HUMANITIES

a. History

B-1. Abu-Nasir, Jamil M. *A History of the Maghrib in the Islamic Period.* Cambridge and New York: Cambridge University Press, 1987.

The book is about the history of the *Maghrib*, a collective name for the four North African countries—Morocco, Algeria, Tunisia, Libya; the name means "Land of Sunset" and was used by the Arabs to refer to the area to the west of Egypt, also called North Africa. The period covered is from the end of the seventh century to the present. The geographical location of the Maghrib has had great significance, mainly because of the interactions of the major powers of the Mediterranean region. The numerous conquerors (Phoenicians, Greeks, Romans, Vandals, Byzantines, Arabs, Ottomans, and various European powers) before World War II came from the Mediterranean region and they sought to impose their hegemony and institutions upon its people, known as Berbers (derives "from the Latin *barbari,* an appellation equivalent to the English 'barbarian,' which the Romans used for peoples who spoke neither Latin nor Greek," although "the Berbers describe themselves as Imazighen [sing. Amazigh], meaning the noble or free-born" [p.2]).

The author points out that "whereas Arabs and Berbers, united through Islam, provided the main ethnic and cultural elements of Maghribi society, it is important to bear in mind that over the centuries the Maghrib has been a melting-pot of many other ethnic groups and cultures," including "Jews coming from Europe in relatively large numbers from the seventeenth century [who] joined the Jewish communities which existed in the Maghrib from before the Arab conquest" (p.5). Further, "the history of the Maghrib outlined in this book provides many instances of how important was the influence of Sufi saints in its political life" (p.24).

There are seven detailed chapters. Following the introductory chapter, there

3

are these chapter titles: (1) The call of the minaret in the "West": The establishment of Islam in the Maghrib and Spain, (2) The Maghrib under Berber dynasties, (3) Ottoman rule in the Central and Eastern Maghrib, (4) Morocco consolidates her national identity, 1510–1822, (5) The age of aggressive European colonialism, 1830–1914, and (6) 1919 to independence. There is an epilogue: The Maghrib after independence.

The book contains several maps and there is a 10-page comprehensive bibliography, classified in terms of specialized catalogs and general bibliography. There is a 15-page name-subject index.

B-2. Ahmad, Aziz. *A History of Islamic Sicily*. Edinburgh: Edinburgh University Press, 1975.

As part of the Islamic Survey series intended to give "the educated reader something more than can be found in the usual popular books," this book describes the history of Sicily, part of the Arab-Islamic world for about 130 years, until 1091 when it came under Norman sovereignty. Next to Islamic Spain, Sicily was also a fertile center for the cultivation and diffusion of science, with Arabic and Latin in constant use as vernacular dialects. The book provides detailed accounts of the Arab incursions into Sicily during various periods (chapters entitled: Early Arab incursions, Arab conquest and the Aghlabid Rule, Sicily under the Early Fatimids, The Kalbites).

There is discussion of the amicable environment in which Muslims, Jews, and Christians lived and interacted under Islamic rule ("Christians were less aggrieved than under the Lombards or the Franks," p.22). There are chapters that describe the efflorescence of an interesting Christian–Islamic culture under the Normans. The Norman kings (some were labeled as "half-heathen" or "baptized sultans") often dressed like Muslims, patronized Arab learning and arts, surrounded themselves with Muslim philosophers, astrologers, and physicians and allowed the non-Christians freedom to follow their religious practices; Frederick II "resisted all ecclesiastical pressure to force conversion to Christianity" (p.105). "Under the splendid patronage of Frederick II, the Spanish and Sicilian streams of transmission of the Arab heritage to Europe combined," though the Spanish stream also continued directly (p.89).

The 150-page book provides detailed footnotes for each chapter, followed by an extensive bibliography and name-subject indexation.

B-3. Ali, Syed Ameer. *A Short History of the Saracens: Being a Concise Account of the Rise and Decline of the Saracenic Power and of the Economic, Social and Intellectual Development of the Arab Nation*. London and New York: Macmillan and Company, 1900.

The book attempts to "trace the affinity of modern civilization" to the Saracens (Arabs, Muslims) in the hope that such a work "might serve to remove many prejudices and some of the bitterness engendered by the conflict and quarrels of centuries" (p.v). Further, "Modern Europe is still working with the legacy they (the Saracens) left behind, with the intellectual wealth they stored for their successors" (p.v). Thus, "Something more is needed than a bare narration of wars and conquests, more especially in the case of a people whose name, unlike the Romans and the Greeks, has not been made familiar from childhood" (p.v). The book is about "the ethical and moral movement that led to the sudden uprise and overflow of the Saracenic race and their extraordinary growth and expansion" (p.vi).

This encyclopedic, fine print, 640-page book has 32 chapters. Chapters 1–3 cover pre-Islamic Arabia up to the time of Prophet Mohammed's migration to Medina. Chapters 4–6 discuss the period of the first four caliphates, followed by chapters 7–14 which cover the Ommeyade dynasties. Chapters 15–25 discuss the Abbasid period. Chapters 26–32 encompass the Saracens of Spain (The Ommeyades). Identified on each page are relevant notations in the margins, which are also noted in the chapters in the table of contents. Also provided are numerous pictures and maps throughout the text, and there are several dynastic charts at the end.

Some footnotes are provided in the text, but there are more detailed notations in an appendix at the end, identified by page numbers in the text. There is a bibliographical index of authorities consulted, followed by a 10-page name-subject index.

B-4. Arberry, A.J. *Aspects of Islamic Civilization: As Depicted in the Original Texts.* Westport, CT: Greenwood Press, 1964.

Intended for students of Islamic history and general readers, the book is a series of documents illustrating the evolution of Islamic civilization, texts translated from languages in which they were originally composed. The objective is to present a panorama of Muslim life and thought and achievements, as depicted from within. The selections are meant to shed light on the literary, intellectual, and religious movements within Islam, as well as illuminating some aspects "of the politics and the sociology, ranging from the origins in the sixth century down to the present day" (p.9). Further, the selections are taken from authoritative sources, and the attempt is to present a balanced picture.

The book contains 14 chapters: (1) Arabia Deserta, (2) The Speech of Allah, (3) The Sunna and the Successors, (4) Wisdom from the East, (5) Science from the West, (6) La Dolce vita, (7) Religious counsels, (8) Mystical movements, (9) Lyrical interlude, (10) Faith and doubt, (11) Parable and anecdote, (12) The Art of Hafiz, (13) Two modern Egyptian poets, (14) The revolt of Islam. The coverage seeks to provide readers some perspective on questions such as, what is meant by the term *Islamic civilization*; what lies at the roots of the movement toward Arab unity and in what relation does that movement stand vis-à-vis the wider aspirations, the long-standing dream of reunion between all the Muslim peoples; how does Islam stand in the contemporary battle of faith and reason, and so forth. The author especially appeals to the Western observers of world politics to examine, with a keener historical perspective than hitherto, the long processes and massive forces which have culminated in the present global situation.

The book provides a short bibliography, followed by a brief name-subject index.

B-5. Armstrong, Karen. *Islam: A Short History*. New York: Modern Library Edition, Random House, 2000.

Intended for the general reader, the book is an excellent introduction to the Islamic world. It is a chronological history that takes the reader through almost 1,500 years of the evolution and impact of Islam as a faith and a civilization. The author states, "No religion in the modern world is as feared or misunderstood as Islam. It haunts the popular Western imagination as an extreme faith that promotes authoritarian government, female oppression, civil war, and terrorism" (p.1). And the book is said to be "a forceful challenge to those who hold the view that the West and Islam are set on a collision course" (p.1).

There are five chapters: (1) Beginnings, (2) Development, (3) Culmination, (4) Islam Triumphant, (5) Islam Agonistes. The table of contents also provides some details about each chapter. The author concludes, "Western people must become aware that it is in their interests too that Islam remains healthy and strong. The West has not been wholly responsible for the extreme forms of Islam, which have cultivated a violence that violates the most sacred canons of religion. But the West has certainly contributed to this development and, to assuage the fear and despair that lies at the root of all fundamentalist vision, should cultivate a more accurate appreciation of Islam in the third Christian millennium" (p.187).

The 222-page book provides a 275-entry historical chronology. There are ten maps depicting various stages of Islamic history. At the end there is a list of key figures in the history of Islam, followed by a glossary of Arabic terms. Chapter-by-chapter notes and references are provided at the end. There is an extensive list of additional reading sources, organized topically, followed by a name-subject index.

B-6. Armstrong, Karen. *Muhammad: A Biography of the Prophet*. New York: HarperCollins, 1992.

Written by a well-known scholar of religion who is "no longer a believing or practicing Christian," nor one who belongs "to any other official religion," the author is motivated to write this book because she has been "revising" her "ideas about Islam," and because she is persuaded by her belief that Muhammad "made a distinctive and valuable contribution to the spiritual humanity of mankind. If we are to do justice to our Muslim neighbors, we must appreciate this essential fact" (p.14). Further, despite being "more in tune with our own Judeo-Christian heritage," success of Islam during the early medieval period "was threatening: had God deserted the Christians and bestowed his favour on the infidel?" (p.11). Such fears have "made it impossible for Western Christians to be rational or objective about the Muslim faith" (p.11). Thus, "The inaccurate image of Islam became one of the received ideas of Europe and it continues to affect our perceptions of the Muslim world. It is a mistake to imagine that Islam is an inherently violent or fanatical faith, as is sometimes suggested. Islam is a universal religion and there is nothing aggressively oriental or anti-Western about it" (p.11).

While other books, the author says, have focused on political and military aspects of the Prophet's life, this book concentrates chiefly on his spiritual vision, representing a study of his life that enables "an important insight into the nature of the religious experience" (p.14). Among other things, the author argues, "Muhammad's spiritual experience bears an arresting similarity to that of the prophets of Israel, St. Teresa of Avila and Dame Julian of Norwich" (p.14–15).

The book contains ten chapters. The first chapter, Muhammad the Enemy, traces "the history of Western hatred for the Prophet of Islam" (p.15). Other chapter titles are: (2) Muhammad the Man of al-Llah, (3) *Jahiliyah*, (4) Revelation, (5) The Warner, (6) The Satanic Verses, (7) *Hijra:* A New Direction, (8) Holy War, (9) Holy Peace, (10) Death of the Prophet. The author concludes: "If Muslims need to understand our Western traditions and institutions more thoroughly today, we in the West need to divest ourselves of some of our old prejudice. Perhaps one place to start is with the figure of Muhammad: a complex, passionate man who sometimes did things that it is difficult for us to accept, but who had genius of a profound order and founded a religion and a cultural tradition that was not based on the sword—despite the Western myth—and whose name 'Islam' signifies peace and reconciliation" (p.266).

The 290-page book includes some maps and genealogical charts. Chapter-by-chapter notes and references are provided at the end. There is a select bibliography, followed by a comprehensive name-subject index.

B-7. Arnold, Thomas. *The Spread of Islam in the World: A History of Peaceful Preaching.* Delhi, India: Goodword Books, 2001; original 1896.

The book is "a record of missionary efforts and not a history of persecutions" and the author has "endeavored to be strictly impartial" (p.viii). Further, he suggests, "It is not in the cruelties of the persecutor or the fury of the fanatic that we should look for the evidences of the missionary spirit of Islam, any more than in the exploits of that mythical personage, the Muslim warrior with sword in one hand and Qur'an in the other," but, it is argued, "the expansion took place through peaceful preaching and missionary activity" (p.5). This work "does not aim at chronicling the instances of forced conversions which may be found scattered up and down the pages of Mohammadan histories. European writers have taken such care to accentuate these, and there is no fear of their being forgotten" (p.7).

There are 13 chapters in this 470-page book: (1) Introduction, (2) Study of the Life of Muhammad Considered as a Preacher of Islam, (3) The Spread of Islam among the Christian Nations of Western Asia, (4) The Spread of Islam among the Christian Nations of Africa, (5) The Spread of Islam among the Christians of

Spain, (6) The Spread of Islam among the Christian Nations in Europe under the Turks, (7) The Spread of Islam in Persia and Central Asia, (8) The Spread of Islam among the Mongols and Tatars, (9) The Spread of Islam in India, (10) The Spread of Islam in China, (11) The Spread of Islam in Africa, (12) The Spread of Islam in Malay Archipelago, (13) Conclusion. The author notes in the concluding chapter that as for the causes that have contributed to the spread of Islam, "foremost among these is the simplicity of the Muslim creed, 'There is no god but God; Muhammad is the Apostle of God'" (p.413).

There are three appendixes at the end. Numerous notes and references are mentioned within each chapter. There is a 17-page bibliography of titles cited in the text, followed by a name-subject index.

B-8. Artz, Frederick B. *The Mind of the Middle Ages, A.D. 200–1500: An Historical Survey.* Chicago and London: University of Chicago Press, 1980; original 1953.

The book is about "the history of the interests of the intellectual classes" during the Middle Ages, for it is "impossible to write a history of the ideas of the masses" (p.vii). Besides, it was only "after about 1100, each century found more of both clergy and the laity reading, and, thus, doing more thinking for themselves," with increasing criticism of the clergy in the successive Latin centuries when "always present in the minds of medieval Jews, Christians, and Mohammedans, [was] God and his influence in this world and the next" (p.ix).

The book is divided into two parts: (1) The Dominance of the East, unto 1000 AD (six chapters—The Classical Backgrounds, The Jewish and Early Christian Sources, The Patristic Age, Byzantine Civilization, Islamic Civilization, the Latin West) and (2) The Revival of the West, 1000–1500 AD (six chapters—two on Learning, two on Literature, one each on Art and Music, and Underlying Attitudes). There is an epilogue at the end.

The chapter on Islamic civilization is quite detailed. Among other things it discusses the evolution of knowledge in subjects such as education, law, philosophy, science, literature, art, and music, and how this knowledge influenced the Latin West. Various medieval Islamic scholastics and their contributions and influence on Latin scholars are discussed; Al-Ghazali "influenced deeply the greatest of medieval Jewish philosophers, Maimonides, and even Christian writers—above all Aquinas, Dante, and Pascal—found an inspiration in his translated works and used his ideas in the defense of their religion" (p.147). Further, "The Muslims kept alive the philosophy, science, and music of the Greeks and added to them. To all these the Latin West turned to learn and to imitate. Latin Christians began to visit the Islamic world in the tenth century, and in the eleventh there began to flow from Spain and Sicily a stream of translations of Greek and Arabic works" (p.177). The author adds, "The whole story of Islamic influence on the West is very extended. Space forbids a full discussion" (p.178). Elsewhere, the author states, "In the whole history of the civilization of the West, the great turning point from medieval to modern is not the Italian Renaissance of the fifteenth and sixteenth centuries; it is, rather, the revival of philosophy, science, education, literature, art, and music that centered in northern France in the twelfth and thirteenth centuries" (p.228).

There are detailed, chapter-by-chapter, notes provided at the end, followed by a comprehensive chapter-by-chapter—even by sections within chapters—bibliography, as well as a detailed name-subject index.

B-9. Benson, Robert L. and Giles Constable, eds. *Renaissance and Renewal in the Twelfth Century*. Cambridge, MA: Harvard University Press, 1982.

The book is the product of a 1977 conference that celebrated the semicentennial of Charles Homer Haskins's best-known work, *The Renaissance of the Twelfth Century* (Harvard University Press, 1927). Even after 50 years, the editors note, the book's "audience and influence have scarcely diminished" (p.xvii). The title of the conference—and this volume—was intended to undertake "not only a fresh survey of the terrain which Haskins charted, but also an inquiry which goes beyond the limits he set for himself" (p. xvii). Aimed not simply to honor Haskins, the conference intended to further assay the continuing vitality and importance of Haskins's historical vision. The conference goal was three-fold: "to assimilate the substantial advances of medieval research in the last fifty years, to deal with topics (such as painting, sculpture, architecture, and vernacular literature) which Haskins had to exclude from his account, and to emphasize certain elements (such as the role of religion in the process of cultural change) to which Haskins devoted little attention" (p.xviii).

Haskins assigned "the largest role in the formation of the renaissance to influences [Greek and Arabic] from outside Latin Christendom." Conference participants dispute that claim, however. "The renaissance made use of content drawn from other cultures, but the central source of its energy lay within Latin Christian culture. The key question for scholars, then, is not to show the existence of external elements but to explain the host culture's receptivity to them" (p.xxii). Further, as for the role of outside influences, the papers emphasize the Greek ancestry, despite observations and references throughout the book that point to the significance of the Arab-Islamic linkages.

The 780-page volume is divided into seven parts, with three or four chapters in each: Part I, Religion; Part II, Education; Part III, Society and the Individual; Part IV, Law, Politics, and History; Part V, Philosophy and Science; Part VI, Literature; Part VII, The Arts. Part V includes the essay "Translations and Translators" by Marie-Therese d'Alverny, which discusses evidence of the translations of Arab-Islamic scholarship into Latin, though somewhat muted. Also there are occasional such references in other essays.

Each essay provides its own notes and references, with a bibliography at the end. There is no index.

B-10. Berkey, Jonathan P. *The Formation of Islam: Religion and Society in the Near East, 600–1800*. Cambridge and New York: Cambridge University Press, 2003.

Written for students and for all those with interest in the emergence and evolution of Islam, the book is a historical analysis that attempts to describe and understand the gradual emergence of a distinctively Islamic tradition over the centuries. Historical factors, it is argued, have always included faith traditions other than Islam, which from the very beginning have bound Muslim identities to those of Jews, Christians, and others, and that Islam did not appear at once, but emerged slowly, as part of a prolonged process whereby it was differentiated from other traditions.

There are four parts: Part I, The Near East before Islam, with four chapters; Part II, The Emergence of Islam, 600–750, with seven chapters; Part III, The Consolidation of Islam, 750–1000, with six chapters; Part IV, Medieval Islam, 1000–1500, with eight chapters. The opening chapter examines the religious scene in the Near East during late antiquity and the religious traditions that preceded Islam. Subsequent chapters investigate Islam's first century and the beginnings of its own traditions, the "classical" period from the accession of the Abbasids to the rise of the Buyid amirs, and thereafter the emergence of new forms of Islam in the middle period.

The period covered in the book is described as one during which "religious affiliation was the fundamental component of an individual's outlook, and of his and others' understanding of his place in the world" (p.261). However, after 1800, as "a result of European imperial penetration and the broader configuration of the global political order, traditional religious identities were subject to extraordinary and unforeseen pressures." Thus, it is argued, from "the late eighteenth century, the construction of religious identify and authority in the Near East would have to take place in a much larger global context" (p.269).

A comprehensive list of bibliographic references is provided at the end, organized by each part of the book; this is followed by a detailed author-subject index.

B-11. Bloom, Jonathan and Sheila Blair. *Islam: A Thousand Years of Faith and Power*. New York: TV Books, L.L.C., 2000.

The book explores the first millennium of Islamic culture, from the revelation to Muhammad to the great Islamic empires. Written in conjunction with a U.S. Public Broadcasting Service documentary *Islam: Empire of Faith*, first aired in May 2000, the authors point out "the constant barrage of inflammatory news reports," that colors "Western perceptions of a faith followed by over a billion people, approximately one fifth of the earth's population" (p.11). Further, they approach the subject "with more than our old stereotypes," with emphasis on "some of the positive aspects of Islamic civilization" (p.13). They hope to counter the stereotypes and enlighten readers to the many sources of contemporary Islamic world.

The 268-page book provides a readable, yet in-depth, narrative explaining the many intellectual and cultural developments of early Islam during the centuries when Europe suffered through the Dark Ages.

After the introduction, the book is divided into three parts, with several chapters in each, totaling 11 chapters. Part I, entitled Muhammad and the Origins of Islam, 600–750, contains chapters: (1) The World at the Rise of Islam, (2) Muhammad and the Revelation of Islam, (3) The Sources of Faith, (4) Muhammad's Successors, (5) The Spread of Islamic Power. Part II, The Golden Age, 750–1250, has the next three chapters: (6) The Crucible, (7) City and Country, (8) The Flowering of Intellectual Life. Part III, The Age of Empires, 1250–1700, has another three chapters: (9) Regional Powers, (10) Consolidation, (11) Expansion. There is an epilogue at the end where the authors suggest, "To stereotype such a multifaceted and vibrant tradition in a few careless images based on the extreme positions of a few is foolish indeed" (p.138).

The book includes a section entitled A Gallery of Islamic Art and Culture, with 50 pictures extending over 32 pages, that is quite representative of Islamic past and present. There is a glossary of terms, along with notes for further reading, a bibliography, and a name-subject index.

B-12. Brice, William M., ed. *An Historical Atlas of Islam*. Leiden, Belgium: E.J. Brill, 1981.

This historical document provides an excellent visual experience as to the progression of Islamic civilization, extending over various regions of the world and covering the period from early Islam to the First World War. There are 57 maps grouped into broad regional divisions, and within each division maps are arranged in chronological order.

The nine broad divisions, with several maps in each, begin with the map of the world compiled by Idrisi in 1154 AD for King Roger II of Sicily. The divisions are: Part I, The Early Muslim Earth and Sky; Part II, The Extension of the Muslim World; Part III, Early Arabia; Part IV, The Near and Middle East; Part V, Anatolia and the Balkans; Part VI, Muslim Spain; Part VII, North Africa; Part VIII, India and the Indian Seas; Part IX, The Far East.

The volume provides an index of place-names and ethnicities. There is also an index of astronomy literature and another is economic, which identifies agricultural products and natural resources, ranging from alfa to zinc.

B-13. Bulliet, Richard W. *Conversion to Islam in the Medieval Period*. Cambridge, MA: Harvard University Press, 1979.

"The book is about Islamic social history," says the author, "and it attempts to tie together the histories of parts of the medieval Islamic world that are more commonly treated as discrete entities," the approach being an "examination of certain quantifiable aspects of medieval Arabic sources" (p.1). Further, this approach "is predicated upon the notion that there is a direct and fundamental relationship between conversion to Islam and the development of what may be called an Islamic society" (p.1). Bulliet attempts to "elucidate this complex relationship" by "first establishing a hypothetical timetable of conversion for six major parts of the medieval Islamic world and then comparing those timetables with the course of historical development in each area" (p.3). Another objective is to encourage the use of quantitative methodology to the phenomenon of religious or ideological conversion, whether Islamic, Christian, or another.

The book contains 11 chapters: (1) Introduction, (2) Regional Variation in Islamic History, (3) The Curve of Conversion in Iran, (4) Conversion as a Social Process, (5) The Development of Islamic Society in Iran, (6) The Curve of Muslim Names, (7) Iraq, (8) Egypt and Tunisia, (9) Syria, (10) Spain, (11) The Consequences of Conversion. In his concluding remarks, the author notes the consequences. Among these are "a dissolution at a certain point of central government and the appearance at a later point of political factions with a religious coloration. A third related phenomenon, which the attainment of a high level of conversion made possible but which was not brought about by conversion alone, was the development of an elite religious establishment or patrician class with great influence among the population at large and minimal subservience to the government—at least until after the thirteenth century" (p.138).

The 158-page book includes considerable quantitative data as well as graphs. Chapter-by-chapter notes and references are appended at the end, followed by a name-subject index.

B-14. Bulliet, Richard W. *The Patricians of Nishapur: A Study in Medieval Islamic Social History.* Cambridge, MA: Harvard University Press, 1972.

This is a book about the city of Nishapur, located in present Iran, "one of the great metropolises of the Middle East, indeed of the world, from the tenth/fourth to the twelfth/sixth century" (p.ix). The urban history of the city is explored on the basis of biographical dictionaries of the city's patricians (the notables, the *ulamas*, the learned in the religious sciences), thus enabling a better understanding of "the social history of medieval Islamic society" (p.xii). The first part of the book is chiefly devoted to an analysis of the composition and functions of the patriciate within the city and in the broader political and social context, enabling an understanding of Nishapur's social structure. The second part provides detailed histories of nine of Nishapur's patrician families. The account of the life and character of Nishapur is reconstructed by the author on the basis of minute examination of available sources, drawn primarily from the classical literary genre of the biographical dictionaries.

The study makes a case for regarding the right to teach (as opposed to the right to learn) as the measuring rod of social prominence in this early medieval (pre-

Mongol) Islamic city. Thus, "the point of control in the system was the determination of who was to get to teach. The certifying apparatus was the very heart of Islamic education at that time" (p.54).

Part One, The Patrician City, includes six chapters: (1) Nishapur, (2) The Patriciate, (3) Hanafi and Shafi, (4) The Education of a Patrician, (5) The Patriciate and the State, (6) The End of the Patriciate. Part Two, Patrician Families, includes nine chapters: (7) Mahmi-Harashi-Balawi, (8) Masarjisi, (9) Bastami-Suluki-Juwaini, (10) Sabuni-Furati, (11) Qushairi-Furaki-Saffar-Farisi-Shahhami-Farawi, (12) Bahiri, (13) Saidi-Nasihi-Ismaili, (14) Haskani, (15) Hasani. There are two appendices: The Madrasa and Qadis of Nishapur.

Each chapter integrates notes and references within the text. The 290-page book provides a bibliography at the end, followed by two indices—names and general.

B-15. Burke, Edmund, III, ed. *Rethinking World History: Essays on Europe, Islam, and World History (by Marshall G. S. Hodgson).* Cambridge and New York: Cambridge University Press, 1993.

The book is a posthumous collection of essays representing "the best of Hodgson's writings on world history," and "an important contribution to current discussions about world history and the place of Europe in it" (p.vii). Hodgson wrote in the context of textual analysis called orientalism, and he viewed the "history of Islamic civilization in the context of world history" (p.x). For him, "Western civilization as a discourse is predicated upon a deeply rooted sense of the moral as well as cultural superiority of Western Europe to the rest of the humanity" (p.xv). And, he "clearly saw that Islamic history was a strategic point from which to undertake a critique of the discourse on Western Civilization. Islam was the vastly richer and more successful Other against which the West defined itself. The study of Islamic civilization thus almost by necessity invites a reexamination of European history in which its development can be placed in world historical context, and in the process de-exceptionalized" (p.xv).

In addition to two "introduction and conclusion" essays by the editor, there are 13 articles authored by Marshall Hodgson; these are grouped into three parts. Part I, Europe in a global context, includes some of Hodgson's most important work on this topic and it challenges adherents of both Eurocentricism and multiculturalism to rethink the place of Europe in world history. Part II, Islam in a global context, covers Hodgson's main statements on Islam where he seeks to locate the history of Islamic civilization in a world historical framework. Part III, The discipline of world history, brings together the content of Hodgson's unpublished work, "The Unity of World History." The argument here is that in the end there is but one unified global history and that all partial or privileged accounts must necessarily be reexamined in a world historical context.

Presently, it seems appropriate to cite the titles of essays in part II: (1) The role of Islam in world history, (2) Cultural patterning in Islamdom and the Occident, (3) The unity of later Islamic history, (4) Modernity and the Islamic heritage. The editor's concluding essay provides his reflections on how the various themes interacted in Hodgson's thought: "Hodgson's most important achievement, and the place where he had the most to teach us all (non-Islamic scholars included), lies in his effort to devise a new [more inclusive] framework for the writing of world history" (p.327).

Notes and references are integrated within each essay. There is no separate bibliography, nor is there an index.

B-16. Burman, Edward. *Emperor to Emperor: Italy before the Renaissance.* London: Constable and Company Ltd., 1991.

Quoting Edward Gibbon, the author begins with noting that from "840 to 1017 the three great nations of the world, the Greeks, the Saracens [Muslims], the Franks, encountered each other" and created the "crucible of modern western civilization," with Italian Renaissance as the consequence. The book emphasizes continuity from the overthrow of Emperor Augustulus to the coronation of Roman Emperor Frederick II in 1220. It is noted that the story of the Italian peninsula from the fifth to the 13th centuries is that of a search for a new social identity, and in this process the contributions of the various invaders were vital.

The cultural mosaic generated by the blend of these apparently heterogenous influences is covered in part I (Benedictine Italy and its enemies 529–1100). Part II (Towards new power and wealth 1100–1250) discusses the sociopolitical and economic thrust of various Italian cities, as well as some monasteries and castles, which together represented the foundation of the Italian Renaissance. And part III (Epilogue 1250–1300) integrates the discussion of the previous chapters.

Given the heterogenous influences, there are references throughout to contacts and linkages with the Islamic civilization. Part I includes two chapters: Muslim Palermo and Norman Cefalu. As for Palermo, while "few traces of pure Islamic architecture can be found today, the urban structure, name of the city and its role as the Sicilian capital are legacies of the new importance acquired during [two centuries of] Muslim rule of the island" (p.82). Further, "It is probably at Granada and Cordova itself, together with al-Qayrawan, that Muslim Palermo may be best imagined; it must have been a truly astonishing capital" (p.95). Similar influences are documented in the chapter on Cefalu. And, King Roger "held the Muslims in great honor, and was always ready to defend them. Moreover, apart from his interest in the Arabic sciences he was ready to introduce features of Muslim rule into his own government" (p.139).

The chapter on Frederick II discusses a variety of Islamic/Muslim connections, but "translation was one of the principal activities in this polyglot court. Translations of the works of Aristotle, Averroes ([Ibn Rushd]—who exercised a profound influence on the emperor's thinking), and Avicenna were made, and copies sent to the universities of Bologna and Paris" (p.239–240). A serious student of mathematics, "Frederick took with him on crusade a Muslim tutor in logic called Ibn al-Giuzi, and astonished his contemporaries by discussing mathematical problems with the 'enemy' during negotiations for the liberation of Jerusalem" (p.240).

The book includes numerous maps, illustrations, and figures. Also there is a chronology of major events (from 493 to 1250), and a list of events from 1260 to 1806. At the end there is a chapter-by-chapter, 18-page select bibliography. There is a detailed index of people and places.

B-17. Cantor, Norman F. *Western Civilization: Its Genesis and Destiny—From the Prehistoric Era to 1500.* Glenview, IL: Scott, Foresman and Company, 1969.

This book is first of a three-volume set (the second covers the period 1300–1815; the third, 1815 to present) intended as a "study of Western civilization in order to communicate a synthesis of prevailing historical knowledge and interpretation in the clearest and most effective way" (p.vii). While cognizant of the need for studying world history, the author mentions several reasons for his focus on Western civilization. He says, "Only in the West did men come to see that the rationality of the universe could be translated into mathematical terms and that the study of natural science could be applied to the development of industrial technology" (p.5). There are some, however, who would suggest that the idea of rationality, having its roots with the Greeks, matured in the early Islamic civilization before traveling to the West; this is evident in the present work as well.

The book is divided into three parts, with several chapters in each. Part One, The Advent of Western Civilization (four chapters); Part Two, The Rise of Western Civilization: From the Roman Empire to the High Middle Ages (four chapters); Part Three, The Expansion of Western Civilization: From the Later Middle Ages to the Reformation (two chapters).

Part Two has a chapter entitled The Foundation of the Medieval World in which there is a ten-page section on Medieval Islam. Here the author notes the linkages with the early Islamic civilization, though a bit remotely. "Alien in spirit as was the Arabic world of the Middle Ages to the Christian West," the author suggests, "its preservation and translation of the classical heritage gave it great significance in European history. The most important agent of cultural transmission to the West was Islamic Spain. European scholars also translated the Arabic commentaries on Aristotle, particularly those written by Avicenna and Averroes. Doctrines propounded by these Muslim thinkers played significant roles in medieval European thought" (p.296). Further, "Even while Islam acted as the great adversary of Christianity, its synthesis of ancient cultures contributed to the development of Christian philosophy in the period of its highest expression" (p.296). There are additional references to the influence of Islamic scholars in the chapter entitled The Rise of Medieval Culture, especially when the author discusses the "medieval synthesis" of St. Thomas Aquinas.

The 520-page book provides numerous diagrams and maps. There is a bibliographic essay at the end, with the purpose of acquainting the reader to some of the historical literature on the subjects discussed in each chapter. There is a detailed name-subject index.

B-18. Carlyle, Thomas. *Heroes, Hero Worship and the Heroic in History*. New York: A.L. Burt Company, n.d.

This is a collection of lectures by an eminent English scholar, delivered between May 5, 1840, and May 22, 1840. In the language of this scholar, it is a "discourse here for a little on great men, their manner of appearance in our world's business, how they have shaped themselves in the world's history, what ideas men formed of them, and on their reception and performance; what I call hero-worship and the heroic in human affairs" (p.1).

The 300-page book contains six lectures about the author's heroes: Lecture 1, The Hero as Divinity: Odin, Paganism, Scandinavian, Mythology; Lecture 2, The Hero as Prophet: Mahomet, Islam; Lecture 3, The Hero as Poet: Dante, Shakespeare; Lecture 4, The Hero as Priest: Luther, Reformation, Knox, Puritanism; Lecture 5, The Hero as Man of Letters: Johnson, Rousseau, Burns; Lecture 6, The Hero as King: Cromwell, Napoleon, Modern Revolutionism.

Of particular interest is lecture 2, delivered on May 8, 1840. The author notes, "From the first rude times of paganism among the Scandinavians in the north, we advance to a very different epoch of religion, among a very different people: Mahometanism among the Arabs. A great change; what a change and progress is indicated here, in the universal condition and thoughts of men!" (p.49). Further, "in the history of the world there will not again be any man, never so great" (p.49). However, "He is by no means the truest of prophets; but I do esteem as a true one. Let us try to understand what *he* meant with the world; what the world meant and means with him, will then be a more answerable question. Our current hypothesis about Mahomet, that he was a scheming impostor, a falsehood incarnate, that his religion is a mere mass of quackery and fatuity, begins really to be now untenable to any one. The lies, which well-meaning zeal has heaped round this man, are disgraceful to ourselves only" (p.51). The author asks, "Are we to suppose that it was a miserable piece of spiritual legerdemain, this which so many creatures of the Almighty have lived by and died by?" (p.51). The rest of the lecture describes many of characteristics of Mahomet that the author admires, along with a brief history of the evolution of Islam among the Arabs.

There is a summary of each lecture at the end, followed by a name-subject index.

B-19. El-Cheikh, Nadia Maria. *Byzantium Viewed by the Arabs*. Cambridge, MA, and London: Harvard University Press, 2004.

This is a study of "the Arab-Islamic view of Byzantium as it evolved through centuries of contact, exchanges, and warfare and as it reflected developments from the first/seventh century to the fall of Constantinople in the ninth/fifteenth century" (p.ix).

After numerous incursions, the author says, the Byzantine empire became part of expanding Islam in 1453. While the warfare between the two empires has given rise to a distorted overview of Muslim-Byzantine relations, "there was also a less adversarial side to the relations between Byzantium and the Muslims" (p.2). Thus, "a semiporous border permitted the exchange of ideas and standards, manners and customs, languages and literatures. The result of this interpenetration was the diffusion of culture, political ideas and institutions, military techniques, material goods, and methods of economic production. In fact, Islamic civilization adopted substantial features from Byzantium, such as concepts of state and administration and elements of its material and intellectual culture. Consequently, any analysis of the various aspects of the Arab Muslim image of the Byzantine empire must acknowledge the effect that Byzantium had on the developing Islamic civilization and also the state of perpetual warfare between them" (p.2–3). The book yields little in new empirical knowledge about Byzantium, but the explorations into "the significance of Byzantium to the Arab Muslim establishment and Muslim appreciation of Byzantine culture and civilization contribute to efforts to find the foundational discourses that underlie Arab Muslim formulations of alterity" (p.5).

The 272-page book contains four rather long chapters, in addition to the introductory and concluding chapters: (1) The Encounter with Byzantium, (2) Confronting Byzantium, (3) Islam on the Defensive, (4) A New Reality: Revisiting Byzantium. The author concludes that this "study has tried to formulate an alternative appreciation to the politics of confrontation and hostility that so often underlies scholarly discourse on Muslim-Byzantine relations. Indeed, the connections between the two states and societies were complex and dynamic throughout, and the discursive production reveals a sophisticated apprehension of Byzantium and a conceptualization that transcends fatal binarisms and essentialist understanding" (p.230).

Notes and references are provided at the end of each chapter. There is a 23-page bibliography, classified in terms of secondary literature and primary Arabic sources. There is a detailed name-subject index.

B-20. Clagett, Marshall, Gaines Post, and Robert Reynolds, eds. *Twelfth Century Europe and the Foundations of Modern Society*, Proceedings of a Symposium. Madison, WI: University of Wisconsin Press, 1961.

Inspired by Charles Homer Haskins's *magnum opus* (*The Renaissance of the Twelfth Century*, Harvard University Press, 1927), this symposium, held at the University of Wisconsin in 1958, chose the 12th century, an "age extending from the eleventh to the thirteenth century, as the principal theme," and "one of the great constructive ages in European history." As with the Haskins book, the various papers in this volume also attribute the European revival to what "Western

Christians found, in Arabic and Greek versions which were rapidly translated into Latin, the main body not only of Islamic but also of ancient Greek learning in Aristotelian and Neoplatonic philosophy, and in medicine, mathematics, astronomy, and the natural sciences" (p.v). There are direct/indirect references to numerous early Islamic scholars throughout.

The book is divided into three parts, with three chapters in each. Written by prominent medievalists, the titles and authors are: Part I, Thought in European Society: (1) The School of Chartres by Raymond Klibansky, (2) Transitions in European Education by Urban T. Holmes Jr., (3) The Representation of the Seven Liberal Arts by Adolf Katzenellenbogen; Part II, Transition in Economy and Society: (1) Economic Aspects of Expanding Europe by Hilmer C. Krueger, (2) The Development of Feudal Institutions by Joseph R. Strayer, (3) Kingship under the Impact of Scientific Jurisprudence by Ernst H. Kantorowicz; Part III, Eastern Influences on European Culture: (1) The Influences of Hebrew and Vernacular Poetry on the Judeo-Italian Elegy by Leo Spitzer, (2) Some Aspects of Byzantine Influence on Latin Thought by Milton V. Anastos, (3) The World of Islam: The Face of the Antagonist by G.E. von Grunebaum.

Footnotes and references are integrated in the text of each essay. The book has a detailed name-subject index.

B-21. Courbage, Youssef and Philippe Fargues. *Christians and Jews under Islam* (translated from French by Judy Mabro). London and New York: I.B. Tauris Publishers, 1998.

This book, written in accessible language for both students and general readers, draws on a large body of scholarly research to set out the political, sociological, and demographic forces that have shaped the history of the Christian and Jewish communities under Islam. The position of these communities in the past and presently is a much discussed but widely misunderstood phenomenon, according to the authors.

Focusing on the Arab world and Turkey, the authors show how Christianity and Judaism survived and even prospered in the region, thus challenging the view of Islam as an unbending radical religion. The authors argue that periods of rapid decline of the minorities occurred in the wake of confrontation with the Christian West, after the first victories of the Spanish Reconquista, at the time of the Crusades, further accelerated by the collapse of the Ottoman Empire in North Africa and of the Balkans as a result of colonialism and the First World War, and with the creation of the state of Israel.

The 242-page book contains eight chapters: (1) The Installation of Islam in the Arab East, (2) The Dechristianization of North Africa, (3) The Crusades: A Confrontation of Two Christianities, (4) The Christian Recovery in the Ottoman Arab East, (5) From Multinational Empire to Secular Republic: The Lost Christianity of Turkey, (6) Islam under Christian Domination: The French Empire in

North Africa, (7) Israel and the Palestinian Population Explosion, (8) Arab Christianity in the Twentieth Century: Decline or Eclipse?

The book contains a wealth of historical, quantitative data. Notes and bibliographic references, chapter-by-chapter, are provided at the end. There is a name-subject index.

B-22. Davies, Norman. *Europe: A History*. New York: Oxford University Press, 1996.

This rather comprehensive book (over 1,300 pages) has 12 chapters that follow the conventional framework of European history, providing the basic chronological and geographical grid into which all other details have been fitted. However, the book has an unusual approach in that it attempts to "counteract the bias of 'Eurocentrism' and 'Western civilization.'" It emphasizes throughout the importance of "contingent subjects such as Islam, colonialism, or Europe overseas" (p. viii). Indeed, the author is rather inclined to emphasize the links between East and West; even the maps in this book subvert the practice of looking at Europe in East–West terms: they appear at a 90-degree angle to the usual layout, with Spain at the top and Russia at the bottom.

The book has an interesting section at the beginning, entitled The Legend of Europa, followed by the introduction. Then there are long discussion chapters (each about 80–90 pages) with titles: (1) Peninsula: Environment and Prehistory, (2) Hellas: Ancient Greece, (3) Roma: Ancient Rome, 753BC–AD337, (4) Origo: The Birth of Europe, AD330–800, (5) Medium: The Middle Age, c.750–1270, (6) Pestis: Christendom in Crisis, c.1250–1493, (7) Renatio: Renaissances and Reformations, c.1450–1670, (8) Lumen: Enlightenment and Absolutism, c.1650–1789, (9) Resolution: A Continent in Turmoil, c.1770–1815, (10) Dynamo: Powerhouse of the World, 1815–1914, (11) Tenebrae: Europe in Eclipse, 1914–1945, (12) Divisa et Indivisa: Europe Divided and Undivided, 1945–1991.

There are frequent references to the links with the early Islamic civilization. However, a large section of one of the chapters is especially devoted to the influence of Islam, and here, among other things, the author makes reference to the famous but controversial Pirenne thesis: "The Frankish Empire would probably never have existed without Islam, and Charlemagne without Mahomet would be inconceivable" (p.258). Above all, Islam "created the bulwark against which European identity could be defined. Europe, let alone Charlemagne, is inconceivable without Muhammad" (p. 258).

In the post-Cold War era, the author warns, there may be a temptation to keep the West as a short-sighted and self-satisfied rich man's club, but the continued exclusion of the East may lead to rebuilding the "Iron Curtain" in another disguise. Further, with the background of the post-Communist environment, he discusses factors such as the shared classical and Christian heritage and argues that the growing international trade in goods and ideas has produced a diverse yet discernible common civilization that may lead to a unified Europe. And, he muses, a crisis in the United States might be what it takes to finally bring the Europeans together.

Chapter-by-chapter notes and bibliographic references are provided at the end. There are three appendices relating to various capsules, maps, and plates, as well as one entitled historical compendium. The 1,350-page book provides a comprehensive name-subject index.

B-23. Dawson, Christopher. *The Formation of Christendom.* New York: Sheed & Ward, 1967.

This book, written by a Catholic scholar who seems keen to forge a unity between Catholicism and Protestantism, contains the author's lectures at Harvard University from 1958 to 1962. The discourse deals with the formation of Christendom, from its origins in the Judeo-Christian tradition through the rise and the decline of the medieval unity, although, as the author suggests, "it is impossible to write the history of Christianity without" the study of Catholicism (p.4).

The book has three parts: (1) Introduction, with four chapters (Introduction, Christianity and the history of culture, The nature of culture, The growth and diffusion of culture); (2) Beginnings of Christian Culture, with six chapters (The Christian and Jewish idea of revelation, The coming of the kingdom, Christianity and the Greek world, The Christian empire, The influence of liturgy and theology of the development of Byzantine culture, The Church and the conversion of the Barbarians); (3) Formation of Medieval Christendom: Its Rise and Decline, with eight chapters (The foundation of Europe, The Carolingian age, Feudal Europe and the age of anarchy, The Papacy and medieval Europe, The unity of western Christendom, The achievement of medieval thought, East and West in the Middle Ages, The decline of the medieval unity).

Part three of the book, especially chapter 16, The Achievement of Medieval Thought, contains numerous references to Arab-Islamic linkages. Such linkages led to the "confidence in the power of reason and that faith in the rationality of the universe without which science would be impossible" (p.230). Further, during the 12th and 13th centuries, "The Schoolmen received them [Greek philosophy and science] from the Arabs as part of a living scientific movement, and their attention was concentrated not on the form but on the content of the newly discovered literature" (p.230). And, "The characteristic feature of this phase of the medieval revival is its humanism" (p.232). "From this *impasse* [of traditionalism where divined omnipotence rules, with no room for a science of things] Western thought was delivered, not by a gradual process of criticism and experiment, but by the importation *en bloc* of the scientific and philosophic tradition of the Moslem world. This was the great intellectual event of the twelfth century" (p.235). The contacts took place in Spain, Sicily, Southern France, and Syria during the Crusades. The epilogue discusses the "Catholic idea of a universal spiritual society" (p.298).

The 310-page book provides some footnotes in the text. There is a detailed name-subject index.

B-24. Dawson, Christopher. *The Making of Europe: An Introduction to the History of European Unity.* New York: Sheed & Ward, 1952.

First published in 1932, the 280-page book is about what the author calls "a neglected and unappreciated subject," the European Dark Ages—the period prior to 13th century that "witnessed changes as momentous as any in the history of Europe," and "the most creative age of all, the root and ground of all the subsequent cultural achievements" (p.xv). To the "secular historian," this period represented "barbarism and ignorance," but to the "Catholic" historian, "they are not dark ages so much as ages of dawn" (p.xvii). But, the book "is not a history of the Church or a history of Christianity; it is a history of a culture, of the particular culture that is ancestral to our own" (p.xx).

The book is divided into three parts: (1) The Foundations, with five chapters (The Roman Empire, The Catholic Church, The Classical Tradition and Christianity, The Barbarians, The Barbarian Invasions and the Fall of the Empire); (2) The Ascendancy of the East, with five chapters (The Christian Empire and the Rise of the Byzantine Culture, The Awakening of the East, The Rise of Islam, The Expansion of Moslem Culture, The Byzantine Renaissance and the Revival of the Eastern Empire); (3) The Formation of Western Christendom, with four chapters (The Western Church and the Conversion of the Barbarians, The Restoration of the Western Empire and Carolingian Renaissance, The Age of the Vikings and the Conversion of the North, The Rise of the Medieval Unity).

There are references throughout to linkages with the early Islamic civilization, but especially so in the second and third parts of the book. "For more than four centuries the intellectual leadership of the world passed to the Islamic peoples," says the author, "and it was from the Arabs that the scientific tradition in Western Europe derived its origin" (p.150). Further, Muslim scholars developed their "Islamic synthesis" with a "vigour of thought and an intellectual ingenuity which render their work one of the most complete and symmetrical philosphical structures that have ever been created" (p.153). And, the author emphasizes, "We are so accustomed to regard our culture as essentially that of the West that it is difficult for us to realize that there was an age when the most civilized region of Western Europe was the province of an alien [Islamic] culture. It is, in fact, hardly accurate to identify Christendom with the West and Islam with the East, at a time when Asia Minor was still a Christian land and Spain and Portugal and Sicily were the home of a flourishing Moslem culture. Western culture grew under the shadow of the more advanced civilization of Islam, and it was from the latter rather than from the Byzantine world that medieval Christendom recovered its share in the inheritance of Greek science and philosophy" (p.168). The author cautions, however, in that "we can no longer be satisfied with an aristocratic civilization that finds its unity in external and superficial things and ignores the deeper needs of man's spiritual nature" (p.290).

The book provides a detailed bibliography, classified in terms of a general listing, plus three listings according to the three parts of the book. Provided also are several illustrative pictures and maps, as well as a detailed name-subject index.

B-25. Dawson, Christopher. *Religion and the Rise of Western Culture.* Garden City, NY: Image Books, A Division of Doubleday and Company, Inc., 1958.

This book, written by an eminent Catholic intellectual, explores the "problem of Religion and Culture—the intricate and far-reaching network of relations that unite the social way of life with the spiritual beliefs and values, which are accepted by society as the ultimate laws of life and the ultimate standards of individual and social behavior" (p.12). He says, "Side by side with the natural aggressiveness and the lust for power and wealth which are so evident in European history, there were also new spiritual forces driving Western man towards a new destiny" (p.17).

The 242-page book contains 12 chapters: (1) Introduction: The Significance of the Western Development, (2) The Religious Origins of Western Culture: The Church and the Barbarians, (3) The Monks of the West and the Formation of the Western Tradition, (4) The Barbarians and the Christian Kingdom, (5) The Second Dark Age and the Conversion of the North, (6) The Byzantine Tradition and the Conversion of Eastern Europe, (7) The Reform of the Church in the Eleventh Century and the Medieval Papacy, (8) The Feudal World: Chivalry and the Courtly Culture, (9) The Medieval City: Commune and Gild, (10) The Medieval City: School and University, (11) The Religious Crisis of Medieval Culture: The Thirteenth Century, (12) Conclusion: Medieval Religion and Popular Culture. There is an appendix entitled Notes on Famous Medieval Art.

At various points throughout the book, especially chapters 7 and after, the author recounts numerous close linkages with the Arab-Islamic civilization. He mentions the "anarchy of the feudal system" that was broken by expansion through the Crusades. And, "So long as the Crusades continued, the unity of Christendom found expression in a dynamic and militant activity which satisfied the aggressive instincts of Western man, while at the same time sublimating them in terms of religious idealism. Thus, the Crusades expressed all that as highest and lowest in medieval society" (p.151).

With the age of the Crusades also evolved a secular ideal through contacts with the Islamic culture in Western Mediterranean, says the author. Further, "The distinctive features of this new movement were the cult of courtesy and cult of love. It was concerned, above all, with the refinement of life—with creating a new pattern of social behavior," which, according to the author, "must have stood out in abrupt and startling contrast to the brutality and violence that still characterized feudal society" (p.152–153). Thus, "The new movement has all the marks of an exotic growth. It has no roots in the earlier medieval culture of the West. It is neither Christian, nor Latin, nor Germanic. It appears abruptly in South-Western France about the time of the First Crusade without any preparation or previous development" (p.153). The author says, he has "argued elsewhere that the origins of the new style are to be found in the rich and brilliant society of Moslem Spain" (p.153).

While discussing the evolution of cities, gilds, universities, and schools, Dawson discusses the "ultimate end" of human civilization, which "in Aristotelian or rather Averroistic terms," is "the continuous actualization of the potential intellect, i.e., the realization of all the potentialities of human mind" (p.178). The ruler, or emperor, says the author, is the formal principle of human unity, "in the same way as God, the First Mover, imparts a single law of uniform motion to the heavens. All this is much nearer to Averroes or Avicenna than to the teaching of St. Thomas" (p.179).

Elsewhere, the author mentions the translations of the works of "great Moslem and Jewish philosophers and men of science: Al-Kindi, Al-Farabi, Al-Battani, Avicenna, Ibn Gebirol and Al-Ghazali" (p.192). Further, "The Aristotelian tradition was represented in its purest and most uncompromising form by the teaching of the Spanish Moslem Averroes (Ibn Rushd, 1126–1198)" (p.193). And, "The result of this influx of new knowledge and new ideas was to provide the universities and the international society of scholars and teachers who frequented them with the materials from which to construct a new intellectual synthesis" (p.193).

Notes and references are integrated within each chapter, and there is a name-subject index.

B-26. Donner, Fred M. *The Early Islamic Conquests.* Princeton, NJ: Princeton University Press, 1981.

The 490-page book "presents a description and interpretation of the early Islamic conquest movement, from its beginnings under the Prophet Muhammad (ca. AD 570–632) through the conquest of the Fertile Crescent" (p.ix). It has two objectives: to provide a new interpretation of the origins and nature of this movement and to definitively establish the sources of the two phases (Syria and Iraq) of the movement. The book differs from other similar studies in its approach to the sources; it relies on the author's understanding of the accounts "collected, synthesized and transmitted by the early Arabic historians," as well as the author's assessment of their reliability (p.ix). The author argues that this view of the sources has freed him from the "exaggerated" and "unwarranted skepticism toward Arabic sources shown by some recent authors" (p.ix). The book "also parts company with many of its predecessors in its attempt to use ethnographic literature, much of it of quite recent origin, to help elucidate economic, social, and political structures that flourished over thirteen centuries ago" (p.ix).

Beyond the introduction, there are six detailed chapters: (1) State and Society in Pre-Islamic Arabia, (2) The Foundations of the Islamic Conquest, (3) The Conquest of Syria, (4) The Conquest of Iraq, (5) Military Organization, Migration, and Settlement, (6) Conclusion. There is a short epilogue that notes, "The Islamic conquests had a profound impact on the Near East and on the general course of world history" (p.274).

The book is extremely well-documented. There are 75 pages of chapter-by-chapter notes and references. There are 14 appendices, covering 72 pages, consisting of lists of individuals mentioned in the book in connection with specific events or belonging to a specific group. There is a 20-page bibliography of "essential" references. There are two indices—one relating to "traditionists" mentioned in the notes and appendices, the other a general name-subject index.

B-27. Douglas, David C. *The Norman Fate, 1100–1154.* Berkeley and Los Angeles: University of California Press, 1976.

The book represents a survey of "the historical process which during the earlier half of the twelfth century went to the making of Europe. Its particular aim is to assess the contribution made by the Normans to the political growth of Europe between 100 and 1154" (p.1).

Throughout there are frequent references to linkages with the Arab-Islamic culture, especially after the conquest of Sicily by Roger, the "Great Count." Most important was "his recognition of what might be the future value to Norman power of the Greek and Moslem institutions and traditions which he found alive in the island he had conquered" (p.2). Further, "His administration, based upon Norman authority but using Greek and Moslem expertise, would serve as a pattern for the future" (p.2).

The 260-page book is made up of three parts: (1) The Norman Kingdoms (four chapters), (2) The Norman Impact upon Europe (four chapters), (3) The Normans in the World's Debate (three chapters). Chapters 6 (Secular Government) and 8 (The Mind of the West) include more focused discussion of the influence of Arab-Islamic institutions and traditions. Some illustrative quotes are appropriate. "Scholars and writers from all over the Latin West mingled in Norman Sicily with Islamic writers who represented the Moslem population from whom the island had so recently been taken. The intellectual and artistic revival which began under Roger the Great in the Norman South was thus derived from Latin, Greek and Arabic traditions" (p.145). Further, "The Arabic influence on the Norman kingdom in the South has been plentifully illustrated in the work of modern historians, who have properly seen in it one of the most remarkable phenomena in the growth of medieval Europe" (p.147). And, the author quotes a Muslim historian of the time: "He [King Roger] adopted the customs of Moslem kings with regard to the officers he appointed. Franks did not comprehend the functions of such officials. He treated Moslems with great honor. He was familiar with many of them and favoured them even against the Franks" (p.147). "Arabic studies, too, particularly in science and mathematics, were vigorously pursued in Sicily between 1130 and 1154 under the king's encouragement. One of the great works of Arab learning, the *Geography of al Idrisi* was undertaken at his [King

Roger's] command for the comfort of those who wish to go round the world" (p.148). "There is of course no question of England before 1154 having the same direct contacts with the Greek and Moslem worlds of culture which were enjoyed in the Norman kingdom of the South," adds the author (p.150).

At the end, the book provides several maps, select genealogies, selected dates of major events, a list of contemporary rulers, and an extensive bibliography. There is also a detailed name-subject index.

B-28. Draper, John W. *History of the Conflict between Religion and Science.* New York and London: D. Appleton and Company, 1902; original 1874.

"The history of science is a narrative of the conflict of the two contending powers, the expansive force of the human intellect on one side, and the compression arising from traditionary faith and human interests on the other. No one has hitherto treated the subject from this point of view. Yet it presents itself to us as a living issue—in fact, as the most important of all living issues," so states the author in the preface (p.vi–vii). Further, it was from the rise of Mohammedanism that the "doctrine of the Unity of God [became] established in the larger portion of what had been the Roman Empire" (p.xiii).

Then the 313-page book discusses four conflicts: (1) the Southern Reformation ("Arabian Reformation"), (2) nature of the soul—"under the designation of Averroism, there came into prominence the theories of Emanation and Absorption," (3) with the emergence of astronomy, geography and other sciences, conflict arose as to the "position and relations of the earth, and as to the structure of the world. In this Galileo led the way on the part of the Science," (4) the Northern Reformation, "respecting the standard or criterion of truth, whether it is to be found in the Church or the Bible." In connection with Reformation and the influence of Averroistic philosophy, the author states, since "philosophy or science was pernicious to the interests of Christianity or pure piety, the Mohammedan literature then prevailing in Spain was making converts among all classes of society" (p.209). Much of the book contains frequent references to Arab-Islamic influences.

The book provides no bibliographic references; however, there is a comprehensive name-subject index.

B-29. Draper, John W. *History of the Intellectual Development of Europe*, revised edition in two volumes. New York and London: Harper and Brothers Publishers, 1876 and 1904.

At the 1860 meeting of the British Association for the Advance of Science, the author spoke of researching "the historical evidence respective the mental progress of Europe." One of the most comprehensive, yet neglected, works of its kind, "this work contains that evidence. It is a history of the progress of ideas and opinions from a point of view heretofore almost entirely neglected" (p.iii).

Volume I has 16 chapters—some of the titles are: Europe's topography and ethnology, Hindu theology and Egyptian civilization, Greeks—age of antiquity, faith, reason, intellectual decline, Roman influences, early European age of inquiry and of faith and reason, age of faith in the East, age of faith in the West (image-worship and the monks), the Arabians and their age of reason. The last chapter includes sections: The Arabs originate scientific chemistry, discover the strong acids, their geological ideas, application of chemistry to medicine, approach of the conflict between the Saracenic material and the European supernatural system. Volume II has 12 chapters, some are: age of faith—three attacks (northern or moral, western or intellectual, eastern or military), intellectual condition of Christendom contrasted with that of Arabian Spain, diffusion of Arabian intellectual influences, overthrow of the Italian system, intellectual condition in the age of faith (supernaturalism destroyed by the Jews and Arabians), age of reason in Europe, the Reformation, and the future of Europe.

The book abundantly documents the influence of the Arab-Islamic civilization and does so rather dispassionately and sympathetically throughout the two volumes. The flavor of the book is evident from the following quotes: "I have to deplore the systematic manner in which the literature of Europe has contrived to put out of sight our scientific obligations to the Mohammedans. Surely they cannot be much longer and national conceit cannot be perpetuated for ever. The Arab has left his intellectual impress on Europe, as, before long, Christendom will have to confess; he has indelibly written it on the heavens, as any one may see who reads the names of the stars on a common celestial globe" (p.42). And, "When Europe was hardly more enlightened than Caffraria is now, the Saracens were cultivating and even creating science. Their triumphs in philosophy, mathematics, astronomy, chemistry, medicine, proved to be more durable, and therefore more important than their military actions had been" (p.412).

The book provides no bibliographic details; however, there is a comprehensive name-subject index at the end of the second volume.

B-30. Dunlop, D.M. *Arab Civilization to A.D. 1500.* New York and Washington, DC: Praeger Publishers, 1971.

Drawing upon original Arabic sources, the book provides a lucid account of the cultural life of the Arab civilization, describing the general history of the Middle East before the rise of Islam and Islamic civilization, as well as the main course of events thereafter. The purpose of the book is to convey an overall picture of the richness and vigor of Islamic culture by concentrating on the literature, history, and philosophy of the early empire. This empire was the most extensive global state during the Middle Ages, stretching to Spain and France in the West and Turkestan and India in the east. The author discusses the historians of Mohammad's time, the sagas of the Persians, the genealogy of Arab tribes, and the early expansion of Islam.

The 368-page book has seven detailed chapters: (1) The Arabs and the Arab world to 1500, (2) Arabic Literature, (3) History and Historians, (4) Geography and Travel, (5) Arabic Philosophy, (6) Science and Medicine, (7) Some Famous Women in Islam. Among other things, interestingly, the author notes the origin of the Robinson Crusoe story with Ibn Tufayl's (d. 1185) well-known work *Hayy b. Yaqzan* ("The Living, Son of the Wakeful") (p. 197). Also, while noting the influence of Ibn Rushd on Latin West, it is mentioned that in Islam, "he had no real successors, in the sense of men who, having sharpened their wits by intensive study of the ancients, proceeded, while keeping within the great assumptions of Islam, to try to give a rational account of the universe and spared no effort in the attempt" (p.201).

There is a comprehensive, 62-page list of chapter-by-chapter notes, including bibliographic references, along with a name-subject index.

B-31. Eaton, Richard M. *Islamic History as Global History*. Washington, DC: American Historical Association, 1990.

Part of a series of essays on global history, the title of this 51-page monograph is self-descriptive and it begins with a brief note on the legacy of Europe's often hostile encounter with Muslim societies and why, beginning with the Crusades, "since the eleventh century, it was the fate of Islamic civilization to serve in the European imagination as a wholly alien 'other,' a historic and cosmic foil against which Europeans defined their own collective identity" (p.2).

The booklet is divided into five brief sections: (1) The Legacy of Europe's Encounter with Islam, (2) The Rise and Growth of Islam and Its Historians, (3) Early Islamic Civilization and Global History, (4) Islam in the Wider World, (5) Dar al-Islam as a World System. Historically, the author suggests, the Islamic rulers chose to "bring all the diverse communities and traditions [Greek Orthodox Christians, Monophysites, Nestorians, Copts, Zoroastrians, Manicheans, Jews, as well as a plurality of linguistic and literary traditions] together into a new cultural synthesis" (p.21).

Thus, the author argues, Islam provides "a sense of civilizational coherence by uniting hitherto separate religious and linguistic communities into a single ethnoreligious identity, initially transcending and ultimately supplanting all other such identities. Because Muslims chose this option, Islam became a world civilization and not just one more parochial, ethnic cult" (p.21). Muslims saw themselves playing this unifying role, as per the Qur'anic passages, "exhorting Jews and Christians to leave aside their differences and return to the pure, unadulterated monotheism of Abraham, their common ancestor" (p.21). As a consequence, therefore, while Marco Polo (d. 1324) was a stranger wherever he went, Ibn Battuta, "in his intercontinental wanderings, moved through a single cultural universe in which he was utterly at home" (p.44).

Footnotes and references are followed by a brief bibliography at the end. There is no index.

B-32. Esposito, John L., ed. *The Oxford History of Islam*. New York: Oxford University Press, 1999.

This compendium offers about the most wide-ranging, authoritative, and recent account available of the Islamic world. The book is part of the process of "redressing of earlier imbalances of coverage and stereotyping" of this religion. Written for the general reader but also appealing to specialists, Esposito aims to present the best scholarship on the subject in a readable style, complemented with several historical and contemporary illustrations and pictures.

The first part of this 750-page volume provides an overview of the origins and development of classical Islam along with a survey of the historic encounter of Islam and Christianity. The next group of chapters tracks the domestic and international challenges faced by premodern and modern Muslim countries, especially movements of Islamic renewal and reform. The final chapters provide perspectives on the contemporary landscape, in particular the late 20th-century resurgence of Islam.

There are 15 chapters: (1) Muhammad and the Caliphate: Political History of the Islamic Empire up to the Mongol Conquest by Fred M. Donner, (2) Fruit of the Tree of Knowledge: The Relationship between Faith and Practice in Islam by Vincent J. Cornell, (3) Law and Society: The Interplay of Revelation and Reason in Shariah by Mohammad Hashim Kamali, (4) Science, Medicine, and Technology: The Making of a Scientific Culture by Ahmad Dallal, (5) Art and Architecture: Themes and Variations by Sheila S. Blair and Jonathan M. Bloom, (6) Philosophy and Theology: From Eight Century C.E. to the Present by Majid Fakhry, (7) Islam and Christendom: Historical, Cultural, and Religious Interaction from the Seventh to the Fifteenth Centuries by Jane I. Smith, (8) Sultanates and Gunpowder Empires: The Middle East by Ira M. Lapidus, (9) The Eastward Journey of Muslim Kingship: Islam in South and Southeast Asia by Bruce B. Lawrence, (10) Central Asia and China: Transnationalization, Islamization, and Ethnicization by Dru C. Gladney, (11) Islam in Africa to 1800: Merchants, Chiefs, and Saints by Nehemia Levtzion, (12) Foundations for Renewal and Reform: Islamic Movements in the Eighteenth and Nineteenth Centuries by John Obert Voll, (13) European Colonialism and the Emergence of Modern Muslim States by S.V.R. Nasr, (14) The Globalization of Islam: The Return of Muslims to the West by Yvonne Yazbeck Haddad, (15) Contemporary Islam by John L. Esposito.

The book has a chronology of Islamic history (570–1998 AD) at the end, followed by a select, chapter-by-chapter bibliography. There is also information about each contributor and a detailed 38-page name-subject index.

B-33. Ezzati, Abul-Fazl. *An Introduction to the History of the Spread of Islam.* London: News and Media Ltd., 1978.

The purpose of the book is to present an introduction "dealing with some of the factors, incentives, and circumstances which have helped the spread of Islam" (p.ii). The author has relied "mainly on Western sources and books for technical and research purposes" (p.iii). He asks the "impartial scholars to follow this subject critically and contribute to the furtherance of public knowledge about Islam and the development of human knowledge in general and to do justice to a religion which has been wronged intentionally and unintentionally by foes and friends" (p.iii).

The 280-page book has 14 chapters: (1) The spread of Islam: Islamic tolerance, (2) Religious and spiritual factors contributing to the spread of Islam, (3) Religious leadership factor: Absence of hierarchy, (4) Intellectual factor: Mental freedom, rationalism, (5) Moral factor: Ethical values of Islam, (6) Cultural factor: Islam and the integration of culture, (7) Humanitarian factor, (8) Political factor, (9) Social and socio-political factor: Inclusiveness of Islam, (10) Economic factor: Islam as the "middle course," (11) Emigration and immigration factor, (12) Educational factor, (13) Civilization: Asia, Africa, Sicily, Spain, and influence on Europe, (14) Islamic dynamism and resilience.

There is a selected bibliography at the end, followed by notes and references listed chapter-by-chapter. There is no index.

B-34. George, Linda. *The Golden Age of Islam.* Tarrytown, NY: Benchmark Books, 1998.

As part of the Cultures-of-the-Past series, this 80-page book is written for the general reader and it explores "a golden age that stretched from the last years of the eighth century—the time of Harun al-Rashid—to the middle of the thirteenth century" (p.6).

The book is divided into five short sections: History, Cultural History, Belief System, Beliefs and Society, The Legacy of Islam's Golden Age. There are five chapters: (1) A Beacon in the East, (2) Life in the Golden Age, (3) Islam, (4) A Vision of Beauty, (5) The Golden Age and the World of Today. The last chapter is of particular interest as it provides a glimpse of the "lasting mark" on the West throughout the Golden Age. In addition to the Europeans' first experience during the Crusades (1095–1270), "Arabic learning and culture filtered into Europe in other ways as well: through Sicily, where a Muslim dynasty ruled from the ninth to the eleventh century, and through Muslim Spain" (p.65).

Described by a Saxon nun as the "jewel of the world," the tenth-century Cordoba "boasted free schools, a university, and an important library, all of which made it an intellectual center, attracting students from Europe as well as from the Muslim world" (p.66). There are briefs on products and technology introduced from the Islam world to Europe: various crops, irrigation methods, paper, decorative arts, tools of navigation and exploration, etc. The author adds, "The Islamic civilization was a bridge across both space and time. It took the classical Western works, mainly those of the Greeks, transformed and preserved them, and passed them on to Europe. Along the way, Islamic civilization added its own original ideas and put its own unique stamp on all it touched" (p.70).

There is a glossary of Arabic words, followed by a list of further readings, a bibliography, and a name-subject index.

B-35. Gimpel, Jean. *The Medieval Machine: The Industrial Revolution of the Middle Ages*. New York: Holt, Rinehart and Winston, 1976.

The "foundations of our present technologically oriented society were laid not in the Italian Renaissance or in the English Industrial Revolution, but in the Middle Ages" (p.viii). That being the main theme, the book examines the "industrial life and institutions of the Middle Ages, and the genius of their inventiveness" (p.xi). Elsewhere, the author argues that what gave rise to the "medieval machine" was the "renaissance of the twelfth century" (see Charles Homer Haskins, *The Renaissance of the Twelfth Century*, Harvard University Press, Cambridge, MA, 1927), not the later, more famous, Italian Renaissance. The former pertained to philosophy and science, while the latter related to literature and art. It was during the 12th-century renaissance, contrary to "St. Bernard's anti-intellectualism," when there was "massive invasion of books from the classical world, works translated from Greek and Arabic in the frontier towns of Christendom, mainly in Sicily and Spain. This influx of books may not have had the impact that was to follow the spread of printing, but it exerted a strong influence on Europe's way of thinking in the 12th and 13th centuries" (p.174). The author provides two tables (pages 176 and 177)—each enumerating Arabic and Greek sources of translations of ancient literature.

There are nine chapters and the titles relate to topics such as development of energy resources, agricultural revolution, environment and pollution, labor conditions, the mechanical clock ("the key machine"), reason, mathematics, and experimental science. Often there are references to Arab-Islamic linkages, especially in the last chapter where the author is more explicit; he discusses Latin-European translators who "learned Arabic" and who "produced Latin translations not only of Greek works but also of original works by Arab scholars, particularly in the fields of medicine, astronomy, arithmetic, algebra, and trigonometry" (p.175).

The book's epilogue concludes with a pessimistic note; for various economic, sociopsychological, and demographic reasons, it is suggested "the whole of Western civilization is approaching the end of its historical cycle" (p.252).

There is a chapter-by-chapter listing of footnotes, including bibliographic references, and a comprehensive name-subject index.

B-36. Goitein, S.D. *Studies in Islamic History and Its Institutions*. Leiden, Netherlands: E.J. Brill, 1966; reprinted 1968.

This is a collection of articles, organized as chapters on various topics, all of which, except those that represent chapters I and III, have been previously published by the author, who is recognized as among the most eminent scholars of Islamic civilization. They provide a general introduction to the Islamic civilization based on specialized research by the author, with a focus on Islamic institutions and social history. The author notes, "The articles presented here have been selected with an eye to their possible usefulness for university teaching" (p.vii).

Further, he suggests the collection reflects three different perspectives about Islam ("understood as a human experience of divine things"): (1) religious and political institutions, as well as the social phenomena, (2) economic, social, and spiritual life of "the man in the street" within Islamic civilization, (3) comparison with Judaism, for "Islam and Judaism, even from the mere topological point of view, betray an amazing degree of affinity" (p.viii).

The 390-page book contains 19 chapters (17 of which were previously published in prominent journals; the author provides a list of original sources). Chapters are grouped into three parts. Part One, The Nature and Development of Islam, with two chapters: (1) The Four Faces of Islam, (2) The Intermediate Civilization/The Hellenic Heritage in Islam; Part Two, Islamic Religious and Political Institutions, with eight chapters: (3) Prayer in Islam, (4) Ramadan: The Muslim Month of Fasting, Its Early Development and Religious Meaning, (5) The Origin and Nature of the Muslim Friday Worship, (6) The Birth-Hour of Muslim Law, (7) The Sanctity of Jerusalem and Palestine in Early Islam, (8) A Turning-Point in the History of the Muslim State, (9) The Origin of the Vizierate and Its True Character (with an appendix), (10) Attitudes towards Government in Islam and Judaism; Part Three, Islamic Social History, with nine chapters: (11) The Rise of the Middle-Eastern Bourgeoisie in Early Islamic Times, (12) The Mentality of the Middle Class in Medieval Islam, (13) The Working People of the Mediterranean Area during the High Middle Ages, (14) The Documents of the Cairo Geniza as a Source for Islamic Social History (with an appendix), (15) The Unity of the Mediterranean World in the "Middle Ages," (16) Medieval Tunisia: The Hub of the Mediterranean, (17) Letters and Documents on the India Trade in Medieval Times, (18) The Beginnings of the Karim Merchants and the Nature of their Organization, (19) The Present Day Arabic Proverb as a Testimony to the Social History of the Middle East.

The chapter on "The Intermediate Civilization" is especially instructive. Concentrating on the period between 850 and 1250 AD, the author insists, among other things, that his concern is with the "*Intermediate,* not *Intermediary,*" for that "civilization created its own works of the spirit and was not a mere transmitter of an ancient heritage" (p.55).

Notes and references are integrated in the text of each chapter, and there is a detailed name-subject index.

B-37. Goldstein, Thomas. *Dawn of Modern Science.* Boston: Houghton Mifflin Company, 1988.

"If we want to study the question of the beginnings of modern science, then, we can't begin with Copernicus and Vesalius as adults with finished thoughts. We must remember the scholars, the thoughts, and the techniques that made Copernicus and Vesalius' work possible," says Isaac Asimov, who wrote the foreword for this book. Thus, the author "goes back beyond the Renaissance, too, to the scholars who translated the Arabic works, and to the Arabs themselves, who preserved Greek science at a time when Europe had forgotten it" (p.vii). The book is written in the spirit of conveying "an integral unity between the Medieval and Renaissance and the modern experience of science: across the differences of the cultures and the boundaries of time, here was the same human mind struggling to grasp nature's laws and enjoying her dual challenge to the intellect and the senses" (p.xiii).

The 300-page book has six chapters: (1) The Idea of the Earth in Renaissance Florence, (2) Ancient Roots, (3) Science and Faith at Chartres, (4) The Gift of Islam, (5) Scholastics, Mystics, Alchemists, (6) Art and Science in the Renaissance. There is a concluding chapter, Epilogue: The Tree of Knowledge.

The 37-page chapter, The Gift of Islam, is particularly interesting. Thus, "Spain, to the intelligentsia of the high Middle Ages—teachers and students or *vagantes*, wandering scholars—represented adventure. The fascination of the enemy culture that had ruled over the Iberian Peninsula had spread secretly and slowly since the tenth century at least. By the twelfth century it attained the proportions of a cult" (p.94). And "the medieval [Latin-European] scholars crossing the Pyrenees ['at first, in a trickle, then, in droves'] found the quintessence of all preceding science distilled by the theorists and practitioners of Islam. Historically, by entering the arena of Islamic civilization they had indeed entered the whole vast vibrant world of antiquity as well" (p.98). Further, "What Islam had to offer them now was not only a spate of enlightening digests of this whole, long, rich evolution but an intelligent discussion of all its essential features, screened and refined through Islam's own intensive experience" (p.102). The chapter discusses various Islamic scholars and their contributions, as well as the impact on Latin Europe. The author emphasizes, "Every single specialized science in the West owes its origins to the Islamic impulse—or at least its direction from that time on" (p.99).

The book provides a 25-page list of chapter-by-chapter bibliographic notes, followed by a detailed name-subject index.

B-38. Guizat, Pierre Guillaume. *General History of Civilization in Europe* (edited, with critical and supplementary notes, by George W. Knight). New York: D. Appleton and Company, 1899.

The book is based on the author's lectures at Sorbonne, Paris, in 1828. Writing in 1899, the editor argued, their intrinsic merit made them valuable. The book is not a recital, but an interpretation, of facts; it is an inquiry into the meaning and the philosophy of history.

While the discussion ranges from early European history up to the French Revolution, with emphasis on European developments, there are sections in the book that are relevant for present purposes. The chapters on the Crusades and the Reformation discuss the impact of the Arab-Islamic civilization, through contacts during the Crusades, that laid the roots for the 16th-century Reformation, leading to the rise to Protestantism. Whatever the causes, the author argues, "the principal effect, then, of the crusades was a great step towards the emancipation of the mind, a great progress towards enlarged and liberal ideas" (p.228). The crusaders were "struck with the riches and elegance of manners observed among Mussulmans," and "it cannot be doubted that the impulse which led to them was one of the most powerful causes of the development and freedom of mind which arose out of that great event and this newly-acquired knowledge inspired many minds with a boldness hitherto unknown" (p.232). And the resultant "insurrection of the human mind against the absolute power of the spiritual order" led to the 16th-century religious revolution called the Reformation, a challenge to the authority of the Church (p.326).

There is extensive footnoting of references and explanations within each chapter and a brief index.

B-39. Hambly, Gavin R.G., ed. *Women in the Medieval Islamic World.* New York: St. Martin's Press, 1999.

This 570-page collection of 23 essays attempts to challenge traditional, monolithic perceptions of women in the Islamic world. It alters significantly our knowledge about women's lives and our understanding of their roles in the early Islamic civilization. The contributors, it is suggested, help to "lift the veil" about Muslim women and Islamic cultures. "For the most part, Europeans and Americans (and some Muslims) have cavalierly stereotyped women in the Islamic world as passive victims of male oppression, without rights, without individuality, and without voices" (p.xi). The essays document a different set of assumptions and roles: women in political roles, sponsoring the construction of public projects, patronizing men of letters, mystics, and saints, leading troops in battle, and as part of the workforce, etc.

The editor's introductory chapter is entitled Becoming visible: Medieval Islamic women in historiography and history. Some illustrative titles of specific essays, along with authors, are: Three queens, two wives, and a goddess: The roles and images of women in Sasanian Iran by Jenny Rose, Zaynab Bint Ali and the place of the women of the households of the first Imams in Shi'te devotional literature by David Pinault, Sayyida Hurra: The Isma'ili Sulayhid queen of Yemen by Farhad Daftary, Heroines and others in the heroic age of the Turks by Geoffrey Lewis, Female piety and patronage in the medieval hajj by Marina Tolmacheva, Timrud women: A cultural perspective by Priscilla Soucek, Conjugal rights versus class prerogatives: A divorce case in Mamluk Cairo by Carl Petry, Invisible women: Residents of early sixteenth-century Istanbul by Yvonne Seng, The "jewels of wonder": Learned ladies and princess politicians in the provinces of early Safavid Iran by Maria Scuppe, Women in Safavid Iran: The evidence of European travelers by Ronald Ferrier, Contributors to the urban landscape: Women builders in Safavid Isfahan and Mughal Shahjahanabad by Stephen Blake, Private lives and public piety: Women and the practice of Islam in

Mughal India by Gregory Kozlowski, Embattled Begams: Women as power brokers in early modern India by Richard Barnett.

Each essay has its own footnotes and references in the text. There is also a comprehensive bibliography at the end. No index is provided.

B-40. Haskins, Charles Homer. *The Renaissance of the Twelfth Century*. Cambridge, MA: Harvard University Press, 1927.

Described by some scholars as the classic account of Arab-Islamic influence on the development of Western European philosophy and science during the Middle Ages, this 437-page book, published in 1927, is known as the author's *magnum opus* among several books written by this prolific medievalist. In contrast to the "not-so-unique" 15th–16th century Italian Renaissance which focused on literature and arts, Haskins argues, the real renaissance that pertained to philosophy and science took place during the 12th century, also known as "the Medieval Renaissance." This is when Europe experienced "the revival of learning in the broadest sense," armed with "new knowledge of the Greeks and Arabs and its effects upon Western science and philosophy" (p.vii–ix).

The book has 12 chapters, documenting the Middle Ages as few other authors have: (1) The Historical Background, (2) Intellectual Centres, (3) Books and Libraries, (4) The Revival of the Latin Classics, (5) The Latin Language, (6) Latin Poetry, (7) The Revival of Jurisprudence, (8) Historical Writing, (9) The Translators from Greek and Arabic, (10) The Revival of Science, (11) The Revival of Philosophy, (12) The Beginnings of Universities.

The last half of the book especially deals with aspects of the 12th-century renaissance that were explicitly Arab-Islamic in origins. Second-half chapter titles are: The translators from Greek and Arabic, The revival of science, The revival of philosophy, The beginnings of universities. It is in these chapters that the author extensively discusses the influence of Arab-Islamic precursors of Latin scholastics. And he states, "The reception of this [Arab-Islamic] science in Western Europe marks a turning point in the history of Western intelligence" (p.282).

Each chapter ends with detailed footnotes, inclusive of bibliographic references, and there is a detailed index. Well-documented, this classic has since generated considerable other literature, some focusing specifically on the 12th-century renaissance.

B-41. Haskins, Charles Homer. *Studies in Mediaeval Culture*. Oxford: Clarendon Press, 1929.

The 295-page book covers various aspects of the medieval culture, the common theme being "the illustration of medieval civilization through the Latin literature of the times" (p.vii). Much of the material in the book has been published in the relevant journal literature, and in discussing medieval culture, "the broad fact remains that the Arabs of Spain were the principal source of the new learning for Western Europe" (p.5).

The first three chapters describe the life of the medieval student as seen in letters (common requests were "for money," professors are referred to as "dictators" [p.7–8]), sermons delivered at universities, and manuals prepared for guidance. The next chapter sketches the various sources through which ideas spread in the Middle Ages. Chapter 5 covers the literature on sports, while chapter 6 discusses the influence of Frederick II, who maintained close contacts with Arabic scholars/scientists of his time, upon his Latin contemporaries. Chapter 7 discusses the development of the science of alchemy, ascribed to Frederick's astrologer Michael Scott. Then, contacts of the Western world with Byzantium are covered in chapters 8 and 9. Chapters 10 and 11 cover the emergence of controversial heresies and the 13th-century Inquisition in Northern France. The last chapter provides brief memoirs of two prominent American medievalists of the time (Henry Charles Lea and Charles Gross).

While there are frequent references to linkages with the medieval Islamic world, chapter 4 in particular (Spread of Ideas) reveals considerable Arab-Islamic influence.

There is an index of manuscripts and libraries at the end, as well as a general index.

B-42. Havighurst, Alfred F., ed. *The Pirenne Thesis: Analysis, Criticism, and Revision.* Lexington, MA: D.C. Heath and Company, revised edition, 1969.

The 195-page book is a collection of papers on the controversial "Pirenne Thesis," a set of ideas developed by Henri Pirenne (1862–1935) concerning the transition from antiquity to early medieval Europe. He concluded that the Roman world essentially continued in all particulars through the centuries of the German invasions. It was rather the impact of Islam in the seventh and eighth centuries which, by destroying the unity of the Mediterrarean, ended the Roman world and led to a strikingly different civilization. "Without Islam the Frankish Empire would probably never have existed and Charlemagne, without Mahomet, would be inconceivable," Pirenne argued in a famous sentence.

Several essays, along with author's name, are: Mohammed and Charlemagne by Henri Pirenne; M. Pirenne and the Unity of the Mediterranean World by Norman H. Baynes; Economic Consequences of the Barbarian Invasions by H. St. L.B. Moss; Mohammed and Charlemagne: A Revision by Robert S. Lopez; Pirenne and Mohammad by Daniel C. Dennett, Jr.; Mohammed, Charlemagne and Ruric by Sture Bolin; The So-Called "Grand Commerce" of the Merovingian Period by Robert Latouche; Commerce in the Dark Ages: A Critique of the Evidence by Philip Grierson; The Pirenne Thesis: Towards Reformulation by Paul Craig Roberts; The Work of Henri Pirenne after Twenty-Five Years by Bryce Lyon.

An additional reading list is provided at the end, followed by a name-subject index.

B-43. Hawting, G.R. *The First Dynasty of Islam: The Umayyad Caliphate AD 661–750.* Carbondale, IL: Southern Illinois University Press, 1987.

This 140-page book is an "introduction to the importance, main events and personalities, and problems of the Umayyad period," different from the "general" surveys of Islamic or Middle-Eastern history and "detailed monographs on particular aspects of Umayyad history" (p.xiv). It is not a substitute for other, more comprehensive works on the subject, nor is it an attempt to provide a wholly new version of the subject.

The book contains eight chapters: (1) Introduction: The Importance of the Umayyad Period and Its Place in Islamic History, (2) The Umayyad Family and Its Rise to the Caliphate, (3) The Sufyanids, (4) The Second Civil War, (5) Abd al-Malik and al-Hajjaj, (6) The Development of Factionalism and the Problems of Islamisation, (7) The Third Civil War and the Caliphate of Marwan II, (8) The Overthrow of the Umayyad Caliphate. There are two appendices: A Note on the Sources, and Modern Developments in the Study of and Attitudes to Umayyad History.

The book provides useful genealogical tables, maps, and a glossary of Arabic terms. Notes and references are provided at the end of each chapter. There is a comprehensive bibliography at the end, followed by a name-subject index.

B-44. Hearnshaw, F.J.C., ed. *Medieval Contributions to Modern Civilization: A Series of Lectures Delivered at King's College University of London.* New York: Henry Holt and Company, 1922.

The editor mentions two medieval contribution to modern civilization: the idealized, magnified, and indirect contributions as reflected in modern man, and the direct and actual contributions of the Middle Ages. Each essay includes references to linkages with the "learning of the Arabs."

There are ten essays: (1) Introductory: The Middle Ages and Their Characteristic Features by F.J.C. Hearnshaw, (2) The Religious Contribution of the Middle Ages by Rev. Claude Jenkins, (3) Philosophy by H. Wildon Carr, (4) Science by Charles Singer, (5) Art by Rev. Percy Dearmer, (6) The Middle Ages in the Lineage of English Poetry by Sir Israel Gollancz, (7) Education by J.W. Adamson, (8) Society by Hilda Johnstone, (9) Economics by E.R. Adair, (10) Politics by J.W. Allen.

The introductory essay identifies the period 600–1300 AD as "the heart of the Middle Ages," with succeeding two centuries as the "period of transition from the medieval to the modern" (p.20). The author discusses contacts with the East during the "heart" centuries, the period 1000–1300 AD being "undoubtedly the culmination and crown of the Middle Ages" (p.33). Several factors are identified. First, "Crusades had brought the semi-barbarians of the West into contact with the more highly cultivated denizens of the East. The rude knights found to their amazement that the infidels were not only soldiers but also men of a culture far superior to their own. Fanatical hostility had given place to respect and even friendship, and not a few Crusaders had accepted Islam as a purer faith than the debased Catholicism of their day. A new tolerance, a new scepticism, a new eclecticism, had resulted from this intermingling of East and West" (p.35–36).

Second, Crusades led to the development of commerce between Asia and Europe and command of the Mediterranean was secured by "monopolies of nobles and priests" (p.36). Third, "the learning of the Arabs began to reach the scholars of the Christian West" (p.36). Thus, "the advent of the modern spirit— secular, rationalistic, individual, adventurous, curious, anti-clerical, and often anti-Christian—was marked by a change of attitude toward the universe and man" (p.37). Thus, "bewildered by the rationalism of the Renaissance," the way was created for "new schism of the Protestant Reformation" (p.39).

Elsewhere, the author of the Science essay notes that the period between 400 and 1500 (identified as the "Age of Arabic Infiltration and Translation") is "divided by an event of the highest importance for the history of human intellect. Between the tenth and the end of the 12th century there was a remarkable out-burst of intellectual activity in Western Islam. This movement reacted with great effect on Latin Europe, and especially on its scientific views, by means of works translated from Arabic which gradually reached Christendom" (p.114).

The 270-page book provides little in terms of notes and references, and there is no index.

B-45. Hell, Joseph. *The Arab Civilization* (translated from German by S. Khuda Bukhsh). Cambridge: W. Heffer & Sons, 1926.

The book is a brief history of Arab civilization. According to the translator, it is written with "wide-mindedness, sympathy and clearness of vision"; moreover, it is "compact, accurate, felicitous in diction, and sound in judgment" (p.vii).

The 135-page book has six chapters: (1) Arabia Before Islam, (2) Mohamed, (3) Muslim Conquests, (4) The Omayyads, (5) Baghdad, (6) Muslim North Africa and Spain. The first chapter provides interesting facts and details as to the part Arabs played in antiquity before Islam and the culture and civilization they evolved. In his foreword, the translator is a bit critical of some aspects of the book. While appreciative of the chapter on the Prophet, he finds some faults. He finds chapters 3 and 4 "accurate, suggestive and well-written." Chapter 5 relates to Baghdad—once the center of learning and explorations, the focus of science and arts, the home of commerce; this chapter seems to receive special attention from the author and the translator. All of Baghdad's many-sided historical attri-butes are touched upon, and the city's resplendent glory is highlighted for the readers. Chapter 6 discusses Islamic Spain's history of achievements in art and architecture, literature and the sciences. The author says little about the decline of Islamic civilization; however, the translator provides his own views in the fore-word, along with some expression of hope and optimism.

The appendix provides a bibliography of literature, linked to each chapter, fol-lowed by a detailed name-subject index.

B-46. El-Hibri, Tayeb. *Reinterpreting Islamic Historiography: Harun al-Rashid and the Narrative of the Abbasid Caliphate.* Cambridge and New York: Cambridge University Press, 1999.

The history of the early Abbasid caliphate in the eighth and ninth centuries has been typically studied as a factual or interpretive synthesis of various accounts preserved in the medieval chronicles. But, argues the author, "the intertwining lines of fiction and fact in these works have never been clearly separated. What did the narratives about the caliphs signify in their times? How did anecdotes convey various levels of thematic meaning? To what extent were literary tropes appreciated and detected by the medieval audience?" (p.2).

This book breaks with the traditional approach in that it adopts a "literary-critical" reading to examine the lives of the caliphs. It differs from contemporary studies on the subject, "in that it is not concerned with establishing one or another picture of historical fact. Nor does it seek to build social, political, and religious interpretations on the basis of the chronicle's information. Rather, it adopts a literary-critical approach to reading the resources, based on a new set of propositions and assumptions aimed at established an originally intended meaning in the narratives" (p.13). By focusing on the reigns of Harun al-Rashid and his successors and the early Samarran period, the book demonstrates how the various historical accounts were not intended as faithful reflections of the past, but as devices used to explain controversial religious, political, and social issues of the period, as well as more abstract themes such as behavior, morality, and human destiny. The study also reveals how the exercise of decoding Islamic historiography, through an investigation of the narrative strategies and thematic motifs used in the chronicles, can uncover new interpretations.

The 236-page book contains six chapters: (1) Historical background and introduction, (2) Harun al-Rashid: Where it all started or ended, (3) Al-Amin: The challenge of regicide in Islamic memory, (4) Al-Ma'mum: The heretic Caliph, (5) The structure of civil war narratives, (6) Al-Mutawakkil: An encore of the family tragedy. There is also a concluding chapter in which the author emphasizes the "central point of this study, namely that the historical accounts of the early Abbasid caliphs were originally intended to be read not for facts, but for their allusive power. Their description of the lives of caliphs may seem realistic, but the narrators intended their anecdotes to form a frame for social, political, and religious commentary" (p.216).

There is a ten-page select bibliography at the end, organized in terms of primary and secondary sources, and a name-subject index.

B-47. Hill, Fred James and Nicholas Awde. *A History of the Islamic World.* New York: Hippocrene Books, Inc., 2003.

This concise book is designed to make the history of the Islamic world accessible to the general readers. It outlines developments from Islam's beginnings in seventh-century Arabia to the present day, including cultural, political, and religious developments. The authors note, however, "Sadly, despite enjoying a shared cultural and historical past, the political relationship between the two worlds [Islamic and Christian] is an uneasy one" (p.7). Further, the "constant flashpoints stemming from centuries-old disagreements detract from the parallel reality of peaceful and constructive co-existence. Islam is, after all, a religion that unites an international community with a way of life that reflects humankind from Morocco to China, from Kazan on the banks of the Volga to Fiji in the Pacific" (p.7).

The 215-page book is divided into three parts, with a total of 14 chapters. Part One, The Rise of Islam, has eight chapters: (1) Cradle of Islam, (2) The Arab Conquests and the Age of Empire, (3) The Abbasids and the Rise of Baghdad, (4) Al-Andalus: Islam in Spain, (5) The Mysticism of the Sufis, (6) The Crusades, (7) From Mongols to Mamluks, (8) Islam on the Periphery: Travels in Africa and Asia. Part Two, The Age of the Three Great Muslim Empires, has three chapters: (1) The Ottomans, (2) The Safavids and Shi'ism: Persia Reunified, (3) The Mughals in India. Part Three, Islam in the Twentieth and Twenty-First Centuries, has three chapters: (1) Creation of the Nation States, (2) Islam and the West: Facing Difficult Times, (3) Afterword: The Challenge of the Future.

The book also points to the numerous linkages between the early Islamic civilization and Latin Europe. In discussing Spain as "a catalyst for Western civilization," the authors discuss the contributions of Islamic Spain to the world of learning and its "vital role in the transference not only of Islamic scholarship to the West, but also Greek philosophical and scientific works that had long been lost to Christendom. These were works that would stimulate the European Renaissance and directly influence the scientific revolution that would lead to the ascendancy of Europe throughout the world" (p.80).

The book includes over 70 illustrations, maps, and photographs. At the end there is a chronological list of key dates in Islamic history (from the birth of Prophet Muhammad in 670 to the U.S. invasion of Iraq in 2003). Also, there is a chronological list of key figures and dynasties in Islamic history, followed by a glossary of Islamic terms. There is a name-subject index.

B-48. Hitti, Philip K. *The Arabs: A Short History.* Princeton, NJ: Princeton University Press, 1943.

"The following pages are addressed not to the scholar but to the general reader. They tell, very briefly, the story of the rise of Islam in the Middle Ages, its conquests, its empire, its time of greatness and decay. The story of the Arabians and the Arabic-speaking people unrolls before us one of the truly magnificent and instructive panoramas of history. Knowledge of the past throws new light on the present—the light of the perspective. It is hoped that this brief history of the Arab world will suggest how intimately a part of our own history it is" (p.iv). Further, "In the international melee today, the Arab often feels that he is the forgotten man. And it is the American, in particular, to whom he looks for under-standing and comprehension" (p.iv).

The 270-page book contains 19 chapters, each about 12–14 pages in length. Some illustrative titles are: Muhammad, the Prophet of Allah; Islam on the March; Conquest of Spain; The Glory That Was Baghdad; Science and Litera-ture; Cordova: Jewel of the World; Contributions to the West; The Cross Sup-plants the Crescent; and The Crusades. The author emphasizes that "between the middle of the eighth and the beginning of the thirteenth centuries, the Arabic-speaking peoples were the main bearers of the torch of culture and civilization throughout the world, the medium through which ancient science and philosophy were recovered, supplemented and transmitted to make possible the renaissance of Western Europe" (p.146). And, during late medieval centuries, "Arabic stud-ies were cultivated in several European universities, including Oxford and Paris, but with an entirely different motive: that of preparing Christian missionaries for the Moslem lands" (p.177).

Footnotes and references are integrated in the text of each chapter. There is a detailed index of names, places, and subject matter.

B-49. Hitti, Philip K. *History of the Arabs.* London: Macmillan and Company, 1943.

Originally published in 1937, this book is a classic on the subject. It furnishes exhaustive details about political events during nine centuries of an Arab-speak-ing world, essentially Islamic history. The author discusses the main features of economic, religious, literary, and artistic developments and points out how pro-foundly the Arab-Islamic civilization that became the heir of the whole legacy of the Ancient East affected the West during the Middle Ages. Throughout, the most conspicuous merit of the book is the author's emphasis that the significance of the Arab-Islamic history lies not so much in politics but in culture. The pages devoted to literature, art, and customs are more than those that extend to history proper. Hitti gives a comprehensive and candid picture of the multidimensional Arab-Islamic cultural life.

The 700-page book is divided into five parts with a total of 49 chapters: (1) The Pre-Islamic Age (seven chapters: the Arabs as semites; the Arabian penin-sula; Bedouin life; early international relations; the Sabaean and other states; the Nabataean and other petty kingdoms; al-Hijaz on the even of the rise of Islam); (2) The Rise of Islam and the Caliphal State (nine chapters: Muhammad the Prophet of Allah; The Koran the Book of Allah; Islam the religion of submission to the will of Allah; period of conquest, expansion and colonization, 632–661; the conquest of Syria; Al-Iraq and Persia conquered; Egypt, Tripolis and Barqah acquired; the administration of the new possessions; the struggle between Ali and Mu'awiyah for the Caliphate); (3) The Umayyad and Abbasid Empires (17 chap-ters: The Umayyad Caliphate; hostile relations with the Byzantines; the zenith of Umayyad power; political administration and social conditions; intellectual aspects of life; decline and fall of the dynasty; the establishment of the Abbasid dynasty; the golden prime of the Abbasids; the Abbasid state; Abbasid society; scientific and literary progress; education; the development of fine arts; Moslem sects; the Caliphate dismembered; sundry dynasties; the collapse of the Abbasid caliphate); (4) The Arabs in Europe: Spain and Sicily (nine chapters: conquest of Spain; the Umayyad amirate in Spain; civil disturbances; the Umayyad caliphate of Cordoba; political, economic and educational institutions; petty states: fall of Granada; intellectual contributions; art and architecture; Sicily); (5) The Last of the Medieval Moslem States (seven chapters: a Shi'ite caliphate in Egypt: the Fatimids; life in Fatimid Egypt; military contacts between east and west–the Crusades; cultural contacts; the Mamluks, last medieval dynasty of Arab world; intellectual and artistic activity; the end of the Mamluk rule).

The period covered is from the pre-Islamic era (BC era until the rise of Islam in 610) to the last medieval Arab-Islamic dynasty, the Mamluks, 1250–1517.

The book is augmented with 58 illustrations and 20 maps. There is an extensive name-subject index, with page numbers highlighted for items first mentioned in the text.

B-50. Hitti, Philip K. *Makers of Arab History.* New York: St. Martin's Press, 1968.

The 268-page book is intended to give students and interested laypersons an introduction to "the religious, political and other cultural movements in Arab-Islamic history through the lives of representative leaders," as selected by the author. While this book draws upon his other works (e.g., *History of the Arabs*), Hitti states that it is based on original sources available from more recent scholarship.

The book is divided in two parts. Part I is devoted to religious and political personalities, with seven chapters. It begins with the Islamic Prophet Muhammad, followed by chapters on Umar ibn-al-Khattab, Mu'awiyah, Abd-Al-Rahman, Al-Mamum, Ubaydullah Al-Mahdi, and Salah-Al-Din. Part II relates to Islamic intellectuals—Al-Ghazali, Al-Shafi, Al-Kindi, Ibn-Sina, Ibn Rushd, and Ibn-Khaldun. Especially with respect to the later, the author discusses not only the contributions of each but also their influence upon various Latin-European intellectuals.

Footnotes and references are integrated in the text of each chapter and there are eight maps indicating various aspects of Islamic history (e.g., Arabian peninsula at the time of Muhammad, 600 AD; Salah-al-din's conquests in Syria, Palestine, and Upper Mesopotamia; places visited by Ibn Khaldun) There is a detailed name-subject index.

B-51. Holt, P.M., Ann K.S. Lambton, and Bernard Lewis, eds. *The Cambridge History of Islam, Volume I, The Central Islamic Lands; Volume II, The Further Islamic Lands, Islamic Society and Civilization.* Cambridge and New York: Cambridge University Press, 1970.

These volumes, written by a group of eminent specialists, provide a comphrensive survey of the Islamic civilization over a period of 13 centuries up to the years following World War II. The purpose is to present Islam as a cultural whole and enable readers to assimilate all of the various threads—historical, theological, philosophical, political, economic, scientific, military, artistic—relevant to the rise, spread, and development of Islamic civilization.

Volume I (over 800 pages) begins with Arabia before the Prophet Mohammad and explores his career and the ensuing formation of the Arab Empire which reached its zenith under the 'Abbasid Dynasty (749–1158 AD). Later chapters describe the spread of Islam northeastward, Syria, Egypt, Turkey, and North Africa, and the transformation of Muslim history and society under the impact of those populations. The final chapters survey the influence of the West on the Central Muslim lands in recent times. This volume has four parts: Part I, The Rise and Domination of the Arabs (four chapters); Part II, The Coming of the Steppe Peoples (four chapters); Part III, The Central Islamic Lands in the Ottoman Period (eight chapters); Part IV, The Central Islamic Lands in Recent Times (seven chapters). There are several expository maps in the text and a glossary of Arabic words at the end. There is also a set of flow-charts of various Islamic dynasties and a comprehensive bibliography, both relevant to this particular volume, and a detailed 60-page name-subject index.

Volume II (about 1,000 pages) deals with Islam in the Indian subcontinent, South-East Asia, Spain, Sicily, and Africa, and brings the history of political developments to the years following World War II. The final chapters cover all aspects of the Islamic social and cultural history and the cultural contributions of the Islamic civilization. This volume is also divided into four parts as continuation of the previous volume: Part V, The Indian Sub-Continent (four chapters); Part VI, South-East Asia (three chapters); Part VII, Africa and the Muslim West (seven chapters); Part VIII, Islamic Society and Civilization (13 chapters). Part VIII especially covers the scholarly and scientific contributions, entitled The Transmission of Learning and Literary Influences to Western Europe.

As with volume I, there are several maps and some dynastic charts, along with a section of photographs (some never published before) illustrating Islamic art and architecture. There is a glossary of Arabic words, a comprehensive bibliography (different from that at the end of the first volume), and a 55-page name-subject index.

The editors suggest that no work of this magnitude has previously been available in the English language.

B-52. Hopwood, Derek, ed. *Studies in Arab History: The Antonius Lectures, 1978–87.* New York: St. Martin's Press, 1990.

The 190-page book is a collection of lectures, delivered at Oxford, England, by well-known scholars, in honor of George Antonius, a scholar of Arab/Middle-

Eastern studies, from 1978 to 1987. These lectures reflect "George Antonius's interests—historical, political, literary, topographical, all to do with some aspect of the Middle East, and more particularly with the relations between that area and the West" (p.ix).

The titles and authors of the 11 lectures are: (1) On the Origin and Development of the College in Islam and the West by George Makdisi, (2) *The Arab Awakening* Forty Years Later by Albert Hourani, (3) The Ottoman Conquest and the Development of the Great Arab Towns by Andre Raymond, (4) Muhammad Ali and Palmerston by Afaf Marsot, (5) George Antonius, Palestine and the 1930s by Thomas Hodgkin, (6) Cairo Memories by Magdi Wahba, (7) Ernest Bevin and Palestine by Harold Beeley, (8) Mouths of the Sevenfold Nile: English Fiction and Modern Egypt by Mahmud Manzalaoui, (9) The Meaning of the Dome of the Rock in Jerusalem by Oleg Grabar, (10) Space, Holiness and Time: Palestine in the Classical Arab Centuries by Tarif Khalidi, (11) Orientalism Again by Norman Daniels.

Each lecture provides its own notes and references at the end. There is no index.

B-53. Hourani, Albert. *A History of the Arab Peoples*. Cambridge, MA: Harvard University Press, 2002; original 1991.

Among the best of its kind, the book is about the history of the Arab-speaking parts of the Islamic world, from the rise of Islam until recently. The book is intended for general readers and students who wish to learn about a region that "is little and poorly understood in the West" (p.xvii). The author explores various dimensions of this rich civilization—the beauty of Alhambra and the great mosques, the importance attached to education, the achievements of the Arab science, and also internal conflicts, widespread poverty, the role of women, and the Palestinian question. Also narrated are topics such as expansion of Islam, the growth of the Ottoman empire, the expansion of Europe through trade and empire, and more contemporaneously, the challenge of Islamic resurgence and integration into the contemporary world dominated by the West. Throughout, social institutions and culture are intertwined with politics and economics, and there are references to prominent historic and contemporary scholars.

The 570-page book is divided into five parts, with several chapters in each, totaling 26. The parts are: (1) The Making of a World (seventh–tenth century)—four chapters (New Power in an Old World, The Formation of an Empire, The Formation of a Society, The Articulation of Islam); (2) Arab Muslim Societies (11th–15th century)—eight chapters (The Arab Muslim World, The Countryside, The Life of Cities, Cities and Their Rulers, Ways of Islam, The Culture of the 'Ulama, Divergent Paths of Thought, The Culture of Courts and People); (3) The Ottoman Age (16th–18th century)—three chapters (The Ottoman Empire, Ottoman Societies, The Changing Balance of Power in the Eighteenth Century); (4)

The Age of European Empires (1800–1939)—five chapters (European Power and Reform Governments, European Empires and Dominant Elites, The Culture of Imperialism and Reform, The Climax of European Power, Changing Ways of Life and Thought); (5) The Age of Nation States (since 1939)—six chapters (The End of the Empires, Changing Societies, National Culture, The Climax of Arabism, Arab Unity and Disunity, A Disturbance of Spirits).

The prologue pays special tribute to Ibn Khaldun (1332–1406), "the Arab philosopher of history whose theories of cyclical renewal and concept of *'asabiyya*—'a corporate spirit oriented towards obtaining and keeping power'— still provide a useful frame through which to view contemporary events" (p.460). There is a post-9/11 afterword written by Malise Ruthven in 2002 which applies the *'asabiyya* concept to various regimes in the Middle East, but which also seems applicable to the post-Iraq invasion of United States. Almost prophetically, this essay notes, "An attack on Iraq by Western countries considered by many Arabs and Muslims to be hostile towards the Islamic world as a whole could lead to further instability throughout the region. For good or ill the Arab experience is now ineradicably bound with that of the rest of the world" (p.469).

The book provides 39 illustrative pictures of various aspects of Arab history— religious, architectural, and sociocultural. Also, there are 12 maps. There is a section at the end that provides information on genealogies and various dynasties. A chapter-by-chapter listing of footnotes is followed by a general bibliography, as well as a comprehensive, 30-page chapter-by-chapter bibliography. There is an index of terms (Arabic and Turkish) and a name-subject index.

B-54. Issawi, Charles. *An Arab Philosophy of History: Selections from the* Prolegomena *of Ibn Khaldun of Tunis (1332–1406)* (translated and arranged by Charles Issawi). Princeton, NJ: The Darwin Press, Inc., 1987.

The purpose of the book is "to introduce the Arab historian and sociologist Ibn Khaldun to English-speaking readers by selecting from his *Prolegomena* passages chosen and grouped so as to present his views on such subjects as: History, Geography, Economics, Sociology, Politics, Metaphysics, and so on" (p.xi). It is intended for students in various fields, especially the social sciences, but also for those interested in the intellectual background of the Arab world. The writer has avoided "literal translation," so that the depth, originality, and "modernity" of Ibn Khaldun's thought is not obscured.

In order to facilitate comparison with corresponding topics in the social sciences, the selections are grouped according to subject matter. The order chosen is different from that provided by Ibn Khaldun, and the main outlines of the original Arabic can be identified from the opening selection in this volume. The author notes in the introduction that Ibn Khaldun's "*Prolegomena* represents the most comprehensive synthesis in the Human Sciences ever achieved by the Arabs, and gives the modern non-specialist reader an accurate picture of the range of knowledge available to the medieval Muslim world . . . and their influence over Europe was immense. But Ibn Khaldun, while profiting from their philosophical speculations, greatly surpassed them in his understanding of social problems" (p.1).

The 190-page book has ten chapters: (1) Method, (2) Geography, (3) Economics, (4) Public Finance, (5) Population, (6) Society and State, (7) Religion and Politics, (8) Knowledge and Society, (9) Theory of Being and Theory of Knowledge, (10) A Turning Point in History.

At the end there is a bibliography of texts, translations, and other studies (books and articles). There is a name-subject index.

B-55. Issawi, Charles. *The Arab World's Legacy: Essays by Charles Issawi.* Princeton, NJ: The Darwin Press, Inc., 1981.

The 375-page book is a collection of essays (all but two previously published), written by the author over a period of more than 30 years. A wide variety of topics are covered—cultural history, economic history, politics, demography—with one common theme: they deal with the Middle East, particularly its Arab component. The author states that some aspects of some of the essays are out of date, but the main conclusions and insights are essentially unchanged. Further, the time range covered is a long one—from the seventh to the 20th century; about half of the book is devoted to the formative period of classical Islamic civilization and the other half pertains to 19th- and 20th-century developments. The author argues, however, the past is intimately related to the present Middle East, and "no one wishing to understand contemporary trends can afford not to ask himself certain questions about the formative period of classical Islamic civilization" (p.9).

There are 22 essays in the book. Some representative titles are: The Christian-Muslim Frontier in the Mediterranean; The Contributions of the Arabs to Islamic Civilization; The Historical Role of Muhammad; Europe, the Middle East, and Shift in Power; Crusades and the Current Crises in the Near East; The Arab World's Heavy Legacy; Economic and Social Foundation of Democracy in the Middle East; The Entrepreneurial Class; Schools of Economic History and the Middle East; and The Change in the Western Perception of the Orient.

Each essay provides notes and references at the end. There is a name-subject index.

B-56. Izzeddin, Nejla. *The Arab World: Past, Present, and Future.* Chicago: Henry Regnery Company, 1953.

While much of this 412-page book focuses on the "current state of affairs" (1950s), with anticipations for the future, there are two chapters that discuss Islamic history and its legacy. Chapters 2 and 3, The Cultural Heritage and The Arabs and the West in the Middle Ages, respectively, provide a wealth of historical material. Other chapters have titles such as The Eclipse, Cross Currents, The

Arab Revolt, Egypt's Political/Social Struggles, Syria and Lebanon, Iraq, Palestine, The Arab Women, and Arab Unity.

In chapter 2 (The Cultural Heritage), the author argues, "The broad humanity of Islam was responsible for its broad success and its hold upon those who embraced it" (p.22). And a Byzantine patriarch is quoted, in that Arabs/Muslims "are not enemies of Christianity. On the contrary they praise our faith and honor the priests and saints of the Lord and confer benefits upon the churches and monasteries" (p.23). The Moslem society "recognized the values of diversity within the general pattern, and was hospitable to a variety of views and concepts" (p.24). There are references to Arabic literature, language, sponsorship of learning, economic pursuits, the role of the individual as his own religious teacher and guide, and so forth.

Chapter 3 (The Arabs and the West in the Middle Ages) provides a fuller description of Arab-Islamic civilization in the medieval period, how it "directly influenced contemporary Europe" and led to "qualities and contributions which have become a permanent possession of all who share the Western heritage" (p.35). The chapter identifies the works of various Arab scholars in different fields, along with the manner and sources of transmission of that knowledge to Latin-European scholars. In addition, there is discussion of cultural transmission through Crusades and other sources. A French medievalist is quoted: "The Arab-Moslem thinkers—Farabi, Ghazali, Ibn Sina, Ibn Rushd, Ibn Khaldun, and many others; the mystics—Ibn Al-Arabi, Al-Hallaj, Ibn al-Faridh; the works of the mathematicians, physicists, music theorists, biologists, physicians, geographers and travelers; the architectural monuments, the Dome of the Rock—'a symphony of lines and colors'; the Omayyad Mosque in Damascus, the Mosque of Cordova, Alhambra; all these and much besides are an integral part of the cultural effort of civilized humanity" (p.56). Further, "The impact of the Arabs upon Medieval Europe was a leaven which liberated the spirit and awakened the dormant creative impulse" (p.56).

There are other chapters with titles such as Egypt since 1918: The Political Struggle, The Arab Island, Palestine, The Arab Woman, The Powers in the Arab World, and The Greater Struggle.

Numerous footnotes, including bibliographic references, are integrated in each chapter, and there is a detailed name-subject index.

B-57. Japan Foundation. *The Islamic World and Japan: In Pursuit of Mutual Understanding.* Tokyo, Japan: Park Building, 3-6 Kioi-cho, Chiyoda-ku, 1981.

This volume represents the proceedings from the sixth annual international symposium, beginning 1975, sponsored by the Japan Foundation, focusing particularly on cultural exchange between Japan and the developing countries. The theme of this gathering was "Islamic Civilization and Japan," partly because, as the keynote speaker acknowledged, "how ignorant we are of Islamic civilization and yet how important that civilization is to us" (p.3). And, further, it is a means to build a framework for understanding, for, "until now, efforts to achieve mutual understanding have by and large been made using frameworks devised by Europeans" (p.4).

The proceedings included 19 papers, grouped in six sections, entitled: (1) Problems in Modernization, (2) Perception of Different Cultures: Cases of Civilization Encounters, (3) Patterns of Thought, (4) Arts: Human Life and Space, (5) The Individual and Society, (6) In Absentia (two papers presented in absentia). While not all papers seem relevant to the present task, three papers in section 2 are especially appropriate: (1) A Contribution to the Cultural and Linguistic Debate on the Contact between the West and the Arabo-Moslem World by Salah Garmadi, (2) Islamic Civilization as Seen from Japan: A Non-Western View by Shuntaro Ito, (3) Perception of Different Cultures: The Islamic Civilization and Japan by Yuzo Itagaki.

Of these, Shuntaro Ito's observations are particularly noteworthy. While studying Latin paleography at the University of Wisconsin in the 1960s, he "was totally shocked to discover that until Europe entered the 'Twelfth-Century Renaissance,' by way of Arabic learning, it had been lurking on the outskirts of world civilization, almost unaware of Euclid, Archimedes, Ptolemy or Aristotle. Like many a western scholar, I had till then thought of the history of the world civilization in terms of a transition from Greece to Rome and to Western Europe. It was this experience with old manuscripts that opened my eyes to the importance and majesty of Arabic civilization" (p.132). Further, "A linear view of a Greco-Roman-Mediterranean-European progression is a Eurocentric view of history, fabricated by European historians after the *fait accompli* of nineteenth-century European world domination. It is biased and does not accurately reflect historical facts" (p.133). And, Ito continues, "Consciously or unconsciously, Europeans have been unable to throw off their colonialist mentality in their understanding of Islam. But we Japanese have the comparative advantage of greater distance and are in a position to examine and evaluate the significance of Islamic culture from the perspective of world history. We can do this fairly and without prejudice, without forcing our own position on anyone" (p.138).

Each paper provides notes and references at the end. There is no index.

B-58. Kapoor, Subodh, ed. *The Muslims: Encyclopedia of Islam*, 11 volumes. New Delhi, India: Cosmo Publications, 2004.

One of the most comprehensive anthologies on Islam and Muslims, this encyclopedia of Islam proposes to give its readers full and authoritative information on the entire spectrum of Islamic religion, history, and civilization: Islamic teachings, Islam's role in the evolution of humankind, Islam's struggles, triumphs, and achievements of its followers, not only for its own immediate benefit but for the broadening and deepening of all true science, literature, and art. This work claims to differ from all previous attempts, in that it is not limited to the geographic and historic knowledge of Islam. It records all that Islam has done, not only in the field of religion and philosophy, but in the intellectual and artistic development of humanity. It chronicles what Islamic artists, educators, poets, philosophers, scientists, and men of action—historic and contemporary—achieved in their several areas. One key reason for this venture is said to be Islam's pervasiveness and widespread influence.

The encyclopedia endeavors to encompass the whole range of Islamic theology and philosophy together with the relevant coverage of its history, economics, politics, sociology, as well as the arts, the music, and the architecture. Also covered are sciences—medicine, alchemy, mathematics, astronomy, astrology, etc. The readers will also find entries concerning Islamic perspectives on a wide range of controversial issues, such as feminism, marriage, eating habits, drugs and drinking, sexuality, abortion, and gambling. There are articles on almost all aspects of Islamic civilization—religious beliefs and customs, ethical movements, philosophical and religious ideas, moral and spiritual practices, etc. All important scholars in the entire spectrum of Islamic philosophical and historical systems have been included in the compendium. Entries have been prepared by a number of eminent Orientalists and Islamic scholars.

Each of the 11 volumes is identified alphabetically in terms of the topics covered: (1) A–Arabic, pages 1–350, (2) Arabs–Buath, pages 351–704, (3) Calendar–Ethic, pages 705–1056, (4) Ethics–Indo-China, pages 1057–1406, (5) Inheritance–Al-Kimiya, pages 1407–1750, (6) Al-Kindi–Mantik, pages 1751–2070, (7) Marriage–Mutawwif, pages 2071–2392, (8) Al-Mutazila–Qur'an, pages 2393–2706, (9) Rabab–Shi'ite, pages 2707–3028, (10) Sin–Turkoman, pages 3029–3390, (11) Turks–Z, Bibliography and Glossary, pages 3029–3390.

There is a comprehensive bibliography and name-subject index at the end.

B-59. Kennedy, Hugh. *The Early Abbasid Caliphate: A Political History*. London: Croom Helm, 1981.

The 240-page book is a narrative on the political history of the early Abbasid Caliphate; it does not pretend to be a general history of the period. The author argues that this period (from the Abbasid Revolution to the restoration of the Ma'mun's authority) "is more than just the backdrop to an age of cultural efflorescence. For the student of politics and political science it is fascinating to see how so many diverse peoples and countries were brought under the control of a single regime. The early Abbasid system also represented a sustained attempt to reconcile the ideals of Islam with the demands and constraints of secular government. The problems faced by the early Abbasid caliphs in this respect are very similar to those faced by some Islamic governments today" (p.17). The purpose of the book, the author says, is twofold: to introduce the period to the readers, both historians and Arabists, and to suggest some new problems and approaches to the expert.

For the most part, the book is arranged in terms of chronological developments. The 12 chapter titles are: (1) The Geographical Background, (2) The Origins of the Abbasid Revolution, (3) Saffah: The Laying of the Foundation, (4) Mansur: The Years of Struggle, (5) Mansur: The Consolidation of Power, (6) The Reigns of Mahdi and Hadi, (7) Harun Al-Rashid, (8) The Great Civil War: I, (9) The Great Civil War: II, (10) Ma'mun: An Age of Transition, (11) Patterns of Provincial Power, (12) Alid Rebellions in the Early Abbasid Period.

The book provides useful genealogical tables, maps, and a glossary of Arabic terms. Notes and references are provided at the end of each chapter, and there is a bibliography of sources at the end, followed by a name-subject index.

B-60. Kennedy, Hugh. *The Prophet and the Age of the Caliphates: The Islamic Near East from the Sixth to Eleventh Century.* London and New York: Longman Group Ltd., 1986.

The 425-page book is an introduction to the history of the Near East in the early Islamic period, from the time of the Prophet to the upheaval with the arrival of the Seljuk Turks in the mid-fifth/eleventh century. The author has tried to balance factual material and speculative interpretation, keeping in mind readers who look for a basic framework of chronological narrative of Near East history. Further, the book attempts "to avoid the impression that Islamic history is full of ephemeral rulers and pointless battles and to devote space to long-term social and economic changes and to positive aspects of Muslim government and the immense achievements of the period which are too often neglected in Western writing" (p.ix).

The first half of the book provides a comprehensive account of the Near East before Islam: the birth of the Islamic state, the life of the Prophet, and the rise and fall of both the Ummayad and Abbasid Caliphates. The second half spans a complex period characterized by the growth and expansion of the Muslim community in the Near East—the community described by the author as the "Muslim Commonwealth," a galaxy of regional centers each developing its own political society and culture. The break-up of the Caliphate, according to the author, was a natural product of its own success—an evolution from a Muslim empire ruled by a small elite to a series of regions dominated by local men, with diminishing loyalty to the Caliph.

The book contains 12 chapters: (1) The Matrix of the Muslim World: The Near East in the Early Seventh Century, (2) The Birth of the Islamic State, (3) Conquest and Division in the Time of the Rashidun Caliphs, (4) The Ummayad Caliphate, (5) The Early Abbasid Caliphate, (6) The Middle Abbasid Caliphate, (7) The Structure of Politics in the Muslim Commonwealth, (8) The Buyid Confederation, (9) The Kurds, (10) The Hamdanids, (11) Bedouin Political Movements and Dynasties, (12) Early Islamic Egypt and the Fatimid Empire. There is a postscript chapter, The Coming of the Seljuks.

There are several useful maps and genealogical tables in the book. While there are no notes and references tied to the text chapters, there is a topical list of suggested readings at the end, followed by a glossary of important Arabic words. There is a detailed name-subject index.

B-61. Kennedy, Hugh. *When Baghdad Ruled the Muslim World: The Rise and Fall of Islam's Greatest Dynasty*. Cambridge, MA: DaCapo Press (Perseus Books Group), 2005.

This 350-page book, originally published as *The Court of the Caliphs: The Rise and Fall of Islam's Greatest Dynasty* (2004), is "intended to tell the story of the Abbasid caliphs and their court in the two centuries that constituted their golden age" (p.ix). Presently, Baghdad is associated with violence and insurgency; but more than a thousand years ago this city was the center of arts and the global sciences, a city of dreams and limitless opportunities.

Chronicling the first two of the five centuries of Abbasid rule (749–1258), the author acquaints readers with an important segment of Islamic history, perhaps best known to Western readers as the period setting for fictional *Arabian Nights*. He recounts the struggles and contests for successions to the caliphate, with details on the accompanying political tensions; yet, he states, the Abbasid caliphate produced a munificent court culture, reveling in its richness of varied scholarship and architecture. Further, "The Abbasid caliphate in the eighth and ninth centuries was as central and pivotal to world history as the Roman Empire was in the first and second." The author hopes "this book will go a little way towards making the world of the Abbasid caliphs a part of the world view of educated people in the way in which the world of ancient Greece and Rome already is" (p.xxiii–xxiv). Combining academic rigor and accessibility, the book is a compelling reading for anyone concerned with the perils of power, the medieval Islamic legacy, and the images that Baghdad continues to conjure in the modern imagination.

There are ten chapters: (1) Revolution, (2) Mansur and His Legacy, (3) Harun al-Rashid: The Golden Prime, (4) The War between the Brothers, (5) Poetry and Power at the Early Abbasid Court, (6) Landscape with Palaces, (7) The Harem, (8) Ma'mun to Mutawwakil, (9) Abbasid Court Culture, (10) High Noon in Samarra.

The book provides several illustrations, maps, genealogy, and a timeline of the Abbasid Caliphate. Chapter-by-chapter notes and references are provided at the end, followed by a bibliography. There is also a name-subject index.

B-62. Khalidi, Tarif. *Classical Arab Islam: The Culture and Heritage of the Golden Age*. Princeton, NJ: The Darwin Press, Inc., 1985.

This short, provocative book is primarily concerned with *Arab* Islamic culture (i.e., Islamic literature written in Arabic, since Arabic was the principal language of Islam) of the classical period—the period roughly stretching from the seventh to the 13th centuries. But it is more; it is about modern "Arab Muslims [who] are locked into Islamic culture far more politically than any modern Western scholar is locked into his own medieval West." Further, the "modern Arab Muslim scholar is constantly forced to come to grips with issues that are a thousand years old or more but that still retain enormous contemporary vividness and polemicability." Thus, there are "'Orientalist' Arab Muslim scholars who see Arab Islamic culture through Western eyes" (p.8).

There are 11 chapters: (1) The Foundations, (2) God and His Message, (3) Muhammad and His Community, (4) Islamic Paideia, (5) Attitudes Towards the Past, (6) The Mystic Quest, (7) The Place of Reason, (8) The World of Nature, (9) The Governance of the *Umma*, (10) Ibn Khaldun: The Great Synthesis, (11) Past and Present in Contemporary Arabic Thought.

The 160-page book ends with a bibliographical essay, a glossary of Arabic proper names and terms, and a name-subject index.

B-63. Knowles, David. *The Evolution of Medieval Thought.* Baltimore, MD: Helicon Press, Inc., 1962.

The book is an "endeavour to present medieval or scholastic philosophy as a direct continuation of Greek thought, colored though it may be by its surroundings, and impoverished by many losses, but also fertilized and enriched by Christian teaching" (p.ix).

The 337-pages are divided into five parts: (1) The Legacy of the Ancient World (five chapters); (2) The Renaissance of the Eleventh and Twelfth Centuries (seven chapters); (3) The New Universities: The Rediscovery of Aristotle (five chapters); (4) The Achievement of the Thirteenth Century (six chapters); (5) The Breakdown of the Medieval Synthesis (five chapters). The book ends with an epilogue.

It is in the second part of the book where, in discussing the numerous early-medieval Latin scholars and monks, there are references to the Arab-Islamic scholars whose influence lurks behind the Latin names. Thus, the Western awakening resulted from "the outward thrust of the northern peoples into south Italy, the East and especially into Spain, brought into contact with centres of civilization, hitherto unfamiliar, which contained treasures from the past of which they hitherto had no knowledge" (p.186). These were Greek and Arabic treasures, but "the broad fact remains that the Arabs of Spain were the principal source of the new learning for Western Europe" (p.187). Further, "The Arabian thinkers handed over a legacy of their own to the Latins. It has often been repeated that the Arabs were not creative thinkers, and it is true that they did not originate a totally new system of thought. It might nevertheless be claimed that the system of Aristotle underwent at their hands a change similar, if not as thorough, to that experienced by Plato's system at the hands of the Neoplatonists, or Aristotle himself in the thirteenth century at the hands of Aquinas" (p.195). The author does not mention that the Aquinas synthesis (*Summa Theologica*) was substantially influenced by several Islamic scholastics, Al-Ghazali in particular but also Al-Kindi, Ibn Sina, Al-Farabi, and Ibn Rushd.

The fourth and fifth parts of the book discuss the "achievement of the thirteenth century" and "the breakdown of the medieval synthesis," respectively. The Franciscan school of thought, in contrast to the Dominican school, was inspired by the Great Commentator, Ibn Rushd (Averroes), and was led by Siger of Brabant, says the author. There is a chapter on St. Thomas Aquinas, but with scant reference to his influential Arab-Islamic sources. And the breakdown of the medieval synthesis was substantially induced by the Aristotelian rationalism, introduced to Latin Europe through the scholarship of Ibn Rushd particularly (some of his writings were condemned in 1277 as "Averroestic heresies").

There is a list of selective readings at the end (however, some key literature on the 12th-century renaissance is not listed; for example, omitted is Charles Homer Haskins, *The Renaissance of the Twelfth Century*, Harvard University Press, Cambridge, MA, 1927). There is a combined name-subject index.

B-64. Lacroix, Paul. *Science and Literature in the Middle Ages and the Renaissance*. New York: Frederick Ungar Publishing Company, 1964; original 1878.

This book on the scientific revival of Europe during the Middle Ages is a classic of its kind. The author begins with pointing out the fifth-century demise of the Greek and Roman civilizations at the hands of the Barbarians, and "everywhere darkness succeeded." The author says, "The religion of Jesus Christ was alone capable of resisting this barbarian invasion, and science and literature, together with the arts, disappeared from the face of the earth, taking refuge in the churches and monasteries" (p.v). And, Europe thus "witnessed a general revival of scholastic zeal; poets, orators, novelists, and writers increased in numbers and grew in favour; savants, philosophers, chemists and alchemists, mathematicians and astronomers, travellers and naturalists, were awakened, so to speak, by the life-giving breath of the Middle Ages; great scientific discoveries and admirable works on every imaginable subject showed that the genius of modern society was not a whit inferior to that of antiquity" (p.vi). While not explicitly mentioned, the revival is the consequence of contacts with the "pagan" world of Islam and the Arabs. This becomes clear as one glances through the rest of this 550-page volume.

The book contains 18 chapters: (1) Universities, Schools, Students, (2) Philosophic Sciences, (3) Mathematical Sciences, (4) Natural Sciences, (5) Medical Sciences, (6) Chemistry and Alchemy, (7) The Occult Sciences, (8) Popular Beliefs, (9) Geographical Science, (10) Heraldic Science, (11) Proverbs, (12) Languages, (13) Romances, (14) Popular Songs, (15) National Poetry, (16) Chronicles, (17) The Drama, (18) Civil and Religious Oratory.

The first six chapters, covering 200 pages, in particular make extensive references to the knowledge acquired from the Arabs and "Mahometan" schools, scholars, and commentators (in particular, Averroes [Ibn Rushd, 1126–1198]). It was in the East, the author notes, "that the pursuit of mathematics, applied to the study of astronomy, had acquired the greatest impetus. The Caliph Haroun Alraschid constituted himself protector of mathematical sciences, which fitted in so well with the genius and tendencies of his people" (p.80). Further, "The exact sciences continued to be taught and to make progress amongst the Greeks, the Eastern peoples, and the Arabs in Spain. Astronomy was still the favourite science in the Mussulman schools, and the wise men of Islam were always drawing up astronomical tables" (p.84). As for Roger Bacon of the 12th century, "he had become a dupe of Arabism of Albumazar and the Aristotelism of Averroes, and that he acquiesced in all the wild conceptions of astrology and alchemy" (p.91). Such developments "were the preludes of the Reformation, which made its presence felt in science by proclaiming the right of free examination before applying it to the dogmas of religion" (p.95). Elsewhere, the author notes, "The light of science emanated chiefly from the Saracen schools in Spain" (p.110). Referring to Avicenna (Ibn Sina), the author states, "Among the numerous works in Arabic which he left behind, that entitled the 'Cannon,' a medical encyclopedia, which testifies to the erudition and sagacity of the author, was translated into Latin, and served as a basis of teaching for six centuries" (p.146). Further, the Baghdad Academy ("House of Wisdom") "gave a great impetus during the ninth century to the sciences of observation, to the experimental methods, and consequently to physics and chemistry" (p.176).

Other chapters provide interesting information as to the "pagan" festivals of the then Catholic hierarchy. The chapter on "Popular Beliefs" describes celebrations such as the Feast of Buffoons and the Festival of the Ass; the latter included a "Mass of the Ass," in which "all the congregation brayed in chorus in imitation of an ass" (p.243).

The book includes sketches of more than 400 fascinating wood engravings (some titles: How Alexander Fought the Dragons with Sheep's Horns upon Their Foreheads; Noah's Ark: Miniature of a Commentary upon the Apocalypse; The Image of Dame Astrology, with the Three Fates; Coronation of Charlemagne in the City of Jerusalem; The Prince of Darkness: After a Miniature of the "Holy Grail"). The author provides no notes or citations, and there is no bibliography. There are some references to other literature in the text, however. There is no index.

B-65. Landau, Rom. *Islam and the Arabs*. New York: Macmillan Company, 1959.

Written by an eminent scholar, the book's introductory statement conveys its purpose. Neither Islam nor the Arabs have been treated over-generously by Western scholars, the author suggests. Yet even a glance at a newspaper reveals how intricately the future of the Western world is bound up with that of the Near East—the cradle of both Islam and Arabism. "Western civilization owes so much to that [Islamic] civilization that unless we have some knowledge of the latter we must fail to comprehend the former," he argues (p.7).

Written at the request of his students, the author says, the book is designed for the general reader. The word "Arabs" and "Muslims" are used synonymously, though it is recognized there are also Arab Christians. He reduces the long, involved history of the Arabs to a clear and absorbing survey of Arab civilization. The Western debt to Islam is traced in the areas of philosophy, mathematics, medicine, agriculture, the arts, the literature, and so forth. The major portion of the book is devoted to the golden age of Arab civilization and linkages with Latin Europe; also covered is a summary of contemporary issues. The author notes the book was completed before the 1958 Iraqi Revolution. The impact of the Islamic philosophy, "the intellectual beacon in the darkness of the early Middle Ages," is noted, which, "apart from transmitting, interpreting and developing the wisdom of the Greeks, it taught Christian thinkers how to reconcile philosophy and religion" (p.160).

The 300-page book contains 13 chapters: (1) Arabia before the Prophet, (2) The Prophet, the Koran and Islam, (3) The Caliphate (Umayyads and Abbasids), (4) From the Caliphate to the End of the Ottomans, (5) The Crusades, (6) The Maghreb (Morocco, Algeria, Tunisia), (7) Muslim Spain, (8) The Sharia, (9) Philosophy, (10) The Sciences, (11) Literature, (12) The Arts, (13) Problems of the Present Arab World. The author presents two chronological tabulations. First, the various philosophical developments are discussed (identified with names such as al-Kindi, al-Farabi, Ibn Sina, al-Ghazali, Ibn Hazm, Ibn Bajjah, Ibn Tufayl, Ibn Rushd, Ibn Arabi). The influence of each on various European scholars (Roger Bacon, St. Thomas Aquinas, Maimonides, Albertus Magnus, Dante, and so forth) is noted (p.161–164). Second, various developments in arts (architecture, pottery and glass, textiles, metalwork, leatherwork, painting, and carpets) and the impact of each on similar developments in the West are discussed (p.235–236).

Each chapter provides a brief list of recommended reading. At the end there is a country-by-country chronology of major events in the modern Arab world. There is a detailed bibliography, followed by a name-subject index.

B-66. Lane, Rose Wilder. *The Discovery of Freedom: Man's Struggle Against Authority*. New York: John Day Company, 1943; third edition 1993.

The book is the expanded version of another book that was derived from this: Henry Grady Weaver, *The Mainspring of Human Progress*, New York: The Foundation for Economic Education, Inc., 1953. Much of the content is about the same. Part One, The Old World, has five chapters: (1) The Pagan Faith, (2) Communism, (3) The Living Authorities, (4) The Planned Economies, (5) War. Part Two, The Revolution, also has five chapters: (1) The First Attempt, (2) The Second Attempt, (3) The Feudal System, (4) The English Liberties, (5) The Third Attempt (with sections: Americans, Without a Leader, The People's War, Democracy, The Rights of Property, The Constitution, The Right to Vote, Republicanism, The Republic Survives, The Industrial Revolution, The World Revolution).

Part One traces the global dismal conditions of life over centuries—and how individual liberty attempted to unleash solutions. Also, there is discussion of approaches that did not work (Paganism, Communism, Planned Economies). Part Two begins with the "Revolution" that almost worked. Here the author talks of the "First Attempt" that began 4,000 years ago with Abraham in Iraq (Ur), but failed because his followers "went back to pagan submission to an imaginary authority" (p.78). Later, the new commandment of Christ emphasized human brotherhood, but while there were glimmers of hope, the author states, nowhere were to be found the God-given rights of freedom.

As with the other book, the author argues that the idea of individual freedom emerged from Islam's religious individualism; this is "The Second Attempt" of Part Two. Europe was still stagnating, and several centuries before Britain had its Magna Carta a dynamic civilization emerged whose prophet insisted that "there be no priests. Each individual must recognize his direct relation to God, his self-controlling, personal responsibility" (p.83). And, during European Dark Ages, "the world was actually bright with an energetic, brilliant civilization, more akin to American civilization. Millions upon millions of human beings, thirty generations, believing that all men are equal and free, created that civilization and kept on creating it for eight hundred years. To them the world owes modern science—mathematics, astronomy, modern medicine and surgery, scientific agriculture. To them the world directly owes the discovery and the exploration of America" (p.86). Further, "Since American scholars and intellectuals in general are European-minded, an American can get only glimpses of the Saracens' world, seen through European indifference and hatred" (p.87). "Through Italy, the Saracens gave Europeans 'the awakening' of Europe," the author adds, and "through Spain, the last flare of their energy gave the world the discovery of America. Of course Columbus did not discover America" (p.114).

And this was the "Third Attempt." The discovery, exploration, and early colonization of America are closely connected with the Spanish Inquisition, the author suggests. And, it is noted, the voyage of Columbus would hardly have been possible except for the magnetic compass developed by the Saracens, as well as maps and navigation charts. The succeeding sections discuss the outstanding material progress of America, based on individual freedom and opportunities. It also talks of the moral dilemma and war potential of this material progress.

While there are occasional footnotes in this 265-page book, there is no bibliography and no index.

B-67. Lapidus, Ira M. *A History of Islamic Societies*, second edition. Cambridge: Cambridge University Press, 2002.

This 1,000-page book is one of the most comprehensive narratives on the history of Islamic societies. In a single volume a vast amount of material is synthesized and presented in a clear and effective style. The author is concerned not so much with defining an essential Islam, but rather with mapping the role of Islamic beliefs, institutions, and identities in particular historical contexts. He explores the origins and evolution of Muslim societies across the world. His over-arching vision brings perspective and coherence to a rich and diverse history, which he has updated and revised in this second edition.

The book is divided into three parts. Part One (The Origins of Islamic Civiliza-tion, The Middle East from 600–1200; 12 chapters) covers the formative era of Islamic civilization from the origins to the 13th century. Part Two (The World-wide Diffusion of Islamic Societies from the Tenth to the Nineteenth Century; 9 chapters) traces the creation of similar societies in the Balkans, North Africa, Central Asia, China, India, Southeast Asia and sub-Saharan Africa. And Part Three (The Modern Transformation: Muslim Peoples in the Nineteenth and Twentieth Centuries; 11 chapters) explores the interface of these societies with European imperialism and describes how they emerged in the twentieth century as independent states.

The concluding chapter examines Islam's most recent history, including a dis-cussion of Islamic secularization and revival. Throughout the author engages the reader with the social structures of these societies, along with numerous illustra-tive expressions of the richness of the Islamic civilization—language, theology, philosophy and law, science, art, and architecture.

There are numerous illustrations, figures, maps, and tables. There is a glossary of terms and concepts at the end, along with a 60-page bibliography and a detailed name-subject index.

B-68. Lapidus, Ira M. *Muslim Cities in the Later Middle Ages*. Cambridge, MA: Harvard University Press, 1967.

The book is a study of the social structure and political processes of several Muslim cities in the late Middle Ages, including the "dynamic interactions between different classes and groups of the populations which created communal and political order" (p.vii). Further, "This book may also serve as a commentary on the problem of why European cities were organized as communes" and why Asian and Muslim cities "were autonomous self-governing associations" (p.vii). The book focuses on Damascus, Aleppo, and Cairo during the Mamluk Empire (1250–1517), with supporting discussion of other cities—Alexandria, Beirut, Tripoli, and some smaller towns. Sources of the study include chronicles, bio-graphies, inscriptions, descriptions of towns, administrative manuals, travelers' accounts, diplomatic communications, treaties, works of art, and archeological and artistic remains.

The 310-page book contains six comprehensive chapters: (1) A History of Cities in the Mamluk Empire, (2) The Mamluk Regime in the Life of the Cities, (3) The Urban Society, (4) The Political System: The Mamluk State and the Urban Notables, (5) The Political System: The Common People Between Vio-lence and Impotence, (6) Conclusion: Society and Polity in Medieval Muslim Cities.

The author concludes that "European and Muslim urban societies had by the late middle ages evolved two differing overall urban social configurations. Muslim society tended to be relatively undifferentiated" (p.185). However, "by contrast, European urban society was much more highly segmented. Strong cultural and emotional underpinnings supported interests and functions in dividing the classes of the society. The nobility was virtually a caste apart, with its own ethic, occupation, and internal system of feudal law and obligations. Even more than the Mamluks the nobles were divorced from contact with urban society. Their ties with the church were close, but ties with the bourgeoisie were scarcely formed" (p.186).

There are five appendices at the end (waqfs; institutional constructions and repairs—Damascus; institutional constructions and repairs—Aleppo; Karimi [merchants in the spice trade]; Tajir-Khwaja [merchants with official ranking]). There is a 25-page detailed bibliography, classified in terms of primary sources, secondary works, and bibliographies, followed by a detailed, 50-page chapter-by-chapter listing of notes and references. There is also a detailed name-subject index.

B-69. Laroui, Abdallah. *The History of the Maghrib: An Interpretative Essay* (translated from French by Ralph Manheim). Princeton, NJ: Princeton University Press, 1977.

The book, written by a Moroccan scholar, presents a history of the Maghrib, usually referring to North Africa and typically inclusive of Algeria, Morocco, Tunisia, and sometimes even Egypt, Libya, and Sudan. This "interpretative essay" contrasts significantly with much that has been written by European scholars (mainly French), especially those of the colonial period. The author is critical of the colonial impressions of the Maghrib that continue to be adopted and adapted rather uncritically by Western scholars. He says, "A familiar theme in the histories written during the colonial period is that the Maghrib has been unfortunate: unfortunate in not having recognized the Roman conquest as a bringer of civilization, unfortunate in having been forced to accept Islam, unfortunate in having undergone the Hilalian invasion, and unfortunate in having served as a base for the Ottoman pirates" (p.3). But, continues the author, "might there not be more reason to speak of a very different misfortune? That of always having inept historians: geographers with brilliant ideas, functionaries with scientific pretensions, soldiers priding themselves on their culture, art historians who refuse to specialize, and, on a higher level, historians without linguistic training or linguists and archeologists without historical training. All these historians refer the reader back to each other and invoke each other's authority. The consequence is a conspiracy which puts the most adventurous hypotheses into circulation and ultimately imposes them as established truths" (p.3).

The 432-page book is divided into four parts, with several chapters in each (a total of 15 chapters, plus the concluding chapter). Part I, The Maghrib under Domination, with four chapters: (1) The Search for Origins, (2) Colonizer Fol-

lows Colonizer, (3) Conqueror Succeeds Conquerors, (4) The Winning of Autonomy; Part II, The Imperial Maghrib, with five chapters: (5) Islam and Commerce:
The Ninth Century, (6) Eastern Forces for Unity: The Fatimid and Zirid Ventures,
(7) Western Forces for Unity: The Almoravid Venture, (8) Western Forces for
Unity: The Almohad Venture, (9) The Failure of the Imperial Idea; Part III, Institutional Stagnation, with three chapters: (10) The Western Crusade, (11) Two
Reactions, Two Powers, (12) The Eve of Foreign Intervention; Part IV, The Colonial Maghrib, with three chapters: (13) Colonial Pressure and Primary Resistance, (14) The Triumph of Colonialism, (15) The Renascent Maghrib.

In the concluding chapter the author is a bit eclectic about the colonial experience and says, "The Maghrib has now been independent for a decade. Despite all
the ideas popularized by government propaganda, the problem remains politico-
cultural. Economic underdevelopment will never be overcome until social and
cultural underdevelopment have been diagnosed and combated, and that calls for
a questioning of the past" (p.385). Among other things, the author says, "Despite
our sometimes justified harangues about democracy and justice in Islam, we must
recognize that the political structure which Islam engendered, and which foreign
pressure solidified or fossilized, was not equal to modern needs and never will
be" (p.385).

At the end an appendix provides a chronology of principal dynasties that ruled
the region. There is a 22-page bibliography of literature in French, Arabic, and
English languages, followed by a name-subject index.

B-70. Lewis, Bernard, ed. and trans. *Islam: From the Prophet Muhammad to the
Capture of Constantinople (Religion and Society).* New York: Walker and Company, 1974.

The book contains selections, in English translation, from the original sources
for the history of Islam in the Middle Ages. As part of the series entitled, The
Documentary History of Western Civilization, this volume (the first volume covered politics and war) consists of narratives on the religious, cultural, and social
life of the medieval Islamic world, with translations that are intended to be "representative examples of the different periods and regions" (p.xiv). The period
covered extends from the beginning of the seventh century to 1453 (when Byzantine Constantinople fell to the Ottomans); and the region extends from Western
Arabia to the Middle East and North Africa, as well as parts of Asia, tropical
Africa, and southern and eastern Europe.

The author notes, "During the centuries of confrontation and conflict, Muslims
and Christians alike were more conscious of their differences than of their similarities. Yet these similarities are very great, for the two religions and two cultures
had much in common" (Abrahamic "fatherhood"; ethical monotheism; prophetic revelations; heritage from ancient civilizations and Greeks; Middle-Eastern origins). Further, "These inherent resemblances were confirmed and
extended by their long cohabitation across the whole length of the Mediterranean

world and by the mutual influences between them" (p.xvii). However, "An appreciation of the affinities between Christianity and Islam should not lead us to overlook the very real differences which divide them or to try and describe Islam by false analogies" (p.xvii).

The 340-page volume is divided into seven parts, some with several chapters. Part I, Religion (four chapters: Scripture and Worship, Belief, Pilgrimage, The Law and Its Upholders); Part II, Heresy and Revolt (one chapter with the same title); Part III, The Lands of Islam and Beyond (three chapters: Capital and Provinces, Travelers' Tales, Neighbors); Part IV, The Economy (one chapter with the same title); Part V, Poets, Scholars, and Physicians (one chapter with the same title); Part VI, Race, Creed, and Conditions of Servitude (five chapters: Social Principles, Ethnic Groups, Black and White, The Status of Non-Muslims, Slaves); Part VII, Social and Personal (three chapters: Personal Documents, Literary Portraits, Humor).

There is a chronological table of historical events at the beginning and a comprehensive bibliography of sources. At the end, there is a glossary of Arabic terms, followed by a detailed name-subject index.

B-71. Lewis, Bernard, ed. *The World of Islam: Faith, People, and Culture*. London and New York: Thames and Hudson, Ltd., 1992.

This is one of the premier volumes on historical Islam, with 490 illustrations, 330 photographs, drawings, and maps. As the editor's note states, for centuries Christians were content to refer to Muslims simply as unbelievers. From the Renaissance onwards, however, European scholars made a serious attempt to learn the language of the Muslims and to understand and interpret their religion and civilization. Presently, there is an impressive body of scholarly literature on different aspects of Islamic religion, history, and culture. Further, this volume is an introduction to some of the distinctive qualities and achievements of the Islamic civilization.

The book begins with an introductory chapter by the editor, followed by 12 others primarily but not exclusively concerned with the central area and period of Islamic greatness—from about the seventh century to the 13th century. The chapters titles with authors are: (1) The Faith and the Faithful: The lands and peoples of Islam by Bernard Lewis, (2) The Man-Made Setting: Islamic art and architecture by Richard Ettinghausen, (3) Cities and Citizens: The growth and culture of urban Islam by Oleg Graber, (4) The Mystic Path: The Sufi tradition by Fritz Meier, (5) Jewelers with Words: The heritage of Islamic literature by Charles Pellat, (6) The Dimensions of Sound: Islamic music—philosophy, theory, and practice by A. Shiloah, (7) The Scientific Enterprise: Islamic contributions to the development of science by A.I. Sabra, (8) Armies of the Prophet: Strategy, tactics and weapons in Islamic warfare by Edmund Bosworth, (9) Moorish Spain: The Golden Age of Cordoba and Grenada by Emilio Garcia Gomez, (10) Land of the Lion and the Sun: The flowering of Iranian civilization

by Roger M. Savory, (11) The Ottoman Empire: The rise and fall of Turkish domination by Norman Itzkowitz, (12) Muslim India: From the coming of Islam to
Independence by S.A.A. Rizvi, (13) Islam Today: Problems and prospects of the
19th and 20th centuries by Elie Kedourie.

At the end, there is an epilogue by the editor, along with a chronological chart
of Islam and a comprehensive bibliography. There is a detailed name-subject
index.

Incidentally, this 360-page book is similar to one published earlier with a
slightly different title but identical contents: Bernard Lewis (editor), *Islam and
the Arab World: Faith, People, Culture*, New York: Alfred A. Knopf, in association with American Heritage Publishing Company, 1976.

B-72. Libby, Walter. *An Introduction to the History of Science.* New York:
Houghton Mifflin Company, 1917.

While the book attempts to provide a chronological history of the evolution of
knowledge (science), there is a chapter that specifically focuses on the Arab-
Islamic sources and their linkages with Latin Europe. There are chapters that
relate this evolution to Egypt and Babylonia, the Greeks and the Romans, followed by a discussion of the classification of sciences attributed to Roger Bacon,
the scientific method attributed to Gilbert, Galileo, Descartes, scientific measurement to Kepler and Boyle, science as it relates to the struggle for liberty (Benjamin Franklin), etc.

There are references to Arab-Islamic linkages throughout several of the 20
chapters, but chapter 4, The Continuity of Science: The Medieval Church and the
Arabs, is especially instructive in this respect. The tone and content are rather
remote and unflattering as to these connections, yet one acquires some interesting
insights. For example, the author acknowledges that Avicenna (Ibn Sina, 980–
1037) "wrote a large work on medicine which was used as a textbook for centuries in the universities of Europe," and further, Averroes (Ibn Rushd,
1126–1198), "the Arab physician and philosopher, was reserved the title 'The
Commentator,' due to his devotion to the works of the Greek(s). It was through
his commentaries of Averroes that Aristotelian science became known in Europe
during the Middle Ages and his influence was perpetuated in all the western centers of education" (p. 51–52). Commenting on the battles between faith and reason, the author mentions that St. Thomas Aquinas (1225–1274), "being familiar
with the works of Greek and Arabian scientists," demonstrated the supremacy of
faith over reason, and reconciled "the truths of revelation" in his synthesis,
Summa Theologica. There is an accompanying sketch that shows St. Thomas as
having been "inspired by Christ in glory, guided by Moses, St. Peter, and the
Evangelists, and instructed by Aristotle and Plato. He has overcome the heathen
philosopher Averroes, who lies below discomfited" (p.54). Throughout the 288-
page book, there are references to linkages of Latin Europe "science" history
with the earlier Arab-Islamic world.

There are no footnotes, but some references are provided at the end of each chapter. There is a name-subject index.

B-73. Lombard, Maurice. *The Golden Age of Islam* (translated from French by Joan Spencer). Amsterdam and New York: North-Holland Publishing Company/ American Elsevier Publishing Company, 1975.

The book focuses on the Islamic Civilization, beginning during early Middle Ages (from mid-eighth to the 11th century), "which provided the driving force behind economic and cultural life; the West was a void—an area in which all commercial and intellectual life had ceased after the decline and fall of Rome and the subsequent barbarian invasions" (p.1).

The discussion is couched in three distinct areas: Islamization (conversion of ancient populations), Arabization (to be understood in purely linguistic sense), and Semitization (the adoption of a set of moral concepts, taboos, cosmogonies, mental and practical systems—urban civilization of the East, the Persian Empire, and the Hellenistic kingdoms, literary and scientific civilization). The Islamic conquests left no trail of destruction, the author argues. "No cities were burned down or sacked, with the single exception of the pillaging of Sassanid palaces filled with gold. There was in consequence no disorganization. The recent Christian, Jewish, or Persian converts, known as *mawali* (clients), were to play a decisive role in the elaboration of this syncretic civilization we style 'Muslim'" (p.4–5). Further, "From Samarkand to Cordoba, Muslim civilization was a remarkably unified urban civilization, with considerable movement of men, merchandise, and ideas within it, a syncretic civilization superimposed upon the original regional system, whether rural or nomadic" (p.10).

The 260-page book is divided into three parts: (1) The Territories of Islam: Regions and Networks (four chapters—The Isthmus Region, The Iranian World, The Muslim West, The Linguistic Factor); (2) Monetary Power and Urban Rythms (three chapters—Monetary Problems, Urban Expansion and Consumer Demand, Social Movements and the Organization of Labor); (3) The Dynamics of Trade (two chapters—Production and Trading Commodities, Commercial Interchange in the Muslim World). There are 30 expository figures and maps.

In the concluding chapter, the author states that the center of gravity moved westwards after the 11th century, and now "economic power, the force of material expansion, and creative activity, were to be for centuries the privilege of Western Europe. However, even during its economic decline, the Muslim World long continued to influence the world in the realms of science, medicine and philosophy. Muslim civilization in its Golden Age, from the end of the ancient Empires to the emergence of the modern States, was a melting-pot in time and space, a great crossroads, a vast synthesis, an amazing meeting place" (p.238–239).

Curiously, the book does not have a single footnote, nor is there any bibliography. There is a detailed name-subject index, however.

B-74. Lunde, Paul. *Islam: Faith, Culture, History.* London and New York: DK Publishing Company, 2002.

The author states that the apocalyptic 9/11 event has "thrown into sharp relief the urgent necessity for Muslims and non-Muslims to confront and overcome the barriers that separate them" (p.6). Further, "Islam and the West share a common history, and their destinies have been linked since the expansion of Islam in the seventh century. Medieval European civilization took shape in the shadow cast by powerful Islamic empires, and the Islamic world entered modernity in the shadow of European imperial powers" (p.6). Thus, the author hopes to correct misconceptions about Islam and contribute toward building a common ground upon which to nurture the future of our shared humanity in the global village. Especially for anyone knowing nothing about the Islamic world, the book is a repository of information, historical as well as contemporary.

The seven chapters are: (1) Islam in Context, (2) The Islamic Faith, (3) History of the Islamic World, (4) Islamic Art and Science, (5) Modernity and Tradition, (6) The Islamic World Today, (7) Chronology. Chapters 3 and 4 trace the emergence of Islam in the early seventh century and its subsequent impact on world history through its spread across Africa, Europe and Asia, and beyond. Chapter 6 provides detailed maps and commentaries on contemporary Islam, plus an in-depth survey, along with some quantitative data, of the 44 countries in which Islam is the dominant faith. Chapter 7 provides a chronology of events in Islamic history, divided into eight periods up to the present.

The 192-page book contains over 300 photographs, historical as well as contemporary. There is a detailed name-subject index.

B-75. Macdonald, Duncan B. *Development of Muslim Theology, Jurisprudence and Constitutional Theory.* New York: Charles Scribner's Sons, 1903.

The author begins with this introduction: "In human progress unity and complexity are the correlatives forming together the great paradox. Life is manifold, but it is also one. So it is seldom possible to divide a civilization into departments. And this is emphatically true of the civilization of Islam" (p.5). Thus, in discussing the development of Islamic theology, jurisprudence, and constitution, the author cautions that this division is purely mechanical and for convenience only. "To aid some little to the understanding of Islam among us is the object of this book" (p.6).

The book is divided into three parts, with a few chapters in each, totaling 11 chapters. Part One, Constitutional Development, has three chapters: (1) From Death of Muhammad to Rise of Abbasids, (2) To Rise of Ayyubids, (3) To Present Situation. Part Two, Development of Jurisprudence, has two chapters: (1) To Close of Umayyad Period, (2) To Present Situation. Part Three, Development of Theology, has six chapters: (1) To Close of Umayyad Period, (2) To Foundation of Fatimid Khalifate, (3) To Triumph of Asharites in East, (4) Al-Ghazali, (5) To Ibn Sab'in and End of Muwahhids, (6) To Present Situation.

Written in 1903, the author implores the readers "to remember that Islam is a present reality and the Muslim faith is a living organism, a knowledge of whose laws may be life or death for us who are in another camp. For there can be little doubt that the three antagonistic and militant civilizations of the world are those of Christendom, Islam, and China. When these are unified, or come to a mutual understanding, then, and only then, will the cause of civilization be secure" (p.7).

The book provides three appendices: (1) Illustrative Documents in Translation, (2) Selected Bibliography, (3) Chronological Table. There is a detailed name-subject index.

B-76. Magoffin, Ralph V.D. and Frederick Duncalf. *Ancient and Medieval History: The Rise of Classical Culture and the Development of Medieval Civilization.* New York and Chicago: Silver, Burdett and Company, 1934.

The book was written with the principal objective of establishing a "real connection between present and past. They all know present-day people," but "the people in history were much like these whom they know and like" (p.iii). In order to understand modern civilization, the authors say "it is best to go back to the beginning and then see what has been added through the ages" (p.iii).

The 880-page book is divided into seven parts, with several chapters in each for a total of 29 chapters. Part I, Civilization begins in the Ancient Near East (four chapters); Part II, Civilization Advances under the Greeks (five chapters); Part III, Civilization is carried on by the Romans (four chapters); Part IV, Civilization is almost forgotten in the West (four chapters); Part V, A New Civilization arises in the West (four chapters); Part VI, Civilization creates new states in the West (four chapters); Part VII, Transition to Modern Civilization (four chapters).

While the authors do not provide a separate part of the book relating to the impact of the Islamic civilization, there are chapters, especially in Part V, that discuss that influence. Chapter 15, The Eastern Roman Empire and the Conquests of the Arabs, discusses the acquisition of knowledge of science from the Arabs and that "we owe a considerable debt to the Greeks and the Mohammedan peoples of the Middle Ages" (p.458). Particularly with respect to the Crusades, the authors state that while this effort failed, "the westerners did establish relations with the East. At the same time, westerners started a slow revival of trade, industry, and town life, which also stimulated agriculture. A new class appeared in medieval society, when men began to make their living in occupations than fighting, praying, and farming. There was also considerable intellectual and artistic progress" (p.527). In a chapter entitled The Crusades: How the Western Christians united to fight the Mohammedans, the authors state, "But neither the church nor the crusaders (the soldiers of the cross) knew what the results would be. For the first time since barbarism had swept over the West, its people were brought

into close contact with the other two medieval civilizations. Whether the westerners, who went forth eager to fight for their faith, wished to learn or not, they did
return with a changed point of view. They became more broadminded and tolerant in spite of themselves. They also acquired tastes for many articles which they
found in the East and this demand for eastern goods promoted commercial relations between the peoples who lived about the Mediterranean Sea. In short, the
crusades, as these expeditions were called, were a liberal education to many westerners who found out that the Greek and oriental peoples knew more about many
matters than they did and lived in more civilized fashion" (p.551).

Referring to the last crusades, the authors mention that in 1228, Frederick II,
though excommunicated by the Pope, "by negotiations with the Mohammedans
secured more privileges for pilgrims than other crusaders had won by fighting"
(p.570). In a section entitled, How the crusades hastened the growth of western
civilization, the authors identify four key factors: (1) the crusades stimulated
trade in spices, carpets, velvets, cotton and silk, sugar, jewels of the East, etc.;
(2) the crusades reduced the strength of feudal lords, and "St. Bernard said that
he sent good men into monasteries, and bad men on crusades" (p.572); (3) the
church gained much influence from the crusades by uniting people "against enemies of their faith" (p.572); and (4) "Most important of all was the influence of
the crusades on western minds. They also found out that much they had always
believed about the Mohammedan peoples was wrong. They also found most of
them to be chivalrous, charitable, and often tolerant. The westerners came home
with new ideas, but what was more important than ideas was the stimulating
effect that their interesting experiences had on their minds. It made them more
ready to learn and use new things, and less inclined to believe all that they were
told" (p.572).

The first three "hastening" forces are discussed in detail in chapter 20, The
Growth of Trade, Industry, and Town; the "mental awakening" factor is discussed in chapter 21, The Awakening of Medieval Minds: Learning, Literature,
and Art. Chapter 21 explores the rise of reason and how "medieval education and
learning made great progress during the twelfth and thirteenth centuries" (p.600).
Various medieval scholars are considered, including Peter Abelard, Roger Bacon,
and St. Thomas Aquinas. Bacon lamented that "scholars did not know the classical Greek and Latin, or the Arabic, languages well enough to understand the old
writers" (p.611). Yet, while he learned much from the Arabs, he "even said that
if he had the means, he could make a sun glass strong enough to burn up all
Mohammedans with its powerful rays" (p.612). The influence of the Islamic
world is clear throughout these chapters.

The book includes numerous maps, pictures, and sketches. There is a list of
selected readings at the end of each chapter, and a detailed 16-page name-subject
index.

B-77. Nawwab, Ismail I., Peter C. Speers, and Paul F. Hoye, eds. *Aramco and Its World: Arabia and the Middle East.* Washington, DC: Arabian American Oil Company, 1981.

This collection, according to the editors, represents a survey of "some of the most crucial events in the history of mankind that took place in the area" (p.vi). Further, "From the broader area we call the Middle East came the basic elements of mathematics, the wheel, the architectural arch, sciences such as astronomy and medicine, and the framework of organized trade and commerce. From this region, too, came the three great monotheistic religions: Judaism, Christianity, and Islam. Indeed, civilization itself—the triumph of human experience over time—began in the land that lies between the valleys of the Nile and the Indus" (p.vi). However, "no one volume can do full justice to such an immense sweep of history" (p.vi).

The 275-page book is divided into four long chapters. Of particular relevance are chapters one and two, "Before Islam" and "Islam and Islamic History." Chapter One covers such topics such as early and later Mesopotamia, Egypt, Other Ancient peoples, the Arabs, the Romans, and the rise of Mecca; also included here are three "box" articles: Quest for the Past, The Art of Writing, Early Times in the Arabian Gulf. Chapter Two focuses on Islamic history, covering topics such as the Prophethood, the four caliphs, the Umayyads, Spanish Islam, the Abbasids, the Golden Age, the Fatimids, the Seljuk Turks, the Crusaders, the Mongols and the Mamluks, the legacy, the Ottomans, the coming of the West, and revival of the Arab East. There are six "box" articles: The Holy Qur'an, The Faith of Islam, Arabic Writing, Science and Scholarship in Al-Andalus, Arabic Literature, Arabic Numerals. There is an excellent chronological chart of Islamic history (p.100–101).

The other two chapters are, respectively, devoted to a detailed history of Saudi Arabia and the discovery of oil, along with the formation, development, and role of Aramco.

Each chapter includes several large and small color pictures, as well as maps and sketches relevant to the topics. There is a detailed bibliography, classified by main topics covered in the book, followed by a name-subject index.

B-78. Nebelsick, Harold P. *The Renaissance, the Reformation and the Rise of Science.* Edinburgh: T&T Clark, 1992.

The book, while essentially completed by the author, was edited and finalized for publication posthumously; the author died in 1989. There are substantial additions and alterations to the original, but "all editorial decisions were based upon the principle of remaining as true to the phraseology and intention of the author" (p.vii). Among other things, the book attempts to contribute to our understanding of the relationship of theology to scientific culture; it is a "significant contribution to the theological renaissance we are experiencing now and toward which he was so deeply committed" (p.vii).

The book argues that when the Greek science came to the West, "the theologico-philosophical concepts so defined God and reality that, while Aristotelian 'science' intrigued the West as a description of nature, it also served to hinder the development of modern science" (p.xii). Further, it argues that rather than "showing that the interaction between theology and natural science was either inevitably salutary or always harmful, the evidence would seem to indicate that at times it was counter-productive and other times beneficial" (p.xii).

Throughout the book, but especially in the earlier chapters, there are extensive references to the Arab-Islamic influences that laid "the foundations for a quite unprecedented revival of learning in Europe" (p.ix). Further, "The Arabs are not only responsible for sustaining modern western industrial civilization with their oil, but in a real sense, are responsible for the transfer to Christian Europe culture of the intellectual basis on which our oil-dependent civilization developed in the first place" (p.2). And, the "results were the Renaissance, the Protestant Reformation in the sixteenth century, and eventually the scientific revolution of the seventeenth century" (p.9).

The 240-page book contains three long chapters; chapter titles and some content are identified herewith: Chapter 1, The Christian Critique of Aristotle, discusses the Arab contributions, the bearers and developers of Greek learning, assessment of Aristotelianism, etc.; Chapter 2, The Renaissance Mind, discusses the roots of Renaissance, place of Plato, the "New Science," etc.; Chapter 3, The Reformation and the Rise of Science, discusses the Biblical faith and the rise of science, the movement toward natural science, Francis Bacon's way of science, etc. There is an epilogue about the deceased author.

Each chapter has its own footnotes and references at the end. There is no index.

B-79. O'Leary, De Lacy. *Arabic Thought and Its Place in History*. London: Kegan Paul, Trench, Trubner and Company Ltd.; New York: E.P. Dutton and Company, 1922.

The book represents an effort "to trace the transmission of Hellenistic thought through the medium of Muslim philosophers and Jewish thinkers who lived in Muslim surroundings, to show how this thought, modified as it passed through a period of development in the Muslim community and itself modifying Islamic ideas, was brought to bear upon the culture of medieval Latin Christendom." And this thought "diverted Christian philosophy into new lines directly leading to the Renascence which gave the death-blow to medieval culture" (p.vi).

Eleven chapters of the 327-page book extensively cover the transmission of Hellenistic thought to the early Islamic world in Syria through numerous translators (many of them Nestorian Christians). Also discussed are the faith–reason controversies surrounding the "hellenization of Islam vs. Islamization of Hellenism," the Latin-Christian and Jewish translators/transmitters of Arab-Islamic scholarship (in Islamic Spain particularly), the interaction of Eastern (Islamic: Al-Kindi, Al-Farabi, Ibn Sina, Al-Ghazali, Ibn Rushd, and others, as well as the influence of Jewish scholars, such as Maimonides) upon Western (Latin) philosophies. There is discussion of the emergence of orthodox scholastism, sufism, and the influence of the Arab philosophers on Latin scholasticism. This influence "attained its final evolution in North-East Italy, where, as an anti-ecclesiastical influence, it prepared the way for the Renascence" (p.295).

The book provides no bibliography, nor an index. However, there is a chronological table that enumerates major events in Islamic history, with Islamic and Gregorian dates, beginning from the death on March 29, 632 AD (11 AH) of Prophet Muhammad to the fall of the Muwahhids dynasty in Spain, on September 10, 1268 AD (667 AH).

B-80. O'Leary, De Lacy. *How Greek Science Passed to the Arabs*, second edition. London: Routledge and Kegan Paul Ltd., 1951.

First published in 1949, the book title suggests the author's objective. The Greek writers who influenced the Arabs "oriental world" were not poets, historians, or orators, but "exclusively the scientists who wrote on medicine, astronomy, mathematics, and philosophy, the type of scientific thought which does not always come foremost when we speak about classical literature" (p. 1). When the Arabs inherited the Greek culture during the eighth century, Greek thought was chiefly interested in science and Hellenism had acquired an entirely "modern" outlook. There are three interwoven threads in this transmission: (1) Greek knowledge was translated and studied by Arabs and was subjected to commentaries; (2) there are conclusions and scientific principles developed by Arabic writers for which the Greek reservoir was a key basis; and (3) there are issues which were explored and resolved by the Arabs with which the Greeks had difficulties.

While the Greek reservoir had been around for a long time, it reached the Arabs through various directions, adaptations, and enhancements. First, it came through translations by the Christian-Syriac (Nestorians) writers. Second, the Arabs applied themselves directly to the original Greek sources and corrected and verified their earlier knowledge. Third, another indirect channel was through India where Greek knowledge on mathematics and astronomy had reached and further developed. Another source for Arab acquisition was the Greek kingdom of Bactria, one of the Asiatic states founded by Alexander the Great; also mentioned are two other relatively minor sources. Regardless of various ethnicities, Arabs shared the same cultural history and "all participated in the scientific heritage derived from the Hellenistic world" (p.3). Baghdad was the center where Greek material was brought together from different directions (Syria, Bactria, India, Persia), and from there the reservoir spread to other parts of the Islamic civilization—Aleppo, Damascus, Cairo, Cordova, and Samarqand. Wherever located, the author argues, the Arabs further developed almost all areas of inherited knowledge. Moreover, the scholarship of the Arabs "made its contributions not only by passing on what others had done, but by a very real development which enabled them to give to succeeding generations more than they had themselves received" (p.5).

The 196-page book provides detailed footnotes at the end, linked to the various pages of the text. There is also a detailed bibliography, followed by a name-subject index.

B-81. Packard, Sidney R. *Twelfth Century Europe: An Interpretive Essay.* Amherst, MA: University of Massachusetts Press, 1973.

In narrating European history, the author asserts, while the 13th and 14th centuries are often identified as "the greatest of centuries" that inspired "the dawn of a new era," the "twelfth century is actually the first European century about which we are reasonably well informed, yet no one seems to have made a clear case for the identification of its distinctive qualities and achievements" (p.1). Indeed, "In the whole history of Western Europe," this century represents the most distinctive break that "separates the earlier from the later Middle Ages" (p.1). This was the century of transfer of knowledge, in all areas known then, from the Arab-Islamic sources to Latin Europe—thus, "the renaissance of the twelfth century." The author alludes to this phenomenon, in that "new ideas, new at least to Europe, in law, in medicine, in philosophy, in theology, and in both economic and political theory came into Europe progressively through the century, but with a rush into western Europe in the second half" (p.4–5). The "book is an attempt to find out what made the twelfth century 'tick' and to present the findings in reasonably brief compass" (p.6).

This "knowledge-transfer" phenomenon is reflected almost throughout the 362-page book. After the introductory chapter that discusses "Why the Twelfth Century?," the book contains six detailed chapters: (1) Europe in 1100: Basic Factors, (2) Twelfth-Century European Economic Developments, (3) The Church, (4) The World of the Mind in the Twelfth-Century Europe, (5) The World of the Senses in the Twelfth-Century Europe, (6) The "States" of Twelfth-Century Europe. The "World of the Mind" chapter discusses details of Arab-Islamic linkages prominently. Thus, contacts "with a much more highly developed civilization produced great changes in the educational system in western and central Europe" (p.158). Referring to various disciplines, the author suggests, "In all these instances the dependence upon Greek and Arabic learning was crucial, largely available through translations made in Toledo" (p.213). These linkages are discussed further in chapter 5.

The book provides bibliographical notes, classified in terms of references (1) that deal primarily with the twelfth century, (2) that cover a wider chronological scope, containing useful material for the period, and (3) that pertain to some articles of special interest. Also, there is a list of modern writings and a detailed name-subject index.

B-82. Peretz, Don, Richard U. Moench, and Safia K. Mohsen. *Islam: Legacy of the Past, Challenge of the Future*. New York: North River Press/New Horizon Press Publishers, 1984.

Written with the background of the 1979 Iranian revolution, this monograph examines some prevailing conceptions of government and society as perceived by Muslims. While many of these expressions of political and social thought are relatively easy to comprehend for the average person, the authors argue, they often tend to be distorted when viewed through the "lenses of Western media and seen against a background of riots, demonstrations, and other media events. We have been left with images of 'Islamic fanaticism,' Muslim 'hatred of the West,' and other similar stereotypes" (p.5).

For those with little or no knowledge, the book attempts to clarify topics such as the meaning of an Islamic state, the Islamic system of law and justice, an Islamic economic system, and the Islamic law of nations. The discussion is presented with a historical perspective.

The three chapters are: (1) Islamic Revival or Reaffirmation by Don Peretz, (2) Islam and Development by Richard U. Moench, (3) Islam: The Legal Dimension by Safia K. Mohsen.

Footnotes and references for each essay are listed at the end. There is no index.

B-83. Peters, Edward. *Europe: The World of Middle Ages*. Englewood Cliffs, NJ: Prentice-Hall, 1977.

The comprehensive, 620-page book is about the settlement of Europe by its historical populations and the formation of a distinctively European material and spiritual culture that "lasted, in some respects at least, until the Industrial Revolution and the political upheavals of the nineteenth and early twentieth centuries" (p.xiii). And this civilization emerged out of the worlds of Mediterranean antiquity and western/central Eurasia and the form it assumed, says the author, requires a wider and more diverse map than that which describes Europe alone. Thus the author chooses a wider frame of inquiry.

Part One (Europe and the Ancient World, four chapters) treats both the general character of Mediterranean expansion and the encounter of Greeks and Romans with Celtic and Germanic people through the history of Roman Empire. Part Two (The Legacy of Mediterranean Antiquity, five chapters), covering 395–650 AD, traces the further division of the Mediterranean world of Hellenism and Rome and the particular forms that the survival of earlier traditions took in the face of new peoples settling in the areas of North Africa, the Near East, and Europe. Part Three (The Book and the Sword, 650–950, four chapters) characterizes the shaping of the first distinctive European culture. By 950, contacts with Byzantium and Islam had produced open and vulnerable societies. Part Four (Christendom: Material Civilization and Culture, 950–1150, four chapters) focuses on the development of the new material civilization and culture of the Latin West and the growing use of the concept of Christendom to designate it on a territorial and cultural basis. Part Five (Christendom: Authority and Enterprise, 1150–1300 AD, six chapters) concentrates on the articulation of the material and cultural world of Christendom. Part Six (The Human Condition, four chapters) discusses, "not the end of the Middle Ages," but the transformation of material life and the roots of traditional Europe.

All but Part One include numerous references to linkages with the Islamic world. Chapter 9, entitled The New Mediterranean World: The Rise of Islam, focuses briefly on the African provinces, the Arab world, and the Islamic Prophet, his successors, the spread of Islam, and the Abbasid Dynasty. Chapter 17 (Christendom, East and West, 1025–1150) covers discussion on Christian–Islam tensions. Thus, "Christian attitudes toward the Moslems were a mixture of curiosity and perverse misinformation. To Bede, the eighth-century English chronicler, the Moslems were the descendants of Hagar and Ishmael, the Old Testament outcasts. To others, they were one of the scourges sent by God as a punishment for the sinful Christian world. To others still, they were a schismatic Christian sect whose doctrines were a perversion of Christian doctrines (some even constructed an imaginary Moslem 'Trinity' consisting of Mohammed, Apollo, and 'Termagant'). For those in Spain, Sicily, and Byzantium who dealt with Islam, however, there was much mutual understanding and cultural sympathy, and Carolingian attitudes toward Islam had been marked, one historian has observed, by 'caution and sobriety'" (p.334). On the other hand, "Islamic views of Christianity were characterized largely by indifference and occasional scorn" (p.334). Further, "The world beyond Europe was filled, for most thinking Europeans, with hostile peoples and strange and mysterious creatures, part human and part beast. Such limited knowledge, fed by new hostility and a new conception of the warrior class within a new ideology of Christian society, heightened the potential militancy with which Latin Christendom regarded Islam" (p.334).

Chapter 18 (The Materials of New Learning) discusses, among other things, the Islamic influences for Latin Europe's intellectual revival. "By the early twelfth century, knowledge of the achievements of the Arabic thought and the Islamic legacy of much of Greek learning had begun to make inroads in the West. Adelard of Bath traveled [to] South Italy, Sicily, Greece, Cilicia, Syria, Palestine, and possibly Spain, seeking out knowledge [and] the wealth of Arabic thought [he acquired] amounted to a torrent of translations from Arabic works, and by the thirteenth century, from Greek works directly as well. The ninth and tenth centuries had witnessed the translation into Arabic of much of the corpus of earlier Greek learning, and westerners began to acquire some of this legacy through translations from Arabic. Both the Greek and Islamic legacies acquired great popularity in the West" (p.367).

There are references to the diversified influence of numerous scholars, such as Ibn Sina, Ibn Rushd ("probably the greatest of all commentators upon Aristotle's scientific works"), Al-Khwarizmi, al-Battani, Alhazen, and Al-Idrisi, and others. The names of numerous translators and translation centers (e.g., Toledo, Sicily,

Salerno) are mentioned; also mentioned is the first translation of the Islamic Qur'an in 1142, sponsored by Peter the Venerable, Abbot of Cluny (p.368). Further, "The new learning that the translators made available to the Latin West was certainly not the only contribution of the great age of translators. Islamic medical, agricultural, and architectural discoveries also passed into western hands during this period, and the prominent role of Jewish translators marks the beginning of a new Christian interest in Jewish literature" (p.368). The increasing sophistication thus acquired "touched all of European society and marks one of the first of the great ages of intellectual cosmopolitanism in modern history" (p.369).

The book includes a detailed bibliography, divided into two parts. Part I is a general bibliography of selected topics, and Part II is a selective bibliography arranged to correspond to the six parts of the book. There is a brief name-subject index.

B-84. Peters, F.E., ed. *The Arabs and Arabia on the Eve of Islam*. Brookfield, VT, and Hampshire, UK: Ashgate Publishing Company, 1999.

This is one of several volumes in the series, The Formation of the Classical Islamic World, under the general editorship of Lawrence I. Conrad. Motivated by the premise that modern scholarship tends to be "compartmentalized" into specific areas, each volume in this series presents a number of previously published recent studies, representing the "best of current scholarship," on a particular topic in early Islamic history (covering approximately 600–950 AD). Articles published in languages other than English have been translated, and the editor has provided critical introductions and select bibliographies for further reading.

This 388-page volume contains 18 essays previously published and written by well-known scholars in the field. These are: (1) The Nature of Arab Unity before Islam by G.E. von Grunebaum, (2) The Role of Nomads in the Near East in Late Antiquity (400–800 CE) by Fred M. Donner, (3) The Bedouinization of Arabia by Werner Caskel, (4) Trans-Arabian Routes of the Pre-Islamic Period byDaniel T. Potts, (5) Al-Hira: Some Notes on Its Relation with Arabia by M.J. Kister, (6) Pre-Islamic Bedouin Religion by Joseph Henninger, (7) Idol Worship in Pre-Islamic Medina (Yathrib) by Moshe Gil, (8) The Origin of the Jews of Yathrib by Moshe Gil, (9) Haram and Hawtah, the Sacred Enclave in Arabia by R.B. Serjeant, (10) Pre-Foundations of the Muslim Community in Mecca by Fazlur Rahman, (11) Mecca before the Time of the Prophet: Attempt of an Anthropological Interpretation by Walter Dostal, (12) The "Sacred Offices" of Mecca from Jahiliyya to Islam by Gerald R. Hawting, (13) *Hanifyya* and *Ka'ba*: An Inquiry into the Arabian Pre-Islamic Background of *Din Ibrahm* by Uri Rubin, (14) Pre-Islamic Monotheism in Arabia by Hamilton A.R. Gibb, (15) Belief in a "High God" in Pre-Islamic Mecca by W. Montgomery Watt, (16) The Ka'ba: Aspects of its Ritual Functions and Position in Pre-Islamic and Early Islamic Times by Uri Rubin, (17) The Role Played by the Organization of the "Hums" in the Evolution of Political Ideas in Pre-Islamic Mecca by Ugo Fabietti, (18) The Campaign of Huluban: A New Light on the Expedition of Abraha by M.J. Kister.

Notes and references are integrated in the text of each essay. The 390-page volume provides a detailed name-subject index.

B-85. Pirenne, Henri. *Economic and Social History of Medieval Europe* (translated from French by I.E. Clegg). New York: Harcourt, Brace and Company, 1937.

Originally published as *Histoire du Moyen Age* (*History of the Middle Ages*), this classic is a composite volume based on the author's widely read but controversial published papers. These writings gave rise to what subsequently became known as the "Pirenne Thesis," the argument being that European socioeconomic revival was stimulated by the pre-11th century contacts with the Islamic world. Thus, the author begins, "In order to understand the economic revival which took place in Western Europe from the eleventh century onwards, it is necessary first of all to glance at the preceding period" (p.1). He further argues, "It was only the abrupt entry of Islam on the scene, in the course of the seventh century, and the conquest of the eastern, southern and western shores of the great European lake, which altered the position, with consequences which were to influence the whole course of subsequent history" (p.2).

Throughout the 252-page book, in addition to frequent references to the disciplinary literature emerging early-medieval Islamic civilization, one observes evidence of direct/indirect socioeconomic influences from that world.

Notes and references are integrated within each chapter. There is a general bibliography, separated by books and journals, at the end. There are two indices, one by authors, another general.

B-86. Powell, James M., ed. *Muslims under Latin Rule, 1100–1300*. Princeton, NJ: Princeton University Press, 1990.

The theme of this book emerged from a session entitled "Medieval Mediterranean Society in Comparative Perspective" at the 1985 American Historical Association conference. While considerable literature exists that documents Muslim tolerance of non-Muslim minorities, much less attention has been paid to the treatment of Muslim minorities in Christian lands. These essays attempt "to place the relations between dominant Christians and subject Muslims into a comparative perspective across a geographical spectrum that extends from Spain to the Near East" (p.4). "Though the kernels for a policy of religious tolerance were always present," the editor observes in the introduction, "their importance was chiefly as a check or restraint on actions based on utter intolerance of the rights of minorities" (p.9).

There are five essays in the 221-page book: (1) The Mudejars of Castile and Portugal in the Twelfth and Thirteenth Centuries by Joseph E. O'Callaghan, (2) Muslims in the Thirteenth-Century Realms of Aragon: Interaction and Reaction by Robert I. Burns, (3) The End of Muslim Sicily by David S.H. Abulafia, (4) The Subjected Muslims of the Frankish Levant by Benjamin Z. Kedar, (5) The

Papacy and the Muslim Frontier by James M. Powell. These essays are followed by a concluding comparative note by the editor.

Each chapter provides notes and bibliographic references in the text. There is a name-subject index.

B-87. Price, B.B. *Medieval Thought: An Introduction.* Cambridge, MA: Blackwell Publishers, 1992.

The book is an introduction to the Middle Ages, designated here as from the late fourth century to the late 15th century; and it touches various aspects, discussed chronologically, in the development of ideas, thoughts, and culture. The basic thrust of the book is the evolution of the Latin-Christian intellect and "how medieval ideas are a product of their context," the context being Christian religious thought (p.2). The author acknowledges that "the variety of cultures—classical-pagan and religious, Christian and Jewish or Muslim, religious and secular, Latin and vernacular—lay the seeds of medieval intellectualization." The book's "necessary compression meant foregoing thorough treatment of Jewish and Arabic religious and cultural influence on western European medieval culture" (p.4).

The 262-page book contains eight chapters: (1) The Christian Impress, (2) Early Medieval Religious Thought, (3) Christianity and Liberal Arts, (4) The Return to Plato and Aristotle, (5) The Vernacular Breakthrough, (6) Scholasticism, (7) The Dictates of Philosophy and the Late Medieval Church, (8) Domains of Abstract Thought. There are references to various Arab-Islamic precursors (Alkindi, Ibn Sina, Al-Farabi, Ibn Rushd, etc.) of various Latin-Christian scholars discussed. In the discussion on reconciling Christianity with Aristotelianism, there is reference to numerous Arabic thinkers who "were frequently received with great relief, for they supplied new works and ideas, many of which filled gaps in the Aristotelian scheme of classified knowledge" (p.87). Further, it is noted that "the scholastic method had already developed in the East before it began to develop in the West" (p.137).

The book provides seven appendixes (glossary of philosophical–theological terms, major primary sources, major journal sources, tools for using manuscripts, bibliographies, chronology of political–intellectual history, and a pedagogical syllabus). Also, there are chapter-by-chapter notes and references and a 10-page bibliography with each reference identified by a brief annotation. There is a detailed name-subject index.

B-88. Reynolds, Robert L. *Europe Emerges: Transition Toward an Industrial World-Wide Society 600–1750.* Madison, WI: University of Wisconsin Press, 1961.

The book is about the "centuries from the late Roman Empire to the global commercial, industrial, and political pattern which was rapidly emerging under European domination by the time of George Washington" (p.vii). There is emphasis on medieval European economic history—banking, bookkeeping, insurance, government finance, mercantile practices. Technology is also stressed, leading to the Industrial Revolution, although the author notes the importance of the medieval craftsmen in the process. There are frequent references to the linkages with the Islamic world, especially during the early medieval period.

The book is divided into five sections (with several chapters in each): (1) Basic Assets: About 600 AD, (2) Medieval Economy and Society: 600 to 1350, (3) Societies Outside Europe, (4) Europe on the Eve of Its Great Expansion, (5) Expansion Before 1750.

Section 3 includes a chapter on the Islamic civilization; however, earlier chapters also include references. An early chapter entitled Crops, Foods, and Livestock talks of Europe's indebtedness to Islam in the matter of citrus fruits. Thus, "The Mohammedans were skilled horticulturists, painstaking in raising all sorts of other things as well. It is to Saracen genius that we owe the development of good varieties of lemons and oranges" (p.55). Referring to the Moorish Spain, the author states, the Moors "came into Spain definitely more civilized, better organized, and in matters of economy much more advanced than the contemporary western Europeans. This was quite clearly an instance of those from an advanced area conquering those in a backward area. The cultural advantages and superiorities of the Islamic peoples over the Europeans lasted from the early seven hundreds until at least into the late eleven and early twelve hundreds" (p.82–83). And during this period, Islam "produced some of the most important of the Saracen scientists and poets, and some of the most prosperous communities, finest manufactures, and ablest, richest merchants. It was a world quite remote in every way from the northern Europeans" (p.84). Furthermore, where Islam extended its reach, "the peoples were still Christian for a long time after the Mohammadens came in. The idea that the latter came with the Koran in one hand and a sword in the other is completely wrong" (p.298–299).

The 530-page book provides no notes, references, or bibliography, although there is a detailed name-subject index.

B-89. Richards, D.S., ed. *Papers on Islamic History: Islamic Civilization, 950–1150, A Colloquium.* Published under the auspices of the Near Eastern History Group, Oxford, and the Near East Center, University of Pennsylvania; Bruno Cassirer (Publishers) Ltd., Oxford, 1973.

The book focuses on the two centuries (950–1150 AD) of Islamic civilization, a period that is sometimes identified as the "age of transition," at least for the central and eastern areas of the Islamic world; the 11th century is often mentioned as the "turning point in the history of Islamic culture" (p.vii). The book is a collection 15 papers, 13 of which were presented at the colloquium held at Oxford in 1969 as part of the series on Islamic history. The papers explore "the nature of the 'transformation' and the degree to which Islamic civilization at their close was really different in kind from what it had been in earlier centuries" (p.vii).

The 285-page book's papers, with titles and authors, are: (1) Barbarian Invasions: The Coming of the Turks into the Islamic World by C.E. Bosworth, (2) Changes in the Middle East 950–1150 as illustrated by the Documents of the Cairo Geniza by S.D. Goitein, (3) Administration in Buyid Qazwin by R. Mottahedeh, (4) The Revival of Persian Kingship under the Buyids by H. Busse, (5) The Political–Religious History of Nishapur in the Eleventh Century by R.W. Bulliet, (6) Nomades et Sedentaires dans le Monde Musulman du Milieu du Moyen Age by C. Cahen, (7) Aspects of Suljuq-Ghuzz Settlement in Persia by A.K.S. Lambton, (8) Nouvelles Orientations des Berberes d'Afrique du Nord 950–1150 by R. Le Tourneau, (9) The Sunni Revival by G. Makdisi, (10) Les Agitations Religieuses a Baghdad aux I'VE and Ve siecles de l'Hegire by H. Laoust, (11) Les Conceptions Imamites au debut du XI siecle d'apres le Shaykh al-Mufid by D. Sourdel, (12) Political Centres and Artistic Powers in Seljuq by R. Schnyder, (13) The 11th Century: A Turning Point in the Architecture of the Mashriq by J.M. Rogers, (14) Renouvellement et Tradition dans l'Architecture Saljuqide by J. Sourdel-Thomine, (15) A Note on Fatimid-Saljuq Trade by G.T. Scanlon.

Notes and references are integrated in the text of each paper. There is a detailed name-subject index.

B-90. Richards, D.S., ed. *Papers on Islamic History: Islam and the Trade of Asia, A Colloquium*. Published under the auspices of the Near Eastern History Group, Oxford, and the Near East Center, University of Pennsylvania; Bruno Cassirer, Oxford, and University of Pennsylvania Press, 1970.

The 266-page book is part of the series Papers on Islamic History, and papers included are those read at the colloquium sponsored in 1967 by the Oxford University and the University of Pennsylvania. Perhaps because one does not discern any general themes, or even a unifying theme, there is no introduction by the editor. Some papers reflect a broad general import (e.g., papers by Maxime Rodinson, G.F. Hudson, and Charles Issawi); others are shorter papers with a narrower focus (e.g., papers by G.T. Scanlon, J. Carswell, M. Rogers, and N. Chittick).

There are 15 papers: (1) Asian Trade in Antiquity by A.H.M. Jones, (2) Trade in the Eastern Islamic Countries in the Early Centuries by B. Spuler, (3) Le Marchand Musulman by M. Rodinson, (4) Commercial Techniques in Early Medieval Islamic Trade by A.L. Udovitch, (5) Archaeology and the Study of Later Islamic Pottery by J. Carswell, (6) China and Islam: The Archaeological Evidence in the Mashriq by M. Rogers, (7) Egypt and China: Trade and Imitation by G.T. Scanlon, (8) East African Trade with the Orient by N. Chittick, (9) Arab Trade with Indonesia and the Malay Peninsula from the 8th to the 16th Century by R.R. Di Meglio, (10) Trade and Islam in the Malay-Indonesian Archipelago Prior to the Arrival of the Europeans by M.A.P. Meilink-Roelofsz, (11) The Medieval Trade of China by G.F. Hudson, (12) L'Empire Ottoman et le Commerce Asiatique aux 16e et 17e siecles by R. Mantran, (13) Trade and Politics in 18th Century India by A. Das Gupta, (14) Persian Trade Under the Early Qajars by A.K.S. Lambton, (15) The Decline of Middle Eastern Trade by C. Issawi.

Each essay provides footnotes and references in the text. There is no index.

B-91. Robinson, Chase F., ed. *Texts, Documents and Artefacts: Islamic Studies in Honor of D.S. Richards.* Leiden, Netherlands, and Boston: E.J. Brill, 2003.

This book of essays, in honor of D.S. Richards of the Oxford University, is part of the series entitled Islamic History and Civilization: Studies and Texts. Written by some leading Arabists and Islamists, "the articles published in this Festschrift range nearly the length and breadth of Islamic studies, but in their close engagement with the written word, they all honor D.S. Richards and his scholarship" (p.ix). The wide range of topics should be of interest to students of Islamic history and culture.

The 420-page book contains 17 essays: (1) The word made visible: Arabic script and the committing of the Qur'an to writing by Alan Jones, (2) Caliphs and their chroniclers in the Middle Abbasid period (third/ninth century) by Hugh Kennedy, (3) A new text on Ismailism at the Samanid court by Patricia Crone and Luke Treadwell, (4) A treatise on the Imamate of the Fatimid Caliph al-Mansur bi-Allah by Wilferd Madelung, (5) The imprisonment of Reynald of Chatillon by Carole Hillenbrand, (6) A conversation on contemporary politics in the twelfth century: Al-Maqama al-Baghdadiyya by al-Wahrani (d. 575/1179) by Geert Jan van Gelder, (7) Les sources d'Ibn al-Adim sur le regne de Sayf al-Dawla en Syrie du Nord (333–356/944–967) by Anne-Marie Edde, (8) An original Arabic document from Crusader Anitoch (1213 AD) by Nadia Jamil and Jeremy Johns, (9) Yaqut's interviewing technique: "Sniffy" by Julia Bray, (10) "Sirat al-Mu'ayyad Shaykh" by Ibn Nahid by Amalia Levanoni, (11) Foot soldiers, militiamen and volunteers in the early Mamluk army by Rewen Amitai, (12) Tribal feuding and Mamluk factions in medieval Syria by Robert Irwin, (13) The collapse of the Great Saljuqs by Julie Scott Meisami, (14) Mamluk Sgfraffiato ware: The power of the new by George T. Scanlon, (15) De passage a Damas en 688/1286: Ibn al-Najib et la transmission du savoir by Jacqueline Sublet, (16) When is a fake a fake and how much does it matter? On the authenticity of the letter of the descendants of Muhammad b. Salih to the descendants of Mu'awiya b. Salih by David J. Wasserstein, (17) Materials for the study of Arabic in the age of the early printed book by David Morray.

The book also provides a bibliography of the scholar honored. Notes and references are integrated in the text of each essay. There is brief index of "selected persons."

B-92. Robinson, David. *Muslim Societies in African History*. Cambridge: Cambridge University Press, 2004.

Examining a series of processes (Islamization, Arabization, Africanization) and relying on case studies from North, West, and East Africa, the book—intended mainly for undergraduate students—gives snapshots of Muslim societies over the last millennium or so. The author says, "Europeans and North Americans have had difficulty understanding Islam and individual Muslims, even greater difficulty understanding Muslim societies in Africa and in African history. And all of these difficulties are compounded in light of the events of September 11, 2001, their revelations and repercussion" (p.xv). The author attempts, among other things, to explain these "difficulties" in terms of Islamic reaction to the Crusades, the "Western domination in the form of colonial rule, technological superiority, and other forms of hegemony over the 'lands of Islam,' and that, "from the perspective of the West and the Mediterranean, Africa is 'black'" (p.xvi–xvii).

The book challenges numerous assumptions and stereotypes about Islam, Muslims, and Africa. The author's narrative throughout the book is couched in terms of the "Judeo-Christian-Islamic" (or "Abrahamic") tradition upon which "so much of European and world history is built" (p.xv). In contrast to the traditions which suggest that Africa is not Muslim, or that Islam did not take root in Africa, the author explains the complex struggles of Muslims in the Islamic states of Morocco and in the Hausaland region of Nigeria. Further, he portrays the manner in which Islam was practiced in the "pagan" societies of Asante (Ghana) and Buganda (Uganda) and in the "ostensibly" Christian state of Ethiopia.

The book is divided into three parts, with a total of 13 chapters. Part I, The Historical and Institutional Background, has two chapters: (1) Muhammad and the Birth of Islam, (2) The Basic Institutions of Islam. Part II, General Themes, has four chapters: (3) The Islamization of Africa, (4) The Africanization of Islam, (5) Muslim Identity and the Slave Trades, (6) Western Views of Africa and Islam. Part III, Case Studies, has seven chapters: (7) Morocco: Muslims in a "Muslim Nation," (8) Ethiopia: Muslims in a "Christian Nation," (9) Asante and Kumasi: A Muslim Minority in a "Sea of Paganism," (10) Sokoto and Hausaland: *Jihad* within the *Dar al-Islam*, (11) Buganda: Religious Competition for the Kingdom, (12) The Sudan: The Mahdi and Khalifa and Competing Imperialisms, (13) Senegal: Bamba and the Murids under French Colonial Rule.

The chapter entitled "Western Views of Africa and Islam" is particularly relevant presently. It briefly discusses the history of the *Reconquest* of Islamic Spain, the Crusades, and the Inquisition, and also why the early Islamic civilization's "intellectual, theological, and military challenge led many Europeans and Christians during the Middle Ages to create a counter-vision—to demonize Islam, the Qur'an, and the Prophet" (p.77). Thus, it became much more difficult "to find situations where Christians and Muslims—and Jews—could live and work together, as they once had in Baghdad and Toledo. The negative images persist to the present day" (p.80). The author also briefly discusses the implications of Orientalism, a phenomenon by "which the West has framed, studied, and ruled the Other, particularly the Middle Eastern Muslim Other" (p.82). The author says, "The book, then, bridges an old and yawning gap. It is about Islam and it is about Africa. It is about North and Sub-Saharan Africa. It draws from Islamic and African studies. It draws from the 'Islamic history' of North Africa, recognized however grudgingly by the West" (p.87).

The 220-page book includes seven maps and 24 black-and-white sketches and pictures, depicting the historical Islamic aspects of life in North Africa. Each chapter ends with several appropriate notes and references. There is a glossary of terms at the end, followed by a name-subject index.

B-93. Robinson, Francis. *Islam and Muslim History in South Asia.* New Delhi, India: Oxford University Press, 2001.

The 300-page book contains nine essays by the author; all but one appeared in print between 1979 and 1997. The exception, published herewith, traces the mutual influence and interdependence of the Muslim and Christian worlds since the seventh century. The remaining papers deal with the past three centuries of Muslim history in South Asia. There are also six major reviews. Four themes are evident: (1) interaction between European and Muslim societies (including a critique of Samuel Huntington's clash-of-civilization thesis); (2) study of religious ideas and change since the British rule in India; (3) the impact of British rule on Muslims and Islamic knowledge in South Asia; and (4) religion and the wider influence of social developments on the Muslim separatist identity in the 19th and 20th centuries.

The nine essays, following the introduction, are: (1) The Muslim and the Christian Worlds: Shapers of Each Other, (2) Islam and Muslim Society in South Asia, (3) Islam and the Impact of Print in South Asia, (4) Religious Change and the Self in Muslim South Asia since 1800, (5) Secularization, Weber and Islam, (6) The Muslims of Upper India and the Shock of the Mutiny, (7) Nation-formation: The Brass Thesis and Muslim Separatism, (8) Islam and Muslim Separatism, (9) The Congress and Muslims. The six review-essays, grouped under Responses to Major Contributions to Indo-Muslim History, are: (10) Sufis and Islamization, (11) Nineteenth-Century Indian Islam, (12) Islam in Malabar, (13) Islamic Revival, (14) The Jinnah Story, (15) Congress Muslims and Indian Nationalism.

Notes and references are appended at the end of each essay, and there is a name-subject index.

B-94. Robinson, Francis, ed. *The Cambridge Illustrated History of the Islamic World.* London: Cambridge University Press, 1996.

This excellent 328-page volume is assembled with the purpose of making the world of Islam readily accessible to the scholar and the general reader. The foreword by an eminent scholar of Islamic studies, Ira Lapidus, emphasizes the importance of the rapidly evolving global relationships between Muslims and non-Muslims. Aided by the advent of modern technology and transportation, the East-West boundaries are fast vanishing, he states. Further, he suggests, even though large numbers of Muslims live in Europe and North America and are part of the pluralistic cultures, for many Westerners, Islam represents the East, outside their own civilization and always problematic, despite the fact that Islam has also been a source of Western enlightenment.

Beginning with an exploration of the problems of understanding between the Islamic world and the West, the succeeding eight chapters, written by well-known scholars, cover a wide spectrum of Islamic history. The first four chapters provide an overview of Islamic history, from the beginning to the challenges and transformations attendant on the expansion of the West in the 19th and 20th centuries. The next four chapters explore major themes—economic foundations, the ordering of the society, evolution of knowledge and its transmission, and artistic expression.

The chapter titles and authors are: (1) The Rise of Islam in the World by Patricia Crone, (2) The Emergence of the Islamic World System 1000–1500 by Robert Irwin, (3) The Islamic World in the Age of European Expansion 1500–1800 by Stephen F. Dale, (4) The Islamic World in the Era of Western Domination 1800 to the Present by Sarah Ansari, (5) The Economy in Muslim Societies by K.N. Chaudhuri, (6) The Order of Muslim Societies by Basim Musallam, (7) Knowledge, Its Transmission and the Making of Muslim Societies by Francis Robinson, (8) Artistic Expressions of Muslim Societies by Stephen Vernoit. There is a concluding chapter by the editor.

Throughout there are numerous pictorial illustrations, maps, and entries on specific topics. Also, there is an excellent glossary and bibliography, followed by a detailed name-subject index.

B-95. Rogers, Michael. *The Spread of Islam.* Oxford: Elsevier-Phaidon, 1976.

The book is a study of the early "history and architecture" of Islam. It covers the period from Islam's origins in the seventh century to the year 1500, when Muslim presence in Spain ended and the Ottomans were laying the foundations of an empire in the Near East.

The introductory chapter narrates the accounts of European travelers to Islamic regions. This is followed by a chapter that surveys the historical development of Islam, thus paving the way for more detailed discussion of the surviving structures and monuments. Using architectural history as a framework, the author builds a picture of the secular and religious life of medieval Islam and concludes with descriptions of palaces, shrines, and mausoleums, notably the Alhambra, the Dome of the Rock and Mecca. Also, there are visual stories that portray in pictures four major monuments of Islamic civilization.

After the introduction, there are six chapters in this 152-page volume: (1) The

Lure of Islam (visual story: Samarkand in the 15th Century), (2) Islam: The History of a Religion (visual story: The Citadel of Aleppo), (3) Town and Country (visual story: The Art of Islamic Calligraphy), (4) Religion, Education and Mysticism (visual story: The Mosque of Sultan Hasan in Cairo), (5) Palaces and Domestic Architecture, (6) Shrines and Mausoleums.

The book is illustrated throughout with numerous pictures, maps, and diagrams. There is a short bibliography at the end, followed by an 11-page glossary of Arabic names and words. Also available is a name-subject index.

B-96. Rosenthal, Franz. *The Classical Heritage in Islam* (translated from the German by Emile and Jenny Marmorstein). Berkeley and Los Angeles: University of California Press, 1965.

The influence of the classical heritage was diverse and comprehensive; it affected religious disciplines, theology, mysticism, law, as well as Arabic philology, grammar, literary studies, and the arts. However, the book is not intended to cover these intellectual and literary activities; it is an anthology of selections "confined to the direct and obvious links between the two cultures which mostly concern other branches of learning" (p.xv). They seek to convey an impression of the extent and quality of Muslim acquaintance with the classical heritage. The author notes that regardless of "how fundamental and undeniable the degree of dependence, the Muslim acquisition, adaptation and development of the heritage of classical antiquity constitute an independent, and historically, an extraordinarily fruitful achievement" (p.xvi). Further, "The principal aim of all but a very few of the Muslims concerned with the Greek heritage was to breathe a new life into their religion. Yet, the process that took place in the Muslim empire between the eighth and tenth centuries is much closer in spirit and character to the European renaissance" and we can "call it the renaissance of Islam" (p.12). And, "More than anything else, it was the intellectual life of medieval Europe that profited from Muslim achievements in the realm of science and scholarship by means of translations from the Arabic" (p.14).

After the introductory chapter, there are 12 main chapters, each with several sections and each identified with the original translator—Jewish, Christian, and Muslim. The titles are: (1) Translation Technique and Textual Criticism, (2) Biography and Cultural History, (3) The Classification of the Sciences and Methods of Research and Teaching, (4) Philosophy (covering Logic, Ethics, Metaphysics, with sections within each), (5) Natural Science, (6) Medicine, (7) Geometry, Arithmetic and Optics, (8) Geography and Astronomy, (9) Musicology, (10) Mechanics, (11) The Occult Sciences, (12) Literature and Art.

Chapter-by-chapter notes and references are appended at the end of this 300-page book, followed by a detailed name-subject index.

B-97. Ross, Frank, Jr. *Arabs and the Islamic World*. New York: S.G. Phillips, Inc., 1979.

The author begins with the assertion: "Centuries ago when Europe was grop-ing through the Dark Ages, there was an Arab empire, a dazzling, vibrant society. They assimilated the intellectual attainments of many peoples, Greek, Persian and Hindu among others, and made these their own. But Arab scholars also made many original contributions in science, literature and the arts. At a time when the Western world lived in the shadow of intellectual darkness, the Arabs' lamps of knowledge burned with an all-pervading glow" (p.10). Thus, "The Arabs' story which this book proposes to tell is a kind of a Cinderella story among the many different stories of the nations of the world" (p.11).

The 225-page book has 11 chapters: (1) Arab Lands, (2) Arabs and Islamic Peoples, (3) Muhammad, (4) The Islamic Faith, (5) Umayyad and Abbasid Dynasties, (6) Arabs in Science, Technology, the Arts, (7) Fall of the Islamic Civilization, (8) Ottomans and the Islamic World, (9) The Arab World Between Two Wars, (10) Arabs and the Modern World, (11) Israel, Oil, and the Arabs.

Chapter 6 ends with this note: "The intellectual, artistic and technical endeav-ors of the Islamic civilization, of which we have only scratched the surface, were impressive. A great store of human knowledge, physical beauty and things of practical usefulness were brought into existence. By their achievement and pre-serving and passing along the priceless knowledge accumulated by other civiliza-tions, plus their own original contributions, the people of Islam rendered an invaluable service to the progress of humanity. Perhaps their greatest impact was on Europeans as the latter entered upon their own brilliant era of the Renais-sance" (p.126). Each chapter includes some illustrative pictures, maps, and/or drawings.

The book ends with a chronology of events, from 1350 BC to 1978 AD. There is a bibliography, followed by a name-subject index.

B-98. Rubin, Uru, ed. *The Life of Muhammad.* Brookfield, VT, and Hampshire, UK: Ashgate Publishing Company, 1998.

This is one of several volumes in the series entitled The Formation of the Clas-sical Islamic World, under the general editorship of Lawrence I. Conrad. Moti-vated by the premise that modern scholarship tends to be "compartmentalized" into specific areas, each volume in this series presents a number of recent studies, representing the "best of current scholarship," on a particular topic in early Islamic history (covering approximately AD 600–950). Articles published in lan-guages other than English have been translated, and the editor has provided criti-cal introductions and select bibliographies for further reading.

This 410-page volume contains 15 essays, previously published and written by well-known scholars. They are grouped into four main topics: (I) Authors of Muhammad's Biography—(1) "Maghazi" and "Sira" in Early Islamic Scholar-ship by Martin Hinds, (2) Ibn Ishaq and al-Waqidi: The Dream of Atika and the Raid to Nakhla in Relation to the Charge of Plagiarism by J.M.B. Jones, (3) Waqi-di's Account on the Status of the Jews of Medina: A Study of a Combined Report by Michael Lecker; (II) Events in the Life of Muhammad—(4) Abraha and Muhammad: Some Observations Apropos of Chronology and Literary *Topoi* in the Early Arabic Historical Tradition by Lawrence I. Conrad, (5) The Sons of Khadija by M.J. Kister, (6) The First Muslims in Mecca: A Social Basis for a New Religion by Miklos Muranyi, (7) The Meetings of al-Akaba by Gertrud Melamede, (8) The *Sunnah Jamiah*, Pacts with the Yathrib Jews, and the *Tahrim* of Yathrib: Analysis and Translation of the Documents Comprised in the So-Called "Constitution of Medina" by R.B. Serjeant, (9) The Chronology of the *Maghazi*: A Textual Survey by J.M.B. Jones, (10) Al-Hudaybia: An Alternative Version by Farrukh B. Ali, (11) Al-Hudaybiyya and the Conquest of Mecca: A Reconsideration of the Tradition about the Muslim Takeover of the Sanctuary by G.R. Hawting; (III) The Idealized Muhammad—(12) The Growth of the Mohammed Legend by Josef Horovitz, (13) Jerusalem in the Story of Muhammad's Night Journey and Ascension by Heribert Busse, (14) Muhammad and the Prophets by A.J. Wensinck; (IV) Muhammad and Christian Apologies—(15) The Prophet Muhammad: His Scripture and His Message According to the Christian Apologies in Arabic and Syriac from the First Abbasid Century by Sidney H. Griffith.

Notes and references are integrated in the text of each essay. There is a detailed name-subject index.

B-99. Sarton, George. *The Normans in European History.* Boston and New York: Houghton Mifflin Company, 1915.

According to Sarton, this book is not about the Norman history, but about the larger characteristics of Norman rulers' "work as founders and contributors to European culture," covering their "achievements in France, in England, and in Italy" (p.vii).

The 260-pages contain eight chapters: (1) Normandy and Its Place in History, (2) The Coming of the Northmen, (3) Normandy and England, (4) The Norman Empire, (5) Normandy and France, (6) Norman Life and Culture, (7) The Normans in the South, (8) The Norman Kingdom of Sicily.

There are occasional references to the Arab-Islamic world linkages from the Iberian Peninsula, but The Norman Kingdom of Sicily, in particular, includes several pages that document this influence; Sicily was part of the Islamic world for almost 200 years prior to the Norman kingdom. Politically, the kingdom was a mixed bureaucratic inheritance of the Lombards, Romans, Greeks, and the Saracens. Thus, the "Normans were profoundly modified by the bureaucratic traditions of the East" (p.227). The central financial body of the kingdom was called the Arabic *Diwan*, in Latin *duana*; and "it kept voluminous registers, called in Arabic *defetir,* and as its officers and clerks were largely Saracens, it seems plain to go back to Saracenic antecedents" (p.228). Further, "The culture of the Norman kingdom was even more strikingly composite than its government. Moreover, in the intellectual field the splendor of the Sicilian kingdom coincides with that movement which is often called the renaissance of the twelfth century and which consisted in considerable measure in the acquisition of new knowledge from the Greeks of the East and the Saracens of Sicily and Spain" (p.235). "The distinctive element in southern learning lay, however, not on the Latin side, but in its immediate contact with Greek and Arabic scholarship, and the chief meeting point of these various currents of culture was the royal court at Palermo, direct heir to the civilization of Saracen Sicily" (p.238).

Some notes and references are integrated in each chapter, followed by a bibliographic-note at the end of chapter. There is a name-subject index.

B-100. Saunders, J.J. *A History of Medieval Islam.* London: Routledge and Kegan Paul, 1965; reprinted 1972.

The book aims "to provide a brief sketch of a vast theme, a rough outline which may serve as an introduction for those wishing to acquire a general view of the Muslim world during the Middle Ages" (p.vii). The author points to the "indifference to Oriental history among the educated public of the West," which has been somewhat diminishing, "with wider perspectives now being opened up," and the historians are become less "Europe-centered" (p.vii). The author seems to have his own limitations, however, when he categorically suggests Islam "knows no distinction between secular and ecclesiastical, and is puzzled by our concepts of representative government and a free society" (p.vii). There have been numerous progressive elements in Islam that would dispute that observation.

The 220-page book begins with a glossary and a chronology of historic dates, followed by 12 chapters: (1) Arabia and Her Neighbors, (2) The Prophet, (3) The First Conquests, (4) The Civil Wars, (5) The Arab Empire, (6) The Abbasid Revolution, (7) The Breakup of the Caliphate, (8) The Isma'ilian Schism, (9) The Turkish Irruption, (10) The Christian Counter-Attack, (11) The Mongol Disaster, (12) The Civilization of Medieval Islam. There is an epilogue.

In discussing the Arab Empire, the author notes that the conquest of Spain was facilitated by the "Jews who especially blessed the tolerance which the Muslims had brought into the land" (p.88). And, "Pursuant to their usual policy, the Arabs permitted the Spanish Christians to be judged by their own laws" (p.88). Moreover, in addition to the acquisition of Arabic treatises on science and philosophy from Islamic Spain, "the sophisticated urban culture of Muslim Sicily also instructed its Christian conquerors, and Oriental art and scholarship radiated its influence deeply into Italy, thereby contributing something to the later Renaissance" (p.167). Further, while Muslims had long been familiar with Christian minorities in their midst, "as for the Western Christians, disappointment with the ultimate failure of the Crusades drove them into an attitude of bitter antagonism, and though the Koran was translated into Latin in 1143, late medieval literature displays small knowledge of Islam but many fantastic errors and misconceptions, not the least whimsical being the belief that Muhammad's iron coffin was suspended in midair at Mecca by the action of powerful loadstones!" (p.167).

Chapter 12 provides a summary of the causes of the rise and decline of Islamic

civilization. "The Shari'a came to dominate Muslim life as the Torah had dominated post-exilic Judaism. The door was closed against further borrowings from
outside: philosophy was repudiated as a danger to Faith" (p.197). Further, Ibn
Rushd's (1126–1198) defense of "pursuit of secular science fell on deaf ears and
exposed him to the charge of atheism" (p.197). In his epilogue, the author
expresses doubt as to the "spiritual and intellectual" future of Islam (p.203).

Each chapter provides a list of "books for further reading" at the end. There
is a name-subject index.

B-101. Sauvaget, Jean. *Introduction to the History of the Muslim East: A Bibliographical Guide.* Berkeley, CA: University of California Press, 1965.

The book hopes to achieve the "broadening of the Western mind on the one
hand, and the growing activity of the native scholars of Islamic lands on the
other" and thereby, "correct a situation that is detrimental to the study of man in
general and that cannot be explained as due exclusively to the difficulties
involved in the study of the sources" (p.6). The cleavage between the historians
and Orientalists must be rectified, the author emphasizes, "as though there were
two kinds of humanity and not a common history," and they "must learn to col-
laborate" (p.6). The book is not about "Muslim East," defined as Syria-Palestine,
Arabia, Mesopotamia, Egypt, Turkey, and neighboring regions. Thus, while the
greater emphasis is on Muslim East, "Muslim West" (North Africa, Spain in the
Middle Ages, and Sicily) is also covered.

This 250-page bibliographic guide is divided into three parts. Part One (The
Sources of Muslim History) contains nine chapters, extending to language and
scripts, archives, narrative sources, travel books, literary and archeological
sources, etc. Part Two (Tools of Research and General Works) covers the main
works of reference and related concerns which could not be classified chronologically and contains four chapters encompassing historical and reference works
(periodicals), special disciplines (geography, historical topography, ethnology),
dynastic series and tribal genealogies, the main outlines of Muslim history (eco-
nomic-social life, religion, slavery, technology and warfare, land tenure, philosophy and science, etc.). Part Three (Historical Bibliography) has 12 chapters
dealing with bibliography of works classified according to period or region (pre-
Islamic Arabia, Muhammad and Qur'an, early Caliphs, Abbasid Caliphate, Seljuks, Mongols, Mamluks, Iran and Muslim East, Ottoman Empire, the Muslim
West, and the Influence of Muslim Culture in Europe).

As to a bibliography guide to the Islamic influences, the author cautions, "The
influence of Islamic culture in Europe is evident, but there is nothing more peril-
ous than the accurate definition of its channels and its exact nature in any given
period or region. Many hasty, exaggerated, or erroneous assertions have been
made, particularly in connection with the Crusades. In this field of study the student cannot be too often advised to exercise the greatest possible caution and to
be as objective as he can" (p.229). As for the book in general, the author sug-

gests, it "must be regarded as nothing more than a guide to the diversity and the richness of the research still to be done" (p.231).

There is a 27-page index of the names of the authors identified in the book.

B-102. Savory, R.M. *Introduction to Islamic Civilization.* Cambridge and New Delhi, India: Cambridge University Press/Vikas Publishing House, 1976.

The book is a wide-ranging, general introduction to the Islamic civilization. What began as 24 radio broadcasts in Canada between 1970 and 1971, it "examines the religious, philosophical, and legal foundations of Islamic civilization and its contributions to world civilization in the field of literature, art, science, and medicine. It also deals with the interaction between the East and the Christian West from the Crusades in medieval times down to the massive encroachment of the West upon the Muslim world at all levels—military, political, economic and cultural—in the modern era" (p.vii–viii). The focus is primarily on the Middle East; Moorish Spain and the Maghrib (Muslim North Africa) are not given special treatment but are mentioned contextually.

The 300-page book has 18 essays written by prominent scholars: (1) Introduction to the Middle East by G.M. Wickens, (2) The Historical Background of Islamic Civilization by C.E. Bosworth, (3) Islamic Faith by Charles Adams, (4) God and His Creation: Two Medieval Islamic Views by Michael E. Marmura, (5) Law and Traditional Society by R.M. Savory, (6) Arabic Literature: A Living Heritage by Ella Marmura, (7) Persian Literature: An Affirmation of Identity by G.M. Wickens, (8) Turkish Literature through the Ages by Eleazar Birnbaum, (9) Islamic Art: Variations on Themes of Arabesque by R. Sandler, (10) The Middle East as World Center of Science and Medicine by G.M. Wickens, (11) What the West Borrowed from the Middle East by G.M. Wickens, (12) Christendom vs. Islam: 14 Centuries of Interaction and Coexistence by R.M. Savory, (13) The Changing Concept of the Individual by R. Sandler, (14) The Modern Arab World by L.M. Kenny, (15) Tribalism and Modern Society: Iraq, a Case Study by Albertine Jwaideh, (16) Iran by W. Millward, (17) Turkey: From Cosmopolitan Empire to Nation State by Eleazar Birnbaum, (18) Khatimah by G.M. Wickens.

The book also contains numerous pictures and maps. There is a list of suggested background reading and a glossary of terms, followed by a name-subject index.

B-103. Sha'ban, M.A. *Islamic History, A.D. 600–750 (A.H. 132): A New Interpretation.* Cambridge: Cambridge University Press, 1971.

The book is a systematic attempt to present "a new interpretation of early Islamic history in light of a detailed scrutiny" of "newly discovered material" and re-examination and re-interpretation of older sources. The author pays special attention to the "way the Arab tribesman were settled in the various provinces, their relationship with the conquered peoples, their varying interests, activities and rivalries, their relations with the central government and the attempts of the latter to establish its authority over the vast conquered territories" (p.vii). The author argues that despite their occasional shortcomings, "Arab statesmen were responsible leaders" and not driven by "hatred and fanatical delusions" (p.vii–viii).

The 200-page book has ten chapters: (1) The Islamic revolution in its environment, (2) The emergence of Abu Bakr, (3) Umar and the conquests, (4) The breakdown of the Madinan regime, (5) Mu'awiya and the second civil war, (6) The age of Hajjaj, (7) Moderate reform, radical reform and reaction: The reigns of Sulayman, Umar II and Yazid II, (8) Hisham: Survival of the empire, (9) The collapse of the Marwanids, (10) The end of an era. Four expository maps are provided.

There is a bibliography of the works cited at the end, followed by a name-subject index.

B-104. Sonn, Tamara. *A Brief History of Islam.* Oxford: Blackwell Publishing Ltd., 2004.

This 203-page book outlines Islamic history, beginning with the life of Muhammad and the birth of Islamic ethos, through Islam's geographical expansion and cultural development, up to the creation of modern states and the current situation in Islamic societies. An attempt is made to enable readers to clearly grasp the interrelated cultural, political, and ideological developments. Throughout the book, representative events, characters, and movements have been selected to highlight the key issues and engage the reader. The book concludes with vignettes of Islamic life that represent current challenges facing Islamic societies.

The book has five chapters: (1) Many Paths to One God: Establishing the Ideals, (2) Pursuit of Knowledge in the Service of God and Humanity: The Golden Age, (3) Division and Organization, (4) Colonialism and Reform, (5) Obstacles and Prospects for Islamic Reform. Among other things, the author notes, "The translations of classical Greek, Persian, and Indian texts, in the intellectually charged atmosphere of medieval Islam, became the basis of the Muslim world's great cultural flowering in the Middle Ages. They were the basis of Europe's, as well, transmitted to Europe via Syria, Sicily, and especially Spain. A school was established in eleventh-century Toledo specifically for translating Arabic texts into Latin" (p.55). Further, "The debt of Europe to the medieval Islamic scholars is impossible to measure. As historian Philip Hitti put it, 'Had the researchers of Aristotle, Galen, and Ptolemy been lost to posterity the world would have been as poor as if they had never been produced'" (p.56).

There are six illustrative pictures in the book. Chapter-by-chapter notes and references are provided at the end, as is a "further reading" bibliography, organized in terms of broad topics (art and architecture, current affairs, history, literature, religion, philosophy, science, women). Also, there is a list of websites and a name-subject index.

B-105. Southern, Richard W. *The Making of Middle Ages.* New Haven, CT: Yale University Press, 1959.

The formation of Western Europe from the late tenth to the early 13th century is the subject of this book. In this evolution the book explores "new views of the world [that] raised problems for scholars as well as statesmen—questions, for instance, about the bounds of the habitable world, or about the right use of force against heretics, schismatics and unbelievers" (p.230). Further, "Students in Arts Faculty were learning about the heavens from Ptolemy and his Arab commentators—the 'real stuff' at last, undebased by the tradition of the Latins" (p.230). And, "It was the same on all the frontiers of knowledge. The extension of the boundaries of knowledge was accompanied by, and indeed made possible by the changing structure of society, by the enlarging of the field of vision beyond the confines of highly localized interests" (p.231).

The 280-page book has five detailed chapters: (1) Latin Christendom and Its Neighbors, (2) The Bonds of Society, (3) The Ordering of the Christian Life, (4) The Tradition of Thought, (5) From Epic to Romance. While there are frequent references to linkages between the early Islamic world and evolving Latin Europe, there is more focused discussion on these aspects in the first chapter. As to the "Crusading" zeal of the West, "certainly it was not born in the border lands where Christian and Moslem met: in these lands we find rather the spirit of live-and-let-live, a certain tentative friendliness even, produced by the desire to avoid unnecessary trouble. The impulse to attack was generated further back, in the power-centers of Europe" (p.49). However, "Despite the Crusades—partly even as a result of the Crusades—Christian and Moslem scholars met on common ground in scientific enquiry" (p.67). Further, between about 1150 and 1200, translations of Greek thought from Arabic entered Latin Europe, and "to this body of scientific works we should add the works of Moslem scholars, who henceforth became familiar in the West under strange names—Albumazar, Alfragani, Alfarabi, Avicenna, and soon, and most potent of all, Averroes" (p.67). The author adds that "the collaboration was of more permanent importance than the hostility" (p.67).

Each chapter has its own page-by-page footnotes. There is a general bibliographic narrative, with references, at the end, as well as chapter-by-chapter bibliographic narratives along with appropriate references. There is a name-subject index.

B-106. Stiefel, Tina. *The Intellectual Revolution in Twelfth-Century Europe.* New York: St. Martin's Press, 1985.

Somewhat revisionistic, the book is intended to offer a fresh interpretation as to the development of "skeptical rationality" during early 12th century that for the first time since antiquity began to see "the world as open to human inquiry" (p.1).

Stiefel argues that the prevailing view of medieval thinking about science is deficient, for, among other things, "productive ideas concerning nature as a fit subject of objective inquiry were articulated in Western Europe before the appearance of the Aristotelian corpus in translation. These ideas and approaches to natural sciences which were expressed then were influenced in part by Arab scientific thought, scattered bits of Greek science and medicine, and the Chalcidius' version of Plato's *Timaeus*" (p.2). Further, "Till now we have two enlightenments to ponder—that of the ancient Greeks and that of the eighteenth century. The evanescent but brilliant flash of intellectual light that made an appearance in the twelfth century is not unworthy of some scrutiny and, in view of the historical circumstances surrounding it, considerable wonder" (p.4). Thus, the book builds upon other works of this type, in particular, "the pioneering work of Charles Homer Haskins and the seminal studies in medieval science of A.C. Crombie" (p.5).

Referring to 12th-century Latin monks such as Adelard of Bath, William of Conches, and Thierry of Chatres, the author says they traveled "to foreign centers of non-Latin culture such as Toledo and Seville, they taught themselves Arabic the better to uncover new ideas and approaches to the world in which they lived," for, heretofore, for a good Christian, "scientific research would be thought of as an unsavory occupation" (p.12–13). And, "Such uses to which a knowledge of nature was being put at this time suggested the possibility of mastery in nature, an idea that probably originated in Islam. (The ancient Greeks did not use it.) For the Arabic treatises now being translated stressed the concept of making nature serve man, of gaining power and control over it" (p.70). The book is interspersed with quotations from Latin-medieval scholars (e.g., Adelard of Bath, addressing his nephew, says, "For I was taught by my Arab masters to be led only by reason, whereas you were taught to follow the halter of the captured image of authority" [p.80]).

The 120-page book has five short but tightly written chapters. After the introduction, these are: (1) The Intellectual Background, (2) The Role of Reason, (3) The New Conception of Science, (4) The Critical Examination of Tradition, (5) The Voice of the Opposition.

Notes and references are appended at the end of each chapter. There is a detailed bibliography at the end; there is no index, however.

B-107. Stewart, Desmond. *Early Islam.* New York: Time Inc., 1967.

The book is part of a series entitled A History of the World's Cultures. It is noted in the introduction that "Islam is a way of life that has religious aspects, political aspects and cultural aspects, and each of the three overlaps and interacts. To do justice to a triple story of this kind presents problems that tax the ingenuity of any author" (p.7). The author has done a rather thorough job of putting together this story, with vivid narrative, illustrations, documentary evidence, and authenticity.

There are eight chapters in this 192-page book and each includes a picture essay: (1) A Messenger from God (Essay: The Prophet's Progress), (2) Five Pillars of Faith (Essay: Desert Sanctuaries), (3) A Time of Conquest (Essay: Reaches of Empire), (4) The Golden Age (Essay: A Muslim's Life), (5) An Art of Many Peoples (Essay: Craftsmen's Treasures), (6) The Scientist–Philosophers (Essay: A Persian Bestiary), (7) From Spain to Sumatra (Essay: Patterns of an Enchanted Place), (8) A Durable Religion (Essay: Islam's Magic Carpets).

Chapters 6 and 7, in particular, discuss the contributions of Islamic scholars and how "modern man—dependent as he is on the drugs of the chemist and the skills of the physician, on the reckoning of the computer and the predictions of the economic planner—owes more of a debt than he might suspect to the Islamic scientists of the Middle Ages" (p.121). And, "While Muslim scholarship had an impact on virtually every field of science, it probably reached a climax in the work of a single historian, Ibn Khaldun, who was the first to examine society scientifically," in that he "gave history a new dimension by trying to find rational laws to explain it and the human behavior that shaped it" (p.130). Further, "Through a series of penetrating commentaries on Aristotle's philosophy, Averroes [Ibn Rushd, 1126–1198 AD] reintroduced Europe to the true nature of Aristotle's ideas. Indeed, he laid the groundwork for one of the great intellectual triumphs of the Middle Ages: St. Thomas Aquinas' *Summa Theologica*" (p.144). Referring to the Crusades, the author states, "In attacking the people it considered its arch-enemies, Christianity did not even hesitate to distort history. A classic case is the saga of the *Song of Roland*" (p.143).

At the end the book provides a chronological listing of significant events during the Islamic era, followed by a bibliography classified in terms of general history, art and architecture, literature, science and thought, and religion. There is a detailed author-subject index.

B-108. Strayer, Joseph R., Hans W. Gatzke, and E. Harris Harbison. *The Mainstream of Civilization*, second edition. New York: Harcourt Brace Jovanovich, 1974.

The authors express their humility about this undertaking, in that "it requires a certain amount of courage to attempt to write a history of civilization in one volume," and, further, that "we trust no one will passively accept our interpretations or believe that our book is an adequate summary of human history" (p.v). Yet, the book is fairly comprehensive and covers "the basic characteristics of each civilization and of different periods in the history of each civilization" (p.v). But, "This is a history of civilization, with emphasis on the civilization developed by the peoples of Europe" (p.xxviii). "There is unbroken continuity between the civilization of the Greeks and the Romans and that of the modern West" (p.xxiv). A remnant of the old Roman Empire, however, became the Byzantine Empire, Christian in belief, Greek in language, but strongly influenced by the East. Once Western Europe achieved its own "independent and consistent civilization," it benefitted from "contacts with the more highly developed civilizations of the Arab and Byzantine worlds" (p.xxiv).

The book is divided into Ancient, Medieval, and Modern components, with several chapters in each, totaling 34. There are two chapters that cover in some detail the role and significance of the Islamic civilization. Chapter 8 (Byzantium and Islam) has a ten-page section on Mohammed and the Rise of the Arab Empire, and the author discusses the "obvious similarities between Islam and Christianity." Further, "Islam had a great advantage. It needed no organized church, for it had neither a priesthood nor a sacramental system. Each individual had to assure his salvation by his own right belief and good conduct. Every essential act of the religion could be accomplished by a man living quite by himself. These advantages often gave Islam the victory in competition with Christianity" (p.172).

In addition, chapter 14 (Western Europe's Neighbors during the Middle Ages) discusses the role of Arabic scholarship and its influence on the West. With the background of the rediscovered Greek heritage, "by the ninth century Moslem scholars had assimilated the work of their predecessors and were beginning to make original contributions of their own. From 900 to 1200 the most important work done anywhere in the world in mathematics, astronomy, physics, medicine, and geography was done in Moslem countries" (p.301). Once these contributions were transferred to the West, the author notes, they "had a decisive influence on the course of western civilization. Certainly the West would not have developed a scientific tradition of its own as rapidly as it did without the assistance of Moslem scholarship, and quite possibly it never would have developed the tradition at all" (p.302).

Each chapter has a topical list of suggestions for further reading. There are numerous illustrations in each chapter and their chapter-by-chapter sources are listed at the end of the book, followed by a detailed name-subject index.

B-109. Thatcher, Oliver J. and Edgar Holmes McNeal. *Europe in the Middle Ages.* New York: Charles Scribner's Sons, 1896; reprint 1920.

"The greatest factor in the progress of man has been his ability to use the experience—the achievements, the successes, and even the failures—of the generations that have preceded him," say the authors (p.v). Early centuries of the European Middle Age (about 350 to 1500) were the result of catastrophic invasions of the barbarians.

The 550-page book provides a comprehensive history of medieval Europe, beginning with the Roman Empire. The coverage includes topics such as the Germanic invasions, the empire of Charlemagne, European feudalism, Papacy and Monasticism, struggles between Papacy and the Empire, Mohammadanism, the Crusades, origins of national states, the Hundred Years' War, decline of the Papacy power, urban life, industry and commerce, civilization and culture, and the Renaissance. The authors suggest, "The life of Mohammad, viewed narrowly, lies outside the field of European history. But in a larger, truer sense it may properly find a place there. The influence of Mohammadans in Europe has been considerable and, many times, good. I have tried therefore to explain Mohammadanism by describing its founder. If I have succeeded in humanizing him, I am content" (p.xi).

While there are occasional references to "Mohammedanism" in various chapters, chapter 14 (21 pages) is devoted entirely to "Mohammed and Mohammedanism," and the first 12 pages are replete with invectives. The "camel-driver" engaged in "mockery," "had acquired all his religious ideas from the Jews," had "shallow theological knowledge" and "demanded" acceptance as a prophet, created "forgeries about Abraham," engaged in "ever-increasing deception and violence," "plundered the Jews," and his "nervous attacks resembled epilepsy," and so forth.

The rest of the chapter has relatively positive content, however. Mohammad was about like "King David, in whom vindictiveness, cruelty, lust, and deceit were found side by side with the noblest qualities," but if "we study Mohammed in a comparative way from the point of view of his age and of his people and surroundings we find that he possessed qualities and virtues which command our respect and admiration" (p.266). While "during his early years Mohammad declared over and over again that there should be no compulsion in religion," later Mohammedans "forced their religion upon heathen peoples, [but] permitted Jews and Christians to retain their faith. But it must not be supposed that Mohammedanism has been spread only by the sword" (p.267).

Further, "After all, the genius of Mohammed revolutionized their [followers'] minds, and started in them a tremendous impulse to achievement" (p.269). "The elements of this civilization they derived from Greece, Persia, and India, but they modified them and improved them, and the resulting civilization they spread from Spain far into central Asia" (p.272). And, "Through them and their translations medieval Europe obtained its first knowledge of Aristotle. They learned medicine and surgery from the Greeks, but added materially to the stock of medical knowledge. . . . They excelled in mathematics . . . and invented the zero" (p.273). Further, "Much of their learning was carried into Europe in the twelfth and thirteenth centuries and hastened there the general awakening which is called the Renaissance" (p.274).

As for the Crusades (chapter 15), among other things, the authors discuss the various positive effects on Europe—commerce and trade which "increased the wealth of Europe," and one "can hardly estimate the civilizing effect of the introduction" of various symbols of Islamic culture, and "most important still was their effect in quickening the intellect and widening the mental horizon of Europe" (p.305). "This growth [of intelligence and knowledge] was accelerated by the learned and scientific books which they [Europeans] derived from the Mohammedans" (p.306).

The book provides a detailed bibliography, first a list of several source books and works of a general character, then a specific chapter-by-chapter list of references. This is followed by several chronological tables listing various popes and emperors, as well as flowcharts enumerating the various European dynasties from the fifth century to the 16th. There is also a comprehensive, 18-page name-subject index.

B-110. Thomas, Bertram. *The Arabs: The Life of a People Who Have Left Their Deep Impress on the World.* New York: Doubleday, Doran and Company, 1937.

Based on a series of lectures at Harvard's Lowell Institute in 1936, this is a "life story of the Arab people, a story of wide scope and varied interest, attempting as it does an outline of their history, religion, medieval civilization and later-day politics" (p.v). It is intended for the general reader.

The 360-page book has four parts, with a few chapters in each: Part One, The Rise, with four chapters: (1) Arabs in Antiquity, (2) The Prophet Muhammad, (3) Conquests—Eastwards, (4) Conquests—Westwards; Part Two, Arab Civilization, with three chapters: (1) The Medieval State, (2) The Arts, (3) The Sciences; Part Three, The Decline, with three chapters: (1) Disintegration and Decline, (2) The Arabs of Arabia, (3) Rise of the West; Part Four, Revival, with three chapters: (1) Arabs, (2) The World War, (3) Palestine.

There is an epilogue at the end that discusses issues confronting the Arab world—modernization, need for general education, oil resources, links with the West, and the status of Palestine. There are 27 illustrations and maps interspersed in the book, followed by an appendix on the "racial origins of the Arabs."

There is a detailed bibliography and a name-subject index.

B-111. Treadgold, Warren, ed. *Renaissances Before the Renaissance: Cultural Revivals of Late Antiquity and the Middle Ages.* Stanford, CA: Stanford University Press, 1984.

The book explores the evolution of the Western culture between the first century AD and the 15th-century Italian Renaissance, the thesis being that this period was not one of continuous decline or stagnation, but instead saw several revivals of culture. There were setbacks, or "dark ages," and there were revivals, the "renaissances." Such issues are explored in a series of papers presented at a 1981 gathering at Stanford University; the 238-page book is a collection of these papers.

After the introductory essay by the editor, the book includes seven "Renaissance" essays, written by well-known scholars. These are: (1) The Second Sophistic (Greek literary activity during the first and second centuries AD) by B.P. Reardon, (2) The Latin Revival of the Fourth Century by Alan Cameron, (3) The Carolingian Renaissance by John J. Contreni, (4) The Macedonian Renaissance by Warren Treadgold, (5) The Anglo-Saxon Monastic Revival by George Hardin Brown, (6) The Twelfth-Century Renaissance by Stephen C. Ferruolo, (7)

The Palaeologan Renaissance (the 1261–1453 period, the reign of the last Byzantine dynasty) by Igor Sevcenko. There is a concluding chapter by the editor.

Of special relevance presently is the essay that discusses the Twelfth-Century Renaissance, "the most widely acknowledged of the pre-Renaissance renaissances," which "was also the one that most resembled the Renaissance proper— not only in time and place but also in extent and originality" (p.17). It was during this renaissance that the "Europeans encountered new ideas and new problems as they learned of and from the two great neighboring civilizations of Byzantium and Islam" (p.136). Further, "The cultural advances they made during this time were undoubtedly influenced by the rediscovery of the classical past, but the greater stimulus probably came from the discovery of Byzantium and Islam, two very different and hostile cultures that shared that same past" (p.137). The Twelfth-Century and Palaeologan Renaissances formed the basis of the subsequent Renaissance proper, according to Treadgold.

Detailed chapter-by-chapter notes are provided at the end, along with a selected/annotated bibliography also tied to each chapter. There is a detailed name-subject index.

B-112. Watt, W. Montgomery. *The Majesty That Was Islam: The Islamic World, 661–1100.* London: Sidgwick & Jackson Ltd., 1974.

This book, written by one of the most eminent 20th-century Islamicists in the West, is a classic. As the author states, it documents the experiences of a large part of the human race over a period of four and a half centuries—the golden age of the Islamic civilization. The story begins after the death of Ali in 661, marking the end of the period of the first four caliphs (that begin from the death of Mohammad in 632) and the beginning of the Ummayyad caliphate. The introductory chapter provides a brief discussion of the early history, beginning with the Prophethood of Mohammad and the end of the period of the first four caliphs.

The 276-page book is divided into five dynastic periods chronologically, with several chapters on various aspects within each: (1) The Umayyad Period, 661–750 (struggle for power, expansion, forms of government, religious aspects of rule, beginnings of Islamic culture); (2) The First Period of Abbasid Century, 750–850 (establishment of rule, political struggle, Arab self-assertion in religion, theology and the stimulus of Hellenism, Arab self-assertion of humanities); (3) The Abbasid Decline, 850–945 (struggle at the center, growing autonomy in the provinces, new forms of Shi'ism, consolidation of Sunnism, intellectual currents—literature, history, geography, rational theology, sufism); (4) The Muwayhid Period, 945–1055 (the empire, the provincial empires, politics and theology, trends in literature, science and philosophy); (5) The Earlier Seljuq Period, 1055–1100 (the empire, the Mediterranean provinces, the intellectual struggle).

There is an extensive bibliography at the end, along with an appendix on Arabic names and Islamic dates. There is also a name-subject index.

B-113. Weaver, Henry Grady. *The Mainspring of Human Progress.* Irvington on Hudson, NY: The Foundation for Economic Education, Inc., 1953; original 1947.

The author, a Baptist minister, wrote this book based on the conviction that "human liberty is the mainspring of progress and that government tends always to tyranny" (p.7). Further, the book is a condensation of Rose Wilder Lane's book *The Discovery of Freedom* (1943).

The book is divided into three parts. Part I, Comparisons and Contrasts, has three chapters; Part II, The Old World Views, has four chapters; Part III, The Revolution, has 14 chapters. Part I traces the poor conditions of life, materially and otherwise, over centuries—and how individual liberty unleashed the solutions. Part II explores some solutions that did not work (Paganism, Socialism, etc.). Part III talks about the "Revolution" that worked. Here the author talks of the "First Attempt" that began 4,000 years ago with Abraham in Iraq (Ur), but failed because his followers "went back to pagan submission to an imaginary authority" (p.83). Later, the new commandment of Christ emphasized human brotherhood, but while there are glimmers, nowhere are found the God-given rights of freedom.

Then, in chapter 10, the author discusses the "Second Attempt" that gave rise to individual freedom, based on Islam's religious individualism. "While Europe was still stagnating in the Dark Ages—and several centuries before Britain had its Magna Carta—a dynamic but little known civilization, based on a recognition of personal freedom, was blazing in the Near East and spreading along the shores of the Mediterranean" (p.98). There is brief discussion of the emergence of Islam, whose "one God judges men but does not control them; each individual is self-controlling and responsible for his own deeds; all men are brothers" (p.100). Further, this chapter discusses the "Saracen's" contributions, their universities, their five centuries of progress, their "bewildering" discoveries, their cleanliness, and so forth. "And for 800 years, during the period when the greater part of Europe was submerged in the Dark Ages, this religion produced the most brilliant progress and the greatest material prosperity than had ever been known to man" (p.119). However, "The days of the Saracens were numbered. Medieval Europeans had broken through the Pyrenees; and the spirit of the Crusaders—a white heat of religious fanaticism—was directed against the Saracens of Spain. At the mercy of the Inquisitors in the West and disrupted at its core by the barbarous attacks of the Turks, the world of the Saracens sank into stagnation. But in the wake of this disintegration, there followed a highly significant result" (p.130).

And this was the "Third Attempt." "Through Italy, the Saracens had given Europeans 'the awakening of science and learning' which lifted them out of the Dark Ages; through Spain, the last of their energy led to the development of a new world. The discovery, exploration, and early colonization of America are closely connected with the Spanish Inquisition" (p.131). And the voyage of Columbus "would hardly have been possible except for the magnetic compass developed by the Saracens. The maps and navigation charts were also based on information supplied by the Saracens" (p.138). And, "Columbus might have come and gone and made no more difference than Eric the Red, if human energy had not leaped from Saracenic Spain" (p.139).

The succeeding chapters discuss the outstanding material progress of America, based on individual freedom and opportunities. It also talks of the moral dilemma and war potential of this material progress.

At the end there are two bibliographies, one pertaining to references used in the text and the other a general bibliography. These are followed by a name-subject index.

B-114. Welch, Alford T. and Pierre Cachia, eds. *Islam: Past Influence and Present Challenge*. New York: State University of New York Press, 1979.

This collection of essays is inspired as a tribute to W. Montgomery Watt of the University of Edinburgh; some of the authors are former students of Professor Watt, others long-time colleagues and friends. The book aims to produce a significant, unified work on Islam, built around a specific theme. The result is said to be not so much a fully integrated survey, but "a number of significant landmarks" (p.v). Commenting on Watt's numerous works, one of the contributors states that Watt "wrote not only for the sake of writing or for eternity but equally for the educated people outside his discipline, who wanted, or needed to be enlightened about the 'Majesty that was Islam' and the reality it *is* in the present world" (p.x). Further, he was concerned with development of concepts "which could make Islam as a religion and Muslim civilization as a whole understandable to an outsider" (p.xii). And "this is why he tried to distill the fundamental notions of Muslim civilization out of a recalcitrant mass of material; he wanted to make clear the alternatives which Islam, growing out of the same roots as Christianity, is able to offer. It is only with the awareness of these alternatives a meaningful and unprejudiced dialogue can be started" (p.xiii).

Thus, here is the list of the essays grouped in four parts of the book: Part I, Islamic Thought: (1) L'influence d'Ibn Taymiyya by Henri Laoust, College de France (Paris), (2) Avicenna's Chapter on Universals in the *Isagoge of His Shifa'* by Michael E. Marmura, University of Toronto, (3) The Pure Brethren and the Philosophical Structure of Their System by Geo Widengren, Uppsala University, (4) Des Reformistes (*islahiyyun*) aux mutations en cours by Louis Garden, College Philosophique et Theologique, Toulouse; Part II, Islam in History and Society: (1) Al-Maqrizi's Exposition of the Formative Period in Islamic History and Its Cosmic Significance: *The Kitab an-niza wa-t-takhasum* by C.E. Bosworth, University of Manchester, (2) The Impact of Islam on the Laity in Europe from Charlemagne to Charles the Bold by Norman Daniel, British Council, Cairo, (3) An Islamic Element in the Early Spanish University by George Makdisi, University of Pennsylvania; Part III, Islam in Literature: (1) The Impact of Islam on Early Arabic Poetry by James A. Bellamy, (2) Kharjas in Arabic and Romance: Popular Poetry in Muslim Spain by James T. Moore, University of California, Berkeley, (3) Ghalib's Qasida in Honor of the Prophet by Annemarie Schimmel,

Harvard University; Part IV, Islam and Other Faiths: (1) Quelques reflexions sur l'apparition de l'Islam dans le milieu du Proche Orient by Claude Cahen, La Sorbonne, Paris, (2) World Religions as Seen in the Light of Islam by Jacques Waardenburg, University of Utrecht, (3) The Art of Theology: Islamic and Christian Reflections by Kenneth Cragg, University of Sussex, (4) Encounter between Islam and the African Traditional Religions by Noel Q. King, University of California, Santa Cruz.

The essays in this 360-page book are followed by an "envoi" section, containing (1) Islam: Challenges and Opportunities by Fazlur Rahman, University of Chicago, and (2) Bibliography of W. Montgomery Watt by Michael McDonald, University of Edinburgh. Each essay ends with a list of footnotes, with bibliographic references integrated. There is a detailed name-subject index.

B-115. Wiener, Leo. *Contributions Toward a History of Arabico-Gothic Culture*, four volumes. New York: Neale Publishing Company, 1917, 1919, 1920, and 1921.

The author argues that Germanic languages have arisen by an influx of Low Latin and Arabic. Further, he challenges the "storm of indignation" provoked by his earlier publications and hopes there would be a "change of heart after becoming acquainted with the sum total of my medieval investigations" (p.ix, vol.I). The evidence in these volumes relates to the author's attempt to demonstrate "how the literary Germanic languages have arisen on a weak Germanic substratum by a sudden influx of Low Latin, Arabic, and ghost words," and that they "arose from the Graeco-Latin glossaries under the influence of Gothic interpretations, which themselves owe their origin to the Graeco-Arabic learning of Spain" (p.ix, vol.I). The author is emphatic about his discovery of new documents and argues that "the manner in which the Arabic words got into the Gothic Bible and into the Keronian glosses has by this discovery been made clear beyond all anticipation, and the subjects surveyed by me have been removed from the field of speculation to that of self-evident facts" (p.x, vol.I). Even the word "gothic" is traced by the author to its Arabic origins. The four volumes include a most comprehensive etymology of various words of Germanic languages, thoroughly traced to their Graeco-Arabic origins, with the use of author's thorough knowledge of the Arabic, Latin, and Greek languages. The author challenges other philologists in that he is concerned, additionally, with history, and argues, "My task is accomplished if I compel the world of scholars to take into consideration the influence of Arabico-Gothic culture upon the history of Europe" (p.xix, vol.I).

Volume II "contains the *Prolegomena* to a work on the Arabic element in the Germanic languages" and attempts to "remove the rubbish of ages which has accumulated in palaeography" (p.vii, vol.II). Volume III relates to "Tacitus' *Germania* and Other Forgeries," and documents the "amazing similarity in method in the *Germania* and the writers who had fallen under the Arabian influence" (p.x, vol.III). Further, "There was no escape—the Spanish Goths of the eighth and ninth centuries not only furnished wholesale literary and documentary frauds to the western world, but also inspired interpolations and more important frauds in Greek literature" (p.x, vol.III). In Volume IV the author challenges his critics further, and he argues that "whether Arabic has had the influence I claim upon the Germanic languages, cannot be settled by any *a priori* reasoning. It is only my investigation which proves it, and my critics are perverted and absurd when they condemn me on general principles. The difference between my critics and me is this. They know in advance what should be and what should not be, whereas I am mustering facts and deduce the logical consequences. My critics would do well to discuss the facts that I adduce and leave theories alone for the present" (p.lxxxi, vol.IV).

Each volume enumerates a detailed list of sources quoted, along with notes and references on almost every page of the four volumes (about 1,600 pages altogether). Each volume provides two indices, one by words (each word identified whether Arabic, Hebrew, Low-Latin, Greek, etc.), and the other by subject.

B-116. Wiet, Gaston, Vadime Elisseeff, Philippe Wolff, and Jean Naudou. *History of Mankind: Cultural and Scientific Development—The Great Medieval Civilizations* (translated from French). New York and London: Sponsored by UNESCO, Harper & Row, 1975.

This is Volume III of the six volumes in the *History of Mankind* series published under sponsorship of the United Nations Educational, Scientific and Cultural Organization (UNESCO). The other volumes are: Volume I, Prehistory and the Beginnings of Civilization; Volume II, The Ancient World; Volume IV, The Foundations of the Modern World; Volume V, The World in the Nineteenth Century; and Volume VI, The Twentieth Century.

This particular volume, about 1,100 pages long, explores the world's cultural development between the sixth and early 14th centuries—the period that saw the splendor of the great Asian empires and the emergence of Western Europe as a major center of civilization, as well as the Golden Age of Islam during the intervening centuries. The book is divided into three parts, with several chapters in each.

Part One, The Historical Background, has four chapters—(1) The Migration of Peoples in Eurasia in the Fifth and Sixth Centuries, (2) The Impact of China and India, and the Arab Progress, (3) The Moslem Zenith, Europe and Byzantium from the Seventh to the Eleventh Centuries, (4) Asia, The Arabs, and the Awakening of Europe, from the Tenth to Thirteenth Centuries.

Part Two, Cultural Achievements, is divided into three sections, with 3–4 chapters in each. Section (a) Technological Development—Language and Learning, with three chapters: (1) Evolution of Techniques, (2) The Evolution of Languages and Writing Systems, (3) Learning and Education; Section (b) Religion and Philosophy, Law and Politics, with four chapters: (1) The Chinese World, (2) The Indian World, (3) The Arabic World, (4) Europe and Byzantium; Section (c)

Scientific Thought, Literary and Artistic Expression, with three chapters: (1) The Development of Scientific Thought, (2) Literary Expression, (3) Artistic Expression.

Part Three, Africa, the Americas, and Oceania, has three chapters: (1) The Prehistory of Africa, (2) Prehistoric New World Cultural Development, (3) The Neolithic Settlements of Oceania. Specifically relevant here are sections in each chapter pertaining to the Arab-Islamic civilization—not only there is extensive discussion of various historical sociocultural developments in early Islam, but there is also discussion of the origins and development of Arab scientific knowledge in various fields, translation, transmission, and impact of that knowledge upon Latin Europe. "Science received a new impetus as a consequence of the discoveries of Arab science," say the authors.

The book provides 64 illustrative plates on various topics (medieval agriculture, Arabic water-clock, Arabic surgical instruments, etc.), 56 figures (Arabian plough, lateen sail, Hagia Sophia, evolution of Gothic churches, etc.), 30 maps, and five tables (including one that shows the translations of various Greek works into Arabic and Latin). There is a 70-page bibliography, with detailed classification according to various topics covered in the text. There is a 36-page name-subject index.

B-117. Williams, John Alden, ed. *Themes of Islamic Civilization.* Berkeley, Los Angeles, and London: University of California Press, 1971.

This book is an "attempt to illustrate, from the writings of the Muslim peoples, certain themes and archetypal ideas that have moulded Muslim minds and found expression in institutions of a civilization that, to them, was Islamic: was engaged with, was committed to, the God of revelation" (p.1). The editor hopes that "the book will be useful to students of Muslim institutions, but it is not a book on Muslim institutions. Rather, it is about the attitudes or the convictions that lay behind those institutions, and so helped to condition characteristic responses of the Muslims of one world civilization to history, and to the world they have encountered in history" (p.1).

The 382-page book draws from the writings of Muslims from Spain to Anatolia and India, where religion is not just part of the structure of faith and society; "it is the structure" (p.2). The Muslims of southeast Asia are not included; in that region religion and culture differ, for the older and preexisting culture is viewed as "satisfactorily Islamic" (p.1). The book's reference is to the historic Islamic civilization, "the most spectacularly fortunate of the three great post-Hellenistic civilizations," and "more vital than either Eastern or Western Christian civilizations" (p.2). Yet, "Islamic civilization appears to have been the first of the three to lose its vital force," but Islam itself continues to be "one of the most vital and expanding forms of faith" (p.2). The editor suggests that by 1950, "the specifically Western Christian civilization was as dead as Islam," replaced "by only one civilization—Modern Technological, as at home in Japan or China as in

England or Brazil—in which men can respond creatively to change, or hope to meet the future" (p.3).

What the editor calls "Themes of Islamic civilization" are clusters of major ideas rooted in Islamic faith, reflecting how the civilization ordered its perceptions and built its world. These clusters are grouped in six chapters: (1) The Community ("Ideas about the Community produced the *millet* system"), (2) The Perfect Ruler ("The dream of a perfect, inspired autocrat continues to haunt Muslim politics"), (3) The Will of God ("Modes of thinking about the will of God brought into being the *shari'a* system, the *'ulama*, and the *madrasa*"), (4) The Expected Deliverer ("The optimism of a once-successful society, coupled with the frustration of history's recalcitrance, have made the hope for a deliverer perennial"), (5) Struggle: Jihad ("The emphasis on struggle expanded the Community, and also at times helped to condemn it to a sterile militarism"), (6) The Friends of God ("The theme of *wilaya*, of the friends of God, helped make the transcendent Lord immanent, and gave the civilization its final justification"). Several narratives from the Scriptures and other sources are quoted in each chapter.

Notes and references are provided at the end of each chapter. There is a bibliography, organized by topics such as the Qur'an, Islam as a Religion, the life of Mohammad, Hadith, institutions and political theory, sufism, culture and literature, etc. There is a name-subject index.

B-118. Wolff, Philippe. *The Cultural Awakening* (translated from French by Anne Carter). New York: Pantheon Books, 1968.

Wolff's work is about the history of the birth of European culture, from the ninth century to the 12th, and the task is approached by "examining the relationship between history in general and the growth of culture," particularly the development of social and economic conditions (p.11). Also explored is how "the psychological process whereby the work of those who were intellectually the most gifted" resulted in the intellectual rise of Europe (p.11). The author has segmented the period in terms of the importance of three individuals: Alcuin, Gerbert, and Abelard.

The book is divided into three parts, with several chapters in each. Part One, The Time of Alcuin, has seven chapters: (1) The Historical Background, (2) The Decline in Classical Culture, (3) Charlemagne and His Followers, (4) The Cultural Foundations of Europe, (5) The Legacy of the Carolingian Renaissance, (6) Gaps and Weaknesses, (7) Conclusion. Part Two, The Time of Gerbert, has six chapters: (1) The Terror of the Millennium, (2) The Historical Background: The Eastern World, (3) The Historical Background: The West, (4) The Heritage of the Carolingian Renaissance, (5) Gerbert, (6) Conclusion. Part Three, The Time of Abelard, has five chapters: (1) The Awakening of the West, (2) The Enrichment of Culture, (3) Abelard, (4) Alongside Abelard, (5) Conclusion. There are extensive references to links with the early Arab-Islamic civilization throughout, but especially in parts two and three.

Part Two includes a large section of a chapter devoted to "The Muslim World"—extending from the "Iberian peninsula to the Indus plain," and "from the Caspian to the borders of the Sahara," which was "a huge world within which men, goods, and ideas circulated freely" (p.132). And, "For two hundred years Baghdad remained the scientific capital of the Mediterranean world," and then it was the Muslim Spain. However, during the tenth century, about the time of Gerbert, began "the transference of Greek ideas from the East to West," and by the end of this century, "the finest fruits of 'Arabic' learning were still in the future but already it had gone beyond the mere handing on of the Hellenistic thought" (p.134–135). While the "Arabic scholars also had their original contributions," the search "for a rational explanation of natural phenomena was no longer as fundamental as in Greek science and the desire to acquire power over nature by means of science played a much larger part. This admittedly utilitarian attitude helps to explain the passionate enthusiasm for these studies both in the Muslim and later in the Christian worlds" (p.135–136).

In a chapter devoted to Gerbert the author traces the "first steps in Western science" to this Latin scholar's learning from the Arabs, and "from the Arabs also Gerbert, with his strong practical sense, borrowed the use of instruments with which to demonstrate the universe and observe the movements of the stars" (p.188–189). Another chapter takes account of "everything that has been said so far about the treasures of science and philosophy accumulated in the Near and Middle East in classical times" (p.271). Further, this 11th-century period "saw the most brilliant flowering of 'Arabic' science. This was the time of al Biruni, Ibn Sina (Avicenna) and Ibn al Haitham, all of whom may be considered among the most remarkable minds of all time" (p.273). The author notes in his conclusion, "From Spain after the Arab conquest a flood of books and scholars found refuge in the West, bringing new and fertile knowledge, while later still *Hispania* became the scene of outstanding collaboration between Muslims, Jews, and Christians" (p.294).

At the end of this 315-page volume there is a section called Bibliographical Hints where the author provides numerous references linked to each part of the book. Then there are some maps identified with the periods of Alcuin, Gerbert, and Abelard, followed by a name-subject index.

B-119. Ziad, Zeenut, ed. *The Magnificent Mughals.* Oxford and New York: Oxford University Press, 2002.

This 320-page volume originated in a lecture series organized by the Smithsonian Institution in Washington, DC, to introduce the Mughal legacy to the American public. It claims to be the first book to present, in one volume, an illustrated and authoritative analysis of the Mughal arts and the social, economic, and political history of the Mughals in the Indian Subcontinent. It is about the Mughal

Rule (1526–1858), "described as one of the greatest periods of human achievement. This Indo-Muslim empire was the exemplar of a vibrant, culturally plural, multiethnic polity—the success of which modern states would do well to emulate" (p.xviii). The aim of the book "is to present a broad view of the Mughal empire that will engender an appreciation of the political, economic, social, and cultural renewal the Mughals brought to the South Asian Subcontinent and for the model of statecraft they gave to the world" (p. xviii).

The editor further states that "the Mughals can rightfully claim a place both within the Subcontinent's history and the wider canvas of Muslim civilization. It is a unique fact of history that wherever Muslims spread—whether to Mali in West Africa, Spain in Europe, Anatolia, Central Asia or South East Asia—they catalyzed the indigenous cultures and created civilizations where artists and intellectuals of every faith and persuasion flourished, producing a rich tapestry of accomplishments" (p.xx). Moreover, "The essays in this volume reveal an often overlooked fact: not only was the pervasive atmosphere of tolerance and respect for other faiths a manifestation of Sufi influence, but the literature, music, architecture, art, and even dance of the Mughal era were inspired by Sufi thought" (p.xx).

The ten essays, written by prominent specialists, are: (1) The Mughal Empire by John F. Richards, (2) The Lives and Contributions of Mughal Women by Ellison B. Findly, (3) Religion by Annemarie Schimmel, (4) Literature by Wheeler M. Thackston, (5) Urdu Literature by Shamsur Rahman Faruqi, (6) Imperial Mughal Painting by Joseph M. Dye III, (7) Architecture by Catherine B. Asher, (8) Music and Dance by Bonnie C. Wade, (9) The Economy by Irfan Habib, (10) Coinage and Monetary System by Aman-ur-Rahman and Waleed Ziad. The foreword is written by Milo Cleveland Beach.

Each chapter is decorated with several reproductions of classic paintings that reflect the Mughal Empire, as well as colored pictures of various monuments of that legacy. There are three maps reflecting the political boundaries of the empire, major architectural sites and cultural centers, and the economics of the empire. The 320-page book also includes, at the end, a genealogical chart and chronology of the Mughal rulers. While notes and references are integrated within each essay, a bibliography is also provided at the end of each. There is a name-subject index.

b. Economics/Commerce

B-120. Allouche, Adel. *Mamluk Economics: A Study and Translation of Al-Maqrizi's* Ighathah (translated from Arabic). Salt Lake City, UT: University of Utah Press, 1994.

The book is about the medieval history of the Middle East, with a particular focus on the economic and monetary conditions of Egypt under the Circassian Mamluks during the 13th–14th centuries. The study is based on a translation of the book, *Ighathah al-Ummah bi-Kashf al-Ghumah* (Helping the Nation by

Examining the Causes of Its Distress), written in 1405 by Taqi al-Din Ahmad ibn Ali al-Maqrizi (d. 1442). Various authors at the time, as typical during medieval centuries, attributed the country's economic decline to moral degradation, but al-Maqrizi went further. While he presents a history of famines in Egypt, more importantly, he "stands out as the most vocal critic of the Circassian monetary policy, which he blames for the impoverishment of the country. The targets for his attack were the excessive coinage of the copper *fulus*, the cessation of silver coinage, and the adoption in 1403 of a money of account: the dirham of *fulus*" (p.ix).

In addition to the translator's introduction and the original author's prologue, the book is divided into eight sections: (1) A Logical Premise, (2) The Years of *Ghala* in Egypt, (3) The Causes of Our Ordeals, (4) Currency, (5) A Description of the Population, (6) Current Prices and Present Ordeals, (7) The Means to Eradicate This Disease, (8) The Merits of This Proposal.

There are nine appendices relating to measures, weights, and currency, exchange rates, and historical data on prices of various staples and commodities (including mutton and beef). Notes and references linked to each component of the book are provided at the end. Also, the translator provides a comprehensive, 15-page bibliography on related topics, and there is a name-subject index.

B-121. Esfandiari, Haleh and A.L. Udovitch, eds. *The Economic Dimensions of Middle Eastern History: Essays in Honor of Charles Issawi.* Princeton, NJ: The Darwin Press, Inc., 1990.

The 370-page book includes 12 papers presented at a conference held at Princeton University in 1986 and organized on the occasion of Charles Issawi's retirement. While the book title focuses on economics, the essays cover a broad range of topics—politics/geopolitics, middle east in the global economy and politics, history, ethics, Islamic economics, and oil industry/petrodollars.

The 12 essay titles and the respective authors are: (1) A Twice-Told Tale: British and American Efforts to Organize the Middle East by L. Carl Brown, (2) Britain and Egypt: Background to Suez by J.C. Hurewitz, (3) Middle East Oil Power: Mirage or Reality by Eliyahu Kanovsky, (4) On the Notion of Economic Justice in Contemporary Islamic Thought by Timur Kuran, (5) The Arab World and the World Economy: An Overview by Samir A. Makdisi, (6) Property Rights and Islamic Revolution in Iran by Fatemeh E. Moghadam, (7) Economics of Petrodollars by Ibrahim M. Oweiss, (8) The Middle East in Nineteenth-Century World Trade by Sevket Pamuk, (9) The Political Economy of Divine Unity: A Critique of Islamic Theory and Practice by Manoucher Parvin, (10) International Commerce and Society in Mid-Eleventh Century Egypt and North Africa by A.L. Udovitch, (11) The Growth of Public Sector Enterprise in the Middle East by John Waterbury, (12) The Trends and Prospects of the Middle Eastern Oil Industry by Mohammed Yeganeh.

Each essay contains its own footnotes and bibliographical references; there is no index.

B-122. Ghazanfar, S.M., ed. *Medieval Islamic Economic Thought: Filling the "Great Gap" in European Economics.* London and New York: RoutledgeCurzon, 2003.

This 320-page book presents a collection of papers, published in national/international journals, that document the origins of economic thought discovered in the writings of several prominent early-medieval Islamic scholars. Their writings date from about the five centuries prior to the Latin Scholastics, such as St. Thomas Aquinas (1225–1274). This period was labeled by the renowned historian of economic thought, the late Joseph Schumpeter, as the "Great Gap" in intellectual history, and this "gap" is well-embedded in almost all relevant literature. However, the editor argues, "Almost precisely during this period, the Islamic civilization represented about the most fertile environment of intellectual activity in almost all areas of then known endeavors, including socio-economic thought" and the transfer of this knowledge facilitated the European Renaissance and Enlightenment (p.2). The book attempts to fill the Schumpeterian "Great Gap." It is also noted that such a discontinuity in mainstream literary history prevails in various other areas of knowledge.

The collection includes 15 papers. Some of the titles, along with the year of original publication, are: Scholastic Economics and Arab Scholars: The "Great Gap" Thesis Reconsidered (1991); Economic Thought of an Arab Scholastic: Abu Hamid Al-Ghazali (1158–1111) (1990); Explorations in Medieval Arab-Islamic Thought: Some Aspects of Ibn Taimiyah's Economics (1992); History of Economic Thought: The Schumpeterian "Great Gap," the "Lost" Arab-Islamic Legacy and the Literature Gap (1995); Understanding the Market Mechanism before Adam Smith: Economic Thought in Medieval Islam (1995); Post-Greek/Pre-Renaissance Economic Thought: Contributions of Arab-Islamic Scholastics during the "Great Gap" Centuries (1998); Economic Thought of Al-Ghazali and St. Thomas Aquinas: Some Comparative Parallels and Linkages (2000); Public-Sector Economics in Medieval Economic Thought: Contributions of Selected Arab-Islamic Scholars (2001); Medieval Social Thought and European Renaissance: The Influence of Selected Arab-Islamic Scholastics (2001).

Appropriate notes and references are listed at the end of each paper. There is a 15-page bibliography at the end, followed by a name-subject index.

B-123. Gran, Peter. *Islamic Roots of Capitalism, Egypt, 1760–1840.* Syracuse, NY: Syracuse University Press, 1998.

The book represents a provocative challenge to the conventional view of the development of modern world economic system, in that a capitalist economy could only emerge in peripheral regions through contact with the European centers. The argument is that a significant development toward capitalism took place in parts of the Middle East during the period 1760 to 1840 and that it was later subverted by outside forces.

The author portrays in detail the period in which Egyptian Muslim merchants and Mamluk rulers began the capitalist transformation. Questions are raised as to the basic premise of modernization theory that argues that no development could have taken place before the emergence of the West. Focusing on the nature of the impending capitalistic transformation in Islamic cultural terms, the author brings to light various heretofore unknown scholars and their writings (particularly Shaykh Hasan al-Attar). These scholars, it is argued, demonstrated a utilitarian approach to knowledge, a naturalistic causality, and a capacity for realism. However, when the processes of capitalist transformation shifted out of indigenous hands, Islamic thought in Egypt assumed a more fatalistic philosophic turn. Throughout the book there is awareness of the growth of forces working against Egyptian capitalism (Greeks, Armenians, and Napoleon's 1878 invasion), eventually dislodging indigenous merchants and producers. Thus, subsequent development of the global industrial system would depend on the struggles over markets which local capitalists in the Middle East had created and sought to hold.

The book contains ten chapters: (1) The Social and Economic History of Egypt: A Study of Merchant Capital and Its Transformation, (2) The Religious Framework of the Eighteenth-Century Revival, (3) The Cultural Revival of the Late Eighteenth Century, (4) The Decline of the Eighteenth-Century Cultural Revival, (5) Turkey and Syria in the Early Nineteenth Century, (6) The Muhammad Ali Period, 1815–1837, (7) The Revival of Theology and *Kalam*, (8) The Reform Period, 1815–1837, and the Development of Neoclassical Culture, (9) The World Market as Limiting Factor in the Development of Neoclassicism. The last chapter summarizes the book.

The 278-page volume has three appendices (20 pages), each devoted to the life and writings of Shaykh Hasan al-Attar. This is followed by 41-pages of chapter-by-chapter footnotes, including bibliographic references. There is a glossary of terms and also an alphabetical, select bibliography, as well as an index of names.

B-124. Ibrahim, Mahmood. *Merchant Capital and Islam.* Austin, TX: University of Texas Press, 1990.

The 246-page book is about the evolution of merchant capitalism in early Islam. The author begins with noting the "orientalist" characterization of Islam, according to which "Islamic history is frozen in time and then compared and contrasted to 'others' across time and space. Consequently, Islamic history is not understood on its own terms, but only in mythified relation to an outside world" (p.4). The study examines the influence of merchants and merchant capital on social development in early Islam. The author focuses on internal social forces and how they changed in an unfolding historical context, and this approach "indicates a history that is creative and dynamic," as opposed to the "archaic notions of sterile and static history" (p.5). Only then, it is argued, one can understand "the foundation of Islamic society within a perspective of historical continuity conditioned by the demands of merchants and merchant capital" (p.5). The author suggests that the Crusaders encountered a part of the Islamic society that was "capitalistic," and "it is with the early history and the formation of this sector that this study is concerned" (p.6). The book concludes that "Islam, as a religion, did not hinder capital accumulation," and further, that various social, economic, and political factors precluded the development of industrial capitalism (p.7).

The book contains seven chapters: (1) Pre-Islamic Arabia, (2) The Development of Merchant Capital in Mecca, (3) Merchant Capital and Mecca's Internal Development, (4) Merchant Capital and the Rise of Islam, (5) Islamic Expansion and the Establishment of the Islamic State, (6) The Emergence of the New Segment, (7) The Civil War and the Struggle for Power. There is an epilogue with two sections: The Umayyed Caliphate and Islam, Capitalism or Feudalism.

Chapter-by-chapter notes and references are appended at the end, followed by a 12-page bibliography, classified in terms of traditional Arabic sources and modern sources. There is a name-subject index.

B-125. Lokkegaard, Frede. *Islamic Taxation in the Classic Period, with Special Reference to Circumstances in Iraq.* Philadelphia, PA: Porcupine Press, 1978; original 1950.

The book's subject is taxation in early Islam, and "however peripheral it might seem to outsiders, [it] is of central and comprehensive importance in the field of Islamic studies" (p.1). However, the author's "orientalistic" bent is obvious throughout. As a European, the author expresses concern about the "legitimacy" of undertaking such a topic in Islamic studies. As a "spiritual luxury," he wonders if "the study of Islamic history is a work in the service of our own culture, digging at the roots of it, or whether it is a mere hobby or a fixed idea." He is aware of "the original contributions to the legacy which Islamic civilization has bestowed upon Europe," although he asks the readers "not to exaggerate the influence" (p.2).

Linking its roots to Judaism and Christianity, the author identifies Islam as a "religious fraud," a "Jewish-Christian sect," "the greatest Christian problem of all times." Thus, to find remedies for this "deep-rooted evil," one must understand "its character and points of differentiation." Such understanding, according to the author, will also facilitate the missionary work so that the Christian creed is "as easily understood as is the simple creed of Islam" (p.3). Further, the author is quite candid in that "as a political necessity the great colonial powers were forced to gather information about the internal organization of the dependent Islamic countries." Thus, "The colonial interest has often caused considerations to be made which otherwise are not to be tolerated in an objective investigation (p.4–5). Labeling any studies which were dependent "upon the views of Arabic jurists and traditionalists as fictitious," the author relies for his explorations on

Islamic taxation upon late-19th century work by several European scholars who, after examining those sources, managed to "dig down to the roots of the problems" (p.5).

Various chapters in the book cover topics such as landed property under individual and collective ownership, influence of the state on property, land classifications for taxation, tax-farming, methods of assessment for rural population, capitation, and administration.

The author provides a summary of Danish-language notes at the end, followed by chapter-by-chapter notes and references. A list of important literature is also provided, and there is a subject index.

B-126. Masters, Bruce. *The Origins of Western Economic Dominance in the Middle East: Mercantilism and the Islamic Economy in Aleppo, 1600–1750.* New York and London: New York University Press, 1988.

The book explores "the question of why the Muslim Middle East was surpassed by western Europe, first economically and then politically," leading to the "demise of the Ottoman Empire and its legacy of lingering political and economic dissonance in the region" (p.3). "Between 1600 and 1750," says the author, "Aleppo was one of the premier cities of the Ottoman Empire and one of those rare locations where two cultures competed for a prolonged period without resorting to violence." Also, "The city was an economic battleground where two distinct commercial traditions struggled to control the trade of the Levant" (p.2).

The vision of English mercantilists sought "to increase exports, limit imports through protective tariffs, and use government power wherever possible to promote the foreign trade of the nation in an attempt to accumulate specie, which, in turn, would guarantee the health and vigor of the state and its people" (p.3). On the other hand, the Islamic philosophy of economics "was based on the centuries-old traditions and institutions of trade" (p.3). By 1750, the European version emerged as dominant, and by the 19th century, "most of the world was becoming economically, and often politically, dependent on one or another of the western European powers" (p.2–3). As a challenge to the arguments of the dependency theory (identified with scholars such as Immanuel Wallerstein and Andre Gunder Frank), the book explores the "internal dynamics of the Ottoman economy," which, the author argues, "propelled the region into the world economy much more rapidly than did the external forces of European greed and ambition." Thus, the transformation was not simply the "unfortunate side effect of the historical necessity of the rise of capitalism" (p.3–4).

The 240-page book contains six chapters: (1) Aleppo and the Caravan Trade, (2) Population, Society, and Merchants in Ottoman Aleppo, (3) Merchant Diasporas and Trading "Nations," (4) Commercial Institutions of a Caravan City, (5) Money, Credit, and Investment, (6) An "Islamic Economy" in an Age of Mercantilism. There is also a concluding chapter in which the author identifies "two important local conditions that seemingly abetted the Western designs more than anything else. The first was strictly economic," whereby, since the Muslim merchants preferred not to invest in trade, Europeans "discriminated against Muslim merchants in favor of Christian ones" (p.220). And, "A second factor lay in a belief in the basic moral rectitude of an Islamic economy policy as it had been interpreted over the preceding centuries" (p.220).

Notes and references are provided at the end of each chapter. There is a glossary of terms (Arabic, Turkish, Frankish) at the end, followed by a ten-page selected bibliography of archival sources, contemporary accounts, and secondary sources. There is a name-subject index.

B-127. Rodinson, Maxime. *Islam and Capitalism* (translated from French, originally published in 1966, by Brian Pearce). Austin, TX: University of Texas Press, 1978.

The book is intended for intellectuals in the Islamic world, so they understand their situation, and for European readers so they appreciate Third World problems. It is intended to elucidate the problem of development in Islamic countries. Some have suggested that the Islamic tradition is conducive to economic progress and social justice; others, "who are hostile to Islam (and who are backed by a horde of publicists who know nothing about the subject), endeavor to show that this religion, by forbidding those who hold it to engage in any progressive economic initiative, dooms them to stagnation. The conclusion to be drawn is that these (Muslim) peoples must be vigorously combated, in the interest of the progress of civilization in general" (p.3). The book explores questions such as: "Why did capitalism triumph in modern times in Europe, and not in the Muslim countries (among others)? In the past and in the present, has Islam, or at least, the cultural tradition of the Muslim countries, favored (or does it favor?) capitalism, or socialism, or a backward economy of the 'feudal' type? Or does it urge those who are influenced by it in a quite different direction, a new economic system specific to Islam?" (p.3).

After exploring the Islamic scriptures and socioeconomic history in detail, the author disputes the traditional explanations, mainly from Weber and Weberian analyses, that have blamed Islamic prohibitions against economic activity. The 310-page book challenges the Weberian notion that capitalism required western Protestantism to inspire it.

The book contains six chapters: (1) The Problem Stated, (2) What Islam Prescribes, (3) Economic Practice in the Muslim World of the Middle Ages, (4) The Influence of Muslim Ideology Generally in the Economic Field, (5) Islam and Capitalism in the Muslim Countries Today, (6) Conclusions and Prospects. There is an afterword written in 1973.

At the end there are several pages of notes and bibliographic references, chapter-by-chapter. There is a name-subject index.

c. Philosophy

B-128. Asin-Palacios, Miguel. *The Mystical Philosophy of Ibn Masarra and His Followers* (translated from Spanish by Elmer H. Douglas and Howard W. Yoder). Leiden, Netherlands: E.J. Brill, 1978; original 1914.

The book is about "the interdependency of philosophical-religious thought of the ninth, tenth, and succeeding centuries," for "human thought is continuous, transcending frontiers of race, language, faith, and nationality. We are heirs of the cultural past and trustees, though unwittingly, of the future" (p.vii). According to the translators, such interdependency in philosophical thought (Sufi'ism)—from the ninth-century Spanish-Muslim, Ibn Masarra and his followers, to others in the Latin-European tradition—is the task undertaken in this book by Miguel Asin-Palacios, who offers "a modest study of the origins of philosophical-theological thought in Muslim Spain" (p.xi).

The 205-page book has eight chapters, plus six appendices. The chapter titles are: (1) Oriental Muslim Thought in the First Three Centuries, (2) Spanish Muslim Thought in the First Three Centuries, (3) The Life of Ibn Masarra, (4) Pseudo-Empedoclean Doctrine of Ibn Masarra, (5) Historical Criticism of the Pseudo-Empedoclean System, (6) The Theological Doctrine of Ibn Masarra, (7) The School of Ibn Masarra, (8) The Influence of the Masarrian Ideas.

There are six appendices: Life, Works, and Ideas of Al-Jahiz; The First Spanish Mutazilites; First Spanish Muslim Ascetics; Arabic Text of Pseudo-Empedocles According to al-Shahrazuri; Life and Doctrine of Dhu'l-Nun the Egyptian and of al-Nahrajuri; and The Theory of the *Hadras* of Ibn Al-Arabi and of the *Dignities* of Raymond Lull and Other Analogies of the Two Systems.

Notes and references are integrated within each chapter; there is a separate bibliography at the end, however. There is an index of names and titles, and another index relates to technical terms.

B-129. Butterworth, Charles E. and Blake Andree Kessel, eds. *The Introduction of Arabic Philosophy into Europe*. Leiden, New York, and Cologne: E.J. Brill, 1994.

This 150-page volume brings together ten of the 12 papers presented at a 1988 conference on the occasion of the 900th anniversary of the establishment of the University of Bologna (Italy). Given the role that the philosophic and scientific works of medieval Arab scholars played in the history of European thought, the participants explored various issues concerning the way these writings came to be known in European universities. Who first introduced Arabic philosophical scholarship into the University of Oxford, the University of Paris, or other European institutions? What prompted the choice of some Arabic authors or works, but not others? Was competence in the Arabic or Persian languages necessary, or was it sufficient to rely on works in Latin translations?

Paper titles and authors are: (1) The Transmission and Reception of Arabic

Philosophy in Christian Spain (until 1200) by Josep Puig, (2) La Reception de la Philosophie Arabe a l'Universite de Paris au XIIIeme siecle by Abdelali Elamrani-Jamal, (3) The Introduction of Arabic Learning into British Schools by Charles Burnett, (4) George Drohobych's Astronomical Treatises and Their Arabic Sources by Iaroslav Isaievych, (5) The Reception of Islamic Philosophy at Oxford in the 17th Century: The Pococks' (Father and Son) Contribution to the Understanding of Islamic Philosophy in Europe by Hans Daiber, (6) Arabic Philosophy and the Universite Catholique de Louvain by Therese-Anne Druart, (7) The Reception of Arabic Philosophy at the University of Budapest by Miklos Maroth, (8) La Premiere Reception de la Philosophie Islamique a l'Universite de Cracovie by Jerzy B. Korloec, (9) La Philosophie de l'Ouest et de l'est dans l'Academie Kiev-Mohyleana by Y.N. Kochubey, (10) La Reception due Soufisme par l'Occident: Conjectures et Certitudes by Michel Chodkiewicz.

The editors conclude that "it is all too evident that however much Arabic philosophy flourished in Latin translation during the Middle Ages and the Renaissance, it quickly dropped out of favor when Latin was no longer the medium of instruction. That Arabic philosophy has never enjoyed a stable place in any single seat of learning in Europe, neither East nor West, also becomes utterly clear from these contributions. Indirectly, they also show how important it is at all times—this one included—for universities to develop the study of the Arabic language" (p.6).

Each essay contains its own notes and references in the text. There is no index.

B-130. Corbin, Henry. *History of Islamic Philosophy* (translated from French by Liadain Sherrard). London: Kegan Paul International, in association with Islamic Publications for the Institute of Ismaili Studies, 1993.

The book is about Islamic philosophy, not *Arab* philosophy, the author insists, and the geographic boundaries extend to Iranian thinkers as well. The discussion is divided into three periods: (1) from the beginning of Islam up to the death of Averroes (Ibn Rushd, 1126–1198), this period is said to be rather insufficiently known; and with Averroes, "something came to an end in Western Islam," and then emerged Al-Suhrawardi and Ibn al-Arabi; (2) the second period extends over the three centuries preceding the Safavid Renaissance in Islam, characterized by the "Sufi metaphysic"—the growth of the school of Ibn al-Arabi; (3) another deriving from Najm al-Din al-Kubra, and it extends to the present, including the centuries when numerous Iranian thinkers wrote in a Shiite milieu.

Part I (From the Beginning Down to the Death of Averroes, 595/1198) contains eight detailed chapters: (1) The Sources of Philosophical Mediation in Islam, (2) Shiism and Prophetic Philosophy (Twelve Shiism, Ismailism, Fatimid Ismailism, and Reformed Ismailism of Alamut), (3) The Sunni *Kalam* (The Mu'tazilites, Abu al-Hasan al-Ashari, Ash'arism), (4) Philosophy and the Natural Sciences (al-Razi, al-Biruni, al-Khwarizmi, ibn al-Haytham, and others), (5) The Hellenizing Philosophers (al-Kindi, al-Farabi, Ibn Sina, al-Ghazali, and others), (6) Sufism (al-Bastami, al-Junayd, al-Tirmidhi, al-Hallaj, and others), (7) Al-Suhrawardi and the Philosophy of Light, (8) In Andalusia (Ibn Hazm, Ibn Bajjah, Ibn Tufayl, Ibn Rushd, and others).

Part II (From the Death of Averroes to the Present Day) has three chapters: (1) Sunni Thought (The Philosophers, The Theologians, The Adversaries of the Philosophers, and The Encyclopedists), (2) The Metaphysics of Sufism (al-Shirazi, Umar al-Suhrawardi, Ibn al-Arabi, Najm al-Din al-Kubra, al-Hamdhani, Jalal al-Din Rumi, Jami, and others), (3) Shiite Thought (Nasir al-Din Tusi, The Ismailis, Sadr al-Din Dashtaki, Mulla Sadra Shirazi, Qadi Said Qummi, Jafar Kashfi, The Schools of Khurasan, and others).

The 450-page book provides a comprehensive chapter-by-chapter bibliography. There is a detailed name-subject index.

B-131. Fakhry, Majid. *Averroes (Ibn Rushd): His Life, Works and Influence.* Oxford, UK: Oneworld Publications, 2001.

This book covers all the key areas of Averroes' life, from transmission of Aristotelian thought to Latin Europe, to conflict with the Ash'arite theologians (Abu Hamid Al-Ghazali in particular), which split the Islamic intellectual world and led to the burning of his books in Cordoba. Emphasizing Averroes' critical role, not only as the "founding father of rational thought" in the West, but also in the development of Islamic philosophy generally, the book explores such topics as Aristotle and Averroes on ethics, physics, and metaphysics; Averroes' achievements as a physician and jurist; and Averroes' influence upon social thought. "Latin scholasticism, prior to the rediscovery of Aristotle, thanks chiefly to Averroes' commentaries, would have been inconceivable. Even the rise of Renaissance rationalism and humanism is closely linked to Averroes' commitment to the primacy of reason in philosophical and theological discourse" (p.xv). The author argues "that Averroes' 'philosophical rationalism' is not only five centuries earlier, but even more comprehensive than the 'mathematical rationalism' of Rene Descartes (d. 1650), generally regarded as the father of modern philosophy" (p.xvi).

The book contains 11 chapters: (1) Life and works, (2) Averroes and the Muslim Neoplatonists, (3) The critique of Ash'arite theology (*kalam*), (4) Logic and theory of knowledge, (5) The physical structure of the universe, (6) The soul and its faculties, (7) God and the creation of the world, (8) Ethics and politics, (9) Averroes as jurist and physician, (10) Averroes and the Latin West, (11) Averroes and Aquinas.

There is a select bibliography on Averroes' works (Arabic), translations and references, and Arabic sources, as well as a detailed name-subject index.

B-132. Fakhry, Majid. *A History of Islamic Philosophy.* New York: Columbia University Press, 1983.

The book is a general historical survey of Islamic philosophy, a subject which, according to the author, has tended to be neglected in Western scholarship, partly because, from the 17th century on, attempts are "continually being made to formulate a coherent world view for modern man, in which the role of the ancient (Greek) and medieval (both Arabic and Latin) thought is progressively ignored or minimized" (p.viii). It discusses the legalism, rationalism, and mysticism of Islamic thought and its impact on the cultural aspects of Muslim societies. While the origins of Western thought and Islamic philosophy lie in the Greek heritage, with close affinities between the two, there are differences in world views, the author suggests (p. viii).

The 395-page book has 12 chapters: (1) The Legacy of Greece, Alexandria, and the Orient, (2) Early Political and Religious Tensions, (3) Beginnings of Systematic Philosophical Writing in the Ninth Century, (4) The Further Development of Islamic Neo-Platonism, (5) Neo-Pythogereanism and the Popularization of the Philosophical Sciences, (6) The Diffusion of Philosophical Culture in the Tenth Century, (7) The Interaction of Philosophy and Dogma, (8) The Rise and Development of Islamic Mysticism (Sufism), (9) The Arab-Spanish Interlude and the Revival of Peripateticism, (10) Post-Avicennian Developments: Illumination and the Reaction against Peripateticism, (11) Theological Reaction and Reconstruction, (12) Modern and Contemporary Trends.

Notes and references are integrated within the text of each chapter. There is a bibliography at the end, classified by Arabic and European language sources, followed by a name-subject index.

B-133. Fakhry, Majid. *Islamic Occasionalism and Its Critique by Averroes and Aquinas.* London: George Allen and Unwin Ltd., 1958.

The 190-page book is addressed to students of medieval philosophy in general and Thomism and Islam in particular. It deals with a significant aspect of the contact between Islamic and Latin Scholasticism in the 13th century, as exemplified by the Thomist critique of the occasionalism ["defined as the belief in the exclusive efficacy of God, of whose direct intervention the events of nature are alleged to be the overt manifestation or 'occasion'" (p.9)] of the Ash'arite theologians (or Mutakallims), Al-Ghazali (d. 1111) being the most prominent. The author suggests that the credit for a systematic statement of this view, which is very close to the Islamic conception, "should be assigned to Malebranche (d. 1715), a disciple of Descartes, with whose name occasionalism is commonly associated" (p.9).

The transmission of Islamic occasionalism to the Latin West happened through the Jewish theologian–philosopher, Moses Maimonides (d. 1204). The Ash'arite view, identified with Al-Ghazali, that God "presided as unchallenged sovereign and in which man played the role of a mere marionette which executed blindly and slavishly the decrees of the Almighty" was challenged by the Aristotelian Averroes (Ibn Rushd, d. 1198). Averroes disputed the fallacies of occasionalism by developing his double-truth thesis; that is, both philosophy and theology are valid in their own sphere. However, the controversy requires reconciliation of the metaphysical and theological interests involved. Such a synthesis must go beyond the metaphysical determinism of Averroes and the theological occasionalism of the Ash'arites. The author states this synthesis was achieved by St. Thomas Aquinas (d. 1274).

The book has four, rather long chapters: (1) The Islamic Metaphysics of Atoms and Accidents, (2) The Repudiation of Causality by al-Ghazali, (3) The Averroist Rehabilitation of Causality, (4) The Causal Dilemma and the Thomist Synthesis. There is a summary chapter at the end.

Each chapter ends with its own footnotes and bibliographic references. At the end there is a chapter-by-chapter bibliography, followed by a name-subject index.

B-134. Flint, Robert. *History of the Philosophy of History.* New York: Charles Scribner's Sons, 1894.

The primary purpose of this 710-page book is to trace the course of human thought in its endeavors to explain human history; that is, to explain the "rise and progress of reflection and speculation on the development of humanity" (p.1). Though unclear from the title, the book's focus is European. There is a long introductory chapter (175 pages), followed by 12 chapters spread over 525 pages, with the main title, The Philosophy of History in France. These chapters cover the historical philosophy, and historiography, in the writings of French scholars such as Bodin, Bossuet, Montesquieu, Turgot, Voltaire, Rousseau, and Condorcet, followed by discussions of the ultramontanist (traditional) and liberal catholic schools, the socialistic schools, the spiritualist movement, the democratic historical school, philosophy of naturalism and positivism, and so forth.

In the introductory chapter, however, there is considerable discussion of the emergence of Islamic civilization and its linkages with Latin Europe. While "medieval Europe produced nothing worthy to be called a philosophy of history," the Islamic civilization "roused and quickened the minds of its believers; and for several centuries Moslem civilization in most respects equaled, and in some surpassed, the Christian civilization which it confronted" (p. 78). Further, "The Christian medieval world was only a part of the medieval world, and a part imperfectly intelligible without acquaintance with its Mohammedan counterpart and complement. It may safely be affirmed that all our universal histories, histories of civilization, and philosophies of history, suffer from their authors' defective knowledge of the history of Mohammedanism" (p. 79). Elsewhere in the same chapter, the author discusses the influence of Ibn Khaldun and states, "As regards the science or philosophy of history, Arabic literature was adorned by one most brilliant name. Neither the classical nor the medieval Christian world can show one of nearly the same brightness. Ibn Khaldun (1332–1406) considered simply as an historian had superiors even among Arabic authors, but as a theorist on history he had no equal in any age or country until Vico appeared, more than three hundred years later. Plato, Aristotle, and Augustine were not his Islamic linkages and influence" (p.87). This chapter also includes a detailed section on Ibn Khaldun's scholarship. Various other chapters of the book are interspersed with references to other Islamic scholars.

The author often cites references within the page of the text although there are also other references and accompanying footnotes on various pages of each chapter. Unfortunately, there is no index; however, the table of contents provides considerable details about each chapter.

B-135. Gilson, Etienne. *History of Christian Philosophy in the Middle Ages.* New York: Random House, 1955.

This rather comprehensive book, written by one of France's most eminent religious ("Thomist") philosophers, provides the readers with an introduction to the history of Christian philosophy from about the second century to the 15th century AD. It is primarily concerned with the history of philosophical ideas in the discourses of Christian writers, although, as is generally the case in the medieval era, such discourses—Jewish, Christian, or Islamic—are typically couched in a theological context.

The 1,000-page book is divided into 11 parts: (1) The Greek Apologists, (2) Early Christian Speculation, (3) From Augustine to Boethius, (4) From Scotus Erigena to Saint Bernard, (5) Arabian and Jewish Philosophy, (6) Early Scholasticism, (7) Theology and Learning, (8) The Golden Age of Scholasticism, (9) The Condemnation of 1277, (10) Fourteenth-Century Scholasticism, (11) The Modern Way. Altogether there are 34 chapters.

The author provides fairly detailed coverage of the Arab-Islamic philosophers and states that while, in Western Europe, "the greatest contributions to philosophy were made by theologians, the greatest contributions to philosophy by Mohammedan thinkers have been made by philosophers" (p.183). He provides some details of the philosophies of Alkindi (Al-Kindi, 801–873), Alfarabi (Al-Farabi, 870–950), Avicenna (Ibn Sina, 980–1037), Averroes (Ibn Rushd, 1126–1198), with some observations as to their influence upon Latin-Scholastics of the era. Most coverage is devoted to Avicenna (29 pages) and Averroes (9 pages). There is little mention of Al-Ghazali (1058–1111), however, whose religious philosophy, unlike that of "Aristotelian" Averroes, was compatible with that of St. Thomas Aquinas (1225–1274) and parallels the latter's *Summa Theologica*. Part 9 (The Condemnation of 1277) is substantially devoted to the "faith-vs-reason" controversies ("219 Averroistic heresies") generated in Latin Europe with the introduction of "Averroisms" (Averroes' Commentaries on Greek Thought). The author states, "The greatest name in Arabian philosophy, along with Avicenna, is Averroes, whose influence spread, in many directions, through the duration of the middle-ages, then in the epoch of the Renaissance and up to the very threshold of modern times" (p.217).

Perhaps as interesting as this classic text itself are the author's meticulous footnotes, with bibliographic references (252 pages), linked to each chapter. Also, there is a list of bibliographic periodicals. There are two indexes—authors and historians—but the book lacks a subject index.

B-136. Gilson, Etienne. *Reason and Revelation in the Middle Ages.* New York and London: Charles Scribner's Sons, 1948.

This 114-page book is a compilation of lectures delivered at the University of Virginia, Charlottesville, in 1937. Known as the "Thomist" philosopher, this French scholar divides the book into three major chapters: (1) The Primacy of Faith, (2) The Primacy of Reason, (3) The Harmony of Reason and Revelation.

The first chapter discusses how during the early Middle Ages (also called the Dark Ages) "the normal use of natural reason was obscured by blind faith in the absolute truth of Christian Revelation" (p.4). Such thinking was grounded in the teachings of St. Augustine; revelation was a substitute for all other knowledge. Thus, the "Greek miracle" was irrelevant, "What indeed has Athens to do with Jerusalem? What (concord is there) between heretics and Christians?" (p.9).

In the second chapter, the author argues that in addition to the "modern rationalism" of the 16th-century Renaissance, there was "another rationalism, much older than that of the Renaissance. It was a purely philosophical rationalism, born in Spain, in the mind of an Arabian philosopher" (p. 37). Referring to Averroes (Ibn Rushd, 1126–1198) as the "herald of rationalism," the author says, he "bequeathed to his successors the ideal of a purely rational philosophy, an ideal whose influence was to be such that, by it, the evolution of Christian philosophy was to be deeply modified" (p.38). His attempts to reconcile rationalism with Islamic faith, based on Aristotelian logic, subsequently influenced similar debates vis-à-vis the Christian revelations—the focus of the third chapter. There are references to other Islamic philosophers (e.g., Avicenna [Ibn Sina, 980–1037] and Gazali [Al-Ghazali, 1058–1111]); however, the main emphasis is upon the influence of Ibn Rushd.

There are chapter-by-chapter notes and references at the end, followed by a name-subject index.

B-137. Grant, Edward. *God and Reason in the Middle Ages.* Cambridge and New York: Cambridge University Press, 2001.

The book has two purposes: to describe how reason was manifested in the curriculum of medieval universities, especially in the areas of logic, natural philosophy, and theology; and to explain how the Middle Ages acquired a reputation as an age of superstition, barbarism, and unreason. The argument is that it was "in the esoteric domain of university scholasticism that reason was most highly developed and perhaps ultimately most influential. Reason in the university context was not intended for the acquisition of power. Its primary purpose was to elucidate the natural and supernatural worlds" (p. 3). From around 1100 to 1500, the author argues, reason became the center of intellectual life and thereby made possible the development of modern science.

While the emphasis is on Latin-European scholars, the book points out that "the achievements of Western society were made possible because of the intellectual gifts it received from the pagan Greeks, the Byzantine Christian Greeks, and the civilization of Islam" (p.9). There are frequent references to the influence of Islamic knowledge. For example, Abelard of Bath (d. 1142) learned "not to trust authority . . . under the guidance of reason, from Arabic teachers" (p.70). As for texts for university education, they were "inherited from the ancient world, from Islamic authors—from Avicenna (Ibn Sina), Averroes (Ibn Rushd), Rhazes (al-Razi), and Alhazen (Ibn Al-Haytham)" (p.103). The scholastic approach "was most evident in the Aristotelian commentaries by Averroes, the Muslim commentator who exercised great influence on the West. Averroes' format was used by such eminent scholastic authors as Walter Burley and Nicole Oresme as did Roger Bacon and Thomas Aquinas" (p.105).

Following the introduction, this 400-page book contains seven chapters: (1) The Emergence of a Transformed Europe in the Twelfth Century, (2) Reason Asserts Itself: The Challenge to Authority in the Early Middle Ages to 1200, (3) Reason Takes Hold: Aristotle and the Medieval University, (4) Reason in Action: Logic in the Faculty of Arts, (5) Reason in Action: Natural Philosophy in the Faculty of Arts, (6) Reason in Act: Theology in the Faculty of Theology, (7) The Assault in the Middle Ages (this chapter also includes a section entitled The Culture and Spirit of "Poking Around").

There is a 20-page comprehensive bibliography at the end, followed by a detailed name-subject index. Footnotes, with references, are integrated within each chapter.

B-138. Grant, Edward. *Studies in Medieval Science and Natural Philosophy.* London: Variorum Reprints, 1981.

The 378-page book is a collection of 16 articles published by the author in various reputable journals or edited volumes during the period 1963 to 1979. The essays are grouped into two parts: Part One, Medieval Cosmology and Physics with Emphasis on Place, Space and Vacuum (12 papers, some entitled: Oresme's Agorismus proportionum; Cosmology; Aristotle, Philoponus, Avempace, and Galileo's Pisan Dynamics; The Concept of *Ubi*, Motion in the Void and the Principle of Inertia) and Part Two, Medieval Natural Philosophy: Conjectures and Interpretations (four papers: The Condemnation of 1277, God's Absolute Power, and Physical Thought in the Late Middle Ages; Late Medieval Thought, Copernicus, and the Scientific Revolution; Scientific Thought in Fourteenth-Century Paris: Jean Buridan and Nicole Oresme; Aristotelianism and the Longevity of the Medieval World View).

Most of the essays include extensive references to the early-medieval Islamic scholars as the forerunners of the Latin-European scholars. Specifically mentioned are Avempace (Ibn Bajja, d. 1138), Averroes (Ibn Rushd, 1126–1198), Avicenna (Ibn Sina, 980–1037), Al-Kindi (801–873), and al-Farabi (870–950), Ibn al-Haytham (Alhazen, 965–1040), and several others. As the "earlier and more ultimate source," the author states, "Galileo's law was enunciated many centuries before by Avempace (p.80 of essay #3). Most references relate to the influence of Ibn Rushd, followed by Avempace, Avicenna, Al-Kindi, and Al-Farabi, in that order. The essay entitled The Condemnation of 1277, God's Absolute Power, and Physical Thought in the Late Middle Ages focuses chiefly on the 219 condemnations—also called "Averroestic heresies"—that "rocked Paris in the 1260s and 1270s" and were condemned by the Bishop Etienne Tempier of Paris at the request of Pope John XXI; also, there are references to Avicennian influence in this essay.

Each essay is reproduced exactly as it appeared in the original source, including the page numbers. Each has its own footnotes and bibliographic references. There is a name-subject index, coded according to the particular essay and its paging scheme.

B-139. Haq, Mahmudul. *Reason and Tradition in Islamic Thought.* Aligarh, India: Institute of Islamic Studies, Aligarh Muslim University, 1992.

The 225-page book is a collection of papers presented at a forum in 1982, the focus being the "tensions that have existed between the two [Reason and Tradition] from the formative period of Islamic thought till today" (p.xi). While "the early followers of Islam became the torch-bearers of knowledge and free-inquiry," that spirit has been dormant and "over the last four centuries a steep decline has taken place in Muslim intellect" (p.xi). Indeed, the earlier Islamic "effervescence of knowledge triggered off and got dovetailed into the European Renaissance" (p.xi). The conflict between orthodoxy and heterodoxy is a continuous theme, and there have been "a number of free-thinkers in Islam who were charged of scepticism and unbelief" (p.xvi).

There are 16 papers in this volume. The titles and authors are: (1) The Remaking of Man by Sayed Barakat Ahmad, (2) Origin and Development of Rationalism in Early Islam by Shabbir Ahmad Khan Ghori, (3) Islam and Rationalism by S.T. Lokhandwalla, (4) Role of Reason in Muslim Culture: A Tentative Analysis by Anwar Moazzam, (5) The Isma'ilis: Harbingers of Protest and Rationalist Movement in Islam by Asghar Ali Engineer, (6) Maturidiya: A Happy Blend of Rationalism and Traditionalism by Fazlur Rahman, (7) Harmonization of Philosophy and Religion in al-Farabi's Imam-State by Sayyid Ali Sajjad, (8) Ibn Sina and Rationalism by M.S. Khan, (9) Criticism of al-Ghazali on the Theory of Emanation Presented by Plotinus and Ibn Sina by Noor Nabi, (10) Reason and Science in Medieval India by Irfan Habib, (11) Sir Syed Ahmad Khan and the Tradition of Rationalism in Islam by Ali Ashraf, (12) Sir Syed's View of Islam by A.A. Suroor, (13) The Salvation of Non-Muslims: Views of Some Eminent Muslim Religious Thinkers by Christian W. Troll, S.J., (14) Rationalism and Traditionalism in the Teachings of Ziya Goklap on the Reform of Turkish Literature by N. Akmal Ayyubi, (15) Asian Muslims in Britain: Tension between Modernism and Traditionalism by S.V. Bhajjan, (16) Origins of Free-Thinking in Arabic Thought by Mahmudul Haq.

It is noted in the last paper that "the problem of conflict or harmony between reason and revelation is not unique to Islam alone: before it two other Semitic religions, Judaism and Christianity, had to face the problem in one phase of its history or the other" (p.217). Moreover, "In Islam independent reasoning continued in the form of *ijtihad*, till about its first two and a half centuries, or about the middle of the ninth century. But from then on the idea began to gain acceptance that only the great imams of the past, and not the 'epigones,' had the right to *ijtihad*, and that it was the duty of the coming generations to blindly follow the past authorities, known as *taqlid*. By the beginning of the fourth century of Islam, that is, about AD900, *taqlid* became an established fact. Henceforth the coming generation was denied to have the bonafides for independent reasoning. The triumph of Ash'arism in the version of Ghazalian doctrines sealed the fate of *falsafa* which was for ever banished from Islam" (p.223).

Each essay ends with its own notes and references; there is no index.

B-140. Haren, Michael. *Medieval Thought: The Western Intellectual Tradition from Antiquity to the Thirteenth Century*. Toronto: University of Toronto Press, 1992.

This 315-page book presents medieval thought as stemming from the combination of the legacy of antiquity with a powerful new religious orientation along with the changed social structures—the products of several medieval minds of Latin Europe. It outlines three major categories of ideas upon which the Latin thinkers drew: Platonism, Aristotelianism, and the Arabic philosophical tradition. Further, it shows how these ideas, often controversial, were received and adapted in various schools and universities in Europe. The book begins with an account of a body of classical ideas and ends with how they have been reabsorbed into the Latin tradition.

There are seven chapters: (1) Masters of Those Who Know: Plato, Aristotle, and the Neoplatonists, (2) From Ancient World to Middle Ages: Adaptation and Transmission, (3) The Central Middle Ages: Logic, Theology, and Cosmology, (3) New Sources and New Institutions, (5) Aristotelian Philosophy in the University: The First Phase of Assimilation, (6) Aristotelian Philosophy and Christian Theology: System Building and Controversy, (7) The Condemnations in Context. These chapters are followed by an epilogue.

While Arab-Islamic linkages are apparent throughout the book, this is particularly true in the second half of the book. "Between the reception of the Aristotelian logical and philosophical systems there has to be considered another strand in which too various perspectives were comprised. This is the Arabic philosophical tradition. It was based on the Greek authorities but contained its own interpretations and insights, some of which were to be congenial, others devastatingly unsettling to the Christian world" (p.4). Further, "The speculative movement in Islam affords several interesting analogies to its Christian counterpart. There is ample evidence in Islam of the tension between reason and faith which is a recurrent feature of Christian thought" (p.118). And, "The formal gap between theology and philosophy was much wider in Islam than in Christianity" (p.119). There is considerable discussion of the philosophical thought of several Islamic scholastics; for example, Al-Farabi, Ibn Sina, Al-Ghazali, and Ibn Rushd. Specifically, the book discusses the "faith over reason" views of Al-Ghazali and the contrary perspective of Ibn Rushd, as well as the influence of these scholars on subsequent Latin Scholastics.

The book provides a 26-page list of footnotes at the end, classified by each chapter; similarly, there is a 23-page bibliography, chapter by chapter, and a supplementary bibliography for the second edition. There is also a detailed name-subject index.

B-141. Hourani, George F., ed. *Essays on Islamic Philosophy and Science.* Albany, NY: State University of New York Press, 1975.

The book is based on papers presented by prominent specialists at two conferences held at the State University of New York (Binghamton) and Columbia University in 1970 and 1971, respectively. The articles are devoted to the writings of eminent medieval Islamic scholars, ranging from Masha'allah of the eighth century to Mulla Sadra in the 17th (whose work is viewed as a continuation of the medieval philosophical thought). The majority of the essays pertain to Persian philosophers and scientists, reflecting "both the facts of intellectual history in medieval Islam and a recent trend in the study of that history" (p.vii). Further, the Persian focus reflects the overwhelming cultural fact that in Islam, "as a religion and a civilization, the national origin and language of expression of individual scholars were generally considered of minor importance in their own times" (p.vii).

The combination of philosophy and science in the volume is argued to be "a natural one in the context of medieval Islam. As in ancient Greece, the boundary between the two fields was not sharply defined; both were included in the learned meaning of the Arabic word *al-hikma*, literally 'wisdom'" (p.vii).

The 261-page book contains 20 essays, beginning with a general introduction by Gustave E. Von Grunebaum. Other essays cover various aspects of the writings of several scholars: Al-Kindi, Al-Razi, Al-Farabi, Ibn Sina, Al-Ghazali, Suhrawardi, Ibn Rushd, Mulla Sadra, Nasir al-din Tusi, and Masha'allah. Also, there are essays on themes such as ethics in medieval Islam, the significance of Persian thought in Islamic philosophy, the methodology of the history of science, and the concept of being.

There is a short bibliography on the principal Islamic scholars covered in the essays. There is no index.

B-142. Hyman, Arthur and James J. Walsh, eds. *Philosophy in the Middle Ages: The Christian, Islamic, and Jewish Traditions.* Indianapolis, IN: Hackett Publishing Company, 1973.

This anthology, not intended as a full-fledged history of medieval philosophy, encompasses the major representative thinkers of the Middle Ages covering a wide range of philosophical thought—ethics, politics, epistemology, metaphysics, and natural theology. The more important names from three groups of philosophers—Jewish, Latin-Christian, and Muslim—are included. It is argued that there is considerable common ground in the three religions on various philosophical issues. But, there are differences—Christianity being less compatible with philosophy than Islam and Judaism; that made the "task of a Thomas Aquinas and Duns Scotus in some ways more difficult than that of an Avicennian or Maimonides" (p.2–3).

The 805-page book is divided into five parts: (1) Early Christian Philosophy (Augustine, Boethius, Eriugena, Anselm of Canterbury, Peter Abailard, John of Salisbury), (2) Islamic Philosophy (Alfarabi, Avicennian, Algazali, Averroes), (3) Jewish Philosophy (Saadia, Solomon Ibn Gabirol, Moses Maimonides), (4) Latin Philosophy in the Thirteenth Century (Bonaventure, Robert Grosseteste, Roger Bacon, Siger of Brabant, Thomas Aquinas, the Condemnation of 1277), (5) Latin Philosophy in the Fourteenth Century (John Duns Scotus, William of Ockham, Nicholas of Autrecourt, Marsilius of Padua, John Buridan).

There is a short bibliography after each section and a longer bibliography at the end, as well as a detailed name-subject index.

B-143. Leaman, Oliver. *Averroes and His Philosophy.* Oxford: Clarendon Press, 1988.

The book is intended to provide an introduction to the philosophical thought of Ibn Rushd (1126–1198), whose name was Latinized to Averroes. It is not an exhaustive account of his philosophy, nor of his work on Aristotle and in other fields (theology, law, medicine, etc.). Leaman is mainly concerned with Averroes' arguments as to the importance of philosophy in understanding the world. The author laments the study of Islamic philosophy as being a "minority" activity; some hesitate to even acknowledge it as such, he says. He argues that Averroes produced "intriguing and complex philosophical theories which require and deserve serious analysis" (p.vii). He hopes that this book will persuade readers to raise "profound and exciting questions" as to the considerable intellectual achievement of Averroes.

The 205-page volume begins with an introductory chapter on the cultural context in which Averroes produced his scholarship. Then there are three parts with two or three chapters in each. Part I, Metaphysics, has three chapters—*The Incoherence of the Incoherence* (Averroes' criticism of Al-Ghazali's philosophical thought), What Can God Do?, and The Soul and Essence. Part II, Practical Philosophy, has two chapters—Divine Law and Human Wishes, and Philosophy and

Shari'a. Part III, Reason, Religion, and Language, has two chapters—Averroism, and Averroes' Philosophical Methodology. The last chapter is especially interesting. The author argues that Averroes' thought "might have been a severe check to the progress of philosophy in the Muslim community, a check which is only today becoming gradually weakened, but it did not hinder the transmission of that approach to philosophy to the non-Muslim world" (p.164). Averroes and Averroes' movement "came to have a significant influence on Christian intellectual life" (p.164).

The book provides a select bibliography at the end, organized in terms of "The works of Averroes," "General introduction to Averroes," "Collection of articles on Averroes" (Averroes' metaphysics; Averroes on the soul; Works in Arabic on Averroes). There is a short name-subject index.

B-144. Marmura, Michael E. *Al-Ghazali's The Incoherence of the Philosophers* (*Tahafut al-Falasifa*; a parallel English–Arabic text translated, introduced, and annotated). Provo, UT: Brigham Young University, 1997.

This 260-page book is an English translation of one of more than 70 books written by Abu Hamid Al-Ghazali (1058–1111 AD), widely acclaimed as among the most important thinkers of medieval Islam. Each page of English-language translation is followed by the corresponding original Arabic text.

When originally written, this Al-Ghazali work represented a challenge to earlier Islamic philosophers (particularly Al-Kindi, 801–873; Al-Farabi, 870–950; Ibn Sina, 980–1037) whose rationalistic interpretations of Aristotle, in trying to reconcile rationalism and revelation, reason and faith, appeared inconsistent with the Islamic ethos. This theology–philosophy conflict (which later prompted similar scholastic controversies in the 12th–13th century Latin Europe) was not entirely new in early Islam, but, according to the translator, one does not encounter anything like the comprehensive, sustained critique contained in this book by Al-Ghazali, devoted entirely to refuting the philosophers. While it remains a brilliant, incisive critique, Al-Ghazali's challenge gave rise to a well-recognized counter by Ibn Rushd (1126–1198), *The Incoherence of the Incoherence* (*Tahafut al-Tahafut*), which led to the emergence of rationalism and renaissance in Latin Europe.

At the end, notes and references, keyed to the main text, are provided, followed by a detailed name-subject index.

B-145. Mazzaoui, Michel M. and Vera B. Moreen, eds. *Intellectual Studies in Islam: Essays Written in Honor of Martin B. Dickson.* Salt Lake City, UT: University of Utah Press, 1990.

The 13 articles, written by well-known scholars, "cover significant achievements of the Muslim intellectual and cultural tradition in history, biography, mysticism, philosophy, and art—achievements which in themselves demonstrate the high caliber attained by Islamic societies in medieval and early modern times" (p.viii). Because of the specialization of the scholar honored, the primary focus of the narratives in this 268-page book is on Persian literature.

The article titles and authors are: (1) The Qizilbash Turcomans: Founders and Victims of the Safavid Theocracy by Hans R. Roemer, (2) The *Kitab-i-Anusi* of Babai Ibn Lutf (Seventeenth Century) and the *Kitab-i-Sar Guzasht* of Babai Ibn Farhad (Eighteenth Century): A Comparison of Two Judeo-Persian Chronicles by Vera Basch Moreen, (3) The Religious Policy of Safavid Shah Ismail II by Michel M. Mazzaoui, (4) The Anthology of Poets: *Muzakkir al-Ashab* as a Source for the History of Seventeenth-Century Central Asia by Robert D. McChesney, (5) Timur's Geneology by John E. Woods, (6) Regicide and "The Law of the Turks" by Ulrich Haarmann, (7) Women and Religion in the Fatimid Caliphate: The Case of Al-Sayyidah Al-Hurrah, Queen of Yemen by Leila al-Imad, (8) A Sentence of Junayd's by Andras Hamori, (9) Khankhanan Abdur Rahim and the Sufis by Annemarie Schimmel, (10) Disorientation and Reorientation in Ibn Sina's *Epistle of the Bird*: A Reading by Peter Heath, (11) Hermes and Harran: The Roots of Arabic-Islamic Occultism by Francis E. Peters, (12) Treatise on Calligraphic Arts: A Disquisition on Paper, Colors, Inks, and Pens of Simi of Nishapur by Wheeler M. Thackston, (13) The Peck *Shahnameh*: Manuscript Production in Late Sixteenth-Century Shiraz by Louise Marlow.

The editors suggest, "The desuetude that befell the tradition in more recent times (say, after 1800) should not keep us blind to the great accomplishments of the past. In fact, modern Western as well as Eastern intelligent and curious readers continue to be fascinated by the tremendous strides in the realms of thought and culture of the common Islamic heritage. On the one hand, the West wants to know more about the not-anymore-so-mysterious East; and the Muslim East, undergoing nowadays an exciting resurgence, wants very much to unfold and expose to the thoughtful world of its intellectual and cultural treasures and build on the glorious past a more meaningful and brighter future" (p.ix).

Each narrative has detailed footnotes and bibliographic references. There is a comprehensive name-subject index.

B-146. Murray, Alexander. *Reason and Society in the Middle Ages.* Oxford: Clarendon Press, 1978.

The book traces the evolution of medieval Europe with linkages chiefly with the Greek and Hebrew traditions, the historical focus being on the "central" middle ages, about 1100–1300 AD. There are, however, references to influences from the Islamic civilization and culture.

The 510-page book is divided into four parts. After the introductory chapter, the four parts include a total of 16 chapters. Part I (Economics and the Mind: The Making of Western Society, four chapters) describes the social mechanism within which the intellectual "renaissance" of 12th and 13th centuries took place and how the "rationalistic culture" evolved. During this period, the author argues, a "generic change in the European economy" took place—and this change represented a lasting shift in the world balance of power, beginning about Charlemagne's time, from the Islamic civilization of the Mediterranean to Europe. Parts II (Arithmetic, three chapters) and III (Reading and Writing, four chapters) explore the evolution of the rationalist culture itself and discuss its relation to the social structure—namely, the culture of the educated (the *litterati*), mathematics, demise of ecclesiastical politics, increasing secularization, and so forth. And Part IV (Nobility and Religion, four chapters) discusses "the distinct intellectual interest hiding in medieval society, challenging the secular and ecclesiastical authorities in the name of the mind" (p.19). Moreover, this part discusses the situation of "people who could not rise, because they were already at the top and will describe their association with the ascetic-religious culture which stood in contrast with the rationalistic" (p.19).

While the author explicitly mentions little about the Islamic influences (except occasional references), one observes those influences lurking in the background throughout. Illustratively, Part I has a chapter on money, which includes two sections that document the economic linkages through flows of money and trade from eastern and western Islam. These interactions "affected Europe in two ways. Firstly, it meant that Islam's first gift to Europe was in silver, now Europe's own currency" (p.43). And, "The second outcome for Europe of Islam's early eastern bias was one which complicated the effect of the first. It was a matter of geography. The economic impulse Islam sent to Europe went from Islam's old world; but it came to Europe's new world" (p.43). Elsewhere, there is a brief reference to the 13th century "rationalist" challenge from Averroes (Ibn Rushd, 1126–1198); his "Averroisms," among other things, the author argues, emphasized the path to God and salvation through knowledge, not grace, faith, sacraments, etc.— knowledge, not external symbolisms, was the supreme authority (p.261).

There is a 16-page bibliography at the end, along with a detailed name-subject index.

B-147. Nasr, Seyyed Hossein. *An Introduction to Islamic Cosmological Doctrines: Conceptions of Nature and Methods Used for Its Study by the Ikhwan al-Safa, al-Biruni, and Ibn Sina.* Albany, NY: State University of New York Press, revised edition, 1993.

In the foreword to this book, one of the foremost 20th-century scholars of Islam, H.A.R. Gibb, says, "This study opens up a relatively unexplored, hence unfamiliar, aspect of Islam. The majority of modern Muslim rationalists will no doubt join chorus with the formalist orthodox theologians to deny that its subject can be identified with Islam" (p.xiii). The 322-page book is "the only book to deal with classical Islamic cosmology as it was formulated by the Ikhwan al-Safa, al-Biruni and Ibn Sina during the 10th and 11th centuries. These schools of thought influenced all the later centuries of Islamic history and in fact created the cosmological framework within which all later scientific activity in the Islamic world was carried out—the enduring image of the cosmos within which Muslims have lived during the past millennium," says the author.

The book is written within the Islamic tradition and demonstrates how, based on the teachings of the Qur'an and the Prophet, these scholars integrated elements drawn from various ancient schools of philosophy and the sciences. The book claims to be unique in its treatment of classical Islamic cosmology as seen from within the Islamic worldview and provides a key for understanding traditional Islamic thought. The author argues that to the extent the rigid hold of "modern science becomes loosened and men begin to view modern science as a science of nature which is able to discover a great deal about the physical world but at the expense of overlooking certain essential dimensions of the cosmos, the significance of traditional cosmologies becomes more evident" (p.xx).

Beyond the prologue, the book is divided into three parts: Part I, The Ikhwan al-Safa (four chapters); Part II, al-Biruni (six chapters); Part III, Ibn Sina (five chapters). There is a concluding chapter, followed by an appendix on astrological symbols. There are two bibliographies, covering 25 pages: a selected bibliography (general, Ikhwan al-Safa, al-Biruni, and Ibn Sina) and another supplementary bibliography with similar classifications. There is a detailed name-subject index.

B-148. Nasr, Seyyed Hossein and Oliver Leaman, eds. *History of Islamic Philosophy (Parts I and II)*. London: Routledge, 1996.

As part of the Routledge series, this volume is the first, the other volume being *The History of Jewish Philosophy*, and in the context of Western philosophy, the two are inextricably linked. This particular two-part volume set, covering more than 1,200 pages, provides extensive analysis of the most important Islamic philosophers and concepts, and the essays are written by some of the most influential scholars. It presents Islamic philosophy from "within," rather than the "Eurocentric" view of Islamic philosophy that "has been taken in the West for Islamic philosophy" (p.12). Further, instead of treating the leading Islamic philosophers "within the context of their own times," the attempt here is to view "Islamic philosophy as a living philosophical tradition," with linkages "to other intellectual developments of Islamic civilization. Islamic philosophy in fact deals with conceptual issues which are not tied to a particular author or period, and which have universal import" (p.xvii).

Part I contains six sections, with several essays in each. The section titles are: (1) Religious, intellectual and cultural context, (2) Early Islamic philosophers in the East, (3) Islamic philosophers in the Western lands of Islam, (4) Philosophy and mystical tradition, (5) Later Islamic philosophy, (6) The Jewish philosophical tradition in the Islamic cultural world. Part II has four sections, with several essays in each. The section titles are: (1) Philosophy and its part, (2) Later transmission and interpretation, (3) Islamic philosophy in the modern Islamic world, (4) Interpretation of Islamic philosophy in the West.

There is a total of 71 essays in the two volumes, and most of the essays provide their own notes and bibliographies. There is a detailed bibliography at the end, followed by separate name and subject indices.

B-149. Peters, F.E. *Aristotle and the Arabs: The Aristotelian Tradition in Islam.* New York and London: New York University Press/University of London Press, 1968.

Part of the New York University studies in near-eastern civilization, the book is intended for three different groups of scholars—the orientalists, the Western medievalists (particularly students of Latin scholastics), and the classicists. Further, the book aims to contribute to Islamic studies (especially Islamic philosophy).

Distinguished as Western and Eastern Hellenism, the 303-page book argues, "The Arabs literally 'took' Hellenic philosophy from the all-but-vanished Greek philosophical tradition of the 7th century A.D. The Arabs assiduously sought out Aristotelian manuscripts in the newly conquered cities of Damascus and Antioch and even over the frontier in Byzantine territory. They learnt from scholars who had somehow preserved the school tradition of Alexandria and arrived in Baghdad about A.D. 900" (p.xviii). The Aristotelian philosophy mainly prevailed in Islamic Spain, "metamorphosed into Alkindus, Alpharabius, Avicennian, and Averroes," and through various channels of transmission, "helped produce thirteenth-century Scholasticism" (p.xxiii). And, "The twentieth-century Westerner modestly accepts the fact that he is a Hellene at root and that his intellectual pedigree runs back to Homer, Sophocles, and Aristotle and he is confronted with the evidences of another Hellenism in which he has no part. It is rather Eastern Hellenism" (p.xxiii–xxiv). "Islam created a synthesis that bears more eloquent testimony to the vitality of Hellenism (and the creativity of Islam) than the moldering heaps of Pergamum or Baalbek, and part of this synthesis, surely its most dazzling part, was the Arabs' reception, adaptation, and assimilation of Aristotelianism" (p.xxiv). The book traces the various dimensions of that phenomenon.

The book has six chapters: (1) The Making of the Aristotelian Tradition, (2) The Ground Prepared: The Hellenic and Iranian Near East, (3) The Eastern Translation Movement, (4) The Transmission of the New Learning, (5) The Diffusion of Aristotelianism, (6) Philosophic Movements in Islam. There is an epilogue (The Eastern and Western Aristotle) and an appendix (Sources for the History of the Aristotelian Tradition in Islam).

There is a detailed bibliography and a primary sources classification by the author, along with a comprehensive name-subject index.

B-150. Qadir, C.A. *Philosophy and Science in the Islamic World.* Kent, UK: Croom Helm Ltd., 1988.

The book traces "the history of philosophy and science in Islamic civilization," and it attempts to demonstrate how "the Muslims, inspired by Qur'anic teachings and influenced by the translations of Greek texts of science and philosophy, rose to the highest pinnacles of glory; and then, after losing their spirit of inquiry due to conformism and orthodoxy and also to the lack of financial support, how they sank to the lowest level" (p.ii). The author suggests that "Muslim philosophers felt that there could be no conflict between the dictates of reason" and revelations. "Any apparent conflict could be resolved by deeper thinking" (p.i).

There are 12 chapters in this 220-page book: (1) The Islamic Theory of Knowledge, (2) Religion, Science and Philosophy in Islam, (3) The Transmission of Greek Science and Philosophy to the Muslim World, (4) Early Religio-Philosophic Thought, (5) Mutazilism, Asharism and Ikhwan-al-Safa, (6) Muslim Philosophers and Their Problems, (7) Muslim Mysticism, (8) Science in the Golden Period of Islam, (9) The Decline of Science and Philosophy, (10) The Renaissance of Philosophical Knowledge in the Islamic World, (11) Contemporary Philosophic Thought in Muslim Lands, (12) The Renaissance of Science and Technology in Muslim Countries.

In the chapter entitled The Decline of Science and Philosophy, the author states, "It is unfortunate that the Muslims took no note of Imam Ghazali's scientific and rational methodology and were impressed only by his denunciation of rational thinking and repudiation of philosophic enterprises. Nor did Muslims take note of Ibn Rushd's *Tahafut al-Tahafut* in which he championed Aristotelianism and disputed the criticism of Muslim philosophers by Imam Ghazali. Had Ibn Rushd's *Tahafut al-Tahafut* come to the notice of the Muslims in the East and been properly appreciated, the decline in rational thinking among the Muslims would not have been so steep" (p.126).

The book provides chapter-by-chapter notes and references at the end, followed by a detailed name-subject index.

B-151. Rescher, Nicholas. *Studies in Arabic Philosophy*. Pittsburgh, PA: University of Pittsburgh Press, 1967.

The 162-page book is a collection of ten studies (some have appeared in journals previously) by the author that document the various facets of Arab-Islamic philosophy and its influence upon the West.

The essays are: (1) Al-Kindi's epistle on the concentric structure of the university, (2) Al-Kindi's treatise on the platonic solids, (3) Yahya Ibn Adi's treatise "on the four scientific questions regarding the art of logic," (4) Avicennian on the logic of questions, (5) Ibn al-Salah on Aristotle on causation, (6) the concept of existence in Arabic logic and philosophy, (7) the theory of temporal modalities in Arabic logic and philosophy, (8) Ibn al-Assal's discourse on logic, (9) Nicholas of Cusa on the Qur'an, (10) the impact of Arabic philosophy on the West.

The concluding essay identifies three major "waves" of impact: "(1) In the 12th and 13th centuries, the first period of European impingement, Arabic philosophical writings exerted a significant stimulative influence on the great synthesis of Christian Aristotelianism by St. Albert the Great and St. Thomas Aquinas; (2)

In the Italian Renaissance of the 15th to mid-16th centuries, Averroism exerted a great influence in the study of the philosophy of nature at Padua and Bologna, with the result that Arabic philosophy was operative as a significance force in the intellectual ferment that underlay the work of Galileo and saw the beginnings of modern science; [and] (3) In the late 16th and 17th centuries the study of Arabic philosophy contributed to a small but significant extent to the intellectual ferment of European Protestantism—with various results, of which one of the most striking is that in one significant instance Arabic philosophy served as a stimulus to the philosophico-religious ideology of English pietism" (p.156–157). Further, the author continues, "This influence has not only been extensive and profound, but relatively continuous and astonishingly diversified" (p.157).

All footnotes and references are integrated in each of the essays. There is an index of names at the end.

B-152. Ross, James F., ed. *Inquiries into Medieval Philosophy: A Collection in Honor of Francis P. Clarke.* Westport, CT: Greenwood Publishing Company, 1971.

Written in honor of a distinguished faculty at the University of Pennsylvania, the 330-page book illustrates "the methods by which contemporary philosophers explicate and criticize medieval philosophy" (p.vii). Three parts of the book are: (1) Displaying the Analytic Method (four essays), (2) Displaying Logical and Formalistic Methods (four essays), (3) Displaying More Traditional Methods (six essays).

While several of the essays include references to numerous medieval Latin-European scholars who were influenced by their Arab-Islamic precursors, two essays specifically focus on those linkages. The essay by Joseph Owens, Common Nature: A Point of Comparison Between Thomistic and Scotistic Metaphysics, provides a comparative discussion on some philosophical issues as developed in the writings of St. Thomas Aquinas and John Duns Scotus. The author states, "Both writers develop their doctrine of essence taken just in itself against a background already laid down by Avicennian (Ibn Sina). Both follow the general divisions of the Arabian thinker, and both use to a large extent the terminology taken from the Latin translation of his works" (p.186).

Further, Ibn Rushd's influence is clear in the essay by Harry Wolfson, The Twice-Revealed Averroes, in that "Averroes was revealed twice to European philosophy: first in the thirteenth century and then in the sixteenth century" (p.211). The essay is devoted to documenting the influence of these Averroistic "revelations" upon Latin Europe. "Despite repeated condemnation of Averroes for his real or imaginary heresies, his commentaries were widely read and studied and copied. Moreover, they were imitated. The very same persons who damned him for his heresy—Albertus Magnus, Thomas Aquinas, and even Giles of Rome—followed his example and wrote commentaries on Aristotle in his style and manner; and they constantly quoted him. By the fourteenth century Averroes came to be recognized as the Commentator *par excellence*, and this reputation he continued to enjoy during the fifteenth century" (p.223). Later, during the 15th–16th centuries, the "old cry of heresy no longer came from the Schoolmen" (p.225). Instead, Ibn Rushd's work was viewed as "most praiseworthy. None of the ancient interpreters seem to hit the sense of Aristotle so happily as this Arabian" (p.225).

Expository notes and biographical references are included at the end of each essay; there is no index.

B-153. Sharif, M.M., ed. *A History of Muslim Philosophy, with Short Accounts of Other Disciplines and the Modern Renaissance in Muslim Lands*, two volumes. Wiesbaden, Germany: Otto Harrassowitz, 1963 and 1966.

This two-volume compendium represents about the most comprehensive English-language text of its kind, covering the pre-Islamic period and extending to the most recent. The editor states in the introduction, among other things, that "every thinker of these two centuries (eighteenth and nineteenth) understood history as if it were Western history. Histories of other civilizations and people did not count, except for those events which could be easily linked with the chain of events in the history of the West. Toynbee justly describes this conception of history as an egocentric illusion, and his view is shared by all recent philosophers of history" (p.7). The editor further asserts that in most such accounts, there are "yawning" gaps, not only with respect to non-Western contributions, but, specifically, there tends to be scant reference to the "well-recognized role of Muslim philosophy in transmitting Greek thought to the West, in advancing human knowledge, in supplying a mould for the shaping of Western scholasticism, in developing empirical sciences, in bringing about the Italian Renaissance, and in providing stimulus to the speculation of Western thinkers from Descartes to Kant" (p.8). Thus, the chief aim of these volumes is to "give an account not of Muslim culture as a whole, nor of Muslim thought in general, but only of one aspect of Muslim thought, i.e., Muslim philosophy" (p.12).

Each volume is divided into books, parts, and chapters. Thus, the 787-page volume one has three books, with parts and chapters on specific topics. Book One, entitled Pre-Islamic Philosophic Thought, has two parts, with chapters devoted to pre-Islamic non-Arabic thought and to pre-Islamic Arabic thought. Book Two, entitled Advent of Islam: Fundamental Teachings of the Qur'an, has several chapters. Book Three, entitled Early Centuries (from the First/Seventh Century to the Fall of Baghdad), has five parts: (1) Theologico-Philosophic Movements (six chapters), (2) The Sufis (five chapters), (3) The "Philosophers" (nine chapters), (4) The Middle-Roaders (three chapters), (5) Political Thinkers (seven chapters).

The 1,005-page volume two is similarly divided into books, parts, and chapters. In continuation of the three books of the previous volume, there are five books in this volume. Book Four, entitled Later Centuries (from the Fall of Baghdad [656/1258] to 1111/1700), has six parts: (1) The Fall of Baghdad (one chapter), (2) Theologico-Philosophical Thought (one chapter), (3) The Sufis (three chapters), (4) The "Philosophers" (two chapters), (5) The Middle-Roaders (two chapters), (6) Political Thought (one chapter). Book Five, entitled Other Disciplines (covering both the early and the later centuries), has four parts: (1) Language and Literature (five chapters), (2) Fine Arts (five chapters), (3) Social Studies (two chapters), (4) The Sciences (six chapters). Book Six, entitled Influence of Islamic Thought, has two chapters: Influence of Muslim Thought on the West, and Influence of Muslim Thought on the East. Book Seven, entitled The Dark Age (1111/1700–1266/1850), has two chapters: Decline in the Muslim World, and The Silver Lining: Development of the Urdu Language, Grammar, and Literature. Book Eight, entitled Modern Renaissance, has two parts: Renaissance in the Near and Middle East (seven chapters) and Renaissance in South and South-East Asia (five chapters).

Notes and bibliographic references are integrated in the text, and each chapter provides a bibliography at the end. There is a concluding chapter in the second volume in which the editor expresses optimism for the future of Islamic world, although he is skeptical about the adoption of Western or Soviet models. This volume also has a combined, 130-page name-subject index.

B-154. Siraisi, Nancy G. *Avicenna in Renaissance Italy: The* Canon *and Medical Teaching in Italian Universities after 1500.* Princeton, NJ: Princeton University Press, 1987.

The author explores the place of Avicenna's (Ibn Sina, d. 1037) *Canon* in medical education through the Renaissance of the 16th century and beyond, and why, despite humanists' criticisms and new medical discoveries, this work continued to be printed, taught, and expounded. Thus, the book has three objectives: (1) to map the extent of Renaissance interest in the *Canon* in order to determine the various aspects of this work and to relate them to specific academic, professional, and commercial milieus; (2) to trace various aspects of intellectual history in order to assess attitude and ideas as to Avicennian and Arabo-Latin medicine, medieval Latin scholastic medicine, contemporary Galenism and medical humanism, etc.; and (3) to determine the way in which the *Canon* was used as a teaching text and, in particular, the question of how the teaching of a scientific subject by means of a medieval text synthesizing ancient sources was accomplished in the Renaissance classroom.

The 410-page book is divided into four parts, with two chapters in each. Part I, The *Canon* as a Latin Medical Book (Text, Commentary, and Pedagogy in Renaissance Medicine; The *Canon* of Avicenna), Part II, The *Canon* in the Schools (The *Canon* in the Medieval Universities and the Humanist Attack on Avicenna; The *Canon* in Italian Medical Education after 1500), Part III, The *Canon* and Its Renaissance Editors, Translators, and Commentators (Renaissance Editions; Commentators and Commentaries), Part IV, *Canon* and the Teaching of

Medical Theory at Padua and Bologna (Philosophy and Science in a Medical Milieu; *Canon* and Renaissance Physiology; Conclusion). There is an appendix that documents the various editions and commentaries on the *Canon*.

Notes and references are integrated within the text of each chapter. There is an 18-page select bibliography at the end, mainly consisting of items cited in the footnotes, and a name-subject index.

B-155. Smith, Margaret. *Al-Ghazali: The Mystic*. London: Luzac and Company, 1944.

This study is concerned with al-Ghazali's mystical teaching and the influences that "moulded that teaching, which were not only Islamic, but also Hellenistic, Jewish and Christian" (p.5). Al-Ghazali's teaching "had an influence upon subsequent writers, not only his fellow Muslims, but Christian writers and also, to some extent Jewish writers" (p.5).

The 248-page book is divided into two parts. Part I, Al-Ghazali's Life and Personality, has seven chapters: (1) Al-Ghazali's birth and early years, (2) The new Al-Ghazali, (3) Al-Ghazali's character and personality, (4) Al-Ghazali's family relationships, (5) Al-Ghazali's literary style, (6) Al-Ghazali as poet, (7) Al-Ghazali as mystic. Part II, Al-Ghazali's Mystical Teachings, also has seven chapters: (8) Al-Ghazali's sources, (9) Al-Ghazali's teachings on the nature of Godhead, (10) The beginning of the soul's ascent to God, (11) The Mystic Path, (12) The end of the Path, (13) Al-Ghazali's influence, (14) Summary of Al-Ghazali's Mystical teaching.

Chapter 13 (Al-Ghazali's influence) is of particular interest presently. The author notes, "Al-Ghazali's influence was great even during his life-time, and the widespread appreciation of both his lectures and his writings made his teaching famous" (p.198). Among the various Muslims influenced by Al-Ghazali, Ibn Al-Arabi is perhaps the best known; Ibn Rushd (d. 1198) was his most bitter critic. Among the Jewish scholars so influenced, there were several, Maimonides being the best known. As for his influence on Latin Scholasticism, "there can be no doubt that Al-Ghazali's works would be among the first to attract the attention of these European scholars. The greatest of these Christian writers who was influenced by Al-Ghazali was St. Thomas Aquinas (1225–1274), who made a study of the Arabic writers and admitted his indebtedness to them" (p.220). Other names mentioned are Raymund Martin, Dante Alighieri, and Blaise Pascal.

Numerous notes and references are integrated in each chapter. There is a bibliography of authors quoted, classified as "General" and "Arabic, Persian, and Syriac Authors." There is a name-subject index.

B-156. Stern, S.M., Albert Hourani, and Vivian Brown, eds. *Islamic Philosophy and the Classical Tradition: Essays Presented by His Friends and Pupils to Richard Walzer*. Columbia, SC: University of South Carolina Press, 1972.

The book is a collection of essays written and assembled as a tribute to Richard Walzer as a scholar and a teacher. Although "driven out of Germany in 1933, he never hesitated in accepting an invitation" to lecture in Germany, and further, "no less striking is the fact that, although of Jewish descent, he has continued to attract Arab students to Oxford to study with him" (p.2).

The 550-page book contains 33 essays on a variety of topics relevant to the book title. Some representative titles, with authors, are as follows: Avicennian and the Christian Philosophers in Baghdad by H.V.B. Brown; The Greek Commentators on Aristotle quoted in Al-Amiri's 'As-Sa'ada wa'l-Is'ad by A.A. Ghorab; The Rationalist Ethics of Abd Al-Jabbar by George F. Hourani; Al-Kindi as Philosopher: The Aristotelian and Neoplatonic Dimensions by Alfred L. Ivry; A Translation of the Arabic Epitome of Galen's Book by J.N. Mattock; Al-Farabi's Introduction to the Study of Medicine by M. Plessner; and Some Observations on Al-Farabi and Logical Tradition by F.W. Zimmerman.

Notes and references are provided at the end of each essay, and there is a name-subject index.

B-157. Umaruddin, M. *The Ethical Philosophy of Al-Ghazzali.* Lahore, Pakistan: Institute of Islamic Culture, Combine Printers, 1988; original 1962.

The purpose of the book is to "present the basic principles and the practical implications of Al-Ghazzali's ethical theory, and to re-construct the whole system of his thought as presented in his works" (p.vii–viii). This exposition is based on Al-Ghazzali's original Arabic-language works, along with some works by ancient and modern writers. The author suggests that "we find anticipations in him of many modern philosophers, e.g., Descartes (Method of Doubt), Hume (Law of Causation), Kant (Antinomies), etc." Further, "The study of Al-Ghazzali is helpful in understanding the culture and civilization of Islam" (p.vii).

The 276-page book is divided into four parts, with 17 chapters altogether. Part I, Background of Al-Ghazzali's Thought, has four chapters: (1) Al-Ghazzali's Times, (2) Theological and Philosophical Movements, (3) Islamic Ethics before Al-Ghazzali, (4) Al-Ghazzali's Inner Development. Part II, Al-Ghazzali's Theory of Ethics: Its Basis, has three chapters: (5) The Psychological Nature of Man, (6) Knowledge and Morality, (7) The Freedom of Will. Part III, Al-Ghazzali's Theory of Ethics (continued): Its Principles, has five chapters: (8) The End, (9) Knowledge of God, (10) Knowledge of God: Intuitive Knowledge, (11) Love of God, (12) The Vision of God. Part IV, Al-Ghazzali's Theory of Ethics: Its Practical Aspects, has five chapters: (13) Virtues and Vices, (14) Vices, (15) Virtues, (16) Social Virtues, (17) Religious Duties and Their Ethical Significance. The table of contents provides considerable detail as to the contents of each chapter.

There is a 42-page, chapter-by-chapter listing of notes and references at the end, as well as three appendices: (1) Synopsis of Intuitive Knowledge of God, (2) Bibliography, (3) Name-Subject Index.

B-158. Urvoy, Dominique. *Ibn Rushd (Averroes)* (translated from French by Olivia Steward). London and New York: Routledge, 1991.

According to Urvoy, the 12th-century philosopher Ibn Rushd (1126–1198), known as Averroes in the West, is one of the most important philosophers of the Islamic Middle Ages. He played a crucial role in the transmission of classical philosophy to Islam, and his work had a profound influence on Western scholasticism and on aspects of Renaissance thought.

Going well beyond the Eurocentric view which sees Ibn Rushd merely as an Aristotelian "intermediary," this 156-page book explores the main elements of his thought in light of the historical and cultural background of Muslim Spain. A full account of his works—scientific, medical, legal, and philosophical—is provided, including the wider movement of Almohadism that Ibn Rushd initiated; this was a rationalistic, politico-religious reform movement with great impact in Muslim Spain but little influence in the larger Islamic world. The book also traces the rise and fall of his reputation in his own Islamic environment.

In addition to the introductory chapter, there are four major chapters: (1) The Major Options (the scientific options, methodological consequences, cultural complements, involvement in the Muslim community), (2) The Interpretation of Almohadism (Rushdian theology, the philosophical implications), (3) A "Human" Knowledge (reasoning, the status of the intellect, the human community and the political community), (4) An Ambiguous Audience (the Muslim milieu, the Jewish milieu, the medieval Christian orientalists).

Footnotes and references to each chapter are provided at the end, as is a detailed bibliographical guide. There is a name-subject index.

B-159. Wahba, Mourad and Mona Abousenna, eds. *Averroes and the Enlightenment*. Amherst, MA, and New York: Prometheus Books, 1996.

The 291-page book is a collection of papers presented at two conferences and the book is divided accordingly: The First Special International Philosophy Conference on "Ibn Rushd (Averroes) and the Enlightenment," held in Cairo in 1994; the second, "Averroes and His Influence: Remembering George Hourani" (Hourani was a former professor of Islamic philosophy at the State University of New York), held at the State University of New York (Buffalo campus) in 1996. The editors state that "the Islamic philosopher of the Middle Ages, Ibn Rushd (Averroes) had contributed to the emergence of the European Enlightenment. His philosophy had been the focus of intensive debate among theologians in religious universities in Europe. He did not perform the same role in the Arab societies, however, for he was persecuted and his books were burned" (p.12).

The book includes 21 essays, with a variety of topics reflective of the conference theme. Some titles and authors are: Intellectual Freedom, Rationality, and Enlightenment: The Contributions of Averroes by Paul Kurtz; Averroes and the West by Oliver Leaman; Medieval Scholasticism and Averroism: The Implication of the Writings of Ibn Rushd to Western Science by Vern L. Bullough; Ibn Rushd in the Islamic Context by Mokdad Arfa Mensia; Enlightenment in the Islamic World: Muslims—Victims of Mnemonic Success by Ghazala Irfan; and The Third World and Enlightenment by Mahmoud Osman. The second part includes five essays, including Averroes on the Harmony of Philosophy and Religion by Therese-Anne Druart. To quote one of the scholars, "Averroism played a large part in establishing a tradition in which it became possible to question the status of religion in comparison with reason" (p.65). However, the essence of the volume is conveyed by a statement in Vern Bullough's essay: "In sum, Averroes, whether as a positive or negative force, was extremely influential in the development of the forces which went into the Enlightenment" (p.50).

Each essay is followed by expository and bibliographic notes; there is no index.

B-160. Walzer, Richard. *Greek into Arabic: Essays in Islamic Philosophy.* Cambridge, MA: Harvard University Press, 1962.

This 255-page book is a collection of papers published by the author in various journals during the 1934–1957 period; all but three of the 14 essays are in English. In tracing the impact of the Greek tradition, the author suggests in the introductory essay, "the understanding of Arabic philosophy is thus intimately linked with the study of Greek philosophy and theology in the early stages of Christianity, the last centuries of the Roman Empire and the contemporary civilization of Byzantium" (p.1–2). Further, it is stressed, "Had the Arabic philosophers done nothing apart from saving Greek philosophy from being completely disregarded in the Middle Ages—and they did more—they would deserve the interest of twentieth-century scholars for this reason alone" (p.2).

In addition to the introduction, there are 13 essays: (1) On the Legacy of the Classics in the Islamic World, (2) Un Frammento nuovo di Aristotle, (3) Aristotle, Galen, and Palladius on Love, (4) New Light on the Arabic Translations of Aristotle, (5) On the Arabic Versions of Books of Aristotle's Metaphysics, (6) Zur Traditionsgeschichte der Aristotelischen Poetik, (7) Arabische Aristoteles ubersetzungen in Istanbul, (8) New Light on Galen's Moral Philosophy, (9) A Diatribe of Galen, (10) New Studies on Al-Kindi, (11) Al-Farabi's Theory of Prophecy and Divination, (12) Some Aspects of Miskawaih's Tahdhib Al-Akhlaq, (13) Platonism in Islamic Philosophy.

The original publication source is identified at the end of each essay. Notes and references are included in the text of each, and there is a name-subject index.

B-161. Weinberg, Julius R. *A Short History of Medieval Philosophy.* Princeton, NJ: Princeton University Press, 1964.

The book is intended mainly for students who are not specializing in medieval thought and for the general educated readers. The author acknowledges that while chapters on Islamic and Jewish philosophy are included, he makes "no claim to any expertness in these areas" (p.vii).

There are 12 chapters in this 304-page book: (1) Introduction, (2) St. Augustine, (3) The Mystical Element in Medieval Thought, (4) Anselm and the Beginnings of Scholasticism, (5) Abelard and the Problem of Universals, (6) Philosophy in the Islamic Middle Ages, (7) The Philosophy of the Jews in the Middle Ages, (8) Philosophy in Thirteenth-Century Christianity, (9) St. Thomas Aquinas, (10) Duns Scotus, (11) William of Ockham, (12) The Critical Tendencies of the Fourteenth Century. There is a concluding chapter.

There are references to influential linkages with the Islamic world in almost all chapters, especially so in the chapters on Islamic philosophy and after. "The kind of philosophy," says the author, "which most influenced the intellectual currents of the thirteenth century in the Christian West is represented by a series of Islamic writers who have been miscalled as Aristotelians" (p.99). Reference is to names such as Al-Kindi, Al-Farabi, Ibn Sina (among other things, "the chief influence on the development of early thirteenth-century Scholasticism," p.111), Al-Ghazali, and Ibn Rushd. Also several Jewish philosophers, who pursued their scholarship in the Islamic milieu and wrote in Arabic, are discussed; they also influenced Latin-Christian philosophy—for example, Isaac Israeli, Saadia ben Joseph Al-Fayyumi, Solomon Ibn Gibrol, and the most significant figure in medieval Jewish thought, Moses Maimonides. St. Thomas found comfort especially in Al-Ghazali, whose thought was criticized later by Ibn Rushd, in that both Al-Ghazali and St. Thomas emphasized the ultimate supremacy of faith over reason (p.171). Further, the author states: "It must be remembered that the subjects to which logic could be applied were greatly increased by the Latin translations of the works of Aristotle, of the Muslim philosophers and scientists, and the translations of works of ancient science and mathematics. Moreover, some of the writings of Muslim philosophers contained logical doctrines new to the Latin West" (p.178).

There is a chapter-by-chapter, select bibliography at the end, followed by a names index.

B-162. Wulf, Maurice de. *History of Medieval Philosophy* (translated from French by P. Coffey). New York, Bombay, and Calcutta: Longmans, Green, and Company, 1909.

This encyclopedic, 520-page book aims "to place in their proper historical setting the numerous philosophical systems of the Middle Ages and to trace their mutual doctrinal relations. The intimate connections of the medieval with the ancient Grecian philosophies are becoming daily more evident: notably the importance of the neo-Platonic influences has been proved by recent works, published since 1905" (p.v).

The book is divided in two major parts, with several sections and chapters in each. The first part is entitled Historical Introduction and is divided into Grecian Philosophy (four chapters) and Patristic Philosophy. The second part, Medieval Philosophy, is more comprehensive. After an introduction, this part is divided chronologically into four sections: (1) First Period—Medieval Philosophy to the End of the Twelfth Century (three chapters), (2) Second Period—Medieval Philosophy in the Thirteenth Century (five chapters), (3) Third Period—Medieval Philosophy during the Fourteenth and First Half of the Fifteenth Centuries (four chapters), (4) Fourth Period—Medieval Philosophy from the Middle of the Fifteenth to the Seventeenth Centuries (three chapters).

There are references to the Arab-Islamic linkages and influences throughout. This is especially so in chapter 3 under the First Period where there is a section on Oriental Philosophies, and references are made to the integration of Grecian thought in the Islamic world, and "under these influences Arabia developed a philosophy which flourished for about three centuries and a half, first in Arabia itself and afterwards in Spain" (p.227). The author discusses some "leading features of Arabian philosophy," followed by some specifics about Alfarabi, Avicennia, Ghazali (identified as part of the "oriental branch of Arabian philosophy"), and especially Averroes who, because of his pronounced influence, is identified as part of the "Western branch of Arabian philosophy" (p.233). The author states: "The line of Arabian philosophers proper may be said to have terminated with Averroes; but their influence continued to be felt in the philosophy of the Jews, and even more perceptibly in the Western philosophy of the thirteenth century" (p.236). The Second Period includes frequent references to Arabic-Islamic precursors of the Latins, including translations from the Arabic works to Latin, and there is specific section on Latin Averroism as part of anti-scholastic philosophy. There is a similar section in the Third Period discussion.

Notes and references are integrated within the text of each chapter, and there is a comprehensive name-subject index.

d. Education/Learning

B-163. Duri, A.A. *The Rise of Historical Writing Among the Arabs* (edited and translated from Arabic by Lawrence I. Conrad; introduction by Fred M. Donner). Princeton, NJ: Princeton University Press, 1983; original 1960.

It is noted in the introduction that "the study of early Islamic history, more perhaps than most historical fields, has been plagued by uncertainties about the reliability of written sources. Under such circumstances it is hardly surprising that drastic reinterpretations both of early Islamic history itself, and of the role of various sources for it, should periodically arise" (p.vii). Thus, the book "represents a first attempt to study the evolution of historical writing among the Arabs, a collection of sketches linked both by chronological period—the first centuries after the Hijra—and by their unity of the subject" (p.10). In referring to the "general crisis" as to how to approach historical writing, the author points out that, "before this crisis, it was customary to view Western civilization as the climax in the development of the civilization of all mankind. It was also customary to regard all the history of mankind from a Western perspective, as if the pivot of world history was the West and all other history was merely prefatory or marginal to that of the West" (p.3). However, the post-World War II perspective has gradually evolved to be more inclusive and one that acknowledges the "inter-relationship of civilizations and the reciprocal exchange of influence in the course of their interactions" (p.5). This perspective, it is noted, "places the primary responsibility for the writing of the history of any people on its own historians if a sound view of its history is to be achieved" (p.5).

The 190-page book has five chapters: (1) The Rise of History Among the Arabs and Its Development During the First Three Centuries A.H., (2) Origins of the Historical School of Medina: 'Urwa–al-Zuhri, (3) The Beginnings of Historical Folklore: Wahb ibn Munabbih, (4) Origins of the Historical School of Iraq: Its Rise and Development Until the Third Century A.H., (5) Motives for the Writing of History and the Historical Views Embodied in the Works of the First Historians.

Each chapter has its own notes and references. There is also a detailed bibliography at the end, followed by a name-subject index.

B-164. Haskins, Charles Homer. *The Rise of Universities.* New York: Henry Holt and Company, 1923.

The focus of this book relates to the rise of universities in Europe during the Middle Ages. Necessarily, the discussion relies heavily on Greek, Roman, and Arabic sources. While the Greeks and the Romans had no universities in the contemporary sense, they had higher education. The occasion for the rise of universities was a great revival of learning stimulated by the renaissance of the 12th century. The author stresses the sources for this revival, in that "during 1100 and 1200 there was a great influx of new knowledge into Western Europe, partly through Italy and Sicily, but chiefly through the Arab scholars of Spain" (p.8).

Then he traces the development of universities at places such as Paris, Bologna, Padua, and Palermo. These early universities had no architecture or buildings of their own and were often located in private halls and churches. Soon, however, curricula were developed, as was the degree/diploma structure with appropriate faculty. Typical subjects were philosophy, ethics, theology, law, arts, and medicine. The author discusses the characteristics of the medieval professor (studies, textbooks, examinations, status, freedom) and those of the students (sources of information, manuals, etc.) There are frequent references to Arabic sources of learning [especially Ibn Sina (Avicenna, 980–1037) and Ibn Rushd (Averroes, 1126–1198)].

There is a bibliography at the end, followed by a name-subject index.

B-165. Lowry, Joseph E., Devin J. Stewart, and Shawkat M. Toorawa, eds. *Law and Education in Medieval Islam: Studies in Honor of Professor George Makdisi.* Published by E.J.W. Gibb Memorial Trust. Oakville, CT: David Brown Book Company, 2005.

This 194-page volume, focusing on legal education and its place in classical and medieval Islamic civilization, comprises 11 articles written in honor of late George Makdisi (1920–2002), all except one by his former students at the University of Pennsylvania. As one of 20th century's most prominent scholars of Islamic law, theology, and education, as well as a historian of Islam's institutions of learning, George Makdisi is quoted: "We cannot hope to understand the nomocracy of Islam if we study the theology of Islam without its relation to Islamic law" (p.xi).

There is a preface, The Trail and Scent of Learning, by Edward Peters. This scholar says, "The focus of this volume on broader kind of legal education and its place in classical Islamic civilization indicates the wide range and technical precision of George Makdisi's scholarship as well as his great pedagogical influence" (p.xi). Other essays and authors are: (1) Colleges of Law and the Institutions of Medieval Sunni Islam by Joseph Lowry, Devin Stewart, and Shawkat Toorawa, (2) *Nomas kai Paideia*: A Bibliography of George Makdisi's Publications by Shawkat Toorawa, (3) Discipline and Duty in a Medieval Muslim Elementary School: Ibn Hajar al-Haytami's *Taqrir al-Maqal* by Sherman Jackson (4) The Etiquette of Learning in the Early Islamic Study Circle by Christopher Melchert, (5) The Doctorate of Islamic Law in Maluk Egypt and Syria by Devin Stewart, (6) A Portrayal of 'Abd al-Latif al-Baghdadi's Education and Instruction by Shawkat Toorawa, (7) Medieval Islamic Legal Education as Reflected in the Works of Sayg al-Din al-Amidi by Bernard Weiss, (8) The Reception of Shafi'i's Concept of *Amr* and *Nahy* in the Thought of his Student al-Muzani by Joseph Lowry, (9) Islamic Education and the Transmission of Knowledge in Muslim Sicily by William Granara, (10) The *Madrasah* and the Islamization of Anatolia before the Ottomans by Gary Leiser.

Notes and references are integrated in the text of each essay. There is a name-subject index.

B-166. Makdisi, George. *The Rise of Colleges: Institutions of Learning in Islam and the West*. Edinburgh: Edinburgh University Press, 1981.

The book attempts to achieve a better understanding of the critical period in early Islamic intellectual history, and it is argued that such understanding requires not only an appreciation of the underlying forces but also the methods of instructions, study, and composition. The book is not a survey of Islamic education; rather, "an attempt is made to concentrate on a particular institution of learning, the Muslim college, especially in its madrasa form, and on the scholastic method that was its product" (p.xiii). The main focus is on 11th-century Baghdad, where the madrasa and the scholastic method flourished. In this setting, it is argued, the scholastic method became the peculiar product in the Islamic tradition and then spread to medieval Latin Europe.

The 380-page book contains four long chapters, followed by a concluding chapter. The first three chapters discuss the history of Islamic institutions of learning, linked inextricably with religious history, including linkages with various legal and theological movements. These linkages, it is argued, "led to the development of the college, informed the methods of instruction and shaped the scholastic community" (p.xiii). Chapter four discusses many parallels between Islam's institutions and those which later developed in the Christian West; at least 18 such parallels are documented (e.g., the faqih-sahib and mutafaqqih vs. fellow and scholar; development of the two dialectics, one legal, the other speculative; the unique status of the mudarris—professor of law in the madrasa and the professor of law in the universities of southern Europe; a long list of Latin technical terms peculiar to Latin scholasticism with their corresponding Arabic antecedents).

The brief concluding chapter is instructive. It summarizes how and why in the Islamic world, "traditionalism [proclaimed] its definitive victory over rationalism, symbolized by both dar al-hikma and dar al-'ilm giving way to dar al-hadith and dar al-qur'an" (p.283). It points out why "closing of the gate to *ijtihad*" (scholarly exertion, debate, discussion), "on the part of the governing powers" took place (p.290–291). And further, "The scholastic method was kept alive in the West long after it had disappeared from the land in which it developed" (p.291). Thus, stimulated by the earlier institutions and methods, as well as knowledge in various fields transmitted from Islam, the Latin West evolved in the opposite directions. Moreover, "From 'borrower' in the Middle Ages, the West became 'lender' in modern times, lending to Islam what the latter had long forgotten as its own home-grown product when it borrowed the university system replete with Islamic elements. Thus not only have East and West 'met'; they have acted, reacted, interacted, in the past, as in the present, and, with mutual understanding and goodwill, may well continue to do so far into the future with benefit to both sides" (p.291).

At the end there is an appendix that reviews selected original scholarship on the subject. Also, there is a 40-page list of notes and references, chapter-by-chapter and by sections within each chapter. There is a detailed name-subject index.

B-167. Murdoch, John Emery and Edith Dudley Sylla, eds. *The Cultural Context of Medieval Learning.* Dordrecht, Netherlands, and Boston: Reidel Publishing Company, 1975.

The book comprises the proceedings of the First International Colloquium on Philosophy, Science, and Theology in the Middle Ages, held at Boston University in August 1974. It "exhibits the confluence not only of historical and sociological contexts of science, but also of the concrete philosophical, theological, political, and legal contents" during the medieval centuries (p.v). As an outgrowth of an earlier gathering devoted to the sociology of science, held in England in 1971, the Colloquium focused on three areas: (1) the interdisciplinary relations of philosophy, science, and theology in the Middle Ages and, where relevant, the linkages of these disciplines to other intellectual endeavors; (2) the institutional and social factors that may have affected the origin, growth, and maintenance of philosophy, science, and theology as viable disciplines; and (3) cross-cultural factors that may be elicited as operative between Islam and the Latin West, and secondly, between each of these and the Greek learning that was absorbed in the formation of their philosophical, scientific, and theological doctrines and traditions (p.2).

There are 12 rather long essays, grouped in three parts, each followed by a discussion session among the participants. Part I, Islam—Renouncements de l'algebre aux Xie et XIIe siecles by Roshdi Rashed; The Influence of Stoic Logic on Al-Jassas's Legal Theory by Nabil Shehaby; The Beginnings of Islamic Theology by Josef Van Ess; Science, Philosophy, and Religion in Alfarabi's *Enumeration of the Sciences* by Muhsin Mahdi. Part II, The Twelfth and Thirteenth Centuries in the Latin West—The Organization of Sciences and the Relations of Cultures in the Twelfth and Thirteenth Centuries by Richard McKeon; La Nouvelle idee de nature et de savoir scientifque au XIIe siecle by Tullio Gregory; Experience, Praxis, Work, and Planning in Bernard of Clairvaux: Observations on the *Sermones in Cantica* by Brian Stock. Part III, The Fourteenth, Fifteenth and Sixteenth Centuries in the Latin West—From Social into Intellectual Factors: An Aspect of the Unitary Character of Late Medieval Learning by John E. Murdoch; Autonomous and Handmaiden Science: St. Thomas Aquinas and William of Ockham on the Physics of the Eucharist by Edith Dudley Sylla; Reformation and Revolution: Copernicus's Discovery in an Era of Change by Heiko A. Oberman; Reflexions sur les rapports entre theore et pratique au moyen age by Guy Beaujouan; Philosophy and Science in Sixteenth-Century Universities: Some Preliminary Comments by Charles B. Schmidt.

Each essay in this 570-page volume provides footnotes and references at the end. There is a detailed name-subject index.

B-168. Netton, Ian Richard. *Seek Knowledge: Thought and Travel in the House of Islam.* Surrey, UK: Curzon Press, 1996.

The author begins with the note, "A love of knowledge and learning has been a *leitmotiv* of Islam from its earliest days" (p.vii). Further, "Travel (*rihla*) in search of knowledge (*talab al-'ilm*) became a cliche of medieval Islamic intellectual life" (p.vii). Thus, the book explores various "facets of the Islamic search for knowledge, or the multifarious dimensions of that knowledge or, by neat contrast, especially in the first essay, the search for knowledge about Islam" (p.vii–viii). Indeed, the author notes, "There is an intimate link between thought and travel which predates even the Prophetic utterance about seeking knowledge even in China" (p.viii).

The book is divided into two sections, with five chapters in each. Section One, entitled Thought, has five chapters: (1) The Mysteries of Islam, (2) Foreign Influences and Recurring Isma'ili Motifs in the *Rasa'il* of the Brethren of Purity, (3) The Neoplatonic Substrate of Suhrawardi's Philosophy of Illumination: *Fal-*

safa as *Tasawwuf*, (4) Theophany as Paradox: Ibn al-Arabi's Account of al-Kha-
dir in His *Fusus al-Hikam*, (5) The Breath of Felicity: *Adab, Ahwal, Maqamat*
and Abu Najib al-Suhrawardi. Section Two, entitled Travel, also has five chapters:
(6) Ibn Jubayr: Penitent Pilgrim and Observant Traveller, (7) Myth, Miracle and
Magic in the *Rihla* of Ibn Battuta, (8) Arabia and the Pilgrim Paradigm of Ibn
Battuta: A Braudelian Approach, (9) Basic Structures and Signs of Alienation in
the *Rihla* of Ibn Jubayr, (10) Tourist *Adab* and Cairene Architecture: The Medieval Paradigm of Ibn Jubayr and Ibn Battuta. All essays are linked together by the
common theme of questing for knowledge in the Islamic tradition.

The 162-page book provides notes and references at the end of each chapter.
There is a name-subject index.

B-169. Rosenthal, Franz. *Knowledge Triumphant: The Concept of Knowledge in
Medieval Islam.* Leiden, Netherlands: E.J. Brill, 1970.

The book is about the critical role of knowledge in medieval Islam, also relevant to our understanding of present Muslim world. While the Arabic word *'ilm*
is a fair approximation of the English word "knowledge," the author states, the
later "falls short of expressing all the factual and emotional contents of *'ilm*. For
'ilm is one of those concepts that has dominated Islam and given Muslim civilization its distinctive shape and complexion. In fact, there is no other concept that
has been operative as a determinant of Muslim civilization in all its aspects to the
same extent as *'ilm*" (p.2). The book is about "how this came about, how it continued to develop and grow, and what it meant historically" (p.2). Referring to
pre-Islamic Arabic vocabulary, it is stated that "a Semitist looking at this vocabulary will be struck immediately by the fact that Arabic roots expressing mental
activity have no clear-cut correspondences in other Semitic languages or appear
to enjoy only a very restricted existence in the one or other of them" (p.5).

Following the introduction, the 360-page book contains eight chapters: (1) The
Knowledge before Knowledge, (2) The Revelation of Knowledge, (3) The Plural
of Knowledge, (4) Definitions of Knowledge, (5) Knowledge Is Islam (Theology
and Religious Sciences), (6) Knowledge Is Light (Sufism); (7) Knowledge Is
Thought (Philosophy), (8) Knowledge Is Society (Education). There is also a
concluding chapter.

The author concludes: "In Islam, the concept of knowledge enjoyed an importance unparalleled in other civilizations" (p.334). Further, unlike medieval Christendom, various areas of knowledge (metaphysical, ethical, scientific) "were
conceived as part of one human–divine attribute called 'knowledge,' which held
sway over all human and divine affairs" (p.337). And, "Islam may be compared
and contrasted with the civilizations of Classical Antiquity and the Christian
West. At the same time, however, these three are branches of the very same tree"
(p.337).

Each chapter contains notes and references within the text. There is a detailed
name-subject index.

B-170. Stanton, Charles M. *Higher Learning in Islam: The Classical Period, A.D. 700–1300.* Savage, MD: Rowman & Littlefield Publishers, 1990.

The author states two purposes for writing this book: "first, to raise the consciousness of professional educators and scholars to the intellectual and institutional heritage bequeathed by scholars and patrons of Islam's Classical Age, the eighth through thirteenth centuries; and second, to examine the enigma why universities as we have to recognize them did not germinate in the rich intellectual soil of classical Islam" (p.x).

It is noted in the introduction that while Islam's role as a "bridge between Greek learning and the medieval West" is accepted, "most histories ignore the monumental task of conservation and transmission of that body of work, much less admit to any Arabic contributions to it. Histories rarely describe the great centers of learning that arose in Islamic society and the impact of those structures on institutions of higher education as they emerged in Europe" (p.ix). Further, the author states, "The omissions and distortions of Western historians, coupled with regional chauvinism, largely account for our present ignorance. For centuries, students educated in European tradition have learned little of the greatness of this Golden Age in Islamic culture" (p.x).

The 205-page book has seven chapters: (1) Islam and Arabic: The Foundations of the Higher Education, (2) Formal Institutions of Higher Education, (3) Hellenistic Influence on Higher Learning, (4) The Flowering of Islamic Science, (5) Spontaneous Centers of Higher Learning, (6) Transmission of Higher Learning to Medieval Europe, (7) The Higher Learning in Classical Islam: Final Thoughts.

In the final chapter, referring to early Islamic scholars, the author notes, "As a society we can repay our debt to them only by honoring their memory and the faith that inspired their search for knowledge, and resolving to live by the humanitarian and intellectual values of openness, tolerance, and integrity so valued by them" (p.186).

Each chapter ends with its own notes and references. At the end of the book, there are chapter-by-chapter guides to further readings, followed by a detailed bibliography. There is a name-subject index.

B-171. Totah, Khalil A. *The Contribution of the Arabs to Education.* New York: Teachers College Press, Columbia University, 1926; AMS Press, Inc., 1972.

This short book, originally written in 1926, begins with remarks about the "western notions about the Arabs" (often identified with "a desert, a tent, horses, camels, and palm trees"). While "the scholars know better," the "number of those who think of the Arab (negatively) is far too great" (p.1).

There are eight chapters: schools; teachers and students; the curriculum; method and school etiquette; Arabic pedagogical literature; Arab women and education; the philosophy of Arab education; and conclusion. The period covered extends, roughly, from the seventh to the 15th centuries (the medieval period), before "scientific knowledge was advanced," before the emergence of "Baconian inductive thinking," and "before Copernicus and Newton appeared" (p.91).

The author also notes several merits, defects, and contributions of Arab education. Among the merits, Arab education produced scores of scholars (e.g., Al-Kindi, Ibn Sina, al-Farabi, al-Ghazali, Ibn Rushd, and Ibn Khaldun) who had a great influence on the Islamic culture and beyond, gave rise to a highly civilized culture and society, founded democratic institutions (among other things, education was open to all), the religious complexion of education gave it a "certain reverence, sacredness, and dignity of which it is worthy; teaching was considered a sacred duty. Scholarship was prized" (p.97). And students were encouraged to journey abroad for knowledge. Among the defects, education was often controlled by dogma ("it looked backward more than forward"), the "Arabic curriculum contained elements of weakness in that theology was too controlling an interest in its constitution," methods of teaching tended to be "formal and dogmatic (though students had full liberty to disagree and challenge), education system was superimposed by the rulers (royal patronage and financing)," and Arabic education did not "thoroughly permeate the masses" (p.95).

Among the influences, "the Arabs contributed a great deal to the *content* of education during the Middle Ages," transmitted knowledge to Latin Europe (including Europe's dependence until the middle of 17th century almost wholly on textbooks on many subjects translated from the Arabic), contributed their share in the Renaissance of Europe, "saved the world for several centuries from ignorance and barbarism," Arabic colleges provided an example for European universities, and Arabic education made a substantial contribution to the sociocultural evolution of Europe (p.103). The author concludes, "The East served the West in many ways and for a long period. Now, Western civilization may return notable service to the ancient seats of culture but, if it is to be done at all, it will have to be done through ideas, scholarship, humanity, rather than through war, injustice, and exploitation" (p.103).

There is a bibliography of references at the end; there is no index.

B-172. United Nations Educational, Scientific and Cultural Organization. *Islam, Philosophy and Science.* New York: UNESCO Press, 1981.

The book is a compilation of five public lectures, by prominent scholars, organized by UNESCO in 1980 in "celebration of the 1400th anniversary of the Hegira, which is the starting point of Islamic civilization and culture" and in recognition of "the rich spiritual, social and cultural contribution of Islamic civilization to humanity" (p.9).

The essay titles and authors are: (1) Tolerance in the Prophet's Deeds at Medina by Muhammad Hamidullah, (2) The Development of Philosophical Thought in Its Relationship with Islam up to Avicennian by Jean Jolivet, (3) Islam and Innovation by Jacques Berque, (4) Modern Muslim Thinkers of the Indian Subcontinent by Rahat Nabi Khan, (5) Islam and the Flowering of the Exact Sciences by Roshdi Rashed. The first essay discusses, among other things, the realization on the part of the nascent community "how much it had to learn, and its zeal for information sprang from its awareness that it did not know everything" (p.12). The second argues that the philosophic speculation was not "unconnected with revelation and alien to Koranic inspiration" (p.12). The paper by Jacques Berque reviews the innovative tendencies in contemporary Islam, inspired by "the will to formulate anew links with the past, to renew the spirit of reflection and to recreate for Islamic societies those solutions of continuity which lie between their image of the past and their present problems" (p.14). The Rashed paper, while focusing on mathematics, discusses how science evolved in Islam: "It began with the translations. Here we find the Greek heritage preserved and extended; the exact sciences, with the Arabic language as their medium of expression, flourished in the setting of Islamic culture and society and enriched the learning bequeathed by antiquity" (p.13).

Each essay is followed by discussion among the participants and others. There is also a listing of each contributor's other works, but there is no index.

B-173. Young, M.J.L., J.D. Latham, and R.B. Serjeant. *Religion, Learning and Science in the Abbasid Period.* Cambridge and New York: Cambridge University Press, 1990.

The book is about the five centuries (749–1258 AD) of "the 'Abbasid caliphate in Baghdad [that] saw the flowering of Arabic writing over an extraordinary variety of literary fields, from poetry and humane letters to philosophy, law, history and the natural sciences" (p.xv). It covers the scholarly disciplines delineated by "religion, learning and science" (p.xv). The literary classifications in Arabic scholarship of the time generally admitted distinction between the "religious sciences" and the "foreign sciences." The former included Qur'anic exegesis, tradition, theology, jurisprudence, and subjects such as philology and historiography; the latter included medicine, the natural sciences, mathematics, astronomy, astrology, geography, alchemy, and mechanics.

Of the 29 chapters, the first five deal with the literature of theology and religious experience. Chapters 6–10 pertain to topics such as philosophy, lexicography, grammar, legal and administrative literature, including the celebrated "quarrel of the *Tahafut*" between al-Ghazali (1058–1111) and Ibn Rushd (1126–1198). Chapters 11–13 are concerned with aspects of Arabic biography and historical writing. Chapters 14–19 are concerned with areas of natural science which are most prominently represented in medieval Arabic literature—mathematics, medicine, astrology, astronomy, alchemy, including scientific experimentation. This "extensive scientific literature in medieval Arabic had a strong influence on European thought, a fact illustrated by those terms from the sciences cultivated by the Muslims which have become part of the European vocabulary" (p.xviii). Influenced by Muslim achievements, the 12th-century English Arabist, Adelard of Bath "is at pains at different points in his book to emphasize the contrast between the learning of the Arabs which, he believed, followed the leadership of reason, and the hidebound reliance on established authority among the savants of Christendom in his day" (p.xviii). Chapters 20–25 deal with the lives of six universal scholars of the Abbasid Dynasty whose careers span 300 years of Islamic history, from ninth to the early 12th centuries—al-Kindi, al-Razi, al-Farabi, Ibn Sina, al-Biruni, and al-Ghazali. Chapters 26 and 27 consider Christian Arabic literature and Judeo–Arabic literature, respectively. Chapter 28 discusses the processes by which Greek themes and thought assimilated into Islamic civilization through translations. Chapter 29 pertains to "Arabic didatic verse, that is verse intended to assist the learning process and aid the student's memory" (p.xix).

All footnotes and references are included within each chapter. The main text is followed by a 15-page glossary of Arabic terms, as well as a 25-page bibliography, classified by broad themes of the book. The 588-page book also includes a comprehensive, 50-page name-subject index.

e. Geography

B-174. Penrose, Boies. *Travel and Discovery in the Renaissance, 1420–1620.* Cambridge, MA: Harvard University Press, 1955.

The book attempts to fill a gap, in that while "the exploration and exploitation of non-European areas by Europeans during the fifteenth and sixteenth centuries form one of the greatest phenomena of the Renaissance," there is no book that tells the story in a concise, satisfactory form, "not only of the great explorers, but of the lesser free-lance travelers, of cartography and navigational knowledge, and of geographical literature, as well" (p.vii).

The 377-page volume contains 18 chapters covering the classical and medieval period, early renaissance travels, African voyages, the Portuguese in the Orient, the Conquistadores, early North American explorations, the search for Northern Passages, English and the Dutch in the Orient, colonization of North America, cartography-navigation of the Renaissance, and the geographical literature of the Renaissance.

The impetus for geographic explorations is credited to the early Islamic world. To wit, "A revival of the science was long in coming, and we must credit the Moslem scholars of the early Middle Ages for keeping alive the learning of the ancients. With this impetus, Christian savants from the newly founded universities of the West traveled in the twelfth and thirteenth centuries to Toledo, Palermo, and Tunis to find the knowledge of Aristotle and Ptolemy awaiting them" (p.8). Further, "The introduction of classical and Islamic geography into the West is epitomized in the career of Edrisi (1100–1166), a brilliant Moor from Ceuta, who spent many years at the Court of King Roger II of Sicily. Edrisi, the most gifted of Moslem geographers, brought Ptolemy up to date, and in his exhaustive *Geography*, he put before Christian scholars the best work in the field written for nearly a thousand years. This book was translated from the Arabic [and] in mid-thirteenth century became the great practical manual of seamanship until the end of the Middle Ages" (p.8). There are references elsewhere to men from Andalusia's "hardy seafaring population" who accompanied various explorers in almost all directions (p.77). Moreover, "In Spain, the sailors seem to have been largely recruited from the seaports of Andalusia, while the conquistadores drew their great strength from the inland province of Estremadura, which was quite depopulated by what was in effect a mass migration" (p.331). Curiously, however, while there are frequent references in the book to Marco Polo's (1254–1324) travels to the East, there is no reference at all to the Moroccan Ibn Battuta (1304–1368), whose travels covered far more places and much longer distances.

The book provides a comprehensive chapter-by-chapter bibliography, followed by a detailed name-subject index. There are several sketches and maps of historical interest.

f. Humanities

B-175. Afsaruddin, Asma and A.H. Mathias Zahniser, eds. *Humanism, Culture, and Language in the Near East: Studies in Honor of Georg Krotkoff*. Winona Lake, IN: Eisenbrauns Inc., 1997.

The book is a collection of essays written in honor of an eminent scholar of Arabic and Middle-East studies, now emeritus-faculty at Johns Hopkins University. The papers are written by scholars, former colleagues, and students of Georg Krotkoff. His own literary contributions are enumerated in the first few pages, as well as in the essay Georg Krotkoff as Scholar and Teacher.

This 440-page book is divided into five parts, encompassing a total of 33 essays. Each part and the essays, along with the author's name, are enumerated below:

Part I, Humanism, Culture and Literature: (1) Inquiry into the Origins of Humanism by George Makdisi, (2) Humanism and the Language Sciences in Medieval Islam by Michael G. Carter, (3) Cosmic Numbers: The Symbolic Design of Nizami's *Haft Paykar* by Julie Scott Meisami, (4) Playing with the Sacred: Religious Intertext in *Adab* Discourse by Fedwa Malti-Douglas, (5) From Revolt to Resignation: The Life of Shaykh Muhsin Sharara by Werner Ende, (6) Sura as Guidance and Exhortation: The Composition of *Surat al-Nisa* by A.H. Mathias Zahniser, (7) The *Hijab*: How a Curtain Became an Institution and a Cultural Symbol by Barbara Freyer Stowasser, (8) The Development of Fictional Genres: The Novel and Short Story in Arabic by Roger Allen, (9) An Arabic Poem in an Israeli Controversy: Mahmud Darwish's "Passing Words" by Issa J. Boullata, (10) *Bi-l'Arabi al-fasih*: An Egyptian Play Looks at Contemporary Arab Society by Asma Afsaruddin.

Part II, Arabic: (1) Learning Arabic by Carolyn Killean, (2) The Alchemy of Sound: Medieval Arabic Phonosymbolism by Karin C. Ryding, (3) Al-Khalil's

Legacy by Karl Stowasser, (4) The Etymology of Muqarnas: Some Observations by Wolfhart Heinrichs, (5) Egyptian Arabic and Dialect Contact in Historical Perspective by Manfred Woidich, (6) On Later and Modern Egyptian Judeo-Arabic by Benjamin Hary, (7) Ein Arabischer Text aus Constantine (Algerien) by Hans-Rudolph Singer.

Part III, Armaic: (1) Zur griechischen Nebenuberlieferung im Syrischen by Anton Schall, (2) Syriac Loanwords in Classical Armenian by John A.C. Greppin, (3) The Modern Chaldean Pronunciation of Classical Syriac by Robert D. Hoberman, (4) Double Polsemy in Proverbs 31:19 by Gary A. Rendsburg, (5) Zum neuaramaischen Dialekt von Hassane by Otto Jastrow, (6) A Preliminary List of Armaic Loanwords in Kurdish by Michael L. Chyet, (7) The Story of Balaam and His She-Ass in Four Neo-Armaic Dialects: A Comparative Study of the Translations by Yona Sabar, (8) A Comparative Study of Pet Names in English and Assyrian by Edward Y. Odisho.

Part IV, Afroasiatic: (1) The Trickle-Down Approach by Carleton T. Hodge, (2) Albaut im Verbalsystem osttschadischer Sprachen by Hermann Jungraithmayr, (3) Akkadian *lisan-u-m,* Arabic *lisan-u-n*: Which Is the Older Form by Werner Vycichl.

Part V, Ancient Egyptian, Ottoman Turkish, and Other Linguistic Matters: (1) You Gotta Have Heart by Yoel L. Arbeitman, (2) The Protean Arabic Abjad by Peter T. Daniels, (3) A Matter of Inconsistency: Variations of Arabic Loanwords in English by Alan S. Kaye, (4) The Language and Prose Style of Bostan's *Suleymanname* by Claudia Romer, (5) Language and Script in Ancient Egypt by Hans Goedicke.

The first two essays of Part I are of special interest. While the essay entitled Inquiry into the Origins of Humanism (by George Makdisi) traces the origins of Italian Renassiance humanism in classical Islam, the other, Humanism and the Language Sciences in Medieval Islam (by Michael G. Carter), similarly argues that "although at first sight the terms humanism and Islam might seem incompatible, there is good evidence that they are not" (p.27). The second essay also argues that various forces, along with "a universal respect for learning, all combined to provide a fertile environment for the emergence of a kind of humanism analogous to that which arose in the West" (p.27). This essay identifies five distinct kinds of Islamic humanism: philosophical, literary, religious, legal, and intellectual.

Each essay contains footnotes and references in the text. A list of contributors is provided at the end, followed by an index of authors cited in the text.

B-176. Ahmed, Leila. *Women and Gender in Islam: Historical Roots of a Modern Debate.* New Haven, CT: Yale University Press, 1992.

The author suggests that throughout Islamic history the "core discourses of Islam have played a central role in defining women's place in Muslim societies" (p.1). This book adds a new perspective to the current debate about women and

Islam by exploring its historical roots, tracing the developments in Islamic discourses on women and gender from the ancient world to the present. The book
also examines the debates between the Islamists and secularists and "the way in
which Arab women are discussed in the West" (including merits and demerits of
Islam or Arab culture), and so forth. Are Islamic societies inherently oppressive
to women? Is the trend among Islamic women to appear once again in veils and
other traditional clothing a symbol of regression or an effort to return to a "pure"
Islam that was just and fair to both sexes? Focusing primarily on Middle Eastern
Arab women, the author explores such issues and pieces together "the history of
women and the articulation of gender in Muslim societies, areas of history largely
invisible in Middle Eastern scholarship" (p.3).

The book is divided into three parts. Part I, The Pre-Islamic Middle East, has
two chapters: (1) Mesopotamia, (2) The Mediterranean Middle East. It outlines
the practices and concepts relating to gender in pre-Islamic societies of the
region. Part II, Founding Discourses, has four chapters: (1) Women and the Rise
of Islam, (2) The Transitional Age, (3) Elaboration of the Founding Discourses,
(4) Medieval Islam. It deals with Arabia at the time of the rise of Islam, tracing
changes that occured when Islam emerged and changes that accompanied its
spread to the wider Middle East. Part III, New Discourses, has five chapters: (1)
Social and Intellectual Change, (2) The Discourse of the Veil, (3) The First Femi-
nists, (4) Divergent Voices, (5) The Struggle for the Future. This part begins with
the 19th century and outlines the socioeconomic, political, and cultural changes
that accompanied the European encroachment on the Middle East, as well as the
impact of socioeconomic changes that have occurred during the 20th century
which also gave rise to renewed feminine discourses. Part III concludes with an
account of the social background of the "return of the veil" phenomenon, along
with an analysis of the accompanying social and intellectual debates on Islamism
and Islamic dress, including the perspectives of feminist women and women
adopting Islamic dress. Further, in the concluding chapter, the author states that
"in the context of the contemporary structure of global power, then, we need a
feminism that is vigilantly self-critical and aware of its historical and political
situatedness if we are to avoid becoming unwitting collaborators in racist ideologies whose costs to humanity have been no less brutal than those of sexism"
(p.247).

Chapter-by-chapter notes and references are provided at the end of the book.
There is a detailed name-subject index.

B-177. Briffault, Robert. *Rational Revolution: The Making of Humanity.* New
York: The Macmillan Company, 1930.

A completely rewritten version of the 1919 edition, this is a classic in its genre;
at the time it provoked considerable discussion and controversy. The author
embarks on exploring the monumental question: "What is the nature of the power
which has enabled brute-born humanity to raise itself from the level of savagery

and barbarism to one which, for all the survivals of savagery and barbarism in its midst, is yet higher than any vapid angelical plane whence it once claimed to have fallen?" (p.8).

The book's 16 chapters explore the answer. After narrating some fascinating details in chapter titles such as "primal stupidity," "civilization and irrationalism," "the secret of the east," "the Hellenic liberation," "barbarism and Byzantinism," the author gives profound credit [chapter 9, Dar al-Hikmet (The Home of Science)] to the early Islamic civilization for the Rebirth of Europe (chapter 10). While Greek thought "laid the foundation of the Western world, the 'miracle of Greece' took place in Asia" (p.65). "The light from which civilization was once more rekindled did not come from the Northern, but from the Southern invaders of the empire, from the Saracens" (p.132). "Never before and never since, on such a scale, has the spectacle (of intellectual culture) been witnessed. [That culture was] given to a frenzied passion for the acquirement of knowledge" (p.137).

Further, the author argues, "It was under the influence of Arabian and Moorish revival of culture, and not in the fifteenth century, that the real Renaissance took place. Spain, not Italy, was the cradle of the rebirth of Europe" (p.138). However, "The debt of Europe to the 'heathen dog' could, of course, find no place in the scheme of Christian history, and the garbled falsification has imposed itself on all subsequent conceptions" (p.138). "Discussions as to who was the originator of the experimental method, like the fathering of every Arab discovery or invention on the first European who happens to mention it are part of the colossal misrepresentation of the origins of European civilization" (p.152). And, "Columbus, writing from Haiti, says that the existence of America suggested itself to him from reading the works of Ibn Roschd (Averroes)" (p.153). "The paramount part of Arab culture in bringing about the (European) awakening, proportionate to the grossness and insistence of traditional misrepresentation, would be difficult to overestimate" (p.176). There are similar observations in these chapters and elsewhere in the book.

While there is no separate bibliography, some footnotes are provided in the text, as are bibliographic references. There is a detailed name-subject index.

B-178. Calder, Norman, Jawid Mojaddedi, and Andrew Rippin, eds. and trans. *Classical Islam: A Sourcebook of Religious Literature*. London and New York: Routledge, 2003.

This sourcebook includes more than 50 authoritative new translations of key Islamic texts. Edited, translated, and contextualized by the three specialists, the book illustrates the growth of Islamic thought from its seventh-century origins to the end of the medieval period. While not attempting to provide "a comprehensive overview of Islam in terms of doctrine," it tries to "illustrate most of the genres of literature in which the development of the doctrines of Islam is expressed and the creative variations within those genres" (p.x). The book is said to be an essential resource for the study of early and medieval Islam and its legacy.

The 275-page book is divided into two parts, with four thematically organized chapters in each. Part One, Formation and Salvation History: (1) The Qur'an, (2) The Life of Muhammad, (3) Hadith, (4) Religious History. Part Two, Elaboration of the Tradition: (5) Qur'anic Interpretation, (6) Theology and Philosophy, (7) Law and Ritual, (8) Sufism. There are several selections in each chapter. Among the selections are Ibn Abbas's account of the heavenly journey, al-Taftazani's discourse about the Qur'an as God's speech, al-Farabi on the faculties of the soul, and extracts from Rumi's *Mathnawi*. Each selection includes an explanatory preface, followed by a listing of its source and a bibliography for further reading.

At the end there is a glossary-index that identifies each scholar covered in the book and defines key Arabic terms and words.

B-179. Ernst, Carl W. *Following Muhammad: Rethinking Islam in the Contemporary World*. Chapel Hill, NC: University of North Carolina Press, 2003.

This 244-page book, written from both historical and contemporary perspectives, attempts "to provide a completely different alternative to currently available books on Islam. What is offered is a sympathetic yet reasoned and analytical view of the Islamic religious tradition and the contemporary issues that Muslims face" (p.xiii). While the author eventually found a publisher, given the post-9/11 environment but despite having initially "commissioned" the manuscript, the original publisher refused "to be associated with any book on a subject that could be used to justify terrorism" (p.xiv). Similar hostile reactions were encountered from other sources. Thus, the author states that "when publishers, religious groups, and politicians are opposed to an impartial and fair-minded discussion of Islam, it is painfully obvious that such a discussion is exactly what we need." Further, he argues that while some unbiased scholarship on Islam is available, it tends to be "couched in impenetrable prose and buried in obscure academic journals." This book attempts to offer readers "the tools to reach an independent understanding of key themes and historical settings affecting Muslims and non-Muslim around the world today" (p.xv).

The book notes that conventional discussions of Islam often begin with two divergent viewpoints: (1) political writings about Islam that focus on the Middle East, collapsing the 1,400 years of history into the last two generations (particularly since the creation of Israel), and (2) writings that tend to be philological in nature and focus on "classical" (pre-modern) legal, Qur'anic, and philosophical texts (usually in Arabic). The author, however, takes a radically different approach: Islam is examined as a religious tradition, one shaped and understood through the human lens of its practitioners, not in a transcendent timeless fashion, nor as a means of understanding the post-colonial trauma of the last 40 years. Instead, the author moves comfortably through the 1,400 years of practices, rituals, institutions, and ideas that have shaped Islam and Muslims. The book has been hailed as a rare work that offers rather sophisticated discussion about Islam, yet it remains completely accessible to the intelligent reader.

The book contains six comprehensive chapters: (1) Islam in the Eyes of the West, (2) Approaching Islam in Terms of Religion, (3) The Sacred Sources of Islam, (4) Ethics and Life in the World, (5) Spirituality in Practice, (6) Postscript. The table of contents provides additional details as to the contents of each chapter. The author notes in the postscript chapter that "for non-Muslims, the larger question remains whether there can be a tolerance of pluralistic ethics. All ethical systems contain elements of reason and authority, but it is tempting particularly for modern Europeans and Americans to regard their own ethical ideas (or idealized versions of their societies) as both rational and universal. The possibility that there might be elements of irrationality, injustice, or the force of customs in our society is not often entertained directly" (p.212).

Chapter-by-chapter notes and references are appended at the end, followed by a list of suggested readings. Also, seven illustrations decorate the book. There is a name-subject index.

B-180. Farmer, Henry G. *Historical Facts for the Arabic Musical Influence.* New York: Benjamin Bloom, Inc., 1971; original 1930.

The author begins with a quote from a 19th-century European scholar: "One of the most deplorable things in history is the systematic way in which European writers have contrived to put out of sight the scientific obligations to the Arabs" (p.v). However, while there have been some explorations of these linkages in three areas of the *quadrivium* (arithmetic, geometry, astronomy), with respect to music, "no one had attempted to demonstrate the definite position of this Arabian science and art in the cultural development of Europe" (p.v). The author proposes to fill this hiatus.

The 375-page book contains eight chapters; these chapters cover only 112 pages. The remainder of the book is devoted to 48 appendices that provide more focused detail on matters that are broadly related but go beyond the topic of the book. The chapter titles are: (1) The Arabian Influence: The Political Contact, The Literary and Intellectual Contact, (2) The True Historical Perspective, (3) The Old Arabian Musical Theory, (4) The Greek Scholastics, (5) The Syllables of Solfeggio, (6) New Data for Notation Origins, (7) Arabian Influence in Instrumental Tablature, (8) The Rise of Organum.

The first two chapters provide a survey of the general nature of Arab-Islamic and Latin-Europe linkages. The author states, "The Arabs outdid their masters (Greeks), and their achievements in art, science and literature dwarf into insignificance anything of a like nature in the East or West. All of this was to be of profound importance to European civilization. Libri, the historian of mathematics, has truly said: 'Efface the Arabs from history, and the renaissance of letters would have been retarded for several centuries'" (p.3). Further, "The cultural influence due to the presence of this Muslim civilization in Europe or in close proximity cannot be over-estimated" (p.8). And, "The facts are these, that while Western Europe was sunk in barbarism following the fall of Rome, the torch of culture and civilization was being held aloft by Muslims. That can scarcely be questioned" (p.47).

Some of the 48 appendices are: Arabian influence on musical instruments; the minstrel class in the Middle Ages; Islamic schools and colleges; the first Arabian-Latin translations; the study of the theory of music in the Middle Ages; the Church and culture; Ibn Misjah and his inventions; Arabic treatises on musical instruments; Villoteau and the Arabian musical influences; the value of the Arabic musical documents; the early notations of Western Europe; Al-Kindi-Ibn Sina and *Organum*; harmony in oriental music; and John Scotus and *Organum*.

Notes and references are integrated in the text of each chapter and appendix. There are two indexes at the end: a persons-works index and a subject-geographical index.

B-181. Goodman, Lenn E. *Islamic Humanism.* New York: Oxford University Press, 2003.

The book seeks "some of the threads of Islamic humanism in the past," so as to present "a fuller picture of Islamic civilization than the headlines and the headline makers can convey" (p.24). There are headlines that depict "the Islam of the Taliban and al-Qa'ida, the Islam of hands severed for theft, adulterers stoned, prostitutes shot, homosexuals crushed under bulldozed walls" (p.22). Yet, "There is another Islam, tolerant, pluralistic, cosmopolitan without triumphalism and spiritual without suppression. It too is authentic expression of Islamic ideals, and worthier expression of the compassion and generosity that flow through the Islamic texts and traditions, as they do through the texts and traditions of the sister religions of Judaism and Christianity" (p.23). It is this "Islam that many Muslims are looking for and that some have never heard of" (p.23).

Thus, one objective of the 273-page book "is to put Muslims as well as non-Muslims in touch with a few of the materials and ideas that might be relevant in that work of rediscovery and reinvention" (p.23). The author hopes "to promote or provoke a fuller self-understanding among Muslims, and among others too, who are interested, intellectually and pragmatically, in the possibilities and pitfalls of a religiously constructed or religiously inspired way of life" (p.24). In quoting a verse from the Qur'an (24:35), the author notes "a cosmopolitan spirit that is authentically Islamic. That is the spirit of Islamic humanism" (p.24). The introductory chapter notes the pressures of modernity encountered by contemporary Islamic scholars, in contrast to the openness experienced and advocated by earlier scholars, such as al-Farabi, Avicennian (Ibn Sina), and others. The author also notes that "secularity plays a role in Islamic humanism, both within and outside the religious sphere, as we shall see, but Islamic humanism is not typically secular" (p.27). Further, "Islamic humanism has a long and sometimes splendid history. But if pursued as an option for today, it does not come ready made, and this book offers neither a recipe nor a prescription" (p.28). And, "The task of forging a new and humanistic Islam lies with thoughtful and progressive Muslims" (p.28).

Beyond the introduction, the book contains four long chapters, with some topical details provided for each in the table of contents: (1) The Sacred and the Secular, (2) Humanism and Islamic Ethics, (3) Being and Knowing, (4) The Rise of Universal Historiography.

Extending more than 35 pages, chapter-by-chapter notes and references are provided at the end, followed by a detailed name-subject index.

B-182. Kraemer, Joel L. *Humanism in the Renaissance of Islam: The Cultural Revival during the Buyid Age,* second revised edition. Leiden, New York, and Koln: E.J. Brill, 1992.

The book "attempts to show that in the Renaissance of Islam, which flourished under the enlightened Buyid dynasty, there was a conscious attempt to assimilate and transmit the intellectual legacy of Greek antiquity" (p.vii). The book investigates the nature of the environment (Buyid dynasty, 945–1055 AD, in the Abbasid Empire) in which the cultural transformation took place, and the cultural elite who were its bearers. Reference is to "a classical revival and cultural flowering within the soil of Islamic civilization, not to a renaissance, or resurgence of Islam itself. The principal expression of this renaissance was a philosophical humanism that embraced the scientific and philosophical heritage of antiquity as a cultural and educational ideal. Along with this philosophical humanism, a literary humanism epitomized in the word *adab*, equivalent in many of its nuances to Greek *paideia*, was cultivated by litterateurs, poets, and government secretaries" (p.vii).

Further, this renaissance "witnessed a powerful assertion of individualism, a burst of personal expression, in the domains of literary creativity and political action. Baghdad, the center of the Abbasid empire, and of Buyid rule, was a microcosm of the Islamic world, the rendevous of scholars from far and wide, of diverse cultural and religious backgrounds. Philosophers belonged to a class of their own, transcending particular loyalties, united by the pursuit of wisdom, the love of reason" (p.vi). This cultural flowering, however, did not survive, says the author, for "the period of receptivity to outside influence is followed by a retreat to entrenched traditional attitudes" (p.viii). In this paperback edition, the author also responds to earlier criticisms which argued that the terms such as "renaissance," "humanism," "individualism," "cosmopolitanism," and "secularism" were "European (Eurocentric) and inappropriate for a foreign culture ('the Other'). European civilization has been taken by some Western historians as a model of superiority and as a universally valid paradigm" (p.xi).

Following the introduction, the 330-page book contains three long chapters (with several subtopics identified in the table of contents). The titles are: (1) Setting the Stage: The Early Buyid Era, (2) Schools, Circles, and Societies, (3) Profiles: Scholars, Patrons, and Potentates. There is a brief concluding chapter in which the author notes: "The contemporary cultural expressions we have noted mark the tenth century as a period of particular openness to fresh currents, a readiness for experimentation. The openness did not last. Once the minority cultural elite succeeded, its role diminished. Moreover, the intellectual atmosphere was created by a courtly culture, sponsored by the ruling establishments and carried out by its lieges. When things went wrong, whether as a result of a foreign invasion, internal threat, or economic disaster, as later in the thirteenth century, solace and serenity were sought in the familiar bosom of tradition" (p.288).

Notes and references are integrated in the text of each chapter. There is a bibliography, followed by a name-subject index. Also reproduced at the end is the author's article, "Humanism in the Renaissance of Islam: A Preliminary Study," *Journal of the American Oriental Society*, 104, no.1 (1984): 135–164.

B-183. Kristeller, Paul Oskar. *Renaissance Thought: The Classic, Scholastic, and Humanist Strains.* New York: Harper Torchbooks, Harper & Row Publishers, 1961.

This short book is an attempt to "show the impact and influence of classical studies and of ancient sources upon the philosophical and general thought of the Renaissance period," defined as "that period of Western European history which extends approximately from 1300 to 1600," with a focus specially on Italy.

The 169 pages contain six chapters: (1) The Humanist Movement, (2) The Aristotelian Tradition, (3) Renaissance Platonism, (4) Paganism and Christianity, (5) Humanism and Scholasticism in the Italian Renaissance, (6) The Philosophy of Man in the Italian Renaissance.

While there are frequent references to the Arab-Islamic precursors of the Latin Europe scholastics of the era in several chapters, this is especially the case in the earlier chapters. Thus, "During the later Middle Ages, and more specifically between the middle of the eleventh and the end of the thirteenth centuries, profound changes occurred in the intellectual culture of Western Europe. A growing professional interest developed in philosophy and in the sciences, which was kindled by the Arabic influences and nourished by a flood of Latin translations from the Arabic and from the Greek" (p.6–7). Further, "When the Arabs began to translate the works of Greek literature, they centered their efforts on the most authoritative writers in such fields as mathematics, astronomy, medicine, astrology and alchemy, and philosophy" (p.27). And, "A large amount of writings on philosophy, on the sciences and the pseudo sciences was translated from Arabic and from Greek that tended to stimulate and transform Western thought" (p.30). There are numerous specific references to the influence of Averroes (Ibn Rushd) and Avicenna (Ibn Sina).

There is a general bibliography at the end and a chapter-by-chapter listing of footnotes, followed by a name-subject index.

B-184. Kritzeck, James. *Modern Islamic Literature from 1800 to the Present.* New York: A Mentor Book from New American Library, 1970.

The author begins with pointing out in the introduction that other than *The Thousand and One Nights* and Omar Khayyam's *The Rubiyyat*, the Islamic literature "remains generally unknown outside the Islamic world" (p.9). While our universities, the author laments, cover some of the literature from other parts of the world, "there is scarcely one modern Moslem author whose name is familiar to most of us" (p.9). Further, "This incredible state of affairs is but a recent manifestation of a very old cultural pattern. Islam and Europe, in particular, have managed to make for themselves a long and cruel history of cultural misunderstanding" (p.9).

The author traces the geopolitical developments of the 19th century and then notes that "the Islamic world came into the nineteenth century without a Renaissance, a Reformation, an Enlightenment, or anything closely resembling those movements of minds and time to assist it in understanding the tangled European thought of the age" (p.12). Thus, modern Islamic literature is in marked contrast to classical Islamic literature, with distinctly different forms, impulses, and messages.

The 334-page book includes excerpts from the works of 30 prominent post-1800 writers from various parts of the Islamic world. Some are: Al-Jabarti, Mirza Ghalib, Muhammad Abduh, Abd Al-Rahman Al-Kawakibi, Ziya Gokalp, Mohammed Iqbal, Omer Seyfettin, Marmaduke Pickthall, Taha Hussein, King Abdullah, Nagib Mahfouz, Muhammed Aga Khan, Gamal Abdel Nasser, Muhammed Kamal Hussein, Mohammed Reza Shah Pahlavi, Taieb Saleh, Mohammad Hejazi.

The name of the translator is noted following each piece. There is a select bibliography at the end.

B-185. Kritzeck, James, ed. *Anthology of Islamic Literature: From the Rise of Islam to Modern Times.* Toronto and New York: Mentor Books, Holt, Rinehart and Winston, Inc., 1966.

This anthology "presents a representative and rich sampling of some thirteen centuries of great Islamic literature. More than forty selections span the period from the rise of Mohammed and the Age of Caliphs (632–1050) to the new world of Islam, which was inaugurated in 1350 by such master poets and chroniclers as Hafiz, Ibn Battutah, and Ibn Khaldun" (p.i).

The editor provides a general introduction where he notes that "Islamic culture is unquestioningly one of the greater cultures in the history of mankind and of the world today" (p.15). Yet, the editor laments, there is an "appalling ignorance on the part of American adults," and "such ignorance, if inexcusable, is at least not inexplicable. It has, in fact, a long and fascinating history of its own, reaching back to the beginning of contact between Islam and Christendom" (p.17–18). Thus, as a "direct result of that attitude and image, one imagines, the Islamic literatures have not, until comparatively recently, been widely studied in the West" (p.18).

The 352-page book is divided into five parts, with several sections in each. Part One, The Koran: Scripture and Literature, has two sections—Meccan chapters and Medina chapters. Part Two, Early Arabic Poetry, has three sections—The Odes of Amru al-Qays, Labid, and Tarafah; Poems from Early Anthologies; Proverbs. Part Three, The Age of the Caliphs (632–1050), has fourteen sections, including Ibn Ishaq, The Prophet Mohammed; Al-Jahiz, Clever Sayings; Al-Hallaj, The Crucification of a Mystic; Firdawsi, Rustam and Sohrab; Al-Maari, Doubts; Ibn Hazm, Falling in Love, and Moorish Poetry. Part Four, Turks, Franks and Mongols (1050–1350), has 15 sections; some are: Nizam al-Mulk, Advice to Governors; Kai Kaus, The Purchase of Slaves; Al-Ghazzali, Confessions of a Troubled Believer; Ibn Tufayl, Alone on a Desert Island; Usamah, A Moslem View of the Crusaders; Ibn Jubayr, A Pilgrimmage to Mecca; Rumi, Love Poems; and Sadi, Morals. Part Five, Islam's New World (1350–1800), has 14 sections; some are: Ibn Battutah, The Maldive Islands; Ibn Khaldun, Group Solidarity; The Thousand and One Nights, The Tale of the Three Apples; Jami, The Women of Memphis; Babar, Memoirs of a Conqueror; and Ottoman Poetry.

Each part of the book begins with an introduction that enables the reader to place the work in its proper historical perspective. The first few pages of the book acknowledge the various publishers of books from which this anthology has extracted some excerpts; also there are brief descriptions of transliterations, Islamic proper names, and Islamic dates. There is a brief bibliography at the end, classified in terms of Islam, Islamic History, and Islamic Literature.

B-186. Makdisi, George. *The Rise of Humanism in Classical Islam and the Christian West: With Special Reference to Scholasticism.* Edinburgh: Edinburgh University Press, 1990.

This 430-page book is a comprehensive, well-documented study of the rise of humanism and scholasticism in classical Islam and Christian Latin-West. The study "treats of the rise of humanism, with its representatives, its institutions, its 'art of dictation,' and its emphasis on books for autodidacts in an attempt to answer the questions *what?* and *who?, when?* and *where?, how?* and, especially, *why?* For it is especially the answer to the question *why?* that holds the key to the origins of these two intellectual movements" (p.ix). In classical Islam, the humanism movement arose due to deep concern for the purity of the classical Arabic of the Qura'an, and scholasticism arose due to a struggle between opposing religious forces; both aimed for orthodoxy—one in language, the other in religion.

Both movements, it is suggested, began in Eastern Islam, and both reached the Christian West during the 11th century, via Iraq, Syria, Egypt, North Africa, Spain, and Sicily; but the sequence was in reverse—scholasticism, followed by humanism. The author argues that "the evidence is overwhelmingly in favor of the reception of both movements, scholasticism and humanism, from classical Islam by the Christian West. It is generally known that this influence existed in such fields as philosophy and medicine, mainly because of the translation of books in those and other fields of science, from Arabic to Latin, as well as the adoption of Arabic terms. It is however not generally known that books in the field of humanistic studies have also been translated from Arabic to Latin and other European languages, and that terms of humanism in the West are terms of classical Arabic humanism" (p.xx).

The book is divided into seven parts, with several chapters in each. Part I, Scholasticism (four chapters); Part II, Typology of *Adab* Institutions (three chapters); Part III, Instruction: The Organization of Knowledge (two chapters); Part IV, Instruction: Major Fields of *Adab*-Humanism (seven chapters); Part V, Instruction: The Methodology of Learning (six chapters); Part VI, The Humanist Community (four chapters); Part VII, Classical Islam and the Christian West (four chapters). There is a concluding chapter in which the author is critical of the Eurocentric historians who, concerning both movements, suggest "'a spontaneous movement of the human mind,' 'a spontaneous and natural development,' 'a self-contained whole which developed on its own accord,' 'something quite new,' and cause some puzzlement over 'the mysterious urge' of the humanists." And, "When *outside* influence was indeed considered a possibility, what was meant was influence from *within* Europe" (p.349). But why bother about influence? "For indeed the centuries-old intellectual culture of our present day is the civilization of classical Arabic Islam and that of the Christian Latin West" (p.350).

There are three appendices, identifying the humanist literature from classical Islam, including a "sample list of prime ministers, chancellors, secretaries of state and other professional humanists" from classical Islam. There is a detailed bibliography, followed by a comprehensive 41-page name-subject index.

B-187. An-Na'im, Abdullahi Ahmed (foreword by John Voll). *Toward an Islamic Reformation: Civil Liberties, Human Rights, and International Law*. Syracuse, NY: Syracuse University Press, 1990.

This 255-page book is almost revolutionary in its approach and content. Written by a Sudanese Muslim scholar–jurist who has been a follower of the teachings of Sudan's well-known Islamic scholar, Mahmoud Mohammed Taha, it provides a challenging statement of one way that the Islamic traditions may provide answers to critical contemporary questions. According to the author of the foreword, the book "provides the intellectual foundations for a total reinterpretation of the nature and meaning of Islamic public law." It is argued that "the Shari'a (Islamic law) as historically developed and understood by Muslims is based on the experience of the Muslim community in Medina in the seventh century.

Although such a foundation may have been appropriate for medieval times," the book's author argues "that other foundations *within* Islam are available for a transformed Islamic law that will be appropriate for modern times. This alternative foundation is the revelation to the Prophet Muhammad in the first stage of his mission, while he was preaching in Mecca" (p.ix–x).

Obviously provocative and controversial, the author, who is sometimes identified as an "unorthodox reformist," advocates a "wholly new system of Islamic law which he believes provides a suitable foundation for Islamic life in the contemporary world" (p.x). This alternative formulation, as presented in the book, deals with political structure, social order, criminal justice, international law, and basic human rights. Yet, while the author believes secularism will not appeal to most Muslims, "intelligent and enlightened Muslims are therefore best advised to remain within the religious framework and endeavour to achieve the reforms that would make Islam a viable modern ideology" (p.xii).

There are seven comprehensive chapters in the book: (1) Public Law in the Muslim World, (2) On the Sources and Development of Shari'a, (3) Toward an Adequate Reform Methodology, (4) Shari'a and Modern Constitutionalism, (5) Criminal Justice, (6) Shari'a and Modern International Law, (7) Shari'a and Basic Human Rights. Also, there is a concluding chapter in which the author states his "conviction as a Muslim that the public law of Shari'a does not represent the law of Islam which contemporary Muslims are supposed to implement in fulfillment of their religious obligation. I also strongly believe that the application of the public law of Shari'a today will be counterproductive and detrimental to Muslims and to Islam itself." Further, he states: "My trust in God leads me to believe that current efforts to implement the public law of Shari'a will fail because they are harmful to the best interests of Islam and the Muslims. These efforts will fail because the public law of Shari'a is fundamentally inconsistent with the realities of modern life. This is my firm conviction as a Muslim. My only concern is to avoid the human suffering which is likely to be caused by this doomed endeavor. May this book, by the grace of God, contribute to minimizing that suffering" (p.187).

At the end, the book provides 40 pages of chapter-by-chapter notes and references. This is followed by 15 pages of select bibliography and a name-subject index.

B-188. Salloum, Habeeb and James Peters. *Arabic Contributions to the English Vocabulary—English Words of Arabic Origin: Etymology and History.* Beirut, Lebanon: Librairie du Liban Publishers, 1996.

This 140-page book offers a list of English words derived from Arabic sources (often available from the English-language dictionaries), although the list is not complete, say the authors. It is intended for "those students of English etymology as well as those scholars who study the interrelationship of Arabic and other cultures and the resultant language of borrowings" (p.vii).

While there are several sources of Arabic words' direct or indirect penetration into English, some other avenues have been "the spread of Islam in the seventh century and after, the converts, the conquered, and the Christians beyond and within the borders, either were Arabized or came under strong Arab influences" (p.viii). Further, trade, administrative practices, agriculture, navigation, mathematics, and science are some of the activities of the Arabs which led to the introduction of related terms into Europe and into Asia.

The authors hope that the book "will serve as a gentle corrective to the mistaken stereotyped notion of the Arabs as nomadic, desert-based people, living in a barren land and in a barren culture. This stereotype is neither valid for the past nor for the present" (p.viii).

There is an extensive bibliography of dictionaries, encyclopedias, and lexicons at the end.

B-189. Sarton, George. *The History of Science and the New Humanism.* New York: George Braziller, Inc., 1956.

Based on lectures delivered at Brown University in 1930, the author begins with a plea: "The exuberant growth of science is steadily obliging the old humanities to withdraw; scientific education ought to be humanized more and more in proportion to that withdrawal" (p.ix). The book attempts to convey "the meaning and purpose of the History of Science, or to understand them better"; further, these studies are intended as "earnest interpretations of the history of mankind and anticipations of its highest destiny" (p.vii–viii).

The book has four chapters: (1) The history of science and the history of civilization, (2) East and west, (3) The new humanism, (4) The history of science and the problems of today. The second chapter is most relevant presently. Referring to the civilizations of Mesopotamia and Egypt, the author stresses, "There is no doubt whatever that our earliest scientific knowledge is of oriental origin," with possible links to the Chinese and Hindu civilizations (p.66–67). Then, there was the "Greek miracle." However, the Greek–Christendom connection was interrupted for centuries; then, says the author, it was recovered and re-established through the "Arabic miracle," this "third wave" of oriental wisdom and creativity also coming from the East (first from Egypt and Mesopotamia; the second from Israel, and through it influenced science only indirectly). While "a major part of the activity of the Arabic-writing scholars consisted in the translation of Greek works and their assimilation, they did far more than that. They did not simply transmit ancient knowledge, they created a new one" (p.87). Further, "It is no exaggeration to say that during the twelfth and down to about the middle of the thirteenth century the foremost activity of Christian scholars was the translation of Arabic treatises into Latin" (p.94).

Some notes and references are provided in each chapter, and there is a name-subject index at the end.

B-190. Steiger, Arnald. *Origin and Spread of Oriental Words in European Languages.* New York: S.F. Vanni Publishers, 1963.

This brief study presents "the outlines of a circumscribed period, to follow the paths of the rays shed during the Middle Ages upon Europe by the Islamic Empire," with special reference to the integration of Arabic language into European languages (p.1–2). While the "contact zone" of the Arabic language extends to numerous other languages (Hebrew and Aramaic, Greek and Persian, Sanskrit, Turkish, and even Chinese and Japanese), the "vocabulary of the Iberian Peninsula, of the Mediterranean islands and, to a lesser degree, of Provencal and Italian is drenched with Oriental [Arabic] elements" (p.5).

The author identifies four "language immigration routes": commercial relationships, cultural contacts, the Crusades, and "the caravan road." As the Islamic civilization expanded, commercial linkages led to the "pouring" of Arabic vocabulary into Europe. This also led to the "migrations of Oriental cultural objects, and therewith the terms denoting them; words traveled with the things and the concepts" (p.7). Areas of cultural contacts were, for example, geographical points and intellectual activities (philosophy, medicine, astronomy, chemistry, etc.). Then, from the twelfth century on, there is "the road of the Crusaders," which leads westward, mainly to Italy, from the Eastern Mediterranean. Further, the integration of Arabism in the European languages happened through another route: "the caravan road, traveled by Arab merchants along the Volga and thence to the coast of the distant Baltic" (p.65).

The author identifies numerous words, along with their etymology, and then adds, "This list is far from being complete. Indeed it could not be, without including terms belonging to the arts and architecture, to commerce and traffic, to medieval warfare, to the animal and plant kingdom, to foodstuffs and plays of Oriental origin; some of these found their way into even German and English" (p.12). Further, "All these categories are to be found the most completely and deeply rooted in Spanish and Portuguese, the first and most important languages to pass on loans from Arabic. But in Spain and Portugal, the symbiosis goes much further: the names of the most commonplace things, of domestic objectives, of the highways and byways, of rural life, come from the Orient [Arabic]" (p.13).

The book provides a bibliography at the end of each chapter. There is no index, however.

g. Social Sciences, General

B-191. Ali, Basharat. *Muslim Social Philosophy.* Karachi, Pakistan: Jamiyatul Falah Publications, 1967.

This short book is a useful introduction to the social thought of several early Islamic scholars. The narratives include the author's own commentaries, as well as some comparisons not only with the discourses of other Islamic writers but also some Western scholars. The Islamic scholars covered—some in more detail than others—are Al-Mawardi (991–1031), Al-Ghazzali (1058–1111), Ibn Jama'a (1241–1333), Ibn Taymia (1263–1328), Ibn Khaldun (1332–1404), Al-Farabi (d. 950), Ibn Sina (980–1033), Ibn Bajja (d. 1138), Ibn Rushd (1126–1198), Al-Dawwani (d. 1386?), and Aurangzeb (1656–1707). The last name seems like a forced entry, for, unlike others who belong to the Arab-Islamic world of the early centuries, Aurangzeb was a Mughal emperor of India during the late-17th century/early-18th century.

There is a short index at the end.

B-192. Atiyeh, George N. and Ibrahim M. Oweiss, eds. *Arab Civilization: Challenges and Responses: Studies in Honor of Constantine K. Zurayk*. Albany, NY: State University of New York Press, 1988.

The book is written in honor of an Arab scholar, Constantine K. Zurayk, a "leader of Arab thought on questions of civilization, nationalism, and the relationship between the two" (p.ix). The contributors are scholars from Europe, the Arab world, and the United States, who have known him as a person and an intellectual. It discusses Arab history, law, philosophy, politics, and literature, analyzing the challenges and responses aroused by the interaction between Western culture and the ancient and modern Arab cultures.

The 365 pages are divided into three parts, with a total of 19 essays. Part One, The Man and His Work, has two essays on Zurayk and his works, with the following titles and authors: (1) Constantine K. Zurayk: Advocate of Rationalism in Modern Arab Thought by Hani A. Faris, (2) Humanism and Secularism in the Modern Arab Heritage: The Ideas of al-Kawakibi and Zurayk by George N. Atiyeh. Part Two, The Classical Heritage, has seven essays: (1) On the Use of Islamic History: An Essay by Muhsin Mahdi, (2) The Expression of Historicity in the Koran by Jacques Berque, (3) Equity and Islamic Law by Majid Khadduri, (4) The Devolution of the Perfect State: Plato, Ibn Rushd, and Ibn Khaldun by Majid Fakhri, (5) al-Khwarizmi's Concept of Algebra by Roshdi Rashed, (6) Ibn Khaldun, the Father of Economics by Ibrahim M. Oweiss, (7) A Mamluk "Magna Carta" by Aziz Sourial Atiya. Part Three, The Modern Age: Challenges and Responses, has ten essays: (1) The Memoirs of Nubar Pasha as a Source for the Social History of Egypt by Charles Issawi, (2) The Neopatriarchal Discourse: Language and Discourse in Contemporary Arab Society by Hisham Sharabi, (3) The Interplay Between Social and Cultural Change: The Case of Germany and the Arab Middle East by Bassam Tibi, (4) Criticism and Heritage: Adonis as an Advocate of a New Arab Culture by Mounah A. Khouri, (5) Ahmad Amin and Abbas Mahmud al-Aqqad Between al-Qadim and al-Jadid: European Challenge and Islamic Response by Ibrahim Ibrahim, (6) Amin al-Rihani and King Abdul-Aziz ibn Saud by Irfan Shahid, (7) A Reinterpretation of the Origins and Aims of the Great Syrian Revolt by Philip S. Khoury, (8) The Social and Economic Structure of Bab-al-Musalla (al-Midan), Damascus, 1825–75 by Abdul Karim

Rafeq, (9) Imperial Germany: A View from Damascus by Samir M. Seikaly, (10) The Egyptian Press under Nasser and al-Sadat by Fauzi M. Najjar.

Each essay has notes and bibliographic references at the end, and there is a detailed name-subject index.

B-193. Banani, Amin and Speros Vryonis, Jr., eds. *Individualism and Conformity in Classical Islam.* Wiesbaden, Germany: Otto Harrassowitz, 1977.

The book represents the proceedings of Fifth Giorgio Levi Della Vida Biennial Conference, sponsored by the Gustave E. von Grunebaum Center for Near Eastern Studies, University of California, Los Angeles, held in May 1975. The Center awards the Della Vida Medal biennially to "an outstanding scholar whose work has significantly and lastingly advanced the study of Islamic civilization." The recipient at this conference was Shelomo Dov Goitein (Princeton University), being the fifth such scholar, "all known for their decisive contribution to an aspect of Islamic studies—so much so that one cannot think of that field without thinking of them—while at the same time the sum of their life's work has a breathtaking range. Theirs is not the versatility of a dilettante nor the perseverance of a mosaic artist, but the ability to grasp a fundamental and causal root of Islamic civilization and to pursue its growth into a mighty and spreading tree" (p.1).

The 165-page book contains seven papers, each consistent with the theme of the conference. The titles and authors are: (1) Individualism and Conformity in Classical Islam by S.D. Goitein, (2) Conversion and Conformity in a Self-Conscious Elite by Amin Banani, (3) "I Am You"—Individual Piety and Society in Islam by Franz Rosenthal, (4) Formalism and Informalism in the Social and Economic Institutions of the Medieval Islamic World by Avrom L. Udovitch, (5) Originality and Conformity in Islamic Art by Richard Ettinghausen, (6) Cultural Conformity in Byzantine Society by Speros Vryonis, Jr., (7) Individualism and Conformity in Medieval Western Europe by John F. Benton. It may be noted that the theme of Goitein's paper is that "the pre-Islamic and early Islamic Arabs were great individualists and had a keen eye for personality and character" (p.3). Further, Benton's paper points out, among other things, the "historiographic tradition to treat the development of individualism as something comparable with the Industrial Revolution, a tendency based on an underlying assumption that it is something that originated in Europe and then spread to the rest of the world" (p.147).

Notes and references are integrated within the text of each essay. There is a detailed name-subject index.

B-194. Coulton, G.G. *Studies in Medieval Thought.* New York: Russell and Russell, 1965.

Written in an informal style, the book is a brief narrative of some of the leading currents of thought during the medieval centuries. Beginning with the Roman ancestry, the author passes on "to a slender historical thread, from St. Augustine to the verge of the Reformation." The book contains 17 short chapters; some titles are Augustine, The City of God, John the Scot, The School of Chartres, Abaillard, Averroism, The Universities, By Whose Authority?, The Lay Revolt, John Wyclif, and Nicholas of Cues.

While the focus is chiefly upon Latin-European scholars, the chapter entitled Averroism discusses the influence of Averroes (Ibn Rushd, 1126–1198). "This Mohammedan became infinitely better known outside than inside his own communion; and Christendom adopted him as the leader, if not actual creator, of a system of thought which in fact he did scarcely more than summarize" (p.121). The author notes this influence in several statements. St. Thomas Aquinas paid Averroes "the compliment of imitating his method in his own commentaries" (p.124). Further, "It is startling to find in Averroes a plea for the emancipation of women, for which we must wait until the fourteenth century in the Frenchman Dubois and the English Ockham" (p.125). And, Averroes' distinction between philosophical and theological truths became part of the vernacular of the time. Later, Averroism spread throughout France and Italy, and by the 16th century it had become "almost the official philosophy of Italy in general" (p.129).

There is a short bibliography at the end, followed by a name-subject index.

B-195. Daniel, Norman. *The Cultural Barrier: Problems in the Exchange of Ideas*. Edinburgh: Edinburgh University Press, 1975.

The book is about "an examination of facts that hinder communication between cultures." Stated as "an historical problem," the author explores three issues: (1) defining the cultural barrier that inhibits communication; (2) identifying a cultural filter that can distinguish between technical and cultural borrowings; and (3) assessing judgements made about situations of the present day by historical parallels. Failure to communicate between cultures is the main subject of the book, the key theme being that "effective communication requires an acceptance of differences which is often unhappily reluctant" (p.v). The problem is analyzed in terms of historical parallels to clarify the issues, in particular "the nature of cultural arrogance and the choice of what to communicate" (p.vi). Throughout, while parallels that "help us to judge the effectiveness today of cultural resistance to intrusion from outside" are discussed, much of the book covers the "problems in the exchange of ideas" between historical Islam and the West (p.vi).

The 230-page book is divided into three parts, with several chapters in each, for a total of 12 chapters. Part One, The Problem, has five chapters: (1) Conditions of Cultural Exchange, (2) Suspicion of the West, (3) Academic Traffic, (4) Cultural Shock and Adaptation, (5) Techniques and Cultures. Part Two, Historical Perspectives, also has five chapters: (1) Evaluation of Cultures, (2) Past and Present, (3) Transmission of Ideas, (4) A Culture Filter in the Middle Ages, (5) A

Cultural Filter in the Modern World. Part Three, Principles, has two chapters: (1) Theorica, (2) Practica.

In chapter 9 the author argues that "it is not so obvious that modernization must create one single culture" (p.80). Further, this chapter discusses the medieval Latin West and Islamic cultural linkages and provides "examples of the successful application of a cultural filter in acquiring knowledge from an alien source considered to be tainted" (p.86). During the 12th century, says the author, Christian and Muslim communities were kept apart and "a clear and unshakeable doctrine, which has largely survived into the present day, of what Muslims must be believed to believe was formed in the West" (p.156). Further, "The dogmatic filter excluded every Islamic idea, except those deformed to 'prove' a Christian argument, so successfully that the only cases of Islamicising that came before the Inquisition were those of unhappy Moors who had been forced or tricked into Christianity. [And], the great interest in attacking Islam may correlate with the translation of scientific learning" (p.166).

The book provides chapter-by-chapter notes and references at the end; there is no index, however.

B-196. Daniel, Norman. *Heroes and Saracens: An Interpretation of the Chansons de Geste.* Edinburgh: Edinburgh University Press, 1984.

The book is about *unofficial* attitudes (in contrast to the official Christian attitude in the Middle Ages) toward Islam and the Arabs, as reflected in the heroic poems of medieval France, the *chansons de geste*, which derived much of their content from the struggle of Christian and Muslim, from Merovingian times to the Crusades, for, according to the author, "much less has been said about ordinary and unofficial attitudes, and most of it relates to the origins of idols imputed to the Saracens" (p.1). In addition to ignorance, prejudice, and hostility, the book uncovers a world of fantasy about Islam and Muslims, like the sagas of "cowboys and Indians" or "Star Wars," the readers are told. The poems, historical fictions mostly set in the time of Charlemagne or his son Louis, are a kind of medieval "pop art" genre, "composed for the benefit of laymen, primarily soldiers, but at all social levels of society interested to hear about courtly adventures" (p.2). They made for propaganda for the chivalry, in which "hero" and "saracen" alike share a common brutality, a common attitude to sex and violence, while their pantheons are total travesties of any actual religious beliefs, says the author.

After the introductory chapter, the book is divided into three parts, with 11 chapters. Part One, The People, has four chapters: (1) Chivalry, (2) Courtly Pastimes, (3) The Family, Women and the Sexes, (4) Violence: Hatred, Suffering and War. Part Two, The Gods, has five chapters: (1) Why the Gods?, (2) Who Are the Gods?, (3) The Cult of Gods, (4) Conversion, (5) Christianity. Part Three has two chapters: (1) Corroboration, (2) Conclusions. The author concludes: "The poets show no interest at all in Saracens, that is, in Muslim Arabs and

Moors, as they actually were; they chose to see them as an extension of Western Christian society as they understood it" (p.263).

Chapter-by-chapter notes and references are provided at the end, followed by plot-summaries of the poetic works covered in this 350-page book. There is a detailed name-subject index.

B-197. al-Faruqi, Ismail R. and Lois Lamya al-Faruqi. *The Cultural Atlas of Islam.* New York: The Macmillan Company, 1986.

This 520-page book represents the worldview of Islam—its beliefs, traditions, institutions, and its place in the cultures in which it has become rooted. It is a comprehensive introduction to the Islamic experience in history and the modern world. The authors state that the book is a clear presentation of the essence of Islamic civilization in all its spheres, from everyday practices of Muslims around the world to the Islamic legacy in art, science, law, politics, and philosophy.

Of the four parts, Part One begins with the ancient setting of Islam, examining the different strands of influence (Judaism, Christianity, classical Greek philosophy, etc.) that were its forerunners. Part Two explains the concept of *Tawhid*, the essence of Islam, the affirmation of God as One, Absolute, and Ultimate. Part Three shows how the core of belief takes shape in scripture, social institutions, and the arts. And Part Four explores the manifestations of Islam in all areas of intellectual, social, artistic, political, economic, and scientific life—its legacy in language, law, theology, philosophy, the social sciences, history, literature, art, architecture, music, and crafts, as well as its impact on other traditions.

Part One, The Origin, has three chapters (Arabia: The Crucible; Language and History; Religion and Culture). Part Two, The Essence, has one chapter (The Essence of Islamic Civilization). Part Three, The Form, has three chapters (The Qur'an; The Sunnah; The Arts). Part Four, The Manifestation, has 15 chapters (The Call of Islam; Al-Fatuhat: The Spreading of Islam; The Methodological Sciences; The Sciences of the Qur'an; The Sciences of the Hadith; The Law; *Kalam* [Theology]; *Tasawwuf* [Mysticism]; Hellenistic Philosophy; The Natural Order; The Art of Letters; Calligraphy; Ornamentation in the Islamic Arts; The Spatial Arts; *Handasah of Sawl* or the Art of the Sound).

The book contains 87 illustrative maps. Each chapter ends with its own notes and references, and there is a detailed, 31-page name-subject index.

B-198. Hallaq, Wael B., ed. *The Formation of Islamic Law.* Burlington, VT, and Hants, UK: Ashgate Publishing Company, 2004.

This is one of several volumes in the series entitled *The Formation of the Classical Islamic World,* under the general editorship of Lawrence I. Conrad. Motivated by the premise that modern scholarship tends to be "compartmentalized" into specific areas, each volume in this series presents a number of previously published recent studies, representing the "best of current scholarship," on a particular topic in early Islamic history (covering approximately AD 600–950).

Articles published in languages other than English have been translated, and editors have provided critical introductions and select bibliographies for further reading.

This particular 420-page volume has 14 essays, written by prominent scholars in the field: (1) The Arab Conquests and the Formation of Islamic Society by I.M. Lapidus, (2) Pre-Islamic Background and Early Development of Jurisprudence by Joseph Schacht, (3) Foreign Elements in Ancient Islamic Law by Joseph Schacht, (4) The Birth-Hour of Muslim Law? An Essay in Exegesis by S.D. Goitein, (5) Two Legal Problems Bearing on the Early History of the Qur'an by Patricia Crone, (6) Unconditional Manumission of Slaves in Early Islamic Law: A *Hadith* Analysis by Ulrike Mitter, (7) The Role of Non-Arab Converts in the Development of Early Islamic Law by Harold Motzki, (8) The Judiciary (*Qadis*) as a Governmental-Administrative Tool in Early Islam by Irit Abramski-Bligh, (9) Islamic Juristic Terminology Before Safi'i: A Semantic Analysis with Special Reference to Kufa by Zafar Ishaq Ansari, (10) Was al-Shafi'i the Master Architect of Islamic Jurisprudence? by Wael Hallaq, (11) Muhammad b. Da'ud al-Zahiri's Manual of Jurisprudence, *al-Wasul ila Ma'rifat al-Usul* by Devin Stewart, (12) Early *Jihad* and the Later Construction of Authority by Christopher Melchert, (14) The Caliphs, the Ulama, and the Law: Defining the Role and Function of the Caliph in the Early Abbasid Period by Muhammad Qasim Zaman.

Notes and references are integrated in the text of each essay. The 417-page book provides a detailed name-subject index.

B-199. Heer, Nicholas, ed. *Islamic Law and Jurisprudence: Studies in Honor of Farhat Ziadeh.* Seattle and London: University of Washington Press, 1990.

This 234-page book is a collection of papers presented at a 1987 conference held at the University of Washington in honor of retiring Professor Farhat J. Ziadeh. There are 11 papers grouped under three main topics. Topic I, Islamic Jurisprudence: (1) On Inductive Corroboration, Probability, and Certainty in Sunni Legal Thought by Wael Hallaq, (2) Interpretation of the Divine Command in the Jurisprudence of Muwaffaq al-Din Ibn Qudamah by Jeanette Wakin, (3) Exotericism and Objectivity in Islamic Jurisprudence by Bernard Weiss, (4) Integrity ('*Adalah*) in Classical Islamic Law by Farhat J. Ziadeh. Topic II, Islamic Law and Its Relation to the West: (1) Lost, Strayed, or Stolen: Chattel Recovery in Islamic Law by David F. Forte, (2) Magisterium and Academic Freedom in Classical Islam and Medieval Christianity by George Makdisi, (3) An Inquiry into Islamic Influences during the Formative Period of the Common Law by John Makdisi. Topic III, Islamic Law in the Modern Period: (1) A Resurrection of the Shari'ah: The Jurisprudence of the Gulf States by William Ballantyne, (2) The Development of Decennial Liability in Egypt by Ian Edge, (3) The Shari'ah: A Methodology or a Body of Substantive Rules? by Ann Mayer, (4) Executive and Legislative Amendments to Islamic Family Law in India and Pakistan by David Pearl.

The second topic in this book, Islamic Law and Its Relation to the West, contains papers of special relevance. Each compares certain aspects of Islamic law with Western law, and two argue that Islamic academic institutions and legal systems had an influence on Western institutions. George Makdisi, in tracing the origins of the doctorate degree of the modern university, argues, among other things, that "the doctorate may have traveled through history under three main designations: (1) the classical Islamic-Arabic *ijazat al-tadris* (permission to teach), (2) the medieval Christian-Latin *licentia docendi* (license to teach), and (3) the modern doctorate" (p.118). This author concludes, "The roots of the doctorate are firmly implanted in the legal scholarship of classical Islam. That is to say that classical Islam's legacy in the realm of intellectual culture is to be found, among other things, in the doctorate and the academic freedom of professor and student. These have come to modern times from the medieval university, which owed them in turn to classical Islam" (p.133). John Makdisi explores Islamic influences on the Western common law, and his analysis leads him to conjecture, "as we begin to lift our eyes from the glories of Roman law to the glories that lay beyond, we may come to realize the tremendous impact which Islam and its legal system must have exercised on the West" (p.146).

Footnotes and references are integrated within the text of each essay. There is a name-subject index.

B-200. Hovannisian, Richard G. and Georges Sabagh, eds. *Religion and Culture in Medieval Islam*. Cambridge and New York: Cambridge University Press, 1999.

This 120-page book represents the proceedings of the Fourteenth Giorgio Levi Della Vida Biennial Conference, sponsored by the Gustave E. von Grunebaum Center for Near Eastern Studies, University of California, Los Angeles, held in May 1993. The Center awards the Della Vida Medal biennially to an outstanding scholar whose work has significantly and lastingly advanced the study of Islamic civilization. The 14th recipient at this conference was George Levi Makdisi (University of Pennsylvania), "in recognition of his internationally celebrated contributions to the study of classical Islamic society and culture" (p.1). He has held professorial positions "at many prestigious academic institutions," and "has published extensively in Arabic, English, and French, not only on various aspects of classical Islamic society and culture but more recently on the Christian West as well" (p.1).

The key paper, "Religion and culture in classical Islam and the Christian West," is presented by Professor Makdisi. The editors suggest this essay to be "more than a brilliant and novel scholarly contribution. It points to a better understanding between Islam and the Christian West. How many academicians in the West are aware that the academic freedom that they cherish and the doctorate that they prize have their origins in Islamic scholastic methods and institutions?" (p.1). To quote Professor Makdisi, "The type of schools, their legal basis of perpetuity, the basic scholarly method, the doctorate as a symbol of academic freedom and authoritative opinion, briefly, the very soul of professional learning" are "the legacy of classical Islam and classical Christendom, a legacy due of interaction of religion and culture" (p.1). The argument is that the Scholastic movement originated in Islam in the ninth century, reached its zenith in the 11th century, and then it spread in the Christian West. Further, in classical Islam, its institution par excellence was the college; in the Christian West, the university. Indeed, it is argued, this movement is at the basis of our current system of higher learning.

Other essays are written by the recipient's long-time distinguished colleagues: The future of Islam by W. Montgomery Watt; Arabic rhetoric and the art of the homily in medieval Islam by Merlin Swartz; Medieval Islam: The literary-cultural dimension by Irfan Shahid; The Ash'arites and the science of the stars by George Saliba; Religion, religious culture, and culture by Roger Arnaldez; Cult and culture: Common saints and shrines in Middle Eastern popular piety by Mahmoud Ayoub.

Each essay ends with notes and references. There is a name-subject index.

B-201. Kincheloe, Joe L. and Shirley R. Steinberg, eds. *The Miseducation of the West: How Schools and the Media Distort Our Understanding of the Islamic World.* Westport, CT: Praeger Publishers, 2004.

The 210-page book is a collection of essays that attempts, among other things, to discuss the "historical dimensions of the Islamophobic miseducation," with a particular focus on the post-9/11 environment. The editors argue that "in the Western tradition of writing about, researching, and representing Islam, Europeans have consistently positioned Muslims as the irrational, fanatic, sexually enticing, and despotic others. This portrayal, as many scholars have argued, has been as much about Western anxieties, fears, and self-doubts as about Islam." Thus, with such historical and contemporary concerns in mind, the editors and authors examine the educational practices—defined broadly to include both schooling and media pedagogy—that help construct these ways of seeing" (p.1). The essays document the evidence for their arguments from numerous historical and contemporary sources, both academic and the general media.

The book contains ten chapters, each provocative and controversial, but with astute and substantial documentation: (1) Introduction by Joe L. Kincheloe, (2) September 11, Terror War, and Blowback by Douglas Kellner, (3) Loving Muslim Women with a Vengeance: The West, Women, and Fundamentalism by Loubna Skalli, (4) Iran and American Miseducation: Cover-ups, Distortions, and Omissions by Joe L. Kincheloe, (5) Consequences of Perceived Ethnic Identities by Christopher D. Stonebanks, (6) The United States and Israel: Double Standards, Favoritism, and Unconditional Support by Mordechai Gordon, (7) The Great European Denial: The Misrepresentation of the Moors in Western Education by Haroon Kharem, (8) Schooled to Order: Education and the Making of Modern Egypt by Yusef J. Progler, (9) The New Bogeyman under the Bed: Image Formation of Islam in the Western School Curriculum and Media by Ibrahim Abdukhattala, (10) Desert Minstrels: Hollywood's Curriculum of Arabs and Muslims by Shirley R. Steinberg.

Extensive chapter-by-chapter notes and references are provided at the end, as is a detailed name-subject index.

B-202. Lacoste, Yves. *Ibn Khaldun: The Birth of History and the Past of the Third World* (translated from French by David Macey). London: Verso Publishers, 1984.

The book is about Ibn Khaldun (1332–1406), "the greatest historian and philosopher ever produced by Islam and one of the greatest of all time"; further, "he has conceived and formulated a philosophy of history which is undoubtedly the greatest work of its kind that has ever yet been produced by any mind in any time or place" (p.1). Such comments are more than justified, the author argues, for "Ibn Khaldun's work marks the birth of the science of history." The book explores Ibn Khaldun's thought as "a means of furthering an analysis of the underlying causes of the most serious of contemporary problems," that is, the study of the underlying causes of Third World underdevelopment (p.2). While Ibn Khaldun's work dealt primarily with North Africa, its significance is universal, the author notes. He raised many of the same questions that modern historians have raised concerning Third World economic, social, and political structures, the author argues. Additionally, while "the great Muslim historian was no thinker of the Enlightenment, in terms of historical analysis, his approach is rational and scientific, and at times he comes close to historical materialism" (p.7).

The 214-page book is divided into two parts. Part One, The Past of the Third World, has seven chapters: (1) General Characteristics and Fundamental Structures, (2) A Politician from a Great Family, (3) From Condottiere to Historian, (4) The Myth of the "Arab Invasion," (5) The Crisis of the Fourteenth Century, (6) The Development of the State, (7) The Case Against the Townspeople. Part Two, The Birth of History, has five chapters: (1) Thucydides and Ibn Khaldun, (2) Historical Materialism and Dialectical Conceptions, (3) The Emergence of the Science of History, (4) Historiography and the Rationalist Heritage, (5) The Effect of Religious Reaction.

The author notes in the final chapter that Ibn Khaldun's *The Muqaddimah* "is thus of contemporary and universal significance in that it sheds light on underlying factors whose importance has been underestimated. It helps to clarify the role of colonialism and modern neo-colonialism. The work of Ibn Khaldun, a brilliant Maghrebian of the fourteenth century, does not only mark the birth of science of history. It is also a major contribution to the history of underdevelopment" (p.201).

Chapter-by-chapter notes and references are provided at the end, followed by a name-subject index.

B-203. Levy, Reuben. *The Social Structure of Islam*. Cambridge, London, and New York: Cambridge University Press, 1962.

This book was originally published in 1931 as the widely acclaimed *The Sociology of Islam*. The underlying theme is that "the Muhammadan communities of the world, possessing certain common characteristics traceable to their religion, are suited for treatment as a unity, and the purpose of this book is an endeavor to investigate the effects of the religious system of Islam on the life and organization of the societies which acknowledge it" (p.v). The basic principles of Islam are examined in a historical context and an attempt is made to ascertain how Mohammadans of different periods and environments have adapted their way of life to them. Incidentally, the term "Mohammadan" is a misnomer.

The 536-page book contains ten detailed chapters: (1) The Grades of Society in Islam, (2) The Status of Women in Islam, (3) The Status of the Child in Islam, (4) Islamic Jurisprudence, (5) Moral Sentiments in Islam, (6) Usage, Custom and Secular Law under Islam, (7) The Caliphate and the Central Government, (8) Government in the Provinces of the Caliphate and in the Succession States, (9) Military Organization in Islam, (10) Islamic Cosmology and Other Sciences.

There is a 17-page bibliography at the end, followed by a 12-page name-subject index. Also included are four maps indicating the geographical extent of Islam at various times.

B-204. Sachedina, Abdulaziz. *The Islamic Roots of Democratic Pluralism*. New York: Oxford University Press, 2001.

The author of the foreword suggests that in the present post-Cold War era, the post-Enlightenment "strong Western bias against studying religion in history" has "effectively blinded scholars, political analysts, journalists, and diplomats to the meaning of religion for the vast majority of humanity. This ignorance, paired with the knowledge that religion had been used by politicians and clergy to justify political violence from the Crusades, the expulsion of Jews and Muslims from Moorish Spain, the Catholic–Protestant wars in Europe, and the endemic genocidal violence by European Christians against Jews, had given religion a bad name among the Western intelligentsia" (p.vii). Thus, the book is motivated by "the necessity of dealing with the consequences of Western ignorance of the basic values of Islam that contributed to fear and destructive stereotyping" and as a step toward contributing "to the closing of the psychological gap between Islam and the West, thereby offering a measure of preventive diplomacy in the service of peace in the Middle East and everywhere Muslims and non-Muslims meet" (p.ix).

As the author says, the book "undertakes to map some of the most important political concepts in Islam that advance better human relationships, both within and between nations. It aims at uncovering normative aspects of Muslim religious formulations and specifying their application in diverse cultures to suggest their critical relevance to the pluralistic world order of the twenty-first century" (p.11).

Further, the "goal here is not to glorify the Muslim past but to remember it, retrace its path, interpret it, and make it relevant to the present" (p.11). And, Sachedina argues that "post-Koranic" considerations have tended to eclipse the "Koranic provision for a civil society" based on freedom of conscience, tolerance, and acceptance of plurality of the communities of belief" (p.81). On a broader historical and sociological level, the author stresses the necessity of bold and earnest efforts to reinterpret Islam along democratic, pluralistic, and humanistic themes.

The book contains five chapters: (1) The Search for Democratic Pluralism in Islam, (2) The People Are One Community, (3) Compete with One Another in Good Works, (4) Forgiveness Toward Humankind, (5) Epilogue. The author concludes: "The challenge for Muslims today, as ever, is to tap the tradition of Koranic pluralism to develop a culture of restoration, of just intrareligious and interreligious relationships in a world of cultural and religious diversity. Without restoring the principle of coexistence, Muslims will not be able to recapture the spirit of early civil society under the Prophet" (p.138–139).

The 180-page book provides 20 pages of detailed, chapter-by-chapter notes and references at the end, followed by a bibliography of relevant literature. There is a name-subject index.

B-205. Vryonis, Speros, Jr., ed. *Islam and Cultural Change in the Middle Ages.* Wiesbaden, Germany: Otto Harrassowitz, 1975.

The book is the product of the Fourth Giorgio Levi Della Vida Biennial Conference, held in 1973, in honor of Professor Della Vida (1886–1967) of the Near Eastern Center, University of California, Los Angeles—"an outstanding scholar whose work has significantly and lastingly advanced the study of Islamic Civilization." The theme of the conference is one that, according to the editor, "has not received the scholarly attention that its importance merits. The military expansion and conquests effected by the Islamic peoples in the Middle Ages brought in their train forces that culturally transformed major regions from the Atlantic to the Indian Oceans and from the Danube to Central Africa" (p.1). The papers explore the primary causes, sequence, and effects of cultural change via religious, linguistic, and other manifestations of the Islamic civilization.

The 150-page book contains seven essays: (1) The Book and the Master as Poles of Cultural Change in Islam by Muhsin Mahdi, (2) Factors and Effects of Arabization and Islamization in Medieval Egypt and Syria by Georges C. Anawati, (3) Muhammad or Darius? The Elements and Basis of Iranian Culture by Alessandro Bausani, (4) Islamization and Arabization of Al-Andalus: A General View by Anwar G. Chejne, (5) Spanish Islam in Transition: Acculturative Survival and Its Price in the Christian Kingdom of Valencia, 1240–1280 by Robert I. Burns, (6) Turk and Hindu: A Poetical Image and Its Application to Historical Fact by Annemarie Schimmel, (7) Religious Change and Continuity in the Balkans and Anatolia from the Fourteenth through the Sixteenth Century by Speros Vryonis, Jr.

Notes and references are integrated in the text of each essay. There is no bibliography, but there is a name-subject index.

B-206. Waines, David, ed. *Patterns of Everyday Life.* Burlington, VT, and Hampshire, UK: Ashgate Publishing Company, 2002.

This is one of several volumes in the series entitled The Formation of the Classical Islamic World, under the general editorship of Lawrence I. Conrad. Motivated by the premise that modern scholarship tends to be "compartmentalized" into specific areas, each volume in this series presents a number of previously published recent studies, representing the "best of current scholarship," on a particular topic in early Islamic history (covering approximately AD 600–950). Articles published in languages other than English have been translated, and editors have provided critical introductions and select bibliographies for further reading.

The essays included in this volume relate to the "patterns" of civilized life, "a viable collective social organism," from the seventh through to the tenth centuries, relating to the classical Islamic civilization. The 21 essays (previously published) are authored by well-known scholars. These are grouped into three topics—Shelter; Textiles and Clothing; Food and Drink. Topic I, Shelter—(1) Pre-Islamic Traditions of Domestic Architecture in Islamic Egypt by Alexandre Lezine, (2) A Mansion in Fustat: A Twentieth-Century Description of a Domestic Compound in the Ancient Capital of Egypt by S.D. Goitein, (3) The Houses of Siraf, Iran by David Whitehouse, (4) The Andalusi House in Siyasa: Attempt at a Typological Classification by Julio Navarro Palazon, (5) The Palm-Front House of the Batinah by Paolo M. Costa, (6) Type and Variation: Berber Collective Dwellings of the Northwestern Sahara by William J.R. Curtis, (7) New Caves for Old: Beduin Architecture in Petra by Pitor Bienkowski, (8) Architectural Provision Against Heat in the Orient by Alexander Badawy; Topic II, Textiles and Clothing—(9) The Tiraz System by R.B. Serjeant, (10) Notes on Costume from Arabic Sources by Reuben Levy, (11) New Data on Islamic Textiles from the Geniza by Yedida K. Stillman, (12) Abbasid Silks of the Ninth Century by Ernst Kuhnel, (13) Covered with Flowers: Medieval Floor Coverings Excavated at Fustat by Louise W. Mackie, (14) A Medieval Face-Veil from Egypt by Gillian Eastwood; Topic III, Food and Drink—(15) The Most Ancient Recipes of All by Jean Bottero, (16) The Arab Agricultural Revolution and Its Diffusion, 700–1100 by A. Watson, (17) Dietic Aspects of Food in Al-Andalus by Expiracion Garcia Sanchez, (18) Pots and Fire: The Cooking Processes in the Cookbooks of al-Andalus and the Maghreb by Manuela Marin, (19) Muzawwar: Counterfeit Fare for Fasts and Fevers by David Waines and Manuela Marin, (20) Al-Razi on When and How to Eat Fruit by Rosa Kuhe Brobant, (21) Abu Zayd al-Balkhi on the Nature of Forbidden Drink: A Medieval Islamic Controversy by David Waines.

Notes and references are integrated in the text of each essay. The 370-page volume provides detailed name-subject indexation.

B-207. White, Lynn, Jr. *Medieval Technology and Social Change*. London: Oxford University Press, 1962.

The author begins with a provocative statement: "History is a bag of tricks which the dead have played on the historians. The most remarkable of these illusions is the belief that the surviving written records provide us with a reasonably accurate facsimile of past human activity" (p.vii).

Then the author proceeds with his explorations with a special focus on the role of early technology in human affairs. First, the 194-page book presents three studies of technology and social change in medieval Europe—the origins of secularism, the dynamism of early peasantry, and the technological context of early capitalism. Second, it shows the kinds of sources and the means which, going beyond mere technological history, have been unexplored heretofore. Third, it demonstrates that the cultures of the eastern hemisphere were far more "osmotic" than most of us have believed. The three long chapters are: (1) Stirrup, Mounted Shock Combat, Feudalism, and Chivalry; (2) The Agricultural Revolution of the Early Middle Ages; (3) The Medieval Exploration of Mechanical Power and Devices.

Thus, the author explores the "osmotic" sources that not only connect the medieval European technological evolution to the Chinese, the Indians, and the Arab-Islamic civilization but also documents the connections among those later sources.

There is a bibliography at the end, followed by a name-subject index.

(II) SCIENCES

B-208. Ariew, Roger and Peter Barker, eds. (translated from French). *Pierre Duhem: Essays in the History and Philosophy of Science*. Indianapolis, IN, and Cambridge: Hackett Publishing Company, 1996.

This book is a collection of selected essays, translated by the editors from French, authored by an eminent French scholar who wrote between 1892 and 1915. The editors note in their introduction that while primarily a physicist, Pierre Duhem's (1861–1916) historical and philosophical work extended "over such diverse topics as the relations between the history of science and the philosophy of science, the nature of conceptual change, the historical structure of scientific knowledge, and the relations between science and religion" (p.xi). This range of scholarship is reflected in the selected essays.

While several of the essays make reference to linkages with medieval Arab-Islamic scholars, this is prominently so in the essay entitled History of Physics (1911). However, Duhem is inclined to view those scholars as mere "commentators," "translators," and "intermediaries." Those Greek "works that escaped the fires kindled by Islamic warriors," he says, "were subjected to the barren interpretations of Muslim commentators and, like parched seed, awaited the time when Latin Christianity would furnish a favorable soil in which they could once again flourish and bring forth fruit" (p.163). Further, the Greek science "was to be much more completely revealed to the Christians of the West through the medium of Islamic tradition," but "there is no Arabic science. The wise men of Islam were always the more or less faith disciples of the Greeks but were themselves devoid of all originality" (p.167). The rest of the essay is replete with numerous references to various Islamic scholars—Al-Farabi, Al-Farghani, Al-Ghazali, Avicenna, Averroes, and others—and clearly, the manner of presentation suggests these names as precursors of their subsequent Latin counterparts. The editors note, however, that Duhem's biases "may be corrected in the light of modern scholarship" (p.163). Some references are provided for further exploration.

The editors provide a biography of Pierre Duhem, along with a selected bibliography of his works as well as a list of selected works on this scholar. Each essay has notes and references at the end, and there is a detailed name-subject index.

B-209. Berggren, J.L. *Episodes in the Mathematics of Medieval Islam.* New York, Berlin, and Tokyo: Springer-Verlag, 1986.

The author states that "no textbook on the history of mathematics in English deals with the Islamic contribution in more than a general way," and that "this is unfortunate, not only from a scholarly point of view but from a pedagogical one as well, for Islam's contributions include some gems of mathematical reasoning, accessible to anyone who has learned high school mathematics" (p.vii). This book is an attempt to fill this need; the subject is described in its proper historical context, with references to specific Arabic texts. However, the author mentions that in recent years, "historians of mathematics have re-learned what our medieval and Renaissance forbears knew: the Islamic contribution affected the development of all branches of mathematics in the West and was of prime importance in many" (p.vii).

The 200-page book has five comprehensive chapters (with well-defined sections in each): Chapter 1, Introduction; Chapter 2, Islamic Arithmetic; Chapter 3, Geometrical Constructions in the Islamic World; Chapter 4, Algebra in Islam; Chapter 5, Trigonometry in the Islamic World. Where appropriate, the author identifies the influence of foreign sources (Greek and Indian in particular) upon Islamic scholars, and there is a map so that the reader may identify the locations where major developments took place. Also, several pictures of places and art relevant to the subject matter are provided.

At the end of each chapter, the author provides some exercises and there is a bibliography as well as a name-subject index.

B-210. Butterfield, H. *The Origins of Modern Science, 1300–1800*. New York: The Macmillan Company, 1961.

The 242-page book is based on author's lectures delivered at the Cambridge University, Cambridge, UK, in 1948, and the objective is to "stimulate in the historian a little interest in science and in the scientist a little interest in history" (p.vii). The "scientific revolution" of the 16th–17th centuries led to the eclipse of the scholastic philosophy, the author suggests, thus reducing European Renaissance and Reformation to the rank of mere episodes, mere internal displacements. There are chapters on developments in medicine, physics, chemistry, astronomy, etc., with frequent references to linkages with the early Islamic civilization. This is especially so in the chapter entitled The Place of the Scientific Revolution in the History of Western Civilization.

The author argues that, in documenting the history of science, we must proceed from the earlier to the later as well as probe deeply into historical processes. It is in this context that despite the book's main focus on Europe, the author often points to the linkages with the earlier Arab-Islamic scholarship. There is reference to "Arabian physicians" when discussing medicine and to the "Averroistic" (Ibn Rushd, 1126–1198) commentaries on the Greeks ("seeing Aristotle in the light of the Arabian commentator, Averroes" [p.48]) that led to the demise of the Latin-Scholastic philosophy. Moreover, the rise of the scientific method became possible only when contact with the science of the ancient world was re-established "by the unearthing of texts and manuscripts, or by the acquisition of translations and commentaries from peoples like the Arabs or the subjects of the Byzantine Empire, who already possessed, or had never lost, the contact." Otherwise, the author suggests, the Middle Ages would have prolonged "many hundreds of years more" (p.77). Further, "Until a period not long before the Renaissance, the intellectual leadership of the globe had remained with the lands in the eastern half of the Mediterranean or in the empires that stretched farther still into what we call the Middle East" (p.176).

There is a list of suggestions for further reading, followed by a name-subject index.

B-211. Casulleras, Josep and Julio Samso, eds. *From Baghdad to Barcelona: Studies in the Islamic Exact Sciences in Honor of Professor Juan Vernet*, Volumes I and II. Barcelona, Spain: Anuari de Filogia (Universitat de Barcelona) XIX, B-2, Instituto Millas Vallicrosa de Historia de la Ciencia Arabe, 1996.

The 830-page two volumes represent a collection of 28 papers presented at a special symposium, "The Transmission of Scientific Ideas, in the Field of the Exact Sciences, between Eastern and Western Islam in the Middle Ages," as part of the 19th International Congress of History of Science, held in Zaragoza, Spain, August 24–26, 1993. Each paper is written by an eminent scholar in the respective field.

The 28 papers are grouped in six categories. Volume One, covering 525 pages, encompasses these three categories (with 17 essays): (1) General (two essays), (2) Matematicas (three essays), (3) Ziyes y Tablas Astronomicas (12 essays). Volume Two, covering 305 pages, includes the remaining three categories (with 11 essays): (4) Astrologia Matematica (three essays), (5) Instrumentos Astronomicos (six essays), (6) Astronomia Popular y Miqat (two essays). Most of the essays are written in English; some are in French and Spanish.

One of the two General essays, Arabic Science and the Greek Legacy by George Saliba, sets forth the main theme of the symposium. He argues that "to most people, even those with more than a casual interest in Islamic civilization, the image that comes to mind when speaking of Arabic science is that of a vague recollection of highly fragmented statements that connect the sciences and cultures of antiquity to those of medieval Europe" (p.19). And, for them, Arabic science essentially means the Greek works, says the author; he calls this the "refrigeration model of cultural transmission, for it does not quite describe the role that Arabic science actually played in the general development of science" (p.36). And, further, when "echoes" of Arabic science, through translations into Latin, are encountered in the study of Medieval Europe, thus triggering the early European renaissance, "it is only then that some mention is made of the scientists of medieval Islam" (p.19). "This picture is not only Eurocentric," according to the author, "it is also an excellent example of bad history" (p.20).

Notes and references are integrated in the text of each essay. Neither volume provides a separate bibliography, nor is there an index.

B-212. Crombie, A.C. *Medieval and Early Modern Science: Vol. I, Science in the Middle Ages, V–XIII Centuries; Vol. II, Science in the Later Middle Ages and Early Modern Times, XIII–XVII Centuries.* New York: Doubleday and Company, revised second edition, 1959.

One of the most eminent medievalists, the author suggests that there have been studies of science in antiquity and in modern times, but there exists no adequate short of history of science in the period that lies between; the book attempts to fill this gap.

Both volumes document Arab-Islamic linkages throughout, though there is greater documentation in the first. The author is a bit apologetic, however: "If I have seemed to give too little attention to the originality of Arabic science in this period, that is not because I underrate the indispensable contribution made by medieval Arabic civilization in developing ancient science as well as in transmitting it to the West"—his focus being specifically the history and evolution of science in the Latin West (p.xii). Chapters II and III (The Reception of Greco-Arabic Science in Western Christendom and The System of Scientific Thought in the Thirteenth Century) of Volume I document the Arab-Islamic linkages quite extensively. Discussion is organized in terms of various knowledge areas (astronomy, optics, geology, chemistry, biology, etc.), as well as by economic activities, such as agriculture, major industries, and medicine.

Volume II covers scientific developments in the later Middle Ages, and while the focus is primarily on Latin-European scholars, the author often identifies numerous Arab-Islamic scholars (Avicenna, Avempace, Averroes, and others) whose influence is evident in the background.

Both volumes provide a chapter-by-chapter bibliography, and there is detailed name-subject index.

B-213. Dalafi, H.R. and M.H.A. Hassan, eds. *Renaissance of Sciences in Islamic Countries.* Singapore, London, and River Edge, NJ: World Scientific, 1994.

The book is a collection of speeches and essays by one of the most eminent scientists of the 20th century—M. Abdus Salam—Pakistani in origin and the recipient of the 1979 Nobel Prize in Physics. The collection should be of historic as well as contemporaneous interest, especially to scholars interested in the Islamic world. The essays present Abdus Salam's views on the role of sciences in early Islamic history and linkages with the Western intellectual evolution, the subsequent decline of sciences in the Islamic world, and the need for the revival of science and technology in Islamic countries.

The book has five sections, three of which are relevant here: (1) Islam and Science (several addresses to Muslim and non-Muslim audiences), (2) New Initiatives (undertaken by Abdus Salam), (3) Science and Muslim Countries (essays documenting the relative dirth of scientists and scientific work in Muslim lands).

Some notes and references are integrated in each essay. Except for the works of Abdus Salam, there is no bibliography, nor an index.

B-214. Dales, Richard C. *The Scientific Achievement of the Middle Ages.* Philadelphia, PA: University of Pennsylvania Press, 1973.

The 180-page book is not intended to be comprehensive, but attempts "to provide an accurate sampling of medieval scientific thought in the context of a historical narrative" (p.v). The themes and topics demonstrate medical scientific thought at its most original, the world of non-material causation, the beginning of science. The author argues that it was the 12th and 13th centuries that came to regard human reason as man's distinctive and unique possession. "The great debt owned by Latin Christian and later European culture to the thought of the world of Islam is centered here, for the 'Arab masters' cited so authoritatively by Adelard of Bath were indeed in a position to criticize the humble scientific and mathematical achievements of the West" (p.15).

The book contains eight chapters: (1) The Early Middle Ages, (2) The Twelfth Century, (3) Robert Grosseteste and Scientific Method, (4) The Tides, (5) Studies of the Rainbow, (6) Studies of Local Motion, (7) Astronomy, (8) The Fringes of Science. Each chapter includes some historical selections and/or selections from modern scholars.

While there are references to linkages with Islamic civilization throughout, chapter 2, The Twelfth Century, establishes the background; this was "a transitional period in the history of medieval science" (p.37). Adelard of Bath is identified as "one of the crucial figures" of this period. "Determined to perfect himself in the wisdom of the Arabs, he spent seven years in travel, visiting Italy and Sicily, Syria, Palestine, and perhaps Spain. He became an ardent exponent of Arabic learning and did much to popularize it in Latin Europe as well as translate several treatises from Arabic into Latin" (p.37–38). In his *Natural Questions*, Adelard of Bath advises his nephew, "I have learned under the guidance of reason, from Arabic teachers; but you, captivated by a show of authority, are led around by a halter, just as brute animals are led about by a halter and are not told where or why, but see the rope by which they are held and follow it alone" (p.41). Based on a selection from an anonymous treatise, the author says, "Within two generations after this treatise was written, the most important writings of the Greek and Muslim scientists became the common property of the European intellectual community" (p.52).

There is a short bibliographic essay at the end which, with some annotations, provides numerous references relevant to the content of the book. There is no index.

B-215. Grant, Edward. *The Foundations of Modern Science in the Middle Ages: Their Religious, Institutional, and Intellectual Contexts.* Cambridge and New York: Cambridge University Press, 1996.

This is a book from which both teachers of university-level history of science courses as well as educated lay-readers, with no knowledge of medieval intellectual life, can benefit greatly. The book has two objectives: first, to provide an introduction to European medieval science; and second, to revivify Pierre Duhem's claim (see his *Le System du monde, histoire des doctrines cosmologiques de Platon a Copernic*, 10 volumes, Hermann, Paris, 1913–1959) that the roots of modern science were planted not in the 17th century but in the ancient and medieval worlds, with the cumulative antecedent efforts of three great civilizations: Greek, Islamic, and Latin. Four essential factors, it is suggested, enabled medieval Europe to plant the seeds for the modern science: (1) translations of Greek and Arab-Islamic scientific texts in the 12th and 13th centuries, (2) the development of universities which absorbed the translations in the science curriculum, (3) the adjustments of Christianity to secular learning, (4) the transformation of Aristotle's natural philosophy.

The 248-page book contains eight chapters: (1) The Roman Empire and the First Six Centuries of Christianity, (2) The New Beginning: The Age of Translation in the Twelfth and Thirteenth Centuries, (3) The Medieval University, (4) What the Middle Ages Inherited from Aristotle, (5) The Reception and Impact of Aristotelian Learning and the Reaction of the Church and Its Theologians, (6) What the Middle Ages Did with Its Aristotelian Legacy, (7) Medieval Natural

Philosophy, Aristotelians, and Aristotelianism, (8) How the Foundations of Early Modern Science Were Laid in the Middle Ages.

While there are references to the Arab-Islamic linkages throughout the book, the second chapter specifically discusses the significance of these influences. "Thus to the Greek legacy," says the author, "must be added the contributions of numerous Islamic authors, a group that includes not only Muslims but also Christians and Jews" (p.22). After the fall of Toledo and Sicily, "a now reinvigorated Western Europe came into possession of significant centers of Arabic learning" (p.23). And, among Muslim scholars whose works were translated into Latin, "the most important were al-Kindi (801–866), Al-Farabi (870–950), Avicenna (Ibn Sina, 980–1037), al-Ghazali (1058–1111), and Averroes (Ibn Rushd, 1126–1198). Of this group, Avicenna, al-Ghazali, and Averroes had the greatest impact on Aristotelian natural philosophy in the West" (p.29). Elsewhere, in chapter 5, there is discussion of the 1277 condemnation of the 219 "faith-vs-reason" heresies, "a list of errors drawn from the works of the non-Christian philosophers Aristotle, Averroes, Avicenna, Algazal (al-Ghazali), al-Kindi, and Moses Maimonides" (p.71).

The author concludes: "If Muslim scholars had assumed that they had nothing to learn from 'Dead Greek Pagans,' and if Latin Christian scholars similarly had assumed that they had nothing to learn from 'Dead Muslim heretics,' the great translation movements of the Middle Ages would never have occurred, impoverishing history and delaying scientific developments by many centuries. Fortunately, this did not happen, and we can look upon Greco-Arabic-Latin science and naturally philosophy as one continuous development. It was truly a progression toward modern science and represents one of the most glorious chapters in human history" (p.206).

The book provides chapter-by-chapter notes and references at the end. This is followed by a two-part, 20-page bibliography: first is an essay in which literature is grouped thematically, and the second lists the relevant books and articles in alphabetical order by author. There is a detailed name-subject index.

B-216. Hall, A. Ruper and Marie Boas Hall. *A Brief History of Science.* Ames, IA: Iowa State University Press, 1988.

The book covers considerable ground on this fascinating topic, from the ancient world to the present, with about two-thirds of the book devoted to the pre-19th century period; the remainder focuses on a small number of major scientific developments since the 19th century.

The 352-page book is divided into five parts: (1) Philosophy and Physics in the Ancient World (four chapters), (2) Philosophy and Physics in Medieval Europe (two chapters), (3) Biological Knowledge before the Microscope (two chapters), (4) The Scientific Revolution (three chapters), (5) The Establishment of Science in the West (seven chapters).

While there are references and citations relevant to Islamic influences throughout the book (especially in the first two-thirds), chapters 5 and 6 (Europe Redis-covers Its Past, and The Rise and Fall of Aristotle) in Part 2 (Philosophy and Physics in Medieval Europe) in particular provide considerable detail regarding these connections. Partly because of the schisms between the Catholic West and Orthodox East, the Greek heritage laid buried for centuries, to be re-discovered in the eight-century by the Islamic world (which "spread by proselytism rather than violence" [p.63]). The author says, "Intellectually it was to Greece and Rome that Islam—like Europe—looked for its inheritance. But what a difference! Islam, from its first conquests, was rich in learned men. Under their stimulus Baghdad became the most mentally vigorous city in the world, and it was not long before other lesser centers of learning graced the whole Islamic empire" (p.64). There were other centers of learning: Cairo, Cordova, Toledo, Seville, Granada, and even Palermo, capital first of Muslim and then of Norman Sicily.

Further, "Christian Europe was necessarily thrust against a rival society towards which it felt the strongest hostility," the author says, "yet whose superi-ority in philosophy, science, and technology it was gradually forced to recognize. Not until the twelfth century were the first efforts made to render this heritage accessible in Latin. The occasion was provided by the slow retreat of Islam; Christians became willing to learn from Muslims and Jews only when they were indisputably their masters" (p.66). And then the transmission of knowledge took place through numerous channels. Islamic scholars and their Latin-Christian and Jewish translators are mentioned, as well as specific areas of knowledge and Latin-scholars who benefitted.

The book provides chapter-by-chapter footnotes at the end, along with a chap-ter-by-chapter list of further reading. There is a name-subject index.

B-217. Haskins, Charles Homer. *Studies in the History of Medieval Science.* Cambridge, MA: Harvard University Press, 1927.

At the time of its writing, this 411-page book was intended to cover two "sides of a consecutive and comprehensive history" of science. The "first phase deals primarily with translation from the Arabic and the Greek, in Spain, Sicily, North Africa, and the East, as a preliminary to the full assimilation of these successive increments of ancient learning and the Arabic additions thereto." He argues, "The full recovery of this ancient learning, supplemented by what the Arabs had gained from the Orient and from their own observation, constitutes the scientific renaissance of the Middle Ages" and "the broad fact remains that the Arabs of Spain were the principal source of the new learning for Western Europe" (p.3). The second phase, more obscure, attempts to "trace the extension of knowledge by such means as the observation of plants and animals, the actual treatment of disease, geographical exploitation, and the growth of the experimental habit." The focus is limited to the 12th and 13th centuries, the period of scientific revival.

The book is divided into four parts. Part One is the longest and covers The Science of the Arabs. It includes seven chapters: (1) Translators from the Arabic in Spain, (2) Adelard of Bath, (3) Hermann of Carinthia, (4) The Translations of Hugo Sanctallensis, (5) Some Twelfth-Century Writers on Astronomy, (6) The Introduction of Arabic Science into England, (7) Translators in Syria during the Crusades.

Part Two, entitled Translators from the Greek, has four chapters; the author states, "This Greek learning came in large measure through Arabic intermediaries, with some additions in the process, so that the influence of the Saracen scholars of Spain and the East is well understood," although "translations made directly from Greek originals" were also important. However, "Less considerable in the aggregate than what came through the Arabs, the Greek element was nevertheless significant for the later Middle Ages" (p.141). Part Three is entitled The Court of Frederick II, and the discussion here documents the considerable affinity and influence of "Jews and Mohammedans" that prevailed during this time; "the hospitality of Frederick II to Arab learning is well known" (p.5). Part Four covers Other Studies, and the four chapter titles are: (1) The Abacus and the Exchequer, (2) Nimrod and the Astronomer, (3) Some Early Treatises on Falconry, (4) A List of Textbooks from the Close of the Twelfth Century.

The book provides three separate indices: manuscripts and libraries (with towns identified), subject, and proper names.

B-218. al-Hassan, Ahmad Y. and Donald R. Hill. *Islamic Technology: An Illustrated History.* Cambridge and New York: Cambridge University Press, 1986.

Partly in commemoration of the 15th century of the Hegira of the Islamic world, this book was sponsored by the United Nations Educational, Scientific and Cultural Organization. An additional motive was to provide engineering students and educators a volume that documents the contributions of the Islamic civilizations to the history of science. The book draws together material from a wide variety of sources. The authors state that "even the leading published histories of technology do not have a chapter on Islamic technology, or if they have, the exposition has been written by an author with little affection for Islamic civilization" (p.xiii).

The 300-page book has 11 chapters. The introductory chapter discusses reasons for emphasis on science and technology in the Islam world, including the transfer of technology to the West. The authors dispute "the traditional view of Western historians," in that "European culture is the direct descendant of the classical civilizations of Greece and Rome" (p.31). Particularly during the 12th century, transfer of knowledge was generated by numerous Islamic scholars "as important as the works of Aristotle himself in forming European scientific and philosophical thought" (p.32). Other chapters are devoted to specific areas of engineering and technology: (2) Mechanical Engineering (water-raising machines, water and wind power, water and mechanical clocks, etc.), (3) Civil Engineering (buildings, roads and bridges, irrigation, dams, surveying, etc.), (4) Military Technology (cavalry, edged weapons, siege engines, fortifications, communications, gunpowder, cannon, etc.), (5) Ships and Navigation (shipbuilding, navigation, navies), (6) Chemical Technology (chemistry, chemical technology, distillation, perfumes, petroleum, acids, soap, glass, ceramics, dyes, etc.), (7) Textile, Paper and Leather (the textile industry, paper, and leather), (8) Agriculture and Food Technology (agricultural revolution, implements, flour and bread, sugar, vegetable oils, food and drink, etc.), (9) Mining and Metallurgy (mines and mining technology, nonferrous metallurgy, iron and steel), (10) Engineers and Artisans (technology as a branch of science, role of engineers and architects, artisans, quality control), (11) Epilogue (reexamination of critical historical issues, factors for decline and obstacles to progress, future Islamic technology).

Among the various critical issues, the authors point out that historians "have for the most part been harsh in their judgement on Islamic technological innovation" (p.280). Further, "Underestimation or even denial of this aspect of Muslim culture may be attributed to a variety of causes," one being that "Islamic science has not been sufficiently studied," but "another factor that may have influenced the judgement of some historians is that of personal prejudice" (p.280–281).

Each chapter includes several relevant illustrations (pictures and drawings). There is a detailed chapter-by-chapter bibliography at the end, followed by a name-subject index.

B-219. Hess, David J. *Science and Technology in a Multicultural World: The Cultural Politics of Facts and Artifacts.* New York: Columbia University Press, 1995.

Motivated by the politics of global multiculturalism, the author suggests, the "story of what constitutes international science and technology today is largely limited to the viewpoint of the experts who are seen to have produced their fundamental principles, and historically those experts have been generally European or of European descent" (p.vii). Thus, as its key premise, this 311-page book seeks "to include historically excluded perspectives" (p.ix). One of the goals is to promote multicultural science-and-technology education. Written as a resource for a variety of research on technoscience, culture, and power, the book is also intended for students and nonspecialists. There are chapters with titles such as "cultural construction of science and technology," "social relations and structures of scientific and technical communities," "other ways of knowing and doing: the ethnoknowledges and non-western medicines," and "cosmopolitan technologies, native peoples, and resistance struggles."

The chapter, The Origins of Western Science, is one that is particularly interesting. The story of the scientific revolution, the author suggests, has been "passed on from one heroic Great White Man to another" and it is the "Western textbook version of the story" (p.60). And in raising the question "How Western is 'Western' science and how revolutionary was the scientific 'revolution'?" (p.63), the author argues that much of "the technical infrastructure" of Western science "rests on borrowings from China and other non-Western cultures" (p.64). Thus, much of this chapter discusses the early-medieval Arab-Islamic linkages and in doing so, dismisses the "ethnocentric idea that Arab-Islamic science served only as a storehouse of Greek science that was activated during the Renaissance" (p.65).

There is a bibliography at the end, followed by a name-subject index.

B-220. Hill, Donald R. *A History of Engineering in Classical and Medieval Times.* La Salle, IL: Open Court Publishing Company, 1984.

This 265-page book represents a concise survey of the many and varied machines and techniques devised between the Hellenistic and early-modern times in the regions comprising Europe, the Mediterranean basin, and western Islam. The author argues that in general, the technical and engineering dimension has been missing in any accounts of the social history of antiquity and the Medieval world. This book attempts to fill that gap, with particular attention devoted to technological developments in the Islamic world, whose early sophistication and wide influence is too little known in the West.

The author says that he has "paid more attention than is usual to Islamic achievements, in an attempt to present a balanced view of engineering developments in the classical and medieval period" (p.xiii). Further, he argues, "The debt owed by Europe, in matters of technology, to Islam and other civilizations has never been fully acknowledged, and it is hoped that some of the material in this book will help to redress the balance" (p.4).

The book contains 12 chapters, grouped into three parts. After the first introductory chapter, Part One, Civil Engineering, has six chapters: (2) Irrigation and Water Supply, (3) Dams, (4) Bridges, (5) Roads, (6) Building Construction, (7) Surveying; Part Two, Mechanical Engineering, has two chapters: (8) Water-Raising Machines, (9) Power from Water and Wind; Part Three, Fine Technology, has three chapters: (10) Instruments, (11) Automata, (12) Clocks.

The book includes several tables, 12 black-and-white figures, and eight black-and-white plates. Each chapter provides notes and references at the end. There is a bibliography, followed by a name-subject index.

B-221. Hill, Donald R. *Islamic Science and Engineering.* Edinburgh: Edinburgh University Press, 1993.

This 250-page book is an introduction to the physical sciences and engineering of the Islamic civilization during the period 750–1150; it is said to be the first to trace the full extent of those achievements, a subject that has received little attention in the past. The author, who relies on original Arabic-language sources as well as others, notes that the "Muslim scientists and engineers contributed enormously to the technology of medieval Europe, both by preserving earlier traditions and by adding their own inventions and innovations"(p.xii). Further, using drawings and photographs as well as iconographic and archaeological evidence to enhance the material from Arabic sources, the book gives explanations of the underlying principles of scientific formulae, machines, and constructions, examining the historical background of Islamic technology and its subsequent effect upon European science and engineering. Four exact sciences are covered, but there is also coverage of irrigation systems, bridge and dam construction, surveying, and mining techniques.

Beyond the introduction, there are 11 chapters: (1) Mathematics, (2) Astronomy, (3) Physics, (4) Chemistry, (5) Machines, (6) Fine Technology, (7) Bridges and Dams, (8) Irrigation and Water Supply, (9) Surveying, (10) Mining, (11) Transmission of Islamic Knowledge to Europe. It is noted that the Church was almost the sole patron of learning in medieval Europe: "It was from the cathedral schools that the universities were to be established, and it was mainly from the cathedral schools and early universities that Islamic knowledge was to enter the Latin West" (p.220). Further, "The great period for the dissemination of Islamic science in the West was the twelfth and early thirteenth centuries. The translation movement from Arabic to Latin, whether the translations were from Greek or Islamic works, gave the necessary impetus to the growth of European science" (p.220).

Numerous pictures and illustrations are included in the book. A selected bibliography, classified in terms of the chapters of the book, is provided at the end. There is also a detailed name-subject index.

B-222. Hill, Donald R. (edited by David A. King). *Studies in Medieval Islamic Technology: From Philo to al-Jazari—From Alexandria to Diyar Bakr.* Variorum Collected Studies Series. Brookfield, VT, and Hampshire, UK: Ashgate Publishing Ltd., 1998.

The book is a bit unusual in that the author (1922–1994) is deceased, and one of his loyal friends (David King) has undertaken the task of collecting 20 major titles from Hill's total production of published articles. Thus, the volume is indeed a memorial dedicated to this scholar who is known not only as the most prolific writer on the subject of Islamic science and technology but was also responsible for spurring others into such explorations.

The articles are grouped into five categories; for each article, the book provides complete details as to its original publication. The category and article titles are: (I) Islamic Technology—General; eight articles: (1) Islamic Fine Technology and Its Influence on the Development of European Horology, (2) Medieval Arabic Mechanical Technology, (3) From Philo to Al-Jazari, (4) Arabic Fine Technology and Its Influence on European Mechanical Engineering, (5) Arabic Mechanical Engineering: Survey of the Historical Sources, (6) Information on Engineering in the Works of Muslim Geographers, (7) Mining Technology, (8) Hydraulic Machines; (II) Greek Technology; two articles: (1) Les oevres de Heron et leur context historique, (2) Construction of a Fluting Machine by Apollonius the Carpenter; (III) Islamic Technology—Specific; six articles: (1) The

Nilometer, (2) The Banu Musa and Their *Book of Ingenious Devices*, (3) Qusta ibn Luqa, (4) Al-Biruni's Mechanical Calendar, (5) Al-Jazari, (6) Notice of an Important al-Jazari Manuscript; (IV) Technology in Andalusia; two articles: (1) A Treatise on Machines by Ibn Mu'adh Abu Abdullah al-Jayyani (the treatise is by Ibn Khalaf al-Muradi, as per editor), (2) Andalusian Technology; (V) Technology and War; two articles: (1) Trebuchets, (2) The Camel and the Horse and the Early Arab Conquests.

While the influence of Islamic technology on medieval Europe is addressed throughout the book, according to the editor, it is significantly noteworthy in connection with the development of clocks in medieval Europe and the relationship of that development in general to the impact of the imported Islamic technology. This major influence is documented in the first and fourth articles in the first category (Islamic Technology—General).

Each article is reproduced exactly as it appeared in the original source, including notes, references, and pagination. Also available is a list of publications by Donald Hill. The editor provides four indices at the end: names of persons, titles of books, topics, technical terms.

B-223. Holmyard, Eric J. *Makers of Chemistry*. London: Oxford University Press, first published 1931; reprinted 1937, 1945, 1946, 1953, and 1962.

The 314-page book tells "the story of chemistry from its remote and obscure beginnings up to the establishment of the modern science" (p.ix). Going back to the Genesis, the author suggests, "Legends were invented, during the Dark and Middle Ages, to meet the needs of the moment: Greeks of Alexandria ascribed the birth of chemistry to Egypt; Muslim chemistry vacillated between the Prophet Muhammad and the Caliph Ali on the one hand and Aristotle, Plato, Pythagoras and Democritus on the other; early Jewish and Christian writers made the first chemists of scriptural figures; and the Chinese asserted that chemistry was an outgrowth of the venerable system of Tao-ism" (p.ix).

The book is divided into 58 short sections, of which 11 are specifically devoted to evolution of chemistry in the early Islamic civilization, beginning with a section entitled, The Origins of Alchemy in Islam, and ending with General Review of Muslim Chemistry. Numerous Islamic scholars and their works are discussed. This is followed by a discussion of the Latin-Europe translators. The author notes: "There seems to be no doubt that chemistry as a science was a definite importation from the civilization of Islam. The role which Islam played as the transmitter of Greek learning to late medieval Christendom is so well known that it need not be emphasized here; but its particular importance in the history of science, especially chemistry, has not always been fully recognized" (p.84). Among the translators, Albertus Magnus (1206–1280) "was well-acquainted with Latin translations of Avicenna, Averrous and other Muslim writers. In his *De Mineralibus* he moulds his views upon alchemy very largely in accordance with Avicenna's opinions" (p.91). As for Roger Bacon (1214–1292), "he accepts the sulphur-mercury theory, which he appears to have taken over bodily from Avicenna. He clearly had a wide knowledge of Arabian authors, whom he read in the original Arabic" (p.97).

The book provides 98 pictures and illustrations, and bibliographic references are integrated within the text throughout. There are two indices: author and subject.

B-224. Huff, Toby E. *The Rise of Early Modern Science: Islam, China, and the West*. Cambridge and New York: Cambridge University Press, 1993.

The book is "about the rise of modern science and how the world got to be the way it is" (p.ii). While there have been collisions of cultures and civilizations, a by-product of newly intensified globalization is also the unprecedented fusion of cultures. However, the author argues, there is insufficient recognition of the fact that the cultural–legal institutions forged in the 12th and 13th centuries in the West laid the foundations for modern science, and the origins were "the new contacts with Arab-Islamic culture in the 12th century [that] produced a renaissance in Europe. This new burst of energy and creativity affected virtually every sphere of intellectual activity" (p.99). Yet, a key question explored is: Why did modern science emerge in the West rather than, say, Islam or China? An underlying assumption of the author, controversial as it is, is that science is universally valid and independent of culture; we do not "create" science; we simply "discover" it (p.60).

The 420-page book has nine chapters, and several pertain to the development of scientific thought in the early Arab-Islamic civilization. Two lengthy chapters are devoted to the "problem of Arabic science" and "the differing philosophies of man and nature found in Arabic-Islamic civilization and the West" (p.5). Similarly, Chapters 4 and 5 elucidate the philosophical and legal foundations of institution building in the two civilizations. Chapter 6 discusses the social and intellectual transformation of the West in the 12th and 13th centuries, with a view also to spelling out the cultural–institutional obstacles that prevented the emergence of the ethos of science in the later Arabic-Islamic world. Chapters 7 and 8 extend the analysis to Chinese civilization. The book conveys a sense of global optimism: "It is somewhat premature to speak of the postmodern era; the conditions of modernity have yet to be achieved among the greater part of the peoples of the world" (p.7).

At the end there is a 20-page bibliography, as well as a rather comprehensive name-subject index.

B-225. Hull, L.W.H. *History and Philosophy of Science: An Introduction*. London and New York: Longmans, Green and Company, 1959.

The 340-page book is an attempt to bridge the gap between science and humanities by considering scientific ideas in a historical–philosophical context. The author argues that specialization has meant that technicians are often lacking in philosophical background while the humanities scholars have little respect for the works of science. Greek science is treated more fully, chiefly because, the author suggests, the most significant ideas behind modern science have their origin in it. The author points out, however, that subjects such as mathematics could not be ignored, "any more than you can afford to ignore Aristotle or Mohammed or the Roman Catholic Church—if you want a balanced picture of human development" (p.4).

There are ten chapters: (1) Early Science, (2) The Athenians, (3) The Alexandrians, (4) The Middle Ages, (5) Celestial Geometry, (6) Celestial Mechanics, (7) Changes of Outlook and Method, (8) Other Developments in the 16th and 17th Centuries, (9) The 19th Century and Evolution, (10) Epilogue: 20th Century Trends.

The chapter entitled The Middle Ages discusses linkages with the early Arab-Islamic civilization. At the time, "Christian thought affected science as adversely as Roman action. It supposed the sole purpose of this life was preparation for another. Unquestioning faith was set up as a greater virtue than intellectual curiosity and effort" (p.105). "Christian unity was further fostered by the Christian attitude toward other religions, which was intolerant. The pagan religions existed together without mutual interference or ill will. But the Christian code involved the denunciation of other religions and the conversion of those devoted to them" (p.107). Moreover, "The course of Western thought was in time deeply influenced" through contacts with the Arab-Islamic world (p.113). These influences gave prominence to the struggle between reason and authority; and "it was a long time before reason could fight on equal terms. It might have been much longer if there had been no Moslem conquests" (p.113). Thus, the "previously dormant intellect of the West began to seek employment. It became susceptible to the influences which were ready to revive humanism. The most important of these influences was that of the south [Moorish Spain], which entered Europe by several ways"—Crusades, Sicily, trade, etc. (p.121). Further, "Men of discernment in Europe were impressed by these glimpses of Mohammedan culture. Among the ablest of those who did so were Gerbert, later Pope Sylvester II, and Adelard of Bath" (p.121). Thus, Latin Europe became increasingly disposed to "free thought" and a "new breadth of outlook and the development of secular learning" (p.122). Throughout this chapter the author discusses, though somewhat hesitatingly, the influence of numerous early Islamic scholars in various fields; there are similar references in succeeding chapters.

This book includes, at the end, a brief list of references for further reading. Also, there is a name-subject index.

B-226. Ihsanoglu, Ekmeleddin and Feza Gunergun, eds. *Science in Islamic Civilization*. Istanbul, Turkey: Research Center for Islamic History and Culture, 2000.

The book is a collection of papers presented at an international symposium, held in 1991, and sponsored jointly with the Turkish Society for History of Science, UNESCO, and the Third World Academy of Sciences. Given the content and quality of the papers, the editors argue, that unlike the common view, "the golden age of Islamic science" did not go into a "steep decline" after the 11th century; considerable scientific activities continued to take place in various parts of the Ottoman lands and in other regions of the Muslim world.

The book is divided into five sections, with several papers in each. The section titles, with selected representative paper topics and authors identified in each, are: (1) Institutions (six papers; The reception of the model of the Islamic scholastic culture in the Christian West by George Makdisi; Ottoman scientific mentality: Formation, development, and decline by Nesimi Yazici); (2) Astronomy (three papers; Islamic geographical coordinates: al-Andalus' contribution to the correct measurement of the size of the Mediterranean by Merce Comes); (3) Mathematics (six papers; Al-Biruni on Trigonometry by Ahmed Salim Saidan; Kamal-al-Din al-Farisi and the fundamental theorem of arithmetic by A. Goksel Agargun); (4) Engineering Technology, Cartography (three papers; Turkish cartography in the 16th century by Dogfan Ucar); (5) Medical Sciences (four papers; Notes on the reception of Darwinism in some Islamic countries by A.H. Helmy Mohammad; Disinfecting stations in Ottoman Empire by Nuran Yuldrun).

Notes and references are integrated within each essay. No index is provided.

B-227. Kennedy, E.S. (and colleagues, former students; David A. King and Mary Helen Kennedy, editors). *Studies in the Islamic Exact Sciences.* Beirut, Lebanon: American University of Beirut, 1983.

The editors suggest, "for any serious student of the history of Islamic science the writings of E.S. Kennedy are required reading," for his writings represented "a model for scholarly investigation on material of scientific, historical, and cultural interest" (p.ix). This 771-page volume includes Kennedy's published articles, most written individually but several with co-authorship. Further, the volume "speaks well for the growing interest in the history of Islamic science" and "all colleagues in Islamic Studies and History of Science and others who are interested in the transmission and development of scientific ideas" will indeed benefit from this collection (p.ix). The collection covers a "wide range of topics within the field of Islamic astronomy, astrology, and mathematics" (p.ix).

There are 70 articles in the volume, grouped under six broad categories, with subcategories in each; within each subcategory are several relevant articles. The categories and subcategories are as follows: (1) General Surveys, (2) Mathematical Astronomy (Planetary Theory; Computation of Solar, Lunar, and Planetary Longitudes and Latitudes; Planetary and Lunar Visibility; Eclipses, Parallax, and Planetary Distances; Spherical Astronomy and Astronomical Timekeeping; Mathematical Astrology; Methodology), (3) Astronomical Instruments (General; Astrodome; Equatorial), (4) Mathematics (Greek Mathematics and Its Influence; Influence of Babylonian Mathematical Techniques; Mathematical Methods), (5)

Al-Biruni (Biographical Studies, Selected Works; Selected Topics), (6) Miscellanea (Mathematical Geography; Calendars; Miscellanea Varia).

The General Surveys category reproduces the author's article, The Arabic Heritage in the Exact Sciences, published in 1970. This summarizes the background of Arabic science, the "mingling of three sources, Iranian, Indian, and Hellenistic, in roughly this order of incidence, and certainly in this order of increasing importance" (p.32). Also discussed here are the auspices under which this scientific knowledge flourished, along with a discussion of the evolution of several individual branches. The article concludes: "When all mental reservations have been made, it is still possible to draw valid general inferences from what has been set down in this essay. There need be no laboring of the conceited notion that the providential function of the Arabs was to preserve Greek science against the time when Western man should awake from his slumbers of the Dark Ages. All societies destroy parts of their heritage and preserve the rest. What can be said with assurance is that the Arab-writing cultures of the medieval Middle East supported scientific work more widely and more intensively than any of the societies which preceded them. Many of the findings of their scientists were transmitted to other regions and contributed directly to the further advance of the subject" (p.47).

All articles are reproduced with the same scheme of notes, references, and pagination as originally published, although continuous, separate page numbers are also indicated in this volume. At the end there is a comprehensive name-subject index, followed by two other indices—decimal numerical parameters and sexagesimal numerical parameters. Also there is a listing of manuscripts cited in the various articles, identified with pages from the articles.

B-228. King, David A. and George Saliba, eds. *From Deferent to Equant: A Volume of Studies in the History of Science in the Ancient and Medieval Near East in Honor of E. S. Kennedy.* Volume 500. New York: Annals of the New York Academy of Sciences, New York Academy of Sciences, 1987.

This is one of a series of volumes, the latest being No. 1050 published in 2005, that are assembled by the New York Academy of Sciences each year, often several in a given year. This particular volume is a collection of papers written on the history of science, with a focus on the ancient and medieval Near East in honor of E.S. Kennedy, who was known affectionately to his students and colleagues as "Kindi."

The honored scholar had spent decades at the American University of Beirut (1946–1976), with several years before and after simply as a "native" of the land he loved. For the editors, Kennedy is "the model scholar, strictly interested in the *Quellen und Studien* approach to the history of science." In addition, they "have savored his humanity and his humor, as well as his concern for justice and peace and his love for the Near East." By way of this volume, they pay "tribute to the idea that a Western scholar can devote the major part of his life to working in the Near East in the service of its people and their cultural legacy" (p.xii).

Kennedy's formal academic background was in mathematics and engineering but, having rubbed shoulders with the likes of George Sarton at Harvard, he developed a passion for Islamic astronomy and mathematics and for the history of science in particular. Thus, scores of his publications (listed in this volume) reflect those interests, as do the 34 rather technical essays contained in this 570-page book. Some representative titles and authors: A Late-Babylonian Procedure Text for Mars, and Some Remarks on Retrograde Arcs by Asger Aaboe; Zoomorphic Astrolabes and the Introduction of Arabic Star Names into Europe by Owen Gingerich; A Survey of Islamic Interpolation Schemes by Javad Hamadanizadeh; An Unknown Treatise by Sanad ibn Ali on the Relative Magnitudes of the Sun, Earth, and Moon by Anton M. Heinen; Some Early Islamic Tables for Determining Lunar Crescent Visibility by David A. King; Al-Khwarizmi as a Source for the *Sententie astrolabii* by Paul Kunitzsch; Kennedy's Geographical Tables of Medieval Islam: An Exploratory Statistical Analysis by Mary H. Regier; Sa'id, the *Toledian Tables*, and Andalusi Science by Lutz Richter-Bernburg; The Height of the Atmosphere According to Mu'ayyad al-Din al-Urdi, Qutb al-Din al-Shirazi, and Ibn Mu'adh by George Saliba; The Influence of Islamic Astronomy in China by K. Yabuuti.

Each essay ends with its own notes and bibliography. There is no index.

B-229. Lindberg, David C. *The Beginnings of Western Science: The European Scientific Tradition in Philosophical, Religious, and Institutional Context, 600 B.C. to A.D. 1450.* Chicago and London: University of Chicago Press, 1992.

Written by a highly regarded historian of science, this book is based on the author's conviction that recent works on the subject do not adequately cover ancient science, and so the present work has three goals: (1) the book incorporates recent research on the subject, (2) by conjoining ancient and medieval science, there is emphasis on transmission and continuity, (3) the present attempt is to place ancient and medieval science in philosophical, religious, and institutional (educational) context, more so than other works (especially the religious context). Built upon accumulated past scholarship, there are new interpretations and fresh judgments on old disputes, but the author admits himself to be an "outsider" with respect to the ancient science and more on his "home ground" concerning medieval science. The book is intended for the classroom, but also for the general educated readers and historians.

The 455 pages contain 14 detailed chapters: (1) Science and Its Origins, (2) The Greeks and Cosmos, (3) Aristotle's Philosophy of Nature, (4) Hellenistic Natural Philosophy, (5) The Mathematical Sciences in Antiquity, (6) Greek and Roman Medicine, (7) Roman and Early Medieval Science, (8) Science in Islam, (9) The Revival of Learning in the West, (10) The Recovery and Assimilation of Greek and Islamic Science, (11) The Medieval Cosmos, (12) The Physics of the Sublunar Region, (13) Medieval Medicine and Natural History, (14) The Legacy of Ancient and Medieval Science.

Beginning with chapter 8, there is coverage of the assimilation of Greek learning in the Islamic civilization as well as almost continuous coverage of the intellectual output of Islamic scholars in various fields. Further, there is discussion as to the "translation movement" and the impact of the "knowledge-transfer" in the Latin West (p.202). Numerous Islamic precursors of Latin-Christian scholars in various disciplines are identified. For example, Alhazen's (Ibn Al-Haytham, 965–1040) influence on Roger Bacon, John Pecham, Johannes Kepler, and others is mentioned; further, Alhazen's optical theory (including his combined physical-mathematical-physiological approach) facilitated Roger Bacon's (1220–1292) "theory of vision in almost all of its details" (p.313). Also, there is reference to the 1277 condemnation of "Averroistic heresies" that "provoked a reexamination of ideas of place and space" among a number of Latin-European philosophers (p.366).

The book includes some maps and numerous figures (pictures and sketches). Detailed chapter-by-chapter notes and references are provided at the end, followed by a 34-page bibliography, and there is a name-subject index.

B-230. Lindberg, David C., ed. *Science in the Middle Ages*. Chicago: University of Chicago Press, 1978.

The book, intended for the non-specialists as well as professional historians, is a collection of 15 essays written by eminent scholars. The papers provide an overall view of the state of knowledge concerning the sources, development, and teaching of science in medieval times, as well as of the medieval achievements in particular sciences. The editor stresses the character of science in the Middle Ages as natural philosophy rather than as a set of autonomous disciplines as it later became. Further, it is emphasized that medieval science "must be viewed within a broad social and intellectual context" and must be explored "with a broad grasp of medieval social and intellectual history" (p.xiv). Although 12th-century developments receive greater emphasis, the surveys encompass intellectual activities of more than a millennium (400–1500 AD), extending over several cultures (ancient Greece and Rome, Islam, and Latin Europe).

The titles and authors of the 15 essays are as follows: (1) Science, Technology, and Economic Progress in the Early Middle Ages by Brian Stock, (2) The Transmission of Greek and Arabic Learning to the West by David C. Lindberg, (3) The Philosophical Setting of Medieval Science by William A. Wallace, (4) The Institutional Setting: The Universities by Pearl Kibre and Nancy G. Siraisi, (5) Mathematics by Michael S. Mahoney, (6) The Science of Weights by Joseph E. Brown, (7) The Science of Motion by John E. Murdoch and Edith D. Sylla, (8) Cosmology by Edward Grant, (9) Astronomy by Olaf Pedersen, (10) The Science of Optics by David C. Lindberg, (11) The Science of Matter by Robert P. Multhauf, (12) Medicine by Charles H. Talbot, (13) Natural History by Jerry Stannard, (14) The Nature, Scope, and Classification of Sciences by James A. Weisheipl, (15) Science and Magic by Bert Hansen. The first four essays (and the essay by Weisheipl) provide general background as to the social and institutional setting, organization, and non-scientific accompaniments of medieval science, and other essays focus on particular sciences.

While almost every essay documents the Arab-Islamic linkages, often with Greek heritage as the backdrop, the second essay particularly focuses on those influences. The author concludes: "Viewed as whole, the translations provided Western Christendom with an adequate knowledge of the Greek and Arabic intellectual achievement—and thus with the basic materials out of which its own system of philosophy and natural science would be constructed" (p.79).

There are numerous illustrations, and each essay provides its own notes and references at the end. There is also a list of suggested readings, organized by broad themes of the 550-page book, and a detailed name-subject index.

B-231. Mason, Stephen F. *A History of the Sciences*, revised edition. New York: Collier Books, 1962.

The book presents a highly readable survey of the evolution of scientific ideas from ancient to contemporary achievements. It includes material not otherwise readily accessible on the contributions of Babylonian, Oriental, and medieval science, including the early Islamic world. The book also provides a historical perspective as to the intellectual and social problems generated by scientific developments.

The 638-page book is divided into six parts, with several chapters in each: Part One, Ancient Science; Part Two, Science in the Orient and Medieval Europe; Part Three, The Scientific Revolution of the Sixteenth and Seventeenth Centuries; Part Four, Eighteenth-Century Science: The Development of National Scientific Tradition; Part Five, The Science of the Nineteenth Century: The Agent of Industrial and Intellectual Change; Part Six, Twentieth-Century Science: New Fields and New Powers.

While several chapters in Part Two include numerous references to the influence of Muslim scholars upon European scientific/intellectual developments, a chapter entitled Science and Technology in the Muslim World discusses scientific developments in the early Islamic world and also points out, though somewhat hesitatingly, linkages with the subsequent Latin-Europe developments. There is discussion of developments in the fields of mathematics, astronomy, medicine, alchemy, optics, paper-making, and printing, etc. There is also reference to the translations of "Muslim science" into Latin. Further, it is noted that it was after the late 11th-century Crusade against Muslim Spain that the "Arabic versions of the Greek scientific works were translated," and "Spain was the most important centre of contact between the Muslim and Christian worlds" (p.113). Sicily is also mentioned as another source. As for the development of experimental method through "Muslim science," there is mention of Roger Bacon's (1214–1294 AD) "experiments in optics, following the works of Al-Hazen" (p.114).

The book provides a 10-page bibliography, grouped by clusters of chapters relevant to specific topics. There is a 20-page name-subject index.

B-232. Nasr, Seyyed Hossein. *Islamic Science: An Illustrated Study* (photographs by Roland Michaud). Kent, UK: World of Islam Festival Publishing Company, Westerham Press Ltd., 1976.

This volume is said to be "the first ever written on Islamic science in which the study and analysis of the texts is combined with illustrations from sources throughout the Islamic world" (p.xiii). It was developed as part of the "first exhibition ever organized of Islamic science anywhere" and was held in London. The author's perspective is one of the Islamic tradition, and the work is "in many ways a complement" to his other writings. It is suggested that Islamic science includes a wide spectrum of intellectual activity, and "its extensive influence upon the Latin and Renaissance West has, since the eighteenth century, caused numerous studies in European languages to be devoted to the various facets of Islamic science" (p.xiii). Further, "No understanding of the Islamic sciences is possible without a comprehension of Islam itself, the life-giving force of a vast civilization one of whose fruits is the sciences" (p.3). Given the Islamic emphasis on unity of knowledge, various forms of knowledge are not allowed to be cultivated independently, the author argues; moreover, there is an organically related hierarchy of knowledge, from the material to the metaphysical.

The 275-page book is divided into five parts, with 2–3 chapters in each for a total of 12 chapters. Part One, The General Background, has two chapters—(1) Islam and the Rise of the Islamic Sciences, (2) The Islamic Educational System. Part Two, The Islamic Sciences: The Qualitative Study of the Universe, has two chapters—(3) Cosmology, Cosmography and Geography, (4) Natural History: Geology, Mineralogy, Botany, Zoology. Part Three, The Cosmos and Its Mathematical Study, has three chapters—(5) Mathematics, (6) Astronomy and Astrology, (7) Physics. Part Four, The Applied Sciences, has three chapters—(8) Medicine and Pharmacology, (9) Alchemy and Other Occult Sciences, (10) Agriculture and Irrigation. Part Five, Man in the Universe, has two chapters—(11) Man and the Natural Environment, (12) Man in the Cosmic Order.

The book contains 135 illustrative plates (pictures, sketches, other depictions) and 94 figures (Qur'anic verses, maps, diagrams of mechanical devices, anatomical illustrations, etc.). Sources of each plate and figure are identified, chapter-by-chapter, at the end. Also, there is a glossary of Arabic words and phrases, followed by a select bibliography in European languages, and a detailed name-subject index.

B-233. Nasr, Seyyed Hossein. *Science and Civilization in Islam*. Cambridge, MA: Harvard University Press, 1968.

The author begins with the statement: "The history of science is often regarded as the progressive accumulation of techniques and the refinement of quantitative methods in the study of Nature. Such a point of view considers the present conception of science to be the only valid one; it therefore judges the sciences of other civilizations in the light of modern science and evaluates them primarily with respect to their 'development' with the passage of time. Our aim in this work, however, is not to examine the Islamic sciences from the point of view of modern science and of this 'evolutionistic' conception of history; it is, on the contrary, to present certain aspects of the Islamic sciences as seen from the Islamic point of view" (p.21). That's what this 385-page book is all about.

The introductory chapter defines the book's focus, as well as the principles of Islam and the perspectives within the Islamic civilization. This is followed by 13 detailed chapters: (1) The Universal Figures of Islamic Science, (2) The Basis of the Teaching System and the Educational Institutions (classification of the sciences; educational institutions; institutions of higher learning; the observatories; the hospitals; the sufi centers), (3) Cosmology, Cosmography, Geography, and Natural History, (4) Physics (Alhazen, Al-Biruni, Al-Khazini), (5) Mathematics (the brethren of purity; al-Khwarazmi; Umar Khayyam), (6) Astronomy (the nature of the heavenly spheres; planetary motion; the distance and size of the planets), (7) Medicine (the historical background; medicine during the early centuries; medicine after Avicenna; the philosophy and theory of Islamic medicine), (8) The Sciences of Man, (9) The Alchemical Tradition (Jabir ibn Hayyan, Rhazes, Al-Iraqi), (10) Islamic Alchemy and Its Influence in the Western World, (11) Philosophy, (12) The Controversies of Philosophy and Theology—The Later Schools of Philosophy (Al-Ghazali; Averroes and Philosophy in Andalusia; Al-Tusi; Suharawardi and Mulla Sadra), (13) The Gnostic Tradition.

The book provides a selected bibliography, organized approximately in terms of the topical scheme of the book. There is a detailed name-subject index.

B-234. Rashed, Roshdi, ed. (in collaboration with Regis Morelon). *Encyclopedia of the History of Arabic Science, Vol. 1, Astronomy.* London and New York: Routledge, 1996.

This is volume one of the 1,100-page comprehensive text, "conceived and realized to make its contribution towards a history of Arabic science," which intends "to accomplish two principal tasks: to open the way to a genuine understanding of the history of classical science from the ninth to the seventeenth century; and to contribute to the knowledge of the Islamic culture itself by according it a dimension which has never ceased to be its own—that of scientific culture" (p.xiii, vol.1). It is argued to be the *first synthesis* ever carried out in this area, the result of research accumulated since the last century and further stimulated from the 1950s onwards. There is a total of 30 essays: nine in this volume, 12 in volume two, and nine in volume three.

The editor argues that while there was considerable mobility of scholars (especially Muslim and Jewish) and ideas relating to Arabic science—from Basra to Cairo, from Cordoba to Cairo, from Tus to Damascus, "such a fundamental and obvious feature of Arabic science remained obscured and escaped the attention of historians." In part, this is attributed to the "oblique viewpoint of an historical ideology which views classical science as the achievement of European humanity alone" (p.xii, vol.1). However, "From the twelfth century onward, Latin science could not be understood without Latin translations from Arabic" (p.xii, vol.1).

Titles and authors of the nine essays are: (1) General survey of Arabic astronomy by Regis Morelon, (2) Eastern Arabic astronomy between the eight and the eleventh centuries by Regis Morelon, (3) Arabic planetary theories after the eleventh century AD by George Saliba, (4) Astronomy and Islamic society: Qibla, gnomonics and timekeeping by David King, (5) Mathematical geography by Edward Kennedy, (6) Arabic nautical science by Henri Grosset-Grange, (7) The development of Arabic science in Andalusia by Janet Vernet and Julio Samsa, (8) The heritage of Arabic science in Hebrew by Bernard Goldstein, (9) The influence of Arabic astronomy in the medieval West by Henri Hugonnard-Roche.

Each essay is followed by footnotes and references. Each volume has its own comprehensive bibliography at the end; there are two indices—proper name and subject.

B-235. Rashed, Roshdi, ed. (in collaboration with Regis Morelon). *Encyclopedia of the History of Arabic Science, Vol. 2, Mathematics and the Physical Sciences.* London and New York: Routledge, 1996.

This is volume two of the 1,100-page comprehensive text, "conceived and realized to make its contribution towards a history of Arabic science," which intends "to accomplish two principal tasks: to open the way to a genuine understanding of the history of classical science from the ninth to the seventeenth century; and to contribute to the knowledge of the Islamic culture itself by according it a dimension which has never ceased to be its own—that of scientific culture" (p.xiii, vol.1). It is argued to be the *first synthesis* ever carried out in this area, the result of research accumulated since the last century and further stimulated from the 1950s onwards. There is a total of 30 essays: nine in volume one, 12 in this volume, and nine in volume three.

The editor argues that while there was considerable mobility of scholars (especially Muslim and Jewish) and ideas relating to Arabic science—from Basra to Cairo, from Cordoba to Cairo, from Tus to Damascus, "such a fundamental and obvious feature of Arabic science remained obscured and escaped the attention of historians." In part, this is attributed to the "oblique viewpoint of an historical ideology which views classical science as the achievement of European humanity alone" (p.xii, vol.1). However, "From the twelfth century onward, Latin science could not be understood without Latin translations from Arabic" (p.xii, vol.1).

Titles and authors of the essays: (1) Numeration and arithmetic by Ahmad Saidan, (2) Algebra by Roshdi Rashed, (3) Combinational analysis, numerical analysis, Diophantine analysis and number theory by Roshdi Rashed, (4) Infinitesimal determinations, quadrature of lunules and isoperimetric problems by Roshdi

Rashed, (5) Geometry by Boris Rosenfield and Adolf Youschkevitch, (6) Trigonometry by Marie-Therese Debarnot, (7) The influence of Arabic mathematics in the medieval West by Andre Allard, (8) Musical science by Jean-Claude Chabrier, (9) Statics by Mariam Rozhanskaya, (10) Geometrical optics by Roshdi Rashed, (11) The emergence of physiological optics by Gul Russell, (12) The Western reception of Arabic optics by David C. Lindberg.

Each essay is followed by footnotes and references. Each volume has its own comprehensive bibliography at the end; there are two indices—proper name and subject.

B-236. Rashed, Roshdi, ed. (in collaboration with Regis Morelon). *Encyclopedia of the History of Arabic Science, Vol. 3, Technology, Alchemy and Life Sciences.* London and New York: Routledge, 1996.

This is volume three of the 1,100-page comprehensive text, "conceived and realized to make its contribution towards a history of Arabic science," and it intends "to accomplish two principal tasks: to open the way to a genuine understanding of the history of classical science from the ninth to the seventeenth century; and to contribute to the knowledge of the Islamic culture itself by according it a dimension which has never ceased to be its own—that of scientific culture" (p.xiii, vol.1). It is argued to be the *first synthesis* ever carried out in this area, the result of research accumulated since the last century and further stimulated from the 1950s onwards. There is a total of 30 essays: nine in volume one, 12 in volume two, and nine in this volume.

The editor argues that while there was considerable mobility of scholars (especially Muslim and Jewish) and ideas relating to Arabic science—from Basra to Cairo, from Cordoba to Cairo, from Tus to Damascus, "such a fundamental and obvious feature of Arabic science remained obscured and escaped the attention of historians." In part, this is attributed to the "oblique viewpoint of an historical ideology which views classical science as the achievement of European humanity alone" (p.xii, vol.1). However, "from the twelfth century onward, Latin science could not be understood without Latin translations from Arabic" (p.xii, vol.1).

Titles and authors are: (1) Engineering by Donald R. Hill, (2) Geography by Andre Miquel, (3) Botany and Agriculture by Toufic Fahd, (4) Arabic alchemy by Georges C. Anawati, (5) The reception of Arabic alchemy in the West by Robert Halleux, (6) Medicine by Emilie Savage-Smith, (7) The influence of Arabic medicine in the medieval West by Danielle Jacquart, (8) The scientific institutions in the medieval Near East by Francoise Micheau, (9) Classification of the sciences by Jean Jalivet.

This volume contains the capstone essay by Muhsin Mahdi, Postface: Approaches to the History of Arabic Science.

Each essay is followed by footnotes and references. Each volume has its own comprehensive bibliography at the end, and there are two indices—proper name and subject.

B-237. Ronan, Colin A. *Science: Its History and Development among the World's Cultures.* New York: Facts On File Publications, 1982.

Recognizing the difficulty in documenting the details of all the scientific and technical knowledge of every age and every civilization, Ronan presents an overview of the evolution of science and scientific thought across major civilizations from early times to the present. The chapters cover a broad spectrum, with titles such as The Origins of Science, Greek Science, Chinese Science, and Hindu and Indian Science.

Following the introduction, the book contains ten chapters: (1) The Origins of Science, (2) Greek Science, (3) Chinese Science, (4) Hindu and Indian Science, (5) Arabian Science, (6) Roman and Medieval Science, (7) From Renaissance to Scientific Revolution, (8) The Seventeenth and Eighteenth Centuries, (9) Science in the Nineteenth Century, (10) Twentieth-Century Science.

Of particular interest presently are the middle three chapters where the author not only discusses the Arab-Islamic contributions but also linkages to the evolving Latin Europe. In documenting these contributions, the author emphasizes that this civilization was not merely a storehouse for inherited Greek knowledge; that sort of argument is "a travesty of truth" (p.203). The Arabs made many original contributions of their own and, thus, it is important to appreciate the "cultural renaissance in Arabia which was later to prove so important for the West and thus to the development of the modern scientific outlook" (p.205).

The 543-page book is well-documented and cross-referenced, with numerous pictorial and graphic illustrations and sketches. There is a detailed bibliography linked to each chapter, followed by a comprehensive name-subject index.

B-238. Saliba, George. *A History of Arabic Astronomy: Planetary Theories during the Golden Age of Islam.* New York and London: New York University Press, 1994.

The book presents a series of articles, written by the author over a period of two decades, devoted to the study of the various aspects of non-Ptolemaic astronomy in medieval Islam (from the 11th to the 15th centuries). The main thesis of the volume is that, contrary to the general view, this period was not one of decline in Islamic intellectual history; indeed, this was a very productive period in which astronomical theories of the highest order were generated, including scientific and mathematical theorems which were identical to those that were employed by Copernicus much later.

The articles explore four fundamental questions. First, to what extent the so-called age of decline in Islamic intellectual history, usually defined as beginning around the end of the 12th century, was applicable to the field of astronomy? Second, what is the relationship between astronomy and the religious sciences in determining if astronomy experienced the same kind of treatment as claimed for philosophy as the cause of the intellectual decline? Third, what was the geographical range of astronomical activities and did the Mongol's destruction of Baghdad in 1258 leave any impact on astronomical activities? And, finally, what were the temporal and geographical boundaries of that intellectual decline? Saliba's general conclusion is that the period from the middle of the 13th century to the middle of the 14th century was the "golden age of Arabic astronomy," and among the key Arabic scholars in this field was Ibn al-Shatir (d. 1375), whose "lunar model was essentially identical to that of Copernicus (1473–1543) thus raising the specter of indebtedness and transmission"; another major link was the contributions of a group of astronomers that "came to be known as the works of the 'Maragha School'" (p.254).

While astronomy is the primary focus, the 350-page book provides considerable details as to the translations of the Greek reservoir in early Islam as well as the various intellectual contributions emerging from the Islamic civilization and the subsequent transmission of that comprehensive heritage to Latin Europe.

There is an extensive bibliography at the end, along with an author-subject index.

B-239. Sarton, George. *A Guide to the History of Science: A First Guide for the Study of the History of Science, with Introductory Essays on Science and Tradition.* Waltham, MA: Chronica Botanica Company, 1952.

The book is divided into two parts, different but complementary to each other. The shorter, first part explains the purpose and meaning of the history of science and is based on lectures delivered at the University of London in 1948. The much longer, second part is a bibliographic summary prepared for the guidance of scholars in the history of science studies.

Part I contains three chapters: (1) Science and Tradition, (2) The Tradition of Ancient and Medieval Science, (3) Is It Possible to Teach the History of Science? Presently relevant is the second chapter; here the author cautions, "Men of science whose retrospective insight does not go much deeper than the last century have no idea of the vicissitudes of tradition" (p.17). There was the "Greek miracle" of ancient science during the sixth and fifth centuries BC, but "the history of ancient and medieval science is a history of traditions. The tradition was oral, written or manual; the last one is the most difficult to deal with, the tradition of each single idea or fact might be symbolized by a line, more or less regular, with ups and downs" (p.26). However, for the "scientific pattern in its totality, the graph would be very different. The roots of western science are Egyptian, Mesopotamian, and to a much smaller amount, Iranian and Hindu. The central line represents the Arabic transmission which was for a time, say, from the ninth to the eleventh century, the outstanding stream, and remained until the fourteenth century one of the largest streams of medieval thought" (p.27). Further, some "will glibly say 'The Arabs simply translated Greek writings, they were industrious imitators, and by the way, the translations were not made by themselves but by Christians and Jews.' This is not absolutely untrue, but is such a small part of the truth, that when it is allowed to stand alone, it is worse than a lie" (p.27). And, "When we try to explain our own culture we may leave out almost completely Hindu and Chinese developments, but we cannot leave out the Arabic ones without spoiling the whole story and making it unintelligible" (p.30).

Then Sarton makes a case for the teaching of history of science. The second part of the book is a guide for the study of the history of science and provides a listing of catalogs of scientific literature, journals, and periodicals, as well as national academies and scientific societies. Also, there are references to primary treatises and handbooks, along with the history of science in various countries of the world. In addition, there is a listing of scientific societies by disciplines.

The bibliographic references are included in the second part of the book, as indicated. There is a comprehensive author index at the end.

B-240. Sarton, George. *Introduction to the History of Science: Volume I—From Homer to Omar Khayam.* Baltimore, MD: Published for the Carnegie Institution of Washington by William & Wilkins Company, 1927.

This volume is part of the widely acclaimed, most comprehensive, authentic, and meticulous scholarship ever on the subject, written by one of the 20th century's most eminent medievalists and historians of science. There is a total of three volumes, but volumes II and III have two parts, covering almost 5,000 pages.

This 840-page volume covers the development of ancient science beginning with the ninth–eighth centuries BC and focusing on the early Greek and Hebrew knowledge; the coverage extends to early Iranians, the Romans, the Chinese, the Hindus, the Buddhists, the Byzantines. The discussion includes development of knowledge by various disciplines—for example, mathematics, astronomy, chemistry, physics, technology, geography, and medicine. About half of the volume is then devoted to the evolution of medieval science, with almost exclusive focus on the Islamic civilization. The author says, "The greatest achievements of antiquity were due to the Greek, Western, genius; the greatest achievements of the Middle Ages (especially during the period covered in this volume) were due to the Muslim, Eastern, genius" (p.16).

Moreover, "The most valuable of all [works], the most original and the most pregnant, were written in Arabic. From the second half of the eight to the end of the eleventh century, Arabic was the scientific, the progressive language of mankind. During that period anyone wishing to be well informed, up-to-date, had to study Arabic. It is not necessary to substantiate these statements, for my whole work is a proof of them" (p.17). From about the first half of the eighth century to the second half of the 11th century, the Arab-Islamic scholars covered, along with their contributions in various fields, are: Jabir ibn Hayan, al-Khwarizmi, al-Razi, al-Masudi, Abu'l-Wafa, al-Biruni, and Omar Khayyam.

There is a comprehensive, 52-page combined author-subject index. A detailed bibliography is provided in Volume III.

B-241. Sarton, George. *Introduction to the History of Science: Volume II, Part I—From Rabbi Ben Ezra to Ibn Rushd.* Baltimore, MD: Published for the Carnegie Institution of Washington by Williams & Wilkins Company, 1931.

Among other things, one of the main goals of the author in writing these volumes is to "discuss the relationship of the three cultures—Jewish, Christian, and Muslim—whose imperfect fusion had gradually created our own European civilization" (p.v).

"The end of the eleventh century was a turning point in the history of mankind," says Sarton (p.109). Further, "From the end of the eighth century to the end of the eleventh century the intellectual leaders had been most of them Muslims, and the most progressive works had been written in Arabic. It is not too much to say that during these centuries the Arabic language had been the main vehicle of culture" (p.109).

Part I relates to the 12th century and it begins with a chapter entitled Survey of Scientific Thought in the Twelfth and Thirteenth Centuries; the focus here is chiefly on developments during the 12th century. This part of Volume II is further divided into Book I and II, with 13 and 14 chapters each, respectively.

Book I (480 pages) covers "The Time of William of Conches, Abraham Ibn Ezra, and Ibn Zuhr (First Half of Twelfth Century)," and the various chapters are devoted to such topics as the religious background of the era, the various translators, the philosophic background, the development of knowledge in various disciplines (mathematics, astronomy, physics, technology, music, chemistry, geography, natural history, medicine, historiography, law and sociology, and philology and education). Book II (1,251 pages) covers "The Time of Gerard of Cremona, Ibn Rushd, and Maimonides (Second Half of Twelfth Century)," and the various chapters provide extensive coverage on topics similar to that of Book I. Each book begins with a survey of scientific–intellectual developments covered in greater detail in the succeeding chapters. With respect to about the most prominent Latin Scholastic of the time, St. Thomas Aquinas (1225–1274), Sarton notes, he "was deeply influenced by Muslim philosophy, chiefly by al-Ghazzali and Ibn Rushd; the aim of his life was to reconcile Aristotelian and Muslim knowledge with Christian theology" (p.914).

For both parts of this particular volume, there is a 94-page author-subject index at the end of Part II (devoted to developments "From Robert Grosseteste to Roger Bacon"). A detailed bibliography is provided in Volume III.

B-242. Sarton, George. *Introduction to the History of Science: Volume III, Science and Learning in the Fourteenth Century, Part I—First Half of the Fourteenth Century; Part II—Second Half of the Fourteenth Century.* Baltimore, MD: Published for the Carnegie Institution of Washington by Williams & Wilkins Company, 1947.

Part I (over 1,000 pages) of this volume covers "The Time of Abu'l-Fida, Levi ben Gerson, and William of Occam (First Half of the Fourteenth Century)," with

14 chapters, beginning with religious background of the era, philosophical and cultural background, and then a discussion of the various translators and translations from Arabic into Latin, from Arabic to Italian, from Arabic to Spanish, from Arabic to Hebrew, from Persian to other languages, from Greek to other languages, etc. This is followed by chapters covering developments in various disciplines: education, mathematics, astronomy, physics, technology, music, chemistry, geography, natural history, medicine, law and sociology, historiography, and philology.

Part II (about 1,200 pages) covers "The Time of Geoffrey Chaucer, Ibn Khaldun, and Hasdai Crescas (Second Half of the Fourteenth Century)," with 14 chapters. While the format of these chapters is similar to that of Part I, the content obviously differs. The history and impact of the Crusades is also part of the discussion in this volume.

This volume provides a detailed general bibliography, covering 38 pages. There is a comprehensive, all-volume, 178-page general index, followed by a 6-page Greek index, a 40-page Chinese index, and a 14-page Japanese index. Any names and words from other languages (English, Latin, Arabic, Hebrew, Hindi) are integrated in the general index.

B-243. Sarton, George. *The Life of Science: Essays in the History of Civilization.* New York: Henry Schuman, 1948.

The book is a collection of author's essays, each attempts a new focus on the history of science, moving beyond the language of the scholars to that of lay persons. There are recurring themes, stressing the unity of mankind, the unity of knowledge, the international character of science and so forth.

There are four parts in the book: (1) The Spread of Understanding (with three chapters), (2) Secret History (five chapters on prominent European scholars), (3) East and West (one chapter—East and West in the History of Science), (4) Casting Bread upon the Face of the Waters (two chapters). The first chapter of Part 1 gives illustrations of early scientific developments whose applications were often delayed "because prejudice sat on the lid" (p.9). Chapter 9 (East and West in the History of Science) traces the evolution of "modern science," and cautions against the misleading idea of the whole evolution; "it is as if he knew a man only in his maturity" (p.131). For studying the history of science, the author suggests, there are two reasons: "a purely historical one, to analyze the development of civilization; and a philosophical one, to understanding the deeper meaning of science" (p.134).

The dawn of science began 3,000 years ago in the East, in Mesopotamia and Egypt, perhaps also in India and China. Borrowing from Egypt and Mesopotamia, the "Greek miracle" evolved; "much of the Greek knowledge was borrowed from eastern sources" (p.140). Then the "Greek miracle" connected with early Christendom, but this connection "ended by being so precarious that it might have conceivably been broken altogether, but for the intervention of another oriental people, the Arabs" (p.145). Having re-discovered the Greek treasure, the Arabs "had no rest until the whole of it was translated into Arabic" (p.147), and "they did far more than that" (p.150). Additionally, "The immense importance of Islam lies in the fact that it finally brought together the two great intellectual streams [Semitic religion and Greek knowledge] which had flowed independently in ancient times" (p.147–148). "The creation of a new civilization of international and encyclopedic magnitude within less than two centuries is something that we can describe, but not completely explain. This movement, as opposed to the Greek, was perhaps more remarkable for its quantity than for its quality. Yet it was creative; it was the most creative movement of the Middle Ages down to the thirteenth century" (p.151). "Indeed the superiority of Muslim culture" was such that one can imagine "their doctors speaking of the western barbarians almost in the same spirit as ours do of the 'Orientals'" (p.152). And, "Toward the end of the thirteenth century some of the greatest doctors of Christendom, Albert the Great, Roger Bacon, Ramon Lull, were ready to acknowledge the many superiorities of Arabic culture" (p.158).

And so, "We must bear in mind two things. The first is that the seeds of science, including the experimental method and mathematics, in fact, the seeds of all forms of science came from the East; and that during the Middle Ages they were largely developed by Eastern people. Thus, in a large sense, experimental science is a child not of the West, but also of the East; the East was its mother, the West was its father" (p.163).

The book concludes with editorial notes, acknowledgments, and sources, followed by a name-subject index.

B-244. Singer, Charles. *A Short History of Science to the Nineteenth Century.* Oxford, London, and New York: Clarendon Press, 1943.

Extending over two-and-a-half millennia, the book "seeks to present, in simple form, the development of the conception of a rational and interconnected material world. It considers, therefore, both physical and biological, but not psychological, social, or abstract mathematical problems" (p.v).

Beyond the introduction, the 399-page book contains eight chapters: (1) Rise of Mental Coherence: The Foundations (about 600–400 BC), (2) The Great Adventure: Unitary Systems of Thought: Athens (400–300 BC), (3) The Failure of Nerve: Divorce of Science and Philosophy (300 BC–200 AD), (4) The Failure of Inspiration: Science the Handmaid of Practice (50 BC–400 AD), (5) The Failure of Knowledge: The Middle Ages (about 400–1400), Theology—The Queen of the Sciences, (6) The Revival of Learning: The Rise of Humanism (1250–1600), (7) The Insurgent Century (1600–1700): Downfall of Aristotle, New Attempts at Synthesis, (8) The Mechanical World: 18th–19th Century, Enthronement of Determinism (17th–19th Century).

While there are references to Arab-Islamic scholarship in much of the book, this is especially so in chapter 5 (The Failure of Knowledge). The author says,

"This millennium is divided unequally by an event of the highest importance for the history of the human intellect. From about 900 to 1200 there was a remarkable development of intellectual activity in Islam. The movement reacted with great effect on Latin Europe through works which reached it, chiefly in the twelfth and thirteenth centuries, in Latin translations from the Arabic. This intellectual event divides the medieval period in the Latin West into two parts, an earlier *Dark Age* which terminates in the twelfth century, and a later *Age of Arabian Influence* which expressed itself characteristically in Scholasticism" (p.126). There is detailed discussion of Arab-Islamic scholarship in various fields of knowledge. The next chapter discusses the rise of humanism. While this development is attributed to the Catholic rationalization of Christianity, associated with the recovery of the Aristotelian texts that took place via interpretive writings in the Islamic environment, references to Arab-Islamic scholars are somewhat muted.

Each chapter provides some footnotes in the text. The book also contains 94 figures of various scientific instruments and illustrations (list is provided at the beginning). There is a names-only index.

B-245. Teresi, Dick. *Lost Discoveries: The Ancient Roots of Modern Science— From the Babylonians to the Maya.* New York and London: Simon & Schuster, 2002.

The author considers this 453-page book as one of "unkempt historical details," in which he explores non-Western roots of science, the unheralded scientific breakthroughs from peoples of the ancient world—Babylonians, Egyptians, Indians, Africans, New World and Oceanic tribes, among others—and the medieval world of Islam. What began as an endeavor to demonstrate that "nonwhite science" was negligible, he says, his embarrassment in that endeavor was overtaken by "the pleasure of discovering mountains of unappreciated human industry, four thousand years of scientific discoveries by peoples I had been taught to disregard" (p.15). In the process, the author has created a rather neat chronicle—and a timely reminder—of how much of the foundation of modern scientific thought and technological knowledge was built by the often-overlooked contributions of Arabs, Indians, Chinese, and others.

The first chapter, A History of Science: Rediscovered, sets the tone for the book. The author traces the roots of 16th-century astronomer, Nicolaus Copernicus' system to medieval Arab-Islamic scholars such as Al-Shatir (d. 1375), Nasir al-Din Tusi (d. 1274), and others, who were not acknowledged "because Muslims were not popular in sixteenth-century Europe" (p.4). Also there is mention of Alhazen (al-Haytham, d. 1040) as the precursor of both Copernicus and Johannes Kepler (d. 1630). Further, as for the Arab-Islamic civilization: "The story goes that the Arabs kept Greek culture, and its science, alive through the Middle Ages. They acted as scribes, translators, and caretakers, with, apparently no thought of creating their own science. In fact, Islamic scholars admired and preserved Greek math and science, and served as the conduit for the science of many non-Western cultures, in addition to constructing their own impressive edifice" (p.5).

There are seven additional chapters on major fields of science: (2) Mathematics: The Language of Science, (3) Astronomy: Sky Watchers and More, (4) Cosmology: That Old-Time Religion, (5) Physics: Particles, Voids and Fields, (6) Geology: Stores of Earth Itself, (7) Chemistry: Alchemy and Beyond, (8) Technology: Machines as a Measure of Man.

Throughout, there are references not only to the ancient civilizations but also to influences from various medieval civilizations, the Arab-Islamic world in particular. Chapter-by-chapter notes and references (50-pages) are provided at the end, followed by a select bibliography, also chapter-by-chapter. There is a detailed name-subject index.

B-246. Turner, Howard R. *Science in Medieval Islam: An Illustrated Introduction.* Austin, TX: University of Texas Press, 1995.

The book is based substantially on research pursued in the course of author's work in organizing "The Heritage of Islam" exhibition, sponsored by the National Committee to Honor the Fourteenth Centennial of Islam, during 1982 and 1983. The author offers a fully illustrated, highly accessible introduction to the Golden Age of Islam (seventh through 17th centuries) when Muslim philosophers, scientists, and humanists created a unique culture that has influenced societies on every continent. This survey aspires to offer students and general readers a window into one of the world's great cultures, which, the author notes, is experiencing a remarkable resurgence as a religious, political, and social force in our own time.

The 262-page book opens with an historical overview of the spread of Islamic civilization. It describes how the passion for knowledge led the Muslims to assimilate and expand the scientific knowledge of older cultures, Greece in particular. It explores medieval Islamic accomplishments in cosmology, mathematics, astronomy, astrology, medicine, natural sciences, alchemy, and optics. Also discussed are the ways in which Muslim scientific achievements influenced the advance of science in the Western world from the Middle Ages to the modern era, something "that is less familiar to us" (p.2). Further, the author states, "Few if any of the scientific disciplines that began to be transformed in the West during the late medieval and early Renaissance centuries could have developed as they did without the clarification, renovation, and enhancement that had been achieved by Muslim scientists" (p.211).

The book contains 16 brief chapters, with 107 illustrative diagrams and figures scattered throughout. Chapter titles are: (1) Islam as Empire, (2) Forces and Bonds: Faith, Language, and Thought, (3) Roots, (4) Cosmology: The Universe of Islam, (5) Mathematics: Native Tongue of Science, (6) Astronomy, (7) Geography, (8) Geography, (9) Medicine, (10) Natural Sciences, (11) Alchemy, (12)

Optics, (13) The Later Years, (14) Transmission, (15) The New West, (16) Epilogue.

At the end there is a section entitled Islam and the World: A Summary Timeline, followed by a glossary. Also, there is a list of works consulted, topically organized, as well as a list of sources for the diagrams and figures. There is a name-subject index at the end.

(B) Islam–West Linkages

B-247. Abu-Lughod, Janet L. *Before European Hegemony: The World System A.D. 1250–1350.* New York and Oxford: Oxford University Press, 1989.

Based on the premise that "in social and cultural sciences, anomalous findings can arise from *what is in the observer*, as well as what is to be observed," the author argues that "several recent transformations in sociohistorical work have forced reformulations of prior knowledge" (p.vii). The author suggests that "the Eurocentric view of the Dark Ages was ill-conceived. If the lights went out in Europe, they were certainly still shining brightly in the Middle East" (p.ix).

The 443-page book challenges the premise that "the first world-economy ever to take shape in Europe was born between the eleventh and thirteenth centuries"; instead, "before Europe became *one* of the world-economies, there were numerous preexistent world-economies. Without them, when Europe gradually 'reached out,' it would have grasped empty space rather than riches" (p.12). Further, the author takes the position that "the century between 1250 and 1350 constituted a fulcrum or critical 'turning point' in world history and the Middle-East heartland region, linking the eastern Mediterranean with the Indian Ocean, constituted a geographical fulcrum on which West and East were then roughly balanced. The main thesis of this book is that there was no *inherent historical necessity* that shifted the system in favor of the West rather than the East" (p.12). Moreover, "In spite of the tendency of western scholars dealing with the 'Rise of the West' to stress the *unique* characteristics of western capitalism, comparative examination of economic institutions reveals enormous similarities and parallels between Asian, Arab, *and* Western forms of capitalism" (p.15).

After the introductory chapter, Studying a System in Formation, the book is divided into three parts, with three chapters in each: (1) The European Subsystem: Emergence from Old Empires (The Cities of the Champagne Fairs; Bruges and Gent: Commercial and Industrial Cities; The Merchant Mariners of Genoa and Venice); (2) The Mideast Heartland: The Three Routes to the East (The Mongols and the Northeast Passage; Sindbad's Way: Baghdad and the Persian Gulf;

Cairo's Monopoly under the Slave Sultanate); (3) Asia: The Indian Ocean System (The Indian Subcontinent: On the Way to Everywhere; The Strait and Narrow; All the Silks of China). There is a concluding chapter: Restructuring the Thirteenth-Century World System.

The discussion in each part documents numerous commercial/trade linkages across the then-known world, from the Middle East to Europe and to Asia. Another aspect of such linkages, the author argues, pertained to "the change in Europe's relationship to the East between the thirteenth and sixteenth centuries" through the absorption of knowledge and scholarship of the "Saracens," especially during the Crusades (p.21).

The book provides an extensive bibliography, organized in terms of "General and Europe," "Middle East," and "Asia." There is a comprehensive name-subject index.

B-248. Adas, Michael, ed. *Islamic and European Expansion: The Forging of a Global Order.* Philadelphia, PA: Temple University Press, 1993.

The book is "intended to provide both professional historians and interested readers with an overview of assessments of developments within a revitalized field of study," that is, comparative and global history (p.x). Unlike some leading exponents of world history, such as Oswald Spengler and Arnold Toynbee, "the great majority of the empirically-minded area specialists who dominated the historical profession" have, until recently, resisted the world-history approach (p.vii). Thus, "One of the central purposes of this collection is to make available much needed background information on the sources and methods essential for effective teaching and writing on cross-cultural history" (p.viii). And, "All of the essays are thematically oriented, and each is organized around a particular historical era, such as the age of Islamic expansion or the centuries of the industrial revolution" (p.ix). Further, "The spread of Islamic civilization, European overseas expansion, the rise and decline of the South Atlantic slave trade, industrialization and the completion of Europe's drive for global hegemony, all have key European (or North American) components. But each of these processes has been grounded in the historical experiences of non-Western societies" (p.x). The book includes essays that "explore key themes in the spread of Islamic civilization, which was the first to bring together the continents of the 'Old World' ecumene—Africa, Asia, and Europe," including a few that examine "the reasons for the rise of western Europe as the civilization that would supplant Islam as the mediator of the process of global unification" (p.xi).

Beyond the editor's introduction, the 380-page book contains ten essays written by prominent scholars: (1) Islamic History as Global History by Richard M. Eaton, (2) Gender and Islamic History by Judith Tucker, (3) The World System in the Thirteenth Century: Dead-End or Precursor? by Janet Lippman Abu-Lughod, (4) The Age of Gunpowder Empires, 1450–1800 by William H. McNeil, (5) The Columbian Voyages, the Columbian Exchange, and Their Historians by

Alfred W. Crosby, (6) The Tropical Atlantic in the Age of the Slave Trade by Philip D. Curtin, (7) Interpreting the Industrial Revolution by Peter N. Stearns, (8) Industrialization and Gender Inequality by Louise A. Tilly, (9) "High" Imperialism and the "New" History by Michael Adas, (10) Gender, Sex, and Empire by Margaret Strobel.

Notes and references, as well as a separate bibliography, are provided at the end of each essay. Each contributor's background is briefly sketched at the end of the book; however, there is no index.

B-249. Agius, Dionisius and Richard Hitchcock, eds. *The Arab Influence in Medieval Europe: Folia Scholastica Mediterranea.* Reading, UK: Ithaca Press, 1994.

The book represents a collection of papers presented at a 1990 Oxford University conference of the same title at the University of Oxford in April 1990. The underlying theme relates to the interactions between the Arabs and Europe during the medieval period. The region covered extends beyond the Iberian Peninsula, although, the editors suggest, Al-Andalus had a major role in the transmission of knowledge. "There was vigorous literary and cultural impact in both Sicily and Italy, and in scientific disciplines Arabic knowledge was widely disseminated, and permeated European monasteries as early as the tenth century" (p.vii).

The 181-page book includes seven papers, each written by a well-known medievalist: (1) The Role of Trade in Muslim: Christian Contact during the Middle Ages by David Abulafia, (2) Arabic Fine Technology and Its Influence on European Mechanical Engineering by Donald R. Hill, (3) The Influence of the Metalwork of the Arab Mediterranean on That of Medieval Europe by James W. Allan, (4) Muslim Sources of Dante? by Phillip F. Kennedy, (5) Christian–Muslim Frontier in Al-Andalus: Idea and Reality by Eduardo Manzano Moreno, (6) An Islamic Divinatory Technique in Medieval Spain by Charles Burnett, (7) Boys, Women and Drunkards: Hispano-Mauresque Influences on European Song? by David Wulsan.

Each essay has footnotes and references listed at the end, and there is a detailed name-subject index.

B-250. Ahmad, Ziauddin. *Influence of Islam on World Civilization.* Delhi, India: Adam Publishers and Distributors, 1996.

The book documents the development of knowledge in various areas (medicine and surgery, mathematics, chemistry, geology, geography, political science, philosophy, mechanical devices, music, literature, etc.) as it evolved in the early Islamic civilization. Further, it discusses three intellectual streams that helped to bring the West out of the Dark Ages: the scientific method, a rationalistic view of life and the universe, and the introduction of humanistic literature. These influences penetrated Europe through Sicily and Spain primarily; European scholars—Pope Sylvester II (1000 AD) being the most important among them—

gathered into the Spanish Arab universities of Cordova and Granada and translated and assimilated Arab knowledge.

The book shows how Europe's eminent scholars were influenced by Arabic
literature. "Only when Islamic learning spread through the universities of Spain
and Sicilian Arab scholars began to adorn Christian courts of Italy did the darkness begin to decrease" (p.xi). Further, "Hitherto the average Western generally
recognizes only the Judeo-Christian tradition and Greece and Rome as his bene-
factor; he must give a place to the achievements of Islam as well in his intellectual
pantheon. This will be a potent instrument in breaking down hostility and erect-
ing tolerance between neighbors who have so much in common without realizing
it" (p.xii).

The 300-page book has 31 short chapters. Some select titles are: channels
through which influence spread; Islam's influence on political thinkers (Francois
Rousseau, John Locke, Thomas Hobbes, Immanuel Kant, Montesquieu, and others); Ibn Khaldun's influence on John Dewey; influence on English literature
(Hawthorne, Shakespeare, Shelley, Carlyle, Longfellow, Emerson, and others);
science of Arabic numerals; medicine and surgery; science of chemistry; science
of geology; science of geography; inventions and mechanical devices; economic
and social influence; development of agriculture; women's contributions; new
horizons of science and learning; decline of Muslim ascendancy.

Footnotes and references are integrated within each chapter. There is a detailed
bibliography, followed by a name-subject index.

B-251. Allison, Robert J. *The Crescent Obscured: The United States and the
Muslim World, 1776–1815.* New York: Oxford University Press, 1995.

The context of the book is the war that the United States fought with the "Barbary pirates" in the early 1800s, as well as other similar episodes (including the
1979 hostage crisis with Iran), which were "more than a struggle for trade routes
or territory" (p.xv). Further, viewed as a contest between the "newly civilized
world" and "barbarism," the "Americans inherited this understanding of the
Muslim world and pursued this enemy more relentlessly than the Europeans had
done" (p.xv). Thus, the Muslim world, presented as the consummate "Other,"
was a lesson for Americans in what not to do, in how not to construct a state,
encourage commerce, or form families" (p.xvii). However, there were contradictions. The image Americans had of Islam and themselves, argues the author, was
divorced from reality. While Americans felt outraged when some citizens were
enslaved by the Barbary states, they were oblivious to the plight of African slaves
in the United States. Thus, the author exposes such gaps between Americans'
rhetoric of ideals and interests-induced action.

The 255-page book contains nine chapters: (1) American Policy Toward the
Muslim World, (2) The United States and the Specter of Islam, (3) A Peek into
the Seraglio: Americans, Sex, and the Muslim World, (4) American Slavery and
the Muslim World, (5) American Captives in the Muslim World, (6) The Muslim

World and American Benevolence, (7) American Consuls in the Muslim World, (8) Remembering the Tripolitan War, (9) James Riley, the Return of the Captive. It may be noted that for the novice, the book can serve as an endorsement of the "clash of civilization" theme, but for the perceptive scholar, it represents a compelling reading that also highlights the superficial nature of current perceptions in the West of Islam and Muslims.

Chapter-by-chapter notes and references are provided at the end, followed by a name-subject index.

B-252. Amin, Samir. *Eurocentrism* (translated from French by Russell Moore). New York: Monthly Review Press, 1989.

This provocative book is a critique of Eurocentrism, a cultural phenomenon that assumes "the existence of irreducibly distinct cultural invariants that shape the historical paths of different peoples. Eurocentrism is therefore anti-universalist, since it is not interested in seeking possible general laws of human evolution. But it does present itself as universalist, for it claims that imitation of the Western model is the only solution to the challenges of our time" (p.vii).

After discussing the notion that precapitalist Europe was part of a broader "peripheral tributary" ideological construct, the author analyzes the "ambiguities" of the new capitalist culture developed from the Renaissance onward and this culture has created a need for universalism that need not be shared by all; that is, "Imitate the West, the best of all possible worlds" (p.xii). He discusses the nature of existing capitalism and questions its universal desirability.

The book has two parts. Part I, Central and Peripheral Tributary Cultures, has two chapters; the longer, more substantive Part II, The Culture of Capitalism, has five chapters.

Chapter 1 (The Formation of Tributary Ideology on the Mediterranean Region) of Part I is especially interesting. Here the author discusses in some detail the evolution of rational thought in early Islam, particularly with Ibn Rushd (1126–1198), who "produced a synthesis of Islamic metaphysics in the course of his polemic against the adversaries of reason, a *summa* that was later taken up almost intact by Christian scholasticism in the West" (p.44). Moreover, this "incipient 'Protestant Reformation' in Islam" did not emerge; Ibn Rushd was condemned by Muslims and, later, by the Christian heirs of his scholasticism. However, the author argues, "Western medieval scholasticism takes shape beginning in the twelfth century, not by chance in regions in contact with the Islamic world: Arab Andalusia and the Sicily of Frederick II" (p.56).

Further, it is argued that "the myth of Greek ancestry [of the culture of capitalism] performs an essential function in the Eurocentric construct. In this myth, the author argues, Greece was the mother of rational philosophy, while the 'Orient' never succeeded in going beyond metaphysics" (p.90–91). Further, "Arab-Islamic philosophy is treated in this account as if it had no other function than to transmit the Greek heritage to the Renaissance world. Moreover, Islam, in this dominant vision, could not have gone beyond the Hellenic heritage; even if it had attempted to do so, it would have failed badly" (p.91).

The book provides some footnotes and references in the text. There is no index.

B-253. Arnold, Sir Thomas and Alfred Guillaume, eds. *The Legacy of Islam.* Oxford: Clarendon Press, 1931.

This 416-page classic is a companion volume to *The Legacy of Greece, The Legacy of Rome, The Legacy of the Middle Ages,* and *The Legacy of Israel.* It seeks to give an account of "those elements in the culture of Europe which are derived from the Islamic world" and, further, the editors state, "it was under the protection and patronage of the Islamic Empire that the arts and sciences which this book describes flourished" (p.v).

Accompanied by numerous illustrations, the book is comprised of 13 essays by some of the most eminent scholars of the era: (1) Spain and Portugal by J.B. Trend, (2) The Crusades by Ernest Barker, (3) Geography and Commerce by J.H. Kramers, (4) Islamic Minor Arts and Their Influence upon European Work by A.H. Christie, (5) Islamic Art and Its Influence on Painting in Europe by Sir Thomas Arnold, (6) Architecture by Martin S. Briggs, (7) Literature by H.A.R. Gibb, (8) Mysticism by R.A. Nicholson, (9) Philosophy and Theology by Alfred Guillaume, (10) Law and Society by David de Santillana, (11) Science and Medicine by Max Meyerhof, (12) Music by H.G. Farmer, (13) Astronomy and Mathematics by Baron Carra de Vaux.

There are detailed notes and bibliographic references within each chapter, and the book provides a comprehensive name-subject index.

B-254. Ascher, Abraham, Tibor Halasi-Kun, and Bela K. Kiraly, eds. *The Mutual Effects of the Islamic and Judeo-Christian Worlds: The East European Pattern.* Brooklyn, NY: Brooklyn College Press, 1979.

This 230-page book is the result of a conference at Brooklyn College, held in May 1976, whose aim is evident from the title. The focus is on the cultural interchange that took place during the early modern period of European history. Among the 12 articles included, all but one concentrate on the Turkish component of the Islamic world, "the only segment that was directly in contact with, and played a major role in the history, in the development of the area under consideration. And even further, nine of the twelve articles deal with Ottoman problems, while two refer to the modern Islamized remnants of the Kipchak Turkic Golden Horde" (p.xi). These papers clearly underline the paramount importance of Ottoman source materials in the evolution of East–West relations.

The book is divided into five parts: Part I—Early Cultural Interactions—The Role of the Bosphorus Kingdom and Late Hellenism as the Basis for the Medieval Cultures of the Territories North of the Black Sea by Omeljan Pritsak; Part II—Communal and National Relations—(1) Servile Labor in the Ottoman

Empire by Halil Inalcik, (2) The Protestant Reformation and Islam by Stephen Fischer-Galati, (3) Western Nationalism and the Ottoman Empire by Dankwart A. Rustow; Part III—The Slavic World and Islam—(1) Social and Legal Aspects of Russian-Muslim Relations in the Nineteenth Century: The Case of the Crimean Tartars by Alan W. Fisher, (2) State and Society in Muscovite Russia and the Mongol-Turkic System in the Sixteenth Century by Jaroslaw Pelenski; Part IV—Danubian Europe and the Ottoman Empire—(1) Serbians and Rumanians in Ottoman Southeastern Hungary: *Detta* by Tibor Halasi-Kun, (2) The Sublime Porte and Ferenc II Rakoczi's Hungary: An Episode in Islamic-Christian Relations by Bela K. Kiraly and Peter Pastor, (3) Muslim, Christians, and Jews in Sixteenth Century Ottoman Belgrade by Allan Z. Hertz; Part V—Mutual Cultural Impacts—(1) The European Influence on Ottoman Architecture by Ulku U. Bates, (2) The Oguz Turkic (Ottoman/Safavid) Elements in Georgian: Background and Patterns by Peter B. Golden, (3) Living Legacy of the Ottoman Empire: The Serbo-Croatian Speaking Moslems of Bosnia-Hercegovina by William G. Lockwood.

Each article contains notes and references at the end. There is no index.

B-255. Asin-Palacios, Miguel. *Islam and the Divine Comedy* (translated and abridged from Spanish by Harold Sunderland). London: John Murray, 1926.

Written by a Catholic priest and a scholar of Arabic at the University of Madrid, this book—written in 1926—challenges the origins of Dante Aligheri's classic. The author argues that Dante received his basic idea for the plot and some of the particulars from the Islamic tradition known as *mir'aaj*, the Prophet Mohammad's descent to hell and ascent to heaven, as documented in the writings of Al-Andalusian, Ibn Al-Arabi (1164–1240). This Muslim tradition is a prototype of Dante's conception, the author suggests. He argues, "A methodical comparison of the general outlines of the Moslem legend with those of the great poem confirmed my impression and finally quite convinced me" (p.xiii). Further, he insists that nothing similar to the features found in *Divine Comedy* appears in Christian legends; thus, "the Moslem element thenceforth appeared as a key" (p.xiv). The author states that he has "sufficiently proved" that "the Moslem models of the *Divine Comedy* may easily have reached Italy and the Florentine poet from Moslem sources" (p.256).

Moreover, the author argues that Dante felt considerable "attraction towards Arabic culture," which also confirms the "imitation hypothesis," for the Muslim culture "at the time was all-pervading. It is inconceivable that he should not have felt the attraction of a science that drew men of learning from all parts of Christian Europe" (p.256–257). The book's key thesis generated considerable controversy, even rejection, among Dante scholars, despite the author's hope that "the greater equanimity of the modern school of Danto-philes will not be moved to ire by the suggestion of Moslem influences in the *Divine Comedy*" (p.xv).

The last part of the book (with five chapters) is primarily devoted to the transmission of Islamic knowledge to Christian Europe and particularly to Dante.

There is a bibliographic section at the end, with a listing of Arabic, Spanish, and English-language literature. Also, there is a combined author-subject index.

B-256. Bammate, Haidar. *Muslim Contribution to Civilization.* Takoma Park, MD: Crescent Publications, 1962.

This brief monograph, written by a French scholar, documents the "fact that Muslims contributed to civilization so expandedly in every walk of life" and how this fact "is the solemn answer of history to the much perpetuated criticism of passivity and fatalism against Islam" (p.ii).

The monograph begins with six brief sections: (1) The Origins of Muslim Civilization, (2) Development of Muslim Civilization, (3) The Golden Age of Muslim Civilization, (4) The Baghdad School, (5) How Did Islamic Civilization Penetrate the West?, (6) Normal Routes of Islamic Penetration. Then follow brief narratives, with appropriate authentication, on "Islamic contributions" in various fields. The subjects covered (about 2–3 pages each) are Astronomy, Mathematics, Physics, Chemistry, Natural Sciences, Medicine, Philosophy, Literature, Geography and History, Political Sciences and Sociology, Architecture and Plastic Arts, and Music.

The author suggests that the influence of the Islamic world during the Crusades must first "distinguish between intellectual and moral culture on the one hand and purely material civilization on the other" (p.13). This distinction aroused "Christianity against Islam in an implacable struggle, [and] by breeding an atmosphere of intolerance and hatred, it created a deep gulf between West and East" (p.13). While the record of the Crusades on the spiritual side is "sad," the West "owes much to the Crusades in the material civilization" (p.13). The author adds, however, that "Muslim science, philosophy, literature and art were known in the West well before the Crusades" (p.15). Also, a 19th-century French scholar is quoted, in that "it may well be that the work of Muslim scholars contributed to the discovery of America. In a letter written from Haiti and dated October 1498, Christopher Columbus names Avcentuez (Averroes; Ibn Rushd, 1126–1198) as one of the authors who led him to guess at the existence of the New World" (p.46).

Notes and references are integrated with the text. There is no index.

B-257. Beckingham, C.F. *Between Islam and Christendom: Travellers, Facts and Legends in the Middle Ages and the Renaissance.* London: Variorum Reprints, 1983.

The 326-page book is a collection of papers published by the author. They are "concerned with the history of travel, some rather with European knowledge of, or illusions about, Islam; two of them illustrate relations between the Muslim and Christian communities in Cyprus where British colonial administration preserved until the middle of this century the plural structure of society characteristic of the great Islamic empires and of the Ottoman in particular" (p.i). Further, the author says, "It is by no means unusual to picture the medieval West as having virtually no accurate knowledge about Asia beyond the small area temporarily subdued by the Crusaders. Even in the notorious book of Sir John Mandeville there is a great deal, which though distorted has been derived from reputable sources. What was difficult for the cosmographer was to find a criterion by which he could distinguish what was trustworthy from what was mythical" (p.i). Throughout these papers the author is documenting, among other things, the "legends" about the Islamic world generated over centuries by European travelers.

The book includes 25 papers; each is published as it appeared in the source of publication or presentation, with original pagination, notes, references, etc., and for each the original source is identified. (1) The Achievements of Prestor John, (2) The Quest for Prestor John, (3) Misconceptions of Islam: Medieval and Modern, (4) Arabic Texts and the Hakluyt Society, (5) Ibn Hauqal's Map of Italy, (6) The Pilgrimage and Death of Sakura, King of Mali, (7) In Search of Ibn Battuta, (8) Ibn Battuta in Sind, (9) The Travels of Pero da Covilha and Their Significance, (10) Some Early European Travellers in Arabia, (11) Some Early Travels in Arabia, (12) Francisco Alverez and His Book on Ethiopia, (13) Notes on an Unpublished Manuscript of Francisco Alverez: *Verdadera Informacam das Terras do Preste Joam das Indias*, (14) Amba Gesen and Asirgarh, (15) A Note on the Topography of Ahmad Grans Campaigns in 1542, (16) Pantaleao de Aveiro and the Ethiopian Community in Jerusalem, (17) The *Itinerario* of Fr. Pantaleao de Aveiro, (18) The Turks of Cyprus, (19) A Cypriot *Wakfiyya*, (20) Hakluyt's Use of the Materials Available to Him—The Near East: North and Northeast Africa, (21) Hakluyt's Description of the *Hajj*, (22) Dutch Travellers in Arabia in the Seventeenth Century, (23) The Travels of Jeronimo Lobo, (24) Jeronimo Lobo: His Travels and His Book, (25) The Date of Pitt's Pilgrimage to Mecca.

There is an index primarily of names, with each entry identified by the article number in the table of contents and the relevant page number in that article.

B-258. Blanks, David, ed. *Images of the Other: Europe and the Muslim World Before 1700*. Cairo Papers in Social Sciences, Volume 19, Monograph 2, Summer 1996. Cairo, Egypt: University of Cairo Press, 1997.

The essays in this 140-page book represent an attempt to "re-evaluate relations between Europe and the Muslim world before 1700" (p.3). Unlike the more recent "superior West/inferior East" phenomena, the situation in the Middle Ages was reversed; "The Medieval European authors were aware of their cultural debt to the Muslim world, but they were also intimidated" (p.3). With no "hidden agenda," the editor states, the approach of the essays is "interdisciplinary, drawing from sociology, anthropology, and political science as well as history and literature" (p.3). The contributors were asked to consider past attitudes, in part, because it was felt that this would shed light on the origins of contemporary stereotypes and biases.

The essays are grouped into three categories: (1) Western images of Islamic culture, (2) Muslim images of Europe, (3) the Arabs and the Byzantines. The editor argues that while cultural differences are a fact of life, "Western attitudes of racism are the result of a long-held inferiority complex vis-à-vis the East; whereas eastern fears of assimilation are primarily the result of a long-held sense of cultural superiority" (p.6).

Following the editor's introduction, there are eight chapters, grouped in the aforementioned three categories: (1) Mirror of Chivalry: Salah Al-Din in the Medieval European Imagination by John Victor Tolan, (2) Renaissance England and the Turban by Nabil I. Matar, (3) Cervantes and Islam: Attitudes Towards Islam and Islamic Culture in *Don Quixote* by John Rodenbeck, (4) Arab Views of Northern Europeans in Medieval History and Geography by Thabit Abdullah (5) Medieval Muslim–European Relations: Islamic Juristic Theory and Chancery Practice by E.M. Sartain, (6) The Religious Other: Christian Images in Sufi Poetry by Omaima Abou-Bakr, (7) Byzantium and the Muslim World by David R. Blanks, (8) An Ambivalent Image: Byzantium Viewed by the Arabs by Nadia M. El-Cheik.

Notes and references are integrated in the text of each essay. There is no index.

B-259. Bosworth, C. Edmund, ed. *A Century of British Orientalists 1902–2001.* Published for The British Academy. Oxford: Oxford University Press, 2001.

The book commemorates some of the prominent British orientalists of the 20th century. "Oriental studies" at the British Academy have included "all regions between Egypt and North Africa and the Levant, and South-east Asia, China, and Japan, and covering chronologically the period of the ancient Near-Eastern civilizations until the present day" (p.2). However, for much of the medieval period and up to the 18th century, the primary focus has pertained to the Near and Middle East; that is, the Islamic world. Further, the editor suggests, since religious passions in Europe have given way to the calmer atmosphere of the Enlightenment, "this study could be undertaken in a more dispassionate fashion and in what we would now consider a more scholarly one" (p.2).

Bosworth suggests that these orientalists would dispute the "Orientalism" thesis of the late Edward Said, the thesis being that "the outsider (in this case, the European) can never enter, with sympathy and understanding, into a religious ethos and a cultural environment alien to his or her own, and that any attempts at understanding will be ineluctably vitiated by the hostility and misconceptions nurtured by past centuries of political and military clashes and of imperialist 'exploitation'" (p.4).

The essays, written by well-known scholars (names in parenthesis), cover 13 British orientalists: (1) Harold Walter Bailey, 1899–1996 (Ronald Emmerick), (2) Alfred Felix Landon Beeston, 1911–1955 (Edward Ullendorff), (3) Edward

Granville Browne, 1862–1926 (C. Edmund Bosworth), (4) Gerard Leslie Makins Clauson, 1891–1974 (C. Edmund Bosworth), (5) Godfrey Rolles Driver, 1892–1975 (J.A. Emerton), (6) Samuel Rolles Driver, 1846–1914 (J.A. Emerton), (7) Alan Henderson Gardiner, 1879–1963 (J. Cerny), (8) Hamilton Alexander Rosskeen Gibb, 1895–1971 (Albert Hourani), (9) Francis Llewellyn Griffith, 1862–1934 (J.D. Ray), (10) Vladimir Fed'orovich Minorsky, 1877–1966 (C. Edmund Bosworth), (11) Ralph Lilley Turner, 1888–1983 (R.H. Robins and others), (12) Arthur David Waley, 1889–1966 (Jonathan D. Spence), (13) Richard Olaf Winstedt, 1878–1966 (John Bastin).

Each essay provides its own notes, bibliographic and others. There is a name-subject index at the end.

B-260. Bulliet, Richard W. *The Case for Islamo–Christian Civilization*. New York: Columbia University Press, 2004.

This thought-provoking, post-9/11 book is a most timely narrative, written by an eminent scholar of Middle-Eastern/Islamic studies, not as "a scholarly book in the purest sense," but with "different perspectives" that "will appeal not just to specialists but to many different audiences" (p.vii). Further, "The four chapters it contains do not add up to a continuous historical exposition, but they all contribute to the idea that the title of the book is intended to evoke: Despite the enmity that has often divided them, Islam and the West have common roots and share much of their history. Their confrontation today arises not from essential differences, but from a long and wilful determination to deny their kinship" (p.vii).

The titles of the four chapters in the 185-page book are: (1) The Case for Islamo–Christian Civilization, (2) What Went Wrong?, (3) Looking for Love in All the Wrong Places, (4) The Edge of the Future. The content of these chapters is provocative and most instructive.

The author argues, among other things, that the Huntington's "Clash of Civilizations" theme "pronounces against Islam the same, self-righteous and unequivocal sentence of 'otherness' that American Protestants once visited Catholics and Jews" (p.5). Further, "Neither the Muslim nor the Christian historical path can be fully understood without relation to the other" (p.10). And, "'Islamo–Christian civilization' involves different historical and geographical roots and has different implications for our contemporary civilization anxieties" (p.10). But, "We are heirs to a Christian construction of history that is deliberately exclusive" (p.14). However, "Looked at as a whole, and in historical perspective, the Islamo–Christian world has much more binding it together than forcing it apart. The past and future of the West cannot be fully comprehended without appreciation of the twinned relationship it has had with Islam over some fourteen centuries. The same is true of the Islamic world" (p.45). The author calls for a fundamental restructuring of Western thinking about relations with Islam and calls for a fresh look at history; and to facilitate this restructuring, "the voices that will enunciate the pivotal ideas for the next great phase of Islamic history have not been heard yet," but they are rapidly emerging (p.138).

Chapter-by-chapter notes and references are provided at the end, followed by a bibliography of works cited. There is a name-subject index.

B-261. Burke, James. *Connections.* Toronto, Boston, and London: Little, Brown and Company, 1978.

The book's objective "is to acquaint the reader with some of the forces that have caused change in the past," because "each one of these is part of a family of similar devices, and is the result of a sequence of closely connected events extending from the ancient world until the present day" (p.vii). The book is an exploration of the ideas, inventions, and "coincidental" developments that have culminated in the major technological achievements of our world.

The 300-page book, written in a simple, lucid style for the educated reader, has ten chapters: (1) The Trigger Effect, (2) The Road from Alexandria, (3) Distant Voices, (4) Faith in Numbers, (5) The Wheel of Fortune, (6) Fuel to the Fame, (7) The Long Chain, (8) Eat, Drink, and Be Merry, (9) Lighting the Way, (10) Inventing the Future. There are numerous illustrative pictures and sketches in almost every chapter.

There are references to links with the East in earlier chapters ("luxuries from the East," various types of textiles and looms ["somebody arrived in Europe, probably from Muslim Spain, with a new kind of loom," p.93], introduction of paper, etc.). However, the intellectual connections between the Arab-Islamic civilization and developments in Latin Europe during the early medieval centuries, especially the 12th century, are much more vivid in the chapter entitled The Wheel of Fortune. The author traces the evolution of the modern computer to such areas of knowledge as mathematics, astronomy, and astrology. Further, with the absorption of Greek heritage, knowledge of astronomy was developed further, and the eighth-century Caliph Al-Mansur had an Indian scholar in his Baghdad court who "claimed to be able to calculate the movement of the stars and predict eclipses" (p.118). And, "The great Arab astronomers brought a sophisticated mixture of Greek and Indian science to the medieval West. To them we owe our system of numbers and the use of the decimal in calculation" (p.115). And there is the author's "wheel of fortune" metaphor: "As the Earth turned, it appeared that the planets and the constellations moved through each of the twelve houses [twelve sections of the sky] in turn, and since each star or planet had significance for almost anything the astrologers could dream up, its influence on a man would depend on whatever house it was passing through at certain critical moments in his life" (p.120).

"As the Arabs moved West, across North Africa and into Spain, they took their knowledge with them," the author notes; the "news of this vast fund of information spread to Europe, and as the continent recovered from the anarchy and confusion of the previous five hundred years," European scholars, beginning mainly with Gerbert in 940 who later became Pope Sylvester II, landed in Spain to absorb that knowledge (p.122). There were also other prominent names—"the early twelfth-century Englishman, Adelard of Bath, and a German, Herman of Carinthia, [who] both made trips to Muslim-held countries and brought back translations of Arab science and philosophy. But the event that must have done more for the intellectual and scientific revival of Europe was the fall of Toledo in Spain to the Christians in 1105. The Spanish libraries were opened, revealing a store of classics and Arab works that staggered the Christian Europeans" (p.123). The rest of the chapter offers similar additional observations.

There is a chapter-by-chapter list of further readings at the end, followed by a name-subject index.

B-262. Burke, James. *The Day the Universe Changed*. Toronto, Boston, and London: Little, Brown and Company, 1985.

The book, written for the curious, well-informed readers, is about change and evolution of social history. The author says, "At any time in the past people have held a view of the way the universe works which was for them similarly definitive, whether it was based on myths or research. And at any time, that view they held was sooner or later altered by changes in the body of knowledge" (p.10). The book explores some of those moments of change, "in order to show how the changes of view also generated major institutions or ways of thought which have since survived to become basic elements of modern life" (p.10).

The 360-page book contains ten chapters: (1) The Way We Were, (2) In the Light of the Above, (3) Point of View, (4) Matter of Fact, (5) Infinitely Reasonable, (6) Credit Where It's Due, (7) What the Doctor Ordered, (8) Fit to Rule, (9) Making Waves, (10) Worlds Without End. The last chapter raises some profound questions: "If all research is theory-laden, contextually determined, is knowledge merely what we decide it should be? Is the universe what we discover it is, or what we say it is? If knowledge is an artefact, will we go on inventing it, endlessly? And if so, is there no truth to seek?" (p.10).

There are references to links with the early Arab-Islamic civilization throughout the book, but especially in the first few chapters. In describing Islamic Spain, the author notes, "This rich and sophisticated society took a tolerant view of other faiths. Thousands of Jews and Christians lived in peace and harmony with their Muslim overlords" (p.39). "To the early medieval mind, the universe of Augustine was static and unchanging. The world had been made for the edification of man in order to bring him closer to God. It had no other purpose" (p.30). Further, the medieval mind "lacked a system for investigation, a tool with which to ask questions and, above all, they lacked the knowledge once possessed by the Greeks" (p.36). Then, "In one electrifying moment it was rediscovered. In 1085 the Arab citadel of Toledo in Spain fell, and the victorious Christians troops found a literary treasure beyond anything they could have dreamed of" (p.36). Further, "The intellectual plunder of Toledo brought the scholars of northern

Europe like moths to a candle" (p.40). And, "The scholars came in a steady flood. Some stayed, some translated the text they were looking for and returned to the north. All of them were amazed by the culture they found" (p.41). Thus, Adelard of Bath, having "acquired rationalism and the secular, investigative approach typical of Arab natural science," implored his contemporaries to abandon "the blind respect for all past authority that he had left in Latin Europe" (p.41). There are numerous similar observations in the book, including references to assimilation of Arab-Islamic material culture, living styles, business practices (including double-entry accounting system [p.61]), and so forth.

Throughout there are numerous pictures and illustrations. There is a chapter-by-chapter bibliography at the end, followed by a name-subject index.

B-263. Burnett, Charles. *The Introduction of Arabic Learning into England: The Panizzi Lectures 1996.* London: The British Library, 1997.

This short book is an *introduction*, the author stresses, of Arabic learning into England, specifically the late "medieval translations of Arabic philosophical texts into Latin by Hermann the German" (p.vii). And the reference is to England in its larger geographic boundaries, "the society of the British Isles in the eleventh to thirteenth centuries which was characterized by several languages and several cultures—among which Arabic should be included" (p.viii). Further, the author places emphasis "on the enjoyable side of this learning as manifest in the playful anecdotes of masters and pupils, and the verses and jingles in which the learning was couched" (p.viii). Three Latin scholars—Welsh Marches, Adelard of Bath, and Waltham Abbey—figure quite prominently in the book. Beginning with noting the "opulence" of tenth-century Cordoba, the author states that this city "outstripped any city in the Latin West, and the contrast between the scientific cultures of al-Andalus and Latin Christendom was just as extreme" (p.3). In his epilogue, Burnett stresses, "I hope I have demonstrated how pervasive the presence of Arabic learning was in medieval England" (p.81).

The 110-page book contains three lectures: (1) The Books of King Harold, (2) The Education of Henry II, (3) The Beginnings of Oxford University. There is an epilogue, followed by the appendix "Didactic Rhymes and Jingles."

For the three lectures combined, notes and references are provided at the end. There is also a name-subject index.

B-264. Campbell, Donald. *Arabian Medicine and Its Influence on the Middle Ages*, Volumes I and II. London: Kegan Paul, Trench, Trubner and Company, 1926.

The two volumes (each about 220 pages) are about "the history of the development of Arabian Medicine which reached its maturity in the ninth century, and its subsequent dominant position in Europe long after the Western or Cordovan Caliphate had ceased to exist" (p.xiii). Medieval Medicine was "but a modification of Arabian Medicine," which in turn relied on Greek texts. The author states that, the "great interest of Arabian Medicine and Science centres on the fact that while Europe was in its Dark Age, the Caliphs of Baghdad and Cordova endowed and fostered education among their subjects (Mohomedan and 'unbeliever') to the extent that in the latter city, which enjoyed a 'golden age' analogous to that of Ancient Greece, every boy and girl of twelve was able to read and write, and this at a time when the barons and ladies of Christendom were scarcely able to write their names" (p.xiii–xiv). Further, "The Arabians raised the dignity of the medical profession from that of a menial calling to the rank of one of the learned professions" (p.xiv).

The main coverage of the subject is in the first volume. There are 12 chapters: (1) Greek Medicine in Its Relation to the Arabians, (2) Arabian Manuscripts, (3) The Historiography of Islam, with Reference to the Development of Arabic Medical and Philosophical Literature, (4) Arabic Medical Writers and Their Works (Eastern Caliphate), (5) Arabic Medical Writers and Their Works (Western Caliphate), (6) The Age of Early Arabian Rumors in the West, (7) The Tide of Arabism in the Intellectual Currents of Medieval Europe, (8) The Latin Translators and the College at Toledo, (9) The Transmutors and the Arabist Dominancy in Latin Europe, (10) The Experimenters and the Effect of Their Work on Arabist Tradition in Europe, (11) Hellenism and Arabism in the Fifteenth and Sixteenth Century, (12) A Review of European Literature and the Medical Curricula of European Universities in the Later Middle Ages. This volume provides footnotes and references in the text of each chapter.

The second volume has two appendices: Latin Translators of the Arabic Work and An Investigation of the Date and Authorship of the Latin Versions of the Works of Galen. This volume also provides a bibliography, organized in terms of the various themes of the book. There is an index, chiefly consisting of historic names and authors cited in the first volume.

B-265. Cardini, Franco. *Europe and Islam* (translated from Italian by Caroline Beamish). Oxford: Blackwell Publishers, 2001.

The purpose of the book is to trace the development of the interactions between Europe and Islam. The period covered is early medieval centuries to the 1990s. The explorations relate to the historical processes, including the "ideas, prejudices, disinformation and anti-information that have formed and coloured Europe's attitude towards Islam" (p.ix).

The book relates primarily to the Mediterranean Islam, for here Europe came into contact with Islam over a long period. As with Christianity, the author suggests, there are varieties of Islam; and "the traditions and historical/philological culture of Southern Europe have been affected solely, or almost solely, by the Islam of Turkey, the Middle East and North Africa, whose versions of the religion are closely related to one another" (p.ix). However, from the 18th to 19th centuries onwards, contacts ranged from the Middle East and Central Asia for Poland and Russia, to India and the Far East for England, Portugal, and Holland.

The book contains 12 chapters: (1) A Prophet and Three Continents, (2) Between Two Millennia, (3) Europe's Response: The *Reconquista* and Naval Exploits, (4) The Role of the Holy City, (5) Conflict and Encounters in the Twelfth and Thirteenth Centuries, (6) The Treasure of the Pharaoh, (7) The Lords of Fear, (8) *'Inimicus crucis, inimucus Europae'*: The Ottoman Threat, (9) Renaissance Europe and the Turks, (10) Sultans, Pirates and Renegades, (11) The Age of Iron and the Enlightenment, (12) From the "Sickness" of the Ottoman Empire to the Third Wave of Islam.

Three chapters particularly focus on Islam–Europe interactions; these are chapters 5 (Conflict and Encounters in the Twelfth and Thirteenth Centuries), chapter 6 (The Treasure of the Pharoah), and chapter 7 (The Lords of Fear). As for the accumulated intellectual reservoir in Spain and elsewhere, "by mid-twelfth century it was beginning to be realized that such treasures were worth acquiring" (p.86). Based on an Old Testament dictum, "it was argued 'Let us therefore rob the pagan philosophers of their wisdom and their eloquence as the Lord commands and with His help; let us rob these infidels and enrich our own faith with the spoils.' 'Philosophers' was the name given by Latin scholars to the Arabs who, to the *illiterati*, were simply 'pagans' and 'infidels'" (p.86–87). Further, "Tradition has it that when St. Albert the Great arrived in Paris [from Spain] in 1245 he was wearing Arab dress. By now the Muslims were 'philosophers' rather than 'pagans'" (p.101).

At the end, the book provides a chronology of Islam–Europe interactions, from 622 to 1996 (for the year 1996: "In Afghanistan, the integralist movement known as the Taliban seizes power" [p.224]). There is a brief bibliography, followed by a name-subject index.

B-266. Chew, Samuel C. *The Crescent and the Rose: Islam and England during the Renaissance.* New York: Octagon Books, Inc., 1965; original 1937.

This 580-page book is about the "anxious thought of the Elizabethan travellers," exploring the "exotic" in the Near and Middle East, "even when their interests were fixed, to the exclusion of the immediate present, upon classical or biblical associations or upon the marvels of the Orient." The period covered (though "occasionally transcended") is from the downfall of the Byzantine Empire (1453) to 1642 ("the downfall of the older English drama")—the period of the English Renaissance. "The point of view is that of a student of English literature, and the focus of the inquiry is upon London, not Stamboul or Baghdad or Isfahan" (p.vii). The book is a critical narrative of the origins/creation of "Oriental" literature and anticipates works such as the late Edward Said's seminal book, *Orientalism* (1979) and Norman Daniel's *The Arabs and the Medieval West: The Making of an Image* (1975).

There are 12 chapters. A listing of the titles provides a flavor of the book: (1) Tales and Tale-Bearers, (2) The Classical and the Biblical Past, (3) "The Present Terror of the World," (4) "The Great Turk," (5) The Sophy and the Shi'a, (6) "A

Great Plotter and Projector in Matters of State," (7) "The Greatest Traveller in His Time," (8) "The Throne of Piracy," (9) The Prophet and His Book, (10) Festivities *Alla Turchesca* and *Alla Moresca*, (11) Moslems on the London Stage. The last chapter is the epilogue.

Additionally, in the epilogue the author offers some interesting observations. The travellers—"whether ambassador, preacher, discharged soldier or ransomed captive, semi-professional vagabond or seeker after exotic sensations—built up in the Elizabethan imagination and passed into English literature a picture of Islam as at once splendidly luxurious, admirable in its serenity, sombre in its cruelty and sensuality, and terrible in its strength" (p.541). And, "In the back of his mind the traveller carried a quantity of superstitions, fabulous lore, and old wives' tales; it was part of the baggage he took with him into the East; and when once there he was generally more desirous to have it all confirmed" (p.542). And, "False prophet? A shadow of uncertainty flits across the thoughts of the returned traveller. Is everything that Christians tell of Mahomet and his followers true? Can it be that God suffered a disreputable impostor, such as he is described in the pulpits of Christendom to mislead so great a concourse of mankind? . . . But a tolerant outlook was beyond the Elizabethan comprehension" (p.545). And consultations with these travellers "helped to shape the public policy of states-man when, confronting Islam, the states of Christendom in times of critical deci-sions had a dim realization of a community of interests transcending political boundaries, uniting them in a common peril, and making them all members of a great society" (p.546).

There are several illustrations in the book. There is no bibliography as such, but extensive notes and references are integrated in the text of each chapter. There is a detailed name-subject index.

B-267. Cobb, Stanwood. *Islamic Contributions to Civilization.* Washington, DC: Avalon Press, 1963.

Having lived and taught in Turkey for several years, the author begins with a brief contextual narrative as to the depth of religious serenity and calmness about life in general that he discovered in Turkey's Islamic culture, for, he argues, the historical nature of his book could "never be appreciated save by those who real-ize somewhat the inner spirit and the effect of this inner spirit in conferring some degree of dignity and tranquility to the life even of the common man" (p.ix). His suggestion to the readers: "To understand a people we have to try to feel as they do; and to understand an epoch we need to imagine ourselves as living in it" (p.ix).

Written for the lay-reader, this short book has ten chapters: (1) A Blind Spot in History, (2) Out of the Desert, (3) The Arabic-Islamic Civilization, (4) New Heights in Spain, (5) How Islamic Culture Was Communicated to the Spaniards, (6) Summary of Arabic-Islamic Contributions (medical science, chemistry, astronomy, geography and navigation, the decimal system, algebra, paper, gun-powder, textiles, agricultural products, rise of the university, machinery), (7)

Greek Science Reaches Europe from the Arabs and Not from Constantinople, (8) Europe Develops the Scientific Attitude, (9) The Rhythm of the Civilization Pattern, (10) History Looks Ahead.

The book provides no footnotes or references, nor is there a bibliography or index.

B-268. Colish, Marcia L. *Medieval Foundations of the Western Intellectual Tradition, 400–1400.* New Haven, CT: Yale University Press, 1997.

The book begins with the claim that "the foundations of western intellectual history were laid in the Middle Ages and not in classical Greece and Rome or the Judeo-Christian tradition" (p.x). The argument is that western European thought "acquired its particular character not only as a result of the cultural components that flowed into it. Equally important were the attitudes that western thinkers took to their sources and the uses to which they put them" (p.x). There were sister civilizations, Byzantium and Islam, as well Jewish thinkers in the Arabic-speaking community. It was Islam, however, that rose to "the challenge of absorbing oriental as well as classical culture as the caliphate expanded into the Near East and Persia, becoming the most dynamic and original of the three sister civilizations in the early Middle Ages. Its scholars made creative and important contributions to the natural sciences, medicine, mathematics, philosophy, art, and literature, as well as elaborating Muslim theology and religious law" (p.xi).

The 390-page book is divided into seven parts, of which the first five primarily focus on early Middle Ages and the last two relate to high Middle Ages. Part I, From Roman Christianity to the Latin Christian Culture of the Early Middle Ages, has six chapters; Part II, Vernacular Culture, has two chapters; Part III, Early Medieval Civilizations Compared, has three chapters (including a chapter entitled Peoples of the Book: Muslim and Jewish Thought); Part IV, Latin and Vernacular Literature, has four chapters (including a chapter entitled The Renaissance of the Twelfth Century; curiously, the author discusses "the desire to make fuller use of available classical sources," but there is no mention of the source of availability); Part V, Mysticism, Devotion, and Heresy, contains four chapters; Part VI, High and Late Medieval Speculative Thought, covers four chapters; Part VII, The Legacy of Scholasticism, has three chapters (including the chapter Economic Theory: Poverty, the Just Price, and Usury). There are numerous references indicating the linkages with and influence of Muslim scholars throughout much of the book, although the author appears a bit hesitant in so doing.

At the end, there is a chapter-by-chapter listing of footnotes and references, followed by detailed bibliographic notes. There is a name-subject index.

B-269. Daniel, Norman. *The Arabs and Medieval Europe.* London: Longman Group Ltd., 1975.

As part of the Arab Background Series, the book is intended to provide the English-speaking, educated reader with some knowledge of the historical past of the Arab-Islamic civilization and interactions with medieval Europe. That civilization, "which reached its height in the ninth, tenth and eleventh centuries, was, for a few centuries that followed, the guiding light for a large part of the world. Its role cannot thus be ignored" (p.xi). The book explores these intercultural linkages. In discussing these linkages, the author notes his concern is not with "what happened, but what was in the minds of Europeans, and asking it, not as a means to an historical judgement of events, but as an end in itself" (p.xiii).

The 380-page book has 11 chapters: (1) Introduction, (2) The Martyrs of Cordova, (3) The Central and Western Mediterranean to the end of the tenth century, (4) Spain in the eleventh and twelfth centuries, (5) European solidarity and the inception of the crusading idea, (6) The Central Mediterranean: Eleventh–thirteenth centuries, (7) Courtly ideals in the East, (8) Adaptation and development in the Latin East, (9) The Arabs, Islam and European Theology, (10) Arabic scientific literature in Europe, (11) The end of the Middle Ages.

Concerning the First Crusade and the crusaders' entry into Jerusalem, the author states, "The undefended men and women they killed exactly as if they had been destroying vermin; this story, more than any other, suggests the denial of a common humanity" (p.135). As for the Arab-Islamic influence, chapter 10 documents the multifaceted aspects of these linkages, in that "the explosion of scientific translations was the product, in practice, of military success. The opening of much of Mediterranean culture to people of the north of Europe was the result of the European conquest of southern Italy and Sicily, and of Toledo and other smaller centres in Spain" (p.263–264). The author concludes: "We cannot stress too much that Arabs and Europeans share a common inheritance, but cousinship does not preclude dislike or reluctance to understand. Arabs and Europeans are too alike in their differences, and too different in their resemblance, for their relationship to be an easy one, but it has developed continuously since their first encounter, and it is still capable of conferring mutual benefits if both sides so wish" (p.325–326).

The book provides detailed, chapter-by-chapter, notes and references. There is also a brief bibliographical note, followed by a comprehensive name-subject index.

B-270. Daniel, Norman. *Islam and the West: The Making of an Image*. Boston: Oneworld Press, 1960; reprint 2000.

This widely-acclaimed, authoritative study explores the political and religious considerations behind distorted Western views of Islam, examining Christian–Muslim interactions from medieval times to the modern world. From the medieval confrontation between the Islamic world and Christendom to the present day, the relationship between Islam and the West has been one of conflict and misunderstanding, the author notes. The prejudices conceived over a thousand years ago have survived the break-up of Western Christianity into Catholic and Protestant, the growth of atheism, and the rise of the multifaith, pluralistic communities. Yet, despite some efforts toward increased mutual understanding, these prejudices continue to permeate Western attitudes toward Islam. The author's main objective is to scientifically establish evidence to support the main theme of the book, and secondarily, to "see what is implied by this unpleasantness and ignorance in men's attitudes towards those they suppose to be their enemies" (p.9).

Some of the key topics covered are revelation, prophethood, and incarnation; the life of Muhammad; the authenticity of the Qur'an; and Western views of violence, morality, and religious practices in Islam. After the introduction, there are ten chapters: (1) Revelation: Christian Understanding of Islamic Belief, (2) Revelation: The Christian Attack upon "Pseudoprophecy," (3) The Life of Muhammad: Polemic Biography, (4) The Place of Violence and Power in the Attack on Islam, (5) The Place of Self-Indulgence in the Attack on Islam, (6) The Relation between Islam and Christianity: Theory, (7) The Relation between Islam and Christianity: Religious Practices, (8) Polemic Method and the Judgement of Fact, (9) The Establishment of Communal Opinion, (10) The Survival of Medieval Concepts. There are five appendices: The imputation of idolatry in Islam, Martyrs and killers, Christ and the Last Day, Shi'ah Islam, and Res turpissima.

The 470-page book has a 58-page, chapter-by-chapter, listing of notes and references. There is a 38-page bibliography, divided as follows: Bibliography A, direct sources (to 1350); Bibliography B, writers on Islam of the period 1350–1850; Bibliography C, modern works. Also, there is a detailed name-subject index.

B-271. Daniel, Norman. *Islam, Europe and Empire.* Edinburgh: Edinburgh University Press, 1966.

"This book is about new ideas of the Islamic world, which took shape in Western Europe during the period of colonial expansion. New images came to be reflected in the old distorting mirror. The inhabitants of modern Europe inherited from their medieval fathers a large and persistent body of ideas about Islam, which only gradually changed as conditions changed at home, and as new and intimate relations began to be established with Islamic powers and cultures" (p.xiii). Thus, the subject of the book "is the movement of Western Europeans among Islamic peoples, with the consequent creation of new attitudes in their minds" (p.xiii). The book is an early study of the clash of cultures, imperialism, and colonialism, as well as a criticism of Europe's distorted attitude toward the Islamic world and Muslims. Islam was Europe's first major encounter with a non-Christian and non-Western culture; attitudes developed in these interactions were extended subsequently to other peoples and cultures of the world. The purpose of the study, thus, is to identify and distinguish the elements of interactions that are new and changing, and those that are old and continuous.

The book is divided into five parts. Part One (Introductory; two chapters) documents the circumstances as they evolved up to the beginning of the imperial age, together with the 19th-century background to imperial thought. Part Two (Revolution and Empire, 1789–1830; seven chapters) is concerned with adaptations in English and French thought about Islam by the wars of the Revolution and the making of the Empire. Part Three (Christian Civilization, 1800–1900; three chapters) discusses several studies relating to the Christian "civilizing" missions in India, Africa, and Turkey. Part Four (The High Imperial Age, 1877–1900; five chapters) treats the classic age of imperialism at the end of the 19th century, with special focus on Afghanistan, Tunisia, Egypt, Sudan, and other African countries. Part Five (Conclusions; one chapter) provides general conclusions.

The author notes that "it is hardly an exaggeration to say that imperialism was an overflow of energy which Africa and Asia absorbed. Throughout the century, British and French alike were occupied with the 'civilizing mission' of Christian 'improvement.' A conservative might regret the passing of the old order in Europe, and consider industrial progress, despite all the improvements in material and social life that result, an epidemic disease that leaves the patient worse than he was before it attacked him. If so, imperialism is the spreading of the infection." Further, "No nation will willingly permit the rule of foreigners for long; and government of the unwilling can only end in tyranny. This was the great discovery at the end of the century in the Muslim countries too [that] brought out a crisis of empire. For a long time European refused to believe that Arabs and Indians were in the same position as those patriotic Europeans who established their independence during the nineteenth century" (p.478–479).

The 620-page book provides 70 pages of chapter-by-chapter notes and references, followed by a 30-page bibliography, which is "neither complete nor a select bibliography," but simply a list of works quoted or referred to in the main text and notes. There is a 25-page name-subject index. The book also contains 34 sketches, pictures, and cartoons, reflective of the major themes of the study.

B-272. Djait, Hichem. *Europe and Islam* (translated from French by Peter Heinegg). Berkeley, CA: University of California Press, 1985.

The book is a reflection on the history of cultures from a global-historical perspective; as the author says, it is a comparative study that brackets "one concept whose origin is purely geographical [Europe] with another whose origin is just as purely religious [Islam]" (p.1). It offers the reader an analysis of the main motifs of European culture within the framework of its relation with other (especially Islam) cultures. This dialectic stresses the disjunction between the historical particularity of Europe and the universality it professes, and places it in a historical perspective where it does not occupy the center. The normative uniqueness of Europe is challenged by recourse to interesting historical sketches. The discussion of Islam, over four chapters, is pursued in terms of categories such as "personality," "identity," "destiny," and their cognates; it also deals with European attitudes toward Islam, along with rebuttals. The book argues that as the world becomes more unified, "individuals from 'non-Europe' (to borrow Laroui's expression) must act as mediators," and their role is "to expose the whole range of European experience, in depth, to other norms, other values, and perhaps other categories. This is the way to hammer out a universal that will not be utopian nor destructive but the outcome of creative synthesis" (p.6).

The 198-page book is divided into two parts, with four chapters in each. Part I, In Another's Eyes: (1) From the Medieval Vision to Modern Visions, (2) French Intellectuals and Islam, (3) European Scholarship and Islam, (4) Islam and German Thought. Part II, Islam and Europe: Two Historical Structures: (5) The Historical Dynamic: Europe and Universality, (6) Islam: Civilization, Culture, and Politics, (7) Europe as a Particular Case, (8) By Way of Conclusion: Islam, the West, and Modernity.

Chapter-by-chapter notes and references are provided at the end, which is followed by a glossary of proper names and Arabic terms. There is a name-subject index.

B-273. Durant, Will. *The Story of Civilization: The Age of Faith—A History of Medieval Civilization, Christian, Islamic, and Judaic, from Constantine to Dante, AD325–1300.* Volume 4. New York: Simon & Schuster, 1950.

This volume is part of a widely acclaimed, monumental 11-volume series entitled, *The Story of Civilization*, each about 1,000 or more pages, written between 1934 and 1975; the last five were written jointly with the author's wife, Ariel Durant. Each represents the very best in literary scholarship. Readers may be aided if each volume is chronologically identified by the title: (1) Oriental Heritage [1934], (2) Life of Greece [1939], (3) Caesar and Christ [1944], (4) The Age of Faith [1950], (5) The Renaissance [1953], (6) The Reformation [1957], (7) The Age of Reason [1961], (8) The Age of Louis XIV [1963], (9) The Age of Voltaire [1965], (10) Rousseau and Revolution [1967], and (11) The Age of Napoleon [1975].

While volumes 4 to 7 are replete with numerous references to linkages with Islam and Islamic scholarship, as well as the impact upon Latin Europe, it is the fourth volume of which Book II, with seven chapters (covering about 200 pages) is devoted to the world of Islam and Islamic civilization (569–1258 AD). Yet, the author, with some humility, cautions the readers, in that "the Christian reader will be surprised by the space given to the Moslem culture, and the Moslem scholar will mourn the brevity with which the brilliant civilization of medieval Islam has been summarized" (p.vii–viii). The seven chapter titles are: (1) Mohammed, 569–632 AD, (2) The Koran, (3) The Sword of Islam, 632–1058 AD, (4) The Islamic Science, 632–1058 AD, (5) Thought and Art in Eastern Islam, 632–1058 AD, (6) Western Islam, 641–1086 AD, (7) The Grandeur and Decline of Islam. Then, Book III is devoted to the Judaic Civilization, 135–1300 AD, with three chapters, followed with Book IV that discusses the European Dark Ages, 566–1095 AD, covering five chapters. Book V, The Climax of Christianity, 1095–1300 AD, is the most detailed, extending over 17 chapters; throughout, there are references to the Arab-Islamic linkages. This is especially so in chapter 23, The Crusades, 1095–1291 AD; chapter 25, The Recovery of Europe, 1095–1300 AD (sections on Spain and Portugal); chapter 26, Pre-Renaissance Italy, 1057–1308 AD (section on Frederick II); chapter 34, The Transmission of Knowledge, 1000–1300 AD (the period broadly identified as representing the "Twelfth Century Renaissance," due to the transfer of knowledge from the Arab-Islamic civilization, the "turning point" for Latin-Europe Enlightenment); chapter 35, Abelard, 1079–1142 AD; chapter 36, The Adventure of Reason, 1120–1308 AD.

The author's emphasis on the significance of medieval Arabic-Islamic / Latin Europe linkages is evident throughout. For example, "The successive waves of translations from the Arabic and Greek in the twelfth and thirteenth centuries brought to the West the revelation and challenge of Greek and Moslem philosophies so different from the Christian that they threatened to sweep the whole theology of Christendom unless Christianity could construct a counterphilosophy" (p.949); and "Thomas Aquinas was led to write his *Summas* to halt the threatened liquidation of Christian theology by Arabic interpretations of Aristotle; indeed, the industry of Aquinas was due not to the love of Aristotle but to fear of Averroes" (p.954). Further, "It was Avicenna and Averrous, as well as Aristotle, who infected Christianity with the germs of rationalism" (p.982). The last chapter is devoted to Italy's Dante Alighieri (1265–1321).

It should be noted that while extensive coverage of the Arab-Islamic linkages is contained in volume 4, there are detailed references to this effect in volume 6, *The Reformation*; among other things, this volume examines the role of "the strangers in the gate: Russia and Ivans and the Orthodox Church, Islam and its challenging creed, culture, and power; and the struggle of the Jews to find Christians in Christendom" (p.viii). There are two chapters that specifically focus on the Islamic world (chapter 30, The Genius of Islam, 1258–1520, and chapter 31, Suleiman the Magnificent, 1520–1566).

There is a bibliographical guide of references, following a 35-page, chapter-by-chapter listing of notes. There is also a 60-page author-subject index.

B-274. Faris, Nabih Amin, ed. *The Arab Heritage*. New York: Russell and Russell, Inc., 1963; original 1944.

The 280-page book is a compendium of lectures delivered by eminent scholars at the 1941 annual summer seminar in Arabic and Islamic Studies at Princeton University. Readers are introduced to the wealth and diversity of Arab-Islamic history and thought, and its cultural development and contributions to the world, particularly the West. A key purpose of the lectures was to convey to the specialist, as well as laypersons, the relevance and significance of Arab and Islamic studies and their bearing on current events and the shape of things to come. That was in 1941, but that purpose is even more relevant presently.

The first chapter, America and the Arab Heritage by Philip K. Hitti, sets the tone for the rest of the chapters. Other chapters are: (2) Pre-Islamic Arabia by Giorgio Levi Della Vida, (3) Islamic Origins: A Study in Background and Foundation by Julian Obermann, (4) Growth and Structure of Arab Poetry A.D. 500– 1000 by Gustave E. Von Grunebaum, (5) Al-Ghazzali by Nabih Amin Faris, (6) Crusade and Jihad by John L. LaMonte, (7) Fourteenth-Century Jerusalem and Cairo through Western Eyes by Henry L. Savage, (8) The Course of Arab Scientific Thought by Edward J. Jurji, (9) The Character of Islamic Art by Richard Ettinghausen.

There are bibliographies attached to each chapter, and there is a detailed name-subject index.

B-275. Farrukh, Omar A. *The Arab Genius in Science and Philosophy* (translated from Arabic by John B. Hardie). Washington, DC: American Council of Learned Societies, 1954.

The 160-page book is intended for the ordinary reader, for whom the story of Arab-Islamic achievements and their influence on the West may be "at once enlightening and stimulating, if sometimes somewhat provocative" (p.vi). "The purpose is not to formulate brilliant sentences and fine phrases in praise of the past, or to laud the days of old; rather, the purpose is to indicate the position held by the Arabs, by presenting their views, their influence and their judgments in relation to the opinions held by some European scientists and philosophers," says the author (p.vii). Further, the book relies heavily on European sources. Arab-Islamic scholars, such as Al-Ghazali, made their contributions in an environment that emphasized "a solid learning which reveals facts in such a way as to leave no room for doubt, and to admit no possibility of error or weakness"; on the other hand, early European scholars, critical of the philosophers, insisted: "First have faith, and then get understanding" (p.10). The book, however, is "not intended to be a history of science and philosophy among the Arabs, or a biographical dictionary of [Arab] philosophers and scientists" (p.11).

The book has six fairly long chapters: (1) Maxims, (2) Theology, (3) The Mathematical Sciences, (4) The Natural Sciences, (5) Mental Philosophy, (6) Social Philosophy. There is an epilogue that explores the question: "But where do we stand today with regard to this outstanding past?"

At the end, the book provides chapter-by-chapter notes and references; there is no index, however.

B-276. Ferber, Stanley, ed. and comp. *Islam and the Medieval West*. Binghamton, NY: State University of New York Press, 1975.

This volume is a compilation of papers presented in connection with an art exhibition at the 9th Annual Conference of the Center for Medieval and Early Renaissance Studies, State University of New York at Binghamton, May 1975, the theme of the conference being "Islam and the Medieval West." The inclusion of "a select number of Western medieval objects is intended to suggest the range of possibilities in examining the types and nature of inter-relatedness and influences at work between East and West during the Middle Ages," says the editor (p.1).

There are five essays in the collection: (1) Muslim Decorative Arts and Paintings: Their Nature and Impact on the Medieval West by Richard Ettinghausen, (2) Islamic Ceramics: A Source of Inspiration for Medieval European Art by Rudolf Schnyder, (3) The Two Sicilies by James D. Breckenridge, (4) Islamic Architecture and the West: Influences and Parallels by Oleg Grabar, (5) Islamic Art and the Medieval West: The State of the Question by Stanley Ferber. Evidence of Islamic influences is presented throughout the essays. As for two Sicilies, reference is "to the Muslim and Christian cultures which encountered each other at this Mediterranean crossroads during four fruitful centuries of the Middle Ages, with results of profound significance to the development of all European civilization" (p.39). Each essay provides its own notes and bibliographic references.

Over half of the book is devoted to a catalog of 132 art exhibits (all black and white), with details as to the artist (where available), country of origin, the period, the source of the collection, and a description of the object. There is also a general bibliography relevant to the art exhibit as well as other general literature. There is no index.

B-277. Frassetto, Michael and David R. Blanks, eds. *Western Views of Islam in the Medieval and Early Modern Europe: Perception of Other*. New York: St. Martin's Press, 1999.

This 235-page edited volume explores the diversity of attitudes of European religious and secular writers toward Islam during the Middle Ages and Early Modern period. By examining works from England, France, Italy, the Holy Lands, and Spain, the essays investigate the reactions of Westerners to the culture and religion of Islam, including the basis of European hostility toward Islam and the creation of negative stereotypes of Muslims. Also, some of the essays document attempts at accommodation and understanding between the two worlds. The editors note that "during the Middle Ages, Islamic civilization was far ahead of its Christian rival, offering enticing advances in architecture, law, literature, philosophy, and, indeed, in most areas of cultural activity. By debasing the image of their rivals, Western Christians were enhancing their own self-images and trying to build self-confidence in the face of a more powerful and more culturally sophisticated enemy" (p.3).

The 11 essays are written by well-regarded scholars in the field: (1) Western Views of Islam in the Premodern Period: A Brief History of Past Approaches by David R. Blanks, (2) Popular Attitudes toward Islam in Medieval Europe by Jo Ann Hoeppner Moran Cruz, (3) The Image of the Saracen as Heretic in the Sermons of Ademar of Chabannes by Michael Frassetto, (4) Muslims as Pagan Idolaters in Chronicles of the First Crusade by John V. Tolan, (5) The Essential

Enemy: The Image of the Muslim as Adversary and Vassal in the Law and Literature of the Medieval Crown of Aragon by Donald J. Kagay, (6) Arabs and Latins in the Middle Ages: Enemies, Partners, and Scholars by Alauddin Samarrai, (7) Islam in the *Glossa Ordinaria* by Ernest N. Kaulbach, (8) "Seven trewe bataylis for Jesus Sake": The Long-Suffering Saracen Palomides by Nina Dulin-Mallory, (9) Noble Saracen or Muslim Enemy? The Changing Image of the Saracen in the Medieval Italian Literature by Gloria Allaire, (10) "New Barbarian" or Worthy Adversary: Humanist Constructs of the Ottoman Turks in Fifteenth-Century Italy by Nancy Bisaha, (11) Early Modern Orientalism: Representations of Islam in Sixteenth-and-Seventeenth-Century Europe by Daniel J. Vitkus.

Each essay provides footnotes, with bibliographic references, at the end. There is a name-subject index.

B-278. Gutas, Dimitri. *Greek Thought, Arabic Culture: The Graeco–Arabic Translation Movement in Baghdad and Early Abbasid Society (2nd–4th / 8th–10th Centuries).* London and New York: Routledge, 1998.

The book is a study of the major social, political, and ideological factors that led to the unprecedented "translation movement" from Greek into Arabic in Baghdad, the capital of the Arab-Islamic Abbasid dynasty, during the first two centuries of their rule. It draws upon an extended line of historical and philological works on Graeco–Arabic studies, which provide evidence that from about "the middle of the eighth century to the end of the tenth, almost *all* non-literary and non-historical secular Greek books that were available throughout the Eastern Byzantine Empire and the Near East were translated into Arabic" (p.1). Two major supportive factors were: intellectual support from the entire Abbasid society—caliphs, princes, civil servants, merchants, scholars, and scientists; and public and private financial support.

Further, Gutas notes, the "translation movement of Baghdad constitutes a truly epoch-making stage, by any standard, in the course of human history. It is equal in significance to, and belongs in the same narrative as, I would claim, that of Pericles' Athens, the Italian Renaissance, or the scientific revolution of the sixteenth and seventeenth centuries, and it deserves to be recognized and embedded in our historical consciousness" (p.8).

Beyond the introduction, the 230-page book is divided into two parts, with four and three chapters, respectively. Part One, Translation and Empire: (1) The Background of the Translation Movement: Material, Human, and Cultural Resources, (2) Al-Mansur: Early Abbasid Imperial Ideology and the Translation Movement, (3) Al-Mahdi and His Sons: Social and Religious Discourse and the Translation Movement, (4) Al-Mamun: Domestic and Foreign Policies and the Translation Movement. Part Two, Translation and Society: (5) Translation in the Service of Applied and Theoretical Knowledge, (6) Patrons, Translators, and Translations, (7) Translation and History: Developments from the Translation Movement. Additional details are provided for each chapter in the table of contents. There is an epilogue, along with an appendix: Greek Works Translated into Arabic—A Bibliographic Guide by Subject.

The author concludes: "On a broader and more fundamental level, its [movement's] significance lies in that it demonstrated for the first time in history that scientific and philosophical thought are international, not bound to a specific language or culture. Once the Arabic culture forged by early Abbasid society historically established the universality of Greek scientific and philosophical thought, it provided the model for and facilitated the later application of this concept in Greek Byzantium and Latin West: in Byzantium, both in Lemerle's 'first Byzantine humanism' of the ninth century and in the later renaissance of the Palaeologoi; and in the West, both in what Haskins has called the renaissance of the twelfth century and in the Renaissance proper" (p.192).

Notes and references are integrated in the text of each chapter. There is a list of bibliography and references at the end, followed by a chronological bibliography of studies on the significance of the translation movement for the Islamic civilization. There is also a general name-subject index and an index of manuscripts.

B-279. Gwatkin, H.M. and J.P. Whitney, eds. *The Rise of the Saracens and the Foundation of the Western Empire.* Cambridge: Cambridge University Press, 1967; original 1913.

As part of the Cambridge Medieval History series, this 890-page volume "covers the stormy period of about three hundred years from Justinian to Charles the Great inclusive" (p.v). There are 22 chapters, written by various European scholars of the early 20th century. Some of the chapters, the editors argue, cover subjects "on which very little has ever been written in English, such as the Visigoths in Spain, the organization of Imperial Italy and Africa, the Saracen invasions of Sicily and Italy, and the early history and expansion of the Slavs" (p.v). The titles range from Justinian's Government in the East by Charles Diehl, Successors of Justinian by Norman H. Baynes, and Germanic Heathenism by Miss B. Phillpotts, to Foundations of Society (Origins of Feudalism) by Sir Paul Vinogradoff.

Three chapters focus specifically on the Islamic civilization ("Saracens"): (1) Mahomet and Islam by A.A. Bevan, (2) The Expansion of Saracens: The East by C.H. Becker, (3) The Expansion of the Saracens: Africa and Europe by C.H. Becker. Rather sympathetically, Bevan concludes his essay: "We must not fall into the error of ignoring the extraordinary influence exerted by the Prophet over his disciples, an influence which was apparently due quite as much to his moral as to his intellectual qualities"; further, "He used his immense power much oftener for the purpose of restraining than for the purpose of stimulating fanaticism" (p.328). Becker begins his discourse with criticizing the "one-sided ecclesiastical and clerical point of view as was bound to obscure the comprehension of historical facts. The popular version of the matter, even among the cultured classes of today, is still under the spell of this tradition; that is, 'inspired by their prophet, the Arab hordes fall upon the Christian nations, to convert them to Islam at the point of the sword'" (p.329). Becker notes that "it is only in recent times that historical research has led away from this line of thought" (p.329). After narrating the expansion of "Saracens," Becker states, "The blessings of culture (from Islamic Spain) which were given to the West by its temporary Islamitic elements are at least as important as the influence of the East during the time of the Crusades" (p.390).

Footnotes and references are integrated in the text of each chapter. The comprehensive, 111-page bibliography is organized by way of a general bibliography (with topical division), and chapter-by-chapter bibliographies (divided by contemporary and modern sources). Also, there is a chronological table of major events mentioned in the text (covering the period 314–1091 AD), and a 67-page name-subject index, followed by several maps (Justinian's Empire, Empire of Charles the Great, England 700 AD, The Caliphate under Harun-er-Rashid, etc.).

B-280. Hamilton, Alastair. *Europe and the Arab World: Five Centuries of Books by European Scholars and Travellers from the Libraries of the Arcadian Group.* Oxford: Oxford University Press, 1994.

This 207-page book is an interesting "catalogue of books" (and pictures) that display "the vacillating relationship between Europe and the Arabs. As objects they cover over four centuries, from the early sixteenth century to the end of the First World War. As repositories of ideas, they illustrate Europe's encounter with its Muslim neighbours from the Middle Ages onwards" (p.11).

The primary objective of the catalogue is clear from the author's observation: "Different cultures have usually been regarded by Christian Europe with a measure of ambivalence in which prejudice and illusions play a significant part, but none for so long as the culture of the Arabs, at times the most influential, at times the most menacing, and always the closest at hand. European views of the Arab world have changed over the centuries yet it is difficult to discern a constant progression from ignorance to enlightenment, even as the means of knowing the Arabs improved. At any moment the prejudices of previous ages could be revived, and the understanding so laboriously acquired by sympathetic orientalists all but completely destroyed" (p.11). During the same centuries, the author notes, as prejudice and illusions developed, "Christian scholars were eagerly reading Latin translations of Arabic texts widely available among the Arabs of Spain and Sicily" (p.11). The catalog includes 75 illustrations of European literature, extending over 200 pages, including pictures of cover pages of original books, numerous other pictures, sketches, and citations of original sources. Illustrations of books also separately identify the author, as well as a brief narrative about the content of each book.

There is a bibliography of relevant references at the end, but no index.

B-281. Hammond, Reverend Robert. *The Philosophy of Alfarabi and Its Influence on Medieval Thought.* New York: The Hobson Book Press, 1947.

This short book is well-documented not only on the essentials of Abu Nasr Alfarabi's (d. 950) philosophical views on various topics, but more importantly, on the close parallels between his thought and that of Latin-European scholastics, especially St. Thomas Aquinas (1225–1274).

The 60-page book is divided into three parts: Part One, Logical, with one chapter entitled Logic. Part Two, Theoretical, has two chapters: Metaphysics and Psychology. Part Three, Practical, has two chapters: Ethics and Political Society. There is also a concluding chapter.

Rather interestingly, the author identifies and reproduces Alfarabi's exact statements on various topics and then reproduces identical statements from St. Thomas Aquinas. For example, on proofs of God's existence, Alfarabi had developed three arguments: the proof of motion, the proof of efficient cause, and the proof of contingence. Thus, for comparison, the author places side by side the exact views of both Alfarabi and St. Thomas on the three proofs and deduces "the great similarity between them" (p.19). Hammond uses the same approach on several other topics (attributes of God, infinity of God, immutability of God, unity of God, omnipotence of God, theory of knowledge, abstractive knowledge, etc.); and he concludes that St. Thomas' statements "are merely repetition of Alfarabi's proofs." However, he says, there is no bias against St. Thomas, but the similarities are "evident to anyone after studying the works of both Alfarabi and of St. Thomas" (p.20). Further, he concludes, "This means that the Saint who came out with the same theory three hundred years later, must certainly have borrowed it from Alfarabi" (p.55).

There is a brief bibliography at the end, followed by a subject index.

B-282. Hayes, John R., ed. *The Genius of Arab Civilization: Source of Renaissance*. Cambridge, MA: The MIT Press, second edition, 1983.

This 260-page book introduces, with numerous illustrations (several diagrams and pictures), the general reader to the cultural achievements of the Arabs, with particular emphasis on the role of classical Arab civilization as a link between the Hellenistic past and the Latin-European Renaissance future. There are also 26 monographs on people and places, the objective being "to convey some idea of the enormous wealth of material that awaits anyone who chooses to pursue Arab studies in greater depth" (p.1).

By providing more knowledge of the Arab past, the author of the foreword states this book "makes us all more civilized and more understanding" (p.2). Further, the editor pointedly remarks, "One of the hallmarks of civilized man is knowledge of the past—the past of an individual's own family, tribe, nation, or culture; the past of others with whom one's own culture has had repeated and fruitful contact; or the past of any group that has contributed to the ascent of man. The Arabs fit profoundly into both of the latter two categories. But in the West the Arabs are not well known. Victims of ignorance as well as misinformation, they and their culture have often been stigmatized from afar" (p.2).

The book contains ten essays, including the introduction and conclusion, written by eminent specialists: (1) Introduction: The Arab Role in Islamic Culture by John S. Badeau, (2) Literature by Mounah A. Khouri, (3) Philosophy and History by Majid Fakhry, (4) Architecture and Art by Oleg Grabar, (5) Music by Ali Jihad Racy, (6) The Exact Sciences by Abdelhamid I. Sabra, (7) The Life Sciences by Sami K. Hamarneh, (8) Mechanical Technology by Donald R. Hill, (9) Trade and Commerce by Ragaei El Mallakh and Dorothea El Mallakh, (10) Conclusion: Past, Present, and Future by Ibrahim Madkour. At the end, there is a "Guide to Further Reading" written by Francis E. Peters.

There are two indices: persons and places, and general.

B-283. Hentsch, Thierry. *Imagining the Middle East* (translated from French by Fred A. Reed). Montreal and Cheektowaga, NY: Black Rose Books Ltd., 1992.

"The book is not about the Orient. It is about us," says the author (p.ix). The 220-page volume is an investigation and analysis of the Western ethnocentricism about the Middle East, from ancient days to the 1991 Gulf War. It stresses the need for an examination of the historical foundations of our collective biases, and argues that our refusal to acknowledge this phenomena will continue to hinder improved relations with that region. It presents "our history's vision of the Arabs, of the Turks, or of Islam. It is also how we viewed—and still view today—these peoples, their cultures and their institutions: in short, what we take to be their 'mentality.' All this has profoundly impregnated our own mentalities, with inevitable political consequences" (p.xiv). The author begins with a discussion of the "mythical frontier" between East and West, including the formulation of a united, anti-Islamic European front during the period following Prophet Muhammad's death (p.1–21).

Hentsch points out that Europe's colonization brought with it depreciation of the region and a belief in Western superiority and that the Crusades, while seen by some as a prelude to subsequent imperialist endeavors, were different. The conquering Christians "never looked upon their adversaries with contempt. No sense of cultural or racial superiority flowed from their religious convictions" (p.130). "Imaginations" were different in subsequent centuries, however. As for attitudes toward Arabic science, "the learned elites of the West realized that they were dealing with a culture considerably more advanced and refined than theirs" (p.38). Further "Adelard of Bath (1070–1150) admitted that 'to gain approval for his own ideas,' he often attributed them to the Arabs; so pervasive was the 'fashion for Muslim science'" (p.38). And, "While deprecating the scientific contributions of the Arabs, who 'did little more than adopt the whole of the Greek encyclopedia which the whole world had accepted in the 7th and 8th century,' Renan admits that 'Arab philosophy, particularly in the 11th and 12th centuries, achieves true originality. Here, I am prepared to make certain concessions'" (p.131).

The book contains seven chapters: (1) The Mythical Frontier, (2) Symbiosis and Conflict, (3) The Genesis of Division, (4) The Faraway Orient, (5) The Orient of Modernity, (6) The Uneasy Orient, (7) The Deadly Frontier. The last chapter describes the 1991 Gulf War as "a dramatic demonstration of the deadly nature of the frontier"; additionally, "Bubbling up blindly, in its dark potency, from a deep well of latent act, myth *acts* upon us collectively in the same way that a repressed urge acts upon an individual: *in our unawareness of it*" (p.211). The discussion centers not on latent Western racism, leading to the devastation of Iraq, but rather on how the West proved so "capable of legitimizing a destructive undertaking wholly out of proportion with its announced objectives, and contrary to its own universally proclaimed standards" (p.212).

The last chapter also discusses some of the contradictions of modern civilization, with its values questioned within and made a mockery beyond. The author says, our resistance of the Middle-East "Other" is rooted in three false premises: (1) our knowledge is purely or essentially Western, relegating the contributions of Arabo-Muslim science to oblivion while annexing as "Western" the achievements of Greco-Roman antiquity; (2) paradoxically, our Western knowledge enjoys universality; and (3) universality of knowledge necessarily means universality of values. But, "The consequences of this triple conviction, in our relations with the Other, are so radical that they escape us altogether in their obviousness" (p.213).

Notes and references are provided at the end of each chapter. There is no separate bibliography, nor is there an index.

B-284. Hodges, Richard and David Whitehouse. *Mohammed, Charlemagne and the Origins of Europe: Archeology and the Pirenne Thesis.* London: Gerald Duckworth and Company, 1983.

Based on new data that "come not from manuscripts, but from archeological research," this book is about the Pirenne Thesis, propounded by Henri Pirenne in his *Mohammed and Charlemagne.*

The archeology of the period 500–1000 relates to the Mediterranean and the Islamic world; also work has been done in north Europe. The new data persuade the authors to take another look at written sources and reconsider the "making of the Middle Ages" (p.vii). Pirenne's classic history of Europe between the fifth and ninth centuries has been challenged, but seldom decisively. The book reviews the thesis in the light of archeological data. There are two objectives: to tackle the major issues of the origins of the Carolingian Empire and to indicate the almost staggering potential of archeological data. The thesis is briefly stated in Pirenne's famous passage: "It is therefore strictly correct to say that without Mohammed Charlemagne would have been inconceivable. In the seventh century the ancient Roman Empire had actually become an Empire of the East; the Empire of Charles was an Empire of the West . . . the Carolingian Empire, or rather, the Empire of Charlemagne, was the scaffolding of the Middle Ages" (p.4).

The book has eight chapters: (1) Mohammed, Charlemagne and Pirenne, (2) The Decline of the Western Europe, (3) The Eastern Mediterranean, 500–850: The Archeological Evidence, (4) North Sea Trade and Commerce, 500–800, (5) Charlemagne and the Viking Connection, (6) The Abbasid Caliphate, (7) The End of an Era, after 830, (8) Four Hypotheses.

The authors conclude: "By removing the critical role of Islam in the Mediterranean in the formation of early medieval Europe we have demolished one of the plans with which Pirenne constructed his historical model. As a result one might be tempted to dismiss Pirenne's thesis as a piece of interesting historiography. But we have little sympathy with the consensus view espoused by some historians, which deliberately under-emphasizes the changes that came about in the period 400–850" (p.175).

The 180-page book provides numerous footnotes and references in the text of each chapter, and there is a name-subject index.

B-285. Hodgson, Marshall G.S. *The Venture of Islam: Conscience and History in a World Civilization—Volume One: The Classical Age of Islam; Volume Two: The Expansion of Islam in the Middle Periods; Volume Three: The Gunpowder Empires and Modern Times*. Chicago and London: University of Chicago Press, 1974; original 1961.

This monumental synthetic work attempts to place the Islamic civilization in a world historical context; the book tries to avoid the Orientalist traps by looking at Islamic world from within in all its complexities. Originally published in 1961, it went through considerable revision, and while the revised version had been substantially completed, the author died at age 47 in 1968; the task then was completed by his colleague and his wife. The book originated to meet the needs of the author's students. However, given Hodgson's realization that far more needed to be explored, he expanded the task into three volumes, covering over 1,500 pages. A major theme of the three works is the capacity of the Qur'anic message repeatedly to inspire men of conscience to confront the dilemma of their age in response to the challenge of its ideals. Thus the work proceeds by a series of meditations on the styles of piety of selected Muslim moral epigones—Hasan al-Basri, Ahmad ibn Hanbal, Abu Hamid Al-Ghazali, Jalaluddin Rumi, and modernists Muhammad Abduh and Muhammad Iqbal.

Volume One contains two books. Book One (The Islamic Infusion: Genesis of a New Social Order) has three chapters on pre-Islam and early Islam; Book Two (The Classical Civilization of the High Caliphate) has seven chapters covering topics such as Absolutism, the Shar'i Islamic Version, Muslim Piety, Speculation, Arabic Literary Culture, and Dissipation of the Absolutism. Volume Two has two books (linked to the previous volume): Book Three (The Establishment of an International Civilization) has seven chapters covering topics such as Formation of the International Political Order, the Social Order, Maturity/Dialogue among the Intellectual Traditions, Sufism, the Sunni Internationalism, Persian Literary Culture, and Cultural Patterning in Islamdom and the Occident; Book Four (Crisis and Renewal: The Age of Mongol Prestige) has four chapters—Mongol Irruption, Conservation/Courtliness in the Intellectual Traditions, the Visual Arts, and the Expansion of Islam. Volume Three has two books (linked to the previous volume): Book Five (Second Flowering: The Empires of Gunpowder Times) has four chapters—Safavi Empire, the Indian Timuri Empire, the Ottoman Empire, and the Deluge of the 18th century; Book Six (The Islamic Heritage in the Modern World) has seven chapters, with titles such as The Impact of the Great Western Transmutation, European World Hegemony, Modernism in Turkey, Egypt and East Arab Lands, Iran and the Russian Empire, Muslim India, and The Drive for Independence.

Each volume begins with a prologue, and there is a provocative epilogue in the third volume entitled The Islamic Heritage and the Modern Conscience. Questions raised convey a flavor of the book; challenges for the world, Islamic and non-Islamic, are posed: "What meaning the [Islamic] heritage can have more generally 'for mankind,' as the Qur'an promised, for people of the Modern world society ask as such, among whom Muslims form an integral part, and from whose destinies the destinies of the Muslims can no longer be disengaged? Is the Islamicate culture to be relegated to the history books and the museums? Is the Islamic faith to merge (after whatever loyalistic but parochial resistance) insensibly into some general ecumenical religiosity, or perhaps to disappear altogether in the face of technicalistic enlightenment? Or will it somehow remain a peculiar possession of those among Modern mankind who happen to be Muslims, but be so circumscribed in effect (unless in the form of communal fanaticism) that to others it needs to be at most an object of curiosity? Or might it prove, by virtue of its inherent vitality, to be of potential significance for all of Modern technicalized mankind, whether they accept an explicitly Islamic allegiance or not?" (p.411–412).

Each volume has an extensive bibliography, a glossary of selected terms and names, and a detailed name-subject index. Also, each volume provides several maps relevant to the narrative.

B-286. Hourani, Albert. *Europe and the Middle East.* Berkeley and Los Angeles: University of California Press, 1980.

The author says in his introduction: "The essays in this book all spring, in one way or another, from a concern with the attitudes of Western thinkers and scholars towards Islam and those who call themselves Muslims, and more generally with the relations of Christians with those who profess other faiths. Some of the essays try to explain the obstacles which confront the Western Christian who has tried to understand Islam" (p.xi). He notes the "uneasy recognition with which the two religions have always faced each other: neither of them is wholly alien to the other, but each finds it difficult to give an intelligible place within its system of thought to the other" (p.xi).

There are eight essays in the 225-page book, all except one published previously: (1) Western Attitudes towards Islam, (2) Islam and the Philosophers of History, (3) Muslims and Christians, (4) Volney and the Ruin of Empires (previously unpublished), (5) Wilfrid Scawen Blunt and the Revival of the East, (6) H.A.R. Gibb: The Vocation of an Orientalist, (7) Toynbee's Vision of History, (8) The Present State of Islamic and Middle Eastern Historiography.

The first essay discusses the main theme of the book. According to the author, the "Crusade and *jihad* do not cover the whole reality of political relations between Christianity and the world of Islam, and still less do they explain the attitude of Christians to Islam and of Muslims to Christianity. The communities which profess the two religions have faced each other across the Mediterranean for more than a thousand years; with hostility, it is true, but with a look of uneasy recognition in their eyes" (p.4). The author adds, "It is uneasy because neither knows quite what to make of the other" (p.4).

Then follows a detailed narrative on errors and omissions in understanding the other, particularly Islam. Islam is sometimes viewed as a barrier to progress, the author says, without realizing the impact of the "profound and powerful experience" of the imperial rule (p.12). However, "There is nothing in Islamic doctrine or law which either prevents or encourages capitalist development—if explanations are to be found, they must be found elsewhere" (p.14). In another context, the author quotes an Oxford scholar who "does not hesitate to call Muhammad a prophet: there *are* prophetic traditions outside Judaism, and Muhammad must be regarded as a prophet" (p.17). In another essay, the author notes that "when Islam first appeared as a challenge to the Christian world, the attitude of Western Christians towards it was one of fear and horror. It continued to be so throughout the early Middle Ages down to the Crusades. In a brilliant study Professor Southern has shown that this attitude was rooted in ignorance; or perhaps it would be more correct to say the opposite, that it was the fear and horror themselves which were the cause of ignorance and prejudice" (p.22).

Other essays contain similar well-documented narratives on the main theme of the book. The last essay on historiography has a somewhat different focus; it is an attempt to "consider how the history of the Middle East should be written in our time" and it provides an extensive bibliography.

The book provides chapter-by-chapter notes and references at the end, and there is a name-subject index.

B-287. Hourani, Albert. *Islam in European Thought*. Cambridge and New York: Cambridge University Press, 1991.

This collection of essays examines the relations between European and Islamic thought and culture, primarily from the late 18th to the 20th century. The author emphasizes that his focus is on "the process by which ideas accumulate and are handed on from one generation to another, changing, developing and acquiring authority as they do so" (p.1). It is argued that this process is based on two facets: (1) the formation of a certain view of Islam and the culture associated with it, based on prior knowledge of Islamic civilization and changing ideas about religion and history; and (2) the development of the scholarly tradition known as 'orientalism,' based on identifying and interpreting texts and their transmission from one generation to another through a chain of teachers and students. The two facets are interconnected, for the "scholars do not work in abstraction, their minds are formed by the culture of their age and previous ages, and they bring to the task of interpreting what they have extracted from their sources principles of selection, emphasis and arrangement derived from the ideas and convictions their lives have taught them" (p.1). Through these processes, the author argues, "Islamic scholarship had developed an organization," thus acquiring "a self-perpetuating authority which has continued to exist until today" (p.2).

The 200-page book contains nine essays, the longest being the first, Islam in European Thought. Others are: (2) Wednesday afternoons remembered, (3) Marshall Hodgson and the venture of Islam, (4) Islamic history, Middle Eastern history, modern history, (5) T.E. Lawrence and Louis Massignon, (6) In search of a new Andalusia: Jacques Berque and the Arabs, (7) Culture and change: The Middle East in the eighteenth century, (8) Bustani's encyclopedia, (9) Sulaiman al-Bustani and the *Iliad*.

Among the several conclusions, the author notes that "western scholarship has been politically motivated: in the period of European power—and now in that of another kind of western ascendancy—it has been used to justify domination over Muslim societies, by creating an image of Muslim societies (or oriental societies in general) as stagnant and unchanging, backward, incapable of ruling themselves or hostile; fear of the 'revolt of Islam' haunted the mind of Europe during the imperial age, and has now come back to haunt it once more" (p.58).

Notes and references are integrated with the text of each essay. There is a detailed name-subject index.

B-288. Hoyt, Edwin P. *Arab Science: Discoveries and Contributions.* Nashville, TN, and New York: Thomas Nelson Inc., Publishers, 1975.

The book is the "story of their [Arab] accomplishments and their times [that] vibrates with human interest and historical adventure, as once again Arabs play a prominent role on the stage of world events" (p.ii). Five hundred years before Columbus, scholars in Baghdad knew the world was round and they knew its size. Between the seventh and 13th centuries, unlike in the Arab world, there was no such thing as scientific inquiry in the West. The Arabs inherited the Greek knowledge, passed it on, but they also added much more. In medicine alone they invented the science of pharmacy and extended the practice of ophthalmology and toxicology; and they established hospitals. There were astronomers, mathematicians, farmers, mechanics, and geographers.

The 160-page book has 13 chapters: (1) The Coming of the Arabs, (2) What the Arabs Conquered, (3) Umayyad Culture, (4) The Glory of Baghdad, (5) The Translators, (6) Islam and Science, (7) The Decline of the Abbasids, (8) The Scientific Change, (9) Egypt and Syria, (10) The Arabs of the West, (11) Other Sciences in Western Islam (and Transmission to the West), (12) The Sum of Arab Science, (13) The Assimilation of Arab Science.

Written for lay-readers, the book provides no footnotes or references; several references are included in the text, however. There is no index.

B-289. Hussain, Iqbal S. *Islam and Western Civilization: Creating a World of Excellence.* Lahore, Pakistan: Humanity International, 1997.

The book is written with the intent of countering "the challenges that operate to dismiss the value of the divine injunctions," which have "made clear that man had a vital role to play in the construction of civilized and humane order" (p.ii). There is considerable historical and "civilizational" content in the book, however.

Following the introductory chapter, the book is divided into five parts, with two or three chapters in each (chapter titles in parenthesis): Part One, Divine Message and Dynamism (The Message and the Messengers; Religion and Science; Islamic Fundamentalism); Part Two, Reconstruction of Thought and Spirit (The Vision of Education; Mystical Manifestation of Islam; The Rationale of Creation and Creativity); Part Three, Conspiracies and Crises (Christianity and Colonialism; Neurosis: A Legacy of Western Civilization); Part Four, The West and Cultural Deception (Patterns of World Cultures; Heritage of Islam in the West); Part Five, Evolution of Society (State and Society in Islam; Discovering the Realities of Islam). The chapter entitled Heritage of Islam in the West especially documents, based on numerous Western sources, the historical links between early Islam and Latin West.

The 330-page book provides a chronology of major events in Islamic history, followed by a bibliography and a glossary of Islamic terms. There is a name-subject index.

B-290. Ito, Shuntaro. *The Twelfth-Century Renaissance: Arabic Influences on the West* (original in Japanese language only). Iwanami Seminar Books, No. 42. Tokyo, Japan: Iwanami Shoten Publishers, 1993.

Available only in Japanese, this is written by an eminent Japanese scholar who says that as a graduate student in the United States during the early 1960s, his understanding, like many other scholars, was that the history of world civilization and science was simply a linear trajectory from Greece to Rome to Western Europe. Later, however, further explorations led to his discovery that the origins of modern science had much to do with the influence of the Arab-Islamic civilization. Ito discusses and documents that phenomena.

The 270-page book has seven chapters. Translated from the original Japanese, the titles are: (1) What Is the 12th-Century Renaissance?, (2) Roots of the 12th-Century Renaissance: Main Contributors, (3) Charter Schools of Natural Philosophers, (4) Hellenism and the Arabic Renaissance, (5) From Arabic to Western Europe, (6) Scientific Renaissance in Spain and Sicily, (7) Birth of Romantic Love (Literature and Poetry).

The author argues that the 12th-century Renaissance was the foundation for the 17th-century Scientific Revolution and that foundation is rooted in the Arab-Islamic civilization. Further, he states, this fact must be given more serious consideration in civilizational history. It may be a minority position, he says, but as a Japanese scholar distanced both from the West and the Islamic Arab world, he observes civilizations fairly and equally without any Eurocentric biases.

Notes and references are integrated within each chapter and there is a name-subject index.

B-291. Khan, M. Abdur Rahman. *Muslim Contribution to Science and Culture*. Lahore, Pakistan: Sh. Muhammad Ashraf Publishers, 1973; original 1946.

The author of this 116-page book argues that accumulated knowledge was gathered and then "disseminated through Khaldia, Babel, Egypt, India, and Phoenicia, and ultimately reaching Ionia and Greece, found there a most congenial atmosphere to develop and systematize for six or seven centuries before the birth of Jesus Christ" (p.7). Subsequently, after the downfall of Rome, "the masterpieces of Greek science and culture lay buried in tottering libraries or museums and might possibly have disappeared altogether but for the miracle of Arab rise to power and its subsequent patronage of learning" (p.8).

Following this introduction, there are ten brief chapters: (1) Cultivation of Medicine, Mathematics and Astronomy in the Abbasid Regime, (2) Patronage at the Eastern Provincial Courts, (3) Encouragement by the Fatimids, (4) Work in Other Departments of Knowledge, (5) *Belles-lettres*, Religious Literature and Philosophy, (6) Early Arab Notions of Chemistry, Biology and Allied Sciences, (7) Mechanical Contrivances and Military Science, (8) Fall of Baghdad and Mongol Response to Islam, (9) Arab Enterprise in Ifriqiya, Sidilliyah, and Andalusia, etc., (10) Transmission of Arab Learning and Culture to Christian Europe. The author notes, however, that "but for al-Ash'ari and al-Ghazzali the Arabs might have been a nation of Galileos, Keplers and Newtons" (p.34).

In the last chapter, by relying on several European scholars, the author documents the transfer of Arab-Islamic knowledge to medieval Europe. Further, "Arabic, being the chief medium of scientific thought practically all over the world, was taught systematically in several European universities and schools, especially at Toledo, Narbonne, Naples, Bologna and Paris" (p.113).

Notes and references are integrated within the text of each chapter. There is no index.

B-292. Landau, Rom. *Arab Contribution to Civilization*. San Francisco: The American Academy of Asian Studies, 1958.

This short book is about "a brilliant culture based upon high religious and moral values, military power, and economic prosperity. This Islamic civilization indeed penetrated Europe itself; the Iberian Peninsula and, to a lesser degree, Sicily and the islands of the Mediterranean flourished for hundreds of years under Muslim rule, and held aloft the torch of learning to the reawakening West," says A.J. Arberry in the preface (p.4). He adds, yet "our forebears were taught to regard Islam as crude and fanatical creed which propagated itself, to the tragic detriment of Christianity, only by the sword" (p.4). The book narrates lucidly the many and diverse contributions to human advancement made by Islamic civilization.

The author argues that during its Dark Ages, Europe evinced "few signs of that spirit of curiosity and of intellectual detachment without which there can be no true scientific discovery" (p.4). Further, "Most Americans and Europeans no longer remember from what store-house the Christian world acquired the tools without which western civilization could not have reached its present level" (p.7). That store-house of knowledge came from the Arab-Islamic civilization, which was a mosaic of Muslims, Jews, Christians, Syrians, Moorish, Persian, Turkish, even Hindus. Their contributions were twofold—they were the transmitters of the legacy of Greece, and "their enrichment of this inheritance, the fruit of their own endeavors, laid the foundations of western culture" (p.9).

The 80-page book offers 15 brief chapters: (1) The Significance of Arab Civilization, (2) The Discovery of the Greeks, (3) What Is 'Arab' Civilization?, (4) The Birth of Arab Civilization, (5) Philosophy, (6) Mathematics, (7) Astronomy, (8) Geography, (9) Medicine, (10) Chemistry, (11) Agriculture, (12) Literature, (13) Music, (14) The Arts, (15) The Arab World Today.

The book contains several maps, sketches, pictures, and drawings that represent contributions of the Arab-Islamic civilization. Some notes and references are integrated in the text of each chapter. There is no bibliography and no index.

B-293. Landau, Rom. *The Arab Heritage of Western Civilization.* New York: Arab Information Center, 1962 and 1972.

This brief (90 pages) book, intended for general readership, is quite similar in content to the author's other book *Arab Contribution to Civilization* (1958). It is organized differently, however. There are eight brief chapters: (1) The way they gave, (2) A philosophical passage, (3) They offered a zero, (4) Roadbook to atlas, (5) From Razi to Pasteur, (6) The compass led West, (7) They wrote in Arabic, (8) Arabesque, abstraction in the arts.

Some interesting observations from the book illuminate the early Arab-Islamic/Latin-Europe linkages: "To enable Western scholars to learn from the Arabs, Frederick II founded, in 1224, the University of Naples" (p.16). St. Thomas Aquinas (1225–1274) studied at this university and relied on "Ibn Rushd in matters philosophical and on Al-Ghazali in those concerning theology" (p.16). "Modern Western scholarship has acknowledged that the Christian scholars who made the coming of the Renaissance possible stood on the shoulders of their Arab predecessors" (p.21). Further, European scholars approached Arab-Islamic influences "with a great and growing enthusiasm combined with a blind trust in its authority. Medieval Europe regarded Arab medicine with superstitious awe, and Cordova was looked upon with admiration by the educated Europeans. As a result, up to the end of the sixteenth century, the medical curricula of European universities demanded a knowledge of Avicenna's *Canon*" (p.51).

The book provides 31 illustrations. Notes and references are integrated within the text of each chapter, but there is no bibliography or index.

B-294. Lane, Rose Wilder. *The Discovery of Freedom: Man's Struggle Against Authority*. New York: John Day Company, 1943; third edition 1993.

The book is an expanded version of another shorter edition, written later by the author with Henry Grady Weaver, *The Mainspring of Human Progress*, The Foundation for Economic Education, Inc., New York, 1953. Much of the content is about the same, however. Part One, The Old World, has five chapters: (1) The Pagan Faith, (2) Communism, (3) The Living Authorities, (4) The Planned Economies, (5) War. Part Two, The Revolution, has five chapters: (1) The First Attempt, (2) The Second Attempt, (3) The Feudal System, (4) The English Liberties, (5) The Third Attempt (with sections: Americans, Without a Leader, The People's War, Democracy, The Rights of Property, The Constitution, The Right to Vote, Republicanism, The Republic Survives, The Industrial Revolution, The World Revolution).

Part One traces the global poor conditions of life over centuries—and how individual liberty attempted to unleash solutions. Also, there is discussion of some approaches that did not work (Paganism, Communism, Planned Economies). Part Two begins with the "Revolution" that almost worked. Here the author talks of the "First Attempt" that began 4,000 years ago with Abraham in Iraq (Ur), but failed because his followers "went back to pagan submission to an imaginary authority" (p.78). Later, the new commandment of Christ emphasized human brotherhood, but while there were glimmers of hope, the author states, nowhere were to be found the God-given rights of freedom.

As with the other book, the author argues that the idea of individual freedom emerged and took hold from Islam's religious individualism; this is "The Second Attempt" of Part Two. Europe was still stagnating, and several centuries before Britain had its Magna Carta a dynamic civilization emerged whose prophet insisted that "there be no priests. Each individual must recognize his direct relation to God, his self-controlling, personal responsibility" (p.83). And, during European Dark Ages, "the world was actually bright with an energetic, brilliant civilization, more akin to American civilization. Millions upon millions of human beings, thirty generations, believing that all men are equal and free, created that civilization and kept on creating it for eight hundred years. To them the world owes modern science—mathematics, astronomy, modern medicine and surgery, scientific agriculture. To them the world directly owes the discovery and the exploration of America" (p.86). Further, "Since American scholars and intellectuals in general are European-minded, an American can get only glimpses of the Saracens' world, seen through European indifference and hatred" (p.87). "Through Italy, the Saracens gave Europeans 'the awakening' of Europe," the author adds, and "through Spain, the last flare of their energy gave the world the discovery of America. Of course Columbus did not discover America" (p.114).

And this was the "Third Attempt." The discovery, exploration, and early colonization of America as closely connected with the Spanish Inquisition, the author suggests. And, it is noted, the voyage of Columbus would hardly have been possible except for the magnetic compass developed by the Saracens, as well as maps and navigation charts. The succeeding sections discuss the outstanding material progress of America, based on individual freedom and opportunities. It also talks of the moral dilemma and war potential of this material progress.

While there are occasional footnotes in this 265-page book, there is no bibliography or index.

B-295. Lewis, Archibald R., ed. *The Islamic World and the West, A.D. 622– 1492*. New York: John Wiley and Sons, Inc., 1970.

Through a judicious combination of original sources and secondary accounts, the book illuminates the panorama of ideas and events that began with a mutual discovery in the early Middle Ages, progressed through the cultural and economic exchange of the High Middle Ages, and led to the alienation and hostility that developed in the Late Middle Ages. It is an attempt to reveal some of the reasons "why these two civilizations, possessing so much in common, had by the late fifteenth century become hostile to one another" (p.v). Yet, thoughtful individuals must not fail to grasp the critical need for mutual acceptance and tolerance for our common future, the editor warns. The book focuses on three issues: (1) an understanding of how differently the Western European and Islamic worlds developed during the Middle Ages; (2) the importance of religion in both civilizations; and (3) "during most of this period, Western European civilization was definitely inferior to Moslem civilization and was, in comparison, underdeveloped" (p. vii).

Accordingly, the 146-page book is divided into three parts (with several appropriate selections in each). Part I, Ignorance and Discovery: From the Hegira to the First Crusade, AD622–1095, has five selections. Part II, Contact and Disillusion: From the First Crusade to the End of the Latin Kingdom of Jerusalem, AD1095–1291, has six selections. Part III, Alienation and Divergence: From the End of the Crusading States in Syria to the Fall of Granada, AD1291–1492, also contains six selections.

The editor notes in the epilogue that "by the eighteenth century it (the Islamic civilization) had relapsed into an age marked by hostility to most manifestations of Western civilization—from which it was not to emerge until the nineteenth and twentieth centuries. This was the tragic heritage of Islamic and Western contacts during the Middle Ages" (p.146).

Notes and references are integrated within each selection. There is no bibliography or index.

B-296. Matar, Nabil. *Islam in Britain, 1558–1685.* Cambridge: Cambridge University Press, 1998.

The book explores the impact of Islam on Britain during the period between the accession of Elizabeth I to the death of Charles II. It provides a new perspective on the transformation of British social thought and society by demonstrating how influential Islam was in the evolution of early modern British culture.

Contrary to common assumptions, the author argues, Christian–Muslim interactions were not necessarily adversarial; rather, there was extensive cultural, intellectual, and missionary engagement with Islam in Britain. There is extensive documentation of conversions of the Britons to Islam and Muslims to Anglicanism, as well as a survey of reactions to such conversions. Further, the book examines the impact of the Islamic scriptures on Anglican-Puritan political discourse. Also examined is the impact of the Qur'an and Sufism, not to mention coffee, on British culture, and the author cites extensive interaction of Britons with Islam through travel, in London coffee houses, in churches, among converts to and from Islam, in sermons and in plays and pamphlets. The book discusses the extent to which Britons engaged the civilization of Islam in a manner that superseded their engagement with any other non-Christian civilization in the early modern period. Finally, there is discussion of the theological representation of Muslims in British eschatological writings, comparing it with the representation of the Jews.

After the introductory chapter, Islam in Early Modern Britain, there are five chapters: (1) "Turning Turke": Conversion to Islam in English Writings, (2) The Renegade on Stage and in Church, (3) "Arabian Britannica": "Alcoran" and the Legacy of Arab Islam, (4) "Baptizing the Turk": Conversion to Christianity in England, (5) Eschatology and the Saracens. There is a concluding chapter, Islam and Britain: Centripetal to Centrifugal.

There is a comprehensive bibliography at the end of this 240-page book, followed by a detailed name-subject index.

B-297. Matar, Nabil. *Turks, Moors and Englishmen in the Age of Discovery.* New York: Columbia University Press, 1999.

The book provides an account of, among other things, how "through trade, piracy, ambassadorial exchanges, friendship and marriage, the Muslim was the most frequently encountered non-Christian" during the Elizabethan period and throughout the 17th century—the period also identified as the "Age of Discovery." The Islamic "civilization was experienced by means of its literature, culture, and languages, chiefly Arabic and Turkish. Such an Islam could be written about, debated, denounced, admired, and scrutinized without bringing the Briton into contact with a single Muslim man or woman" (p.ix).

The 270-page book attempts to show how the earlier "centripetal relation" governing Islam and Britain became "centrifugal and oppositional" by the end of the 17th century (p.ix). Further, the author explores this development "in the light of England's concurrent encounter with another non-Christian people—the American Indians. Students of the English Renaissance have ignored the importance of the fact that Britons encountered Muslims at the same time they encountered American Indians" (p.ix). Further, within the "discourse of Otherness and empire, the two encounters were superimposed on each other so that the sexual and military construction of the Indians were applied to the Muslims" (p.x). Thus, in examining the English–Muslim–American Indian triangle, the author argues, especially in the concluding chapter, how English renaissance writings and practices laid the foundations for modern colonialism and racism. Further, viewing "Indians through the lens of his Muslim/Turkish antipathy," and "Muslims through the lens of Indian antipathy," just as "the lands of North American Indians had been 'allotted' to the French, the English, and the Spanish, the lands of the Muslims were to be allotted to 'new [European] nations'" (p.180).

In addition to the introduction, the book has five chapters: (1) Turks and Moors in England, (2) Soldiers, Pirates, Traders, and Captives: Britons Among the Muslims, (3) The Renaissance Triangle: Britons, Muslims, and American Indians, (4) Sodomy and Conquest, (5) Holy Land, Holy War. The final chapter is entitled Conclusion: Muslims, and the Shadow of the American Indians. There are three appendices.

The book provides a 24-page bibliography, classified in terms of primary and secondary sources. There is a name-subject index.

B-298. Matar, Nabil, ed. and trans. *In the Lands of the Christians: Arabic Travel Writing in the Seventeenth Century*. New York and London: Routledge, 2003.

This book gathers together for the first time translated accounts by early modern travelers from the Islamic world to Western Europe and the Americas. The author argues that "Western historians, cultural analysts, and literary critics have viewed the record of early modern travel and exploration as exclusively Euro-Christian, demonstrative of modernity, superiority, and advancement" (p.xiii). However, "For the Renaissance interlocutor, totally ignorant of the Arab-Islamic heritage of geography and cartography, a well-traveled Muslim seemed an anomaly" (p.xiii).

Such a perception has persisted into modern scholarship. Among some names mentioned is that of Bernard Lewis, who has claimed "that the Arabs showed the same lack of interest [about Europe] as in medieval times," and further, "he accused Muslims of a total lack of 'curiosity' toward Europeans" (p.xiv). By relying on travelogues, diplomatic reports, and letters by Muslim and Christian Arabs from the early to the late 17th century, the book challenges the orientalist myth that cross-cultural exchanges in the early modern period were invariably dominated by the more "curious" West. These travelers "wrote with precision and perspicacity, producing the most detailed and empirically based information about the way in which non-Europeans viewed Europeans in the early modern period. No other non-Christian people—neither the American Indians nor the sub-Saharan Africans nor the Asiatics—left behind as extensive a description of the Europeans and of *bilad al-nasara* (the lands of the Christians), both in the European as well as the American continents, as did the Arabic writers" (p.xxii). Thus, the 230-page book enacts a genuine paradigm shift, possibly a timely and essential corrective to the "clash of civilization" thesis.

Beyond the introduction and a note on translations and selections, there are four chapters, each documenting the writings of Arab travelers, Muslims, and non-Muslims to various parts of Europe. Each chapter is entitled by region: (1) France and Holland, (2) Europe and South America, (3) Spain, (4) France.

There are two indices: names and places.

B-299. Menocal, Maria Rosa. *The Arabic Role in Medieval Literary History: A Forgotten Heritage.* Philadelphia, PA: University of Pennsylvania Press, 1987.

The book's fundamental theme is a historical criticism as to why the colossal influence of early Arab-Islamic civilization on medieval Europe has been ignored or marginalized in the mainstream literature for the last two centuries. Yet, the author argues, the evidence indicates that the highly fertile, intellectual contributions of Arab (and Hebrew) culture, especially from Islamic Spain, were central in shaping medieval Europe and stimulating Enlightenment. However, for ideological reasons, she suggests, the "anxiety of influence" has created "resistance to a consideration of this different story of our parentage, of a displacement of our conception of our fundamental cultural lineage, [that] is quite deep-rooted" (p.3).

In presenting her argument, the author reviews the Arabic cultural presence in a variety of major medieval settings: the courts of William of Aquitaine and Frederick II; the universities in London, Paris, and Bologna; and Cluny under Peter the Venerable. Further, Menocal examines how literary perceptions of specific works and themes currently studied within a purely "western" framework would be altered by an acknowledgment of the Arabic culture. In discussing what is called "the myth of westernness in medieval literary historiography," the author agues that while there have been scholars who argue for integrating the Arab-Islamic scholarship as part of medieval European studies, such a possibility "of our paradigmatic view of the Middle Ages has always remained incidental; it has never been systemic" (p.9).

The 180-page book has six chapters: (1) The Myth of Westernness in Medieval Literary Historiography, (2) Rethinking the Background, (3) The Oldest Issue: Courtly Love, (4) The Newest "Discovery": The *Muwashshahat*, (5) Italy, Dante, and the Anxieties of Influence, (6) Other Readers, Other Readings.

There is an extensive 16-page bibliography, followed by a name-subject index.

B-300. Metlitzki, Dorothee. *The Matter of Araby in Medieval England.* New Haven, CT, and London: Yale University Press, 1977.

The book is concerned with the diffusion of Arab-Islamic influences—philosophical, scientific, literary, and cultural—primarily in medieval England, but also in western European civilization generally. Extremely well-documented, the book's contribution is its concentration on English writers. In order to discern the 'matter of Araby' in the making of the Middle Ages through its role in the literary history of medieval England, the author divides the book into two parts.

Part One, Scientific and Philosophical Learning, includes four chapters: (1) The Transmission (the Crusades, Arabian culture in Sicily, Arabian culture in Spain), (2) "Arabum studia" in England (early translators, Petrus Alfonsi, Adelard of Bath, Robert of Ketton, Daniel of Morley, Roger of Hereford, Alfred the Englishman, Roger Bacon, Michael Scot), (3) "Dotrina Arabum" in England (the introduction of Aristotle, Adelard's "Quaestiones Naturales"), (4) "Arabum sententiae" in Middle English Literature ("The Owl and the Nightingale," scientific imagery in Chaucer).

Part Two, The Literary Heritage, also has four chapters: (1) Arabian Source books ("Disciplina Clericalis," The "Secret of Secrets," "The Diets and Sayings of the Philosophers"), (2) History and Romance (The marriage theme as a portrayal of Christian–Muslim relations, the treatment of the Saracens in the English Medieval romances, The converted Saracen, the defeated Sultan, the Saracen giant, "Mahomet and Mede": The Treatment of Islam, The Muslim paradise as the Land of Cockayne), (3) The Voyages and Travels of Sir John Mandeville, (4) The Matter of Araby and the Making of Romance.

"On the rational level," Metlitzki suggests, "in science and philosophy, the assimilation of Arabic material proceeded deliberately and systematically because it was the work of individual scholars who recognized the Arabs as mediators of Greek philosophy and science. In this process, the Arabs did not only transmit and interpret the knowledge and ideas of classical antiquity, but became the teachers and inspirers of the West at the very heart of its cultural life: its attitude to reason and faith. The migration of literary works, as well as concepts, images, themes, and motifs, was a natural by-product in this work of transmission. The literary material brought Islamic modes of thought within the reach of a far wider circle of readers than the intellectual elite, for it was widely translated into the vernacular" (p.249).

The 320-page book provides 50 pages of chapter-by-chapter notes and references at the end, followed by a detailed name-subject index.

B-301. Myers, Eugene A. *Arabic Thought and the Western World in the Golden Age of Islam.* New York: Frederick Ungar Publishing Company, 1964.

This 156-page book begins with the premise that the Islamic world became the center of world learning once "knowledge accumulated by other peoples had been translated into Arabic." Reference here is to the Greek and Hindu knowledge, translated between the eighth and tenth centuries. While the first period of translation into Arabic was between 650–800 AD, the "golden age of translation from Greek into Arabic was the ninth century" (p.74). There is a brief discussion of the works of pre-11th and 11th-century Islamic scholars (e.g., Al-Kindi, Al-Razi, Al-Farabi, Al-Biruni, Ibn Al Haitham, Ibn Sina), followed by documentation of their influence upon various Latin scholastics (Albertus Magnus, Raymund Lull, St. Thomas Aquinas, Roger Bacon, and others).

Then follows a discussion of the works of 12th–14th century Islamic writers (Al-Ghazali, Ibn Tufail, Ibn Rushd, Ibn Arabi, Ibn Khaldun) and their influence on Latin scholastics. The author also documents how, through various Jewish and Christian translators, this knowledge transferred to the Latin West. "Just as translations had lifted Islam to cultural leadership, so translations shocked Europe out of its long slumber and ignited the explosive development of the West," says the author (p.78). A multitude of Latin translators are chronologically identified, covering the period between the 11th and 14th centuries, along with the names of various Arab-Islamic scholars whose works in various disciplines were translated. By the middle of the 13th century, the author asserts, "there had finally developed in Western Europe the core of a new civilization, a core essentially Greco-Arabic-Latin" (p.132). He concludes that while works from various sources were translated, "the translations from Arabic into Latin were far more important than all others" (p.133). Moreover, "The cultural importance of the work of Islamic scholars and translators for the development of science and humanities can hardly be overestimated" (p.134).

There is a selected bibliography at the end, followed by two indexes: authors and translators, and titles-subject.

B-302. Naskosteen, Mehdi. *History of Islamic Origins of Western Education.* Boulder, CO: University of Colorado Press, 1964.

This is a rare book, extremely rich in content; a well-documented and comprehensive narration of the scope and extent of scholarship in the early Islamic civilization. The word "education" in the title is misleading and could as well be interpreted as "knowledge." It covers the development of Muslim learning, including educational institutions, during the medieval centuries, from about 750 to 1350. The author states, "There is no important aspect of the development of Western civilization since the twelfth and thirteenth centuries in which the decisive impact of Islamic culture is not discernible" (p.viii). Considering his own origins in Iran (Persia), Naskosteen specifically points out the contributions of the Persians, before and after the advent of Islam. Further, he asserts, the medieval Islamic scholarship was sustained by a spirit of scholasticism, similar to that of the Christian West in latter centuries; both attempted to reconcile Greco-Hellenistic thought with their respective religious doctrines.

Among other things, the book explores four key concerns: (1) transmission channels of classical scholarship and the extent to which this scholarship—

Greco-Hellenistic and also Syriac-Alexandrian, Zoroastrian, Indian—reached the Islamic world; (2) creative additions, modifications, and adaptations to the classical learning that took place in the Islamic world during these centuries; (3) channels of transmission to the Western world of the results of classical scholarship so preserved, enriched, and enlarged by the Muslims; (4) major contributions of this transmission to the expansion and reconstruction of Latin-West learning. The author also provides a glimpse of the political, religious, and geographic background in which these developments took place.

After the introductory note, the 361-page book contains nine chapters (with page-coded topical details of each provided in the table of contents). Titles are as follows: (1) The Cultural, Political, and Religious Setting, (2) Classical Foundations of Muslim Education, (3) The Nature and Scope of Muslim Education, A.D.750–1350, (4) The Library as an Educational Center in Islam, (5) Muslim Educational Classics, A.D.750–1350, (6) Sa'di's Reflections on Education and the Art of Living, (7) The Creative-Adaptive Period of Muslim Education, (8) Creative Scholarship in Muslim Education, Continued to A.D.1300, (9) The Transmission of Muslim Learning and Europe's Intellectual Awakening.

The book also contains five comprehensive appendices: (1) an adapted Muslim-Christian calendar and important Islamic cultural events and political dynasties, (2) partial list of early translators of Greco-Hellenistic works into Syrian, Arabic, etc., (3) the Al-Fihrist of al-Nadim, (4) partial list of Islamic scholars and works, A.D.700–1350, (5) translators (list of translators: Arabic to Latin, Arabic or Greek to Hebrew, Arabic to Spanish, Arabic to Catalan, Persian to Greek).

At the end, the book provides chapter-by-chapter notes and references. There is an extensive bibliography of Islamic culture by topics, including references classified by various disciplines. There is also a comprehensive selected general bibliography, followed by a detailed name-subject index.

B-303. Pirenne, Henri. *Mohammed and Charlemagne.* New York: Barnes & Noble, Inc., first published, 1939.

Completed in May 1935, this book was published posthumously by the author's son. There is considerable duplication of material between this book and the author's other works (e.g., *The Economic and Social History of Medieval Europe*, 1937). However, the focus here is on a detailed discussion of the socioeconomic conditions in Europe prior to contacts with the Islamic civilization—for example, Mediterranean civilization in the early Christian centuries, economic and social conditions after the Germanic invasions (navigation, commerce, monetary conditions, etc.), and intellectual life after the invasions. However, the author argues, while the "plurality of states had replaced the unity of the Roman State, the fundamental character of life remained the same" (p.142). That is to say, "The Mediterranean unity which was the essential feature of this ancient world was maintained in all its various manifestations." And, the author goes on, "There was nothing, in the 7th century, that seemed to announce the end of the community of civilization established by the Roman Empire" (p.143). During this period of Dark Ages, "no new principles made their appearance, neither in the economic or social order, nor in the linguistic situation, nor in the existing institutions" (p.284).

The second half of the 294-page book develops Pirenne's main thesis, known as the "Pirenne Thesis," that is subject to considerable controversy and debate. This thesis argued that "the cause of the break with the tradition of antiquity [in Mediterranean Roman State] was the rapid and unexpected advance of Islam. The result of this advance was the final separation of East from West, and the end of the Mediterranean unity" (p.284). Thus, the author asserts, this phenomenon began the Middle Ages in Europe (around the eighth century), induced externally through direct/indirect links and confrontations with the Islamic world and internally due to pressures from Islamic invasions, leading to transformations in economic, social, political, and intellectual environments of the region. "It was during this period of anarchy that the tradition of antiquity disappeared, while the new elements came to the surface," the argument goes (p.285).

The book provides footnotes and bibliographic references within each chapter and there is a name-subject index.

B-304. Ragep, F. Jamil and Sally P. Ragep, with Steven Livesey, ed. *Tradition, Transmission, Transformation: Proceedings of Two Conferences on Pre-Modern Science Held at the University of Oklahoma*. Leiden, New York, and Cologne: E.J. Brill, 1996.

The essays contained in this volume are the result of two conferences held in 1992 and 1993 at the University of Oklahoma. The 1992 conference focused on mathematical traditions in Greek, Islamic, Jewish, and Latin-Christian cultures and their interactions; the 1993 gathering pertained to the transmission of sciences (broadly conceived) between different cultures and their consequent transformation, with "transmission, appropriation, and naturalization" as the organizing theme.

The 600-page book contains 21 essays, beginning with an opening chapter by A.I. Sabra, The Appropriation and Subsequent Naturalization of Greek Science in Medieval Islam—A Preliminary Statement. The other 20 papers are organized into six parts.

Part I, Appropriated Transmission and Traditions, with five chapters, along with authors, as follows: (1) Transmission, Transformation, and Originality: The Relation of Arabic to Greek Geometry by Jan P. Hogendijk, (2) The Transformation of Aristotle's "Physical Philosophy" in Ibn Bajja's Commentaries by Paul Lettinck, (3) Hebrew Mathematics in the Middle Ages: An Assessment by Tony Levy, (4) Regiomontanus' Role in the Transmission and Transformation of Greek Mathematics by Menso Folkerts, (5) The Classical Scientific Tradition in Fifteenth-Century Vienna by Michael H. Shank.

Part II, Selective Transmission and Transformations, with three chapters, along with authors, as follows: (1) On Babylonian Astronomy and Its Greek Metamorphoses by Alexander Jones, (2) Kalam Atoms and Epicurean Minimal Parts by Alnoor Dhanani, (3) The Occult and the Manifest Among the Alchemists by William R. Newman.

Part III, Transmission and Linguistic Transformations, with three chapters, along with authors, as follows: (1) The Relevance of Non-Primary Sources for the Recovery of the Primary Transmission of Euclid's *Elements* into Arabic by Sonja Brentjes, (2) The Arabic "Version" of Euclidean Optics: Transformations as Linguistic Problems in Transmission by Elaheh Kheirandish, (3) Transcriptions of Arabic Treatises into the Hebrew Alphabet: An Underappreciated Mode of Transmission by Y. Tzvi Langermann.

Part IV, Naturalization and Cultural Acceptance, with three chapters, along with authors, as follows: (1) Islamic Acquisition of the Foreign Sciences: A Cultural Perspective by J.L. Berggren, (2) On the Role of the Muezzin and the *Muwaqqit* in Medieval Islamic Society by David A. King, (3) Roger Bacon's Appropriation of Past Mathematics by A. George Molland.

Part V, Naturalization and Cultural Resistance, with four chapters, along with authors: (1) Liminal Perils: Early Roman Receptions of Greek Medicine by Heinrich von Staden, (2) Intercultural Transmission and Selection: Greek Toponyms in Arabic Geography by Marina Tolmacheva, (3) Decline and Fall: Arabic Science in Seventeenth-Century England by Mordechai Feingold, (4) Indian Reception of Muslim Versions of Ptolematic Astronomy by David Pingree.

Part VI, Philosophical Perspectives on Transmission, with two chapters, along with authors, as follows: (1) Was the Scientific Revolution Really a Revolution in Science? by Gary Hatfield, (2) Understanding Change and Continuity by Peter Barker.

Notes and references are integrated within each paper, along with a bibliography. Also, conference programs and participants are listed at the end, as well as a detailed, 38-page name-subject index.

B-305. Reeves, Minou. *Muhammad in Europe: A Thousand Years of Western Myth-Making*. New York: New York University Press, 2000.

The premise of this book is that generations of Western writers, from the Crusades down to the present day, have depicted the life and personality of Muhammad, the Prophet of Islam, in a perennially distorted manner. Over the course of 13 centuries, stubbornly biased representations have persisted, depicting images which bear no resemblance to the noble figure familiar to Muslims. The 307-page book traces this tradition of distortion and provides an account of the reasons behind it. It is a riveting story of Muhammad's reception in the West, a story of rivalry and confrontation.

Prefaced by a biographical sketch of Muhammad's life based on original sources, this book traces the defining eras of historical Western writings, showing how Muhammad and Islam have been used as foils to Western thought. It is

argued that most Westerners have inherited the assumption that there was something wrong with Muhammad's character and behavior, a belief that has helped
to kindle the suspicion and resentment toward the West manifested in what is
popularly called Islamic Fundamentalism. Drawing on works dating from the
Middle Ages to the end of the 20th century and spanning Latin, Italian, French,
German, and English language sources, the book culminates with a critical analysis of Salman Rushdie's controversial novel, *The Satanic Verses.*

The book contains 11 chapters: (1) Muhammad the Prophet of Mecca, (2)
Muhammad's Rule in Medina: The Making of Islam, (3) Muhammad's Quest for
Spirituality, (4) Muhammad as Mahound: Medieval Europe and the Fear of Islam,
(5) The Turkish Threat: Muhammad in the Europe of the Renaissance, (6)
Muhammad as an Anti-Christ: The Fate of Muhammad and Islam in the Reformation, (7) Humanist or Fanatic: The Enlightenment Divided—Hero or Impostor?,
(8) Muhammad in the Age of Hero Worship, (9) Fantasies of Sensuality and Cruelty: Muhammad and Islam in Nineteenth Century European Imagination, (10)
The Return of the Crusades and Jihad: Islam at the End of the Ottoman Empire,
(11) From Reverence to Travesty: Muhammad in the Twentieth Century.

Reeves argues that the impact of Islam "has been so great in recent years that,
even as more balanced pictures of Muhammad and his religion have begun to
appear in Western writings, they have been eclipsed by images of radical and
anti-Western and violent Islam that once again bears the hallmarks of the age-old
prejudices. It is as if the wheel of history has turned full circle back to the age of
the Crusades and Holy Wars" (p.xii).

Footnotes and references are integrated within each chapter of the book. There
is also a bibliography, classified by main topics (e.g., life of Muhammad, history
of Arabia and Islam, translations and commentaries on the Qur'an, Muhammad
and Islam in European writings).

There is a ten-page bibliography at the end but no index.

B-306. Rodinson, Maxime. *Europe and the Mystique of Islam* (translated from
French by Roger Veinus). Seattle, WA: University of Washington Press, 1987.

The book is about the "orientalist" debate and, among other things, it presents
an analysis of how the West has perceived the East, especially the Islamic world,
through its own intellectual prism; it is an extension of a paper Rodinson wrote
for Joseph Schacht, editor of *The Legacy of Islam* (Oxford University Press,
Oxford, 1974). Not intended to be a "detailed history of the images and ideas of
Islam," the book attempts to "sketch a picture of the more general trends that
inspired these images and studies, directed their course, and prejudiced, distorted,
and colored the ideas, research, and findings" (p.xi). The author extends some
sympathy for such scholars, however; after all, "scholars are *in* the world, in their
world" (p.xii). Further, "There are many people who are now afraid of Islam. It
is terribly true that many frightening acts are committed in the name of Islam,

but these are no worse than those committed in the names of Christianity, Judaism, Freedom, and so on" (p.xii). The 164-page book argues that it can be instructive to understand how others of different persuasions have reacted to Islam and Muslims, "to their virtues and their crimes" (p.xv).

There are two long essays. The first is entitled Western Views of the Muslim World and covers the period from the Middle Ages to the 19th century and includes subtopics such as "from coexistence to objectivity," "the birth of Orientalism," "the enlightenment," and "challenges to eurocentrism." The second is entitled Toward a New Approach to Arab and Islamic Studies and covers topics such as "traditional orientalism," "the continuance of the past impetus," "regional influences in Islamic studies," "the modalities of future progress."

There is a list of notes and references at the end, keyed to each essay, followed by a comprehensive bibliography, alphabetically organized. There is also a detailed name-subject index.

B-307. Russell, G.A., ed. *The "Arabick" Interest of the Natural Philosophers in Seventeenth-Century England*. Leiden, Netherlands: E.J. Brill, 1994.

This volume is the product of a 1986 symposium, dubbed as "interdisciplinary, pioneering," held at the Wellcome Institute for the History of Medicine in London. It deals with the widespread interest in Arabic in 17th-century England among biblical scholars and theologians, natural philosophers, Fellows of the Royal Society, and others. The editor's introductory chapter sets the focus of the book: "The medieval transmission from Arabic into Latin helped transform European intellectual and scientific development. By the Renaissance, however, it had served its purpose. As Christendom gradually moved into the Age of Scientific Revolution, there was no longer any need or grounds for Arabic to be of interest to the West" (p.1). Institutionalization of Arabic studies is reflected, among other things, by the fact that Arabic was a required language at Cambridge and Oxford (p.1). Despite this "second wave" of interest in Arabic, "in the intensively scrutinized intellectual and social landscape of the period, it seems to have remained somewhat invisible to the historian outside specialized studies" (p.1). Further, "The roots of the 'second wave' of interest in Arabic lie, in fact, in the very movements which seemed to rule out any possible basis for its existence: the Protestant Reformation, the Humanist classical revival, and the 'expansion' of Europe and its emergence as the center of world trade" (p.3). However, "The fact that, in the face of religious intolerance and deeply ingrained prejudice, a detached inquiry into Arabic culture could emerge is a measure, more than any other area, of the fundamental change in the social and intellectual outlook of the period" (p.10).

The 320-page volume contains 14 essays: (1) Background to Arabic Studies in Seventeenth-Century England by H.M. Holt, (2) The English Interest in the Arabic-Speaking Christians by Alastair Hamilton, (3) Arabists and Linguists in Seventeenth-Century England by Vivian Salmon, (4) Edmund Castell and His *exicon Heptaglotton (1669)* by H.T. Norris, (5) The Medici Oriental Press (Rome 1584–1614) and the Impact of Its Arabic Publications on Northern Europe by Robert Jones, (6) Patrons and Professors: The Origins and Motives for the Endowment of University Chairs—in Particular the Laudian Professorship of Arabic by Mordechai Feingold, (7) Arabic Manuscripts in the Bodleian Library: The Seventeenth-Century Collections by Colin Wakefield, (8) Arabick Learning in the Correspondence of the Royal Society 1660–1677 by M.B. Hall, (9) English Orientalists and Mathematical Astronomy by Raymond Mercier, (10) The Limited Lure of Arabic Mathematics by George Molland, (11) The Impact of the *Philsophus autodidactus:* Pocockes, John Locke and the Society of Friends by G.A. Russell, (12) English Medical Writers and Their Interest in Classical Arabic Medicine in the Seventeenth Century by Andrew Wear, (13) Arabo-Latin Forgeries: The Case of the *Summa perfectionis* by William Newman, (14) Coronary Flowers and Their 'Arabick' Background by John Harvey.

The 11th essay is particularly revealing; it documents John Locke's (1632–1704) heavy reliance for his most influential book, *Essay Concerning Human Understanding,* upon Ibn Tufayl's (d. 1185) *Hayy ibn Yaqzan* ("Alive, Son of Man," or "The Self-Taught Philosopher"). Such 17th-century "Arabick" influence, tantamount to plagiarism, exemplifies how "a major figure can be seen from an entirely new perspective which brings out an aspect of his intellectual development that had formerly been unknown" (p.253).

Each essay ends with its own notes and references, and there is a detailed name-subject index at the end.

B-308. Said, Edward. *Orientalism.* New York: Vintage Books Edition, Random House, 1979.

The 370-page book represents a critique of how the Orient, in particular the Islamic world, has been historically represented by Western scholars. It is one of the most widely read and controversial books of the 20th century. Ever since its publication, it has continued to inspire conferences and forums throughout the world, in addition to having given rise to voluminous literature in various disciplines. *Orientalism* is defined as "a way of coming to terms with the Orient that is based on the Orient's special place in European Western experience," "a style of thought based upon an ontological and epistemological distinction made between 'the Orient' and (most of the time) 'the Occident'" (p.2–3). The book has also spawned a field of Occidentalism, which explores how writers in the Middle East have tended to look at the West.

Historically and materially defined, the author says, "Orientalism can be discussed and analyzed as the corporate institution for dealing with the Orient— dealing with it by making statements about it, authorizing views of it, describing it, by teaching it, settling it, ruling over it: in short, Orientalism as a Western style for dominating, restructuring, and having authority over the Orient" (p.3). Moreover, the author contends, "Without examining Orientalism as a discourse one cannot possibly understand the enormously systematic discipline by which European culture was able to manage—and even produce—the Orient politically, sociologically, militarily, ideologically, scientifically, and imaginatively during the post-Enlightenment period" (p.3). He attempts to expose the agendas and assumptions of the scholars who have written about the Middle East.

The "nineteenth-century academic and imaginative demonology of the 'mysterious Orient,'" says the author, is "nowhere more true than in the ways by which the Near East is grasped" (p.26). Three things have contributed to this: (1) "history of popular anti-Arab and anti-Islamic prejudice in the West"; (2) "the struggle between the Arabs and Israeli Zionism, and its effects upon American Jews as well as upon both the liberal culture and the population at large"; and (3) "almost total absence of any cultural position making it possible either to identify with or dispassionately to discuss the Arabs or Islam" (p.26–27).

In addition to the introduction, there are three long chapters: (1) The Scope of Orientalism, (2) Orientalist Structures and Restructures, (3) Orientalism Now. The author concludes with the hope of having "shown readers that the answer to Orientalism is not Occidentalism. If the knowledge of Orientalism has any meaning, it is in being a reminder of the selective degradation of knowledge, of any knowledge, anywhere, at any time. Now perhaps more than ever before" (p.328).

Chapter-by-chapter notes and references are provided at the end, followed by a detailed name-subject index. There is no separate bibliography.

B-309. Sardar, Ziauddin, ed. *The Revenge of Athena: Science, Exploitation and the Third World*. New York and London: Mansell Publishing Ltd., 1988.

The book "explores just how science perpetuates violence against the people, societies, economies, environments, traditions, cultures, ontologies and epistemologies of the Third World; and what possibilities the Third World can itself develop to meet the challenge of western science" (p.3).

The edited book is a collection of papers, written by well-known international scholars, that were presented at the symposium "The Crisis in Modern Science" held in Penang, Malaysia, in 1986. Athena, the daughter of the Greek God Zeus, personified the Hellenic ideal, the goddess of both war and reason; Greek Athena represents the intellectual and social ideal of our time, the editor argues, and modern science, as it is practiced today with origins in the 17th-century European Enlightenment, "is based on extreme use of reason directed towards the extreme use of violence. Reason is exclusive in the sense that there is no place in science for issues of morality or values for it is pure, clinical and neutral" (p.3).

The 360-page book is divided into three parts. Part I, What's Wrong with Science, has three chapters and the discourse relates to the "The Crisis in Science." Part II, Science and Third World Domination, has 13 chapters and the focus is on the impact of science and technology on the Third World—issues such as science and control, science and efficiency, science and health, science and hunger, and science and development are discussed. Part III, Third World Possibilities, explores the prospects of indigenous science in the Third World.

Two chapters in Part III carry special interest: Islamic Science, Western Science: Common Heritage, Diverse Destinies by Seyyed Hossein Nasr and Islamic Science: Current Thinking, Future Directions by Munawar A. Anees and Merryl W. Davies. The first of these argues that while the "Medieval Christianity shared with Islam a world-view based at once upon revelation and a metaphysical knowledge drawn from the sapiential dimension of the tradition [Christian or Islamic]," once this world-view "was eclipsed and for all practical purposes lost, there was no means whereby a science based on metaphysical principles could be cultivated or even understood" (p.13). Also the rise of nominalism, the author argues, "denied the very meaning of universals (an act of reduction) and based religious truth upon faith rather than upon both faith and knowledge" (p.13). The second chapter, concerned with the rediscovery of Islamic science, presents an overview of the current literature, argues for the revitalization of *ilm* (knowledge), "a multi-dimensional, integrative concept that regards knowledge as an organic unity that can be pursued only within the framework of values, a whole system of knowledge that questions and evaluates what constitutes wisdom based upon its own holistic definition of human betterment" (p.15).

Each essay ends with its own footnotes and bibliography. At the end there is also an appendix, "The Penang Declaration on Science and Technology," and there is a detailed name-subject index.

B-310. Sarton, George. *The Incubation of Western Culture in the Middle East.* George C. Keiser Foundation Lecture, Library of Congress. Washington, DC: U.S. Government Printing Office, 1951.

This 45-page booklet is the first Keiser Foundation lecture, delivered on March 29, 1950, and it is extracted from the scholar's other monumental works on the history of science (synonymous to history of knowledge, according to the author). He begins by stating that he has devoted his "life to harmonizing the differences obtaining between Science and the Humanities, and to explaining the misunderstandings between East and West" (p.7). And he argues that the "tree of knowledge" and the "history of science begins definitely in what we are agreed to call the Middle East" (p.10). That is the region that influenced "our civilization" most directly, not "India, China, or even Indochina" (p.10). Further, while America functioned as a melting pot for over two centuries, "the Middle East operated like that for a period at least twenty times longer" (p.14).

The Greek knowledge was closed shut by the Roman Emperor Justinian in 529 AD. By the end of the eighth century, the author notes, the division and antagonisms between Greeks and Latins were so intense that the latter went to the Arab sources to learn. And then happened "one of the most fruitful events in the history of mankind: the birth of Islam" (p.15). The author talks of the "wonders" of Islam and "greatness of the Prophet" (p.18). He emphasizes the point by stating, "No prophet has ever been vindicated as completely as he was" (p.24). As for the spread of Islam, "Christian faith had been undermined for centuries by theological quarrels and by mutual excommunications, and many of the Christians of the Middle East welcomed the Muslim invaders as deliverers from orthodox tyranny" (p.26). And, "The Muslim empire was created with the willing collaboration of Greeks, Persians, Copts, etc.—Christians, Magians, Sabeans, and Jews" (p.27). Then the "miracle of Arabic science" happened, beginning in Baghdad; reference is to the assimilation of Greek knowledge and building upon it; and, Sarton emphasizes, "there is nothing like it in the whole history of the world" (p.27). Those historians who suggest that "the Arabs were nothing but imitators" are blinded by prejudice (p.29). Further, "The achievements of the Arabic speaking peoples between the ninth and twelfth centuries are so great as to baffle our understanding" (p.35). The author also notes, "Islam in its phenomenal rise had raised the Arabs to great heights, in its decadence it let them down to the abyss" (p.41).

The author concludes: "The Middle East was the cradle of our culture, and from it came the means of salvaging it during the Middle Ages when an Iron Curtain was cutting the world asunder. We look to its past with gratitude, and to its future, with loving hope" (p.45).

There is no bibliography or index.

B-311. Schacht, Joseph, ed. (assisted by C.E. Bosworth). *The Legacy of Islam,* second edition. Oxford: Clarendon Press, 1974.

Similar to the 1931 volume of the same title (edited by Sir Thomas Arnold and Alfred Guillaume), this 530-page book includes some chapters with the same titles. However, the authors are different and there are substantial changes in scope and content. Others have been replaced with essays "on the general course of cultural, ideological, and economic interaction between Islam and the outside world, above all, between Islam and the western Christian world" (p.vi). Also included is coverage of the political–military challenge and response, as is the discussion of the impact of Islam on Africa and Asia. The second group of essays incorporates newer approaches to the study of Islamic civilization, notably those drawing upon the historical and social sciences. The editor argues, however, that while "there are still important gaps to be filled," the objective is the same as that of the earlier volume; that is, to document the "contribution of Islam to the achievements of mankind in all their aspects, and the contacts of Islam with and its influences on the surrounding non-Islamic world" (p.vii). Additionally, this collection attempts to update and reformulate the problems and reconsiders the solutions in the light of modern scholarship in Islamic studies.

There are ten distinct topics covered in the book, with separate essays in four of them; thus, a total of 18 essays, each written by eminent scholars in Islamic studies (e.g., Maxime Rodinson, Francesco Gabrieli, Aziz Ahmad, Bernard Lewis, Oleg Grabar, Franz Rosenthal, Joseph Schacht, C.E. Bosworth, Martin Plessner). Topics covered are: (1) The Western Image and Western Studies of

Islam, (2) Islam in the Mediterranean World, (3) Islamic Frontiers in Africa and Asia, (4) Politics and War, (5) Economic Developments, (6) Art and Architecture, (7) Literature, (8) Philosophy, Theology, and Mysticism, (9) Law and the State, (10) Science.

Notes and references are integrated within each essay, with a bibliography at the end of each. There are 63 illustrative pictures of historical structure and artifacts, and there is a comprehensive name-subject index.

B-312. Semaan, Khalil I., ed. *Islam and the Medieval West: Aspects of Intercultural Relations.* Albany, NY: State University of New York Press, 1980.

The book is the second of two volumes and contains six of the 13 papers presented at the 9th Annual Conference of the Center for Medieval and Early Renaissance Studies, held at Binghamton, New York, in May 1975. The first volume, edited by Stanley Ferber with a similar title, covered Islamic art and architecture and their impacts on the medieval West, and was also published by the State University of New York Press.

The papers deal with six different topics; they have in common only the fact that each represents a sample of "orientalist" research with medieval Islam as its cultural axis. The topics provide a flavor of the book's content, and titles and authors are: (1) Commercial Relations between the Near East and Western Europe from the 7th to the 11th Century by Claude Cahen (University of Paris), (2) On the Origin and Development of the College in Islam and the West by George Makdisi (University of Pennsylvania), (3) Islamic Sciences and the Medieval West: Pharmacology by Albert Dietrich (University of Gottingen), (4) Early Islamic Theologians on the Existence of God by Joseph van Ess (University of Tubingen), (5) The Spanish Reconquest: A Classic Holy War against Islam? by Vicente Cantarino (University of Texas), (6) The Role of al-Andalus in the Movement of Ideas between Islam and the West by Anwar Chejne (University of Minnesota).

The last chapter consists of a "Disputatio" section led by George F. Hourani of State University of New York at Buffalo; in addition to tying together the general topic of the volume, it provides an overall view of some of the problems and prospects in the field of Islamic and Medieval European Studies.

The 170-page book provides a select bibliography on topics covered in the papers, and there is a name-subject index at the end.

B-313. Sha'ban, Fuad. *Islam and Arabs in Early American Thought: The Roots of Orientalism in America.* Durham, NC: Published in Association with Duke University Islamic and Arabian Development Studies, The Acorn Press, 1991.

This study, according to the author of the foreword (Ralph Braibanti of Duke University) has special relevance in the context of "contemporary millenarianism, which has become enmeshed in the web of a Christian quest of Zion, thereby contorting our perception of Islamic and Arab affairs" (p.i). This is the phenomenon of *Orientalism,* "explored in greater depth by analysis of both literary and religious texts and behavior from our colonial beginnings to the time of Ulysses S. Grant" (p.i). Added to the "legacy of suspicion, if not hostility" that goes back to the Crusades, says this author, there are contemporary factors: Arab-Israeli conflict ("which results in massive campaigns of disinformation and vituperation damaging to Islam and to the Arab image"), Arab militancy due to that conflict and other humiliations, and American evangelical fundamentalism and "Judaiza-tion of Christianity" (p.iii). Such factors together have strengthened "earlier mis-conceptions by linking Judaism and Christianity and, by implication, isolating Islam as the enemy of both" (p.iii). This is despite the fact that the mainstream Catholic and Protestant groups "show a greater appreciation of Islam and an affinity with Arab culture" (p.iii).

Relying on European and native sources, the book explores and analyzes the factors in American history and culture responsible for the evolution of "Ameri-can Orientalism"; the period extends to the 19th century. Definitionally, "Orien-talism" is described as an institution that treats the Orient "by making statements about it, ruling it: in short, Orientalism is a Western style for dominating, restruc-turing, and having authority over the Orient" (p.vii). The basis of this Oriental-ism, according to the author, lies fundamentally in the fact that the immigrants to the New World "considered themselves chosen people and America the land of promise," the new state being the "Kingdom of God," later translated into extending "American values and beliefs to the rest of the world" (p.viii–ix).

The 242-page book has an introductory essay by Louis Budd, another Duke University faculty member, followed by eight main chapters: (1) A Place for My People, (2) The Star in the West, (3) The Prophet's Progress, (4) The Shores of Tripoli, (5) The Great Commission, (6) Eastward Ho, (7) The Vision of Zion, (8) The Dream of Baghdad. There is also a concluding chapter. The author notes: "As an Arab Muslim, I have approached this subject with some trepidation. Much of the material I have dealt with is obnoxious to me, but I hope that I have not allowed my feelings to interfere with an objective treatment of the subject" (p.xi).

Chapter-by-chapter notes and references are provided at the end of the book, followed by a comprehensive bibliography and a name-subject index.

B-314. Sinor, Denis, ed. *Orientalism and History*, second edition. Bloomington, IN, and London: Indiana University Press, 1970.

Studies of European history, while fairly broad in a geographical sense, still remain narrow, in that mainly the Ancient Near East is usually covered as the key link to "our own civilization"; for other "extra-European studies interest remains very limited" (p.ix). Further, the question remains "whether scholars representing the intellectual tradition of Europe are willing and able to write world history, with Western methods to be sure, but without the Western provin-cialism that mars all too many of the supposedly objective studies of social scien-tists" (p.xiv).

The 124-page book contains five essays written by well-known specialists: (1) The Ancient Near East by H. Frankfort, (2) Islam by Bernard Lewis, (3) India and Its Cultural Empire by J.E. van Lohuizen-de Leeuw, (4) China by Edwin G. Pulleyblank, (5) Central Eurasia by Denis Sinor. The first essay traces European history to the earliest civilized societies of Egypt and Mesopotamia, called the "Ancient Near East," the area from "Greece to Iran, with an offshoot in the Indus Valley" (p.2). More relevant for our purpose is the essay on Islam civilization, which the author says, "forms an interesting and significant subject of study for itself—but not only for itself. Its wide extent, its many contacts, its civilizing role and its rich documentation make it important for many other fields" (p.22).

Further, "The great clash between Christendom and Islam in the Crusades has for long been one of the major concerns of the medieval historian. Yet to this day Western scholars have studied it almost entirely on the basis of Western sources . . . most of them incomplete and inaccurate" And, "The Muslim regimes of Spain and Sicily are important not only because of the European territories over which they ruled, but also because of the influence they exerted on the rest of Europe, [they] started a kind of renaissance in the twelfth century. All this is usually studied only from Western sources" (p.23).

Each essay provides some bibliographic notes; however, there is no index.

B-315. Southern, Richard W. *Western Views of Islam in the Middle Ages*. Cambridge, MA: Harvard University Press, 1962.

Written by one of the most eminent scholars of medieval history, this 115-page book is based on three invited lectures delivered by the author at Harvard University in 1961, in order "to put into shape some thoughts on the problem of Islam as it was viewed in western Europe in the Middle Ages" (p.i). Thus, the three chapter titles are indicative of the content: (1) The Age of Ignorance, (2) The Century of Reason and Hope, (3) The Moment of Vision.

The author's main task is to present a discourse that aims to "understand the contribution of Islam to the development of Western thought and the effect on Western society of the neighborhood of Islam" (p.2). The 12th century was one of "reason and hope," the century of renaissance during which the process of acquisition and adaptation of Greek learning in Islam was "the most astonishing event in the history of thought" (p.8–9). Islam being the "most far reaching problem in medieval Christianity," the spirit of detailed and academic or humane inquiry was seldom pursued in the West; instead, distortions about Islam were created. For many Western writers, the ignorance of Islam was "like a man in prison who hears rumors of outside events and attempts to give a shape to what he hears, with the help of his preconceived ideas" (p.14). Further, "If they saw and understood little of what went on around them, and if they knew nothing of Islam as a religion, it was because they wished to know nothing" (p.25). There were some, to be sure, who recognized "the strength of the Moslem insistence on the unity of God," and who admired and assimilated the works of numerous Muslim scholars (p.36).

As for the multidimensional linkages with the Islamic world, the more relevant section of the book is the chapter entitled Reason and Hope. Here the author notes, "It would be difficult to exaggerate the extent to which these influences changed the outlook of learned Europeans in the half century after 1230" (p.54). Southern cautions, however, in that, having evolved over several centuries, "the Western sense of superiority in every sphere of endeavor has scarcely been challenged. It has become part of our heritage, most painful to abandon" (p.2).

The book provides notes and references in the text of each chapter. There is a name-subject index.

B-316. Tolan, John V. *Saracens: Islam in the Medieval European Imagination.* New York: Columbia University Press, 2002.

The author begins with noting that "countless Christians, throughout the Middle Ages and beyond, found themselves in Riccoldo's [a 13th-century Christian missionary to Baghdad] predicament: confronted by an expanding, dynamic Muslim civilization, they needed to make sense of it" (p.xiv). While some accepted the logic of Muslim expansion, others formulated biblical explanations and "redeployed and reinterpreted" biblical passages "to make sense of Muslim victories" (p.xv). Further, says Tolan, in the face of Islamic successes, "many Christians embraced the faith of the prophet Muhammad. Among those who did not, a number assigned to Islam a place in the pantheon of God's enemies in order to discourage fellow Christians from converting to Islam or to justify military action against Islam" (p.xv). The last chapter clearly defines "two goals of the book: first, to examine these Christian writings about Islam on their own terms, placing them in their particular (and multiple) contexts, rather than on a time line showing, say, the inexorable rise of orientalism or of ideologies justifying colonial expansion; second, to present a number of examples of the social and ideological uses of denigration and contempt, examples that should be of interest to nonmedievalists: historians, anthropologists, sociologists, and others" (p.280).

The author acknowledges some other studies on medieval Christian–Muslim relations, but they do not adequately explore "why Christian writers presented Islam in this way or what ideological interests these portrayals might have served" (p.xvi–xvii). However, there is "no general study on medieval Christian images of Islam" (p.xvi). This book attempts "to fill this gap: to examine how and why medieval Christians portrayed Islam—or rather, portrayed what they preferred to call the 'law of the Saracens'" (p.xvi). Further, "A sentiment of Western superiority over Muslims and over Arabs runs deep in European and North American culture: this sentiment has its roots in the Middle Ages" (p.xvii). The book is also meant to complement Edward Said's 1979 classic, *Orientalism*, a phenomenon defined as "the ideological counterpart to the political and military realities of British and French empires in the Near East" (p.xviii).

The 372-page book is divided into three parts, with 11 chapters altogether, in addition to an introduction and a concluding chapter. Part One, Foundations (Seventh–Eighth Centuries), has three chapters: (1) God and History in the Christian West, c.600, (2) Islamic Domination and the Religious Other, (3) Early Eastern Christian Reactions to Islam. Part Two, Forging Polemical Images (Eighth–Twelfth Centuries), has three chapters: (4) Western Christian Responses to Islam (Eighth–Ninth Centuries), (5) Saracens as Pagans, (6) Muhammad, Heresiarch (Twelfth Century). Part Three, Thirteenth-Century Dreams of Conquest and Conversion, has five chapters: (7) The Muslim in the Ideologies of Thirteenth-Century Christian Spain, (8) Apocalyptic Fears and Hopes Inspired by the Thirteenth-Century Crusades, (9) Franciscan Missionaries Seeking the Martyr's Palm, (10) The Dominican Missionary Strategy, (11) From Verdant Grove to Dark Prison: Realms of Mission in Ramon Llull.

The author concludes: "The Saracen was reputed for his learning, seen as eminently rational; he (like the Jew) became the object of philosophical polemics and impassioned preaching. When, toward the end of the thirteenth century, it became clear that the Saracen was (like the Jew) impermeable to such 'rational' argument, he was relegated to the subrational world of carnal, semibeastly humans. The Saracen (and more generally the non-Christian, be he Jew or Cathar or, in the centuries that followed, an African animist or an Inca priest) was different, was inferior, precisely because he refused the universal and rational message of Christianity" (p.283).

The book provides 63-pages of chapter-by-chapter notes and references at the end. There is also a topical, select bibliography, followed by a name-subject index.

B-317. Toomer, G.J. *Eastern Wisedome and Learning: The Study of Arabic in Seventeenth-Century England.* Oxford: Clarendon Press, 1996.

The book is about the rise and fall of Arabic studies in 17th-century England particularly, but also in Europe generally. With Edward Pococke and others at Oxford, Arabic studies flourished in the late 16th century and much of the 17th century. However, during the late-17th century, decline began to happen, and by 1680 Arabic studies virtually disappeared. During the Middle Ages the study of Arabic was motivated by two factors, the author notes: the acquisition of scientific knowledge and Christian missionary and apologetic activities.

The decline is argued to be due to three factors: (1) with modern innovations in science, Arabic sources became less relevant; (2) the original Arabists were concerned with the use of Arabic for biblical exegesis, but after the Restoration such textual analysis gave way to larger ethical and moral dimensions of Christianity; and, most importantly, (3) the original Arabists engaged in Arabic studies for the love of learning but after the Restoration this interest dwindled. For this last argument, the author maintains that the decline is chiefly the result of diminished scholarly interest in disseminating "knowledge of a civilization about which ignorance and prejudice were still the general rule in Europe" (p.314). And the pursuit of Arabic studies was now increasingly driven by national-interest motives.

The 381-page book has ten chapters: (1) The Medieval Background, (2) The Study of Arabic in Europe during the Sixteenth and Seventeenth Centuries, (3) The Earliest Period of Arabic Studies in England, (4) Laud and Arabic at Oxford, (5) The Early Career of Pococke, (6) Greaves and Pococke in the East, (7) Arabic Studies during the English Revolution, (8) Arabic Studies after the Restoration, (9) The Decline of Arabic Studies in England, (10) Epilogue.

Notes and references are integrated in the text of each chapter. There is a 40-page bibliography, followed by a detailed name-subject index.

B-318. Turner, Bryan S. *Weber and Islam.* London and Boston: Routledge and Kegan Paul, 1978; original 1973.

The book represents a study of Islam that "grew out of the context of teaching comparative sociology of religion against the background of scarce, inadequate and over-specialized literature on Islam," with Max Weber's sociology of civilizations as a starting point (p.1). Another motivation, according to the author, is the fact that most textbooks on sociology of religion "show the recurrent and depressing fact that sociologists are either not interested in Islam or have nothing to contribute to Islamic scholarship" (p.1).

There are three elements to this study. The first task is to outline Weber's views on Islam, Muhammad, and Islamic society. Weber argued that the Luther-Calvin Protestantism led to the rise of European capitalism, and that the patrimonial nature of Muslim political institutions precluded the emergence of capitalistic pre-conditions (e.g., rationality, free markets, money economy, etc.). Also, Weber argued that "Islam as a religion of warriors produced an ethic which was incompatible with the 'spirit of capitalism'" (p.2). Turner challenges these assertions. The second task relates to Weber's response to Marxism; Marx stressed the importance of the monopoly of economic power, whereas Weber argued in favor of concentration of political power. The third task relates to Weber's discussion of the problem of the relationship between Islam, colonialism, and the rise of modern society. The author disputes Weber's view that capitalistic ethic and secularization suited the Middle East due to the link between industrial society and secularization; instead, the author reasons, "These world-views have been imported by Muslim intellectuals who had accepted a Western interpretation of history" (p.3).

The 212-page book is divided into three parts. Part One has four chapters: (1) An interpretation of Weber on Islam, (2) Charisma and the origins of Islam, (3) Allah and man, (4) Saint and sheikh. Part Two also has four chapters: (1) Patrimonialism and charismatic succession, (2) Islam and the city, (3) Weber, law, and Islam, (4) Islam and Ottoman decline. Part Three has three chapters: (1)

Islamic reform and the sociology of motives, (2) Islam and secularization, (3) Marx, Weber, and Islam.

Chapter-by-chapter notes and references are provided at the end, followed by a name-subject index.

B-319. Watt, W. Montgomery. *The Influence of Islam on Medieval Europe*. Edinburgh: Edinburgh University Press, 1972.

The short, concisely written book explores the various ways in which Islamic world influenced medieval Europe in its "totality" and "to assess the importance of its contribution to Europe and Europe's response to it." Further, "It has been recognized for some time that Medieval Christian writers created an image of Islam that was in many respects denigratory. For our indebtedness to Islam, however, we Europeans have a blind spot. We sometimes belittle the extent and importance of Islamic influence in our heritage, and sometimes overlook it altogether. We must acknowledge our indebtedness to the full. To try to cover it over and deny it is a mark of false pride" (p.1–2).

The 125-page book contains six chapters: (1) Islamic Presence in Europe, (2) Commerce and Technology, (3) Arab Achievements in Science and Philosophy, (4) Reconquista and Crusade, (5) Science and Philosophy in Europe, (6) Islam and European Self-Awareness. The book ends with the observation: "Not merely did Islam share with western Europe many material products and technological discoveries; not merely did it stimulate Europe intellectually in the fields of science and philosophy; but it provoked Europe into forming a new image of itself. Because Europe was reacting against Islam it belittled the influence of the Saracens and exaggerated its dependence on its Greek and Roman heritage. So today an important task for us western Europeans, as we move into the era of one world, is to correct this false emphasis and to acknowledge fully our debt to the Arab and Islamic world" (p.84).

There is an appendix that provides a list of numerous English words derived from Arabic. This is followed chapter-by-chapter footnotes (which also provide details on additional references) and a name-subject index.

B-320. Watt, W. Montgomery. *Muslim–Christian Encounters: Perceptions and Misperceptions*. London: Routledge, 1991.

Relations between Christianity and Islam have been strained, almost from the beginning of Islam's emergence, and recent events, especially the apocalyptic nightmare of September 11, 2001, have further widened the gulf. The negative views of Islam, relatively dormant until recently, have revived the historic antagonisms, as has the Muslim resentment against the West, aggravated by events in the Middle East and elsewhere. The author, who is one of the leading authorities on Islam in the West, shows that throughout history, Muslim–Christian encounters, have been marred by myths and misperceptions, many of which survive today. The book is viewed as of particular interest to students of Islam, religion, history, and intercultural relations.

The 165-page book discusses how the myths originated, how they nurtured, and how they continue to blight mutual perceptions. Further, the need for more accurate knowledge on the part of both Muslims and Christians is emphasized, so that there is a more positive appreciation of the other religion. There are suggestions as to how useful cooperation for global peace between Muslims, Christians, and members of other religions may be achieved.

The book contains nine chapters: (1) The Christianity encountered by Islam, (2) The Qur'anic perception of Christianity, (3) The elaboration of Qur'anic perceptions, (4) The encounter with Greek philosophy, (5) Encounters under Muslim rule, (6) Encounters with medieval Europe, (7) The background of the modern encounter, (8) The modern encounter, (9) Towards the future.

In chapter 5, the author concludes that whether in al-Andalus where there was an amazing flowering of culture as, under Muslim rule, Jews and Christians fully participated in the intellectual artistic and spiritual life of the community, or in the later Muslim empires, "Islamic colonialism was relatively benign" (p.62). In chapter 6, the author discusses, among other things, the differences between the distorted perceptions of Islam and "the more objective perception of today's western scholars" (p.85). Four such perceptions are elaborated (falsehood of Islam; spread by violence and sword; self-indulgent religion; Mohammad as the Anti-Christ). The last chapter emphasizes the need for mutual acceptance; Christians must accept other religions "as being on equal footing, that is, as being just as much religions as Christianity" (p.145). And, "For Muslims also, if they are to live alongside other religions, it will be necessary to abandon their exclusivism" (p.149).

The book provides chapter-by-chapter notes and references at the end, followed by a name-subject index.

(C) General

(I) SPAIN/AL-ANDALUS

B-321. Altamira, Rafael. *A History of Spanish Civilization* (translated from Spanish by P. Volkov). London: Constable and Company, 1930.

The book describes the history of Spain during various periods, including political background and international relationships, as well as the Spanish institutions in existence at various times and the functions they performed. Also covered is the evolution of Spanish art and architecture, and what was thought and written. Unlike some other authors, the coverage of the Spain's Moorish civilization is said to be objective.

Beyond the introductory chapter, the 280-page book has ten chapters: (1) The Primitive Age, (2) The Roman Influence, (3) Christianity, (4) The Domination of the Visigoths (5th–8th centuries), (5) Muslim Domination (8th–11th centuries), (6) Hegemony Passes to the Christian Kingdom (11th–15th centuries), (7) End of the Reconquest (1479–1517), (8) Political and Spiritual Supremacy of Spain in Its Decline (1517–1700), (9) The Revival in the 18th Century (1701–1808), (10) The 19th and Beginning of the 20th Centuries (1808–1914).

Chapters 5 and 6 provide considerable detail concerning the Islamic civilization in Spain ("the most brilliant perhaps that the Muslim world has ever known" [p.xvii]). "In spite of the intransigent character of certain Muslims," it is stated, "in general, they respected the religious ideas and practices of the Spanish people, their laws, customs, and, to a great degree, even their property. Thanks to this tolerance, and to the liberty conceded to all their subjects and slaves who embraced the religion of Islam, they did not meet with much resistance on the part of the inhabitants" (p.48). Further, although the Muslims inherited various areas of knowledge from classical antiquity, "they gave them an original and very powerful development, and so became the most cultivated people of those times" (p.50).

As for the Islamic cultural influence, the author quotes a ninth-century monk,

San Alvaro de Cordoba, who complained: "Many of my co-religionaries read the poems and stories of the Arabs, and study the writings of Muhammadan theologians and philosophers, not in order to refute them, but to learn how to express themselves most elegantly and correctly in the Arabic tongue. Alas! All the young Christians who become notable for their talents know only the language and literature of the Arabs" (p.55). Elsewhere, Altamira notes, "The sphere in which the Muslims chiefly shone" during the period 11th to 13th centuries "was that of science and literature, and more especially in philosophy, medicine, astronomy, and mathematics, and in poetry and history. The Jews, numerous in Muslim districts, contributed greatly to this scientific and literary movement, which flourished most brilliantly in the 12th and 13th centuries. Their most illustrious representatives, both by reason of the importance of their doctrines and the influence they exerted all over Europe, were the Muslim philosophers Averroes, Avempace, and Abentofail (Ibn Tufail), with the Jewish savants Ben Gabriol (known to the Latins as Avicebron), Ben Ezra, and Maimonides" (p.71).

The book is interspersed with 50 illustrative pictures in various chapters. An appendix provides a detailed bibliography, with some annotations, classified by 36 topics relevant to the chapters of the book. There is a name-subject index, followed by a brief glossary of several key Spanish words.

B-322. Atkinson, William C. *A History of Spain and Portugal.* Baltimore, MD: Penguin Books, Inc., 1960; reprinted 1961 and 1965.

The 382-page book "attempts to deal selectively with the crowded, perhaps overcrowded, pageant of events, spanning two thousand years and more, in virtue of which Spain and Portugal, Spaniard and Portuguese, are today what they are." The author notes, "It is one of the paradoxes of their history that these two peoples have consistently seemed surer of themselves when imposing their will on others beyond their frontiers than when at the helm of their own affairs" (p.11).

There are 15 chapters (The Setting; Roman Foundations; Visigothic Overlay; Irruption from Africa; The Reconquest; Patterns of Society; The End of the Middle Ages; Literature and the Arts—I; Involvement in Europe; The Age of Retribution; Literature and the Arts—II; "No More Pyrenees"; The Great Experiment; Disillusion; Literature and the Arts—III). Chapter 3 (Visigothic Overlay) concludes that early in the eighth century some Visigoth rulers conspired with the Arab leaders in "overthrowing Roderic," and thus began "the betrayal of the Peninsula to the infidel" and "close to eight centuries were to pass before its final expiation" (p.44).

More relevant presently is chapter 4 (Irruption from Africa) which discusses, among other things, the evolution of Al-Andalus into a "stable civilization which materially and intellectually was centuries in advance of anything else to be found in Europe outside of Byzantium" (p.58). Further, "The Jews, bitterly persecuted under the Visigoths, [were] encouraged in the professions and employed in the highest offices of state and the Talmudic school of Cordoba ranked among the greatest centres of Hebrew learning" (p.59). And, "Al-Andalus, seemingly the negation of European values, thus played a pivotal role in conserving, developing, and transmitting to medieval Christendom that earlier Greek heritage that Roman Spain had already largely forgotten" (p.59). There are frequent references to the impact of Islamic civilization on Spanish/Portuguese culture.

At the end there is a chronological table of major events about the history of the region, followed by a bibliography arranged in terms of histories in Spanish and Portuguese languages; general surveys in English; studies on particular themes and periods. There is detailed name-subject index.

B-323. Brann, Ross, ed. *Languages of Power in Islamic Spain.* Bethesda, MD: CXDL Press, 1997.

The book includes papers presented at a 1994 conference at Cornell University. Focusing on Al-Andalus (Islamic Spain) during the period 711 to 1492, the papers discuss, among other things, various aspects of the cultural interaction and explore "the significance of some of the contested cultural boundaries erected between and within the three monotheistic communities" (p.vii). The editor notes that whether one ascribes to the notion of conflict-ridden Iberian society or to the notion of *convivencia*, "Spain was unique in the history of medieval Europe for its religious and ethnic diversity" (p.vii). The papers also explore "how various discourses mediated tensions between pietists and members of the courtly class, conflicts and rivalries among and within religious communities, and ethnic or socio-economic cleavages within the Andalusi society and in Christian Spain" (p.viii).

The eight essays in the 220-page book are: (1) The *Qasidah* and the Poetics of Ceremony: Three 'Id Panegyrics to the Cordoban Caliphate by Suzanne Pinckney Stetkevych, (2) Philologians and Poets in Search of the Hebrew Language by Angel Saenz-Badillos, (3) Representation and Identity in Medieval Spain: Beatus Manuscripts and the Mudejar Churches of Teruel by D. Fairchild Ruggles, (4) Textualizing Ambivalence in Islamic Spain: Arabic Representations of Ismail Ibn Naghrilah by Ross Brann, (5) The Arabicization and Islamization of the Christians of Al-Andalus: Evidence of Their Scriptures by Hanna Kassis, (6) Ambivalence in Medieval Religious Polemic: The Influence of Multiculturalism on the *Dialogues* of Petrus Alphonsi by Barbara Hurwitz Grant, (7) Longing, Belonging, and Pilgrimage in Ibn Arabi's *Interpreter of Desires (Tarjuman al-Ashwaq)* by Michael A. Sells, (8) Practical Intelligence: Don Juan Manuel by Ciriaco Moron Arroyo.

Notes and references are integrated in the text of each essay, and there is a name-subject index.

B-324. Burckhardt, Titus. *Moorish Culture in Spain* (translated by Alisa Jaffa). New York: McGraw-Hill Book Company, 1975.

Burckhardt states, "In order to understand a culture, it is necessary to feel affinity for its values. These are fundamentally the same in all cultures, at least in those which meet not only the physical but also the spiritual requirements of man, without which life is meaningless" (p.7). Further, the Moorish culture (synonymous with Arab-Islamic culture) lasted over 800 years. This book offers a selection of certain aspects which are relevant to those fundamental values and which, according to the author, "are of more than mere historic interest" (p.7).

The 230-page book contains 13 chapters: (1) Cordoba, (2) Religion and Races, (3) The Caliphate, (4) The City, (5) Heaven and Earth, (6) Language and Poetry, (7) Chivalric Love, (8) Spain in Check, (9) The Philosophical Outlook, (10) Faith and Science, (11) The Mystics, (12) Toledo, (13) Granada.

In discussing the "philosophical outlook," the author notes, the Arab philosophers "have often been accused with having inextricably woven Platonic elements into the Aristotelian heritage, which they passed on to the Christian West, as if by so doing they were guilty of misrepresentation. In reality, this 'mingling' for which they are censured, represents a splendid work of adaptation, a synthesis in the truest sense of the word without which the intellectual flowering of the Christian Middle Ages would have been inconceivable" (p.129). Elsewhere, referring to Ibn Rushd (1126–1198), the author notes that once this scholar's "most comprehensive rendering of Aristotelian philosophy" reached the Christian West, "it caused an absolute upheaval in academic thought. The Cordovan philosopher was without question the most penetrating and faithful exponent of the great Greek thinker" (p.145).

The book contains 90 pictures and sketches (listing provided at the end). There is also a chronological table of dates and events in the history of Moorish Spain (from 711 to 1492). This is followed by a selected bibliography, organized in terms of (1) History, (2) Islamic-Moorish Culture in General, (3) Fine Arts, (4) Languages and Literature, (5) Philosophy, (6) Mysticism, (7) Science. There is also a name-subject index.

B-325. Burns, Robert Ignatius, S.J. *Medieval Colonialism: Postcrusade Exploitation of Islamic Valencia.* Princeton, NJ: Princeton University Press, 1975.

The 394-page book approaches the "colonialized Muslim via his tax burden. As the church volumes revealed the European society in its exploitation of religious dynamism for expansionist practicalities, the present study will explore the dying or at least traumatically transculturating Islamic society as reflected in the tax system and its ambience" (p.xi). It is a socioeconomic monograph that may be viewed "as an indepth study of Mudejar (Muslims under Christian rule) taxation, as an usual approach to crusade history, as an essay in medieval revenues over the spectrum of feudal, royal, and seignorial, as a rare glimpse into the obscure subject of late Almohad society, or finally as crossroads for examining the converging societies of Christendom and Islam" (p.xii).

The book contains 11 chapters: (1) The Crusader Kingdom of Valencia, (2) The Economics of Crusade Victory, (3) Public Monopolies and Utilities, (4) Life and Work: Household, Community, Commercial, and Agrarian Charges, (5) Spectrum: Water, War, Salt, Moneyage, Livestock, (6) Labor Services, Hospitality and Fines, (7) Treasure, Tithe, Fees, and Miscellany, (8) Harvesting the Taxes, (9) Collectories: Muslims, Christian, and Jews, (10) Delinquents, Anomalies, and Exemptions, (11) The Human Factor.

There is a 25-page bibliography at the end, divided into primary and secondary sources. There is a name-subject index.

B-326. Calvert, Albert F. and Walter M. Gallichan. *Cordova: A City of the Moors.* London and New York: John Lane Company, 1907.

The book is a historical account of the city of Cordova, "the beautiful, powerful, and wise Cordova, 'the City of Cities,' 'the Pearl of the West,' 'the Bride of Andalus,' as the Arabian poets have variously named it; the ancient capital of Mohammedan Spain," which still continues to be "one of the most curious and fascinating monuments of this singularly interesting country" (p.vii). "No longer the center of European culture," the authors state, "'the brightest splendour of the world' has been lost in centuries of neglect and decay, and the new light of a modern civilization has not shone upon the remains of its medieval grandeur" (p.viii). The book is part of The Spanish Series; some other titles are *Toledo*, *Seville*, *Granada and the Alhambra*, *Madrid*, *Alhambra*, and *Moorish Remains in Spain*.

The book contains nine chapters: (1) The Bride of Andalus, (2) The Moorish Capture, (3) The Omeyyad Dynasty, (4) The Building of the Mosque, (5) In the Court of Oranges, (6) The Splendours of the Mosque, (7) The Cathedral and Churches, (8) The Palace of the Khalifs and the Moorish Bridge, (9) Illustrious Natives of Cordova. In chapter 9 are identified several prominent historical names—Seneca, Lucan, Averroes, Maimonides, and others. As for Averroes, "he rises far above Seneca in the conduct of life and the application of his principles to action" and his philosophy "was regarded as highly dangerous among the Moors of Cordova. It was considered equally injurious to the Christian faith, for all the works of the Arab doctor were placed upon the Catholic Index" (p.89).

There is an appendix about the "Great Mosque of Cordova," and in referring to the Cathedral built within the Mosque during the 16th century, the authors refer to "the mournful requiem over the departed glories of the Mosque," and quote a 16th-century Catholic king "who rebuked the Bishop, Alonso Manriquez, who had erected the incongruous edifice, in no measured terms. When the king saw the extent of the mischief, he said: 'You have built here what you or any one might have built elsewhere; but you have spoilt what was unique in the world'" (p.97). Another appendix on Cordova describes the historical city as "the repository of science, the minaret of piety and devotion, the abode of magnificence, superiority, and elegance: neither Baghdad nor Damascus can compete with it" (p.106).

The 108-page text is augmented by 155 pictures of the city along with some maps. There is a name-subject index.

B-327. Chejne, Anwar. *Islam and the West: The Moriscos—A Cultural and Social History.* Albany, NY: State University of New York Press, 1983.

The 250-page book is intended to survey and explore the "self-expression of the Moriscos as contained in their own literature" (p.viii). Contemporary histories, archival material, recent scholarly literature, and a variety of published and unpublished Aljamiado manuscripts, found in various original Spanish sources, were classified into broad categories as religious works, polemics, history and legends, divination and sciences, wisdom sayings, and poetry, and then synthesized into this fascinating narrative. The Moriscos are the former Mudejars, those "allowed to remain" as Muslims under the Christian rule, after the gradual Catholic reconquest from 1085 to 1492, while preserving many Arabic customs and their religion. After the fall of Granada in 1492, the descendants of Mudejars became Moriscos, "little moors" (also called Moros, Muhammadans, Hagarians, Saracens) who were forced to baptize and relinquish their identity in all respects—religion, language, literature, customs and traditions, dress, etc.

The book examines the life of the Moriscos from within, drawing upon their experiences recorded and viewed in their literature written in Aljamiado, Spanish dialect with Arabic script. It assesses the status of a minority struggling for survival, with reference to ideological conflict, the clash of religions and cultures, and the differing mutual perceptions. It is a narration that "parallels the imbalance between Europeans and Indians or between whites and blacks in the United States in the similar complexity of reconciling Christian doctrine with the attitudes and practices of Christians" (p.2).

The book contains ten chapters: (1) The Moriscos in a Hostile Environment, (2) Morisco Reaction: A Self-Image, (3) Morisco Education and Literature, (4) Religion, Beliefs and Observances, (5) The Polemics of the Moriscos, (6) History, Legends, and Travel, (7) Sorcery, Talisman, and the Sciences, (8) Secular Literature, (9) Morisco Poetry, (10) Conclusion.

There is a 40-page, chapter-by-chapter, listing of footnotes with bibliographic references, followed by a list of abbreviations of journals cited. Also, there is a 22-page bibliography of literature, followed by a name-subject index.

B-328. Chejne, Anwar G. *Muslim Spain: Its History and Culture.* Minneapolis, MN: The University of Minnesota Press, 1974.

This book is one of the most comprehensive studies of the history of Al-Andalus, although the author modestly states that it "is not intended to be a definitive work on the subject, but rather a general study of the history, culture and intellectual life of Muslim Spain" (p.v). It is an attempt to provide a panoramic view of the entire field of Hispano-Arabic culture, encompassing its nature, scope, and importance, and assessing its relation to the mainstream of Islamic world.

The volume attempts to fill a gap in Hispanic-Arabic studies and stresses the importance of such studies for "cultured persons, students, Islamists, and Romance scholars" (p. vi). The Arabs were present in Spain for almost eight centuries, from 711 to 1492, and during much of this period, Spain was by far the most advanced country of Europe. It was culturally a bridge between Asia, Africa, and Europe—and a melting pot for many diverse ethnicities. As an Islamic enclave in Europe, Al-Andalus played the "greatest role in the transmission of ideas from Arabic into Latin and other European languages" that contributed to the "appearance of a new intellectual perspective in Europe which manifested itself in the European Renaissance" (p.vi–vii).

The 560-page book has 21 detailed chapters: (1) The Conquest of Spain and the Emirate, (2) The Caliphate, 929–1031, (3) The Party-Kings, 1031–1090, (4) The Berber Dynasties, 1056–1269, (5) The Nasrid Dynasty of Granada, 1231–1492, (6) Social Structure and Socio-Religious Tensions, (7) Society and Administration, (8) Acculturation and Self-Appraisal, (9) The Sciences and Education, (10) Arabic and Linguistic Studies, (11) Prose and Belles Letters (*Adab*), (12) Poetry: The Classical Tradition, (13) Poetry: The Popular Forms, (14) Courtly Love, (15) History, Geography, and Travel, (16) The Religious Sciences, (17) Philosophy and Mysticism, (18) The Natural Sciences, (19) Architecture, the Minor Arts, and Music, (20) *Aljamiado* Literature, (21) The Islamic Legacy.

At the end, the book provides an appendix that lists some literature on Spain's Christian rulers, along with a chronological list of those rulers' reign. There is also a list of abbreviations of journals used in the text. Further, there is 60-page, chapter-by-chapter, listing of footnotes, with bibliographic references. Three bibliographies (covering 45 pages) are provided: catalogues and manuscripts; western works; eastern works. There is a comprehensive name-subject index.

B-329. Chiat, Marilyn J. and Kathryn L. Reyerson, eds. *The Medieval Mediterranean: Cross Cultural Studies.* St. Cloud, MN: North Star Press of St. Cloud, Inc., 1988.

The book contains papers presented at the third biennial conference of Medieval Studies at the University of Minnesota in 1987. While three faiths—Jewish, Christian, and Muslim—became dominant religions of western civilization during the Middle Ages, with great cultural and ethnic diversity, the present volume examines the cross-cultural contacts that stress "the positive forms of interactions that mark the long history of coexistence in the Mediterranean world" (p.xi). To understand and evaluate current developments in the region, the editors argue, "we must know the history and culture of the region and the many shared traits and values that arose from significant borrowings among diverse religious groups" (p.xi). With the exception of a paper on prostitution of Muslim women by Christians in Valencia (Spain), the papers generally have positive overtones.

The 133-page book begins with a keynote-paper, The Meaning of the Dome of the Rock, by Oleg Grabar. The remainder of the collection is divided into five sections (with a total of 15 essays): (1) Religion—two essays (Golden Age and the End of the World: Myths of Mediterranean Life from Lactantius to Joshua the Stylite by Oliver Nicholson; Two Early Anecdotes Concerning Gregory the Great from the Greek Tradition by Ivan Havener); (2) Art History—six essays (The Public Baths of Medieval Spain: An Architectural Study by Catherine Asher; The Revival of Early Islamic Architecture by the Umayyads of Spain by Jonathan Bloom; Scenario for a Roman Provenance for the Mosque of Cordoba by Marvin Mills; The Carpet Pages of the Spanish-Hebrew Farhi Bible by Sybil Mintz; The Three Hebrew Children in the Fiery Furnace: A Study in Christian Iconography by Ann Thorson Walton; Pre-Carolingian Concepts of Architectural Planning by Eugene Kleinbauer); (3) History—two essays (Iberia and North Africa: A Comparative View of Religious Heterodoxy by Clara Estow; Prostitution of Muslim Women in the Kingdom of Valencia: Religious and Sexual Discrimination in a Medieval Plural Society by Mark Meyerson); (4) Learning and Technology—three essays (Arabic Books in Jewish Libraries: The Evidence of Genizah Booklists by Moshe Sokolow; Coptic Alchemy and Craft Technology in Islamic Egypt: The Papyrological Evidence by Leslie MacCoull; Technology Transfer between Byzantium and Eastern Europe: A Case Study of the Glass Industry in Early Russia by Thomas Noonan); (5) Literature—two essays (Black and White: Contact with the Mediterranean World in Medieval German Narrative by Stephanie Van D'Elden; The Pilgrim as Tourist: Travels to the Holy Land as Reflected in the Published Accounts of German Pilgrims between 1450 and 1550 by Gerhard Weiss).

The book includes several maps, figures, and picture plates. Each paper ends with its own notes and references. There is no separate bibliography, nor is there an index.

B-330. Collins, Roger. *Early Medieval Spain: Unity in Diversity, 400–1000.* London: Macmillan Press, 1983.

The author suggests that Spanish history has not been covered adequately outside the Iberian peninsula. A major reason is that "for the medieval centuries the complications of a period unfamiliar, and inevitably alien in many aspects of its people's life and thought, are multiplied in Spain by the simultaneous existence of three, or occasionally more, Christian states, each with its own distinct history, culture and institutions, not to mention the one or more Muslim powers that dominate the south" (p.vii). Further, it has been assumed, Collins says, "that Spain, its history and culture, have been isolated from the mainstream European development; that the peninsula has remained an exotic backwater, giving little, and little influenced by events beyond the Pyrenees" (p.vii).

Beyond the introductory chapter, the 320-page book contains seven chapters: (1) The Emergency of New Order, (2) The Imposition of Unity, (3) A Church Triumphant, (4) The Seventh-Century Kingdom, (5) The Arab Conquest: The New Masters, (6) The Umayyad Regime, (7) The Christian Realm. There is a chronological table of events over the period 376–1037 AD, as well as six maps of the region relevant to this period.

The chapters on Islamic Spain are particularly relevant. There is discussion of the development of the Islamic religion and the 711 AD Arab conquest of Spain. In doing so, the author is skeptical as to his sources, for "in the western historical tradition it is highly unlikely that much credence would be given to a seventeenth-century account of events in the eighth to tenth centuries." However, "The character of Islamic historiography gives even quite late sources considerable value" (p.146). The author notes that the spread of the Islamic civilization "from the Pyrenees to the Punjab during the course of the seventh and eighth centuries" represented "arguably, the most important developments in Europe and western Asia during the whole of the first millennium AD" (p.154). Further, "Several of the Umayyads were themselves highly cultivated men," in particular Al-Hakem II (961–976) (p.173). However, "The philosophical, scientific and astronomical collections were burnt publicly" by his successors in order "to please orthodox opinions" (p.173–174). And, "Although these Umayyad scholars are not as well known or preserved as such famous later masters as Ibn Rushd ('Averroes'), philosopher, physician and astronomer, who died in 1198, they led the way to that flowering of intellectual culture in Islamic Spain, which had such an important influence upon Christian Europe in the twelfth and thirteenth centuries" (p.178). Subsequent chapters include numerous references to the Islam–Europe linkages.

There is a 15-page bibliography at the end, organized in terms of general, political and legal history, social and economic, and culture and the church, as well as by English and non-English sources. This is followed by a detailed, chapter-by-chapter, listing of notes and references. Then there is a list of rulers, along with genealogical tables of dynasties, and a detailed name-subject index.

B-331. Constable, Olivia Remie. *Trade and Traders in Muslim Spain: The Commercial Realignment of the Iberian Peninsula, 900–1500.* Cambridge and New York: Cambridge University Press, 1994.

This well-documented book is concerned primarily with medieval international trade, not with the internal Andalusi (Spanish Islam) economy. However, international trade is distinguished by its own profession and the book deals with the activities of merchants specialized in buying and selling over long distances between the internal Andalusian economy and the wider European–Mediterranean sphere.

The 320-page book is a testimony to the evolution and functioning of commercial capitalism, with an international structure of linkages that took traders long distances within the then-Islamic world and to the regions around the Mediterranean and North Europe. Having little in terms of primary sources that deal specifically with Andalusi commerce, the author views "the spectrum of routes, merchants, and commodities in Andalusi trade only by combining many sources." Among these are Arabic-language "works of geography and travel, legal materials, and biographical dictionaries (*tarajim*)," which "yielded the most useful data, with supportive information added from chronicles, poetry, and professional treatises" (p.xix). Further, the author suggests, Andalusi trade was cross cultural in that it extended "across a multiple frontier of language, religion, cultural heritage, and ethnicity," and it "involved traffic with northern Spain, Europe, or Byzantium. In contrast, trade with other areas of the Islamic world was often long distance and international without being cross cultural" (p.xxiii).

The book is comprised of nine chapters, somewhat chronologically developed: (1) The market at the edge of the west, (2) Al-Andalus within the Mediterranean network: Geography, routes and communications before the thirteenth century, (3) The merchant profession in Muslim Spain and the medieval Mediterranean, (4) The merchants in Andalusi trade, (5) Merchant business and Andalusi government authority, (6) Commodities and patterns of trade in the medieval Mediterranean world, (7) Andalusi exports before 1212, (8) Communities and changes in Iberian exports after 1212, (9) Spain, northern Europe and the Mediterranean in the Late Middle Ages.

The book contains two maps, showing trading routes, and nine plates showing trading ships, various commodities being traded, etc. There is an extensive (67 pages) bibliography, organized in terms of primary (unpublished, published) and secondary sources, followed by a comprehensive name-subject index.

B-332. Constable, Olivia Remie, ed. *Medieval Iberia: Readings from Christian, Muslim, and Jewish Sources*. Philadelphia, PA: University of Pennsylvania Press, 1997.

The book is a collection of original texts that provides unparalleled access to the individual cultures and to the multicultural complexity of Al-Andalus, later to become modern Portugal and Spain. The peninsula was remarkable for its political, religious, cultural, linguistic, and ethnic diversity. Some historians have emphasized this *melange* of peoples (Jews, Christians, Muslims) as one of harmonious coexistence, or *convivencia*; others attribute a hostile scenario to this history, eventually leading to the expulsion of Jews in the late 15th century and Muslims in the 16th.

The collection attempts to show the diversity among peoples living in the Mediterranean Iberia during medieval centuries, as well as commonalities and contacts among them. The texts written in medieval Iberia are as diverse as the people who wrote them. Translated into English from Latin, Arabic, Hebrew, Castilian, Catalan, and Portuguese languages, all selections are chosen for their historical content, but they also represent a wide variety of genres. They include chronicle materials, poetry, and legal and religious sources, and each is accompanied by a brief introduction.

The texts included are presented under nine chronologically sequenced sections: (1) The Visigothic Kingdom (6th–7th centuries), (2) The Muslim Arrival and Christian Reaction (8th century), (3) Umayyad Al-Andalus and the Northern Kingdoms (9th–10th centuries), (4) The Taifa Period in al-Andalus (11th century), (5) Christian Expansion (11th–12th centuries), (6) Al-Andalus under the Alomoravids and Almohads (12th–13th centuries), (7) Christian Conquest and Resettlement (13th century), (8) Society under Christian Rule (12th–14th centuries), (9) The Christian Kingdom and Muslim Granada (15th century). The documents are also keyed so as to be accessible to readers interested in specific topics such as urban life, the politics of the royal courts, interfaith relations, women, marriage, and the family.

At the end, the book provides useful guides for the reader. There is a chronology of major events in the peninsula; genealogical tables of various Christian and Muslim rulers; and a glossary of Arabic, Latin, and Hebrew terms. There is a good bibliography on various topics covered, as well as a detailed name-subject index.

B-333. Crow, John A. *Spain: The Root and the Flower: An Interpretation of Spain and the Spanish People*. Berkeley, CA: University of California Press, 1985.

The book "is a history and an interpretation of the civilization of Spain from its earliest beginnings," with chapters on the Romans, the Jews, and the Moors in Spain and particular attention to Spanish art, literature, architecture, and music (p.iv). While the history of political events is covered, there is greater emphasis on "the underlying feelings and *mores* which bring about those events" (p.ix).

The 455-page book contains 17 chapters: (1) The Land: The People, (2) The Dark Beginning, (3) The Cross, the Crescent, and the Star, (4) The Christian Kingdoms: Cross and the Sword, (5) Life in the Medieval Towns, (6) The Golden Age: Politics and the Social Order, (7) Belles-Lettres in the Golden Age, (8) The Fine Arts: End of the Golden Age, (9) The Bourbons, (10) Main Currents of Spanish Thought (1870–1931), (12) The Political and Social Backgrounds of the Second Republic, (13) The Spanish Republic (1931–1939), (14) Communism and Fascism in Spain, (15) Valley of the Fallen, (16) Franco's Legacy: Order and Progress, (17) Spain Today: The Impossible Dream—A Society in Transition.

Early chapters contain frequent references to the several centuries of presence of the Islamic civilization. While Islam is mentioned as "mostly a fusion" from Judaism and Christianity, it "was the spark that resulted in the birth of Arabian civilization, which reached its greatest flowering in Spain in the cities of Cordoba, Seville, and Granada, and left its indelible mark in the blood and culture of emergent medieval Spanish society" (p.47). Further, "By the tenth century, while the rest of Europe lay in the shadow of the Dark Ages, their brilliant civilization in Spain far outshone anything elsewhere on the Continent" (p.47). The author notes, "The intellectual pursuits of the Arabs in Spain gave them the unquestioned leadership of the medieval world in this regard. The Jews, too, who had been bitterly persecuted among the Visigoths, flourished under Moorish rule" (p.48). Moorish writers, however, also feared plagiarization; thus, a 12th-century scholar is quoted, "We should not sell to Jews or Christians books of science except those by their own authors, because they translate these works of science into their languages and attribute them to their people and to their bishops, despite their being the works of Moslem writers" (p.67). Also noted is the discomfort of ninth-century monks who worried about "young Christians" who were attracted to the Arabic literature and language.

As the Reconquest progressed, there was fervent "catholicization" of the population, resulting in the phenomenon known as the Inquisition (not abolished until 1820). "The presumptive proofs of an accused person's being a Judaiser were rather curious: if he wore better clothes or cleaner linen on the Jewish Sabbath than on the other days of the week"; and so forth (p.146). The fate of the Muslims and Moriscos (Muslims forced to baptize) was similar. While the expulsion or conversion of Jews and *marranos* (Jews forced to baptize) began earlier than 1492, that of Muslims started in 1502. "The Moriscos were forbidden to wear any distinctive garb, and the women were to appear with their faces uncovered. They were not allowed to have locks on their doors, their warm baths were made illegal; and above all, they might use no other language but Castilian, and acknowledge no other faith but the Christian. The edict was to be enforced with brutal penalties" (p.173).

In the following centuries, "while the other European nations made of the Renaissance an epoch of the arts, literature, painting, sculpture, and building—all exaltations of the new pagan spirit—the Iberian peninsula made of it an epoch of religion and conquest, of prolonging the Middle Ages" (p.159). Spain remained an "almost medieval economy" until the late 20th century (p.371).

The 450-page book provides a bibliography of relevant literature, followed by a glossary of Spanish words. There is also a chronological listing of important dates in Spanish history and a name-subject index.

B-334. Dozy, Reinhart. *Spanish Islam: A History of the Moslems in Spain* (translated from German, with a biographical introduction and additional notes, by Francis Griffin Stokes). London: Chatto & Windus, 1913.

One of the most comprehensive early works on this topic, and a source for numerous subsequent works, the book was originally published in 1861. This translation is "entirely unabridged, and aims at being faithful without being baldly literal" (p.xi). At the time of his writing, the author claims "to have examined all the manuscripts extant in Europe which bear upon the history of the Moors" (p.xxxv). The translator notes in the introduction, "Early in the eight century a fresh invasion took place, of a wholly different character. Across the

Straits of Gibraltar there poured a strange host from the South and East—a multitude of dark-skinned warriors from Arabia, Syria, Egypt, and Northern Africa,
who found Spain an easy prey. [They] threatened all Western Europe until
checked by the great Christian victory of Tours. But in Spain itself their dominion
seemed destined to endure, fostering as it did, a civilization in many respects
higher than Europe then knew" (p.xxv).

This 750-page compendium is divided into four books (as the translator calls
them). Book I (The Civil Wars), extending over 16 chapters, sketches "the character of pre-Islamic Arabs, the blood-feuds of Yemenites and Ma'addites, the
career of the Prophet, the rapid spread of the Moslem empire—the occupation of
Spain by Arabs and Berbers, and the resulting jealousies and rivalries which
arose between them" (p.xxvi). Book II (Christians and Renegades), extending
over 18 chapters, deals primarily with the conquered people, going back to the
Visigothic dominion, and describes the settlement of the country, the ineffectual
efforts of Christians and Renegades to cast off the Muslim conquest, the episode
of the Martyrs of Cordova, and the attainment of power of the great Caliph Abd-
er-Rahman III. Book III (The Khaliphate), also covering 18 chapters, continues
the history of Spain under the Omayyad Khalifs, describes the reign of the scholarly and peace-loving Hakam II, discusses the victorious campaign to the North,
and narrates the disastrous reigns of the "puppet Khalifs." Book IV (The Petty
Tyrants), spread over 15 chapters, describes the story of the republics and dynasties, inter-tribal jealousies, the decay of the Muslim power, the fatal invitation
sent to the Almoravides, and so forth.

The book provides chronological tables of the Muslim princes of the 11th century. There is a bibliography at the end; there is no index, however.

B-335. Echevarria, Ana. *The Fortress of Faith: The Attitude towards Muslims in
Fifteenth Century Spain*. Leiden, Netherlands: E.J. Brill, 1999.

Focusing on the period before the "Reconquest" (i.e., prior to 1492 when Granada fell), the 255-page book (which is the revised version of the author's doc-
toral thesis at the University of Edinburgh) discusses the approach to the
"Muslim matter" that provides some clues to "understanding the political
thought of Isabel and Fernando" (p.1). The process of transformation—from
"total" Arab-Islamic religious culture, coexisting with two micro-cultures
(Christians and Jews) to "total" Christian religious culture imposing itself on the
other two—had begun with the conquest of Toledo in 1085. Thus, "Islam was not
just an enemy in crusade," the author states, "but also an intellectual adversary to
be defeated by arguments" (p.2).

In evaluating the Christian attitude toward Muslims during the period covered,
the book focuses on information contained in religious treatises, chronicles, and
royal legislation; this material is compared with legislative and other contemporary documents. It is argued that while Christians were asked to be steadfast in
their faith, Muslims and Jews "had to be kept apart" to avoid proselytization

by them. Then, conversation was the next step as a way of assimilation, before declaration of the "last crusade against Muslim power, which would finish with the end of the world and the triumph of Christianity" (p.5).

There are seven chapters: (1) The Political Approach to Muslims, (2) The Intellectual Approach I: The Authors, (3) The Intellectual Approach II: A Style for a Public (Sermons, Disputes, Letters, Reports, Treatises), (4) Tradition and Polemics: Sources for Fifteenth-Century Authors, (5) *Contra Errores Machometi*, (6) Islam in the Treatises, (7) The Religious Argument: Tolerance and Acculturation. The brief concluding chapter suggests, during the period covered, (1) an "evolution towards intolerance and violence [against Muslims] which was common to the society and its rulers," and (2) most writings were negative and "only served the ultimate objective: persuasion of the final triumph of the Christian church" (p.210). Further, the author concludes: "The relation between the defeat of Islam and the end of the world had been pointed out in the seventh century, but the imminence of the fall of Granada produced more literature on the subject. The same happened on the Muslim side, where Isa ibn Djabir thought the time had come to defeat the Christians, and even the Jews had their own prophesies about the end of the world coming around 1453/1492" (p.210).

At the end there is a chronology of events, from 1410 to 1468, followed by Appendix I, "Sources of Fifteenth-Century Treatises," and Appendix II, "External Structure of Fifteenth-Century Treatises." There is a comprehensive, 10-page bibliography, followed a name-subject index.

B-336. Fierro, Maribel and Julio Samso, eds. *The Formation of al-Andalus, Part II (Language, Religion, Culture and the Sciences)*. Brookfield, VT: Ashgate Publishing Company, 1998.

This is second of the two-part anthology of the Iberian peninsula during the Middle Ages, published as the 46th volume in The Formation of the Classical Islamic World series on Islamic studies; the other is Manuela Marin (editor), *The Formation of al-Andalus, Part I (History and Society)*. Both volumes include previously published articles written by prominent scholars in various specific areas, focusing on the formative period of Islamic history (approximately 660 AD–950 AD). Editors provide a comprehensive introduction to the selections, as well as bibliographies for further reading. Most of the articles are written by Spanish scholars and published in Spanish sources, and the reason for this is stated to be that, heretofore, few Spaniards have worked on "an historical phenomenon that has not been easy to integrate into the 'national' history of their own country" (p.xiii). Reflecting new perspectives from Spanish sources on Andalusian historiography, the key theme of both volumes is "revisionist"; that is, "the progressive surmounting of the old concept of 'Spanish Islam' as the defining characteristic of al-Andalus" (p.xvi). Thus, the editors argue, the traditionalist interpretation of al-Andalusian history is being reassessed, with the gradual disappearance of the image of "Spanish Islam" from the overall scholarship, replaced gradually "with the ideological stand which emphasizes the Christian and Hispanic elements." In these respects, these volumes are distinctly at odds with those identified with other medieval scholars such as Maria Rosa Menocal, Salma Khadra Jayyusi, Luce Lopez-Baralt, and others.

There are 21 essays in this 520-page volume encompassing three main sections: (1) Language and Religion (three essays), (2) Intellectual and Artistic Developments (nine essays), (3) The Exact and Natural Sciences (nine essays). Illustratively, some titles (and authors) in each section are: (1) Language and Religion: The Christological Consequences of Muslim–Christian Confrontation in Eighth-Century Spain (Dominique Urvoy), (2) Intellectual and Artistic Development (divided into five subsections—the traditional Islamic sciences, mysticism and philosophy, history, literature, art and architecture): Reflections on Malikism under the Umayyads of Spain (Hady-Roger Idris); Egypt and the Origins of Arabic Spanish Historiography: A Contribution to the Study of Earliest Sources for the History of Islamic Spain (Mahmud Ali Makki); An Oriental Tale in the History of al-Andalus (Fernando de la Granja), (3) The Exact and Natural Sciences (divided into four subsections—astronomy: the Arab tradition, astronomy: the Indian tradition, astronomy and mathematics: the Greek heritage, medicine and pharmacology: the Greek tradition): Abd al-Malik ibn Habib's *Book on the Stars* (Paul Kunitzsch); The Mathematical Works of Maslama of Madrid (Juan Vernet and Maria-Asuncion Catala); Medicine in al-Andalus until the Fall of the Caliphate (Margarita Castells).

There is a 100-title bibliography at the beginning of this two-part volume. Each essay integrates its own notations and references; there is no index, however.

B-337. Fletcher, Richard. *Moorish Spain.* Berkeley, CA: University of California Press, 1993.

The book serves as an introduction to the history and culture of Islamic Spain between the Berber invasion of the early eighth century and the expulsion of the Moriscos (Muslims who were forced to baptize) in the early 17th century. Intended for the general reader, the book is also suggested for appropriate university courses. For nearly a thousand years, the Islamic presence survived in the Iberian peninsula, the author states, flourishing at times and at times dwindling into warring fiefdoms. But the culture and science of this civilization, including the revival of the long-buried knowledge from Greece, forgotten during Europe's Dark Ages, forever transformed the course of the Western civilization.

The 190-page book has nine chapters: (1) Romance and Reality, (2) The Secret of Tower, (3) The Curve of Conversion, (4) The Caliphate of Cordoba, (5) The Party Kings, (6) The Moroccan Fundamentalists, (7) *Convivencia*, (8) Nasrid Granada, (9) An August Pomegranate. Chapter 7 specifically documents the intellectual contributions of Muslim scholars and how that scholarship influenced the awakening of Latin Europe. In the last chapter, however, the author concludes: "The simple and verifiable historical truth is that Moorish Spain was more often a land of turmoil than it was a land of tranquility" (p.172). Further, "Moorish Spain was not a tolerant and enlightened society even in its most cultivated epoch" (p.173). And thus, *convivencia*, or co-existence, was not convenient. Most scholars of the subject will dispute these assertions, it seems; and Fletcher mentions this "tone of intemperance" has been pointed out by some of his critics (p.xiv). Yet, he acknowledges, "The interaction between Islamic and Christian civilizations in the medieval west was an extremely fruitful one" (p.173). And this "traffic was all one way. Moorish Spain was the donor, western Christendom the recipient" (p.174).

There is a list of suggested readings at the end, followed by a name-subject index.

B-338. Glick, Thomas F. *Islamic and Christian Spain in the Early Middle Ages.* Princeton, NJ: Princeton University Press, 1979.

This 376-page book is a comprehensive "analysis of central issues and phenomena that contributed to the formation of Islamic and Spanish cultures in the Iberian peninsula and guided the interaction among both peoples" during the early Middle Ages (p.4). It discusses the processes whereby distinctive cultures and societies are formed—presently, the adaptation of the Christian culture to the dominant Islamic culture. Because the book is cast in a civilizational perspective, the contact of cultures and the diffusion of discrete elements among them plays a major part in the narrative. The book covers the period from the middle of the ninth century to around 1300. During this period the contact was between peoples not only of different cultures, but of different socioeconomic systems—Islamic, "urban-artisanal" society, well implanted in the larger economic network, the Mediterranean and beyond, and the Christian, heavily rural, characterized by the author as "static-agrarian" (p.6).

The book is divided into two parts. Part One, Society and Economy, has six chapters—(1) At the Crossroads of Civilization (the conquest, collapse of the Visigothic state, conversions, Christian north, eleventh-century reversal), (2) Agriculture, Settlement, and the Moving Frontier (two cultures/ecologies, landscape change, settlement and growth—Al-Andalus, settlement and growth—Christian kingdoms, forests and timber), (3) Urbanization and Commerce (urban structure, growth/morphology of towns, urban market, trade and investment), (4) Social Structure (stratification, kinship, lower classes, middle classes, nobility and social mobility), (5) Ethnic Relations (cleavages and boundaries, "protected" minorities, ethnic competition in Al-Andalus, assimilation of neo-Muslims, ethnicity in Christian Spain), (6) Structure and Stability (stability and continuity, structural gains and losses, state systems of the eleventh century, feudalism). Part Two, Movement of Ideas and Techniques, has three chapters—(1) Technology (innovation and change, continuity and change, shared technologies, bilateral diffusion, flow of techniques from East to West), (2) Science (science and cultural values, diffusion and synthesis, social bases of transmission, unity of scientific knowledge, patterns of cultural influence), (3) Cultural Process in Medieval Spain (the linguistic model and cultural continuity, cultural crystallization, modalities of cultural change, balance-sheet of cultural exchange).

The book has a comprehensive 16-page bibliography, classified in terms of (1) The Mediterranean World, (2) The Iberian Middle Ages, (3) Al-Andalus, (4) Christian Spain, (5) Urbanism, (6) Technology, (7) Science, (8) Philology and Linguistics, (9) The Polemic of Spanish History. This is followed by detailed 40-page listing of footnotes tied to each chapter. There is comprehensive name-subject index.

B-339. Harvey, L.P. *Islamic Spain, 1250–1500.* Chicago: University of Chicago Press, 1990.

The 370-page book covers the history of the Iberian Peninsula after 1250 when two distinct categories of Muslims lived in the region: the independent Muslim kingdom of Granada, and the small minorities of Muslims who lived in the Christian kingdoms of Castile, Aragon, Valencia, and Navarre. The history of the first is often seen as an appendage to the Middle East and that of the second group of minorities is viewed as almost irrelevant footnotes to a story that is not their own. The author argues that a quarter of a millennium of the history of Islamic Spain at the end of the Middle Ages has been subjected to a double process of marginalization, and as a consequence, not always well understood, giving rise to even contemporary misunderstandings about Islam.

Thus, the author argues, the experience of Islam in Spain needs to be understood in a more objective and dispassionate light. The Muslims of the peninsula were deeply divided, even during the days of the Caliphate of Cordova, but they were also intensely conscious of an underlying religious–cultural unity and the sociocultural heritage of their al-Andalus. In the 16th century, when Granadans and minorities in the Christian kingdoms were condemned to forcible conversions, they still retained their pride in their religion and culture. And they took this heritage with them into exile in North Africa and elsewhere.

Extended over 20 chapters (some titles: enclaves and anomalies; Mudejar status; Mudejar communities [Castile, Aragon, Valencia, Navarre]; reigns of Muhammad III, Nasr, Yusuf II; the final decade of Granada; Mujedars now [1492–1500]), the book attempts to cover the history of both the Granadans and the Muslim minorities of the rest of Spain. The Christian conquest of Granada in 1492 spelled disaster for all Muslims in the peninsula and by 1500 not only had the last independent enclave been overwhelmed, but the process of forcible conversion and the destruction of the distinctive Andalusia culture was under way. However, underlying the great diversity of the phenomena examined in the book, there is one constant: all the communities, despite encountering formidable challenges, struggled to preserve their identity and pass it on to their descendants. Eventually Spanish Islam failed, but this study is not conceived as a narration of failure, rather as a record of a courageous and stubborn defense, the author asserts.

The book provides an extensive bibliography and there is a name-subject index.

B-340. Hess, Andrew C. *The Forgotten Frontier: A History of the Sixteenth-Century Ibero-African Frontier*. Chicago and London: University of Chicago Press, 1978.

This 278-page book is about how "this once famous borderland reflected a formalization of relations between two Mediterranean civilizations and thereby attained the status of a forgotten frontier" (p.10). Reference is to the interactions between the Turko-Muslim and emerging Latin-Christian civilizations. "Western civilization, armed with the sailing ship, encircled Turko-Muslim empires. Unlike Japan, however, the House of Islam did not find the appearance of Western sailors and merchants on its fringes sufficient cause for modifying its society through any substantial acquisition of the foreigner's institutions. Instead, an introverted Islamic civilization suffered a devastating invasion by the armies and merchants of Europe during the nineteenth century" (p.3).

The book has ten chapters: (1) The Ibero-African Frontier, (2) A Military Revolution, (3) North Africa and the Atlantic, (4) Islam Resurgent, (5) The Clash of Empires, (6) North Africa in Revolt, (7) Islam Expelled, (8) Once Again the East, (9) The Forgotten Frontier, (10) The Mediterranean Divided.

There are several illustrative maps and genealogical tables of Latin-Christian and Muslim dynasties. The book provides chapter-by-chapter notes at the end. Also, there is a glossary, followed by a note on unpublished sources, a bibliographical essay, and a name-subject index.

B-341. Hintzen-Bohlen, Brigitte. *Andalusia: Art and Architecture*. Cologne, Germany: Konemann Verlagsgesellschaft, 2000.

While intended as a guide to travelers, the book also offers deeper insights into the art and architectural history of the region. There are several essays that cover various sociocultural aspects of the history of Andalusia.

The 536-page book has eight chapters, covering each province as well as major cities within each; these provinces are Seville, Huelva, Cadiz, Malaga, Almeria, Granada, Jaen, and Cordoba. In addition to the art and architecture landscape of each, the chapters also provide considerable historical background, including coverage of such topics as the Spanish Inquisition, the scholarship of Maimonides and Averroes, Moorish Gardens, and Islamic calligraphy.

The introductory essay, Andalusia-Europe's Orient, provides some focused background for the book. The region "has a uniqueness in its art and culture incomparable to anywhere else on earth. This uniqueness results from it being located where several very different civilizations meet" (p.9). As for the Islamic civilization, the Arabs "established great mosques and universities, as well as schools and libraries open to the public, all of which enabled Andalusia develop into one of the great intellectual centers of Europe. It is thanks to Arab scholars that classical philosophy and culture were preserved and developed. Here also were laid the foundations of modern scientific disciplines, such as mathematics, physics, geography, mathematics, and astronomy" (p.9). Further, "While Europe was languishing in the depths of the Middle Ages, a far superior culture was thriving in Andalusia. With its climate of total tolerance, it enabled Moslems, Christians and Jews to live peacefully together; and by transmitting classical and oriental knowledge it prepared Europe's passage into the modern world" (p.10).

Elsewhere, the author states, the Arabs [Berbers] "could never have gained a foothold so quickly however, if they had not received massive support from the population," which "was being oppressed by a minority, the Visigothic nobility. The Jews, for their part suffered under the pressure of the Church, the channel through which the Visigoths exerted their power. Both groups helped the Berbers in their conquest of the peninsula" (p.230). Further, while discussing Islamic tolerance and "creative diversity," Hintzen-Bohlen notes, this "unique tolerance was to pave the way for a new culture, strongly Moorish in character, which influenced all aspects of life in medieval Europe" (p.232).

The book includes hundreds of colorful pictures, reflecting both the Islamic as well as Christian traditions of the region; there are also numerous maps and sketches. There is a 76-page appendix at the end that includes an overview of Andalusian history, glossary, Andalusian architectural forms, artists' biographies, literary references, a name-subject index, and photo credits.

B-342. Hole, Edwyn. *Andalus: Spain under the Muslims.* London: Robert Hale Ltd., 1958.

The book begins with a brief historical outline. This is followed by a detailed discussion of Andalusian Spain, covering the mixture of various races that made up the population. The narrative extends to government and diplomacy, role of women, the treatment of slaves, sports and recreation, and the passion for poetry. Also included is a "portrait-gallery" of five prominent but dissimilar Andalusians (Abd al-Rahman, the Founder; Umar Ibn Hafsun, the Rebel; Ziryab, the Musician; Ibn Ammar, the Poet-King; Ibn Abdun, the Censor). The 190-page book provides a well-informed account of a country that is unique in Western Europe, as well as a "civilization in comparison with which the contemporary Christian kingdoms of Western Europe were still in the dark ages" (p.xv). Among other things, the book attempts to fill a gap in that "few historical periods of comparable interest and importance have been so neglected by English scholars as the seven centuries of Muslim rule in Spain" (p.xvii).

There are ten chapters: (1) History, (2) The Capital, (3) The People, (4) Administration, (5) Foreign Relations, (6) Poetry, (7) Slavery, (8) Love, (9) Fun and Games, (10) Portrait Gallery. The chapter on history discusses, among other things, the ease with which the invading Berbers succeeded: the Goths were hopelessly divided; the elected King Roderic deserted on the battlefield; the Bishop of Seville, brother of the late king, fought on the Muslim side. Further, much of the population had less to lose—Muslim rule was lighter and taxes less oppressive. And, given their oppressed status, "the large Jewish population in particular who made up perhaps a third of the population, had everything to gain" (p.21). Moreover, "A century or so ago, when the history of the Muslim domination began to be a subject of research, students whose romantic admiration outstripped their intellectual equipment discovered in it the origin of most of the culture and institutions of modern Europe. Medicine, natural science, philosophy, music, Gothic architecture, epic and lyric poetry, textiles, mathematics, everything was traced back to that magical hothouse" (p.31).

The book provides a brief bibliography (most in Spanish) at the end, followed by a name-subject index. Also, there are 18 illustrative pictures.

B-343. Hook, David and Barry Taylor, eds. *Cultures in Contact in Medieval Spain: Historical and Literary Essays Presented to L.P. Harvey.* Exeter, UK: King's College London Medieval Studies; Short-Run Press, 1999.

This 218-page edited volume, with essays written by colleagues and former students, is to honor the continuing work, even after retirement, of a scholar whose extensive scholarship in the area is eminently recognized. Both in terms of theme and periodicity, there is a wide range of papers exploring various aspects of the contact between the three main cultural and religious communities in the Peninsula (Jewish, Christian, and Muslim). There is a curriculum vita of the honored scholar, along with a list of his publications.

There are 13 brief essays: (1) An Anecdote of King Jaume I and Its Arabic Congener by Samuel G. Armistead, (2) The Morisco Expulsion and Diaspora: An Example of Racial and Religious Intolerance by Roger Boase, (3) Divination from Sheep's Shoulder-blades: A Reflection on Andalusian Society by Charles Burnett, (4) Uses of the Bible in the *Poema de Fernan Gonzalez* by Alan Deyermond, (5) Bishop Juan Arias Davila of Segovia: 'Judaizer' or Reformer'? by John Edwards, (6) The Death of Antar: An Arabic Analogue for the Cid of Cardena by Brenda Fish, (7) Back to Ibn Quzman by T.J. Gorton, (8) Arabic Proper Names in the Becerro de Celanova by Richard Hitchcock, (9) Some Problems in Romance Epic Phraseology by David Hook, (10) Notes al Azar: Para Simultanear lo Par y lo Impar by Francisco Marcos Marin, (11) Labiodental/f/, Aspiration, and /h/-dropping in Spanish: The Evolving Phonemic Value of the Graphs f and h by Ralph Penny, (12) Raimundus de Biterris's Liber Kalile et Dimne: Notes on the Western Reception of an Eastern *exemplus*-Book by Barry Taylor, (13) Jimena "Rverguencas malas" (*Poema de Mio Cid*, l, 1596) by Roger M. Walker and Milija Pavlovic.

Each essay ends with its own notes and references, but there is no index.

B-344. Imamuddin, S.M. *Some Aspects of the Socio-Economic and Cultural History of Muslim Spain, 711–1492.* Leiden, Netherlands: E.J. Brill, 1965.

The book presents an outline of the sociocultural history of Muslim Spain. The author argues that there has been a paucity of knowledge of this part of the history and that until recently, only a few have had the knowledge of the existence of the high civilization of Medieval Spain. This civilization played a great role in the making of the Christian Europe, and there were three routes to this transformation—Spain, Sicily, and Syria.

The author draws considerably on the works of other writers, supplemented by his own independent research. There are 12 chapters: (1) Introduction, (2) Society, (3) Civil Administration, (4) Military Organization, (5) Agriculture, (6) Minerals and Industries, (7) Commerce, (8) Literary Activities, (9) Science, (10) Architecture, (11) Art and Music, (12) Spanish Muslim Civilization and Its Influence on Europe. The discussion in the last chapter is organized in terms of various topics such as Christian Kings and Latin-Arabic Schools; Science; Literature; Philosophy; Civil Organization; The Army; Economics; Architecture and Art; Music. The author notes: "It was easier for the Christians to destroy the mosques and monuments of the Muslims than to remove the effect of Arab culture in Spain. Muslim influence is still perceptible in the manners and customs of Spaniards" (p.200). Further, "The Muslim culture of medieval times remained shining for long as a beacon of light in the cultural darkness of contemporary Europe" (p.200).

Several illustrative maps are provided in the 248-page book. Also, 15 pictures of Spanish architecture are at the end, along with an appendix enumerating a chronology of dates, beginning with the expedition of Tariq ibn Ziyad in 711 AD to the final expulsion of the Moriscos (Muslims baptized forcibly) at the order of Philip III in 1609–1610 AD. Another appendix provides a detailed bibliography, and there is a name-subject index.

B-345. Irving, Thomas B. *Falcon of Spain: A Study of Eighth-Century Spain.* Lahore, Pakistan: Sh. Muhammad Ashraf Publishers, 1991.

The book explores the period when Arabs first held the Iberian peninsula, with special emphasis on the life of the Umayyad ruler, Abdurrahman I (756–788 AD). The author argues that under this ruler's reign the Islamic culture reached its finest flowering, transforming Spain into a great nation, and his descendants ruled longer than any Spanish dynasty of any faith. Further, while other scholars have explored this subject, "no one has made a proper biography of this European ruler who controlled the destinies of Spain throughout thirty-two critical years. Dozy is moreover inclined to interpret Abdurrahman as an oriental despot and to consider any non-Christian as a renegade. I feel he should rather have compared Abdurrahman's reign with that of Charlemagne, and Spanish Islam with contemporary European Christianity" (p.v). Thus, among other things, this study attempts to explore "the environment from which he came, and to disentangle the wretched quarrels which beset Spain the decades before and immediately after the Arab conquest of that country" (p.v). Further, the author has, in general, "tried to take the Arab point of view, because the European, especially in the attitude toward Charlemagne, is overabundant" (p.vi).

The 190-page book contains 24 short chapters. Some selective titles are: Course of Empire, Visigothic Spain, Desert Feuds, First Advances, Lord of Andalusia, Organizing Arab Spain, The Abbasids Intervene, Government and Trade, Distractions from Europe, The Song of Roland: Arab Version, Cordoba: The Bride of Andalus, Umayyad Culture, The Amir's Last Years and Death, Falcon of the Quraysh. The author concludes, "Abdurrahman was the most cultured and civilized of Europe's rulers during the eighth century, notwithstanding the great Charles himself" (p.172).

While each chapter provides notes and references in the text, there is a bibliography of major works consulted, followed by a name-subject index.

B-346. Jayyusi, Salma Khadra, ed. *The Legacy of Muslim Spain*, two volumes. Leiden, Netherlands, New York, and Cologne: E.J. Brill, 1994.

These two volumes, covering over 1,100 pages combined, represent the culmination of a monumental task undertaken by the editor: the documentation of the legacy of Muslim Spain, spread over several centuries (711–1492 AD) of early Islamic civilization that dominated the Iberian Peninsula. Sponsored by the Aga Khan Trust for Culture (Geneva, Switzerland), the work was designed to coincide with the 500th anniversary of the end of Islamic rule in Al-Andalus: "It embodied what came before, illuminated what came after" (p.x). The spirit behind this project is reflected in the editor's words: "What greater cause can a Muslim intellectual have at the present time than to help put the history of the illustrious Islamic civilization back in its rightful place on the map of the world?" (p.xi).

That spirit is eminently reflected in these volumes. They provide a wealth of material, not only for specialists but also for those curious about the evolution of early Islamic civilization and its intellectual links with Europe. The 39 essays, written by well-known scholars, cover the broad topics of Islamic Spain's history (cities, social history and literature, economic history), language and literature, music, art and architecture, philosophy, religious studies, science and technology, agriculture. Some representative titles and authors may be identified here: The Political History of al-Andalus (92/711–897/1492) by Mahmoud Makki; "The Ornament of the World": Medieval Cordoba as a Cultural Center by Robert Hillenbrand; The Jews in Muslim Spain by Raymond P. Scheindlin; Al-Andalus and 1492: The Ways of Remembering by Maria Rosa Menocal; An Islamic Background to the Voyages of Discovery by Abbas Hamdani; The Legacy of Islam in Spanish Literature by Luce Lopez-Baralt; The Mudejar Tradition in Architecture by Jerrilynn Dodds; Muslim Merchants in Andalusi International Trade by Olivia Remie Constable; The Philosophy of Ibn Rushd by Jamal Al-Din al-Alawi; Ibn Tufayl and His *Hayy Ibn Yaqzan*: A Turning Point in Arabic Philosophical Writing by J.C. Burgel; Heresy in Al-Andalus by Maria Isabel Fierro; Hydraulic Technology in al-Andalus by Thomas F. Glick; The Translating Activity in Medieval

Spain by Charles Burnett; Islamic Civilization in al-Andalus: A Final Assessment by Margarita Lopez Gomez.

Each chapter ends with a listing of notes, references, and/or bibliography. The second volume identifies each contributor, along with a brief bibliographic note about each; this is followed by a comprehensive name-subject index.

B-347. Jones, Catherine E. *Islamic Spain and Our Heritage: Al-Andalus, 711–1492 A.D.* Austin, TX: Middle East Outreach Council, University of Texas, 1996; second edition 1997.

The book begins with five quotations, indicating "Why study about Al-Andalus?" Written primarily for pre-college students and teachers, this booklet on Islamic Spain aspires to "provide more background information about the region, persons, history and contributions of the world that Christopher Columbus had left" (p.iv). The author encourages "users to add the contributions of the Arabic culture and Islamic Spain to their study of the European Middle Ages and Renaissance" (p.iv). She also notes, "Multiculturalism is a fairly recent designation in our time, but it existed in part in al-Andalus" (p.136).

After an introduction (West Meets East), the book is divided into three parts. Part I (Islamic Spain) starts with a brief essay, The Case of Christopher Columbus, followed by three chapters: (1) The Land and the People, (2) History, (3) Civil Life and Travel. Part II begins with an introduction, followed by five chapters: (1) Our Heritage in Food and Agriculture, (2) Our Heritage in Science, (3) Our Heritage in Technology, (4) Our Heritage in the Arts, (5) Our Heritage in Language and Literature. The concluding chapter, Beyond al-Andalus, discusses Europe's encounter with Islam, mixed with "fear and admiration." There was "fear that such secular (meaning 'not Christian') knowledge, beyond the sanction of the Church, would be destructive to Europe's Christian values" (p.102). Yet, there was admiration, as "Europe awakened when it accepted the secular with the religious. Europe was able to reap learning not only via the bridge of al-Andalus, but also from Sicily, from the scholars coming from Byzantine, from the learning of the crusaders, and from contacts throughout the Mediterranean" (p.103). The author ends with a quote from the Spanish philosopher, George Santayana (1863–1952): "Those who cannot remember the past are condemned to repeat it." Part III includes some chapter-by-chapter suggestions for learning activities.

The 164-page book provides several maps, illustrations, and pictures. Chapter-by-chapter sources of literature consulted, with a topical breakdown and exact pages, are listed at the end, followed by a general bibliography. Additionally, there is an appendix that enumerates selected events and an annotated list of relevant audiovisual sources, followed by a name-subject index.

B-348. Kamen, Henry. *The Spanish Inquisition.* London: Weidenfeld and Nicolson, 1965.

This "small book on a big subject," intended for the general reader, is "not an account of the Inquisition so much as a tentative interpretation of its place in Spanish history," by tracing "the career of the Holy Office" (p.ix). The author argues that the Reconquest "destroyed the racial and religious coexistence, which despite incessant armed conflict had distinguished the society of medieval Spain" (p.2). Heretofore, "For long periods in medieval Spain, close contact between the peoples of the peninsula had led to a mutual tolerance among the three communities of Christians, Jews and Moors" (p.2). The author asserts that the Reconquest Spain "refused to compromise with the new age" of the Renaissance, thus Spain made a truce "with traditionalism, the traditionalism of scholastic Catholicism" (p.12). The author concludes that "the problem of the Inquisition remains no longer exclusively a religious one, but becomes a sociological one, something to be considered as part of a totality and not as an isolated phenomenon" (p.305). Further, "The spirit which brought it [The Holy Office] to birth still roams abroad, and the problem it was created to solve—preservation of the faith— remains more urgent and intense than it has ever been" (p.305).

The 340-page book has 16 chapters: (1) Introduction, (2) The Great Dispersion, (3) The Coming of the Inquisition, (4) A Minority Opposition, (5) "Silence Has Been Imposed," (6) The End of the Morisco Spain, (7) Race Purity and Racialism, (8) The Spanish Inquisition: Its Organization, (9) The Spanish Inquisition: Its Procedure, (10) The Spanish Inquisition: Trial and Condemnation, (11) Special Features of Jurisdiction, (12) The Last Days of the Conversos, (13) Political Conflict, (14) In Defense of the Ancien Regime, (15) The Abolition of the Inquisition, (16) A Final Assessment.

There is a chapter-by-chapter listing of notes and references at the end, followed by a glossary of Spanish terms and a name-subject index.

B-349. Kennedy, Hugh N. *Muslim Spain and Portugal: A Political History of al-Andalus.* London: Addison Wesley Longman Ltd., 1996.

The book is an account of the political history of Muslim Spain and Portugal from the arrival of the Arabs from North Africa in 711 AD, through to the fall of the last Andalusian state, Granada, in 1492. It is said to be the first serious study and incorporates much of recent Spanish and Portuguese scholarship on the subject. By political history, the author means more than mere narration of events; it also includes understanding of the structures behind those events. "The most important of these structures," says the author, "were the ruling dynasties, where they came from, who their most powerful supporters were and how they attempted to secure a justification and legitimacy for the exercise of power" (p.xiv). Further, "This is not a history of the Reconquista," nor is it "an intellectual and cultural history of al-Andalus" (p.xiv). Those aspects are important, but they are outside the purview of this book. The book should prove to be a useful resource for the specialists, but it is accessible to those outside the field as well.

The 340-page book contains 11 chapters: (1) The Conquest and the Age of the Amirs, 711–756, (2) The Umayyad Amirate, 756–852, (3) Muhammad, al-

Mundhir and 'Abd Allah: The Slide into Anarchy, 852–912, (4) The Golden Age of the Umayyad Caliphate, 912–976, (5) The 'Amirids and the Collapse of the Caliphate of Cordoba, (6) The Taifa Kingdoms, (7) The Empire of the Almoravids, (8) The Second Taifas, (9) The Early Almohad Caliphate, (10) The Later Almohad Caliphate, (11) The Nasirids of Granada. There is a short "Farewell to al-Andalus" chapter at the end.

The author suggests the book should be particularly useful for western medievalists, for the history of the region has been generally neglected in comparison with its Christian neighbors—and when considered, it has been written largely from Christian sources, with a focus on the Reconquest. Yet, this region had a major impact in the transmission of Arab science, culture, and technology to the West.

Notes and references are integrated within the text of each chapter. There are two appendices at the end, one is a listing of the various rulers of al-Andalus and the other provides family trees of the ruling dynasties. There is a bibliography of Arabic and non-Arabic sources, followed by a name-subject index.

B-350. Lane-Poole, Stanley. *The Story of the Moors in Spain* (introduction by John G. Jackson). Baltimore, MD: Black Classic Press, 1990; original 1886.

The book is a chronicle of splendor and tragedy of Moorish Spain. According to the introduction, "No one has told the story better than Stanley Lane-Pool." All serious students of history should read this book, he says. Up to 1886, this was among the few English-language histories of the non-Christian civilizations. The author notes that the book endeavors to "present the most salient points in the eight centuries of Mohammedan rule without prejudice or extenuation" (p.ix).

The author states: "The story of Spain offers us a melancholy contrast. For nearly eight centuries, under her Mohammedan rulers, Spain set to all Europe a shining example of a civilized and enlightened state. Art, literature, and science prospered, as they prospered nowhere else in Europe. Students flocked from France and Germany and England to drink from the fountain of learning which flowed only in the cities of Moors" (p.vii). Then, "In 1492 the last bulwark of the Moors gave way before the crusade of Ferdinand and Isabella, and with Granada fell all Spain's greatness. Then followed the abomination of desolation, the rule of the Inquisition, and the blackness of darkness in which Spain has been plunged ever since" (p.viii). It was in 1570 when the "Moriscos were at least subdued [and] those taken in open revolt were enslaved, the rest were marched away into banishment under escort of troops, while the passes of the hills were securely guarded" (p.278-279). The Spaniards "did not understand that they had killed their golden goose" (p.280).

The book has 14 chapters: (1) The Last of the Goths, (2) The Wave of Conquest, (3) The People of Andalusia, (4) A Young Pretender, (5) The Christian Martyrs, (6) The Great Khalif, (7) The Holy War, (8) The City of the Khalif, (9)

The Prime Minister, (10) The Berbers in Power, (11) My Cid The Challenger, (12) The Kingdom of Granada, (13) The Fall of Granada, (14) Bearing the Cross.

There are several historic pictures throughout the book and a name-subject index.

B-351. Lea, Henry Charles. *The Moriscos of Spain: Their Conversion and Expulsion*. New York: Haskel House Publishers Ltd. (Publishers of Scarce Scholarly Books), 1968; original 1901.

This 460-page book documents the post-Reconquest history of Muslims in Spain, more specifically, the history of Moriscos (Muslims, or "Moors," forced to baptize). The author relied on documentary evidence of the "final catastrophe" that "embodied the Inquisition." The book is based on this evidence, made public by Spanish scholars, and further supplemented by other original Spanish-language sources (several reproduced in the appendix). While there are several recent books on the subject, this is a rare, early account of the history of the Spanish Inquisition of Muslims; there are, obviously, frequent references to a similar plight encountered by Jews.

The book has 11 chapters, each with a detailed topical listing of the contents: (1) The Mudejares, (2) Ximenes, (3) The Germania, (4) Conversion by Edict, (5) The Inquisition, (6) Conversion by Persuasion, (7) Condition of the Moriscos, (8) The Rebellion of Granada, (9) Dangers from Abroad, (10) Expulsion, (11) Results. The second chapter is devoted almost entirely to the life, motivations, policies, and practices of the Inquisitors, with major attention given to the Grand Inquisitor, Cardinal Ximenes, nephew of another inquisitor-general, Cardinal Torquemada (more famous for brutalities inflicted upon Jews). Another provides details of the nature and character of the Inquisition—"ferocious and inhuman as were all these projects, they evoked no scruples of conscience" (p.297). Other chapters document the persecution of those who resisted conversion. The longest (chapter 10; 74 pages) documents the details of expulsion of Muslims, and the last chapter discusses the consequences and effects of the Inquisition upon the Spanish society at the time.

Notes and references are integrated within each chapter. The book also provides seven appendices at the end, each with a listing of the original, Spanish-language documents referenced in the main text. There is a detailed name-subject index.

B-352. Lopez-Baralt, Luce. *Islam in Spanish Literature: From the Middle Ages to the Present* (translated from Spanish by Andrew Hurley). Leiden, Netherlands: E.J. Brill, 1992.

The book is written in the tradition of Miguel Asin-Palacios who, in early 20th century, initiated a series of comparative studies of Hispano-Arabic literature in Spain. While not exhaustive, according to the author, the book begins with a survey of the general phenomenon of the integration of Semitic threads, Arabic and Hebrew, into the fabric of Spanish culture; the impress of the Islamic culture is "the very essence of Spanish culture" (p.ix). The author hopes that "the essays collected here might serve to show how widespread and significant the impact of Islam has been on Hispanic literature throughout its long history," and further "to serve as an index of all that remains to be done in comparative studies of these two traditions" (p.ix).

However, says the author, "It seems, then, that a great part of the supposed 'originality' of some Spanish writers consists not in 'inventing,' but rather in adapting it, in their own unique way, to their own literary ends" (p.x). This also creates difficulties in clearly identifying the sources of borrowing. Among other things, concerning the "Christianized reformulations," the author argues, "the danger presented by this type of cultural borrowing throughout the years of the flourishing of Spanish culture and into the years of the Inquisition, is self-evident and makes more difficult the identification of sources of the loans" (p.xv). The author notes that "it is no exaggeration to state that the book redefines the grounds of the study of Spanish literature; it will be hard for the contemporary reader ever again to read it with innocence, as a literature exclusively 'European.'" Further, "Yet even against the most elementary historical common sense, it has been very hard for most historians and literary critics who have dealt with Spain to accept the existence of these possible Semitic traces in Spanish culture" (p.23).

The 324-page book contains eight chapters: (1) Introduction: The Qualified Westernness of Spain, (2) On the Astrological Sign of the Archpriest of Hita, (3) On the Genesis of the 'Solitary Bird' of St. John of the Cross, (4) Santa Teresa and Islamic Mysticism: The Symbol of the Seven Castles of the Soul, (5) Anonymity and Possible Islamic Mystical Roots for the Sonnet *"No me mueve, mi Dios, para quererte,"* (6) A Chronicle of the Destruction of a World: Moorish *Aljamiado* Literature, (7) The Two Sides of the Coin: The Moor in Spanish Renaissance Literature, (8) Toward a "Mudejar" Reading of Juan Goytisolo's *Makbara*.

There is a 14-page, comprehensive bibliography at the end, followed by a name-subject index.

B-353. Lowney, Chris. *A Vanished World: Medieval Spain's Golden Age of Enlightenment.* New York: Free Press, 2005.

This 340-page book is a compelling story of the 800 years of Spanish history when the main monotheistic religions of Islam, Christianity, and Judaism interacted and religious tolerance was by and large the norm. At a time when the West is dealing with the complexities (Lowney begins with a reference to the March 2004 terrorist attack in Madrid) associated with the joining of Muslim and Western cultures, the author offers enduring lessons learned from medieval Spain, covering an instructive period when Islam ruled Spain where Muslims, Christians, and Jews rubbed shoulders on a daily basis.

The vanished history that the book explores included an intellectually vibrant community of Jewish, Christian, and Muslim philosophers, mathematicians, poets, mystics, and scientists that proved to be the fount of Spain's Golden Age of Enlightenment. Moses Maimonides, Ibn Arabi, Ibn Tufail, Ibn Rushd, and Cardinal Gerbert (later Pope Sylvester II) were just a few of the Spanish intellectuals who breathed enlightenment into Europe's struggle out of the Dark Ages. This environment of religious tolerance ended in 1492 with the rule of Isabella and Ferdinand; and Jews and Muslims were subjected to the wrath of Inquisition.

Beyond the introduction there are 20 chapters: (1) Spain Before Islam, (2) The Moors Conquer Spain ("Our God and Your God Is One"), (3) Santiago Discovered in the Field of Stars, (4) Martyr-Activists (Determined to Die in a City "Piled Full of Riches"), (5) The Pope Who Learned Math from Muslim Spain, (6) Europe's Busiest Highway, (7) A Jewish General in a Muslim Kingdom ("I Am the David of My Age"), (8) The Frontier (Jihad, Crusades, Cowboys, and Sheep), (9) Charlemagne ("God, How Wearisome My Life Is"), (10) El Cid ("Born in a Fortunate Hour"), (11) The Second Moses and Medieval Medicine, (12) Rethinking Religion ("To Long with an Exceeding Longing"), (13) A Muslim Commentator Enlightens Christendom ("You Who Have Eyes to See, Reflect"), (14) Sufism ("My Heart Has Become Capable of Every Form"), (15) The Kabbalah ("An Instrument for Peace in the World"), (16) Fernando III ("Who Broke and Destroyed All His Enemies"), (17) A Common Life Shared Among Three Faiths ("Damnable Mixing"), (18) Alfonso the Learned King, (19) The End of Spanish Judaism ("The Razor That Rips the Membrane of My Aching Heart"), (20) Columbus, a New World, and the End of History ("A Dead Forbidden by Every Faith"). There is an epilogue.

According to the author, three intertwined stories unfold in these chapters. First is Spain's passage from ancient kingdom to flourishing Islamic state to the broad outlines of the Spain we observe today. Secondly, there is the unique collaboration and collision of the three monotheistic religions on European soil. And third is the struggle to engage religious faith with rediscovered reason. "Human history was forever changed by the encounter of three religions; each religion was forever changed by encountering the others; and each in turn was changed by its confrontation with human reason" (p.9). And, while "Medieval Spain's Muslims, Christians, and Jews embraced and rejected each other's faith traditions and customs," Islamic Spain "somehow forged a golden age for each faith." Further, "They haltingly blazed humanity's trail toward tolerance and mutual respect before finally veering into an overgrown thicket of religion enmity and intolerance. Humanity has never completely found the way back. Medieval Spain might help point the way" (p.14).

In the epilogue, the author reminds readers of commandments that are "reverenced in the faith proclaimed by today's Muslim, Christian, and Jewish descendants of Isidore, Tariq, El Cid, Maimonides, Almanzor, Alfonso, Averroes, whether in Cordoba, Jerusalem, Bethlehem, or New York. To dishonor those commandments in God's name is to dishonor the One God who uttered them" (p.268). The author thus leads the readers to the conclusion that there is indeed a historical precedent for the three major religions to once again establish a similar symbiotic relationship in the 21st century.

The book includes several maps and historical pictures. Chapter-by-chapter notes and references are provided at the end. There is a topical list of suggested readings, followed by a detailed name-subject index.

B-354. Mann, Vivian B., Thomas F. Glick, and Jerrilynn D. Dodds, eds. *Convivencia: Jews, Muslims, and Christians in Medieval Spain.* New York: George Braziller, Inc., in association with The Jewish Museum, 1992.

Produced in conjunction with an exhibition with the same title, the book "explores the interaction of three religious groups and looks at the resultant material culture in the period that begins in 711 with the Muslim conquest and ends in 1492 with the expulsion of the Jews and the defeat of the last Muslim ruler" (p.vii). During this period (identified as the "Golden Age of Spanish Jewry"), "the experience of Jews living in medieval Iberia, particularly in the period of Muslim rule, provides a model of achievement for simultaneously flourishing Jewish religious and secular life" (p.vii). The cultural and social dynamics underlying *convivencia* (coexistence) influenced the creation of poetry, art, architecture, and the material culture of Spain, as well as the transmission and absorption of scientific ideas and technology from East to West. It may be noted that the Islamic presence did not encompass the entire peninsula during this period; it diminished geographically as the Catholic *Reconquista* gradually took place and the coexistence prevailed in Al-Andalus and Christian Spain.

The 265-page book contains eight essays: (1) *Convivencia*: An Introductory Note by Thomas F. Glick, (2) Jews, Christians, and Muslims in Medieval Iberia: *Convivencia* through the Eyes of Sephardic Jews by Benjamin R. Gampel, (3) Hebrew Poetry in Medieval Iberia by Raymond P. Scheindlin, (4) Social Perception and Literary Portrayal: Jews and Muslims in Medieval Spanish Literature by Dwayne E. Carpenter, (5) Science in Medieval Spain: The Jewish Contribution in the Context of *Convivencia* by Thomas F. Glick, (6) Mudejar Tradition and the Synagogues of Medieval Spain: Cultural Identity and Cultural Hegemony by Jerrilynn D. Dodds, (7) Hebrew Illuminated Manuscripts from the Iberian Peninsula by Gabrielle Sed-Rajna, (8) Material Culture in Medieval Spain by Juan Zozaya.

There is a 75-page catalogue of historical manuscripts at the end, with the following titles: biblical, prayer books, science, law, and philosophy, poetry, documents, printed books, architectural elements, ceramics, ivory and wood, metal work, stone, and textiles. The book contains numerous pictures and plates relating to the exhibition and reflecting the sociocultural content of the *convivencia* history. There is a bibliography at the end, but no index.

B-355. Marin, Manuela, ed. *The Formation of al-Andalus, Part I (History and Society)*. Brookfield, VT: Ashgate Publishing Company, 1998.

This is first of the two-part anthology of the Iberian peninsula during the Middle Ages, published as 46th volume in The Formation of the Classical Islamic World series on Islamic studies; the other is Maribel Fierro and Julio Samso (editors), *The Formation of al-Andalus, Part II (Language, Religion, Culture and the Sciences)*. Both volumes include previously published articles written by prominent contemporary scholars in various specific areas, focusing on the formative period of Islamic history (approximately 660 AD–950 AD). Editors provide a comprehensive introduction to the selections, as well as bibliographies for further reading. Most of the articles are written by Spanish scholars and published in Spanish sources, and the reason for this is argued to be that, heretofore, few Spaniards have worked on "an historical phenomenon that has not been easy to integrate into the 'national' history of their own country" (p.xiii). Reflecting new perspectives from Spanish sources on Andalusian historiography, the key theme of both volumes is "revisionist"; that is, "the progressive surmounting of the old concept of 'Spanish Islam' as the defining characteristic of al-Andalus" (p.xvi). The editor argues that the traditionalist interpretation of al-Andalusian history is being reassessed, with the gradual disappearance of the image of "Spanish Islam" from the overall scholarship, replaced gradually "with the ideological stand which emphasizes the Christian and Hispanic elements." In these respects, these volumes are distinctly at odds with those identified with other medieval scholars such as Maria Rosa Menocal, Salma Khadra Jayyusi, Luce Lopez-Baralt, and others.

There are 19 selections in Part I of this 510-page volume, focusing on various aspects of al-Andalusian history during the period covered. Some titles and authors are: The Itineraries of the Muslim Conquest of al-Andalus in the Light of a New Source: Ibn al-Shabbat by Emilio de Santiago Simon; The Social Structure of al-Andalus during the Muslim Occupation (711–755) and the Foundation of the Umayyad Monarchy by Miguel Cruz Hernandez; The Population of the Region of Valencia during the First Two Centuries of Muslim Domination by Pierre Guichard; Mozarabs: An Emblematic Christian Minority in Islamic al-Andalus by Mikel de Epalza; Cities Founded by the Muslims in al-Andalus by Leopoldo Torres Balbas; Considerations with Respect to "al-Thaghr in al-Andalus" and the Political-Administrative Division of Muslim Spain by Jacinto Bosch Vila; The "Zalmedina" of Cordoba by Joaquin Vallve Bermejo; Eastern Influences in al-Andalus by Juan Zozaya; The Structure of the Family in al-Andalus by Maria Luisa Avila.

There is a bibliography at the end of the introductory chapter, "deliberately limited to 100 titles." Each essay integrates its own notations and references in the text; there is no index.

B-356. McCabe, Joseph. *The Splendour of Moorish Spain*. London: Watts and Company, 1935.

The book is intended for the general reader and is based on the findings of other scholars who have studied the Arab-Islamic civilization and discovered the facts which vindicate John W. Draper's argument in his 1862 *History of the Intellectual Development of Europe*, in that "the real meaning of the medieval awakening if there was in fact, in the darkest centuries of European life, a stimulating, and indeed brilliant, world [belonged] just on the borders of Christendom, in Spain, South Italy, and the East. Here, in this brilliant Arab civilization, was the lost clue to that mystery of the reawakening of Europe. Yet English and American scholarship remained in a remarkable degree indifferent to this profoundly important revolution" (p.vii).

Further, "One historical writer borrows the *cliche* from another, and it is made an excuse for continuing to represent that the medieval Church was the inspiration of the progressive life of Europe, when it did (after seven centuries of barbarism) begin to make progress" (p.viii). Those who emphasize the deep significance of the Arab civilization are dismissed as "anti-Christian" writers, says the author (p.viii). Yet, this civilization, "which the Spaniards, with strange pride in their vandalism, thrust into the cemetery of dead empires, was one of the happiest, most prosperous, most advanced in fine feeling and culture that had yet appeared on the earth" (p.vi).

The 298-page book contains 21 chapters: (1) The World's Darkest Hour, (2) The Arab Vandals, (3) Damascus and the New Civilization, (4) The Renaissance in Persia, (5) The Light Spreads to Spain, (6) The Brilliant Abd-er-Rahman III, (7) A Royal Patron of Learning, (8) The Romance of Al-Mansur, (9) The Princely City of Cordoba, (10) The Fall of the Caliphate, (11) The Real Moors of Spain, (12) The Christian Reconquest, (13) The Saracens of Sicily, (14) The Intellectual Life, (15) Arab-Persian Science, (16) The General Ideal of Life, (17) The Ministry of the Jew, (18) How the Arabs Educated Europe, (19) The Kingdom of Granada, (20) The Final Tragedy, (21) The Sequel in Spain.

While the Arab-Islamic linkages are noted in almost every chapter, chapter 18, How the Arabs Educated Europe, is of particular interest. The author laments that "there is still much reluctance to admit the full share of the Spanish Arabs in the re-education of Europe" (p.235). Yet, he argues, it is the Arab culture which "directed or stimulated the intellectual, aesthetic, and social advances which slowly made an end of the barbarism of the Middle Ages" (p.237). And, "All the research of the last twenty years," reveals that "Europe borrowed almost all its science until the fifteenth century from the Arabs, and originated almost nothing of importance" (p.240).

The book provides very few footnotes and any bibliographic references are integrated within the text. There is a detailed name-subject index.

B-357. Menocal, Maria Rosa. *The Ornament of the World: How Muslims, Jews, and Christians Created a Culture of Tolerance in Medieval Spain.* Boston, New York, and London: Little, Brown and Company, 2002.

This widely acclaimed 320-page book tells the story of a vibrant civilization of Medieval Spain. Both historical and literary studies often depict the Middle Ages as a dark and barbaric period, characterized by intellectual backwardness and religious intolerance. However, the author focuses on how a "remarkable turn of events" in the Near East "affected the course of European history and civilization" (p.9). "Many aspects of the story," she suggests, "are largely unknown, and the extent of their continuing effects on the world around us is scarcely understood, for numerous and complex reasons" (p.9). The book brings together a different vision of this part of medieval Europe, where tolerance was often the rule, and literature, science, and art flourished in a climate of cultural openness. The story begins in the Iberian peninsula: Al-Andalus. For 300 years, Cordoba was the "ornament of the world."

In a series of interesting vignettes, the reader travels through time and space to discover the often paradoxical events that shaped the Andalusian world and continue to affect our own. One encounters several intriguing characters: the brilliant Jewish vizier of a powerful Muslim city-state; the Christian abbot who commissions the first translation of the Qur'an; the converted Jew who, under a Christian name, brings a first glimpse of Arabic scholarship and storytelling to Europe. Combined with the best of what Muslims, Jews, and Christians had to offer, al-Andalus and its successors influenced the rest of Europe, giving it the first translations of the Greeks, a tradition of love songs and secular poetry, advances in mathematics, and outstanding feats of architecture and technology. This rich and complex culture shared by the three faiths thrived, sometimes in the face of enmity and bigotry, for nearly 700 years. Ironically, it was on the eve of the Renaissance that puritanical forces finally triumphed over Spain's long-standing tradition of tolerance, ushering in a period of religious repression. In the centuries since, the memories of that vital and sophisticated culture have largely been overlooked or obscured, the author argues.

The book contains 20 chapters. Some titles are: a brief history of a first-rate place; the palaces of memory; the mosque and the palm tree; a grand vizier and a grand city; the gardens of memory; love and its songs; the church at the top of the hill; an Andalusian in London; the Abbot and the Qur'an; banned in Paris; visions of other worlds; foreign dignitaries at the courts of Castile; in the Alhambra; epilogue: Andalusian shards.

There is a poignant post-9/11 postscript at the end, written after the book was complete. This is followed by a listing of footnotes and other readings tied to the relevant pages of the book. Also, there is a list of additional readings, with annotations about each, and a name-subject index at the end.

B-358. Menocal, Maria Rosa, Raymond P. Scheindlin, and Michael Sells, eds. *The Literature of Al-Andalus*. Cambridge: Cambridge University Press, 2000.

This volume explores the culture of Iberia (present-day Spain and Portugal) during the period when it was part of the Islamic civilization—from the eighth to the 15th century—and in the centuries subsequent to the Christian conquest, when the Arabic language continued to be widely used. Path-breaking in its approach to the study of Arabic literature, the book embraces many other related aspects of Arabic-Islamic culture, including philosophy, art, architecture, music, and other literatures, especially Hebrew and Romance literatures that flourished alongside Arabic and thus created the distinctive pluralistic culture of medieval Iberia. The editors are, respectively, an Arabist, a Hebraist, and a Romance scholar, and the chapters are compiled by a team of leading scholars of Islamic Iberia, Sicily, and related cultures. The volume is truly interdisciplinary and the comparative literature it offers represents a distinctly new approach to the field.

The 508-page book begins with two introductory essays: Visions of al-Andalus by Maria Rosa Menocal, and Madinat al-Zahra and the Umayyad Palace by D.F. Ruggles. These are followed by 29 chapters, grouped into five parts: (1) The shapes of culture (language, music, spaces, knowledge, love); (2) The shapes of literature (the muwashshah ["strophic poetry quintessentially Andalusian," p.165], the maqama ["collections of independent narratives written in ornamental rhymed prose," p.190], the qasida ["formal multithematic ode addressed to a member of the elite in praise, in admiration, or in quest of support," p.211]); (3) Andalusians (Ibn Hazm, Moses Ibn Ezra, Judah Halevi, Perrus Alfonsi, Ibn Quzman, Ibn Zaydun, Ibn Tufayl, Ibn 'Arabi, Ramon Llull, Ibn al-Khatib); (4) Sicily (poetries of Norman courts, Ibn Hamdis and the poetry of nostalgia, Michael Scott and the translators); (5) marriages and exiles (the mozarabs, the Arabized Jews, the sephardim, the moriscos). The book ends with the poem "To Al-Andalus, would she return the greeting?"

There is a comprehensive bibliography, as well as a detailed name-subject index.

B-359. Meyerson, Mark D. *The Muslims of Valencia in the Age of Fernando and Isabel: Between Co-Existence and Crusade*. Berkeley and Los Angeles: University of California Press, 1991.

The book "focuses on the Muslim minority of the kingdom of Valencia during the reign of Fernando II (1479–1516), some 240 years after the kingdom was conquered from Islam" (p.4). It investigates the situation of the "Valencian Mudejars (Muslims living under Christian rule) of this era," with the objective of comprehending "more fully the reasons for the breakdown of *convivencia*, which for the most part occurred under the Catholic Monarchs, Fernando and his wife, Isabel I of Castile. It was the Monarchs who set about taking care of Spain's 'Jewish Problem,' first by establishing a national Inquisition (1478–1483)," and by eradicating the Conversos (Jews forced to baptize) and then by expelling the Jews (1492) to prevent contamination of the Conversos (p.4). After ten years of Granada's conquest (1492), Muslims here were given the same choice (baptism or expulsion), as were the Muslims of Isabel's Castile (1502). However, by the end of the Fernando's rule, "only the Muslims living in the lands of the Crown of Aragon still retained their dissident religious status" (p.4). The book explores why this was so, even though Fernando's Inquisition could have been extended to Mudejars in Aragon as well. This particularly issue has not been adequately explored in other studies, the author argues.

After the introduction, the 375-page book contains six detailed chapters: (1) Fernando II and the Mudejars: The Maintenance of Tradition, (2) The War against Islam and the Muslims at Home, (3) Mudejar Officialdom and Economic Life, (4) Taxation of the Mudejars, (5) Mudejars and the Administration of Justice, (6) Conflict and Solidarity in Mudejar Society.

In the concluding chapter, the author notes that contrary to the Catholic Monarchs' crusades against Jews and Muslims elsewhere, "Fernando's policy toward the Muslim subjects of the Crown of Aragon, particularly toward those in the kingdom of Valencia, has produced conclusions that defy our expectations" (p.270). The essential explanation, based on this study, is economic: in this kingdom, "where Fernando alone ruled, the king made a considerable effort to augment the population of royal *morerias* by drawing Muslim vassals away from seigneural lands, by constructing new *morerias*, or by settling Muslims from the conquered sultanate of Granada in Valencia. The Catholic Monarch saw no need to change in any way the centuries-old tradition of Mudejarism, and was most concerned to ensure that the Crown received as great a share as was possible of the economic benefits accruing from the Mudejars' labor and enterprise" (p.270). Yet, Fernando the pragmatist was not particularly enamored by Islam; in reaction to some show of Christian accommodation he would pounce on displays of tolerance and angrily called for "the oppression of the disorders of the pestiferous and infernal Mahometan sect" (p.45).The conclusion of this study is at odds with other studies which have argued that the Catholic uniformity of Spain was the chief objective of Catholic Monarchs.

The book provides 75 pages of chapter-by-chapter notes and references at the end. There is an 11-page bibliography of primary (archival, printed) and secondary sources, as well as a detailed name-subject index.

B-360. Meyerson, Mark D. and Edward D. English, eds. *Christians, Muslims, and Jews in Medieval and Early Modern Spain: Interaction and Cultural Change*. Notre Dame, IN: University of Notre Dame Press, 1999.

The book is a collection papers presented at a conference, with the same title, held at the University of Notre Dame in 1994. Recognizing the "marginalization of Jewish, Islamic and Byzantine studies from the field of medieval studies," the editors organized this gathering as a means of integrating the history of medieval Spain, "the land of three religions," into the field of medieval studies. This marginalization, say the editors, is "due in no small part to the unwillingness or inability of many Europeanists to give careful attention to a country in whose history and sociocultural formation Muslims and Jews played such a significant role" (p.xii). With the infusion of multiculturalism in North America, the "land of medieval multiculturalism, once deemed as a handicap, is "now viewed as a virtue, its allure" (p.xii). Thus, the conference was intended to develop "a more refined understanding of the dynamics of social and cultural interchange, whether the result was brilliant literature or horrible violence" and to "provide a framework for a comparative analysis of, for instance, different social and political conditions and the degree to which they facilitated fruitful social and cultural interchange between religious groups or enhanced mutual hostility and aversion" (p.xv–xvii).

The 322-page book is divided into five parts, each with several essays, for a total of 15. Part I, Christians and Jews in Muslim Spain, with four essays: (1) Muhammad as Antichrist in Ninth-Century Cordoba by Kenneth Baxter Wolf, (2) Reading the *Repartimientos*: Modeling Settlement in the Wake of Conquest by Thomas F. Glick, (3) Maimonides and the Spanish Aristotelian School by Joel L. Kraemer, (4) Jewish–Muslim Relations in the Context of Andalusian Emigration by Steven M. Wasserstrom. Part II, Muslims and Jews in Christian Spain, with five essays: (5) Mudejar Parallel Societies: Anglophone Historiography and Spanish Context, 1975–2000 by Robert J. Burns, (6) Muslim–Jewish Relations in Crusader Majorca in the Thirteenth Century: An Inquiry Based on Patrimony Register 342 by Larry J. Simon, (7) Religious and Sexual Boundaries in the Medieval Crown of Aragon by David Nirenberg, (8) History and Intersexuality in Late Medieval Spain by Eleazar Gutwirth, (9) Undermining the Jewish Sense of Future: Alfonso of Valladolid and the New Christian Missionizing by Robert Chazan. Part III, Conversos, with three essays: (10) Crypto-Jewish Women Facing the Spanish Inquisition: Transmitting Religious Practices, Beliefs, and Attitudes by Renee Levine Melammed, (11) Relations Between Conversos and Old Christians in Early Modern Toledo: Some Different Perspectives by Linda Martz, (12) Conversion and Subversion: Converso Texts in Fifteenth-Century Spain by Dayle Seidenspinner-Nunez. Part IV, Moriscos, with three essays: (13) The Moriscos: Loyal Subjects of His Catholic Majesty Philip III by Stephen Haliczer, (14) Moriscas and the Limits of Assimilation by Mary Elizabeth Perry, (15) The Moriscos and Christian Doctrine by Consuelo Lopez-Morillas. Part V includes the epilogue After 1492: Spain as Seen by Non-Spaniards by J.N. Hillgarth. (Note: In contrast to "Moriscos," the word "Moriscas" refers to Muslim women forced to baptize; "conversos" refers to forcibly baptized Jews.)

Each essay provides notes and references at the end. There is no index.

B-361. Monroe, James T. *Islam and the Arabs in Spanish Scholarship (Sixteenth Century to the Present)*. Leiden, Netherlands: E.J. Brill, 1970.

Writing in 1970, the author laments the lack of satisfactory books on Oriental studies in the Western world and if there are some, they do not discuss the manner in which those works succeed in "modifying and influencing the ideas of Western intellectual circles" (p.ix). The author argues that the history of Western Orientalism requires prior nation-by-nation studies, and then a more comprehensive study could be derived. Thus, "It is the purpose of this book to fill the lacuna insofar as Spanish Orientalism is concerned" (p.ix). There have been some studies of Spanish Arabism, but they represented "an anti-Islamic propagandistic and crusading movement closely related to the Spanish *Reconquista*" (p.ix).

This book outlines the cultural references for the Orientalists to understand the intellectual milieu in which the Arabists of Spain were working. Thus, the purpose of the book "is to serve as a guide to those students interested in Spanish Islam" (p.x). Further, in addition to the knowledge of the eight-century-long Spanish crusade known as the *Reconquista*, we also know "how the philosophy of Muslim Spain influenced the Scholastics; how the Oriental prose tale affected medieval European narrative art; how Dante reflects the influence of the Muslim eschatological literature in the *Divine Comedy*; and how the origins of European lyrical poetry seem to be inextricably connected with the lyrics sung by the Arabs in the courts of Muslim Spain" (p.2). Such connections originated in Spain, "thus constituting one of the significant contributions of Spain to contemporary Western scholarship" (p.2).

In addition to the introductory chapter, the 300-page book has ten chapters, grouped into three parts. Part One, The Study of Grammar and Lexicography, has one chapter: (1) Peculiar state of Arabic studies in the seventeenth century. Part Two, The Study of Political History, has four chapters: (2) Early nineteenth-century Arabism, (3) Arabism in the second half of the nineteenth century, (4) Arabism in the second half of the nineteenth century (continued), (5) The precursor of contemporary Spanish Arabic studies. Part Three, The Study of Cultural History, has five chapters: (6) The Arabism of the Generation of 1898, (7) The Arabism of the Generation of 1898 (continued), (8) The school of Asin: His disciplines, (9) Twentieth-century Arabic studies in Spain, (10) Attitudes of twentieth-century Spanish intellectuals toward the Arabs in Spain.

With respect to Islamic civilization, the author says, "To argue tendentiously, as I fear not a few non-Muslims have done, that all that in their view is good in Islam is of foreign origin, and must be traced to one or another non-Islamic source, is not so much honest scholarship as the worst form of sectarian bigotry" (p.192). The last chapter summarizes the views of various Spanish Arabists—some suggesting the impact of Arab-Islamic presence as decidedly negative, others as cautiously positive. The author concludes by quoting the words of Montgomery Watt: "Catholic Spaniards have sometimes tended to regard the period of Islamic domination as a mere interruption in the continuing life of a single entity, Catholic Spain. A more exciting and apparently more balanced treatment of the complex questions at issue—and one more congenial to the Islamist—is that of Americo Castro in *The Structure of Spanish History*. His general thesis is that there was no continuity between Visigothic Spain and later Christian Spain, but that the latter was something new which was born and grew up in the mixed culture (largely Arab) which developed under the Muslims" (p.262–263).

Notes and references are integrated in the text of each chapter. There is 22-page bibliography at the end, followed by an index of authors' names.

B-362. O'Callaghan, Joseph F. *A History of Medieval Spain*. Ithaca, NY, and London: Cornell University Press, 1975.

"Until recently American and most northern European scholars have paid scant attention to the history of the Iberian peninsula in the Middle Ages and have often been content with superficial judgments founded upon antiquated and inaccurate works or on opinions clouded by the prejudices accumulated over the past four hundred years," says the author (p.iii). Thus, the book is intended to contribute to a clearer understanding of the formation of medieval Spain. Chronologically, the book extends from the coming of the Visigoths in the fifth century until the conquest of Granada and the discovery of America in 1492; geographically, it covers the entire peninsula, including both Spain and Portugal.

The book is divided into five parts, with several chapters in each: Part I, The Visigothic Era, 415–711; Part II, The Ascendancy of Islam, 711–1031; Part III, A Balance of Power, from the Fall of the Caliphate to Las Navas de Tolosa, 1031–1212; Part IV, The Great Reconquest and the Beginnings of Overseas Expansion, 1212–1369; Part V, The Struggle for Peninsular Union, 1369–1479. There is an epilogue entitled The Catholic Kings and the Perfect Prince.

As for the Islamic presence, Part II has four chapters: The Emirate of Cordoba; The Caliphate of Cordoba; Government, Society, and Culture in al-Andalus, 711–1031; Government, Society, and Culture in Christian Spain, 711–1035. These chapters, among other things, describe the problems encountered by non-Muslim groups; however, "They enjoyed freedom of worship and the right to live according to their own law and customs" (p.152). Also, there is mention of the imitation of Muslim coinage, with Latin inscription that testified to "the oneness of the Diety," in the 11th century as "only one example of the impact of al-Andalus upon the economy of Christian states" (p.157). Further, there is reference to the bemoaning of the ninth-century monk, Paulus Alvarus, who "decried the impact of Islamic culture upon young Christians" (p.187).

However, chapter 13 of Part V, Religion and Culture (1031–1212), provides more details as to the Islamic influences and linkages. The author states, "Toledo attained fame for its school of translators who turned into Latin the writings of Arabic scholars as well as those of the ancient Greeks. In this way the wisdom of the Greeks and the Arabs, especially in the fields of philosophy, science, and medicine, was made known to western Europe and profoundly influenced the development of western civilization" (p.306). O'Callaghan refers to Ibn Abdun's fear of plagiarism: "Books of science ought not to be sold to Jews or Christians, except those that treat of their own religion. Indeed, they translate books of science and attribute authorship to their coreligionists or to their bishops, when they are the work of Muslim" (p.313). There is also reference to the influence of Averroes (Ibn Rushd, 1126–1198) upon Latin Europe, although "Muslim scholars had little enthusiasm for Averroes, whose approach they found too rationalistic" (p.323).

The 730-page book has numerous illustrations and maps, as well as several genealogical charts. There is a comprehensive bibliography, organized in terms of the five parts of the book, and a detailed name-subject index.

B-363. Pick, Lucy K. *Conflict and Coexistence: Archbishop Rodrigo and the Muslims and Jews of Medieval Spain.* Ann Arbor, MI: University of Michigan Press, 2004.

The book is about Rodrigo Jimenez de Rada, archbishop of Toledo between 1209 and 1247. Rodrigo "was an instrumental force in turning back the tide of Muslim attacks on Christian Spain and restarting the process of Christian conquests of the peninsula" (p.vi). The purpose of the book is "to examine his relations with Muslims and Jews, a crucial part of his career, both as he idealized these relations on paper and as he worked them out in real life" (p.x). The author argues that Rodrigo's "program was aimed at containing threats, both internal and external, Christian and non-Christian, using practical means both derived from and reinforcing a vision of the world as essentially unified under God, although currently fractured by sin and history. The intended and actual consequences of this program were to allow Christians, Muslims, and Jews to live together under Christian hegemony" (p.x). Further, Rodrigo "was bound by practical necessity to find a means of accommodating these groups that was both effective and theologically satisfactory" (p.xi). The book studies this process of accommodation in relation to Rodrigo's other goals as archbishop.

The 240-page book contains six chapters: (1) Introduction: Themes and Arguments, (2) Conquest and Settlement, (3) A Theology of Unity, (4) Rodrigo and Jews of Toledo, (5) Polemic and Performance: The *Dialogus* and the *Auto de los Reyes Magos*, (6) Epilogue. The last chapter summarizes how this "*convivencia* could ever be maintained" and "how it collapsed" (p.204). Rodrigo talked in terms of his "theology of unity" and argued that "their [referring to Jews and Muslims] economic skills and financial resources could be utilized, and their eventual conversion could be hoped for. Any threat they posed of treacherous acts against Christian policies could best be contained by keeping them within those policies, rather than by casting them out" (p.205). However, the fate of Rodrigo's program weakened after his death; "subsequent holders of the archbishopric of Toledo continued to assert the primacy of their see over all the

Spain," and thus, "the equilibrium in Spain between Christians and Jews, and then Christians and Muslims, was being shattered for good" (p.206–207).

The book includes an appendix at the end, Two Charters from the Cathedral Archive of Toledo (June–October 1211), with polemics against Muslims (Saracens) and Jews, and warning those who might align with them. There is a 15-page bibliography of manuscripts consulted as well as primary and secondary sources, followed by a name-subject index.

B-364. Read, Jan. *The Moors in Spain and Portugal*. London: Faber & Faber, London, 1974.

Finding "no general history in English which satisfied" the sort of questions that arouse one's curiosity when visiting Spain and Portugal, the author chose to write this book for the general reader; it is also useful for medieval-history specialists—students, academics, others. The book is broadly chronological (beginning with 710 AD and ending with 1492), although occasionally it describes parallel events in Al-Andalus and the Christian north. The last two chapters go beyond 1492 and describe the conversion/expulsion of Moriscos during 1492–1614, as well as the Moorish legacy to Spain and Porugal. The 268-page book incorporates accounts of sociocultural developments at about the time when they were most significant, summing up trends over a period. To the extent possible, the author has also incorporated material from early and contemporary Islamic chroniclers.

Chronologically arranged, the 15 chapter titles are as follows: (1) Moorish landings, 710–714, (2) Romans and Visigoths in Iberia before the invasions, (3) al-Andalus, 714–741, (4) Thrust and counterthrust: Christian resistance, 718–801, (5) Power and Glory of the Caliphate, 912–916, (6) The Decline and Fall of the Caliphate, 1002–1031, (7) Christians on the move: Beginnings of the Reconquest, 1017–1072, (8) The Almoravids, the resurgence of Al-Andalus, 1102–1145, (9) The origins of an independent Portugal, 1087–1179, (10) The Translators: Toledo and the transmission of knowledge to Western Europe in the 12th and 13th centuries, (11) The Mudejars, their skills and the Reconquest, 1212–1481, (12) The Splendid Capital, Granada, 1245–1481, (13) The conquest of Granada, 1481–1492, (14) The Moriscos: The conversion and final expulsion, 1492–1614, (15) Moors and Christians: The Moorish legacy to Spain and Portugal.

At the end, the book provides a comparative chronological list of major events identified with Moorish Spain-Portugal and Christian Europe. There is a bibliography by broad topics (The History of Moorish Spain, The Fall of Granada and Jewish and Moorish Expulsions, The History of Medieval Spain, The History of Portugal, Literature and Fine Arts, Religion, Philosophy and Science, Moorish Influences in Modern Spain and Portugal). There is also a detailed name-subject index.

B-365. Samso, Julio. *Islamic Astronomy and Medieval Spain.* Brookfield, VT: Ashgate Publishing Company, 1994.

The book is a collection 20 articles, published in various journals by the author, individually or jointly, between 1977 and 1992. Eight of the papers are in Spanish. Each paper is reproduced as originally published, with original page numbers.

Samso argues in the preface that "nothing can be understood in Andalusian and Maghribi (Western) Astronomy without a thorough knowledge of its Oriental (Eastern) counterpart. It took me a long time to understand that there is a cultural unity between the Mashriq (East) and the Maghrib (West) and that only from the eleventh century onwards did al-Andalus develop a set of characteristics of its own which, even though they may have an Oriental origin, created points of emphasis which characterized Andalusian Astronomy and became influential not only in the whole of Maghrib but also in the Mashriq towards the end of the Middle Ages" (p.x–xi).

The book is divided into five parts, with one or more articles in each: (1) General (one key essay, Andalusian Astronomy: Its Main Characteristics and Influence in the Latin West); (2) The Survival of the Latin Astronomy and Astrology in Al-Andalus (three articles); (3) Eastern Influence in Andalusian Astronomy (three articles); (4) Mathematical Astronomy and Astronomical Theory (five articles); (5) Alfonso X and Arabic Astronomy (eight articles).

Almost all articles provide notes and references within the text; a few provide notes, references, and a bibliography at the end of the paper. There is a name-subject index as well.

B-366. Scott, S.P. *History of the Moorish Empire in Europe*, volume one. Philadelphia, PA, and London: J.B. Lippincott Company, 1904.

One of the most comprehensive early studies on the history of the Moorish Spain, this widely acknowledged study (2,400 pages altogether) is similar to an earlier compendium on the subject written by Reinhart Dozy (*Spanish Islam: A History of Moslems in Spain*, Chatto & Windus, London; 1913; original, 1861), whose "learning, accuracy, impartiality, and critical acumen" is acknowledged by the author (p.v, vol.1). Scott suggests that his objective is "to depict the civilization of that great race whose achievements in science, literature, and the arts have been the inspiration of the marvelous progress of the present age. The review of this wide-spread influence, whose ramifications extend to the limits of both Europe and America, has required the introduction of some matter apparently extraneous, but which, when considered in its general relations to the subject, will be found to be not foreign to the purpose of these volumes" (p.v, vol.1).

This volume has 14 chapters: (1) The Ancient Arabians, (2) The Rise, Progress, and Influence of Islam, (3) The Conquest of Al-Maghreb, (4) The Visigothic Monarchy, (5) The Invasion and Conquest of Spain, (6) The Emirate, (7) Foundation of the Spanish Monarch, (8) The Ommeyades: The Reign of Abd-al-Rahman

I, (9) Reign of Hischem I; Reign of Al-Hakem I, (10) Reign of Abd-al-Rahman II; Reign of Mohammed, (11) Reign of Al-Mondhir; Reign of Abdallah, (12) Reign of Abd-al-Rehman III, (13) Reign of Al-Hakem II, (14) Reign of Hischem II.

Throughout the book, the author presents a picture of the harmonious medieval Moorish pluralism of Islamic Spain, along with a detailed discussion of this civilization's influence upon Latin Europe.

At the beginning of this volume there is a 26-page list of "authorities consulted," classified by the language of the publications (English, French, Spanish, Portuguese, Italian, German, Dutch, Danish, Swedish, Limousin and Catalan, Latin, Greek, Hebrew, and Arabic). A combined name-subject index is provided at the end of volume three.

B-367. Scott, S.P. *History of the Moorish Empire in Europe*, volume two. Philadelphia, PA, and London: J.B. Lippincott Company, 1904.

One of the most comprehensive early studies on the history of the Moorish Spain, this widely acknowledged study (2,400 pages altogether) is similar to an earlier compendium on the subject written by Reinhart Dozy (*Spanish Islam: A History of Moslems in Spain*, Chatto & Windus, London; 1913; original, 1861), whose "learning, accuracy, impartiality, and critical acumen" is acknowledged by the author (p.v, vol.1). Scott suggests that his objective is "to depict the civilization of that great race whose achievements in science, literature, and the arts have been the inspiration of the marvelous progress of the present age. The review of this wide-spread influence, whose ramifications extend to the limits of both Europe and America, has required the introduction of some matter apparently extraneous, but which, when considered in its general relations to the subject, will be found to be not foreign to the purpose of these volumes" (p.v, vol.1).

This volume has eight chapters. Continuing from volume one, which has 14 chapters, the titles are: (15) The Moslem Domination in Sicily, (16) The Principalities of Moorish Spain, (17) Wars with the Christians; The Almoravides, (18) The Empire of the Almohades, (19) The Progress of the Christian Arms, (20) Prosecution of the Reconquest, (21) The Last War with Granada, (22) Termination of the Reconquest.

Throughout the book, the author presents a picture of the harmonious medieval Moorish pluralism of Islamic Spain, along with a detailed discussion of this civilization's influence upon Latin Europe.

At the beginning of volume one, there is a 26-page list of "authorities consulted," classified by the language of the publications (English, French, Spanish, Portuguese, Italian, German, Dutch, Danish, Swedish, Limousin and Catalan, Latin, Greek, Hebrew, and Arabic). A combined name-subject index is provided at the end of volume three.

B-368. Scott, S.P. *History of the Moorish Empire in Europe*, volume three. Philadelphia, PA, and London: J.B. Lippincott Company, 1904.

One of the most comprehensive early studies on the history of the Moorish Spain, this widely acknowledged study (2,400 pages altogether) is similar to an earlier compendium on the subject written by Reinhart Dozy (*Spanish Islam: A History of Moslems in Spain*, Chatto & Windus, London; 1913; original, 1861), whose "learning, accuracy, impartiality, and critical acumen" is acknowledged by the author (p.v, vol.1). Scott suggests that his objective is "to depict the civilization of that great race whose achievements in science, literature, and the arts have been the inspiration of the marvelous progress of the present age. The review of this wide-spread influence, whose ramifications extend to the limits of both Europe and America, has required the introduction of some matter apparently extraneous, but which, when considered in its general relations to the subject, will be found to be not foreign to the purpose of these volumes" (p.v, vol.1).

This volume has eight chapters, and continuing from the 22 chapters of the previous two volumes, the titles are: (23) Influence of the Moors on Europe through the Empire of Frederick II and the States of Southern France, (24) The Spanish Jews, (25) The Christians under Moslem Rule, (26) The Moriscos, (27) General Condition of Europe from the Eighth to the Sixteenth Century, (28) The Hispano-Arab Age of Literature and Science, (29) Moorish Art in Southern France, (30) Agriculture, Manufactures, and Commerce of the European Moslems: Their Manners, Customs, and Amusements.

Throughout the book, but particularly in this volume, the author presents a picture of the harmonious medieval Moorish pluralism of Islamic Spain, along with a detailed discussion of this civilization's influence upon Latin Europe. He states: "The extraordinary impulse to scientific investigation, to historical research, to the development and perfection of industrial arts, to the extension of commerce, to the improvement of social and economic conditions which was so intimately connected with the comfort and happiness of mankind, [was] imparted by the Saracen kingdoms of Southern Europe. The progress of their humanizing influence upon other nations had been slow and imperceptible. The philosophical ideas and principles advanced by the Arab universities were necessarily hostile to the doctrines of Christianity, to the opinions of the Fathers, to the infallibility of the Pope, to the imperious claims of ecclesiastical supremacy. In consequence of their heretical tendency, they were perused in secret" (p.1–2, vol.3). However, "The spirit of resistance to Papal aggression, corruption, and tyranny, temporarily checked, in time revived, and found permanent expression in the bold and revolutionary theories of the Reformation" (p.2, vol.3). And, "In almost every European monastery, whose inmates, corrupted by wealth and depraved by sensual indulgence, had abandoned the ascetic habits of the cloister, the infidel works of the Arabian philosophers were studied with curiosity and delight by jovial monks, long strangers to the vows inculcated as cardinal precepts by the regulations of their order" (p.3, vol.3).

At the beginning of volume one, there is a 26-page list of "authorities consulted," classified by the language of the publications (English, French, Spanish,

Portuguese, Italian, German, Dutch, Danish, Swedish, Limousin and Catalan, Latin, Greek, Hebrew, and Arabic). A combined name-subject index is provided at the end of volume three.

B-369. Sertima, Ivan Van, ed. *Golden Age of the Moor.* New Brunswick, NJ, and London: Transactions Publishers, 1993.

The collection of articles included in this 475-page volume represents a special edition of the *Journal of African Civilizations,* vol. 11, Fall 1991. The focus is exclusively on the Moorish civilization of Islamic Spain (Al-Andalus). The contents are rather revealing, provocative, well-documented—and also controversial.

The book is divided into three parts, with several articles in each. Part I, Race and Origin of the Moors, has three articles: (1a) The Moor in Africa and Europe: Origins and Definitions by Ivan Van Sertima, and (1b) The Moor in Europe: Influences and Contributions by Ivan Van Sertima, (2a) "The Moors in Antiquity by James E. Brunson and Runoko Rashidi, and (2b) The Empire of the Moors by John G. Jackson, (3) The African Heritage and Ethnohistory of the Moors: Background to the Emergence of Early Berber and Arab Peoples, from Prehistory to the Islamic Dynasties by Dana Reynolds. Part II, Moorish Contributions to European Civilization, has six essays: (1) The Moor: Light of Europe's Dark Age by Wayne Chandler, (2) Moorish Spain: Academic Source and Foundation for the Rise and Success of Western European Universities in the Middle Ages by Jose V. Pimienta-Bey, (3) Moorish Culture-Bringers: Bearers of Enlightenment by Jan Carew, (4) The Music of the Moors in Spain (Al-Andalus, 711–1492 AD)— Origin of the Andalusian Musical Art: Its Development and Influence on Western Culture by Yusef Ali, (5) The Moors and Portugal's Global Expansion by Edward Scobie, (6) Africans in the Birth and Expansion of Islam by Mamadou Chinyelu. Part III, The Science of the Moors, contains three essays: (1) Cairo: Science Academy of the Middle Ages by Beatrice Lumpkin and Siham Zitler, (2) The Egyptian Precursor to Greek and "Arab" Science: (a) The Judgement, and (b) Supplements to the Indictment by Ivan Van Sertima, (3) An Annotated Bibliography of the Moors, 711–1492 AD by James Ravell.

Notes and references are listed at the end of each essay. All the contributors, along with a brief biographical note, are listed at the end, and there is a detailed name-subject index.

B-370. Sordo, Enrique. *Moorish Spain: Cordoba, Seville, Granada.* New York: Crown Publishers, 1963.

The book, originally written in Spanish, examines the achievements of the Islamic civilization as seen in the three principal cities of Andalusia: Cordoba, Seville, and Granada. Also explored is the sociopolitical history and progress of the art in these cities, two elements that often intermingled in this land of contrasts, where beauty and refinement existed side by side with cultural refinements and conflicts. The detailed account of the Moorish art and architecture is also captured in brilliant black-and-white and color pictures. The book should interest all those attracted to Islamic Spain and Arab past, as well as designers and craft workers looking for ideas.

The author suggests, "It is necessary to live for a time amid the subtle and exciting atmosphere that pervades the Arabic monuments of Cordoba, Seville and Granada in order to grasp the extent and importance of a very alien culture, many facets of which survive still" (p.11). Further, "Whatever the state of its political fortunes, one can say the land of al-Andalus never lost its spiritual sovereignty," and the "essence of this land is distilled in three cities: Cordoba, Seville and Granada" (p.11). And, while "Cordoba seems to be immersed still in the warm atmosphere of Islam," Seville is different—"few traces remain of the city's greatest period under Almoravid and Almohad rule" (p.12). As for Granada, "If there exists in the Iberian Peninsula a city that epitomizes the essential Moorish spirit, without a doubt that city is Granada" (p.12).

After the introduction, there are three chapters, each devoted to one of the three cities. The book includes 87 black-and-white and color pictures of various aspects of each city. Also provided are plans of famous structures (Cordoba Mosque, Granada's Alhambra Palace, etc.), as well as genealogical tables of various dynasties that ruled the cities. The 225-page book includes a glossary of terms at the end, followed by a brief bibliography. There is a name-subject index.

B-371. Watt, W. Montgomery. *A History of Islamic Spain.* Edinburgh: Edinburgh University Press, 1965.

Addressed to the educated reader, the book is part of the Islamic surveys series, designed to provide "something more than can be found in the usual popular books" (p.v). It should also be valuable to university students and others whose interest is of a more professional nature, states the author. Islamic Spain, he says, "offers an important example of the close contact of diverse cultures, and one that has contributed to making the European and American historian what he is" (p.1).

The page book explores three questions: (1) Islamic Spain "must be looked at in itself," but what were its great achievements? (2) Islamic Spain must be looked upon as part of the Islamic world, but how and in what ways? (3) Islamic Spain was in close contact with its European neighbors, but what exactly did it contribute to European neighbors, and how was Europe influenced by reacting against Islamic Spain?

The 200-page book has 11 chapters: (1) The Muslim Conquest, (2) The Province of the Damascus Caliphate, (3) The Independent Umayyad Emirate, (4) The Grandeur of the Umayyad Caliphate, (5) Cultural Achievements under the Umayyads, (6) The Collapse of the Arab Rule, (7) The Berber Empires: The Almoravids, (8) The Berber Empires: The Almohads, (9) Cultural Greatness in Political Decline, (10) The Last of Islamic Spain, (11) The Significance of Islamic Spain.

Particularly interesting is the last chapter. As for cultural achievements, the author points out that "nothing of the Christian intellectual culture of pre-Islamic Spain made any real contribution. On the contrary great numbers of local inhabitants became Muslims, and in course of time were assimilated to the Arab section of the population" (p.168). However, over time, Western Christendom felt "both strong attraction and strong repulsion. Islam was at one and the same time the great enemy and the great source of higher material and intellectual culture" (p.172). Further, could one consider "the Islamic period of Spanish history as being among the great ages of mankind"? (p.173). The author answers affirmatively, in that given all the various and sundry contributions, the "life of al-Andalus is indeed a noble facet of the total experience of mankind," despite the "fear of the Saracen" and the fact that "even now few western Europeans can regard Islam with impartiality" (p.174–175).

The book contains 17 pictures of Islamic Spain and two maps, one showing the extent of Islamic influence and the other showing the main trading routes. Chapter-by-chapter notes and references are provided at the end, followed by bibliographic notes and references. There is a name-subject index.

B-372. Wright, Thomas E. *Into the Moorish World*. London: Robert Hale, 1972.

Written for the lay-public, the 240-page book reads like a travelogue, written in an informal, conversational style; but it offers considerable historical content. It begins with a tribute to the Moorish people, "the legendary men of the desert, those who have had the wilderness for a pillow and called a star their brother" (p.11). And, then emerged the man who "composed a record, or some spirit dictated a record to him, that remains one of the world's strangest, most extra-ordinary, and some say greatest, books. This man, the Prophet, and his book changed the entire course of history" (p.11). "'Islam' they called their religion and their group and more loosely their whole culture. They left behind one of the world's great religions and left behind also social and political institutions, art, language, literature—in short, Islam" (p.12–13). Further, "Christian travellers saw Moorish religious colleges, schools with students-in-residence, and after returning home founded the first European universities. From Moorish lands, medieval Europe learned of arabic numerals, algebra, silkmaking, glassmaking, tile-work, leather-work, citrus fruits, geography books, animal husbandry and much else" (p.14).

The book is divided into two parts: Part One, Andalusia, has eight chapters: (1) Arabesques and Flashing Eyes, (2) Sun-Drenched, Passion-Drunk Seville, (3) Beyond the Barbary Walls, (4) The Strange Tale of the Sacred Crocodile, (5) Across the Andalusian Heartland, (6) The World's Most Beautiful Building, (7) The Alhambra by Moonlight, (8) Cordoba and Its Mosque. Part Two, Morocco, has ten chapters: (1) Tangier: Legend and Reality, (2) The Alleys of Tetuan, (3) Rabat: White, Imperial, Clay-Walled City, (4) Barbary Pirates and Moslem Saints, (5) Sacred Storks and Overladen Donkeys, (6) The Golden Minarets of

Fez, (7) O' Glorious Red-burnt Desert City, (8) Beyond Marrakesh Lies the Legendary, (9) Past the Gates of Sun, (10) Camel Bells and Slaves.

The book includes 24 representative pictures of the Moorish culture, from Andalus as well as Morocco. There is a name-subject index at the end.

(II) THE CRUSADES

B-373. Atiya, Aziz S. *Crusade, Commerce, and Culture.* Bloomington, IN: Indiana University Press, 1962.

The book is based on a series of lectures by the author as a distinguished visiting faculty at Indiana University in 1957 and they reflect his passion for studying the history of "relations between the East and the West" (p.9). Over the years he had delivered similar lectures at various European and U.S. universities, culminating in the present volume (which is a companion volume to the author's *The Crusade: Historiography and Bibliography*, published simultaneously by the Indiana University).

The book attempts to fill the gap, in that, while there are historical books on Crusades, there "exists virtually no satisfactory survey" of "East–West relationship in its triple phase of Crusade, Commerce, and Culture" (p.10–11). The book presents an outline of "the general structure of three great historical movements in the relations between the Near and Middle East on the one hand and the states of European Christendom on the other" (p.13).

The key theme of the book is that the three phases of the medieval society—Crusade, Commerce, and Culture—followed one another in successive stages and represented the genesis of medieval society and medieval mind. These movements, the author argues, contributed to the shaping of modern world and form part of the "story of mankind in general and in the history of the Eastern Question," which "goes far back into antiquity" (p.13). And, "The Crusade should be viewed as only one of many phases or attempts at a solution of the Eastern Question" (p.13).

The first four chapters are devoted primarily to exploring the Crusade, its antecedents and its repercussions. The consequences of the Crusades gave rise to commerce in the Levant, a topic explored by relying on Eastern and Arabic sources. These two movements were necessarily followed by ideas from East to West—thus, the cultural impacts that are discussed in a chapter entitled Arab Culture and the West in the Middle Ages. In the epilogue, the author brings the earlier developments to modern times and discusses "the basic factors at work in the interminable East–West conflict, which has been changing only in milieu and motivation" (p.14).

An appendix entitled Dante's Sources and Muslim Legend (see Miguel Asin-Palacios, *Islam and the Divine Comedy* [translated and abridged by Harold Sunderland], John Murray, London, 1926), is followed by a bibliography of general references, as well as three others classified in terms of the title of the book. The author urges readers to "consult these works for further bibliographic information, because a wealth of material exists in past and current periodical literature, in the languages of almost all countries" (p.262). There is a detailed name-subject index.

B-374. Atiya, Aziz S. *The Crusade in the Later Middle Ages*, second edition. New York: Kraus Reprint Company, 1970.

Disputing the view expressed by several scholars that the crusade movement ended in 1291, the author examines "extensive masses of unpublished material" and argues that the movement did not terminate until about the end of the 14th century or early 15th century (p.v). Other scholars have covered this period, but their work is mainly biographical in character; the present book deals with the crusading impulse and its expression based on a "thorough and comprehensive examination of the western as well as the eastern sources" (p.vi).

The 610-page book is divided into four parts, extended over 20 chapters. The first part (Background) consists of a general view of the later medieval world in the context of the crusades; and the second (Propaganda and Projects, with eight chapters) includes treatment of the enormous volume of propagandist literature in the West, the accounts of the pilgrimages being the main source here. In the third part (The East and the Crusade, two chapters), the author surveys the state of the Eastern Christendom, the relations between Europe and the Mongols, and Latin missionary activities in the Middle East and Far East, as well as the relevance of these otherwise neglected subjects upon the crusade movement in the period covered. The fourth part (The Crusades, with nine chapters) traces the history of the crusading movement itself, expedition by expedition. The closing section briefly outlines what the author calls "counter-propaganda" and "counter-crusades"; that is, the reaction of the East to Western attacks (as manifested from the age of Saladin to that of Suleiman the Magnificent).

The book includes five appendices (pro recuperatione terrae sanctae, petitio raymundi pro conversione infidelium; pilgrims and travellers; Aragon and Egypt; lists of the crusaders; chronological tables). There is a 32-page bibliography of literature in various languages, plus a 10-page bibliography for the second edition of the book. There is also a comprehensive 32-page name-subject index.

B-375. Burns, Robert Ignatius, S.J. *Islam under the Crusaders: Colonial Survival in the Thirteenth Century Kingdom of Valencia*. Princeton, NJ: Princeton University Press, 1973.

This book is about "Islam's predicament under a crusader regime, and the mystery of its acculturative devolution from a proud, celebrated community into a provincial appendage of Aragon, by analyzing the elements of its survival in a series of steps" (p.xvi). The topics discussed are: pre-crusader political, geographical, economic, and social contours of Islamic Valencia; post-crusader constitutional setting that surrounded all Spanish Mudejar (Muslims under Christian rule) life; analysis of social processes and forms evolved through the religious, educational, and juridical matrices; and the position of the Mudejar in his political dimension as he finds his place in the Christian feudal order at the nobility and patrician levels. The book ends with a chapter that probes the community's innermost strength.

The book is divided into three parts. Part I (The Physical–Historical Milieu) has five chapters: (1) The King's Other Kingdom, (2) Death of an Islamic Empire, (3) The Physical Setting, (4) Human Geography, (5) City and Country Classes; Part II (The Juridical–Religious Milieu) has six chapters: (1) Surrender Terms: Universality and Pattern, (2) Burriana-Valencia and the Townsmen, (3) Incorporation: Motives and Mechanisms, (4) Islam: An Established Religion, (5) The Law and Its Interpreters, (6) Christians and Islamic Judiciary; Part III (The Political–Military Milieu) also has six chapters: (1) The Muslim in the Feudal Order, (2) The Military Aristocracy, (3) Patriot Mudejar Lords, (4) Horizontal Power: The Rulers, (5) The City-State Polities, (6) The Islamic Establishment. The author notes in the final chapter: "A civilization may decline and disappear, though remnants remain alive. The crusaders did not kill Islamic Valencian culture, though they dealt it mortal wounds. Unwittingly, without intending final damage, they gave these wounds to a body already in its last throes from self-inflicted injuries" (p.420).

There is a 35-page bibliography, divided into primary and secondary sources; this is followed by a detailed name-subject index.

B-376. Gabrieli, Francesco, ed. *Arab Historians of the Crusades: Selected and Translated from the Arabic Sources* (translated from Italian by E.J. Costello). Berkeley and Los Angeles: University of California Press, 1969.

As the title suggests, the book is written to help the Western readers to see the period of the Crusades from "the other side," from the perspective of those who at that time were the enemy. Such an experience is especially informative since the two civilizations have had a great deal in common; however, their common struggle for universality brought them into conflict and fanaticism (something that seems to have resurfaced in the early 21st century!). The author argues that the Arab/Muslim historians compare favorably with their Christian counterparts in their well-documented accumulation of material and in their faithful characterization; their "general level of scholarship is probably higher than that of their Christian contemporaries" (p.xx).

While the book includes passages from two other similar European sources, most excerpts are taken directly from the original Muslim sources. Seventeen important Muslim authors are represented, plus others; the criteria for inclusion being historical importance, human or literary interest, and some picturesque detail. The book is organized in four parts: (1) From Godfrey to Saladin; (2)

Saladin and the Third Crusade (the largest section); (3) The Ayyubids and the Invasion of Egypt; (4) The Mamluks and the Liquidation of the Crusaders.

The editor confesses in his introduction, in that having studied the Islamic world for many years, "never before have I experienced such a sympathetic comprehension and respect for a civilization whose faults and failings need no emphasis but which possessed inspiring qualities of endurance, dedication and self-sacrifice, amazing elasticity and powers of recuperation, and an unyielding faith in the absolute and supreme Law" (p. xxii).

Any footnotes and references are included within each reading. There is a name-subject index at the end.

B-377. Goss, Vladimir P. and Christine V. Bornstein, eds. *The Meeting of Two Worlds: Cultural Exchange between East and West during the Period of the Crusades.* Kalamazoo, MI: Medieval Institute Publications, Western Michigan University, 1986.

This 450-page volume is a collection of papers presented at a symposium held at Western Michigan University in 1977. As the title suggests, the focus is primarily on the impact of the Crusaders on the West and "the discovery, by Westerners, of new places, peoples, and ideas" (p.4). Also explored are phenomena such as pilgrimages, trade, colonization, and new spiritual and military undertakings, the goal being the investigation of cultural exchange and the transmission and absorption of cultural assets. The editors acknowledge that in spite of their "interdisciplinary and cross-cultural interests and inclinations, all six organizers and consultants are scholars of Western culture and probably even subconsciously Europocentric" (p.4). Thus, the issues explored are couched in terms of West encountering the "Other," the latter being mainly Islam, but also Eastern Christianity. Despite this Western bias, the editors note, some scholars of Byzantine and Muslim civilizations also participated.

There is a total of 33 essays, the first five being introductory statements intended to provide background for the major themes of the symposium and raise some fundamental philosophical and methodical questions. Some "introductory" titles are: Byzantine and the Crusades by Sir Steven Runciman—it covers the political, economic, and ideological roots of mistrust; and The Roots of Medieval Colonialism by Joshua Power—it discusses the problem of the Crusaders' attitude, nurtured by "Messianic" zeal and anticipation of "the Day of Judgement," toward the native population of the Holy Land, both Christian and Muslim, and "paints a picture of a colonial society based on a strict 'apartheid' between the colonists and the original inhabitants" (p.5).

The four major themes of the symposium are: Part I, Western Presence in the Eastern Mediterranean (seven essays), focusing on the impact of Western presence in the Mediterranean, attitude and image about the natives, monuments of Crusader art; Part II, Reaction to the Western Presence in the Levant (six essays), relating to the response of the peoples of the eastern Mediterranean (Christian and Muslim) to the Western presence; Part III, "Materia Orientalis" and Western Medieval Culture (10 essays), pertaining to the impact of the East on Western medieval culture in its various manifestations—political, economic, art and architecture, literature, etc.; Part IV, Crusaders and the Outskirts of Europe (three essays), dealing with the impact of the Crusades on two specific areas: the two bridges between the East and the West, the Iberian and the Balkanic peninsulas. There are two concluding essays and the period covered is primarily the 12th and 13th centuries.

Each essay provides its own footnotes and references at the end. There is no separate bibliography, nor is there an index. There are 75 black-and-white pictures of historical–religious sculptures, however, at the end.

B-378. Hillenbrand, Carole. *The Crusades: Islamic Perspectives*. Chicago and London: Fitzroy Dearborn Publishers, 1999.

Written by an eminent British scholar of Islamic Studies, this widely acclaimed 650-page book is about the most comprehensive work of its kind. It provides Western historians a guide to source material, through translations and otherwise, and it introduces the readers to the mindset of medieval Muslims, providing an entirely different perspective from which to view the Crusades. By putting modern ideas into context, the book enables readers to dispassionately understand events that are shaping the current global environment as well.

Unlike some other chronological narratives of the Crusades, this is a general book intended to introduce some of the broader aspects of the history of the Crusades from the Islamic perspective. Within the modern currents, especially the environment generated by the post-9/11 tragedy, which permeate the contemporary Arab-Islamic world in particular, the Crusades are among the most important and live phenomena, not least because they involve momentous happenings. Such historical events evoke the painful realities and wounded hopes of a present that is deeply steeped in the past. Further, the author claims to have written for a wider audience—general readers, students, and specialists. The book is accompanied by well over 500 illustrations of medieval Islamic art, illustrations, and sketches, which provide a visual reinforcement for the author's attempt to view the Crusades from "the other side."

There are nine detailed chapters: (1) Prologue, (2) The First Crusade and the Muslims' Initial Reactions to the Coming of the Franks, (3) *Jihad* in the Period 493–569/1100–1174, (4) *Jihad* in the Period from the Death of Nur al-Din until the Fall of Acre (569–690/1174–1291), (5) How the Muslims Saw the Franks: Ethnic and Religious Stereotypes, (6) Aspects of Life in the Levant in the Crusading Period, (7) Armies, Arms, Armour and Fortifications, (8) The Conduct of War, (9) Epilogue: The Heritage of the Crusades.

Given that this book attempts to view the Crusades phenomenon through the prism of medieval Muslim sources, such a deliberate bias is salutary, says the author. This is particularly justified in view of the cumulative impact of centuries of Eurocentric scholarship in this field, "with only a perfunctory nod at some Muslim sources. Many a lesson derived from an analysis of Islamic perspectives on the Crusades will help towards better understanding between the West and those lands where Islam is still very much a political rallying-cry and a predominant religious ideology" (p.613). Further, "Those who support the present 'demonisation' of Islam in the Western media would thus do well to bear in mind this history of psychological damage and religious affront" (p.614). Thus, the author argues, the book should help to create a more balanced picture of the present momentous period of Christian-West/Islamic confrontation and interaction.

Each chapter ends with an extensive list of notes. There is 17-page bibliography of primary and secondary sources at the end and a detailed name-subject index.

B-379. Jones, Terry and Alan Ereira. *Crusades*. New York: Facts On File, published by arrangement with BBC Books, 1995.

An accompaniment to a television series by the same title, this book is sponsored by the British Broadcasting Corporation. It is about the "forces of bigotry and righteous savagery [that] were unleashed by Pope Urban II when he preached what later came to be called 'the Crusades.' These forces are still with us," the authors note (p.9). Further, they suggest, "The Crusades have never been without a contemporary significance. Right now, that significance is associated with the emergence of Islamic fundamentalism, and the new confrontations between Christian and Moslem societies in our post-Communist world. It is important to know how the old confrontation affected Christian and Islamic society and how it contributed to the present mess" (p.9).

The book attempts "to break away from a purely Euro-centric outlook and to tell the story of the Crusades from the Moslem point of view as well as from the Christian" (p.9). While "killing was wrong in the eyes of the Church," a penance could be done for that sin, "but killing, the Pope now declared, need not be a sin after all. It depended on who you killed. In fact, if you killed the enemies of Christ, killing did not require a penance—it *was* a penance" (p.24).

Beyond the introduction, the 256-page book has 15 chapters: (1) The World of a Crusader, (2) The Great Adventure, (3) War in Anatolia, (4) The March in Jerusalem, (5) The Arab Response, (6) The Fight Back Begins, (7) St. Bernard's Dogs, (8) Arab Unity, (9) Saladin the Upstart, (10) The Fall of Jerusalem, (11) To the Rescue, (12) The Battle of the Heroes: Richard vs. Saladin, (13) The Fourth Crusade, (14) A New Kind of Crusade, (15) Mongols and Mameluks.

The book includes numerous historical sketches and drawings, mostly in color, taken from original sources (listed at the end). Also, there are five maps. Chapter-by-chapter footnotes are provided at the end, followed by a bibliography, and there is a name-subject index.

B-380. Kedar, Benjamin Z. *Crusade and Mission: European Approaches toward Muslims*. Princeton, NJ: Princeton University Press, 1984.

The book is intended as "an attempt at the clarification of one specific issue: the relationship between crusade and mission as two Catholic approaches to Muslims in medieval times. Did one supersede the other, the rising missionary idea gradually replacing the declining idea of the crusade? Were the two complementary or competitive, with mission implying a criticism of crusade and undermining support for it?" (p.ix). Such concerns, the author notes, have not been sufficiently explored by historians thus far. The book also explores the relations between warfare, conversion, and mission in the history of the crusades; all three, it is argued, were carried out in the crusader East as well as in other areas where Catholics and Muslims clashed. The author notes that "apologetic prefaces to learned surveys of Christian anti-Islamic polemic merely indicate how emotionally charged the subject remains, as does the fact that the translator of a fourteenth-century *itnerarium*, published in Dublin in 1960, simply skips over some of the more extreme anti-Islamic remarks" (p.xi).

The 250-page book has five chapters: (1) The Early Christians: The Muslims beyond the Bounds of European Mission and Polemics, (2) Christian Conquest and Muslim Conversion, (3) The Espousal of Mission: A Criticism of the Crusade?, (4) The Mendicants: Preaching the Gospel to Saracens, Preaching the Cross to Christians, (5) A Contested Linkage: Crusading for the Advancement of Missions.

Each chapter provides notes and references in the text. At the end there are seven appendices (on topics such as information about Muhammad, Urban IV asking Saracens and Jews to convert, Raymon Lull's three questions on preaching, warfare, and conversion). There is also a list of secondary literature, followed by a name-subject index.

B-381. Lewis, Archibald R. *Nomads and Crusaders, A.D. 1000–1368*. Bloomington and Indianapolis: Indiana University Press, 1988.

The book attempts to explain "why Western Europe was able to develop in such a way that her civilization could prevail, in modern times, over others which earlier had seemed to be just as vigorous and just as promising" (p.vii). Instead of focusing on the Western Europe of 15th–16th centuries, or even the earlier medieval period, one must "try to grasp why those other great civilizations of medieval times—the Byzantine-Russian, the Islamic, the Indic, and the East Asian—failed to match the medieval performance of Western Europe, for their failures obviously explain in part the successes of the later" (p.vii). Concentrating on the High Middle Ages, the author places heavy emphasis upon geographical, demographic, economic, technological, and military factors, which in his opinion were more decisive than political, religious, and cultural elements.

The first part of the 215-page book examines the five great civilizations of the Old World: the East Asian, the Indic, the Islamic, the Byzantine-Russian, and the Western European, as they existed around the year 1000. The second part is concerned with "explaining how two major forces, nomadic peoples and Western European Crusaders, played a role in changing, modifying, and, at times, even weakening these civilizations during the nearly four hundred years of the High Middle Ages until 1368" (p.194). Among the nomadic peoples were the Berbers, the Arabs, and the Turks, followed by the Mongols during the 13th century. The Crusades enabled the territorial expansion of Western civilization during the High Middle Ages. The two great movements affected each of the older civilizations and by the end of the 14th century, Western Europe prevailed as the dominant power and continues as such in modern times, while the others fell behind. Yet the author suggests that "there can be no assurance that the Western European civilization which now seems so dominant in the world is more than a temporary phenomenon" (p.viii).

The book provides an excellent bibliography, arranged according to the five civilizations covered, as well as by the nomadic and crusading periods. Also, there is a comprehensive name-subject index.

B-382. Maalouf, Amin. *The Crusades through Arab Eyes* (translated from French by Jon Rothschild). New York: Schocken Books, 1985.

Written by a Lebanese Christian (a journalist/novelist, residing in France since 1976, who professes no particular faith), the book has a simple purpose: to tell the story of the Crusades (or Frankish wars or invasions, as the Arabs called them), as seen, lived, and recorded on "the other side," that is, by the Arabs/Muslims. The well-documented content is based almost exclusively on the testimony of Arab historians and chroniclers and, unlike a history book, the narrative is written like a "true-to-life novel" of the Crusades, spanning two centuries of turmoil that shaped—and still affects relations between—the West and the Arab/Islamic world.

The 295-page book has six parts, with two or three chapters in each (total of 14 chapters), and the narrative is chronologically organized. Part One, Invasion (1096–1100), has three chapters: (1) The Franj Arrive, (2) An Accursed Maker of Armour, (3) The Cannibals of Ma'arra. Part Two, Occupation (1100–1128), with two chapters: (1) Tripoli's Two Thousand Days, (2) Turban-Clad Resistance. Part Three, Riposte (1129–1146), also has two chapters: (1) The Damascus Conspiracies, (2) An Emir Among Barbarians. Part Four, Victory (1146–1187), has three chapters: (1) Nur al-Din, the Saint-King, (2) The Rush for the Nile, (3) The Tears of Saladin. Part Five, Reprieve (1187–1244), has two chapters: (1) The Impossible Encounter, (2) The Perfect and the Just. Part Six, Expulsion (1244–1291), also has two chapters: (1) The Mongol Scourge, (2) *God Grant That They Never Set Foot There Again!*

There is an epilogue in which the author notes, among other things, that "at the time of the Crusades, the Arab world, from Spain to Iraq, was still the intellectual and material repository of planet's most advanced civilization" (p.261). And,

"What they [Europe] learned from the Arabs was indispensable in their subsequent expansion. The heritage of Greek civilization was transmitted to Western Europe through Arab intermediaries, both translators and continuators" (p.264). The author further adds that "in the popular mind, and in some official discourse too, Israel is regarded as a new Crusader state" (p.265). Thus, "In a Muslim world under constant attack, it is impossible to prevent the emergence of a sense of persecution, which among certain fanatics takes the form of a dangerous obsession. And there can be no doubt that the schism between these two worlds dates from the Crusades, deeply felt by the Arabs, even today, as an act of rape" (p.265–266).

At the end, Maalouf provides a listing of chapter-by-chapter notes, sources, and a chronology, followed by a glossary and a note on pronunciation. There is a detailed name-subject index.

B-383. Zacour, Norman P. and Harry W. Hazard. *A History of the Crusades: The Impact of the Crusades on the Near East.* Madison, WI: University of Wisconsin Press, 1985.

This is the fifth volume of the six-part series on the History of the Crusades. Published over a period of 30 years, other titles are: The First Hundred Years; The Later Crusades; 1189–1311; The Fourteenth and Fifteenth Centuries; The Art and Architecture of the Crusader States.

This 600-page volume deals less with the battle cry of the Crusades than with the daily affairs of the Near East and its inhabitants—Muslims, Christians, and Jews—whose lives were wrenched by more than two centuries of violence. It is about crusaders too, especially those who stayed "for the love of Christ" and "put their fighting blood at the disposal of king and magnates" (p.xv). Among other things, it examines the Arab-Islamic culture of the 12th century and the "lasting impact that crusading belligerence had on Moslem lands and peoples; the social structure of the crusaders' states whose problems were as stubborn as they themselves were ephemeral; the long, tenacious exploitation of the eastern Mediterranean, especially by the Venetians, surely the most fortunate heirs of the crusading inheritance; and finally the new direction given to the European drive eastward by missionaries rather than warriors" (p.xv). The devotion of missionaries brought increased knowledge and a deeper understanding of Islam and Muslims, but "not, alas, any real awareness of the futility of warfare against Islam" (p.xv).

There are ten long essays: (1) Arab Culture in the Twelfth Century by Nabih Amin Faris, (2) The Impact of the Crusades on Moslem Lands by Philip Khuri Hitti, (3) Social Classes in the Crusader States: The "Minorities" by Joshua Power, (4) Social Classes in the Latin Kingdom: The Franks by Joshua Power, (5) The Political and Ecclesiastical Organization of the Crusader States by Jean Richard, (6) Agricultural Conditions in the Crusader States by Jean Richard, (7) The Population of the Crusader States by Josia C. Russell, (8) The Teutonic

Knights in the Crusader States by Indrikis Sterns, (9) Venice and the Crusades by Louise Buenger Robbert, (10) Missions to the East in the Thirteenth and Fourteenth Centuries by Marshall W. Baldwin.

Footnotes and bibliographic references are included in the text of each essay. The book contains four illustrations and 13 maps; there is a 33-page gazetteer and note on maps at the end, followed by a 46-page name-subject index. The sixth volume includes a comprehensive bibliography on the complete series.

(III) MISCELLANEOUS

B-384. Armstrong, Guyda and Ian N. Wood, eds. *Christianizing Peoples and Converting Individuals*. Turnhout, Belgium: Brepols Publishers, 2000.

The book contains selected proceedings of the 1997 International Medieval Congress (University of Leeds, England). While "christian conversion" during the Middle Ages was the central theme, two related issues were also addressed: (1) the interface between Christians and Muslims in Spain and in the Holy Land, and between Christians and Jews in Spain and Europe; and (2) the theological question of the nature of conversion. The collection presents current research on christianization and conversion history.

The 28 essays, written by medievalists from various countries, are grouped under nine topics: (1) The Early Medieval East, (2) The Early Medieval West, (3) The Conversion of Scandinavia, (4) The Conversion of Central and Eastern Europe, (5) The Conversion of the Jews, (6) Crusade and Conversion in the Mediterranean Region, (7) Competing Faiths in Asia: Muslims, Christians, Zoroastrians, and Mongols, (8) The Theology of Conversion, (9) Conversion in Art.

An essay, Platonism and Plagiarism at the End of the Middle Ages, by Peter O'Brien is of particular interest. In probing the medieval origins of European esotericism ignored by Leo Strauss and his followers, the author argues that a centuries-long encounter with the superior non-Christian, Islamic civilization fostered esotericism ("the one-way traffic of ideas from Islam to Christendom at the end of the Middle Ages was nothing short of staggering" [p.308]). It is argued that Western medieval intellectuals, in order to avoid persecution, not only distorted the truth ("employed untruth and half-truth" [p.313]) about their knowledge of Islam and borrowed without explicit admission of reliance on the "alien source," but their encounter with the Islamic culture led them to cast doubt about—not merely disguise—their notion of universal truth.

Notes and references are provided in the text of each essay, but the 350-page volume provides no indexation.

B-385. Bloom, Jonathan M., ed. *Early Islamic Art and Architecture*. Burlington, VT, and Hampshire, UK: Ashgate Publishing Ltd., 2002.

This is one of several volumes in the series entitled The Formation of the Clas-

sical Islamic World, under the general editorship of Lawrence I. Conrad. Motivated by the premise that modern scholarship tends to be "compartmentalized"
into specific areas, each volume in this series presents a number of previously
published recent studies, representing the "best of current scholarship," on a particular topic in early Islamic history (covering approximately AD 600–950).
Articles published in languages other than English have been translated, and editors have provided critical introductions and select bibliographies for further
reading.

This particular volume focuses "on the central region between the Nile and the
Oxus in the first four centuries of Islam" (p.xi). There are 13 essays, previously
published and written by prominent scholars: (1) Notes on Arabic Archeology by
Max van Berchem, (2) The Genesis of Islamic Art and the Problem of *Mshatta*
by Ernst Kuhnel, (3) The Lawfulness of Painting in Early Islam by K.A.C. Cres-
well, (4) The Mosque and the Palace by Jean Sauvaget, (5) *Mihrab* and *Anazah*:
A Study in Islamic Iconography by George C. Miles, (6) The Greek Sources of
Islamic Scientific Illustrations by Kurt Weitzman, (7) Deacon or Drink: Some
Paintings from Samarra Re-examined by David Storm Rice, (8) The *Umayyad*
Dome of the Rock in Jerusalem by Oleg Grabar, (9) *Zandaniji* Identified by D.G.
Shepherd and W. Henning, (10) The Throne and Banquet Hall of Khirbat al-
Mafjar by Richard Ettinghausen, (11) *La Dolce Vita* in Early Islamic Syria: The
Evidence of Later *Umayyad* Palaces by Robert Hillenbrand, (12) The Origins of
the *Mihrab Mujawwaf*: A Reinterpretation by Estelle Whelan, (13) Al-Mamun's
Blue Koran? by Jonathan M. Bloom.

Notes and references are integrated in the text of each essay. The 420-page
book also provides a name-subject index.

B-386. Hattstein, Markus and Peter Delius, eds. *Islam: Art and Architecture*
(translated from German). Cologne: Konemann Verlagsgesellschaft mbH, 2000.

This 640-page volume is a majestic document on the subject. The book follows
the historical development of the Islamic civilization and the ruling dynasties in
various regions, and it illustrates the greatly varied forms of artistic expression
from the birth of the religion to the present day. Basic architectural elements,
in their diverse modes of expression, demonstrate the independence of regional
traditions. Further, the decoration and ornamentation of buildings and everyday
objects display profound creativity. There is the inventive brick and tile decoration of Uzbekistan, the bright, naturalistic arabesque of India or Iran, and the
ubiquitous geometrical ornamentation of Spain and the Maghreb. The book presents all of this in colorful illustrations and calligraphy, with pictures of tapestries,
metalworks, ceramics and jewelry produced in various Islamic cultures.

The book begins with four historical chapters: (1) Islam: World Religion and
Cultural Power by Markus Hattstein, (2) Art and Culture in the Islamic World by
Oleg Grabar, (3) The Mosque by Oleg Grabar, (4) Science in Islam by Markus
Hattstein. These chapters briefly cover the evolution of the Islamic civilization,

and, among other things, it is noted that "contrary to what is generally thought in the West, where the achievements of Arab and Persian science are seen as consisting almost exclusively in the preservation and transmission of the inheritance of the classical antiquity, these scholars adopted an intellectually original and independent approach to the texts of antiquity; the Greek inheritance was not simply copied and read, but revised, brought into line with the requirements of Islamic culture (and religion), supplemented, and expanded" (p.54).

Then there are 13 detailed chapters concentrating on various Islamic dynasties and cultures. These chapters focus on history, architecture, and the arts, and are written by prominent scholars in the field. (1) Syria and Palestine: The Umayyad Caliphate, (2) Iraq, Iran, and Egypt: The Abbasids, (3) Tunisia and Egypt: The Aghlabids and Fatimids, (4) Syria, Palestine, and Egypt: Ayyubids, Mamluks, and Crusaders, (5) Spain and Morocco, (6) The Maghreb: From Morocco to Tunisia, (7) Early Empires of the East: Ghaznavids and Ghurids, (8) Central Asia and Asia Minor: The Great Seljuks, the Anatolian Seljuks, and the Khwarzm-Shahs, (9) Islamic Mongols: From the Mongol Invasions to the Ilkhanids, (10) Central Asia: The Timurids, the Shaybanids, and the Khan Princedoms, (11) Indian Subcontinent: From Sultanate to Mughal Empire, (12) Iran: Safavids and Qajars, (13) The Ottoman Empire. There is a final chapter, Islam in the Modern Age.

The appendix includes a list of authors (with some detail as to their credentials), bibliography (classified in terms of the various chapter titles of the book), Islamic calendar and transliteration details, glossary of various Islamic dynasties, glossary of terms, name-subject index, picture credits, and acknowledgments.

B-387. Lowick, Nicholas (edited by Joe Cribb). *Coinage and History of the Islamic World*. Aldershot, UK: Variorum-Grower Publishing Group, 1990.

This volume and its companion, *Islamic Coins and Trade in the Medieval World*, have been compiled, posthumously, with the intention of presenting the main areas of the author's work; both volumes contain 36 articles (17 in this). While the other volume focuses on the author's interest in "coin hoards and finds as evidence of international trade, in northern Europe during the Viking period, in the Persian Gulf and in Iran and Afghanistan" (p.xi), this book "concentrates on the use of coins as primary sources for Islamic political history, in the Yemen, in the Middle East under the pre-Ottoman Turkish and other dynasties, and in Central Asia under the Shaybanid Mongols and their early Mughal successors" (p.xvii). Three main themes underlie this work on Islamic coins: the accurate reading of inscriptions, the recording of coin hoards and finds, and the linkage of numismatic data to literary sources. The author brings together these three "approaches to use coins as a structure for reviewing the movement of coins in international trade during the medieval period" (p.xii). Beyond a study of the coins, there are descriptions of their historical context, political and economic; and such interpretations, says the editor, enable clarification, augmentation, and even correction of the accepted historical accounts.

The 260-page book contains articles published by the author between 1964 and 1985. Each article is identified as to its source of publication and each is reproduced as it originally appeared, including pagination, notes, references, and bibliography. Numerous pictorial representations of coins are provided.

The articles are grouped into three parts. Part I, Coins in the History of the Yemen, contains four articles: (1) The mint of San'a: A historical outline, (2) Coins of the Najahids of Yemen: A preliminary investigation, (3) Some unpublished dinars of the Sulayhids and Zuray'ids, (4) The mansuri and the mahdawi dirham: Two additions to Sauvaire's 'Materiaux. Part II, Coins of Medieval Turkish and Other Dynasties in the Middle East, contains six papers: (5) A gold coin of Rasultegin, Seljuk ruler in Fars, (6) Seljuk coins, (7) A hoard of Seljuk dirhams, (8) Les premieres monnaies artuqides: Une exhumation tardive, (9) The religious, the royal and the popular in the figural coinage of the Jazira, (10) Feudalism in Syria: An Ayyubid silver hoard. Part III, Coins of Late Mongol Dynasties in Central and South Asia, contains seven articles: (11) Shaybanid silver coins, (12) Some countermarked coins of the Shaybanids and early Moghuls, (13) Coins of Sulaiman Mirza of Badakhshan, (14) More on Sulaiman Mirza and his contemporaries, (15) Joint coinage of Humayun and Shah Tahmasp at Qandahar, (16) Humayun's silver coinage in Bengal and the introduction of the rupee, (17) The horseman type of Bengal and the question of commemorative issues.

The book provides a name-subject index.

B-388. Lowick, Nicholas M. (edited by Joe Cribb). *Islamic Coins and Trade in the Medieval World*. Aldershot, UK: Variorum-Grower Publishing Group, 1990.

This volume and its companion, *Coinage and History of the Islamic World*, have been compiled, posthumously, with the intention of presenting the main areas of the author's work; both volumes contain 36 articles (19 in this). This volume "focuses on his interest in coin hoards and finds as evidence of international trade, in northern Europe during the Viking period, in the Persian Gulf and in Iran and Afghanistan" (p.xi). Three main themes underlie this work on Islamic coins: the accurate reading of inscriptions, the recording of coin hoards and finds, and the linkage of numismatic data to literary sources. The author brings together these three "approaches to use coins as a structure for reviewing the movement of coins in international trade during the medieval period" (p.xii). Beyond a study of the coins, there are descriptions of their historical context, political and economic, and such interpretations, says the editor, enable clarification, augmentation, and even correction of the accepted historical accounts.

The 310-page book contains articles, published by the author between 1968 and 1988. Each article is identified as to its source of publication and each is reproduced as it originally appeared, including pagination, notes, references, and bibliography. Numerous pictorial representations of coins are also provided.

The articles are grouped into three parts. Part I, Islamic Coins in Europe, includes four articles: (1) A new type of *solidus mancus*, (2) The Kufic coins from Cuerdale, (3) The Kufic coin fragments [from a Viking period hoard at Dysart, County Westmeath], (4) Un ripositglio di monete d'oro islamiche e normanne da Agrigento. Part II, Coinage of Central Asia during the Tenth and Eleventh Centuries, includes five articles: (5) An early tenth-century hoard from Isfahan, (6) Silver from the Panjhir mines, (7) On the dating of Samanid outsize dirhams, (8) A Samanid/Kakwayhid "mule," (9) The wandering die of Nisabur: A sequel. Part III, Coin Finds and Hoards and the Trade of the Gulf and the Indian Ocean, has ten articles: (10) Recent coin finds in the Arabian peninsula, (11) Trade patterns on the Persian Gulf in the light of recent coin evidence, (12) Further unpublished Islamic coins of the Persian Gulf, (13) The Sinaw hoard of early Islamic silver coins, (14) A hoard of dirhems from Ra's al-Khaimah, (15) An eleventh-century coin hoard from Ra's al-Khaimah and the question of Sohar's decline, (16) A fourteenth-century hoard from eastern Arabia, (17) Islamic coins and weights [from Julfar], (18) Une monnaie 'alide d'al-Basrah datee de 145 H (762-3 apres J.C.), (19) Fatimid coins of Multan.

There is a name-subject index.

B-389. Pereira, Jose. *The Sacred Architecture of Islam.* New Delhi, India: Aryan Books International, 2004.

The 494-page book encompasses one of the most prolific traditions in the history of Islamic architecture, including four major strands: Arab, Iranian, Turkish, Indian. It is a panoramic survey that conveys a cultural phenomenon within the ambit of Islamic civilization. The author suggests that the first three strands appear separated from the last by what he calls the Hindu-Kush barrier. The Indo-Islamic monuments appear to baffle the scholars, as though the South-Asian structures have a singular character conditioned by the impact of styles that had served the Buddhist stupa and the Hindu temple, styles unfamiliar to most students of Islamic architecture. Conversely, says the author, historians specializing in Indo-Islamic architecture seem somewhat unfamiliar with monuments west of the Hindu Kush.

Pereira's wide exposure to the monuments of Eurafroasia and the Americas enables him observe the sacred architecture of Islam in its totality. Further, "One reason for Islam's ecumenicity was its situation in the very centre of the *oikoumene*, straddling as it does three continents, Asia, Africa, and Europe. It thus became the heir of the region's great architectural traditions, and itself possessed the imaginative power to use their resources to create traditions of its own that impacted on other contemporaneous and subsequently originating styles" (p.xiii–xiv).

The preface not only introduces the book but also provides background perspectives, with brief narratives on aspects such as polarities of Islamic civilization, the fourfold method in studying Islamic architecture (historical, idiomatic, axiomorphic, aesthetic), and impact of other styles. Focusing on each of the four strands, then follow five major chapters: (1) Basic Concepts, (2) History (276 pages), (3) Idiomatics (30 pages), (4) Axiomorphics (36 pages), (5) Aesthetics (72 pages). There are numerous black-and-white and color plates, photographs, and illustrations.

There is an appendix entitled A Comprehensive Classification of Muslim Sacred Structures, and there are 14 select bibliographies: a general bibliography plus 13 others covering the various traditions within the four strands (Arab, Iranian, Turkish, Indian). A list of illustrations is also provided at the end, followed a name-subject index.

B-390. Sahai, Surendra. *Indian Architecture: Islamic Period, 1192–1857.* New Delhi, India: Prakash Books (India) Ltd., 2004.

This 164-page book, with text and photographs by the author, attempts to showcase the history of Islamic architecture in India, from the founding of the Delhi Sultanate in 1193 to the end of the Mughal Rule in 1857. The book traces how, during these centuries, various Islamic dynasties evolved and created their own unique architectural tradition. The early Turkish Sultans introduced the forms of the dome and arch into the Indian architectural tradition. The Sharqi rulers of Jaunpur, the Ahmad Shahi's of Gujarat, the Bahmani Sultans of Gulbarga and Bidar, the Qutb Shahi's of Golconda, and the Adil Shahi's of Bijapur all created great regional variations of the imperial architectural style of Delhi. The Mughals erected glorious monuments in Delhi and Agra, incorporating elements from indigenous architectural forms.

The book covers the architecture of the entire period of Islamic rule until it was replaced by the British. It explains complex architectural forms in a lucid style and represents one of the best introductions to Islamic architecture in India.

Beyond the introduction, the book contains 18 chapters: (1) Early Turkish Sultans and the Khiljis, (2) The Tughlaqs, (3) The Sayyids and the Lodis, (4) Kashmir and Multan, (5) Bengal: The Ilyas Shahi and Hussain Shahi Rulers, (6) Gujarat: The Ahmad Shahi's, (7) Jaunpur: The Ahmad Shahi's, (8) Mandu: The Ghuri and the Khilji Sultans, (9) Gulbarga, Bidar and Daultabad: The Bahmani Sultans, (10) Golconda and Hyderabad: The Qutb Shahi's, (11) Bijapur: The Adil Shahi Rulers, (12) Sher Shah, (13) The Great Mughals: Babur, Humayun and Akbar, (14) Fatepur Sikri, (15) Jehangir, (16) Shahjahan, (17) The Taj Mahal and Shahjahanabad, (18) Aurangzeb: The Decline of a Great Tradition.

The book provides a glossary and bibliography at the end, followed by a name-subject index.

B-391. Seherr-Thoss, Sonia P. and Hans C. Seherr-Thoss, eds. *Design and Color in Islamic Architecture: Afghanistan, Iran, Turkey.* Washington, DC: Smithsonian Institution Press, 1968.

The editors suggest this book "is not intended as a historical survey of Islamic architecture, nor does it include all the fine monuments in this style. The U.S.S.R., Iraq, Syria, Egypt, India, Pakistan, North Africa and Spain possess outstanding buildings, but due to space limitations, many Afghan, Iranian, and Turkish monuments have been omitted. This is no reflection on their beauty or merit, but the selections included were chosen because other examples were chosen to show a particular design or use of color, or because they were especially relevant to the Western architecture. And, "It is this pertinence of Islamic architecture and design and aesthetics which is the particular concern of this volume" (p.9).

The 312-page book illustrates this kinship by way of 138 full-color photographs, each reflecting a panorama of 700 years of architectural development—a tribute, as the editors state, to the Muslim builders whose designs seldom overpowered the basic architectural forms but, instead, served to define and enhance them (p.8).

A list of the photographs is provided, with exact location and description, as well as a brief explanation of its cultural history (including Islamic dynasties) and architectural temperament. At the end there is a glossary of terms, followed by a chronology of various Islamic dynasties. There are bibliographic notes for the various photographs, followed by a bibliographic list of the literature consulted. There are also 14 architectural drawings, identified with relevant photographs.

B-392. Sweetman, John. *The Oriental Obsession: Islamic Inspiration in British and American Architecture, 1500–1920.* Cambridge and New York: Cambridge University Press, 1988.

While the impact of Islam on the West has taken many forms, the author notes, this book is about the "role of the visual arts in the relationship between the Islamic Orient and the West, particularly in regard to the English-speaking world and the period 1500–1920, when the appeal of the gilded dream was at its brightest" (p.xv). Further, "If 'obsession' means having a passion of a sustained kind," the word describes "the growing attention to Islamic art that was also part of this European feeling" (p.xv). It is noted that the book "has grown out of an interest in the English 'orientalist' painter, John Frederick Lewis, an unconventional and unmoralising Victorian, whose almost exclusive concern from early middle age was to paint the life of Cairo" (p.1).

The plan of the book is chronological. In addition to the introduction and concluding chapters, the intervening six chapters are: (1) 1500 to 1660: The growing impetus, (2) 1660 to 1750: The connoisseurs of spectacle, (3) 1750 to 1820: Models east of Rome, (4) After 1820: The painters' vision, (5) After 1850: The design reformers, (6) The American story. There are 12 color plates and 148 black-and-white figures. Several are "self-evident pairs" of Islamic art or architecture works and works by British or American artists; most, however, are works by "Western artists which reflect unmistakable Islamic stimulus" (p.xv). Three considerations determined these selections: aesthetic merit, the extent of "Islamic ingredients," and "works which show a distinguishable Islamic reference" (p.xvi). The concluding chapter notes "two developments relevant to us in regard to painting after

1750, in which the British contribution is significant. First came the orientalising tendencies of the English Romantists. Secondly, and more fundamentally, there is the first-hand discovery of Islamic ways of life as a serious and positive alternative to European society and European prejudices, and as a source from which to develop artistic initiatives" (p.245).

There are two appendices: Buildings with Islamic associations in Britain and America, and Note on collections. The 330-page book provides 44 pages of chapter-by-chapter notes and references at the end, followed by a comprehensive bibliography classified in terms of primary and secondary sources. There is a detailed name-subject index.

II
ARTICLES

(A) Sciences/Humanities

(I) SOCIAL SCIENCES/HUMANITIES

a. History

A-1. Gomez, Michael A. "Muslims in Early America." *Journal of Southern History* 60, no.4 (November 1994): 671–710.

This essay is "a preliminary study of Islam in early African American history" (p.671). During the post-1492 formation of the New World, while Christianity and Judaism migrated with European colonizers, this transformation was "at the expense of non-European systems of belief that were also imported into the New World" (p.671). One of these belief systems was Islam. However, the author argues, "The dawn of Islam in the Americas and its association with Africans have yet to receive the scholarly attention that is merited" (p.671). The author mentions that "one of America's most illustrious sons, Frederick Douglass, may have himself been a descendant of Muslims" (p.671).

Based on this detailed exploration, the author derives four conclusions: (1) the number of Muslims was substantial in early African American history; (2) "Muslims made genuine and persistent efforts to observe their religion; and even though they perpetuated their faith primarily within their own families, in some cases they may have converted slaves who were not relatives"; (3) "Islam and ethnicity were important in the process of social stratification within the larger African American society"; (4) "cultural phenomena found in segments of the African American community, such as ostensibly Christian worship practices and certain artistic expressions, probably reflect the influence of these early Muslims" (p.672). The author notes, however, the "scarcity of primary data" for two reasons: first, the "colonial and antebellum observers, who were ignorant of Islamic faith, did not accurately record the variegated cultural expressions of African slaves," and, second, the "reluctance of the descendants of these early Muslims to be forthright in answering questions about their ancestors" (p.672).

The author also explores the influence of Islam on some Christian practices;

for example, congregation of some churches praying to the east, individuals being instructed to pray to the east, the deceased to be buried facing the east, etc. And, some evidence points to "Africans [who], while ostensibly practicing Christianity, were in reality reinterpreting Christian dogmas in the light of Islamic precepts" (p.708). Further, he concludes, "Islam in America never really disappeared but rather underwent a brief hiatus and has reemerged under more appropriate conditions to resume its place as an important aspect of the history of the African experience in America" (p.710).

A-2. Gran, Peter. "Political Economy as a Paradigm for the Study of Islamic History." *International Journal of Middle East Studies* 11, no.4 (1980): 511–526.

The paper explores and compares two frameworks of analyzing the history of long struggles between the West and the Islamic world: (1) the modernization theory of the "American type," also identified with the "older" orientalism, and (2) the theory of political economy which, since the 1970s, has become part of the intellectual life in America as well as in Europe and Islamic countries. The author discusses numerous variations of the two and suggests the differences in "epistemology and metaphysics" are fundamental. Whereas the modernization theory, with West as the example, presents itself as the "universal model" of development through the actions of reform-minded elite, the political economy framework disputes the underlying assumptions of the modernization theory and suggests "it limits history" and "lacks a theory of change comparable to class struggle in political economy" (p.512).

The author argues that Islamic history has tended to be studied by orientalists who, for development in the Islamic world and elsewhere, advocate their "structuralist model of nineteenth-century culture, positing a collective self and other, superior and subordinate, built into the reality of Western identity" (p.514). Relatedly, there is also the "concept of the 'normal' socio-psychological characteristics of the Muslim, no doubt again part of the colonial baggage" (p.515). "Political economy is the most hopeful alternative to the dominant but problem-ridden modernization theory and the older orientalism for the study of the various societies that follow Islam. Political economy is a holistic theory, that is, it seeks to explain, or suggests how to explain, all historical phenomena," the author argues (p.518).

A-3. Granara, William. "*Jihad* and Cross-Cultural Encounter in Muslim Sicily." *Harvard Middle Eastern and Islamic Review* 3, no.2 (1996): 42–61.

The article is about a ninth-century ruler of *Ifriqiya* (now Tunisia), Ziyadat-Allah, who was faced with the decision whether to invade Sicily where, in violation of a previous peace treaty with the Byzantine, Muslims were held captive. The dilemma, according to the author, represented the ruler's "reluctance to break a peace treaty and violate the law, and his willingness to invade Sicily only when given a legal excuse—all of which point to a critical fact of political life in medieval Islam; that is, that Islam law was not merely an intellectual imagining of the ideal *umma*, but a corpus of rules and regulations must apply in the governing of their community" (p.43).

The author also discusses the various features of the survival of the Arab-Islamic culture in Norman Sicily, as well as the legacy of the cross-cultural encounters. It is noted that "the defeat of the Muslims of Sicily in 1091 reflected the military failure of Islamic *jihad*. Yet the fact that Arabic and Muslim culture survived, flourished, and interacted harmoniously with other cultures long after the political defeat of the Muslim community, suggests the success of the spiritual *jihad*, the higher form of the two, whose testimony lives on in the arabesque floors and stalactite ceilings of the great Norman synthesis" (p.58).

A-4. Haskins, Charles H. "The Spread of Ideas in the Middle Ages." *Speculum: A Journal of Medieval Studies* 1 (1926): 19–30.

This paper documents and illustrates how ideas, broadly defined, spread during the Middle Ages, especially after the Western "unity of life and ideas" ended with Germanic invasions, and with "Saracen" conquests in the Mediterranean region. During early Middle Ages, the chief centers of intellectual life were the monasteries, and the spread of knowledge was mainly from one center to another; but it was largely local. Later, however, the author suggests, other sources emerged—courts, towns, universities, travel, migration of books, translations.

Subsequently, "The intellectual influence of the cathedral centers reached its height in the revival of the twelfth century, as seen in the spread of translations from the Arabic under Archbishop Raymond of Toledo" (p.23). And, there was the migration of books, for "Daniel of Morley toward 1200 returned to England from Spain with a 'precious multitude of books'" (p.26). Further, ideas also spread through interactions among the ruling hierarchy, as with Frederick II's "scientific correspondence with various Saracen sovereigns" (p.24).

A-5. Hodgson, Marshall G.S. "Modernity and the Islamic Heritage." *Islamic Studies* 1, no.2 (June 1962): 89–129.

This long paper, originally presented at the Social Thought Seminar series at the University of Chicago (1960), poses several issues and offers a thorough discussion and analysis, specifically from the point of modernity in general and its relationship to the Islamic heritage. What can historical processes mean for the moral individual? In particular, what are the moral implications of the accelerated pace of modernization in the contemporary world? The author deals with the "acceleration of history as it confronts concerned Muslims in particular, not just as believers but rather as participants in a great cultural heritage prevalent in a wide part of the modern world" (p.89).

The discussion is organized in terms of ten detailed sections of the paper: (1) The Modern acceleration of history as a worldwide event, (2) The nuclear, evolutional aspect of the Modern Transformation, (3) The Modern Transformation in its irruptive and interactive aspects, (4) How the initial "interactive" effects of the Transformation limited the development of its "evolutional" effects, (5) The individual in historical acceleration, (6) Modern individual in Islamic lands, (7) The dilemma of discontinuity between the Islamic heritage and Modernity, (8) The attempt to develop the Islamic heritage in terms of Modernity, (9) The frustration of the concerned Muslims, (10) The similarity between Islamic and Western problems in maintaining the heritage.

The author concludes with this note: "If it is true that we must come to solve all such questions cooperatively, Europeans, Muslims, Hindus, Chinese together, then concerned Westerners will have to learn to see the problem of the great gulf created by the Modern Transformation as its own problem too, and learn somehow to reach across it, envisaging our common problems in terms that allow for the divergent effects of Modernity on both sides of it. And the concerned representatives of other traditions likewise will have to forgive the West its guilt and accept it as a partner in solving the common dilemmas" (p.127).

A-6. Kagaya, Kan. "Changing Muslim Views of Islamic History and Modernization: An Interpretation of Religion and Politics in Pakistan." *The Developing Economies* 4 (June 1968): 193–202.

With Pakistan as a case study, the article pursues a sociological analysis of the *romantic-Islamic* interpretation of this nation's history, the historical context being "the Restoration (*tajaddud*) Movement of late medieval Islam and the various intellectual movements of Modern Islam in pre-partition Muslim India" (p.193). The author argues that "although the modern view of Islamic history functions as an ideological force for the reintegration of society, it cannot be concluded that there exists an established fundamental national consensus on the issues of the relation between Islam and the state, or between Islam and society" (p.194).

The article reviews the perspectives of some Islamic "modernists" and "traditionalists" of Muslim India; also there is discussion of Ibn Khaldun's "secularized political theory." It is argued that the Modernists, such as Sir Sayyid Ahmad Khan (d. 1898), "categorically rejected traditional Islam as the residue of the old age (*rasm wa riwaj*). They argued against the conformist position (*taqlid*) of traditional Islam and claimed that true Islam was a principle of *Nature* like the mechanistic rationalism of modern West" (p.200).

The author says, "In conclusion, as another problem of modernization, we wish to point to the general condition of disruption of the traditionalists and the Western-oriented Modernists: this disruption occurred under colonial capitalism in Muslim lands, but even after political independence, the problem has continued to exist and there is no indication that it will be resolved either by the Muslim national elite or the traditionalists in the near future" (p.206).

A-7. Lapidus, Ira M. "The Separation of State and Religion in the Development of Early Islamic Society." *International Journal of Middle East Studies* 6, no.4 (October 1975): 363–385.

The purpose of this article "is to recount the socioreligious history of the Umayyad and Abbasid periods, to trace the progressive differentiation of state and religion, and to evaluate its significance in the evolution of Islamic societies" (p.365). The article explores questions such as: What is the relationship between state and religion in Islam? In particular, what was this relationship in classical Islam, and what is the heritage of early Islam for later Islamic societies?

Based on the experience of the Muslim community of Medina under Prophet Muhammad's leadership, the prevailing view "does not distinguish between the religious and political aspects of communal life" (p.363). Yet, despite such origins, "Islamic society has evolved in un-Islamic ways. In fact, religious and political life developed distinct spheres of experience, with independent values, leaders, and organizations. From the middle of the tenth century effective control of the Arab-Muslim empire had passed into the hands of generals, administrators, governors, and local provincial lords; the Caliphs had lost all effective political power" (p.364).

The author concludes with this question: "Given the fundamental differentiation of state and religion which we have explored, and its ramifications in later Islamic centuries—given the differences in values, in personnel, in organization, and in functions between Muslim sectarian communities and Muslim states—may we not speak of a distinction between church and state in Islam?" (p.385).

A-8. Mottahedeh, Roy. "Some Islamic Views of the Pre-Islamic Past." *Harvard Middle Eastern and Islamic Review* 1 (1994): 17–26.

The article explores the pre-Islamic past, documented from the writings of Muslim writers in the tenth and 11th centuries. The focus is not so much on what they wrote, but the "attitudes or points of view that influenced these authors in their approach to the pre-Islamic past" (p.17).

One key orientation emanated, says the author, from the Qur'an which points "towards a theory of history," in that "there never has been a community that did not ultimately owe its origin to a prophet" (p.17). Explorations through travel represented another means for learning about others—"Many were the ways of life (*sunan*) that passed away before you: travel through the earth and see what was the end of those who reject truth" (p.18, quoted from Qur'an, 3:137). This emphasis is viewed by commentators "as a positive injunction to study the history of communities that preceded Islam, at least insofar as moral lessons were to be derived from their example" (p.18). Further, these writers adopted a "linear and quasi-genealogical approach to the pre-Islamic past," notes the author, which led to an examination of the inherited chronologies of the "Greeks, the prophets of the Jews, and the kings of the pre-Islamic empires, especially of the Iranian empires" (p.20).

The author concludes, "Of all its meanings for writers of this age, perhaps the pre-Islamic past was most significant as a locus of poignancy, for the consolation, the moral warning, and the amazement at the world's mutability which contemplation of that poignant past evoked" (p.25).

A-9. Munro, Dana Carleton. "The Renaissance of the Twelfth Century." *Annual Report of the American Historical Association* (1906): 43–50.

This essay draws a contrast between the 15th–16th century Italian renaissance and the earlier "Renaissance of the Twelfth Century"; one being the "revival of classical arts and literature" and the latter the "period of wonderful advance along very many different lines" (p.45).

What were these "different lines?" "The most marked characteristic of the twelfth century was the evolution of the spirit of independence. Above all, men became less subservient to authority. They began to doubt whether what they had been taught was entirely true" (p.46). This was the "Aristotelian" century (with penetration chiefly of Averroes' [Ibn Rushd, 1126–1198] commentaries). Second was the "devotion to science," as "experimentation and observation were fostered in Christian Europe, as they had been in Arab Spain, by researches of the pseudo-scientists, and the study of science was far more cherished because it was believed to be the key to the interpretation and control of natural phenomena" (p.48). The third factor was the "practicality of the age. They wanted to apply everything as soon as they learnt it" (p.48).

"All of these factors were the product of the restlessness of the age," says the author. Further, he adds, referring to contacts with the Arab-Islamic world, "mixture, or at least contact, of races is essential to progress, and the countries of western Europe, after several centuries of comparative isolation, now experienced the advantages of this mixture or contact. Wealth increased, new tastes were formed and gratified, learning advanced, life became fuller, the spirit of nationality was awakened" (p.49).

A-10. Rahman, Fazlur. "The Religious Situation of Mecca from the Eve of Islam up to the Hijra." *Islamic Studies* 16, no.4 (Winter 1977): 289–301.

The religious conditions in pre-Islamic Arabia have interested many Western scholars. The article critically assesses the arguments by some of these scholars who have argued that "the main historical sources of the Qur'an's teachings was Christianity," and others who have insisted "that it was Judaism that was the chief historical antecedent of the Qur'an" (p.289). The article attempts to briefly "outline the career of Islam in Mecca in relationship to the Meccans as well as to the Judeo-Christian tradition" (p.289).

The author suggests that this analysis will "materially contribute to providing us with a clearer picture of the career of Islam in Mecca both vis-a-vis the 'People of the Book' and the Meccan pagans and significantly alter some crucial views commonly held by Western scholars on what developments are Madinan and what Meccan, including certain key-terms used in the Qur'an" (p.290). In doing so, three points are stated: (1) there were pre-Islamic contacts between Arabs and the People of the Book, (2) but Meccans had rejected the old Semitic religions and had hoped for a new Prophet and a new scripture whereby they could excel the two older communities, and (3) from the early days of Islam some Jews and/ or Christians had supported the Prophet's mission.

The author concludes that the assessment offered, though brief, "has far-reaching implications for the general modern prevailing view of the nature of the nascent stage of Islam and, indeed, of the formal emergence of the Muslim Community" (p.300).

A-11. Rosenthal, Erwin J. "Some Reflections on the Separation of Religion and Politics in Modern Islam." *Islamic Studies* 3, no.3 (September 1964): 249–284.

"The great question in contemporary Islam is really *what* is Islam," says the author, and the answer depends upon the "basic attitude to and understanding of classical Islam and its relevance to the practical problems" of today (p.249). As a Western student of Islam, the author presents himself as a "sympathetic observer" who "is interested in what his fellow human beings, who profess Islam, are thinking, because on their conclusions the future of Islam depends" (p.249). During the transitional phase, how can the "political survival, economic viability and growth, the emergence of a new [Islamic] society on an equal footing with its former 'imperialistic' and 'colonialist' masters" take place? "The roots of the problem," states the author, "are to be found in two movements," external and internal—the former refers to the Western model of separation of religion and politics, and the later refers to inner-Islamic movement of modernization.

The article discusses both, but there is more detailed focus on the internal debates. The author explores and analyzes the views of three recent Muslim scholars, each identified with the modernization movement: Rashid Rida, Ali Abd Al-Raziq, and Muhammad Al-Ghazali. Whereas Rida and Al-Ghazali emphasize "the religious and political unity of Islam and consequently stress the Muslim's duty to apply the teachings of Islam to political and social life," al-Raziq "seems to provide the theoretical basis for the radical separation of Islam as religion from the affairs of state which are the concern of man" (p.275). Thus, "The vital question for Islam, it would appear, is how can it better contribute to an urgently needed solution: as a religious and moral force in a modern *lay* state, or through its *Shari'ah*—howsoever modified by believers—in an *Islamic* state" (p.282).

A-12. Shah, Tahir. "The Islamic Legacy of Timbuktu." *Saudi Aramco World* 46, no.6 (November–December 1995): 1–5.

"No word in English connotes remoteness more than *Timbuktu*," says the author. Yet, Shah notes, this city, located in today's Mali, for Muslim travelers and scores of European explorers, as well as a host of rulers, dignitaries, and scholars from various parts of the North Africa and Middle East, held riches of another sort: it was the starting point for African pilgrims going on the Hajj, and a center of some of the most profound Islamic scholarship of the Middle Ages.

The region was colonized by the French in the 19th century. Presently, Timbuktu stands isolated by sand and heat; yet, the author suggests, some of the richest parts of the legacy of Islam that captivated both West and East "lie only just beneath the city's baked-mud surface, waiting silently to be rediscovered, and perhaps reawakened" (p.5).

A-13. Watt, W. Montgomery. "Pre-Islamic Arabian Religion in the Qur'an." *Islamic Studies* 15, no.2 (Summer 1976): 73–79.

The article states that "while the Qur'an is chiefly concerned with presenting to men the religion of Islam, the fact that it is 'an Arabic Qur'an' means that it incidentally contains some information about conditions in Arabia at the time of its revelation" (p.73). The article thus provides some insights as to the religious outlook of the pagan Arabs at the time. The author points to evidence from the Qur'an that "some Arabs at least adopted a form of belief half-way between paganism and the strict monotheism to which a few were attracted" (p.76). Several illustrations are discussed.

One of the pre-Islamic nomadic beliefs related to the element of time, that is, time determining events of life—the date of one's death (*ajal*) and provisions (*rizq*). The Islamic form from the Qur'an says these events are willed by God, the Provider, *ar-Razzaq*. Also, the nomadic Arabs talked of *Allah*, the "high-god," but often with other deities associated.

The author identifies some other practices in pre-Islamic religion mentioned in the Qur'an—for example, offerings of grain and cattle to pagan deities, prayers at Ka'ba as whistlings and clapping hands, sacrifice of children for fear of want, and some magical practices.

b. Economics/Commerce

A-14. Ahmad, Imad-ad-Dean. "Economy, Technology, and the Environment: The Islamic Middle Way." *Journal of Faith and Science Exchange* 3 (1999): 55–61.

The paper examines some specifics of the ways in which the Qur'an, the Prophetic traditions, and Islamic law lead toward a path of moderation between extremes, in terms of both belief and behavior; in favor of free markets, but with property rights clearly defined to prevent fraud and unfairness; in favor of technology, but not excessive materialism; and with a concept of trusteeship of the environment that accommodates both development and stewardship.

A-15. Ahmad, Imad-ad-Dean. "Islam and Markets." *Religion and Liberty* 6, no.3 (May–June 1996): 1–3.

The article argues that the "relationship between Islam and trade is not well appreciated in the West" (p.1). Not only were the Prophet Mohammad and his wife merchants, but, further, the Islamic scriptures are "filled with parables using the language of trade. It was merchants, not soldiers, who were mainly responsible for the spread of Islam through the world" (p.1). Notwithstanding the anti-market rhetoric among some Arab intellectuals, the author argues, "one cannot be a Muslim and opposed to freedom of enterprise" (p.1). Further, "Islam enshrines private property as a sacred trust" (p.1).

Historically, "The Islamic analysis of markets reached the level of economic science by the time of the great fourteenth century historian Ibn Khaldun. He rejected the utopianism of the Greek-influenced philosophers" (p.3). Indeed, "Markets antedate the mission of Mohammad. They are especially strong in the Semitic world. Like their cousins, the Jews, the early Arabs had a strong commitment to trade and bargaining" (p.3).

A-16. Ahmad, Imad-ad-Dean. "Islam and the Progenitors of Austrian Economics." Pages 77–82 in *The Contributions of Murray Rothbard to Monetary Economics*, edited by C. Thies. Winchester, VA: Durrell Institute, Shenandoah University, 1996.

In his posthumously published survey of the history of economics, Murray Rothbard traced the origins of free market thought as understood by the "Austrian" school back to the 13th-century scholastics and 16th-century Spanish economists. The paper traces interesting parallels to these views in the contemporaneous and preceding Islamic tradition and calls for an extension of Rothbard's work to the Islamic contemporaries and predecessors of the Christian scholars that he studied.

A-17. Ahmad, Imad-ad-Dean. "An Islamic Perspective on the Wealth of Nations." Pages 55–67 in *The Economics of Property Rights: Cultural, Historical, Legal, and Philosophical Issues*, edited by S. Pejovich. Cheltenham, UK: Edward Elgar Publishers, 2001.

This paper is concerned with the politico-economic policies that account for why some nations are wealthier than others and why nations, or dynasties, may be wealthy at one phase of their existence and poor at others. An overview of the rise of early Islamic economies under the influence of the *Shari'a* is presented. Further, a parallel analysis of the development of economic theory in the same period demonstrates that the gradual devolution of Islamic economic practice, though distanced from the *Shari'a* principles of decentralization, hard currency, and private property, continued to be relevant, even as Islamic economic principles, reaching their apex in the work of Ibn Khaldun (1332–1406), justified the market principles enunciated in the Qur'an.

The author argues that economic reform based on evolving understanding was abandoned (called the closing of the door to *ijtihad*) and the Muslim world began its decline into intellectual darkness and economic stagnation. Economic development and technical innovation was taken over by the Western civilization. The knowledge that Ibn Khaldun enunciated went neglected or misunderstood by the Islamic world, while the principles that he and his Islamic predecessors identified found their way into Western economic theory of economic progress. The paper elucidates the specific implications of this analysis for modern economic policy, with a focus on the Islamic world.

A-18. Ahmad, Rafiq. "Ibn Khaldun: A Great Pioneer Economist." *University Economist: Journal of the Punjab University* 2, no.1 (March 1953): 52–61.

After a brief sketch of Ibn Khaldun's (1332–1406) life, the author begins by pointing out the "widespread misunderstanding about the Arabs. It is generally believed that nothing was written on economics in the Arab period which roughly extends from the seventh to the sixteenth century" (p.53). Further, "There was hardly any notable Arab thinker of the period who did not express his views on economic problems" (p.53). Among the several names identified, "perhaps Ibn Khaldun, whose ideas form the subject of this article, contributed most to economic theory" (p.53).

Based on Ibn Khaldun's *Al-Muqaddamah*, the paper briefly discusses several theoretical and descriptive aspects of his economic thought. While other Arab scholars talked in terms of "political economy" (*siyasat-e-mudun*), according to the author, Ibn Khaldun prefer the word "economics" (*ma'ash*), defined as "a science which deals with the management of the household or city according to the dictates of reason as well as ethics" (p.54). He also discussed other topics, such as the forces of demand and supply in a voluntary-exchange setting, money and its characteristics and functions, interdependence of prices, labor, and value, productive and unproductive occupations, economics of population growth, stages of economic development, rural and urban economies, taxation rates, economic benefits of public expenditures, and reasons for the development and decay of industries.

The author argues that, given the scientific-positive content of his economic thought, Ibn Khaldun deserves "the title of 'pioneer economist,' and no history of modern economic thought can claim to be complete without assigning him a proper place" (p.61).

A-19. Ahmad, Rafiq. "The Origin of Economics and the Muslims: A Preliminary Survey." *Punjab University Economics* 7, no.1 (June 1969): 17–49.

One of the early papers that disputes the origins of economic thought exclusively in the West and that "prior to the eighteenth century, it is said, there did not exist a separate science of economics" (p.17). Further, the paper challenges literary history that "omits [a] nearly 1,000-year long Muslim (or Arab) period whose impact on the then known world was as widespread as that of the western culture today" (p.19).

The author briefly surveys economic thought among the ancient orientals, the Greeks, the Romans, and the medieval Europe. However, during the period 625 to 1550 (which overlaps with Europe's Dark Ages), economic ideas in the Islamic civilization emerged from three sources: the Qur'an, the post-Qur'anic religious literature, and writings of numerous Muslim scholars. There is a brief survey of the economic content from these sources, with greater detail from the last. Islamic scholars discussed economics in terms of *tadbir-e-manzil* (management of households and businesses), *siyasat-e-mudun* (political economy), and *al-ma'ash* (economics). Economic ideas of the following scholars are discussed: Nasir al-DinTusi (d. 1274), Ibn Khaldun (1332–1406), Abu Yusuf (d. 798), al-Farabi (d. 950), al-Ghazali (1058–1111), and others.

The author concludes, "It is very likely that the early European schools of economic thought, including Mercantilism and Physiocracy, were stirred into intellectual activity by the Muslim writings on *siyasat-al-madaniya* (political economy) and *al-ma'ash*" (p.49).

A-20. Ali, Syed Ahmad. "Economics of Ibn Khaldun: A Selection." *Africa Quarterly* 10, no.3 (October–December 1970): 251–259.

Based on Ibn Khaldun's (1332–1406) magnum opus, the *Muqaddimah*, this paper briefly explains several aspects of his economic thought. Noted as a forerunner of Ricardo and Marx, Ibn Khaldun recognizes labor as the only source of value.

Incorporated in Ibn Khaldun's economics is a society that is driven by voluntary-exchange behavior, guided market forces of demand and supply. Profit and gain are driving forces and capital formation takes place through surplus. Commercial activities give rise to profits. Hoarding also gives rise to profits, but hoarding of food is an evil. Nationalization is not favored by Ibn Khaldun, but regional trade contributes to prosperity.

Ibn Khaldun also discusses the role of money, taxes, and public expenditures. He recognizes the importance of division of labor and the author suggests, "Adam Smith (1723–1790) may have got his ideas from Ibn Khaldun" (p.257).

A-21. Alrefai, Ahmed and Michael Brun. "Ibn Khaldun: Dynastic Change and Its Economic Consequences." *Arab Studies Quarterly* 16, no.2 (Spring 1994): 73–86.

Referring to the 20th-century recognition that societies are subject to cyclical behavior, the authors note a Russian scholar whose analysis of historical cycles was inspired by Ibn Khaldun's *Muqaddimah*. It is suggested that Ibn Khaldun (1332–1406) developed a comprehensive theory of the dynastic cycle, describing how various features of society evolve during the rise and fall of a civilization.

The paper is divided into two parts. The first part discusses Ibn Khaldun's views on factors of production, with labor as the main input. Also, there is discussion of his views on fiscal policy and public finance, including expenditures and direct/indirect taxes; population cycle is also discussed. The second part discusses Ibn Khaldun's cycle theory, especially in its economic dimensions, and its similarities with the modern business cycle theories are identified. Based on various aspects of Ibn Khaldun's economic thought, the authors identify Ibn Khaldun's views as resembling those of "modern conservatives" (p.85).

A-22. Andic, Suphan. "A Fourteenth Century Sociology of Public Finance." *Public Finance/Finances Publiques* 20, nos.1–2 (1965): 22–44.

Claimed as a forerunner of several Western scholars (Vico, Montesquieu, Comte, Marx, and others), the paper argues that Ibn Khaldun's analysis of economics and public finance represents an integral part of his all-comprehensive "science of culture"; thus, the approach of the paper is in sociological terms.

The paper begins with Ibn Khaldun's discussion of the development of civilizations, followed by his views on public finance and an evaluation of his contribution to knowledge in that discipline. Public finance is discussed in the context of Ibn Khaldun's theory of growth and decline of civilizations. Various aspects of public finance in Ibn Khaldun's thought are examined in terms of how they relate and interact within the context of the stages of development of a civilized state. Thus, the discussion includes public expenditures (their growth and effects on the economy) and taxation (revenue, types, principles, incentive effects, and burden distribution). Specifically, the author notes, for Ibn Khaldun "one effect of changes in government expenditure is the rise in the rate of taxation which in due course leads to the destruction of the entire civilization" (p.39). This notion, it may be noted, became known as the Laffer Thesis in the 1980s United States.

A-23. Baeck, Louis. "Ibn Khaldun's Political and Economic Realism." Pages 83–99 in *Joseph A. Schumpeter, Historian of Economics: Perspectives on the History of Economic Thought, Selected Papers from the History of Economics Society Conference 1994*, edited by Laurence S. Moss. London: Routledge, 1996.

This paper is about Ibn Khaldun (1332–1406), "a detached scholar with a long-term view on the sociopolitical and economic determinants that have had an impact on history" (p.83). The author quotes Franz Rosenthal: "To my knowledge Ibn Khaldun was the first medieval thinker to see the importance of economics for politics and for the whole life of any society organized in a state" (p.83). Various scholars have compared him to Vico, Montesquieu, Rousseau, Marx, Hegel, Nietzsche, and Weber.

The paper is divided into four sections: (1) The Contours of Ibn Khaldun's World-View ("his profound humanism, with underpinning of ethical norms of reason"), (2) A Treatise on Non-Sustainable Development (the rise and fall of civilization due to internal dynamics of the society), (3) The Social Core of Political Change (the *asabiyaa*, the group-mind, weakens, then detribalization; but religion as a cohesive impulse critical), (4) The Mechanics of the Long-Term (cultural, societal, and material unfolding of history; the long-term historical cycle due to dynamic change from *badawa* [nomadic, backward] and *hadara* [urban, civilized, modern]).

The author concludes that in comparisons with other Latin humanists and Ibn Khaldun, "the economic concepts and determinants are more forcefully developed than with any other medieval author. Today we would call Ibn Khaldun's oeuvre a perfect example of the interdisciplinary approach. In this genre the *Muqaddimah* is a masterpiece" (p.97).

A-24. Bass, George F. "A Medieval Islamic Merchant Venture." *Archeological News* 7, nos.2–3 (Fall 1979): 85–94.

The paper relates to the archeological discovery of shipwrecks, which helps identify the nature and history of medieval trade. The author had earlier excavated a tenth-century Byzantine ship which, based on a study of some of its contents ("pottery, lamps, and about 70 coins") "sailed from the Black Sea or Constantinople before she sank after striking a reef" (p.86). This study relates to a "similar distillation of the evidence from our eleventh-century shipwreck at Serce Liman (Sparrow Harbor), Turkey, which "was a popular anchorage in antiquity," and the ship, about "30-tonner," apparently "capsized or driven against the rocky shore by unpredictable gusts" (p.86–87).

According to the author, the cargo content (primarily glass) suggests that it was likely taken from an Arab port, and the ship "was sailed by a crew from one of the Muslim countries, for the eating wares used on board seem mostly or totally of Islamic types" (p.90–91). Further, "The ship probably was owned by one man, probably a merchant" (p.91). "Tyre was the export center for fine glass around 1000," so that was perhaps the destination. Evidence from coins ("three gold quarter dinars of al-Hakim, and several copper coins of Basil II [976–1025]") also suggests the approximate period to be around tenth–eleventh century (p.91). Also, some of the decoration on iron swords and on wooden sheaths found in the shipwreck suggest their Indian origin (p.92).

A-25. Boulakia, Jean David C. "Ibn Khaldun: A Fourteenth-Century Economist." *Journal of Political Economy* 79, no.5 (September–October 1971): 1105–1118.

This paper is about Ibn Khaldun (1332–1406), "a fourteenth-century thinker who found a large number of economic mechanisms which were rediscovered by modern economists" (p.1106). The author notes that while Ibn Khaldun's *Muqaddimah* is mainly a book of history, he is an interdisciplinary scholar who understands the influence of multiple forces on history. Further, "Like most of the authors of the fourteenth century, Ibn Khaldun mixes philosophical, sociological, ethical, and economic considerations in his writings," and he "is remarkably well organized and always follows an extremely logical pattern" (p.1106).

The paper's discussion is organized into four sections: theory of production (including human and social aspects as well as international); theories of value, money, and prices; theory of distribution (including compensations, profits, taxes, optimum income distribution); and theory of cycles (population cycle and public finance cycle). As part of the public finance cycle, the author discusses Ibn Khaldun's views on public expenditures and taxation and notes his anticipation of the Keynesian fiscal policy analysis for mitigating business cycles. Similarly, in discussing taxation, among other things, Ibn Khaldun's views on incentive–disincentive effects of low–high tax rates and the eventual links to national prosperity and depression are discussed; this thesis is what became known as the Laffer Curve in the 1980s United States.

The author concludes (quite erroneously, it may be noted), while "Ibn Khaldun is the forerunner of many economists, he is an accident of history and has had no consequences on the evolution of economic thought. He is alone, without predecessors and without successors. Without tools, without preexisting concepts, he elaborated a genial economic explanation of the world. His name should figure among the fathers of economic science" (p.1118).

A-26. Chapra, M. Umar. "Socioeconomic and Political Dynamics of Ibn Khaldun's Thought." *American Journal of Islamic Social Sciences* 16, no.4 (Winter 1999): 17–38.

This article explores Ibn Khaldun's (1332–1406) theories and ideas about the causes that lead to the rise and decline of civilizations, with emphasis on the dynamic and interdisciplinary nature of this scholar's methodology. Unlike other studies, the author notes, this article frames Ibn Khaldun's ideas in contemporary terminology (in terms of causal relationships, possibly quantifiable) and thus making the analysis relevant; for example, political authority is described as a function of these interacting variables: *Shari'ah*, welfare/happiness of the people, wealth/resources needed for ensuring justice and development, national development, and social justice. The article also examines the central role of welfare, justice, and development in the context of a contemporary Islamic welfare state that encompasses the material and moral well-being of the citizens.

Also discussed are other aspects of Ibn Khaldun's economics—supply–demand forces, public finance (expenditures and taxation). The author briefly notes the economic ideas of "a few isolated scholars like al-Maqrizi (d. 1442), al-Dawwani (d. 1501), and Shah Waliyullah (d. 1762)" (p.33). And, these scholars, in the manner of Ibn Khaldun, "combine moral, political, social, and economic factors to explain the economic phenomena of their times and the rise and fall of their societies" (p.35).

A-27. Desomogyi, Joseph. "Economic Theory in Classical Arabic Literature." Pages 1–10 in *Studies in Islamic Economics, Series 8, Encyclopedic Survey of*

Islamic Culture, edited by Mohamed Taher. New Delhi, India: Anmol Publications (Private) Ltd., 1997.

The article suggests that "from the outset, Islam had a more favorable opinion of economic life than Medieval Christianity. Trade has ever been an occupation 'pleasing Allah,' and also the theoretical 'Inquiry into the Causes of the Wealth of Nations'—to use the title of Adam Smith's fundamental work published in 1776—started much earlier in Islamic literature than in the European" (p.1). Further, the Islamic practical philosophy, with background from the Greeks, falls into three categories: ethics (*'ilm al-akhlaq*), economics (*'ilm tadbir al-manzil*), and politics (*'ilm al-siyasa*). The second category, literally called "the science of the regulations of household," deals with economic issues. One finds considerable discussion on economic issues, both normative and positive, in the early Islamic writings.

The article then traces some economic content in the writings of mainly three prominent Arab-Islamic scholastics: (1) Ali al-Dimishqi's *Kitab al-Ishara il mahasin al-tijara wa-ma'rifa jayyid al-a'rad wa-radi'iha wa-ghushush al-mudallisin fiha* ("The Book of Hint at the Beauties of Commerce and the Knowledge of Good and Bad Merchandise and the Swindlers' Falsifications in Them"; written between ninth and 12th centuries), (2) Ibn Khaldun's *Al-Muqaddima* (written 1407 AD), especially the section entitled *Fi'l-ma'ash wa-wujubihi min al-kasb wa'al-sana'i wa-ma ya'rid fi dhalika kullihi min al-ahwal wa fihi msaa'il* ("On Various Aspects of Livelihood Such as Profit and the Crafts; What sort of Conditions Occur in Them; With Pertinent Problems"), with 33 chapters in this section, plus another section that deals with industry, agriculture, and commerce, (3) Al-Ghazali's (1058–1111 AD) *Ihya' 'Ulum al-Din* ("The Revival of Religious Sciences"), with considerable discussion on economic issues, similar to Adam Smith's *Wealth of Nations* (1776).

The author concludes that several centuries before Adam Smith, these Arab-Islamic scholars "investigated such fundamental elements of economic theory as value, price and money" (p.10).

A-28. Essid, M. Yassine. "Islamic Economic Thought." Pages 77–102 in *Pre-Classical Economic Thought*, edited by S. Todd Lowry. Boston: Kluwer Academic Publishers, 1986.

While referring to the literary history of Western European and near-eastern literature, the book editor states: "Most of the histories of economics that give attention to the pre-Smithian background ignore Judaic and early Christian thought, as well as Islamic economic ideas, although the Mediterranean crucible was the parent of the Renaissance while Muslim learning in the Spanish universities was a major source of light for non-Mediterranean Europe" (p.4).

As with all medieval literature, the author argues that "economics has never been regarded as a separate discipline in Islamic writings." Then, he attempts to overcome the neglect pointed out by the editor by presenting a brief survey of economic thought in early Islam. While market-exchange and competitive markets are emphasized, the practical aspects must operate within the requirements of ensuring socioeconomic justice, as envisaged by the Islamic scriptures. The author discusses the "naturalness" of the market, as covered in detail in the *hisbah* handbooks, chiefly in the writings of Ibn Taimiyah (1263–1328), and identifies the place Muslim writers accorded economic thought in shaping man's economic environment. Also discussed are the links of several early Islamic scholastics (Abu Yusuf, Al-Farabi, Ibn Sina, Al-Ghazali, Tusi, Dawwani, Al-Makrizi, Miskawayah, Ibn Khaldun, etc.) to their Greek predecessors (e.g., Aristotle's *Nicomachean Ethics* and other works).

A-29. Ghazanfar, S.M. "The Economic Thought of Abu Hamid Al-Ghazali and St. Thomas Aquinas: Some Comparative Parallels and Links." *History of Political Economy* 32, no.4 (2000): 858–888.

The paper explores some major parallels and similarities in the economic thought of two major medieval scholastics: St. Thomas Aquinas (1225–1274), the most prominent of the Latin Schoolmen, and Abu Hamid Al-Ghazali (1058–1111), an eminent Arab-Islamic scholastic. It is argued that the evidence of considerable intellectual interaction between the Latin schoolmen and Arab scholastics is abundant.

Further, it is suggested that while at the time there was no specialized discipline of economics, scholars pursued rather sophisticated discussion of economic issues. St. Thomas Aquinas was one such scholar and his writings reveal considerable linkages with various Arab precursors, Al-Ghazali in particular. "Thomistic economics" covered numerous topics, such as (1) value and prices, (2) nature of money (including usury, currency debasement, counterfeiting, etc.), (3) distributive and commutative justice, (4) private property and voluntary exchange, (5) organization of production and markets, and (6) illicit gains and unethical business practices. Interestingly, one finds almost similar topical coverage with Al-Ghazali; and the paper provides considerable comparative analysis of parallels and similarities.

Based on historical evidence, the paper documents the linkages from Arab-Islamic to Latin-Christendom, and in particular, from Al-Ghazali to St. Thomas Aquinas. In conclusion, it is argued that "clearly, medieval Latin Scholastics lived in a sociocultural environment where intellectual linkages among diverse groups, despite religious antagonisms, represented a way of life for centuries. And those links make the cherished ancestry of our literary history, covering almost all areas of knowledge, a rather mixed ancestry" (p.883).

A-30. Ghazanfar, S.M. "Post-Greek/Pre-Renaissance Economic Thought: Contributions of Arab-Islamic Scholastics during the 'Great Gap' Centuries." *Research in the History of Economic Thought and Methodology* 16 (1998): 65–89.

The article explores the economic thought of selected Arab-Islamic scholars who wrote on economic issues during the medieval centuries. The primary stimulus for the paper comes from the well-known "great gap" thesis, proposed by the late Joseph Schumpeter in 1954; this thesis argued that for over 500 years prior to the Latin Scholastics (especially St. Thomas Aquinas, 1224–1274), not much in economics or about any other subject was written anywhere. This thesis is disputed by the author.

The paper presents some details as to the economic ideas of four Arab-Islamic scholastics who wrote during these "gap" centuries: Abu Yusuf (731–798), Alberuni (973–1048), Al-Ghazali (1058–1111), Nasir al-Din Tusi (1201–1274). Their writings covered issues such as price determination through supply and demand, voluntary market-exchange, specialization and division of labor, monetary matters, public finance and taxation, regional/international trade, ethics of the market, etc. The content of their discussions, it is argued, is quite similar to that found in the writings of subsequent Latin-European scholastics. The paper further discusses the various sources through which the "miracle of transmission" of Arab-Islamic intellectual output to Latin Europe took place.

The paper concludes that the notion of the "great gap" is an unfortunate mishap in literary history and must be abandoned.

A-31. Ghazanfar, S.M. "Public Sector Economics in Medieval Economic Thought: Contributions of Selected Arab-Islamic Scholars." *Public Finance/ Finances Publiques* 53, no.1 (1998): 19–36.

The paper focuses (based partly on original writings in Arabic) primarily on the public-sector economics, in a voluntary-exchange environment, of three early Arab-Islamic scholars: Abu Yusuf, 731–798; Abu Hamid Al-Ghazali, 1058–1111; and Ibn Taimiyah, 1263–1328. The paper notes that similar discussion is also provided by numerous other Muslim scholars, especially Ibn Khaldun.

Additional impetus for the paper arises from the well-embedded "great gap" thesis propounded by the late Joseph Schumpeter, which argued that during the centuries between the Greeks and Latin Scholastics, not much in economics or about any other discipline was written anywhere.

The general societal context of these scholars was a free-market voluntary exchange economy, with state regulation to promote the common good. Among the various public finance issues, topics covered are: (1) public expenditures (including elementary cost-benefit analysis, socioeconomic infrastructure, promotion of social justice, security, stability), (2) taxation (various "canons" of taxation—convenience, simplicity, burden distribution, incentive effects, types of taxes, administration), (3) public borrowing as a source of revenue, the institution of *hisba* (from which derives *muhtasib*, the impartial public official with various regulatory responsibilities similar to the present *ombudsman*), etc.

The paper concludes with noting the influence of such Arab-Islamic scholars on the evolution of socioeconomic thought among Latin-European scholastics.

348 *Part II: Articles*

A-32. Ghazanfar, S.M. "Scholastic Economics and Arab Scholars: The 'Great Gap' Thesis Reconsidered." *Diogenes: International Review of Humane Sciences* (Paris) no.154 (April–June 1991): 117–139.

This paper represents the first major challenge to the "great gap" thesis, deeply embedded in the relevant literature, which was propounded by late Joseph Schumpeter in his *History of Economic Analysis* (1954). This thesis argued that "economic analysis begins with the Greeks, not to be reestablished until the Scholastics emerged with St. Thomas Aquinas (1225–1274)," the intervening centuries being "blank" concerning any writings on economics, or for that matter, about any other discipline. This is notwithstanding the fact that Schumpeter insisted on "doctrinal continuity" and "filiation of ideas," according to the paper.

The paper begins with describing the thesis, followed by some analysis that attempts to invalidate the argument. Then, as evidence against the "gap," illustrative synopses of the economic thought of four selected Arab scholastics (Abu Yusuf, 731–798; Ibn Hanbal, 780–855; Ibn Hazm, d. 1064; Al-Ghazali, 1058–1111) are presented. This is followed by a discussion of the transmission of Arab-Islamic socioeconomic thought to Latin Europe and the assimilation of that stream into Scholastic economics. Various sources of transmission are briefly noted. Also, the paper points out that almost all Latin scholars identified by Schumpeter had their direct or indirect Arab-Islamic precursors.

The paper concludes with the plea that "along with the Greeks and Romans, the Arab contributions to economic thought and to the discipline of economics in general should be recognized in the literature. Such indeed is the professional imperative, in order for the history of economic ideas to achieve the doctrinal continuity that any discipline deserves" (p.132).

A-33. Ghazanfar, S.M. and A. Azim Islahi. "Economic Thought of an Arab Scholastic: Abu Hamid Al-Ghazali (AH450–505 / AD1058–1111)." *History of Political Economy* 22, no.2 (1990): 381–403.

This is one of the early papers on the origins of economic thought among early-medieval Arab-Islamic scholastics. The paper, among other things, attempts to fill the "gap" otherwise assumed to prevail in intellectual history. Reference here is to the "great gap" thesis, perpetuated by late Joseph Schumpeter, the argument being that during the several centuries between the Greeks and the Latin scholastics, there were no writings on economic issues anywhere.

This paper focuses specifically on the economic thought of Abu Hamid Al-Ghazali, acclaimed "by general consent, the most important thinker of medieval Islam" (p.381). Like all medieval scholastics, it is suggested, his scholarship was not dominated by economic aspects of life but only as part of the broader discourses on various scholastic issues. For Ghazali, the Islamic scriptures not only made economic pursuits desirable but required as part of "one's calling," which meant working for self-sufficiency for family and for "assisting others in need" (p.384). The paper then discusses Ghazali's economics in four topics: (1) voluntary exchange and the evolution of markets (including, demand, supply, prices, and profits; ethics of market behavior), (2) production activities (production of necessities as a social obligation; hierarchy of production; stages of production, specialization, linkages), (3) barter and evolution of money (including functions of money, money "useless," hoarding, counterfeiting, and currency debasement; prohibition of usury), (4) role of the state and public finances (economic progress through justice, peace, stability; revenue sources; public expenditures; public borrowing).

The authors also argue that Ghazali's social thought influenced various medieval Latin scholastics, particularly St. Thomas Aquinas whose *Summa Theologica* parallels Ghazali's *Ihya Ulum al-Din* (The Revival of the Religious Sciences). Further, the paper concludes: "Clearly Ghazali must be acknowledged as a distinguished pioneer of modern economic thought, with several predecessors as well as successors, deserving at least as much (if not more) disciplinary recognition as Aquinas, the best-known of medieval Europe's scholastics" (p.402).

A-34. Ghazanfar, S.M. and A. Azim Islahi. "Explorations in Medieval Arab-Islamic Economic Thought: Some Aspects of Ibn Qayyim's Economics (691–751 AH / 1292–1350 AD)." *History of Economic Ideas* (Italy) 5, no.1 (1997): 7–25.

The paper explores the economic thought of a medieval Arab-Islamic scholastic, Ibn Al-Qayyim al-Jawziyyah (691–751 AH / 1292–1350 AD). It is suggested that this scholar is one among several medieval Arab-Islamic scholars who wrote on various specific issues.

The authors note that part of their motivation is to point out the irrelevancy of the "great gap" thesis, propounded by the late Joseph Schumpeter in the 1950s, according to which, during the centuries between the Greeks and the Latin scholastics, not much in economics, or about any other field, was written anywhere. During this period, it is suggested, Ibn Qayyim was one among numerous medieval Islamic scholars who wrote on various economic issues. This scholar authored 11 books, but much of his economic thought is found in his *al-Turug al-Hukmiay* (The Rules of Governance).

Based on his original works, the paper explores (a) his economic philosophy, (b) views on affluence and poverty, (c) significance of public charity, (d) prohibition of usury, and (e) marketing exchange and the need for public intervention.

The article concludes that while none of the medieval scholars discussed economics in terms of self-regulating market economy of more recent times, Ibn Qayyim developed several concepts that are similar to those found in contemporary literature. In that sense, "Ibn Qayyim deserves to be acknowledged as among the pioneers of modern economic thought" (p.22).

A-35. Ghazanfar, S.M. and A. Azim Islahi. "Explorations in Medieval Arab-Islamic Economic Thought: Some Aspects of Ibn Taimiyah's Economics." Pages 45–63 in *Perspectives on the History of Economic Thought: Selected Papers from the History of Economics Conference 1990*, edited by S. Todd Lowry. Brookfield, VT: Edward Elgar Publishing Company, 1992.

The paper explores the economic thought of a medieval Arab-Islamic scholar, Taqi al-Din Ahmad bin Abd al-Halim, known as Ibn Taimiyah (661–728 AH/ 1263–1328 AD). It is noted that Ibn Taimiyah is one among numerous such scholars who wrote on a variety of specific economic issues; unfortunately, however, their scholarship is unfamiliar in the profession, nor incorporated in the literature. Parenthetically, the paper also notes the unfortunate Schumpeterian "great gap" tradition, embedded in the literature, which argued that nothing was written elsewhere on economic issues during the period between the Greeks and the Latin scholastics.

Following a brief biographical sketch, the paper discusses Ibn Taimiyah's economic thought. The discussion is organized into three sections: (1) operations of the free-markets (market demand and supply; various factors affecting demand and supply; need for public sector intervention), (2) administration of markets through the institution of *hisbah* (promoting good, forbidding evil; public official entrusted with these tasks called *muhtasib*, or "ombudsman," a contemporary equivalent), (3) some other aspects in Ibn Taimiyah's economic thought ("price of the equivalent," or "just price"; also "just wage," "just profit"; meaning of property rights; barter, evolution/functions of money, currency debasement, prohibition of usury; socioeconomic justice, functions of the state [including public expenditures, taxation]).

The paper concludes, "Clearly, Ibn Taimiyah deserves to be recognized as among the distinguished pioneers of modern economic thought" (p.60).

A-36. Goitein, S.D. "The Rise of the Near-Eastern Bourgeoisie in Early Islamic Times." *Journal of World History* 3 (1957): 583–604.

The key theme of this interesting article is that business-entrepreneurial activities that later became identified with capitalism emerged in the earlier Islamic world and such practices were in accordance with the Islamic scriptures. The author argues that the teachings of Islam nurtured the merchant class of traders, in contrast to the European Christianity at the time, which showed "deep-seated religious prejudices against making money" and encouraged asceticism (p.586). During its early centuries, Islamic civilization developed a favorable attitude toward economic activities, capital accumulation, and even condoned luxuries. During this time, "the merchant class attained a social position and, correspondingly, a self-esteem, which it secured far later in Europe" (p.586). Relying on a book by Muhammad Shaibani (d. 804), the author quotes, "The vigorous striving of the new Muslim trading people for a decent living was not only not opposed by Islam, but was actually regarded as a religious duty" (p.586). Further, "Seeking one's livelihood is a duty incumbent on every Muslim, just as the seeking of knowledge" (p.587). Numerous Islamic scholars who extol the virtues of business activities are quoted.

The author concludes: "The 'bourgeois revolution' of the Near East during the early centuries of Islam had many repercussions on world history. To mention just one: through it the Jewish people, which up to that time had been engaged mainly in agriculture and other manual occupations, was converted into a people predominantly commercial" (p.603).

A-37. Gusau, Sule Ahmed. "Economic Views of Ibn Khaldun." *Journal of Objective Studies* (Aligarh, India) 3 (1990): 48–60.

Following a brief biographic sketch, the paper gives a narrative on this—Ibn Khaldun's (1332–1406)—scholar's economic ideas that covered the "ideals of justice, hard work, cooperation, moderation and fairness" (p.49).

The discussion is divided into four sections: theory of market system and market regulation (including discussion of demand and supply under free markets, market regulation by the state under certain conditions, etc.); theories of value and money (labor as the source of value, functions of money, etc.); theory of growth and business cycle (various stages of growth, trade cycle, taxation and production cycle (incentives/disincentives from taxation and effects on production), theory of international trade, and public finance (lower taxes lead to higher revenue, and vice versa, due to effects on national economy; public expenditures are discussed in terms of effect on the economy—high expenditures during a business slump, etc., reminiscent of the 20th-century Keynesian economics).

A-38. Hosseini, Hamid. "Contributions of Medieval Muslim Scholars to the History of Economics and Their Impact: A Refutation of the Schumpeterian Great Gap." Pages 28–45 in *A Companion to the History of Economic Thought*, edited by Warren J. Samuels, Jeff E. Biddle, and John B. Davis. New York: Blackwell Publishing Company, 2003.

The paper begins with disputing the Schumpeterian "great gap" argument, based on studies by Ghazanfar and others. The paper then briefly documents the nature and significance of economic activities in medieval Islam, followed by a discussion of Islamic views of the economy and economic policy prior to the ninth century, with roots in the Islamic scriptures.

This is followed by a reference to a 1964 paper by Joseph Spengler on Ibn Khaldun's economic thought, and it is argued that this paper stressed the Greek thought and background, and thus helped to perpetuate the "gap" thesis. The paper then proceeds with its main task; that is, discuss the contributions of medieval Muslim scholars, along with their motivations for that scholarship. From this scholarship, some topics are elaborated: (1) wealth, poverty, and acquisitiveness,

(2) division of labor; barter and money, (3) demand, supply, and the market mechanism. The last section discusses the transmission of knowledge from the Islamic world to Latin Europe, along with various sources of transmission. Also discussed is the impact of this transferred knowledge on successive generations of Latin-European scholars.

The paper concludes by raising some questions about the persistence of the "gap" in literary history. After offering several reasons why Schumpeter should have been aware of the Islamic contributions, the question is asked: "Why did Schumpeter not include non-Europeans, particularly medieval Muslims, among the writers who made contributions to the development of economics?" (p.42).

A-39. Hosseini, Hamid. "The Inaccuracy of the Schumpeterian Great Gap Thesis: Economic Thought in Medieval Iran (Persia)." Pages 63–82 in *Joseph M. Schumpeter, Historian of Economics: Perspectives on the History of Economic Thought—Selected Papers from the History of Economics Society Conference 1994*, edited by Laurence S. Moss. London and New York: Routledge Publishers, 1996.

The paper begins with a brief review of studies by Ghazanfar and others which have challenged the Schumpeterian "great gap" thesis. This thesis, proposed by Schumpeter in 1954 and well-embedded in the relevant literature, argued that during the centuries between the Greeks and Latin scholastics, not much was written in the field of economics anywhere. Yet during this period, numerous Muslim scholars wrote considerably on economic issues.

Hosseini then argues that numerous Persian writers "were able to understand and to a remarkable degree analyze the economic realities of their age. The contributions of these writers were substantial, and in many ways their discussions and economic assumptions sound quite modern" (p.65). The discussion is divided into three sections: (1) Islamic, economic activity, and the history of economic analysis, (2) Persian-speaking Iranians and medieval Islamic intellectual history, (3) medieval Persian scholars and their understanding of the economic problem. This last section being critical, the author discusses the following topics: (a) wealth, poverty, and acquisitiveness, (b) division of labor, evolution of markets, and voluntary exchange, (c) production stages and efficiency, (d) economic role of the state, (e) medieval Persian writers as precursors of Malthus and Darwin.

The author points to the diversity of Islamic civilization, as evident from the contributions to Islamic thought by a variety of scholars—Arab as well as non-Arab Muslims, and even non-Muslims. In conclusion, the paper argues that these scholars understood various economic concepts well: the market mechanism, demand and supply, division of labor, economic efficiency, the Malthusian theory of population, economic functions of money, social welfare function, and even the notion of conspicuous consumption.

A-40. Hosseini, Hamid. "Medieval Islamic (Persian) Mirrors for Princes Literature and the History of Economics." *Journal of South Asian and Middle Eastern Studies* 24, no.4 (2001): 13–36.

Hosseini argues that there is considerable evidence of economic thought in the medieval "mirrors for princes" literature in Persian language, with origins in the Seljuk dynasties of Iran. This article is yet another challenge to the "Schumpeterian Gap" thesis, which argued that little or nothing was written on economic issues anywhere during the centuries between the Greeks and the 13th-century Latin-European scholastics.

These "mirrors," influenced by pre-Islamic Sassani works, were written as manuals of counsel for princes and included discussion of practical economic issues. The paper documents discussion of economic content from three "representative" mirrors, from among many, written during the 11th–12th centuries. These three are: (1) *Qabus Nameh* (The Book of Qabus), by an Iranian prince (Kai Kavus) of the Caspian region, written in the 11th century, (2) *Siasat Nameh* (The Book of Politics), composed in 1086 by Nezam al-Mulk (1019–1092), (3) *Nasihat al-Muluk* (The Counsel for the King), written in Persian by Abu Hamid Al-Ghazali (1058–1111).

The article documents from this literature considerable evidence that demonstrates the functioning of the markets, various nuances of economic activities, and appreciation for the accumulation of wealth.

A-41. Hosseini, Hamid. "Seeking the Roots of Adam Smith's Division of Labor in Medieval Persia (Iran)." *History of Political Economy* 30, no.3 (Winter 1998): 653–681.

This article disputes the origins of the "division of labor" proposition assumed to have originated with Adam Smith; this notion is, of course, critical to Smith's discussion of economic growth. It is argued that medieval Muslim scholars, in particular some Persian-speaking Iranian writers, were aware of this concept. Several scholars are identified, such as Ibn Sina, Nasir al-Tusi, Kai Kavus, al-Ghazali, and others. Further, it is noted that al-Ghazali explained this concept by using a needle-factory illustration, similar to Smith's example of a pin-factory more than seven centuries later.

The last section of the article briefly discusses the transmission of Islamic scholarship to the Latin-Christian scholastics. While referring to this influence, the question is raised: "Could Adam Smith have been influenced by al-Ghazali and other Iranian scholars?"

A-42. Hosseini, Hamid. "Understanding the Market Mechanism before Adam Smith: Economic Thought in Medieval Islam." *History of Political Economy* 27, no.3 (1995): 539–561.

The paper begins with briefly disputing the Schumpeterian "great gap" thesis proposed by the late Joseph Schumpeter, which postulated that during the centuries between the Greeks and the Latin scholastics, nothing was written on economic issues anywhere.

Thus, the purpose of the paper is to demonstrate that various medieval Muslim scholars had a sophisticated view of the market mechanism, for, among other reasons, the Islamic civilization "sprang from a mercantile society" (p.541). Then, after discussing some aspects of medieval Islamic trading and mercantile activities, the paper discusses two "distinct theories of exchange (trade)"; one "praising wealth for its own sake," the other "an ethical theory."

The economic ideas of two Arabic Muslim scholars (Dimishqi and Ibn Taimiyah) and two Persian Muslim writers (Al-Ghazali and Kay Kavus Ibn Iskandar) are discussed. It is argued that "medieval Muslim writers had a thorough understanding of the market mechanism long before the eighteenth century" (p.543).

The author concludes that the "the 'Great Gap' thesis in the history of economic thought is patently untenable" (p.559).

A-43. Labib, Subhi Y. "Capitalism in Medieval Islam." *Journal of Economic History* 29 (1969): 79–96.

The author begins, "He who looks for the term 'capitalism' in the Islamic sources of the Middle Ages will look in vain." However, the detailed evidence provided in this paper suggests the presence of capitalistic institutions, ethos, and practices since the beginning of Islamic culture. The Islamic scriptures approved and encouraged business practices, and the Islamic Prophet and many of his companions and successors were traders and merchants.

The article mentions that in the Middle Ages, "a *Pax Islamica* was the foundation of an economic golden age of which the protagonists in the field of trade were Arabs, Persians, Berbers, Jews, and Armenians. Islamic trade reached from Gibraltar to the Sea of China. Oriental and Occidental (Frankish) merchants together created a phase of activity which can be called commercial capitalism" (p.80). The cradle of Islamic capitalism, which encouraged the accumulation of capital for production, was in the major cities of the Islamic world.

The author discusses numerous prominent merchants and traders, as well as the commodities traded and the routes of trading activities. Prominent in this medieval capitalistic trade were institutions such as the *funduqs*—"specialized large-scale commercial institutions and markets which developed into virtual stock exchanges" (p.85). This early capitalism was motivated by the "strong urge for gain, to be sure, but it was different from the factory production and the calculation of modern capitalism" (p.96).

A-44. Mirakhor, Abbas. "The Muslim Scholars and the History of Economics: A Need for Consideration." *The American Journal of Islamic Social Sciences* 4, no.2 (1987): 245–275.

This article, like several others during the last 15–20 years, explores the omissions in literary history in general, and in the history of socioeconomic thought in particular. The author points out the "great gap," argued by the late Joseph Schumpeter, in that nothing was written on economic issues anywhere prior to the 13th-century writings of St. Thomas Aquinas (1225–1274). Yet there are several Western scholars who acknowledge the scholarship of Muslim scholars as "looming in the background" of medieval Western intellectual evolution.

The paper notes that one finds considerable discussion on economic issues in the writings of numerous early Muslim scholars, such as al-Ghazali, Ibn Al-Ukhuwa, Kai Ka'us Ibn Iskander, Nizam al-Mulk, Al-Farabi, Al-Dimishqi, Al-Diwwani, Ibn Bajja, and Ibn Rushd. Also, the author asserts, one finds considerable economic content in Islamic scriptures.

The article also emphasizes that, as in other disciplines, the contributions to economic thought of early Muslim scholars, once transmitted to Latin Europe, facilitated European enlightenment. Numerous Latin scholars, identified by Schumpeter and others, were influenced by the knowledge gained from Muslim scholars. Such knowledge transfer took place through various means— translations en masse particularly, but also travels to Islamic regions by Latin-European scholastics.

A-45. Newby, Gordon D. "Trade in the Levant and the East Mediterranean in the Early Islamic Period: A Search for the Early Muslim Merchant." *Archeological News* 7, nos.2–3 (Fall 1979): 78–83.

The article begins with noting the commercial/trading environment in which Islam emerged, and, further, that Prophet Muhammad himself was a successful trading entrepreneur; much of this trading activity took place in and through the East Mediterranean. However, "There is surprising little direct evidence for the character and extent of this trade until the beginning of the second Islamic century" (p.78).

The article examines "what evidence we have for trade in and through Arabia a little before and during Muhammad's lifetime, shows how the Islamic expansion changed the character of East Mediterranean trade, and explores the question of who was actually engaged in trade" (p.78). The author notes that "Muhammad was born and developed the religion of Islam within this economic context. Some of his first preachings to the Makkans urge them to be grateful to the supernatural source of their good fortune, the *rabb* or lord of the Ka'bah" (p.80). Nonetheless, "Trading activity under the early Caliphs among the Arabs, who retained their ethnic identity into the third Islamic century, was not highly esteemed, and in the East, as in the Iberian Peninsula, they preferred to live, when possible, in villas on their estates" (p.82).

A-46. Oran, Ahmad and Salim Rashid. "Fiscal Policy in Early Islam." *Public Finance/Finances Publiques* 44, no.1 (1989): 75–101.

The paper provides some insights concerning fiscal policy in early Islam, which tended to be guided by the Qur'anic prescriptions and guidelines, with interpretative flexibility. Questions are explored as to how those interpretations evolve and how do they compare with standard Western criteria?

The paper questions some of the historical work in this context that reflects the post-Ibn Khaldun Hellenistic aspects of Islamic civilization. Then follows a discussion of various elements of fiscal policy—the role of the government, various reasons for taxation (income distribution, administrative reasons, financial-economic reasons, political reasons, general welfare). Then there is a discussion of the fiscal system in the first period of Islam—alms tax (or zakat), jizya, monetary system (with emphasis on sound monetary system for purposes of taxation as well as encouragement of commerce). During the second period (beginning with Caliph Umar), there was the emergence of a new administrative apparatus; the notion of diwan emerged, referring to a more refined financial system. However, "The Beit al-Maal, public treasury, provides the general framework of Muslim fiscal policy" (p.81). The paper explores in some detail the four types of taxes as part of the Islamic Tax System: zakat, kharaj (land tax), jizya (poll tax), Ushr (trade tax). Also discussed are various types of expenditures, which are generally linked with the revenue sources.

The authors conclude that the "high standards of honesty and impartiality were stressed during the early years" and that the first four caliphs of Islam set standards "worth emulating" (p.96).

A-47. Oweiss, Ibrahim M. "Ibn Khaldun, the Father of Economics." Pages 112–127 in *Arab Civilization: Challenges and Responses—Studies in Honor of Constantine K. Zurayk*, edited by George N. Atiyeh and Ibrahim M. Oweiss. Albany, NY: State University of New York Press, 1988.

While Ibn Khaldun (1332–1406) "laid the foundations of different fields of knowledge, in particular the science of civilization (*al-umran*)," argues the author, "his significant contributions to economics, however, should place him in the history of economic thought as a major forerunner, if not the 'father' of economics" (p.112). Further, the author argues that "centuries later these same ideas were developed by the Mercantilists, the commercial capitalists of the seventeenth century—Sir William Petty A.D.1623–1687), Adam Smith (A.D.1723–1790), David Ricardo (A.D.1772–1823), Thomas R. Malthus (A.D.1766–1834), Karl Marx (A.D.1818–1883), and John Maynard Keynes (A.D.1883–1946), to name only a few" (p.113).

Some of the topics relating to economics explored from Ibn Khaldun's writings are: (1) labor theory of value, (2) labor as the source of growth and capital accumulation, (3) demand, supply, prices, and profits, (3) macroeconomics and growth, (4) taxes and role of government, (5) role of money, (6) foreign trade. In comparing Ibn Khaldun's thought with that of Adam Smith, the author argues that "even though Adam Smith did not explicitly refer to Ibn Khaldun's contributions, it may well be argued that there were several channels through which he may have encountered the latter's pioneering and original economic thought" (p.123). Several such channels are identified, but the author also notes that "ever since the Crusades, which lasted from the eleventh to the thirteenth centuries, most Western philosophers attempted to discount the impact of Muslim scholars through a multiplicity of approaches, which included using Muslim ideas without mentioning the name of a Muslim author" (p.124).

A-48. Oweiss, Ibrahim M. "A View on Islamic Economic Thought." *Occasional Paper Series*, Center for Contemporary Arab Studies. Washington, DC: Georgetown University, 2000.

"While the Dark Ages lingered in Europe, there was light somewhere else. During that era, Islamic civilization contributed significantly to many fields of knowledge, including economics and its related disciplines," so begins this 28-page monograph. The paper argues that the breadth and depth of economic thought originating in the early Islamic world, while not widely recognized, "warrant recognition, investigation, and analysis" (p.1).

The paper states that Islamic economic thought planted the early seeds of the economics of public finances, and it contributed to what later became known as classical economics, covering areas such as consumption and utility, production and costs, trade and gains from trade, income distribution, and general welfare.

The author reviews the economic thought of several medieval Islamic scholastics—for example, Abu Yusuf, Al-Ghazali, Ibn Taimiyah, and especially, Ibn Khaldun. Focusing on such scholars, several specific topics are also elaborated, such as labor theory of value, labor as source of growth, capital accumulation, demand–supply forces, role of profits, role of government and taxation, money and credit (including interest and usury), and foreign trade. By presenting some circumstantial evidence, the author argues that Ibn Khaldun's work strongly influenced Adam Smith's *Wealth of Nations.*

A-49. Rozina, Parveen. "Ibn Khaldun as an Economist: A Comparative Study with Modern Economists." *Pakistan Journal of History and Culture* 15, no.1 (1994): 111–130.

Referring to Ibn Khaldun (1332–1406) as a "forerunner of Machiavelli, Bodin, Vico, Comte, and Curnot," and quoting George Sarton, "as the greatest theoretician of history, the greatest philosopher of man's experience," the paper begins with a biographical sketch of this scholar. The purpose is to document Ibn Khaldun's economic thought as part of the Muslim legacy in this field, and also to compare his ideas with that of modern Western economic theories. It is suggested that while Ibn Khaldun's contributions in sociology and history have been acclaimed, his economics has not received due attention.

The paper discusses Ibn Khaldun's economic views in several areas: stages of economic development, occupational classification, labor and value, market forces of demand and supply, price determination, generation of wealth (output), functions of money, and public finance issues (including expenditures and effects on national income; taxation and incentives). The author then briefly compares Ibn Khaldun's views with some Western economists.

A-50. Samarrai, Alauddin. "Medieval Commerce and Diplomacy: Islam and Europe, A.D. 850–1300." *Canadian Journal of History* 15, no.1 (April 1980): 1–21.

This essay is a narrative primarily on commercial links between medieval Islam and Europe. While during the period prior to about 1100 AD, commercial links were mainly private, then such activities were formalized with treaties and agreements, the author notes. Contrary to some opinion, trading relations existed throughout, though more limited with Western Europe than Slavonic Europe.

Based on the chronicles and itineraries of merchants and diplomats, the author documents the nature and extent of trade between the Islamic world and Western Europe, as well as the Byzantium. Much of this commerce related to luxury items. Arabs encountered the Volga Rus people and were appalled by the "unsanitary habits of the Rus and their moral laxity" (p.7). Similar observations are noted about the Slavs. Also, Muslim merchants engaged in commercial links with Bohemia—Prague being an important trading center of Central and Eastern Europe.

Beginning with the First Crusade, the paper states that Muslim historians looked at this armed phenomena as a counteroffensive against Islam, motivated, among other things, by commercial expansionism. Such motivations, especially economic, became prominent in subsequent Islam–West relationships. The author concludes that "in spite of the violence and carnage committed during the Crusades, this period witnessed great cooperation in the economic field throughout the Mediterranean world" (p.21).

A-51. Sattar, M. Abdus. "Ibn Khaldun's Contribution to Economic Thought." Pages 121–129 in *Contemporary Aspects of Economic Thinking in Islam*, Proceedings of the Third East Coast Regional Conference of the Muslim Students Association of the USA and Canada, 1968. Baltimore, MD: American Trust Publications, 1976.

While the article is a bit polemical, it identifies several strands of economic concepts and principles discovered in Ibn Khaldun's (1332–1406) *The Muqaddimah*, recognized by the historian Arnold Toynbee as "the greatest work of its kind that has ever been created by any mind in any time or place" (p.122). "Like Adam Smith," the author argues, "Ibn Khaldun tried to discover the nature and underlying causes of the development of nations founded by man and maintained by human law" (p.122). The driving force of the state is "*Asabiyyah*, the common bond, social solidarity and collective awareness," with its creative content and sustaining power coming from religion (122).

States go through cycles of growth and decline and, according to Ibn Khaldun,

growth and development pass through stages—nomadic life, followed by sedentary life, then urban life with security of life and property. Khaldun talks in terms
of a market economy, with hierarchy of needs (necessities, conveniences, luxuries); labor is the key determinant of value. He anticipates Keynesian-type intervention to maintain aggregate demand for growth, but also recognizes the
disincentive effects if taxes are too high. While there is a role for government, he
would want to rely more on the private sector for the operations of the economy.
He discusses division of labor and specialization and also identifies the role and
functions of money in the economy.

A-52. Sharif, M. Raihan. "Ibn-i-Khaldun, the Pioneer Economist." *Islamic Literature* (Lahore, Pakistan) 6, no.5 (May 1955): 33–40.
    The article begins with the suggestion that "had Ibn-i-Khaldun been known to
Adam Smith, he would have probably unhesitatingly acknowledged his debt to
the former. There are reasons to believe that Ibn-i-Khaldun did much to shape
the climate of thinking that helped the seventeenth and eighteenth century economists" (p.33). Further, while Ibn Khaldun (1332–1406) is an interdisciplinary
scholar, he acknowledges economic science as an independent field, with objective principles.
    Ibn Khaldun discusses the labor theory value, usually attributed to Adam
Smith and Ricardo. He discusses market forces of demand and supply in determining prices. He provides a theory of money, including identifying the functions of money, and discusses international trade as a vehicle for progress.
Various occupational classifications are also identified. His theory of population,
among other things, suggests that "the standard of living and wealth depend on
the number of its members," with an implication of what may be called "optimum" population (p.277). Further, he says the wealth of a society is goods, not
"possessions of gold mines."

A-53. Sherwani, H. "Ibn-i-Taimiyah's Economic Thought." *Islamic Quarterly*
(Lahore, Pakistan) 8 (1956): 9–21.
    This article documents the economic thought of an early Islamic scholastic,
Ibn Taimiyah (1263–1328 AD). The author argues that while Ibn-i-Taimiyah
upholds individual property as the foundation of economic activity, he does not
believe in unrestricted property rights. The Sharia-ordained principle of common
good must prevail in the exercise of property rights. Consistent with Islamic principles, pursuit of profits and wealth is preferable to living in poverty.
    Ibn-i-Taimiyah suggests there should be no control of the markets and mer-
chants should be free to dispose of their goods in any way they like; the only
exception may be when necessities are involved and common good must be
ensured. The "role of the state is to serve as an instrument of superintendence
and arbitration for the purpose of harmonizing economic activities" so that the
economic system functions according to Islamic principles (p.20). His is a system

of economic individualism tampered by a sense of responsibility for the common good.

A-54. Siddiqi, M. Nejatullah and S.M. Ghazanfar. "Early Medieval Islamic Economic Thought: Abu Yusuf's (731–798 AD) Economics of Public Finance." *History of Economic Ideas* (Italy) 9, no.1 (2001): 13–38.

The paper, after pointing to the vast literature on economic issues written by numerous Arab-Islamic scholastics during the medieval centuries, focuses on the economic thought of Abu Yusuf (731–798 AD). Specifically based on his book, *Kitab al-Kharaj* (The Book of Taxation), the paper discusses several major public finance issues. Parenthetically, the paper disputes the Schumpeterian "great gap" thesis, which argued that during the centuries between the Greeks and Latins, not much was written in the area of economics or about any other field.

Alongside the private exchange-economy, the paper argues that Abu Yusuf viewed the state as active in promoting socioeconomic welfare. Further, anticipating Adam Smith nine centuries later, he discusses similar "canons of taxation": fairness (ability-to-pay and benefits-received principles), simplicity, convenience, types of taxes, administration, etc. Concerned about economic incentives, he proposes a proportional tax on land output, as opposed to a fixed-amount tax. Further, he has the elements of cost-benefits analysis; depending upon benefits of public projects, he identifies principles concerning sharing of public expenditures.

The article concludes that given the depth of his scholarship on economic matters (especially public finance issues), "Abu Yusuf deserves to be acknowledged among the distinguished early pioneers of modern public finance as a field in the science of economics" (p.36).

A-55. Soofi, Abdol. "Economics of Ibn Khaldun Revisited." *History of Political Economy* 27, no.2 (1995): 387–404.

The author notes that Ibn Khaldun's (1332–1406) "rationalistic approach to economic reasoning" and "his theories bear striking resemblance to those later developed independently by Thomas Malthus and John Maynard Keynes" (p.387–388). However, it is argued that other studies are confined to some general statements as to his theory of politico-economic cycles; but "they neglect his many other contributions to economic theory" (p.288). This article proposes to "develop a searching, critical evaluation of the economic aspects of the Khaldunian system" (p.388). The attempt is to "place Ibn Khaldun's economics in the context of the intellectual history of economics by taking an inventory of his knowledge of economic theory" (p.388).

It is suggested that unlike other Muslim scholars, Ibn Khaldun talked in terms of "the universe governed by an accurate system through which prevails the law of cause and effect," and not simply in terms of "the will of Allah" (p.390). Then follows a discussion of Ibn Khaldun's economics, divided into four sections: (1)

value theories (labor theory of value and subjective value theory), (2) theory of income distribution and growth ("income which a man derives from the crafts is the value of labor," and "he recognized the contribution of circulating capital to the productive process"), (3) theories of economic development and 40-year cycles ("Ibn Khaldun saw aggregate demand as an important determinant of national income"), (4) monetary theory ("his monetary theory, in general, contradicts the quantity theory of money").

The article concludes: "It is regrettable Ibn Khaldun's work was not known to Western economists in the late fourteenth century. Translation of *al-Muqaddimah* into European languages would have expedited the progress of economics, potentially obviating a great deal of work on the part of Western writers" (p.403).

A-56. Spengler, Joseph J. "Alberuni: Eleventh Century Iranian Malthusian?" *History of Political Economy* 3, no.1 (Spring 1971): 93–104.

England's Thomas Malthus is known for his "population–food dilemma" proposition, in that population tends to grow exponentially and food grows arithmetically, thus the long-run dilemma for the human race. Also, there are traces of the evolution theory in Malthus' writings. This article argues that one can find traces of those ideas in the writings of Alberuni, an 11th-century Muslim of Iranian origin. Alberuni is quoted, "The life of the world depends upon sowing and procreating. Both processes increase in the course of time, and this increase is unlimited, whilst the world is limited" (p.95). In contemporary terms, one may interpret this statement as equivalent to "scarcity relative to needs" foundation of modern economics.

Further, the author notes, "Alberuni observed, much as did Charles Darwin upon reading Malthus, that the pressure of increasing numbers would give rise to natural selection, though not to selection so favorable as that carried on under human guidance" (p.95). Also noted are Alberuni's views on taxation, expenditure patterns, and other economic issues.

A-57. Spengler, Joseph J. "Economic Thought of Islam: Ibn Khaldun." *Comparative Studies in Society and History* 6, no.3 (April 1964): 268–306.

This long essay concerns "mainly with the economics of Ibn Khaldun (1332–1406), historian and statesman of prominent Arab descent and medieval Islam's greatest economist" (p.268). His economic observations, derived from *The Muqaddimah* ("undoubtedly the greatest work of its kind that has ever yet been created by any mind in any time or place"), "flowed principally from his concern with the rise and fall of ruling dynasties" (p.269).

The paper begins with a survey of "economics in the Islamic scheme of science." Economics was classified as a practical science, along with politics and ethics, and economic matters are discussed in the Islamic scriptures as well as in the writings of various early Islamic scholars. How these writers influenced Ibn Khaldun is unknown, but "his superior handling of economic matters certainly

warrants Plessner's observation that Islamic economics began with Ibn Khaldun"
(p.283).

Given Ibn Khaldun's main concern being the rise and fall of "civilizations,"
economics occupied a high place in his analysis and he approached his arguments
in terms of "causation and causality" (p.287). Then follows a discussion of Ibn
Khaldun's "cycle theory," which is "political and sociological as well as economic in nature" (p.289). Thus, according to Ibn Khaldun, "Growth is halted by
the inevitable weakening and collapse of the ruling dynasty, usually after three
or four generations, a process that is accompanied by deterioration of economic
conditions, decline of the economy in complexity, and the return of more primitive conditions" (p.290). The author discusses Ibn Khaldun's views as to the
process of how this cycle evolves, the life span of a dynasty, or state, "subdivisi-
ble into four or five stages," etc. (p.291).

While Ibn Khaldun's "essentially economic observations" are not quite sepa-
rable from his "civilization" discussion, the author identifies and briefly discusses six topics: (1) population growth, (2) supply, demand, and price, (3)
profits and their role, (4) rank, obsequiousness, and profit, (5) surplus, luxury,
and capital formation, (6) consumption patterns, expenditures.

Spengler concludes that unlike the Greeks, Ibn Khaldun's ideas "extended far
beyond the household, embracing market, price, monetary, supply, and demand
phenomena, and hinting at some of the macro-economic relations stressed by
Lord Keynes" (p.304). Further, "One is compelled to infer from a comparison
of Ibn Khaldun's economic ideas with those set down in Muslim moral-philo-
sophical literature that the knowledge of economic behavior in some circles was
very great indeed" (p.304).

A-58. Udovitch, Abraham L. "Bankers without Banks: Commerce, Banking,
and Society in the Islamic World of the Middle Ages." Pages 255–273 in *The
Dawn of Modern Banking*, Center for Medieval and Renaissance Studies, University of California, Los Angeles. New Haven, CT: Yale University Press, 1979.

This essay argues that while banking institutions in the contemporary sense
did not appear in the Islamic Middle East until recently, "we encounter extensive
and ramified banking activities" in the medieval Islamic world (p.255).

The author provides an overview of the various types of banking activities
practiced in the medieval Islamic world, even when there were no "banks" in
the contemporary sense. The discussion includes "elements of banking," such as
deposits, credit, loans, and bills of exchange within the Islamic setting. Usurious
transactions were forbidden, as in the Christian West, and "such loans were an
infrequent means of extending commercial credit" (p.257–258).

The essay discusses evidence that "as early as the late eighth century, credit
arrangements of various types were an important feature of both trade and industry in the Near East" (p.261). Credit instruments such as *hawala* (payment of
credit through the transfer of a claim) and *suftaja* (letter of credit or bill of

exchange) were common, as was the credit partnership called *sharikat al-mafalis*—"the partnership of the penniless," or "the partnership of good reputations," whereby, in good faith, "people formed a partnership without any capital in order to buy on credit and then sell" (p.263). Further, Udovitch suggests, "We encounter in eleventh century Egypt and North Africa an elaborate system of banking and money exchange to accommodate the various needs and circumstances" (p.265). There were money-changers and merchant banks—the former performed exchange, "central feature of the money market," and the later undertook "banking activities closely related to private trading and commercial activities" (p.267).

The author concludes that "a wide assortment of credit techniques were known and practiced in the Islamic world from the earliest medieval world—techniques similar to those which began to appear in Europe only in the thirteenth century" (p.271).

A-59. Udovitch, Abraham L. "Labor Partnership in Early Islam." *Journal of Economic and Social History of the Orient* 10 (1967): 64–80.

The article discusses the various characteristics of the institution of partnership in the medieval Islamic world. This institution was one of the chief means that enabled merchants to combine their resources and skills for investment in commercial capitalism. According to the various schools of Islamic jurisprudence, "resources could take the form either of a cash investment or of goods and merchandise, and skills, of commercial know-how and/or of a particular skill on the part of one or all of the partners in some type of trade or craft" (p.64). The primary function of such partnerships, "like that of any other type of medieval partnership, was to perform economic tasks that were beyond the capabilities of a single person" (p.79).

Three categories of partnerships are discussed: (1) complete partnership, in which all partners contributed both capital and services, (2) the *commenda* arrangement (Arabic: *mudaraba, muqarada, qirad*) in which one party supplied capital and the other provided services, (3) a labor partnership, in which each partner provides only skill or labor—capital consisted solely or primarily of the labor of the partners. Each is discussed from the perspective of two major schools of jurisprudence (Hanafi and Malaki). Also included are narratives on the experiences of individuals who engaged in such business practices.

A-60. Udovitch, Abraham L. "Reflections on the Institutions of Credit and Banking in the Medieval Islamic Near East." *Studia Islamica* 41 (1975): 5–21.

The article begins with reference to other studies which have demonstrated that "credit transactions and institutions of credit assumed a major role in the trade and economic life of medieval Christian Europe as well as that of the medieval Islamic Near East" (p.5). The article argues, however, the pattern has been quite different in the Islamic Near East: (1) the widespread use of various

types of credit evolved "at least three or four centuries before anything comparable is recorded for medieval Europe," and (2) while in the Near East these institutions and practices remained rather static, they evolved "into the kind of credit
and banking institutions which were so seminal in the economic growth of
Europe" (p.6–7). The article explores the second premise further, and it is argued
that the answer lies in the social setting of medieval Near Eastern economic life.

The author discusses various types of Near Eastern credit institutions—
commenda (credit partnership), *hawala* (payment of debt through transfer of
claim), *suftaja* (letter of credit, bill of exchange), and others. Also, there is a survey of various merchants and traders involved in credit and money-changing
operations. The author concludes that banking "specialization" did not develop
partly because banking activities were mainly an extension of commercial activities. Further, the answer lies in the social context of economic life. There is the
paradoxical conclusion: "The very factors—status and personal–social relations—which ensured the smooth and successful functioning of credit and mer-
chant-banking activities in the Islamic Mediterranean world were the very
elements which effectively confined their growth, elaboration into independent,
stable organizational forms" (p.20). Thus, "The possibility of integration into a
larger, more cohesive structure was precluded by the comparatively narrow social
basis on which economic life was conducted" (p.21).

A-61. Weiss, Dieter. "Ibn Khaldun on Economic Transformation." *International
Journal of Middle East Studies* 27 (1995): 29–37.

The article explores the relevance of this 14th-century scholar's historical
analysis of the rise and decline of civilizations to the contemporary Arab world
and beyond. The author argues that "considering the mounting social tension that
results from continuing population growth, urban agglomeration, and unemploy-
ment, it would be naive to expect—with Fukuyama—an 'end of history,' as most
countries try to adopt market regimes and to strengthen civil society and parlia-
mentary democracy. As Ibn Khaldun (1332–1406) well knew, economic and
social change is a never-ending process" (p.29). Thus, in search for viable and
sustainable strategies, the author explores the insights of this scholar who wrote
600 years ago.

The author argues that Ibn Khaldun's insights are strikingly modern and have
relevance for contemporary economic transformation. His key emphasis was on
asabiya, social cohesion based on sociocultural consensus, but he also emphasized other forces: commitment to development by the ruling elites and cultural
disposition and enhancement of the human factor. Thus, the article concludes:
"The Arab countries in the process of structural adjustment cannot evade the old
lessons of development: to allocate scarce resources to meaningful goals within
a framework of suitable incentives embedded into a broad social consensus.
These were already the early insights of Ibn Khaldun. His general observations

are still timely for contemporary economic reformers both within the Arab world and outside it" (p.36).

A-62. Zaid, Omar Abdullah. "Were Islamic Records Precursors to Accounting Books Based on the Italian Method?" *Accounting Historians Journal* 27, no.1 (June 2000): 73–90.

The paper argues that "it is most likely that the commercial links between Muslim traders and their Italian counterparts [during the Middle Ages] influenced the development of accounting books in the Italian Republics" (p.73). Further, it is argued that some of the records and reports in different parts of the Islamic state are comparable to modern-day books and reports. The religious requirement of *Zakat* (charity) and expanding responsibilities of the State represented forces behind the development of proper accounting records and reports. Such records were further developed in the Abbasid Caliphate (750–847 AD) whereby "seven accounting specializations were known and practiced," including auditing methods (p.73). Among other things, the author provides evidence to corroborate a Western scholar's assertion that "the Italians borrowed the concept of double entry from the Arabs" (p.74).

The author concludes that "the development of accounting records and reports in the Islamic State have most likely contributed to the development and practice of accounting in the Italian Republics as documented by Pacioli in 1494" (p.89).

c. Philosophy

A-63. Fakhry, Majid. "Philosophy and Scripture in the Theology of Averroes." *Medieval Studies* 30 (1968): 78–87.

The Aristotelian commentaries of Averroes (Ibn Rushd, 1126–1198) during the 13th-century Latin Europe established him as "the greatest Peripatetic" philosopher, but "his original contribution to the perennial problem of the relationship between philosophy and scripture, in which his own deepest convictions appear to have been involved" has been ignored (p.78). Based on Averroes' original works, the article explores this contribution in some detail.

The author reviews this problem in the writings of other Muslim scholars (Al-Kindi and Avicennia [Ibn Sina]); it is suggested that "Al-Kindi and Averroes are perhaps the two philosophers who best illustrate the possibility of 'marriage' of philosophy and dogma in Islam" (p.82). However, "Despite the harmony of philosophy and scripture where the fundamentals of belief are concerned, religion has a wider scope than philosophy" (p.88).

The article points to similar "problem of reason and revelation" in the writings of St. Thomas Aquinas. Both Aquinas and Averroes, according to the author, recognized the two spheres as "distinct and complementary" (p.89).

A-64. Schleifer, Aliah. "Ibn Khaldun's Theories of Perception, Logic, and Knowledge: An Islamic Phenomenology." *American Journal of Islamic Social Sciences* 2, no.2 (December 1985): 225–231.

The article discusses Ibn Khaldun's (1332–1406) theories about perception, logic, and knowledge, which, it is argued, are influenced by Aristotelian thought. However, as an ecclectic, he also develops his own perspectives. Further, his writings demonstrate the underlying metaphysical source of all knowledge.

The author says, for Ibn Khaldun, "the phenomenological approach is opposed to explanatory hypotheses; it confines itself to the direct evidence of intuitive seeing. Thus, in understanding the spiritual world and its essences (intellects), the conditions of logic do not apply. Ibn Khaldun concludes that man must rely on religious law, and like Kant, on faith. Logic, then, is best used as a tool to sharpen the mind" (p.227). Further, according to Ibn Khaldun, "The experimental intellect represents man's ability to acquire useful knowledge from his fellow men. The speculative intellect is man's ability to perceive existent things, whether present or absent" (p.230).

A-65. Shah, Shafqat A. "Aristotle, Al-Farabi, Averroes, and Aquinas: Four Views on Philosophy and Religion." *Sind University Research Journal* (Hyderabad, Pakistan) 19 (1980): 1–20.

The paper begins with noting the extreme views of philosophers and theologians, the former arguing that everything (including the divine law and its political teachings) is explainable through reason, and the latter stressing that all things are "contained and taught through divine law" (p.1). Yet, the author notes, the finer points of both are often overlooked and the extremists sometimes prevail.

The author then focuses on the "moderates," who have attempted to bridge the differences based on their convictions that the teachings of philosophy and religion are not necessarily contradictory. Aristotle represents the ancient philosophy. Al-Farabi and Ibn Rushd (Averroes) formulated the Islamic perspective, and St. Thomas Aquinas developed the Christian thought.

According to the author, "Al-Farabi believes that religious truth and philosophic truth are both the radiation of divine illumination," and the two are complementary (p.12). Averroes elaborates his argument by relating to three classes of people: philosophers, theologians, and the common people. And, "It is the task of the philosophers to reveal the identity of the revealed law and its infallible truth" (p.15). However, prophets are more successful, for they have the revelation "to teach the masses and lead them to happiness" (p.15). Thus, "The Shari'a as a revealed prophetic law is superior to the nomos, as revelation is superior to myth" (p.15). St. Thomas considers the domain of religion and philosophy as distinct. Human mind is limited, so truth could not be deduced through reason; thus faith is a safe guide to rational truth and an infallible warning against philosophical error. Each of these "moderate" sages seems to extend ultimate supremacy to faith.

A-66. Sharif, M.M. "Muslim Philosophy and Western Thought." *Iqbal: A Journal of the Bazm-I-Iqbal* (Lahore, Pakistan) 8, no.1 (July 1959): 1–14.

This brief essay begins with this statement: "Muslim philosophy influenced Western thought in several ways: (a) it initiated the humanistic movement; (b) introduced the historical sciences and the scientific method in the West; (c) helped the Western scholastics in harmonizing philosophy; with faith; (d) stimulated Western mysticism; (e) laid the foundation of Italian Renaissance; (g) influenced the modern European thought down to the time of Emanuel Kant" (p.1).

Then follow some details to elaborate each premise. In the process, the contributions of numerous Arab-Islamic (and Jewish) scholars (Al-Farabi, Ibn Sina, Ibn Tufail, Maimonidies, Al-Ghazali, Ibn Rushd) are noted, as well as their influence on various Latin-European scholastics and others, such as Spinoza, Descartes, Kant, and Leibniz. However, "No Muslim thinker influenced the West more than Ibn Rushd" (p.4).

The author concludes that this influence "ended with Kant but influence has not been all one-sided. Since the beginning of the twentieth century, the West has been paying the debt it owed to the Muslim East with compound interest. There has hardly been a Muslim thinker since then who has not owed a deep debt of gratitude to Western thinkers. In fact Muslim philosophers have drunk so deep at the fountain of Western learning that most of them have lost the taste for appreciating the learning of their ancestors. Now we are all veritable disciples of the West" (p.13).

A-67. Stone, Caroline. "Doctor, Philosopher, Renaissance Man." *Saudi Aramco World* 54, no.3 (May–June 2003): 8–15.

This is a biographical essay on Ibn Rushd (1126–1198). The author states: "A man can be adopted by a civilization other than his own and can therefore become a symbol of something very different from what he signifies to his own civilization. This was the case with Abu 'l-Walid Muhammad ibn Rushd, who came to be known to the West as Averroes. And just as the medieval Arab world and the medieval European world knew him by two names, so did they value two different aspects of his scholarship. In the Arab world, he is remembered primarily as a medical pioneer, while the West esteemed his philosophy" (p.8).

The article includes a note, "Ibn Rushd the Jurist," by Greg Noakes; and it is noted, "Despite his enemies' charges to the contrary, Ibn Rushd did not attempt to subvert religion using philosophy, but rather used analytical methods to better understand the message and tenets of Islam. Far from being irreconcilable opposites, Ibn Rushd saw revelation and reason as complementary, God-given gifts to mankind" (p.8).

The essay includes a chronology of Ibn Rushd's life, as well as some illustrations.

A-68. Tolan, John. "'Saracen Philosophers Secretly Deride Islam.'" *Medieval Encounters* 8, nos.2–3 (2003): 184–208.

Appropriate to the theme of this paper, the title is cited in quotes by the author. The paper argues that while the work of Muslim scholars was an integral part of the curriculum of European universities, "the thirteenth-century mendicant missionaries deployed rationalist arguments to attempt to prove the irrationality of Islam" (p.184). This created a problem, says the author: if Islam is as "irrational" as the polemicists and missionaries claimed, how could the sophisticated Muslim (Saracen) scholars adhere to the Islamic doctrines?

This article examines the response to this problem by various medieval writers, in particular four 13th-century writers (Ramon Marti, Roger Bacon, Ramon Lull, and Ciccoldo da Montecroce). According to the author, these scholars claimed that the learned Saracens did not really believe in the doctrines of the Qur'an, that they "secretly derided Islam," and that only the fear of physical punishment made them publicly claim their adherence to Islam. All four Christian polemicists were familiar with Islamic philosophy and they based their claims on their misreading of Ibn Sina, al-Ghazali, and Ibn Rushd. Further, the various Christian writers "denounced Islam as irrational, while affirming that Christianity was rational. In order to maintain this, they created a stereotypical image of fanatical, anti-intellectual Muslim leaders who prohibited the study of philosophy and science. In order to cling to the belief in the rationality of their own religion, Christian intellectuals had to relegate the religious 'other' to the realm of the irrational" (p.208).

A-69. Wippel, John F. "The Condemnations of 1270 and 1277 at Paris." *Journal of Medieval and Renaissance Studies* 7 (Spring 1977): 169–201.

The article discusses the background and the impact of the "condemnation of some 219 propositions" by Bishop Tempier of Paris in 1277, an "event widely acknowledged to be the most severe and most significant doctrinal condemnation of the thirteenth century, even of the entire medieval period" (p.170). These propositions, part of what was known as the school of Latin Averroism, originated from the Aristotelian writings of Averroes (Ibn Rushd, 1126–1198).

The author notes, "The previous fifty or sixty years had witnessed the gradual absorption of a mass of recently translated scientific and philosophical literature of non-Christian origin" (p.174). Also called "Averroestic heresies," the propositions challenged various aspects of Christianity and were part of the dominant faith-vs.-reason controversies of the time. Despite these condemnations, the author concludes, "a more rigidly Averroistic version would reappear in Paris and then in Italy in the fourteenth century" (p.101).

d. Education/Learning

A-70. Government of Saudi Arabia. "Islamic Science and Learning." Washington, DC: High Commission for the Development of Arriyadh, Culture Center (July 1989): 2–20.

This brochure is based on an exhibition of a collection, "Saudi Arabia, Yesterday and Today," in Washington, DC, with illustrations depicting the importance of the contributions made by Islamic scientists to various branches of knowledge. It is stated that the collection "shows how throughout the Islamic World scholars learned from the past, preserved this knowledge, extended it through their own observations and discoveries and transmitted what they knew to following generations" (p.1).

The document is divided into four sections: (1) An Introduction: Islamic Science and Learning, (2) Astronomy, (3) Hospitals and Medical Education, (4) Geography and Cartography.

There are several pictures and sketches in each article. The most detailed essay pertains to astronomy, with a comprehensive account of the development of the astrolabe.

A-71. Makdisi, George. "Muslim Institutes of Learning in Eleventh-Century Baghdad." *Bulletin of the School of Oriental and African Studies* 24, no.1 (1961): 1–56.

This long essay pertains to the history of institutions of learning in 11th-century Baghdad, in particular the Nizamiya colleges, which were patterned after the original Shafi'ite Nizamiya of Baghdad, founded in 1065. It is argued that historians of Muslim education in the Middle Ages, typically beginning with this college, have identified with Nizamiya colleges the "dogmatic theological movement" (p.2–3). And, "This image of the Nizamiya has had some unfortunate consequences on our understanding of fifth/eleventh century Islamic history, both in the field of education as well as in the development of dogmatic theology" (p.3). Part of the problem, the author argues, has to do with the role and characteristics assigned "to the eleventh-century Nizamiya in this history," which are "based on an interpretation of sources," and this requires closer scrutiny (p.4). Thus, this article undertakes "an analysis of eleventh-century institutions in Baghdad according to types and characteristics, using it as a background against which to place the Nizamiya in order to determine its role and re-examine the major claims which have been made for it" (p.4).

The detailed discussion covers various topics, such as unrestricted and exclusive institutions, teaching personnel, student characteristics, law (or *fiqh*) colleges (specializations, characteristics, administration), various colleges according to the Islamic schools of jurisprudence (hanafite, shafi'ite, and hanbalite), and patrons of learning. This is followed by a comprehensive discussion of the original Shafi'ite Nizamiya College. The author concludes, among other things, that, while this college, unlike the Hanafite institutions, "had no official religious character which would bring it in some way under the supervision of the Caliph," subsequently, "the Nazimiya experiment failed in its attempt to develop an institution free from caliphal jurisdiction" (p.56).

A-72. Makdisi, George. "The Scholastic Method in Medieval Education: An Inquiry into Its Origins in Law and Theology." *Speculum: A Journal of Medieval Studies* 49 (1974): 640–661.

The article explores the role played by Islam in the revival of Western learning, and, further, the influence of this role "as regards the crowning intellectual achievement of medieval Western Christianity: the scholastic method" (p.641). It is argued that "the intellectual contact between Islamic and Western cultures perhaps went deeper than we have generally allowed" (p.641).

It is argued that in the writings of several Muslim writers, "the scholastic method had already been used a century or so" prior to its adoption by St. Thomas Aquinas and others (p.648). Two Islamic scholars mentioned are Ibn Aqil (1040–1119) and Abu Hamid Al-Ghazali (1058–1111). Ibn Aqil, like St. Thomas, also had written a *Summa*, and the author finds several parallels in the writings of the two. Like St. Thomas, earlier Ibn Aqil had embodied "the synthesis which made possible a harmony between faith and reason" (p. 657). Despite "the difference in culture and religious persuasion," the author notes, the two "belonged to the same spiritual family" (p.657).

As for the transmission, the author concludes, "it is interesting enough to note that the Arab-Islamic experience was not one of mere transmission; that having received the Greek legacy, it carried an operation of 'creative assimilation' not only in the realm of philosophy and science but also in that of religion" (p.661). Further, as for religious influence, "the circumstantial evidence is quite impressive" (p.661).

A-73. Newby, Gordon D. "The Foundation of the University of Naples: Typological Parallels with Arab Institutions of Higher Learning." *Medieval Encounters* 3, no.2 (1997): 173–184.

The article explores a proposition suggested over two decades by Richard Southern—that is, the possibility of Islamic influence on the formation of the University of Naples in 1224. Thus, having explored "the complex relations between Islamic and European educational institutions," the author discovered "a stronger typological and circumstantial relationship between the foundation of the University of Naples by Frederick II and the institutions of higher learning in the Islamic world" (p.173).

The author suggests, "It is with the *Madrasas* that we find the greatest typological correspondence with Frederick's university" (p.180). And apart from typological similarities (including the institution of endowment, *waqf* in Arabic), Arabic knowledge, with its Greek heritage, constituted the main curriculum at Naples, and "this material had profound impact on the thinking of thirteenth-century Europe, just as the model of the University of Naples had a far reaching influence on the European educational systems" (p.183). The author concludes with a reference to this university's most illustrious graduate and "Europe's foremost critic of Arab Aristotelianism": St. Thomas Aquinas; and, he says, "If he had been the only graduate of achievement, there would be sufficient credit to Frederick's efforts to bring the new learning from Islam to the West through his University of Naples" (p.183).

e. Geography

A-74. Bullis, Douglas. "The Longest Hajj: The Journeys of Ibn Battuta." *Saudi Aramco World* 51, no.4 (July–August 2000): 2–39.

The three-part essay is about the travels of this 14th-century Muslim from Morocco, over a span of some 30 years, covering some 120,000 kilometers (75,000 miles), that took him from Tangier to Mecca for pilgrimage, then to Africa, and by weaving through various parts of India and the Far East he went as far as Beijing, China. He saw more of the world than anyone else in his time. The author narrates that as this scholar of Islamic law roamed three continents, he earned his living as a judge, advisor, and diplomat in the service of local rulers in the vast arena of *Dar al-Islam*.

Each of the three parts is described as follows. Part One, From Pilgrim to Traveler—Tangier to Makkah: In 1325, Ibn Battuta (1304–1377) went to Makkah along the North African coast, passing through Cairo and Damascus; and after performing the Hajj, he continued east. Part Two, From Riches to Rags—Makkah to India: From Arabia, by the least direct route to the Volga, and across the Mongol-ruled steppe to the Hindu Kush, Ibn Battuta reached India in 1334, where the Sultan made him a judge and an ambassador, but the "sea made him a pauper." Part Three, From Traveler to Memoirist—China, Mali and Home: Ibn Battuta sojourned in Bengal and Sumatra before reaching China, and after returning to Morocco, he visited Andalusia and Mali; and in 1354, the Sultan of Fez commissioned the recording of his travels.

The author states that Ibn Battuta's *Rihla* is the most detailed and fascinating travelogue of the Islamic middle ages, a turning point in Arab literature. It is noted also that the while the book is commonly known as *Rihla*, the proper title is *Tuhfat al-Nuzzar fi Ghara'ib al-Amsar wa-'Aja'ib al-Asfar* (A Gift to Those Who Contemplate the Wonders of Cities and the Marvels of Traveling).

A-75. Gabriel, Judith. "Among the Norse Tribes: The Remarkable Account of Ibn Fadlan." *Aramco World* 50, no.6 (November–December 1999): 36–42.

Based on the records kept by Arab scholars, the most meticulous being penned by the ninth-century scholar, Ibn Fadlan, the article presents a cultural synopsis of the Vikings' network of trade routes from Scandinavia and the Baltic across European Russia to the Muslim Abbasid and Samanid Empires. Trading in silver was the commercial goal which fueled the Viking expansion during the ninth and tenth centuries; Muslim traders paid for the Norse wares (various types of furs primarily) with silver coins, which the Vikings coveted. The article argues that "the Scandinavian traders found an emporium beyond their wildest dreams," but for "the Arabs of Baghdad, the presence of the Norsemen probably did not come as much of a surprise, for the Arabs were long accustomed to meeting people from different cultures and civilizations" (p.37). Further, "Abbasid historians and caliphal envoys put to paper eyewitness accounts of the roving Scandinavians, leaving a historical legacy that is shedding new light both on Viking history and on a little-known chapter of early Islamic history" (p.37). For the Arabs, the "Vikings" were the ethnonym *Rus*, perhaps from the original *Ruotsi* for Sweden, also the source of the modern name of Russia.

The author suggests that "in western Europe, journal entries about Viking raids were often penned by monks and priests whose interests lay in painting them in the darkest, most savage colors. But in the East, the story was different. There the Rus were primarily explorers, colonizers, and tradesmen, and although they were well-armed, Muslim accounts describe them as "merchant-warriors whose primary business was trade" (p.38).

A-76. Lunde, Paul. "The Middle East and the Age of Discovery." *Aramco World* 43, no.3 (May–June 1992): 2–64.

This special issue of the magazine is devoted to the historic linkages of the early Arab-Islamic civilization with various aspects of the Age of Discovery. There are nine essays, each written by historian and Arabist, Paul Lunde. The following statement introduces the essays: "It was, of course, from Portugal and Spain, and particularly from Seville, that the voyages of the westward Age of Discovery set out, but the intellectual spark that set off those world-changing ventures had been kindled long before and far to the east of the Iberian Peninsula. French economist and historian Jacques Attali, in his provocative book *1492*, describes that year as the beginning of the modern era, and so it was. But the hinge on which history turned was forged by the technical and philosophical achievements of the Muslim civilizations of previous centuries. This issue is about those achievements and their effects as the new era swung open—as well as about the Middle East's widening view of the world" (p.1).

The essays are: (1) Voyages of the Mind, (2) Pillars of Hercules, Sea of Darkness: The Eternal Isles, Al-Farghani and the "Short Degree," (3) Piri Reis and the Columbus Map, (4) A Muslim History of the New World, (5) American Silver, Ottoman Decline, (6) Muslims and Muslim Technology in the New World, (7) Ponce De Leon and an Arab Legend, (8) New World Foods, Old World Diet: Questionable Origins, (9) The New World through Arab Eyes.

Each essay contains several pictures and maps as well as references.

A-77. Nadvi, S. Sulaiman. "Arab Navigation, Part I" (three-part essay). *Islamic Culture* (Hyderabad, India) 15 (October 1941): 435–448.

Surrounded by water in three directions and barrenness of desert elsewhere, Arabs have been known for their commercial enterprises and travels by land and water, even before the birth of Christ. This three-part essay is concerned with the navigation history and innovations of the Arabs.

This first part provides information on Arab navigation from three sources: old Arabic lexicons, pre-Islamic poetry, and religious books of the pagan Arabs. Numerous terms are noted for navigation, sea voyages, boats, ships, etc., including some foreign words derived from naval contacts with other regions. Also identified are Arabic words in European languages (Arabic *amir-al-bahr:* French *Amiral,* English *Admiral,* etc.). Also words from pre-Islamic Arab poetry are mentioned. Further, the Qur'an provides references to ships, boats, and seas in its verses (for example, the deluge of Noah is narrated); there are similar references in the Torah and the Bible. Then during the reign of Caliph Omar, a canal was dug from the River Nile to the Red Sea for naval trade between Egypt and Arabia.

A-78. Nadvi, S. Sulaiman. "Arab Navigation, Part II" (three-part essay). *Islamic Culture* (Hyderabad, India) 16 (April 1942): 181–198.

This second part of the three-part essay discusses the geography of oceans and seas, which were once thought to be "separate and different." The fact that they together represent one community of waters, surrounding various countries, was a great discovery, apparently by an eighth-century Arab. Other Muslim scholars provide descriptions of various coastal areas in different countries. However, "The brightest picture of oceans has been drawn by Abu'l-Fida (d. 725 AH), and Ibn Khaldun (d. 808 AH) even excels in his descriptions" (p.184). Relying on the 12th-century Cordovan Al-Idrisi's geography, Ibn Khaldun described the length and the distance of the Red Sea more accurately than found in *Ptolemy's* geography. Similar discussions are provided concerning the Bering Sea, the islands of the Atlantic Ocean, the islands of the Chinese Sea, the Philippines, Australia, and Madagascar. The author states that "Vasco de Gama reached India with the help of an Arab (Moor) sailor," a fact corroborated also by the Portuguese and Arab authorities (p.194).

The last section of this part discusses various types of navigational equipment and implements developed by the Arabs for facilitating travel, including maps, compasses, lighthouses, minarets, long bars, etc. As the knowledge of astronomy developed and astrolabes became available, "Arab navigation had become a science in the tenth century A.D., the mathematicians pointing out direction by latitude, longitude, and the stars" (p.197).

A-79. Nadvi, S. Sulaiman. "Arab Navigation, Part III" (three-part essay). *Islamic Culture* (Hyderabad, India) 17 (January 1943): 72–86.

This final part of the three-part essay begins with a discussion of "nautical" activities during early Islam—shipbuilding, canal digging, naval expeditions, etc., during the Umayyad period. During the Abbasid caliphate, the rivers Tigris and Euphrates and the Persian Gulf facilitated seaborne trade and communications to the East, and Baghdad became a major trading link with every part of the world. Similarly, ports such as Basra and Siraf became prominent, and Arab ships sailed to India and China. There were other locations, such as Aden, Suhar, Shihr, Kaish, Bahrain, Hurmuz, and Jedda. There is discussion of various navigational routes to the East, with descriptions of cultural contacts en route; similarly, with respect to the African coasts and the Mediterranean sea.

There is also discussion of ocean-trading activities, shipbuilding, and harbors in Arab Sicily, as well as the various harbors of Islamic Spain. And, the author mentions, "It may be strange to hear now that just as the origin of Gibraltar is Jabl-al-Tariq, so the origin of the famous French port Marseilles is *Marsa Ali*, meaning the port of Ali. This name is found in Idrisi's geography" (p.86).

A-80. Tolmacheva, Marina. "Bertius and al-Idrisi: An Experiment in Orientalist Cartography." *Terrae Incognitae* 28 (1996): 36–45.

The paper discusses the unusual case of a 17th-century French scholar, Pierre Bertius (1565–1629), who developed a global map, representing the three continents of Europe, Asia, and Africa. The author points out, however, that "not noted in the literature, this undated rectangular map, drafted in black on a white sheet of paper 47 x 64 cm., represents Europe, Asia, and Africa according to the unique system of the Arabo-Islamic geographer al-Idrisi, the *Geographus Nubiensis* of the Bertius title" (p.36). This was the Latin translation of 12th-century al-Idrisi's *Kitab nuzhat al-mushtaq* (commonly referred to as "Geography"), composed at the Norman court of Sicily; this was the first Arabic geographical work to be printed in Europe in 1592.

The author argues, with considerable documentary evidence, that the Bertius reconstruction is a replication of al-Idrisi's work, but without acknowledgement. Further, it is pointed out that "unquestionably, Bertius must have seen some al-Idrisi maps to effect such a faithful reconstruction. The Bertius map is instantly recognizable as an Idrisi derivative, even without the helpful title crediting the Geographus Nubiensis" (p.40).

The author concludes: "But the fact that selective borrowing, or 'sampling' of al-Idrisi's data continued for almost a century after 1592 seems to indicate the great respect the humanists of modern Europe still felt for Islamic science" (p.45).

A-81. Tolmacheva, Marina. "Ibn Battuta on Women's Travel in the Dar al-Islam." Pages 119–140 in *Women and the Journey: The Female Travel Experience*, edited by Bonnie Frederick and Susan H. McLeod. Pullman, WA: Washington State University, 1993.

While "it may be difficult to imagine pre-modern women in the Abode of Islam leading a life not subject to strict confinement," the reality, especially when explored in historical perspective, is quite different. Further, "The Western stereotype of the heavily veiled, male-dominated Muslim female becomes overlaid and complicated by Western preconceptions concerning female travel" (p.119). However, "It is not difficult to discover in medieval sources evidence of physical mobility and travel by Islamic women or women residing in areas governed by Islamic law" (p.120). The author notes that "the attempt is not to plot out the geography of women's journeys, but rather to explore the range of women's spatial mobility. The effort is directed at exploring the historical patterns of medieval Muslim women's journeys and redefining our own notions of female travel" (p.122).

The article explores illustrations of women's travel from the testimony of the Arab traveler of North African origin, Ibn Battuta (1304–1377), known as the "greatest traveler of the Middle Ages," who traveled three times as far as Marco Polo. He left an extensive record of his excursions in Africa, Asia, and Europe (the English version of his book is commonly known as *Travels*). As a well-educated legal scholar, "very few of his remarks are openly critical or disparaging of women or of society's 'permissiveness' in regard to their social manner or mobility in public space," and his "tales are remarkably free of religious prejudice, although not of all Islamic sensibilities" (p.120–121). He discusses the attractions and dangers of travel for free and slave women at a time when the rulers of western Mongol Empire were undergoing Islamization and the Byzantine empire was in the last century of its existence. Also included are instances of Christian women traveling in Muslim lands and Muslim women traveling in Christian Europe.

A-82. Tolmacheva, Marina. "The Medieval Arabic Geographers and the Beginning of Modern Orientalism." *International Journal of Middle East Studies* 27, no.2 (1995): 141–156.

The essay begins with noting that while 19th–20th century European Orientalism is well documented, the study of earlier Orientalism has been neglected. The paper focuses "on the early Orientalist efforts in the West, which preceded the establishment of formal Oriental studies" (p.141). Further, while "as a field Orientalism has long had a strong awareness of geography," the concerted study of "Oriental geographical works dates only to mid-19th century. Nevertheless, Arab geography represents an important chapter in the emergence of European Orientalism at the turn of 17th century" (p.141). The author thus examines the "contribution that arose largely out of 'reappropriation' by Europe of the work of the most important Arab geographer al-Idrisi (12th century), whose book *Kitab nuzhat al-mushtaq* (commonly referred to as 'Geography'), composed at the Norman court of Sicily, became the first Arabic geographical work to be printed in Europe in 1592" (p.141–142).

This examination of the "reappropriation" is pursued by references to several writers in Italy and France who, while relying on al-Idrisi's work, tended to dismiss it "as inadequate and possessing 'merely historical interest'" (p.144). Among other things, the author points to a translation of al-Idrisi's book by the

Italian Bernardino Baldi in 1592, but it "never mentions the author's name" (p.145). Also, there is reference to a 17th-century French scholar, Pierre Bertius, who developed a map representing the "three continents of Europe, Asia, and Africa according to al-Idrisi's system" (p.146). He relied on *Geographus Nubiensis*, a 1619 Latin translation of al-Idrisi's book. However, there is no acknowledgement. The author points out, "Bertius must have seen al-Idrisi's maps to make such a faithful reconstruction, which is instantly recognizable as an Idrisi derivative, even without the title crediting the *Geographus Nubiensis*" (p.148).

A-83. Tolmacheva, Marina. "On the Arab System of Nautical Orientation." *Arabica* 27, no.2 (1980): 180–192.

The paper explores the astronomical theory and terminology of orientation by the stars, as used by the Arab navigators of the West Indian Oceans where weather and sea conditions were quite different from those on the Mediterranean. Relying on the 15th–16th-century nautical manuals of two prominent Arab explorers, Ahmad ibn Majid and Sulayman al-Mahri, the documents detail the sailing directions and rules of navigation and astronomical observation, as well as theoretical knowledge necessary for determining the course and location of the ships relevant to travels in the West Indian Oceans.

For this eastward travel, the Arab navigators also assimilated the Persian maritime practices. The author also notes that the "most important feature of this traditional system of navigation which distinguishes it from the modern methods now widely accepted by the Indian Ocean seamen was the use of stars (in preference to the sun) for all purposes of orientation, including measurement of latitude" (p.181). Further, the fact that "the techniques of navigation described therein remained in popular use until the present century is attested by European travelers, colonial servants and army officers, etc." (p.180–181).

A-84. Tolmacheva, Marina. "Ptolemaic Influence on Medieval Arab Geography: The Case Study of East Africa." Pages 125–141 in *Discovering New Worlds: Essays on Medieval Exploration and Imagination*, edited by Scott D. Westrem. New York and London: Garland Publishing, 1991.

Based on data relevant to the historical geography of East Africa, this essay is a reexamination of the Greek influence—Ptolemy's *Geography* in particular—on Arabic geography. In general, "maps which reappear in the West in the fifteenth century are commonly attributed to Ptolemy in part because they share the cartographic feature of medieval Arabic texts and maps" (p.126). However, the author argues that already in the ninth century, Al-Khorezmi had "corrected and augmented Ptolemy's data with new information then being obtained through scholarly efforts sponsored by the early Abbasids," and "this reworking of Ptolemy" becomes "dominant in later sources even where no other Greek influence is noticeable" (p.126–127).

The paper is a significant corrective to the more usual Eurocentric orientation of not only canonical medieval texts, but modern discussions of them as well. The essay emphasizes the element of rationality as an important component of early geographical thinking among medieval Arabic-Islamic thinkers.

f. Humanities

A-85. Dannenfeldt, K. "The Renaissance Humanists and the Knowledge of Arabic." *Studies in the Renaissance* 2 (1955): 96–117.

The paper explores the various factors that led to the study of Arabic language during the medieval centuries. After considerable early interest, "the language of Islam, a religion branded as a Christian heresy by the medieval Church, fell into discredit, though interest was revived in the eleventh and twelfth centuries with the transmission to Europe of Arabic science and philosophy in Latin translation" (p.96).

The author notes several contributing factors (also several names who learned Arabic are identified): the failure of the Crusades necessitated Arabic language for preaching, the acquisition of Arabic knowledge for the sake of translations, betterment of commercial, judicial, and international relations, etc. Also, several Spanish, German, French, Dutch, English, and Portuguese humanists are identified who learned the Arabic language. Numerous European universities where Arabic was taught are mentioned. The author concludes, "Some of those who learned Arabic were well aware of its value in opening up a vast body of excellent literature in many fields" (p.117).

A-86. Kraemer, Joel L. "Humanism in the Renaissance of Islam: A Preliminary Study." *Journal of the American Oriental Society* 104, no.1 (January–March 1984): 135–164.

The author notes that the "integration of alien cultural elements within a highly developed [Islamic] civilization was a process that proceeded through three discernible stages" (p.135). These were: (1) the fusion of Jewish–Christian materials with the substance of local Arab traditions, (2) the assimilation of "local administrative techniques, local practices, artistic forms and religious tenets under the arch of the new empire," (3) the integration of the "appanage of the 'Graeco-Arabic renaissance,' at the apogee of the Abbasid epoque, in the third/ninth and fourth/tenth centuries" (p.135).

It was during the third stage, the article notes, when "during the Renaissance of Islam that humanism unfolded in its luxuriant expression. This branch of humanism was essentially the offspring of the *humanitas* ideal which germinated in the period of Hellenism and Graeco-Roman antiquity" (p.135–136).

The article explores "the career of the *humanitas* ideal in antiquity, to survey scholarly opinion on its absorption in medieval Islam, and then to support the thesis that this ideal was creatively assimilated within the orbit of Islamic civilization" (p.136). Various dimensions of humanistic thought are identified and surveyed from several early Islamic scholars. The article ends with a quote from Aristotle's letter to his disciple, Alexander the Great, which reflects how the "notion of a world state was known in medieval Islam" at the time (p.164).

A-87. Smith, Wilfred Cantwell. "The True Meaning of Scripture: An Empirical Historian's Nonreductionist Interpretation of the Qur'an." *International Journal of Middle East Studies* 11 (1980): 487–505.

The author focuses on "one matter only: the meaning of scripture. Even that is a generic problem: the specific instance of the Qur'an may illuminate the universal issue—and may serve, I hope, for deepening our understanding globally" (p.488). The various interpretative principles, are not "convincing. All are beginning to be seen as idiosyncratic, and limited" (p.488). The author argues that "Muslims have held the Qur'an to be the word of God. One may not agree with them; but this hardly justifies one in dismissing that fact as not important, not relevant" (p.489).

Thus, the author argues, "If the prime fact about the Qur'an, in historical reality, escaped for a time the West's capacity to grasp and to digest—the fact of its having existed for thirteen centuries and more primarily as a scripture—the second historical fact about it did not escape the Western academic's notice: namely, it had been interpreted differently by different groups at different times. This fact was known and recognized. Yet it too was not really grasped, and certainly was not digested. Rather, it too tended to be dismissed" (p.495).

Further, the author suggests, "Muslims themselves have sensed in Western Islamic scholarship an hostility and antagonism, out to undermine their faith. I am not sure that they are not in part right in this. Quite possibly it could be shown, and one day perhaps will be shown, that the hostility of the West, Christian-and-Jewish on the one hand, secularist on the other, played some part in these attempts to break up their religious system, intellectually. Yet the matter is much more wide-ranging and deep-delving than that. Enlightenment rationality was founded, no doubt in significant part, on a critique of religion, so that Western academic mentality was for a good while inherently skewed against an intellectual understanding of human spiritual traditions, especially as institutionalized" (p.497).

Therefore, the author's essential "thesis would be this, which correlates with my general affirmation (recognition?) that the study of religion is the study of persons. The meaning of the Qur'an as scripture lies not in the text, but in the minds and hearts of Muslims. And this is not a fancy interpretation; it is a statement of observed facts" (p.504–505).

g. Social Sciences, General

A-88. Chejne, Anwar G. "Intellectual Revival in the Arab World: An Introduction." *Islamic Studies* 11, no.4 (December 1973): 410–437.

The article begins by noting the earlier achievements of Arab-Islamic civilization, which were "echoed and reproduced in the West," but, the author notes, "after a time something went wrong and the Arab people came to a standstill, even losing most of what they had at one time possessed" (p.410). Further, "This process of decline was taking place at a time when Europe was undergoing a chain reaction of social and intellectual revolutions without parallel in the history of mankind" (p.415).

The author reviews various developments during the 18th–19th centuries that represent "turning points" in stimulating an intellectual revival. As a result, "the Arab world has become a permanent host to many ideas and innovations which have affected the thinking and the way of life of the Arabic-speaking peoples" (p.416). Some of these events, elaborated in some detail, are: (1) Arab awakening due to the Napoleonic expedition to Egypt in 1798, (2) revival of Arabic literature via missionary contacts—despite their religious orientation—with the West, (3) introduction of the printing press, (4) reform movements, (5) nationalism.

The author notes further, that at the beginning of the First World War, Arab consciousness was strong and "they had a unity of purpose at the time and were psychologically ready to live in unity" (p.431). However, after the war, "one morning they woke up to find that their hopes had been destroyed, and their dream had come to nought. For the French and the British, with complete disregard of former pledges and the principle of self-determination as enunciated by President Wilson, divided Arab territories between themselves. Worse still, each one of those two powers divided her sphere of influence into small states creating a situation which became in the long run not only detrimental to an enlightened self-interest of the West, but to the Arabs who have been still suffering from its effects" (p.434). Thus, while "the Arabic-speaking peoples have made great strides, "they have not so far succeeded in integrating many ideas borrowed from the West into a definable whole, say, comparable to that achieved by their ancestors in medieval times. This may be explained in their not having been in full command of their affairs" (p.434).

A-89. Coulson, Noel J. "The Concept of Progress and Islam Law." Pages 74–92 in *Religion and Progress in Modern Asia*, edited by Robert N. Bellah. New York: The Free Press, 1965.

The article begins by postulating a major problem in contemporary Muslim countries, one that has its historical origins in classical Islam, in that "the classical Islam concept of law and its role in society constitutes a most formidable obstacle to progress," and thus, "the clash between the dictates of the rigid and static religious law and any impetus for change or progress that a society may experience poses for Islam a fundamental problem of principle" (p.74–75). Several Muslim countries have "sought the solution in a process that may be generally termed 'legal modernism'" (p.75). The article explores the efficacy of that solution by focusing on the case of major legal reform instituted in Tunisia in 1957: "the outright prohibition of polygamy, which represented a complete break with the legal tradition of some thirteen centuries" (p.76).

Among other things, the author suggests that scholars have recently "shown that the genesis of Islamic religious law lay in a complex process of historical growth intimately connected with current social conditions and extending over the first three centuries of Islam" (p.76). He argues that there was "wide scope for the use of reason—or *ijtihad*, as it came to be called," which allowed for the influence of particular social conditions (p.77). However, such historical evolution was foreclosed by the "process of ossification" induced by "the principle of *ijma*, the consensus of the legal scholars" (p.82).

Thus, "There was no longer any need or scope for *ijtihad*, and ultimately this attitude was expressed as an infallible consensus of opinion that 'the door of *ijtihad* was closed.' Thenceforth all jurists were known as followers or imitators, bound by the doctrine called *taqlid* to follow the law expounded in the authoritative manuals" (p.83). The case of Tunisia suggests the "legal modernism has at least infused new life and movement into Shari'a law and freed its congealed arteries from a state fast approaching *rigor mortis*. The era of *taqlid*, or blind adherence to the doctrines of the medieval scholars, now appears as a protracted moratorium in Islamic legal history. Stagnation has given way to new vitality and potential for growth" (p.92).

A-90. Cox, Robert W. "Toward a Post-Hegemonic Conceptualization of World Order: Reflections on the Relevancy of Ibn Khaldun." Pages 144–173 in *Approaches to World Order*, edited by Robert W. Cox and Timothy J. Sinclair. Cambridge and New York: Cambridge University Press, 1996.

Defining global politics as a substitute for other expressions to minimize the ontological implications (i.e., assumptions about the basic structure and relationships of various entities), the author mentions that while embedded structures may survive over long periods, when new problems arise, old ontologies cannot accommodate and uncertainties arise. Thus, "One reason to reexamine the thought of Ibn Khaldun is that he confronted this kind of situation," as the Islamic civilization was in its decline at the time. Further, his thought "provides a point of access to the understanding of Islamic civilization; and Islamic civilization is asserting its presence in the shaping of any future world order. There are also some reasons that derive from analogies between Ibn Khaldun's times and our own. He enables us to examine a differently constituted mind confronted with similar problems to those we now face and what factors shaped his understanding of and response to those problems" (p.157).

After discussing other recent "revisionistic" ontologies, the author describes the "political ontology" of medieval Islam. Further, in discussing Ibn Khaldun's world-history analysis, he notes, "The enquiry was directed, not to individual historical actions, but to collective human action in history," in which, while "prophecy played a critical role," it "is not a sufficient cause. It is inoperative in the absence of *asabiya*" (p.162). This concept, meaning "group feeling or solidarity," is similar to Machiavelli's *virtu*. And here the political role of religion, be it Islam or another, is critical, and "Ibn Khaldun could remain a devout Muslim while being pessimistic about the prospects of the Islamic world" (p.165).

The author concludes with questions: "Can there be distinct, thriving macrosocieties, each with its own solidarity, each pursuing a distinct *telos*, which could coexist through a supra-intersubjectivity? Or is the only model of the future one in which differences become absorbed into a new unity, a new global hegemony, perhaps the creation of a new global Mahdi? Ibn Khaldun does not answer, but perhaps his skepticism concerning the coming of a Mahdi and his apparent preference for action at the level of local societies can give us a clue" (p.168).

A-91. al-Hibri, Azzizah Y. "Islamic Constitutionalism and the Concept of Democracy." *Case Western Reserve Journal of International Law* 24, no.1 (Winter 1992): 1–27.

This article contributes to the debate among Muslims and non-Muslims about the possibilities of introducing democratic changes among Arab-Islamic countries. It analyzes Islamic constitutionalism's position on democratic governance, without necessarily suggesting that "Western democratic principles provide the ultimate criteria in determining the democratic character of alternative systems of government" (p.1).

The article begins with a brief historical overview of Islamic law, including its various sources, as the foundation for the rest of the discussion. Then, the Islamic system of government is analyzed from the standpoint of two principles: (1) will of the people as the basis of the authority of the government, and (2) the principle of separate of powers. After discussing the connections between the Western democratic principles (specifically the "will of the people" principle) from an Islamic perspective, the author analyzes the "compatibility of divine law with a democratic form of government." Further, it is suggested that the Islamic jurisprudence and other sources leave the system of government for "Muslims to develop in accordance with (i) the dictates of their own epoch, customs, and needs, and (ii) the few basic but flexible and democratic divine rules" (p.25). Moreover, the author argues, the principle of *shura* (consultation), "combined with the supremacy of Islamic law and the fact that the interpretation of such law rests with the *mujtahids* points to a *de facto* if not *de jure* separation of powers" (p.27).

A-92. Rahman, Fazlur. "Islam: Legacy and Contemporary Challenge." *Islamic Studies* 19, no.4 (Winter 1980): 235–246.

The article begins with the premise that "Islam arose in the early seventh century Mecca as a response to certain spiritual-moral and social problems," and, further, there is evidence in the Qur'an that the two, monotheism and humanitarianism, i.e., human egalitarianism—were organically linked from the beginning" (p.236). The constant interaction of these factors "is ideally the source of all Islamic dynamism," says the author (p.236). Thus, the individual must not only work toward constant reform, but also he "surrenders himself to God."

Referring to the fundamentalists of the 18th and 19th centuries, the author argues, they have deprived themselves of the earlier medieval legacy of Islam's emphasis on forward-looking *ijtihad*. They are "not trained scholars of Islam; in fact, a vast majority of them are not at all scholars of Islam in any sense of the word" (p.246). Such fundamentalism is likely to be a "very transitory phenomenon and will be replaced either by Modernism or some form of Secularism," says the author (p.246). The likely scenario is, according to the author, "some kind of neo-modernism" (p.246).

A-93. Rahman, Fazlur. "The Status of the Individual in Islam." Pages 217–225 in *The Status of the Individual in East and West*, edited by Charles A. Moor (with assistance from Aldyth V. Morris). Honolulu, HI: University of Hawaii Press, 1968.

Contrary to the general belief among non-Muslims (and even many Muslims) that Islam as a religion emphasizes the society rather than the individual, this essay argues that the "primary locus of responsibility in Islam is the individual" (p.217).

The author first identifies the status of the individual in Islam and then it attempts to place the individual in relation to society in its proper perspective in the religious teachings of Islam. It is argued that while Islam stresses the importance of the community and the society, it does not follow that the individual is secondary. Verses in the Qur'an are quoted to emphasize the point ("Man shall come to us alone as an individual" and "Every soul earns but for itself, and no soul shall bear the burden of another"). Historically, the author suggests, "From the twelfth century onward, when Sufism became the religion of the masses, the individualist trend became universal in Islam" (p.222). However, during more recent times, there are forces which suggest the supremacy of the society, but that is due to two transitory factors: collective social efforts to gain freedom for colonialism, and the emphasis on socioeconomic development in the post-colonial period. Once a certain level of development is reached, the author argues, "the individual will regain its true perspective" (p.224).

This paper also appeared in *Islamic Studies* 5, no.4 (December 1966): 319–330.

A-94. Samarrai, Alauddin. "The Idea of Fame in Medieval Arabic Literature and Its Renaissance Parallels." *Comparative Literature Studies* 16, no.4 (December 1979): 279–293.

Some scholars have argued that the "idea of fame," corresponding to the

Sciences/Humanities 383

"inward development of the individual," with a "tendency toward worldly fame and glory," was perfected in the Italian Renaissance, thus largely excluding any such notion during the earlier medieval centuries. This paper argues that not only "the European Middle Ages are not entirely lacking in examples which manifest" this idea, more importantly, there is "continuity of the idea of fame and glory in Arabic literature throughout the Middle Ages" (p.279–280). Further, "Some parallels in this regard between Arabic literature and the literature of the Italian Renaissance" are pointed out (p.280).

The paper then proceeds to develop evidence from various Arabic literary sources, relating to poetry, music, and literary traditions. Also noted is the tenth-century period of Spanish-Arab civilization, "the period of Hispano-Arabic scholarship and originality" (p.283). As for parallels, the author reproduces some poetry stanzas written by Italian poets, quite similar to those earlier written by Arab poets. Also, there were the troubadours, preserved in Italy, later transmitted to France and England, but originated from Islamic Spain.

The author concludes that "although the men of the Renaissance took as their model the ancient classics, the expression of the idea of fame and worldly glory was introduced in Europe in the later Middle Ages from the world of Islam" (p.291).

(II) SCIENCES

A-95. Aramco Services Company. "Science: The Islamic Legacy." *Aramco World Magazine* 33, no.3 (May–June 1982): 2–64.

This 62-page special issue of the magazine is devoted entirely to the scientific legacy of Islam. The editors state: "No one issue could possibly cover the full history of Islamic science, of course; the scientific achievements of the Gold Age of Islam are too numerous and too diverse. Nor is it easy to summarize the scientific revival in the Islamic world today, since it includes elements from technology as well as science and seems to be cropping up in most unexpected ways—and places—and since the data is too diffuse and too raw to evaluate. Instead, therefore, we have chosen to present highlights from history and samplings of present developments. We are fully aware they are neither complete nor comprehensive, but hope that they will suggest, nonetheless, the accomplishments of the past and the hopes of the future" (p.1).

There are six essays: (1) Science: The Islamic Legacy by Paul Lunde, (2) Science in the Golden Age by Paul Lunde, (3) The Book of Animals by Paul Lunde, (4) Science in Al-Andalus by Paul Lunde, (5) The Bodleian Remembers (Oxford University's Bodleian Library Collection of Arab Manuscripts) by Charis Waddy, (6) Science in the Modern Age by Richard Hobson. Each essay is enriched by several illustrations, some copies of the originals.

A-96. Dawson, Christopher. "The Origins of the European Scientific Tradition: St. Thomas and Roger Bacon." *The Clergy Review* 2 (September 1930): 193–205.

The article traces the origins of scientific thought in the West and suggests that St. Thomas' synthesis provided the background against which others were able to develop scientific knowledge. The author says, "In reality St. Thomas was far less representative of medieval thought than is usually supposed. His philosophy is not the mature fruit of the old medieval tradition, but the first fruits of the new scientific thought" (p.193).

Throughout, there are references to the Arab-Islamic precursors; for example, St. Thomas grew up in an environment which provided "one of the main channels through which Arabic science reached the Christian world" (p.195). Further, he was educated at the University of Naples, where his teachers had "come under the influence of Averroistic thought" (p.195). Robert Grosseteste is mentioned as one of the most original minds of the 13th century who was influenced by "the Arabic works on optics and perspective of the great eleventh century mathematician, Ibn al-Haitam (Alhazen)" (p.199). And Roger Bacon is mentioned as one among many who was "responsible for the introduction of Arabic science into the West" (p.200). Further, while St. Thomas vindicated the "rights of reason and scientific enquiry against the theological absolutism," Bacon's intervention ensured "the independence of science from metaphysical absolutism of philosophers" (p.203). Thus ended "the period of dependence upon the Arabs" and emerged the "independent development of Western science" (p.205).

A-97. Gross, Charles G. "Ibn al-Haytham on Eye and Brain, Vision and Perception." *Bulletin of Islamic Medicine* 1 (1981): 309–312.

The article summarizes Ibn al-Haytham's (965–1040 AD) "major contributions to the physiology and psychology of vision"; he was "the major figure in the study of optics and vision in the middle ages," and his "influence was pervasive and usually recognized well into the 17th and 18th centuries" (p.309). It is suggested that this scholar's work represented "the first major advance in optics after Euclid and Ptolemy of Alexandria and in visual physiology after Galen" (p.309). Further, he "was a polymath, contributing to astronomy, mathematics, philosophy as well as a variety of other subjects" (p.309).

The author concludes that "this remarkable man deserves much further study," since "his insights into the psychology of perception and their influence remains an important and potentially fertile field of research" (p.311).

A-98. Hill, Donald R. "Mechanical Engineering in the Medieval Near East." *Scientific American* 264, no.5 (May 1991): 100–105.

The author argues that "the West is accustomed to seeing its own intellectual development as having been shaped, in the main, by internal factors. This view of history traces our heritage back from the Industrial Revolution to the Enlightenment and Renaissance" (p.100). The picture is incomplete, however, says the author; it ignores the intermediation of other civilizations, in particular Islam.

The subject of the article is "the technology of medieval Islam—the knowledge it preserved, the new ideas it contributed to the medieval world and the inventions by which it anticipated later developments" (p.100). Several developments are discussed: (1) utilitarian technology, such as water and waterpower technology, including different types of waterwheels/shipmills to grind corn and other seeds into flour, and (2) fine technology involving the use of delicate mechanisms and controls, such as water clocks, candle clocks, astronomical instruments, other devices for amusement and aesthetic pleasure (e.g., musical instruments), etc.

The author concludes that "the diffusion of the elements of machine technology from the lands of Islam to Europe may always remain partly conjectural. This should not in any way be allowed to devalue the achievements of the Muslim engineers, known and anonymous" (p.105).

A-99. Lindberg, David C. "Medieval Science and Its Religious Context." *OSIRIS* 10 (1995): 61–79.

The author disputes the common portrayal of "the Middle Ages as a period of catastrophic decline, a time of intellectual darkness and decadence" (p.61). Then, after discussing four "critical issues in the history of medieval science," the paper argues for the "proposition that the primary patron of scientific learning throughout the Middle Ages remained the church" (p.67). Referring to the "Thomist synthesis," the author disputes the claim that "the triumph of Christianity was the signal for the complete decadence of philosophy and science" (p.67).

It is argued, on the other hand, that "the condemnation of 219 propositions" in Paris in 1277 was an attack on entrenched Aristotelian natural philosophy, based on Averroes' (Ibn Rushd, 1126–1198) commentaries; and this phenomenon resulted in the eventual "birth certificate of modern science" (p.68). In discussing the medieval "encounter between Christianity and Science," the author discusses the "process by which Western scholars received, assimilated, criticized, modified, and extended the fruits of Greek and Muslim thought about nature; and the intellectual products of this process, expressed in lectures and texts" (p.71). This is how "scholars in Western Christendom learned how to do science—that is, how to think about nature—largely by imitating their Greek and Muslim predecessors" (p.71).

And in the 13th century, "Franciscan Roger Bacon devoted a scholarly lifetime to reclaiming pagan learning for the faith—that is, demonstrating that, purged of a few errors, Greek and Arabic science and mathematics could serve as the disciplined handmaidens of the church" (p.72). Later, the author says, instead of being a hostile observer of the classical tradition, the Church became "a patron of Greek and Arabic natural philosophy," and various 13th–14th century Latin philosophers and theologians "tackled the problem of accommodating Greek and Arabic natural philosophy to Christian theology, *and* vice versa" (p.77).

A-100. Meyerhof, Max. "The 'Book of Treasure,' an Early Arabic Treatise on Medicine." *ISIS: Journal of the History of Science in Society* 14, no.43 (May 1930): 55–76.

This paper is about the 1920s discovery of a ninth-century Arabic manuscript on medicine in Cairo's Patriarchical Library, later translated into English. The manuscript title is "The Book of Treasure in the Science of Medicine" (*Kitab adh-Dhakhira fi Ilm al-Tibb*), written by Thabit Ibn Qurra (835–901 AD), a "polymathist" (i.e., "at the same time, physicist, mathematician, astronomer, physician, and translator from Greek and Syriac into Arabic") of Islamic civilization, as were many others. It is a collection that includes quotations from other Arab and Greek scholars with similar knowledge.

The author then briefly describes the contents of each of the 31 chapters of this 383-page volume. Some of the chapter titles are: skin-diseases of the head; diseases of skin; eye-diseases; apoplexy and paralysis; epilepsy; diseases of mouth and nose; diseases of the stomach; diseases of liver, spleen, kidneys, bladder, and male genitals and anus; female diseases and treatment of obesity; gout and sciatica; diseases of hand and feet; tumors; leprosy; wounds, contusions, and poison; small-pox, measles, and fainting; plague and local conditions that produce it; fractures; uses of milk; uses and abuses of wine; sexual relations. The book concludes with a chapter on the treatment of pollution.

The author ends with the note: "Scholars who intend to study the development of Greco–Arabic medicine will have to take into consideration" this book "as being one of the earliest Arabic medical books composed by one of the most eminent scientists of the Islamic world" (p.74). Also mentioned at the end is a long glossary of Arabic medical terms and their English language equivalents.

A-101. Moody, Ernest A. "Galileo and Avempace: The Dynamics of the Learning Tower Experiment." Part I, *Journal of the History of Ideas* 12, no.2 (April 1951): 163–193; Part II, *Journal of the History of Ideas* 12, no.3 (August 1951): 375–422.

This two-part paper is a fascinating study in the history of the evolution of ideas, including scientific ideas. The author refers to Galileo's (1564–1642) famous Leaning Tower Experiment (allegedly performed in 1589) as a "sheer myth," about which "we may be assured on the incontestable authority of Galileo himself that its physical meaning was totally different from that which is ascribed to it by the tradition of our physics books" (p.163). He explores, more closely than done so far, the question whether Galileo's Pisan dynamics, known as an alternative to Aristotle's dynamics, were "connected, either theoretically or historically, with the fourteenth tradition" (p.165).

The first part contains an analysis of Galileo's Pisan dynamics, as presented in his dialogue *De Motu*, and the author traces the roots to a medieval antecedant of the law of motion, later defended by Galileo, in a criticism of Aristotle by the Arab philosopher Avempace [Ibn Bajah, d. 1138] in the early 12th century. As for the second part, the influence of Avempace's dynamics (and that of Ibn Tufayl [d. 1185], Averroes [d. 1198], and others) in the Christian Middle Ages is traced, along with its relation to the mechanics of the 14th century, and to that of Galileo's Pisa period. The author provides extensive notes and references.

A-102. Omar, Saleh. "Ibn Al-Haytham's Theory of Knowledge and Its Significance for Later Science." *Arab Studies Quarterly* 1, no.1 (1979): 67–82.

That science or scientific method did not "explode" into being in 17th-century Europe is accepted among Western historians and philosophers. However, the author disputes the view that in the 13th century "the medieval Latin scholastics made certain crucial advances in the methodology of science over their Greek and Arab predecessors," which laid the foundation for modern science. Identifying such views with medievalists such as A.C. Crombie, the author mentions that "Arab influence looms large throughout Crombie's book" (p.68).

The article proceeds to establish the case by tracing the scientific works of pre-13th-century Arab-Islamic scientists like Ibn al-Haytham (Alhazen), al-Razi (Rhazes), and others. Focusing especially on Ibn al-Haytham, the question is asked, "Why is it that the rise of experimental science in the thirteenth and fourteenth centuries was associated almost exclusively with the work in optics by men who all were influenced by Alhazen's *Opticae*?" (p.68). Several Latin names, cited by Crombie, are mentioned.

Furthermore, the article associates the origins of the inductive method of science with Ibn al-Haytham, with examples from this scholar's writings. The author concludes that Crombie's claim, shared even by many Arab "modernizers," that scientific thought originated in the works of the medieval Latin writers "reflects a more pervasive Western prejudice which attempts to confine the intellectual origins of scientific thought within the geographic bounds of Western Europe" (p.81).

A-103. Rashed, Roshdi. "Science as a Western Phenomenon." *Fundamenta Scientiae* (Paris) 1 (1980): 7–21.

The author challenges the literary postulate that science, in its origins as well as in its classical modernity, is essentially Western; this premise, he argues, continues to condition contemporary scientific thinking. Citing mainly French historians (Renan, Duhem, Tannery, and others), he examines and challenges the historical validity of this premise and then counters it with pointing out the non-Western scientific contributions: science written in the early Arab-Islamic world.

As though being "outside history," the Arabic science is viewed, according to the author, as essentially consisting of a conservatory of Greek patrimony. "Even until our time, the names of Bacon, Descartes and Galileo (sometimes omitting the first, and, according to circumstances, adding a number of others), are cited as so many markers on the road to a revolution, return to Greek science and philosophy, or as so many stages in the resumption of this march which was interrupted by the centuries of decadence" (p.7).

In this literary history, it is argued that "the image given of Arabic science constitutes an excellent illustration of this approach: essentially it consists of a conservatory of Greek patrimony, transmitted intact or enriched by certain technical innovation to the legitimate heirs of ancient science" (p.8). The author discusses several disciplines which were developed as part of the Arabic science, with a detailed focus on the Arabic contributions to mathematics. He concludes with a plea for "restoring to the profession of the historian of science the objectivity required of it" (p.21). "In brief," the question is posed, though "without excessive optimism": "Hasn't the moment come to write history without recourse to the false evidence of which nationalistic cultural motivations are scarcely concealed?" (p.21).

A-104. Rubenstein, Rheta and Randy Schwartz. "Arabic from A (Algebra) to Z (Zero)." *Math Horizons* (September 1999): 16–18.

The article briefly traces the origins of modern mathematics with Arab scholars, particularly Muhammad ibn Musa al-Khowarizmi (family roots from Khowarizm, Uzbekistan) of ninth-century Baghdad. The authors trace the origin of this word to this scholar's name, so al-Khowarizmi was "translated into Latin as *algorizmi*, and eventually took the form 'algorithm' in English" (p.16). Further, "Much of what we now accept as arithmetic, algebra (from *al-jabr*, a mathematics book of this title written by al-Khowarizmi), and trigonometry was developed by Arab scientists" (p.16).

The article notes that while the Arabic numerals originated from the Hindus, the "Arabs were the first to use them systematically in arithmetic and by using ciphers the Arabs became the founders of the arithmetic of everyday life" (p.17). Additionally, the derivation of several common quantitative terms is traced to Arabic words—ream (*rizmah*), tariff (*ta'rif*), tare (*tarh*), carat (*qirat*), zero (*sifr*), and caliber/caliper (*qalib*).

The authors conclude: "We are indebted to the Arabs for learning and preserving so much mathematics and other aspects of culture from many parts of the world, and for developing and communicating knowledge to others. From 'algebra' to 'zero,' mathematical words are like valuable fossils, showing how our science and our history have developed" (p.18).

A-105. Sabra, A.I. "The Appropriation and Subsequent Naturalization of Greek Science in Medieval Islam: A Preliminary Statement." *History of Science* 25 (1987): 223–243.

The paper discusses various issues concerning the cultural transmission of knowledge from the Greeks to medieval Islam. The discussion is divided into four sections: appropriation and reception; the marginality thesis; the process of naturalization; and the problem of decline. The focus is the transmission of Greek science to medieval Islam, which "was an important event in the history of civilization; it had far-reaching consequences for the history of the classical heritage, for the development of Islamic thought and culture, and for the European Renaissance of the twelfth and later centuries" (p.224). Distinguishing between two extreme interpretative approaches, the author states that concerning Islamic science, *reductionism* interprets the Islamic scientists' achievements as merely a reflection (faded or altered) of Greeks mainly; and the *precursorism* reads the future into the past (p.223–224). And, a counter approach calls for exploring the "cultural context'" of transmission.

The author argues that "reception" suggests a passive, kinematic event, and this reinforces "the image of Islamic civilization as a receptacle or repository of Greek learning. This, however, was not quite what happened; the transmission of ancient science to Islam would be better characterized as an act of appropriation performed by the so-called receiver. Greek science was not thrust upon Muslim society any more than it was later upon Renaissance Europe" (p.225). Further, the author discusses what he calls the "marginality thesis," referring to some interpretations that "science and philosophy" was a "foreign object in the body of Islamic civilization" and that "scientific and philosophic activity" was subject to antagonism, with only marginal relevance to any central social concerns, and that only a few kept the Greek legacy alive (p.229). The author disputes this thesis and argues that in contrast, "what we see in the history of Islamic science is a process of assimilation ending in a complete naturalization of the imported sciences in Muslim soil" (p.236). And, despite that process, the decline of science in Islam occurred, among other things, "when the sciences came to be accepted and practiced only to the extent that they were legitimated by the instrumentalist view," identified with al-Ghazali (p.240).

A-106. Wasserstein, David J. "Greek Science in Islam: Islamic Scholars as Successors to the Greeks." *Hermathena* 147 (1998): 57–72.

The main purpose of the article is to analyze Claude Levi-Strauss' labeling of Islamic civilization as having affected Europe "with uncouth clumsiness," cutting the "more civilized world in two" (p.57). The author argues such views reflect "uninformed and prejudiced view of a culture that he [Levi-Strauss] clearly has not properly or adequately attempted to understand than to be describing a reality known to scholarship or to life" (p.57).

This is misreading of history, says the author, for Islam represents both change and continuity. Contacts with other civilizations, Byzantium in particular, "served to generate among Muslims of Arabic language scientific endeavors and achievements of independent worth and wide significance" (p.61). Further, "The medieval Western tradition depends as much on the Islamic study of Aristotle (particularly in the huge sections of Al-Farabi, Ibn Sina, and Ibn Rushd made available to the Schoolmen) as on the late Greek and Byzantine exposition of his thought" (p.67).

This scholarly continuity also meant change, "because the needs which all these people and activities represent were in fact different" and "Islam clearly was a society which began with such initiative, though later, perhaps like Byzantium, it appeared to retire into encyclopaedism" (p.68). Further, by the time Constantinople fell to Ottomans in 1453, "both Greek learning and that of the Islamic world, in Arabic or in Hebrew dress, were contributing their share to developments in countries at the other end of the Mediterranean" (p.70).

(B) Islam–West Linkages

A-107. Alonso, Manuel Alonso. "Influencia de Algazel en el Mundo Latino" ("The Influence of Algazel in the Latin World"). *Al-Andalus* 23 (1958): 371–380.

Written on the occasion of the 900th anniversary of Al-Ghazali's (1058–1111) birth, the article states, "The Latin world owes much to the *Maqasid al-Falasifa* of Al-Ghazali, a notable work that infiltrated as ripened fruit in all of the scholastic and scientific spheres of the thirteen and fourteenth centuries and continues so, perhaps unwittingly, in the heritage of that medieval science" (p.371).

The author then documents the integration of Al-Ghazali's thought in the writings of numerous Latin scholars; he even provides a quotation from Domingo Gundislavo that parallels one from Al-Ghazali. More than 45 Latin names (St. Thomas Aquinas, Robert Grosseteste, Raymund Martin, Raymund Lull, Duns Scotus, and others) are identified and for each the author mentions the number of times the particular Latin scholar has cited the authority of Al-Ghazali's ideas; the author says this is the minimum count. Also, there is reference to several other anonymous Latin scholars who borrowed similarly.

A-108. Archer, John C. "Our Debt to the Moslem Arab." *The Moslem World* 24, no.3 (July 1939): 248–254.

Noting the tendency among many to preserve the "native" and reject the "foreign," the article presents an exposition of "our own indebtedness" to the Islamic civilization. The author states, "The Christian and the Moslem have yet to reach a constructive understanding by means of mutually sympathetic and objective study" (p.248).

The article is divided into two sections. The first section discusses the emergence of Islam as an "original" religion and as a "definite contribution of the Arabs," the notion of Unity of God, the importance of the Arabic language, the development of Islamic thought in various disciplines, various inventions, the origins of the dialectic method, etc. The second section discusses the influence of the Islamic world on the West, which "profited more from the Arab's transmission of culture than his originality" and "through the instrumentality of 'enemies' of Christendom came new cultural forms of art, architecture, science, literature and philosophy" (p.257).

The author explores several aspects of these connections. In conclusion, he says, "We may then, as Westerners and Christians, continue, with profit to many of us and justice to some others, our review and reappraisal of the Moslem's, especially the Arab's, role in western history" (p.264).

A-109. Baldwin, Marshall W. "Western Attitudes Toward Islam." *The Catholic Historical Review* 27, no.4 (January 1942): 403–411.

The paper is the author's presidential address at the American Catholic Historical Association (December 1941) and the task is "to contribute from a study of past events some thoughts and ideas significant to a situation which is still with us" (p.404). The "situation" is the "menace of a hostile Islamic world," even though "we have long since ceased to regard Islam as a danger to our civilization" (p.403). However, the author notes, "In one important respect, the relations between the Christian and Mohammedan worlds have remained constant. From the beginning of Mohammadenism to our own day, Islam has proved surprisingly resistant to missionary efforts" (p.403).

While noting "Europe's great cultural debt to Islam," the author's main purpose "is to examine the reactions of western Christendom to the presence of Islam, to explain if possible the measures devised to meet this ever present problem, and to show how those measures reflected the organic character of European society" (p.404). The author discusses the role of the Crusades as a "just war," even though it represented a fusion of "the warlike spirit with the Christian ideal" (p.407). Nonetheless, secularization of Christendom weakened the religious zeal and resulted in the failure of the Crusades. There were, however, "a few missionaries who insisted on the incompatibility of the two methods: force and persuasion" (p.410). And some early 19th-century pundits were concerned about "the influence of the Crusades upon the civil liberties of the peoples of Europe"; and such are "still slogans to conjure with. But they reveal little preoccupation with Islam as a religion and culture competing with that of Europe" (p.411).

The author states, "The medieval missionaries to the Muslims met with frustrations and martyrdom" and "modern missionaries" continue to encounter similar problems. Then the author concludes: "The historian of the crusades may assert that the age of the holy war is past. The student of missions, on the other hand, must remind us that the problem of Islam is still very much with us" (p.411).

A-110. Beckingham, C.F. "Misconceptions of Islam: Medieval and Modern." *Journal of Royal Society of Arts* 126 (September 1976): 606–611.

The article begins, "For several reasons it is surprising that Islam should have been so often and so seriously misunderstood in Europe," even though, as the youngest of the great religions, "Islam emerged in the full light of history" (p.606). Yet, the author argues, "In spite of the long and close contacts with Europe, and especially with the most sophisticated part of Europe, the Byzantine Empire, we find from the earliest times misrepresentations of the grossest kind, even among men of unquestionable intellect, intelligence and integrity" (p.606).

The author cites numerous examples of medieval and modern distortions and "extraordinary mistranslations." During the ninth century, the first Sura of the Qur'an ("Read! In the name of thy Lord who created man from clots of blood"), for example, was distorted to suggest "that Muhammad had taught that God had created man from a leach or lamprey" (p.607). And the God of Islam is translated as "made of beaten metal," represented as a "metal idol." Also, St. John of Damascus, "one of the great theologians of the Orthodox Church," translated the Arabic *Allahu Akbar* ("God is most great") as *Alla wa Koubar* and said that Koubar meant Aphrodite's star, the planet Venus; thus he associated the black stone of Ka'aba as the "carved head of Aphrodite" (p.607). Further, in the *Chanson de Roland* and other works of fiction, strange names are given to the "idols supposedly worshiped by Muslims," such as "Apollin, Termagant, Manduquin and the rest" (p.607). Other distortions presented Islam as requiring the killing of "anyone who does not believe in it, a particularly absurd allegation about a religion which from the first allocated a secure if subordinate status in society to the adherents of other revealed religions" (p.608).

Later, even eminent 20th-century scholars such as Sir William Muir attributed "bloodshed and tyranny" and "lack of progress of the Muslim peoples" to Islamic laws and institutions, but those scholars were "perhaps less astonishing, if no less disgusting, to the contemporaries of Hitler and Stalin than they were to a Victorian official. There were, however, important aspects of Muslim government which, it seems to me, men like Muir did not perceive. Very few Europeans until quite recently understood the extent to which the *shari'a*, the religious law of Islam, restricted the authority of the ruler" (p.609).

The author concludes by criticizing the view "commonly held in the last century that Islam was an admixture of degraded pagan Arab notions and 'higher' concepts which Muhammad had derived from Jews and Christians whom he had met" (p.611).

A-111. Benz, Ernst. "The Islamic Culture as Mediator of the Greek Philosophy to Europe." *Islamic Culture* (Lahore, Pakistan) 35 (1961): 147–165.

The paper discusses the "very strong influence of Islamic culture upon the Christian philosophy and theology in Europe," the former having served as a "mediator of the great philosophical tradition of the classical antiquity" (p.147). That tradition was considered as "pagan and useless for the purpose of Christian religion" (p.147). The Islamic culture, on the other hand, "accepted and preserved just this classical tradition which was suppressed by the Christian church, and developed it in a very original and creative manner" (p.147). This phenomenon is the theme of the paper.

The discussion is divided into three major sections: (1) emigration of the classical philosophy from the West to the East, (2) the "return of this classical philosophical heritage through the Islamic philosophers from the East to the extreme West in Spain," (3) "the history of the translations of Aristotle in the 12th to 14th century as the basis of the development of the Christian theology, philosophy and sciences of the medieval scholastic" (p.148).

The author concludes that instead of engaging into polemics of the past, "we should, instead, enter into a further discussion of common sources as a fruitful method to abolish gradually the mass of misunderstandings, traditional polemics and prejudices of the former centuries which have hindered till today that better mutual understanding which alone can be the basis of a new spiritual, ethical and cultural cooperation in our modern world in all freedom of mutual criticism and mutual respect" (p.165).

A-112. Berggren, J.L. "Islamic Acquisition of the Foreign Sciences: A Cultural Perspective." *American Journal of Islamic Social Sciences* 9 (1992): 310–324.

The paper's main focus is to assess the sociocultural context in which the Islamic civilization was receptive—and the Byzantine Empire was not—to the classical Greek scientific tradition. The author's premise is that "no account of the transmission of scientific knowledge can be complete if it does not recognize that it is, at root, an account of the activities of the *Homo sapiens* in a social context" (p.310).

According to the author, four factors affected Islamic assimilation of that knowledge: (1) religion as a unifying force, (2) Arabic language, (3) diversity in unity, given the widespread tolerance of other religions, (4) variety within the larger unity, in terms of smaller kingdoms that encouraged scientific competition. Further, knowledge was divided into two categories: "(1) the religious, traditional, or Arabic sciences, and (2) the sciences of the ancients, the philosophical sciences, or the foreign sciences" (p.314). This division was also reflected in the educational system.

The author concludes that "Muslim scientists were responding to the needs, concerns, and criticism of a civilization profoundly different from that of classical Greece and therefore directed, as they saw fit, the growth of their science in certain directions and away from others" (p.324).

A-113. Burns, Robert I. "Christian–Islamic Confrontation in the West: The Thirteenth Century Dream of Conversion." *American Historical Review* 76 (1971): 1386–1412; 1432–1434.

This long essay not only provides a detailed account of early Christian–Islamic relations, but also conveys insights for our contemporary world. The Crusaders entertained some hope of converting enemy Muslims, but "as the twelfth century wore on, dissent against armed crusading grew"; and there were echoes "with references to Muslims [being] converted singly and en masse, and the first stirrings of a literary and intellectual rapproachment with Islam made themselves felt" (p.1386). The author provides extremely well-documented history of this approach with scores of related notes and references.

The author narrates "the Christian fever for converting Muslims," in various regions of reconquered Spain and in North Africa. In the 13th century, he suggests, "the overall strategy of Christendom underwent modification; the battle now was not only military but doctrinal, through a dialogue of controversy" (p.1387). Pope Innocent III believed "the world might end around 1284, envisioned a final crusade effort in East and West to prepare the mass conversion of both Jews and Muslims" (p.1390). But, "Crusading alone was ineffective against Muslims and must be supplemented by an army of learned men; these men wise in all knowledge should preach by persuasion" (p.1391). The medieval missionary had the option of "five tactics: secret conversions, via commercial, chaplain, or other contacts; fanatic confrontation, designed to precipitate a dramatic response; infiltration via metaphysical dialogue with whatever Islamic savants came to hand; diplomatic maneuvers toward winning a potentate, in whose footsteps many subjects could drift into Christianity; or finally, cracking the military carapace by conquest, to expose an Islamic region to public proselytism" (p.1395). Numerous medieval scholastics, monks, and priests are identified (including their polemical writings): St. Francis, Raymund Lull, Raymund Martin, Roger Bacon, and others.

In conclusion, the author mentions that these medieval polemicists "never really entered the Islamic mind as sympathetic ecumenists" and "they assumed that the Muslim intellectual at bottom could hardly take the dogmas of Islam seriously" (p.1433). Further, "As time passed the dream of conversion flickered, fitfully dimmed, and died" (p.1434). It rested on shallow foundation and "aggressive optimism," the author argues. He notes: "By the end of the century, though Christendom had put on an armor of inquisition and was entering an era of punitive harshness, the memory of the century-long effort remained quiescent in mendicant tradition" (p.1434).

A-114. Butler, Pierce. "Fifteenth Century Editions of Arabic Authors in Latin Translation." Pages 63–71 in *Macdonald Presentation Volume: A Tribute to Duncan Black Macdonald.* Bridgeport, NY: Books for Libraries Press, 1933.

"No historical student of the culture of western Europe can ever reconstruct for himself the intellectual values of the later Middle Ages unless he possesses a vivid awareness of Islam looming in the background," the author begins (p.63). The article makes several similar observations.

The author then proceeds with providing a "bibliographical history of the late fifteenth century [that] might be used for evidence of the influence of Arabic books on the scholarship of Europe" (p.65). There is a list of numerous 15th-century editions of translations from the Arabic and it is noted that these were of "established reputation and formed a part of traditional scholarship [for] preceding generations" (p.65). Various fields and the Latinized names of relevant Arab scholars are identified; three fields are covered—astrology, philosophy, and medicine. Also, the author provides three historic plates, showing a 1514 Arabic script of a Qur'anic verse (erroneously written), Arabic alphabets and their Latin equivalents, and 228 Arabic words, in transliteration, with their Latin equivalents.

A-115. Darling, Linda T. "Rethinking Europe and the Islamic World in the Age of Exploration." *Journal of Early Modern History* 2, no.3 (1998): 2230–2246.

The article begins: "Our image of early modern Europe is one of religious wars, intellectual and scientific discoveries, and global explorations that 'circumvented' the Islamic world and left it behind in the dust of progress. The Islamic world in the same period is pictured as stagnant and declining, unable or unwilling to adopt technologies or profit from discoveries made by a dynamic Europe. However, the idea of eastern mobility reflects not the reality of the east but the persistence of ancient western stereotypes" (p.223). This essay explores such stereotypes, and then, based on recent research, challenges them.

Although the Islamic world was once central to the evolution of the European identity, the author argues, encounters with the New World accompanied a disregard for that world; thus, the Islamic world ceased to be studied, the pervasive assumption being that nothing happened there and that internal stagnation and inadequacy of Islam led to that civilization's decline. This thesis is challenged. Among other things, says the author, "it was the development of capitalism, not the decay of the east, that finally allowed the Europeans, particular the British, to emerge into global predominance" (p.241). Further, "The idea that the west is eternally opposed to the east, that the east stood still while the west progressed, should be related to the horse-and-buggy era as something once believed but no longer credible, like the flat earth, spontaneous generation, or the medical use of leeches" (p.246).

A-116. Dennett, Daniel C., Jr. "Pirenne and Muhammad." *Speculum: A Journal of Medieval Studies* 23, no.2 (April 1948): 165–190.

This article, after delineating the Pirenne thesis, disputes the basis of this thesis, although not necessarily its conclusion. Briefly, the thesis argued that the Muslim expansion during the seventh century placed two hostile civilizations on the Mediterranean and thus "the hitherto centre of Christian frontier and the Mediterranean unit was shattered" (p.166). In this exploration, he states, among other things the "Muslims themselves were more tolerant and placed few obstacles in the path of Christian traders who came to their territory" (p.168).

The author concludes, "There is no evidence to prove that the Arabs either desired to close, or actually did close the Mediterranean to the commerce of the West either in the seventh or eighth centuries. Islam was hostile to Christianity as a rival, not as a completely alien faith, and the Muslims were invariably more tolerant than Christians" (p.189). Further, "The crude Western barbarians were not able to develop—indeed, they were ignorant to preserve the state and the culture they took by conquest, while the Arabs on the contrary not only preserved what they took but created from it a culture which the world had not known for centuries, and which was not to be equaled for centuries more" (p.189–190).

A-117. Druart, Therese-Anne. "Medieval Islamic Thought and the 'What Is X?' Question." *American Catholic Philosophical Quarterly* 73, no.1 (Winter 1999): 1–8.

Socrates raised this question and then the same question is raised with respect to Medieval Islamic Thought—and it is fraught with some complications, for although most were Muslims, there were also Christian and Jews writing in Arabic; and there were not only philosophers but theologians as well. The question relates to what is Islamic or Arabic philosophy? This issue of the journal explores this question and provides some suggestions to get acquainted with the field.

The author describes "the breadth and philosophical sophistication of the Islamic philosophers as well as the liveliness of contemporary scholarly debates in the field. Some papers show the link between Greek, Arabic, and Medieval Latin philosophy but all highlight the originality and intrinsic philosophical worth of Islamic philosophy" (p.2). It is noted that the influence of Islamic philosophy on the West is not history; some have claimed that "Kant's transcendental subject constitutes a revival of Averroism" (p.3). This task is pursued by providing "some guidelines, using in particular material generally not well-known in philosophical or Medievalist circles and often not mentioned in the usual sources of information" (p.3). Numerous references are listed under the following titles: histories of Islamic philosophy; bibliographies; sourcebooks; and important basic books, collective works, journal issues, and recent studies.

The author concludes with this note: "May these far from exhaustive guidelines incite the reader to explore some themes and texts in Medieval Islamic philosophy and, therefore, to have some ground to suggest some way of answering the 'what is *Medieval Islamic Philosophy*?' question" (p.8).

A-118. Fakahani, Suzan J. "Islamic Influences on Emerson's Thought: The Fascination of a Nineteenth Century American Writer." *Journal of Muslim Minority Affairs* 18, no.2 (1998): 291–303.

Ralph Waldo Emerson (1803–1882) was one of several American writers during the 19th century who were fascinated by the Muslim literature. Influenced by what he found in this literature, Emerson "sprinkled his writings with abundant quotations and references to Islamic sources and Muslim personalities and used them to express his own thoughts" (p.291).

This paper documents several dimensions and sources of this influence upon Emerson, who was once an ordained minister. He journeyed to Europe where he befriended Thomas Carlyle whose admiration of Muhammed impressed Emerson. He used references to "Islamic metaphysics in a unique manner to express his own mood, and spiritual experiences. He turned to them as a means of guidance and inspiration" (p.292). Among the various sources, he read numerous articles and books on Islamic culture and values, some translations of the originals. Also, he read the works of various Muslim Persian poets. Finding Islam as the "natural religion," he quotes from the Qur'an in his *The Representative Man*. He views "Islamic simplicity as the key to the soundness of body and soul whereas extravagant Western lifestyle is a hindrance" (p.298).

The author concludes, "Emerson found Islam congenial, for it represented and confirmed his own ideas" (p.301).

A-119. Forget, J. "De l'influence de la philosophie arabe sur la philosophie scholastique." *Revue Neo-Scholastique* 4, no.3665 (October 1894): 385–410.

The article begins with a brief documentation as to the influence of Arab-Islamic scholarship on scholastic philosophy. While such influence had been generally recognized up to the 17th century, later literature raised some questions. These issues are explored further and the author reviews the literature on the Greek heritage and its assimilation in the Islamic world. He mentions, however, that the Christians initiated the translations (although Caliph al-Mamoon, who established the House of Wisdom in 813 in Baghdad, is identified as the sponsor).

While the author discusses the Arab-Islamic linkages and influences, there is reluctant acknowledgment. Numerous Arab-Islamic philosophers and some of the content of their writings are mentioned, but their theories were of "foreign origins," not natural product of the Arab genius. Numerous translators and texts are also identified.

A-120. Gabrieli, Francisco. "Frederick II and Moslem Culture." *East and West* 9 (1958): 53–61.

The article explores the influence of Islamic culture upon Frederick II, the 12th-century emperor of Norman Sicily, which was part of the Islamic empire for about 200 years. Born among Muslims, Frederick II grew up in Sicily, where "he imbibed the first elements of his intellectual personality and culture" (p.53). While he liquidated Islam in Sicily, he was attracted to the Arab-Islamic culture and was indifferent toward Papacy and Christianity. Among the various avenues, the Crusades gave him ample opportunities to interact with and learn from the Arabs.

The author argues that "the central point of his relations with Moslem culture [was] in its purely scientific and intellectual aspects" (p.58). His interests centered in two areas: technical attainments of the Arabs and acquisition of the ancient Greek knowledge through the Arabs. At the end, the author notes the major role that the "Oriental [Islamic] civilization played in Frederick's life from, one may truly say, cradle to the grave" (p.61).

A-121. Gaudiosi, Monica. "Comment: The Influence of the Islamic Law of *Waqf* on the Development of the Trust in England—The Case of Merton College." *University of Pennsylvania Law Review* 136 (April 1988): 1231–1261.

This article notes that while some other studies have been confined to abstract comparison between the Islamic *waqf* and the English trust, this study explores the possibilities of Islamic influence in the development of the English trust. It is argued that in its early phases of development, Oxford University (incorporated as Merton College in 1274) might have owed much to the Islamic legal institution of *waqf*, or charitable trust.

The discussion is divided into three parts. Part I explores key features of the Islamic law of charitable trusts. Part II discusses various views as to the origin of the English trust and argues in favor of Islamic influences, compared to the prevailing view based on Germanic law. Part III consists of a reading of the 1264 Statues of Merton College, identifying many similarities between that document and the typical *waqf* instrument that support the premise of Islamic influence. The author expresses the hope that this research may stimulate further work into the influence of Islamic law on the development of Western law.

The author concludes that while this paper has demonstrated similarities between the Islamic *waqf* and the English trust, it does not necessarily "prove" influence. On the other hand, "Merton College was established during the Crusades, and it would not have been wise for a prominent clergyman and government servant [Walter de Merton] to announce his adoption of an Islamic institution" (p.1255).

A-122. Ghazanfar, S.M. "Civilizational Dialogue: Medieval Social Thought, Latin-European Renaissance, and Islamic Influences." *Encounters: Journal of Intercultural Perspectives* 9, no.1 (2003): 21–36.

The paper argues that the European Renaissance depended critically upon the intellectual armory, itself built upon the rediscovered Greek heritage, acquired through "knowledge transfer" from the early Islamic civilization. The mainstream literary paradigm, however, it is argued, tends to neglect these connections, or at best, grudgingly acknowledges them. Further, the paper documents the extensive influence upon Latin-Europe scholarship provided through the writings of several key Islamic scholastics. Briefly covered are the works of Al-Kindi, Al-Razi, Al-Farabi, Ibn Sina, Al-Ghazali, and, especially, Ibn Rushd, the Islamic "Aristotle," whose contributions revolutionized the Church-dominated, authoritarian social structure of medieval Europe.

With extensive documentation and appropriate quotes from well-known medievalists, the paper calls for greater integration and acknowledgement of such civilizational connections in literary history so that, among other things, there is greater understanding of the contemporary confrontational global environment. The author notes the 1998 UN declaration of the year 2001 as the "UN Year of

Dialogue among Civilizations," and further, that such a dialogue, "more than ever, is necessary for the enhancement of civility, whether at national or international level" (p.34).

A-123. Ghazanfar, S.M. "Medieval Islamic Socio-Economic Thought: Links with Greek and Latin-European Scholarship." *Humanomics* (Special Volume: Comparative Political Economy) 13, nos.3–4 (1997): 33–60.

The paper has three objectives: (1) a brief description of the classical heritage of the Arab-Islamic scholars upon which they developed their own Islamic synthesis, (2) a brief survey of the socio-economic thought of a few early-medieval Islamic scholastics, (3) to provide evidence as to the historical linkages of the Arab-Islamic thought with the Latin-European scholastics. An underlying premise of the paper is that the classical heritage is part of the long historical continuum that represents the inextricably linked Judeo-Christian-and-Islamic tradition of the West.

The first section of the paper argues that once the Greek heritage was rediscovered in Islam, it gave fresh impetus to the scholarly examination of the dogma of the new Islamic faith which sparked faith-vs.-reason controversies, just as there were similar battles in Latin Europe once the Arab-Islamic scholarship, with its Greek rationalism, reached medieval Europe. Then the economic thought of four early Muslim scholastics (Abu Yusuf, 731–798; Hanbal, 780–855; Ibn Hazm, d. 1064; Al-Ghazali, 1058–1111) is briefly discussed. The paper documents the "miracle of transmission" of Arab-Islamic scholarship built upon the "Greek miracle"; various sources of transmission are noted.

Yet, the paper concludes, "It is an anachronism to project into the Western Middle Ages the contempt for the Near East that characterized the Occident in more recent centuries" (quote from an eminent medievalist) (p.51).

A-124. Gibb, H.A.R. "The Influence of Islamic Culture on Medieval Europe." *Bulletin of the John Rylands Library* 95 (1955): 82–98.

This paper discusses some general principles and conclusions concerning the intellectual aspects of Islamic culture and its influence on medieval Europe. It is argued that the Islamic culture was a collective achievement of several groups, including non-Muslims, but religion and language gave it unity and cohesion.

As for the influence of Arab-Islamic achievements, such "cultural achievements are always preceded by an already existing activity in the related fields, and that it is this existing activity which creates the factor of attraction without which no creative assimilation could take place" (p.85). As for the absorption of the Greek heritage, there was nothing in the "Arab tradition or in the Koran" to encourage it, the author suggests; they were confronted by it and were forced to absorb it (p.85). The author acknowledges the "great ingenuity" of Arab scientists in the practical application of scientific theory and the improvement of scientific instruments, and "their works were eagerly sought after in the eleventh and twelfth centuries" (p.90). However, these scientists (except for physicians) oper- ated on the margins of Islamic society; "empirical science scarcely, if ever, entered into its educational structure" (p.90).

The author concludes: "On the whole, therefore, the contributions to the west from Arabic sources, although at first some of them seemed to be alien and dan- gerous, tended ultimately to reinforce the medieval Catholic culture rather than to disturb it" (p.98).

This article also appeared in Sylvia L. Thrupp (editor), *Change in Medieval Society: Europe North of the Alps, 1050–1500*, University of Toronto Press, Toronto, Canada, 1988.

A-125. Goitein, S.D. "Between Hellenism and Renaissance: Islam, the Interme- diate Civilization." *Islamic Studies* 2, no.2 (June 1963): 216–233.

The author argues that the Islamic world, between 850 and 1250 AD, was an *intermediate* civilization that characteristically ignited in Latin Europe the spirit of scientific inquiry and objectivity, combined with a deep-seated interest in reli- gion. That "period is characterized by the predominance of the middle class, which thrived on a free enterprise economy, and by the all-pervading influence of Greek science in both matter and spirit" (p.218). It is not an *intermediary* civilization, he insists, that served as a "mere transmitter of then ancient heri- tage" (p.218).

The article explores the scope, quality, and diversified influence of this inter- mediate civilization which, with Greek heritage as the background, contributed to the 12th-Century European Renaissance. This civilization, the author argues, was intermediate in time, character, and space, thus "forming for the first time in history a strong cultural link between all parts of the ancient world" (p.222). In our own time, he concludes, the cultural process is in reverse.

A-126. Gomez, Reverend Eusebio. "Muslim Theology in Its Bearing on Scho- lasticism." *Clergy Review* 6 (1933): 99–109.

The author discusses the evolution of science in the early Islamic culture and begins with statements such as "Islam is the parent that begat and nourished European civilization," and that Muslims are "not the race they have been depicted, indulgent in every pleasure except intellectual and the artistic. Their love of science was unparalleled at that time in Europe" (p.99–100).

Among other things, the author points out the "hardly deniable" indebtedness of Dante to Muslim models, referring to "the thesis of Asin-Palacios backed by prodigious learning, presented with an amazing acuteness of critical perception and logical coherence [that] seems to us irresistible" (p.101). "Despite fanati- cism, philosophical studies flourished among Arabs to an extent unequal then in Western civilization, and the debt that European philosophy owes to it is over- whelming" (p.101). St. Albert the Great and St. Thomas Aquinas relied on the philosophies of Ibn Sina and Ibn Rushd. And, "Roger Bacon can find no adequate

words to extol the importance of Arabic philosophy, especially when he compares it with that of Latins" (p.101).

However, the author states, "Islam is rather a Christian heresy, a mixture of
antitrinitarian and arian elements, than a different religious system" (p.103). At
the end, he further says, "Whilst we recognize that the Scholastics largely utilized Arabian philosophy and that, in general, Medieval scholars owed a great
deal to Moslem writers in many branches of science, we refuse to acknowledge
any theological influence, least of all on St. Thomas" (p.109).

A-127. Gran, Peter. "The Middle East in the Historiography of Advanced Capitalism." *Review of Middle East Studies*, no.1 (1975): 135–154.

The author starts with the premise that hardly any attempts have been made to
relate the evolution of "Middle-East studies in the U.S. to the general development of American culture or to the history of capitalism" (p.135). The essay then
investigates the argument that the factors that have isolated Middle-East studies
from the mainstream academia were themselves historically conditioned by the
development of industrial-monopoly capitalism.

This argument is approached by summarizing the main periods of the history
of American capitalism, and then for each period the characteristic tendency
which premised the writing of American history is used as a perspective with
which to judge the development of Oriental (Middle East) history. At the end,
among other things, the author notes, "A real stumbling block in the analysis of
scholarship of the Middle East, particularly after 1947, derives from the apparent
absence of a framework of analysis which can accommodate the reality of Zionism" (p.152).

A-128. Hamilton, Bernard. "Knowing the Enemy: Western Understanding of
Islam at the Time of the Crusades." *Journal of Royal Asiatic Studies* 7, no.3
(1997): 373–387.

While the Crusade movement lasted for many centuries, this article focuses
"on the period from c. 1100 to c. 1300 in Spain, Sicily and the Latin Kingdom
of Jerusalem" (p.374). In 1076, says the author, Pope Gregory VII, in emphasizing God's love for humanity, wrote to a Muslim ruler, "Most certainly you and
we ought to love each other in this way more than other races of men, because
we believe and confess one God, albeit in different ways" (p.373).

The main thesis of the article is that during the Crusades, "it became possible
for Western Catholics to obtain a more accurate picture of the Islamic faith," but
this was not a common phenomena (p.374). For example, "Western Christians
who lived in frontier societies like Spain, Sicily and the Latin Kingdom of Jerusalem, came to know Muslims as human beings, and to feel affection and respect
for some of them" (p.379). Further, there were Western scholars, such as Adelard
of Bath, who "studied under Arab masters" and who "were indebted to Arabic
scholarship in the twelfth and thirteenth centuries" for access to Greek texts

through Arabic versions, including many "original works of Arabic scholarship. In this way, at a time when the crusades were at their height, the scholars of western Europe came to have a great respect for Islamic learning" (p.379). However, despite some enhanced respect and understanding, the author recognizes, "this enlightened view of Islam was not widely shared in Latin Christendom at that time, nor was it rooted in any very profound knowledge of the Muslim religion" (p.373). This was despite the fact that "educated Western opinion knew that these stories were born of wishful thinking, not rooted in reality" (p.386).

A-129. Haskins, Charles H. "Arabic Science in Western Europe." *ISIS: Journal of the History of Science in Society* 7 (1925): 478–485.

Writing in 1925, the author explores the Arabic additions to the Greek heritage, as well as further exploration of the scientific writings preserved in Arabic. In general, it is noted, "this contribution was considerable" in areas such as medicine, mathematics, and astronomy. However, "Arabic science remains a significant and profitable field of exploration," and this paper attempts "a provisional statement of this process and its results for European learning" (p.479).

The process began in "Spain, the most continuous point of contact between Arab and Christian civilization," from about 1125 to 1280 (p.479). Translators came from various parts of Europe and several knew Arabic, Gerard of Cremona being the most prominent but there were others, such as Michael Scot, Albertus Magnus, Roger Bacon, Raymund Lull. Italy and Sicily are mentioned as next in importance. Several disciplines of such learning are identified: physics, metaphysics, chemistry, medicine, astrology, zoology, and geography. Also mentioned are the various Arab-Islamic sources.

The author notes, "The Latin world *could* have got its" Greek science "through Greco–Latin versions," but "for the most part, it *did* not. The current language of science was by this time Arabic" and "to their translations must be added the science of the Arabs themselves, assimilating and often going beyond the Greek" (p.485).

A-130. Haskins, Charles H. "The Reception of Arabic Science in England." *English Historical Review* 30 (January 1915): 56–69.

The paper explores the 12th-century diffusion of the science of the "Saracens" in Latin Europe, with a special focus on England. Adelard of Bath is noted as the "chief pioneer" in this "movement of study and translation," and his work "remains comprehensive and fundamental, alike with reference to geometry, astronomy, astrology, philosophy, and his advocacy of the experimental method" (p.61). It is noted that there were numerous others who followed the same path.

The author documents evidence with respect to several subjects (astronomy, mathematics, natural philosophy, metaphysics, etc., but with greater detail concerning the first two) and numerous English scholars, along with their precursors. Toledo in Spain is mentioned "as the most famous center of Arabic science" where scholars went to "hear the wiser philosophers of the world" (p.67). Roger Bacon is mentioned as another major intermediary "between Arabic and western learning. With him, however, the movement passes from its mathematical and astronomical phase to that which occupied itself primarily with natural philosophy and metaphysics" in the 13th century (p.69).

A-131. al-Hibri, Azzizah Y. "Islamic and American Constitutional Law: Borrowing Possibilities or a History of Borrowing." *University of Pennsylvania Journal of Constitutional Law* (Symposium Issue: Contextuality and Universality—Constitutional Borrowing on the Global Stage) 1, no.3 (Spring 1999): 492–527.

According to the author, notwithstanding the commonly held erroneous perceptions about Islam, there have been historical interactions between the West and Islam; and recently, the United States has been encouraging efforts to export its democratic principles and human-rights values to Muslim countries. Thus, the question of constitutional borrowing gains special prominence.

The article is organized into five sections: (1) American View of Islam, (2) Views of the Founding Fathers, (3) Islam and Its Basic Constitutional Principles, (4) The Charter of Madinah: Further Constitutional Principles, (5) The Demise of Democracy in Muslim Societies. Writings on Islam, chiefly from Europe, have been available in the United States, the author notes, but they reflect the typical historical distortions and inaccuracies. Yet, some Founding Fathers made serious efforts to educate themselves about Islam and its civilizations (p.497). Their sources also included knowledgeable African-Muslim slaves. Thomas Jefferson in particular was keen to acquire this knowledge for the purpose of developing the American model of political governance.

The author then discusses the constitutional principles in Islam, including knowledge from the Charter of Madinah; also the question whether the Islamic state is a theocracy is explored. Then there is discussion of why democracy, despite the democratic ethos of Islam, could not thrive in Muslim societies. Several historical reasons are elaborated.

The paper concludes that "whether Jefferson's views were affected at all by Islamic thought through the writings of European thinkers, his own readings of a translated Qur'an, or discussions with Muslim slaves, the fact remains that fundamental similarities exist between the American and Islamic constitutional systems" (p.526). It is further suggested that the present efforts to export democratic principles to the Islamic world should be predicated on a sound understanding of those principles inherent in Islam and why they failed historically in Muslim societies.

The article is extremely well-documented, with 231 notes and references. Numerous English and non-English sources are cited.

A-132. Huff, Toby E. "Science and the Public Sphere: Comparative Institutional Development in Islam and the West." *Social Epistemology* 11, no.1 (1997): 25–37.

The paper discusses the reasons why modern science developed in the West and not in Islam (or India or China), "despite the fact that Arabic science was the most advanced science in the world from roughly the eighth to the thirteenth century, while China's technological base was superior to that of the West up until the fifteenth or sixteenth century, and its science was second to that of the Arabs" (p.26).

The argument is that the emergence of the "idea of legally autonomous entities, governed by their own laws and regulations, laid the foundation for a domain of discourse and participation protected from the incursions of religious authorities—in effect the rudiments of a public sphere. Nothing like this legal revolution ever occurred in Islamic law, and that is one of the major reasons why Arabic science failed to give birth to modern science" (p.29). The author argues that *madrasas* (i.e., Islamic colleges) excluded logic and natural sciences; they "were pious endowments (religious trusts), and as such they could not encompass the teaching of anything that was inimical to the spirit of Islam" (p.31). In essence, "The idea and reality of a free and unfettered public sphere" are the keys to the development of modern science (p.34). Such forces lacked in Islam (and in China and India), the author argues.

A-133. Hunt, R.W. "English Learning in the Late Twelfth Century." *Transactions of the Royal Historical Society* 19 (1936): 19–42.

The paper explores various late-12th-century England scholars who pursued various avenues of learning; the author's premise is that these writers have "on the whole been neglected" (p.19). Also identified are various schools of learning.

Among other things, the author notes, "There is a flood of translations from Greek and Arabic works, scientific and philosophical. The work of Haskins has shown how many Englishmen took part in this movement" (p.23). Daniel of Morley is mentioned, as are several others; Alexander Nequam is mentioned as "being the first person in the West to know both the Greco-Latin and Arabic-Latin translations of Aristotle" (p.25).

A-134. Isani, Mukhtar Ali. "Cotton Mather and the Orient." *New England Quarterly* 43, no.1 (March 1970): 46–58.

The article is a narrative on the "general Puritan awareness of the Orient," specifically that of Dr. Cotton Mather, during the 18th century, who "kept abreast of current news from the East, especially from the Turkish Empire" (p.46). His library included books such as *Persia* (by Johannes de Laet) and Richard Knolles' *History of the Turks*; the latter also included a translation of the Qur'an. The diversity of various references in Mather's works indicates the breath of his interests. His writings include references to "the Talmud and the Koran," and "besides citing an unnamed 'Arabian commentary upon the Al-Choran,' he quotes the mystic Algazal [Abu Hamid Muhammad al-Ghazzali]" (p.46). He also mentions "Avicen" (Ibn Sina) and "Rhazes" (al-Razi). Since the "Near East and Islam attracted particular attention in America," Mather noted the "disturbed state of the Turkish Empire, viewing the Turkish difficulties as signs of the '*Second Wo Passing away*,' and heralds of the approaching fall of Anti-Christ" (p.49–50).

The article notes that "the lack of friendliness toward Islam is in keeping with the orthodoxy of New England at a time when Islam was mentioned in discussions of heresy and apocryphal stories such as those about Sergius the monk or Mohammad's 'trained pigeon' were still current in such esteemed books in America as the Knolles and Rycaut *History of the Turks*" (p.50). Yet, Mather's view of the Orient had its practical side also, for "learning from Oriental experience was desirable because smallpox, described by him as one of the new scourges inflicted by God upon a sinful world, was Oriental in origin" (p.51). Further, "Mather did not see Islam as devoid of virtue. Muslim abhorrence of idolatry caution his attention and received his approval" (p.53). Elsewhere, Mather talked "of the Orient as an object for comparison, sometimes holding the Christian world to scorn. If belief in the Messiahship of Jesus is all that is required of a good Christian, he challenges, then why should not one accept the Koran? Such a belief in Christ 'is a thing many times over expressly acknowledged in the *Alcoran!*" (p.56).

The article concludes that Cotton Mather's "sustained interest which spans most of his adult years shows another side of his extraordinary inquiring nature and, in part, reflects the global awareness of Puritan America" (p.58).

A-135. Ito, Shuntaro. "Islamic Civilization as Seen from Japan: A Non-Western View." Pages 131–138 in *The Islamic World and Japan: In Pursuit of Mutual Understanding*, Proceedings of the 1980 International Symposium, the Japan Foundation. Tokyo, Japan, 1981.

The paper provides an appreciation of the history and influence of Islamic civilization, as seen by a Japanese historian of science. While studying Latin paleography at the University of Wisconsin in the 1960s, the author "was totally shocked to discover that until Europe entered the 'twelfth century Renaissance,' by way of Arabic learning, it had been lurking on the outskirts of world civilization, almost unaware of Euclid, Archimedes, Ptolemy or Aristotle. Like many a western scholar, I had till then thought of the history of the world civilization in terms of a transition from Greece to Rome and to Western Europe. It was this experience with old manuscripts that opened my eyes to the importance and majesty of Arabic civilization" (p.132). Further, "A linear view of a Greco-Roman-Mediterranean-European progression is a Eurocentric view of history, fabricated by European historians after the *fait accompli* of nineteenth-century European world domination. It is biased and does not accurately reflect historical facts" (p.133).

And, the author continues, "Consciously or unconsciously, Europeans have been unable to throw off their colonialist mentality in their understanding of Islam. It will be difficult for them to break out of their habit of dealing, from an ethnocentric viewpoint, only with that part of Islam that has been absorbed by Europe. But we Japanese have the comparative advantage of greater distance and are in a position to examine and evaluate the significance of Islamic culture from the perspective of world history. We can do this fairly and without prejudice, without forcing our own position on anyone. We can adopt a position truly representative of all mankind" (p.138).

A-136. Joubin, Rebecca. "Islam and Arabs through the Eyes of the *Encyclopedie*: The 'Other' as a Case of French Cultural Self-Criticism." *International Journal of Middle East Studies* 32 (2000): 197–217.

This provocative paper begins with the premise that as the French Enlightenment confronted the contest between reason and faith, with risks of censorship and persecution for the heretics, one "can see the philosophies' use of the Oriental motif emerge as one of the leading methods of subterfuge by which they tried to avoid the heavy hand of censorship" (p.197). The author focuses on a single feature of the encyclopedists' ideology: "their advocacy of science and reason over religion using the topos of the Oriental as Other" (p.198).

The author discusses the encyclopedists' "dichotomous presentation of an 'irrational' Islam and 'glorious' Arab science, in which Arab science blossomed only after Arab intellectuals and leaders" abandoned "the oppressive irrationality of Islam" (p.199). It is further argued that their "failure to recognize that scientific and rational Arab civilization was connected to their hidden agenda of presenting Muhammad and his Islamic revelation as a surrogate for Christ and Christianity, a central component of which involved exalting science at the expense of religion" (p.199).

The article documents how, in various ways, the encyclopedists distorted available information and presented "Muhammad as a false prophet, an impostor, who was entirely averse to reason and science and who took advantage of the credulity of the masses to deceive them into following his religion" (p.200). Thus, keen to "deflect the censors' attention," the encyclopedists "used irony, subterfuge, and other clever evasions to attack Christ and Christianity while allowing it to appear as if the Judeo-Christian revelation adhered to their avowed system of prophecy and religious revelation based on reason and science" (p.200). On the other hand, Arab science is exalted, "the ulterior motive [being] to reveal the impossibility of science and reason's association with Islamic civilization" (p.207). The author argues that "in contrast to their presentation of an irrational Islam," the encyclopedists "unreservedly acknowledge their [Arab] contribution to Europe's Renaissance" (p.207).

A-137. Khalidi, Tarif. "Islamic Views of the West in the Middle Ages." *Studies in Interreligious Dialogue* 5 (1995): 31–42.

Citing the example of negotiations, 800 years ago, between Saladin and Richard the Lionheart over the status of the Holy Land, the article suggests that "several distinguished Western historians have turned their attention to Western perception of Islam in the Middle Ages, but little has been done in the opposite direction" (p.31). Further, the author views this example not as an episode in a negotiating process, "but rather of those transparent, rarefied entities that historians call perception, images or mental constructs" (p.31).

The article argues that given the successes of early Islam, "the Qur'anic concept of the Muslim as the community of the center, the *ummatan wasatan*, was now endowed with proofs from nature and history," and non-Muslim nations, including the Byzantines, were perceived by the civilization of classical Islam within this geographic and cultural framework (p.32–33). "The Muslim-Byzantine encounter," says the author, "is a long and very rich example of two cultures locked in combat, and yet, from the Muslim point of view at any rate, an encounter in which fear and hatred were often mixed with a great deal of grudging admiration" (p.34). Further, the universal vision of Islam "gave medieval Muslim civilization an unparalleled capacity to learn from other cultures, an open and oft-expressed willingness to acknowledge its cultural debt to Indians, Persians, Greeks, and so forth" (p.35).

The article concludes: "As one surveys some six hundred years of Muslim perceptions of Europe, from the ninth to the fifteenth centuries, it is clear that it was the geography and society of Europe that interested Islam rather than its history or its culture. At the level of scientific scholarship, the Muslims felt that Europe had nothing to teach them. Nevertheless, the astonishing curiosity of Islamic culture, its readiness to learn about its enemies and to live at peace with them in the Holy Land, is a chapter in human history perhaps worth reading as another peace process begins to unfold almost exactly eight hundred years after the peace of Saladin and Richard" (p.42).

A-138. Khan, M. Abdur Rehman. "A Survey of Muslim Contribution to Science and Culture, Part I." *Islamic Culture* 14 (January 1942): 1–20.

The author begins by suggesting that "the masterpieces of Greek science and culture might possibly have disappeared altogether from the face of the Earth but for the miracle of Arab rise to power and its subsequent patronage of learning" (p.1). In this two-part essay, the author surveys the contributions of science and culture in the early Islamic civilization, along with "the transmission of Muslim culture and learning to distant countries and nations" (p.1).

The paper discusses the cultivation and development of medicine, mathematics, and astronomy, especially during the Abbasid Caliphate. Among the Greek treasures were manuscripts on geometry, astronomy, medicine, and philosophy. Also discussed is the encouragement of learning in the Fatimid dynasty (909–

1171 AD). Contributions in historiography and geography are identified. The last section covers contributions in literature, poetry, and grammar, as well as religious literature and philosophy. Among the prominent names mentioned are Al-Kindi, Al-Farabi, Ibn Sina, and Al-Ghazali. With respect to Al-Ghazali, the author states, "his masterpiece *Ihya al-Ulum al-Din* and other similar works were widely read by the Muslims, Jews, and Christians and contributed to the spread of scholasticism in Asia and Europe, as may be judged by their influence on Thomas Aquinas and even Blaise Pascal" (p.20).

A-139. Khan, M. Abdur Rehman. "A Survey of Muslim Contribution to Science and Culture, Part II." *Islamic Culture* 14 (April 1942): 136–152.

This second part of the two-part essay begins with a narration of the Arab-Islamic contributions in chemistry, biology, and related sciences (animal husbandry, botany, geology, agricultural sciences, and minerals). While the Arabs "do not seem to have added very much to the engineering sciences," they "improved the theory of the hydrostatic balance, the usefulness of the Alexandrian hydrometer and the efficiency of the Syrian water-wheels" (p.138).

The author discusses the "importance of the Norman patronage of Arab learning on European civilization" (p.142). This is followed by a detailed discussion of learning in Islamic Spain, "The Jewel of the World" (as a German Nun Hrostsvitha called it). Numerous scholars of Islamic Spain and their contributions are discussed, along with the output of several Jewish scholars (Yahya Ibn Daud, Maimonides, Ibn Gabirol—the "Jewish Plato," and others).

As for the transmission of Arab learning and its influence upon Latin Europe, the author cites some Western scholars to corroborate the argument. He concludes that "even a cursory acquaintance with Muslim history cannot fail to impress one with admiration for Arab enterprise and achievement in all fields of human activity." Further, "It is interesting to see how Arab learning and culture spread through Europe. Sicily and Spain were the principal sources of propagation. From Sicily, its two 'baptized Sultans' Roger II and Frederick II Hohenstaufen, especially the latter, carried Arab culture through Italy across the Alps. Lotharingia (Lorraine), Liege, Gorze and Cologne become centers of Arab learning. From Spain it penetrated beyond the Pyrenees into Western and South-Western France, slowly but surely" (p.150).

A-140. Kidd, Thomas S. "'Is It Worse to Follow Mahomet Than the Devil?' Early American Uses of Islam." *Church History* 72, no.4 (December 2003): 766–790.

The article argues that the early uses of Islam in America was "essentially discursive. Knowledge of Islam in early America represented a rhetorical strategy of power. Anglo-Americans used the knowledge of Islam that they produced both to reinforce the superiority of their brand of Protestantism over its challengers such as Deism or Catholicism, and to delegitimize Islam and Muslims religiously, morally, and racially" (p.767). Thus, Anglo-American writings, such as those of Benjamin Franklin, represented a "well-established tradition: citing the similarities between an opponent's views and the 'beliefs' of Islam as a means to discredit one's adversaries" (p.766). There were two sources of knowledge: first, impressions acquired from the enslavement of Europeans and Americans in North Africa, and second were "the widely circulated books and sermons related to Islam" (p.767). This "knowledge," says the author, appeared "regularly in the print cultures of seventeenth and eighteenth century Anglo-America" (p.767).

The article's discussion is divided into seven sections, with rather suggestive titles: (1) Fierce Monsters of Africa, (2) That Abominable Imposture of Mahometanism, (3) The Kingdoms of Antichirst and Mahomet, (4) Was Not Mahometanism Founded in Enthusiasm?, (5) With That Overthrow the Millennium Shall Begin, (6) Mahomet Called in the Use of the Sword; Jesus Did Not, (7) They Hate Our Freedoms. The last title is reflective of the post-9/11 rhetoric in the United States.

After noting the anti-Islamic rhetoric of several contemporary Christian evangelicals, the author concludes, "We may ultimately wonder, however, whether both the political and religious uses of Islam still have much more to do with American discourses of power than any 'true' knowledge of various Islamic churches, states, movements, or indeed, whether such 'true' knowledge is even possible in the American public sphere" (p.790).

A-141. Lewis, Archibald R. "The Islamic World and the Latin West, 1350–1500." *Speculum: A Journal of Medieval Studies* 65, no.4 (October 1990): 833–844.

The article clarifies the importance of the 150 years before Europe experienced the age of discovery that began with Columbus, for it was during this period that the two great civilizations—Latin West and the Islamic world—"formed attitudes towards each other that still govern much of how they interact today" (p.833). Two forces had adversely impacted the Islamic world, the author argues; one was the expansion of the crusading Europe, along with the European penetration into North Africa and the Islamic world (Asia, India, and China), and the other was the devastation inflicted by the Mongols.

In the next hundred years, however, three factors contributed to the possible re-emergence of Islamic strength—military, religious revival, and economic. Among these, the author suggests, the religious revival "was essentially hostile to philosophical and speculative thought that had been the glory of earlier medieval Islam" (p.837). On the other hand, despite some difficulties, "Western Europe during these years was laying the basis for its worldwide expansion and domination of overseas areas" (p.840). Further, while the Islamic world was eschewing science it had once prized, "the Latin West was laying the basis for the secular intellectual world of modern times" (p.841). Thus developed "the schism between Moslem East and European West in the world of late fourteenth- and fifteenth-century civilizations," and it "was to remain so for centuries to come" (p.842).

A-142. Makdisi, George. "Interaction between Islam and the West." *Revue des etudes Islamiques* 44 (1976): 287–309.

There was the "Arab Awakening" during early ninth century, "brought on by the translations of Greek works into Arabic," and then there was the "European Awakening," "brought on by the impact of Islam on the Latin West" (p.287). And, since Islamic culture was more advanced, the author suggests, "it is reasonable to expect that Islam influenced the West especially since the number of parallels goes beyond what can reasonably be considered as mere parallels" (p.288). The paper documents numerous parallels in the field of humanities, and this influence is mentioned as "one of the factors in the rise of universities in the West" (p.289). Further, "What the humanists of the Renaissance later referred to derisively as the 'scholastic method,' was referred to by Ibn Aqil as the 'method of disputation,' *trariqat al-nazar*" (p.290).

Other parallels mentioned relate to various types of the *Summa* genre of literature. Specifically mentioned are the *Summas* of Ibn Aqil and St. Thomas Aquinas (1224–1275). There are strong similarities "in the arrangement of the article *(articulus)*. All the essential elements are present in both works" (p.299). Further, "In both Islam and the West, the three essential elements of the scholastic method or method of disputation are found in the same sequence of development" (p.299). In addition, "The very terms used have much in common" (p.299). Several other parallels are also mentioned.

The author concludes, "In the middle ages, writers were not particularly fond of citing their sources. Nor were they particularly loathe to borrow from other writers without citing them or otherwise giving them credit for using their materials. Add to this that Western writers were not particularly anxious to cite Islamic writers, especially in anything having to do with religion, unless they were doing so in order to refute them" (p.308).

A-143. Makdisi, John A. "The Islamic Origins of the Common Law." *North Carolina Law Review* 77 (June 1999): 1635–1739.

This 104-page article begins with the statement that the origins of the common law, created over seven centuries ago in England, are shrouded in mystery, though some historians have traced its roots primarily to the civil law tradition of Roman and canon law. This extremely well-documented article, with 620 notes and references, argues that the origins of the common law are found in the Islamic jurisprudence.

The paper is divided into five parts. The first three parts examine institutions that helped to create the common law in the 12th century by introducing concepts that were totally out of character with existing European legal institutions; for example, (1) contract law permitting transfer of property ownership on the basis of offer and acceptance through the action of debt, (2) property law protected possession as a form of property ownership through the assize of novel disseisin, and (3) the trial-by-jury institution for settling disputes.

The article explores the origins of these three institutions by tracing their unique characteristics to analogous institutions in the Islamic law. Part IV examines the characteristics of the legal systems known as Islamic law, common law, and civil law and demonstrates the resemblance between the first two in terms of function and structure and their dissimilarity with the civil law. Part V traces the transmission path from the Maliki school of Islamic jurisprudence in North Africa and Sicily to the Norman legal system of Sicily and then to England, and thus demonstrates the social, political, and geographical connections that made transplants from the Islamic civilization possible.

The author concludes that the evidence presented as to the origins of common law must not be a surprise, for other writers have also suggested such possibilities. However, none have suggested that the common law as an integrated whole was a product of Islam, and given the evidence provided, the author asserts, such a conclusion is most plausible. "This article barely has begun to explore the wealth of material that needs to be studied to establish the true nature of the transplants between Islam and England that established the foundations of the common law" (p.1730).

A-144. Matar, Nabil. "Muslims in Seventeenth-Century England." *Journal of Islamic Studies* 8, no.1 (1997): 63–82.

The article argues that while "hundreds of Muslims were present on English soil" in the early modern period, there is no comprehensive study that documents their interactions with the Elizabethan/Stuart England, for "Muslims were not permanent residents in England (and the rest of the British Isles); nor were they subjects of the Crown because of their adherence to a non-Christian religion" (p.63). It is noted that Queen Elizabeth I (1558–1603) was the first English monarch "to cooperate openly with the Muslims—and to grant liberty to her subjects to trade and interact with them without being liable to prosecution" (p.64).

These encounters, almost always in southern England, related to three categories of Muslims (always called "Turks" or "Moors"): merchants/refugees, pirates, and ambassadors. While the English-Scottish traveled to the Muslim lands, Muslims seldom visited England on their own initiative. These interactions, the author notes, show little friction between the Muslims and the English; further, "While Muslim pirates, like their English counterparts, were gaoled or punished, ex-slaves were helped, merchants were welcomed to trade, refugees were allowed to work, and ambassadors were honored" (p.82). "Unlike in contemporary literary and theological writings, the actual English interaction with Muslims is remarkable for the absence of racial or religious prejudice. Evidently in the Elizabethan and Stuart periods, and before the beginning of British colonialism and Orientalism, the interactions between Britain and Turks were cordial, open, and devoid of 'domination' and construction" (p.82).

A-145. Matar, Nabil. "The Traveler as Captive: Renaissance England and the Allure of Islam." *Literature Interpretation Theory* 7 (1996): 187–196.

In contrast to "an interpretation of texts on Islam from within the Western literature discourse—where Islam is a 'constructed' image without its own self-presentation" and where it is depicted "from the perspective of domination of power," this article documents "other material about the Muslim dominions which reverses the premises of power that have been presumed to inform the British encounter with Islam. This is the captivity literature produced by men who experienced the domain of Islam not as Mandevillian imaginary wanderers, nor as London playwrights appealing to sensationalism and melodrama, but as Britons who had been enslaved and 'dominated' by Muslims" (p.187–188). Such literature, argues the author, represents a distinct category of cultural encounter in which "Christians encountered the non-Europeans without the accouterments of their theological certitude and military power" (p.188). This literature of direct encounter with Islam, the author posits, provides a "hitherto ignored perspective on the meeting between Britons and Muslims" (p.188).

The author concludes that for the captives, Islam and Muslims did not represent "exoticism, with its wonders, strange creatures and natural prodigies," but that "Islam was real, and Muslims were neither strange nor stereotypical because they were men whom the captives had served, had eaten and hunted and lived with, and most strikingly, had conversed with in their native language" (p.194).

A-146. Menocal, Maria Rosa. "Pride and Prejudice in Medieval Studies: European and Oriental." *Hispanic Review* 53 (1985): 61–78.

As a critique of medieval studies, the paper argues that the "segregation of European (or Spanish, Italian, Provencal) from Arabic when we are discussing many aspects of the Middle Ages and its cultural history is an anachronistic and misleading one" (p.61). The author mentions her entry to this discourse when, as a graduate student, she linked the etymology of the word *troubadour* to the Arabic *taraba* (to sing, to entertain by singing), thus, suggesting a "magnificent connection in the sphere of literary history" (p.63).

This "Arabist" connection was well accepted until the early 19th century, as argued by some European scholars, then "prejudice on the part of Europeans and Europeanists, which is 'Orientalism' of sorts" emerged, and these scholars were "appalled that other Europeans did not understand the extent to which Spain, and that included Arabic Spain, had been the center and stimulus of culture and intellectual advancement in medieval Europe" (p.66–67). And, by "the middle of the nineteenth century, it would have been inconceivable or very difficult for most Europeans to imagine, let alone explore or defend a view of the 'European' as being culturally subservient to the 'Arab'" (p.68). And, "Our views as Westerners vis-a-vis the Arabs have not much improved in the century and a half since then nor are our attitudes about the possibility of interaction in literary history radically more favorable" (p.68). Further, the author argues, when confronted, the modern medievalist responds: "no proof that such cultural-literary borrowing ever took place or that it could have taken place" (p.68). But, the author states, the "standards of proofs" are quite different.

The article then goes on to document "proof" of both these phenomena, and concludes with the suggestion that "it is possible to rekindle the pride in a part of our European ancestry that has too long been kept in the dark, an ancestry that includes the most eminent of medieval Europeans, Averroes, Maimonides, and Ibn Hazm, among many others" (p.78).

A-147. Meyerhof, Max. "On the Transmission of Greek and Indian Science to the Arabs." *Islamic Culture* 11, no.20 (January 1937): 17–29.

The author notes that "it is more than two centuries since orientalists began to take a more lively interest in the transmission of Greek science to the Arabs," and his purpose is "to give a brief account" based on the results of their studies, as well as to add his own findings (p.17).

It is noted that "the growing orthodox fanaticism of the Byzantine governors was a serious obstacle to free scientific work and contributed to give science its decidedly scholastic turn which destined to remain as a legacy in the Arabic and in the European Medieval periods" (p.19). Then, the transfer of the Hellenistic science "from Alexandria to Antioch, and then to Harran" through various sources is documented. And, "In the fifth century A.D., Greek learning had begun to invade Mesopotamia and Persia, not in Greek but in the Syriac language" (p.21). Several scholars involved in this transmission were Muslims, Jewish, and Christians (mainly Nestorians but some Catholics). "But translation work on a vast scale was accomplished under the rule of the Abbassid Caliphs," with the establishment of the "*Bait al-Hikma*, House of Wisdom, in Baghdad by al-Mamum about 830 A.D." and Yuhanna b. Masawaih as the director and Nestorian Hunain b. Ishaq as the chief translator (p.23).

As to the Indian influence on the Arabic scientific development, the author notes, "an Indian influx existed in the pre-Islamic Persian Academy of Gonde-Shapur, in the sixth century," and "it is certain that it began again under the rule of the first Abbasid Caliph" (p.24). But this influence was "very restricted." On the other hand, as for the Islam and West interactions, the author concludes with another medievalist's observation that "the Islamic civilization had always in the first instance a Western, and not an Eastern, orientation" (p.27).

A-148. Millas-Vallicrosa, J.M. "Translations of Oriental Scientific Works (to the End of the Thirteenth Century)" (translated from Spanish by Daphne Woodword). *Journal of World History* 2, no.2 (1954): 395–428.

The article documents the translations of Oriental (Arab-Islamic) works, for, in order to comprehend "the idea of the importance and significance in the cultural development of medieval Europe of the scientific translations derived from the Orient, we must remember that the European science of that period, as heir to the classical culture of Rome, was handicapped from the outset by a radical and irremediable deficiency" (p.395). Further, several centuries "elapsed before that genuine tradition fertilized the virgin soil of medieval European thought, and when it did so, the contact was made through translations of Oriental and above all of Arab origin, which, after serving as a medium for the transmission of Greek, Persian, and Indian original material—to which they sometimes added a great deal—were translated in their turn into Latin or one of the Romance languages" (p.396).

The article is divided into 13 sections: (1) Importance of Translations in Compensation for the Deficiencies of the Latin Scientific Tradition, (2) Arab Culture as the Continuator and the Integrator, (3) Arab and Christian Spain as a Cultural Meeting, (4) The Tenth Century, First Translations from Arabic into Latin, (5) Eleventh Century, Diffusion of Earlier Translations, (6) Constantino Africano and the School of Salerno, (7) Translators Working in the Late Eleventh Century and the First Half of the Twelfth Century, (8) Latin Translators Who Worked Mainly in the Pyrenees or the Ebro Valley, (9) The Toledo Group of Translators, (10) Translators from Arabic to Hebrew, (11) Other Translators from Arabic to Hebrew, (12) The Group of Translators at the Court of Alfonso the Wise, (13) Other Thirteenth-Century Groups of Translators.

This article is also reproduced (English version) in Guy S. Metraux and Francois Crouzet (editors), *The Evolution of Science: Readings from the History of Mankind*, for the International Commission for a History of the Scientific and Cultural Development of Mankind, United Nations Educational, Scientific and Cultural Organization (UNESCO), published by the New American Library of World Literature, New York, 1963: 128–167.

A-149. Moorhead, John. "The Earliest Christian Theological Response to Islam." *Religion* 11 (1981): 265–274.

With respect to the Islamic religion, the paper concentrates "on the early response of Oriental authors, a problem which has been the subject of little discussion." Further, it is argued that "the line taken by these early Oriental thinkers found echoes in the thought of later Christian commentators on Islam" (p.265).

The article refers to an Armenian bishop Sebeos, who "reports that both Jews and Arabs accepted that the Arabs were descended from the patriarch Abraham" (p.266). Also, an anonymous Nestorian monk, writing in Iraq in the 670s, reported that "Arabs' worship of God is a direct continuation of the worship offered by Abraham. As was the case with Sebeos, he seems to accept that the Muslims are indeed worshipers of God" (p.267). Similar references are noted from the work of a Monophysite author writing in about 775. On the other hand, an extreme view thought of "Muhammad as an apostate cardinal who, out of spite at failing to be made pope, founded his own religion" (p.270).

More significantly, however, the testimony of a positive attitude comes from a letter written during the Central Middle Ages, by Pope Gregory VII to Anazir, King of Mauretania, in which Gregory thanks Anazir "for releasing captives," and "accepts Muslim worship and belief in God, and neatly turns a text of St. Paul (Ephesians 2:14) to suggest unity, and consequently peace, between the two faiths." The author quotes from the letter; Pope Gregory says, "May God lead you (Anazir) into the bosom of the most holy patriarch Abraham" (p.271). The author credits Gregory "with the belief that the Islamic faith is a road to salvation" (p.271).

The author concludes: "In short, there is within Christianity a tradition which goes some way towards seeing Islam as 'of God.' It is to be hoped that these theological resources present in the Christian tradition will be mobilized in any future rapprochement with Islam" (p.272).

A-150. Moosa, Matti I. "Al-Kindi's Role in the Transmission of Greek Knowledge to the Arabs." *Journal of the Pakistan Historical Society* 15 (January 1967): 1–18.

This paper explores the question of whether al-Kindi relied on original Greek and Syriac sources, or whether his studies were based on translations from these two languages. And relatedly, how much Greek and Syriac he knew and to what extent he relied upon the works of professional translators. In general, medievalists have credited Al-Kindi with the translation of Greek works into Arabic.

In addition. the article explores the evidence from the writings of other scholars whose works are cited by Al-Kindi and concludes that while he must have had some knowledge of the Greek language, he also "relied on the translation of others in his study of Greek philosophy" (p.18).

A-151. Myers, Eugene A. "Legacy of Arab Culture to the Western World." *The Muslim Digest* 19, no.5 (December 1968): 61–65.

The paper is a brief narrative on "the story of the immense contributions which the Arabs made to the West," which was "actually the *third* great wave of oriental wisdom, the third time that the creative impulse came from the East." "There is no doubt whatever now that our earliest scientific knowledge is of Mesopotamian and Egyptian origin"; this being the *first* wave, according to the author (p.61). Thus, the foundation of a considerable body of Greek science was "wholly oriental," and "while the Greek genius was creating what might be called the beginning of modern science, . . . the Hebrew prophets were establishing the moral unity of mankind upon the notion of one God" (p.62). And, "This marks the *second* impact of the East on the West" (p.62).

But, then the "Greek miracle" ended when the "famous Academy of Athens was closed in 529 by the order of Justinian" (p.62). And then, some centuries later, emerged the *third* wave of Eastern impulse and the most significant, the author argues. This was "the Arab intervention [that] literally saved Greek knowledge from being destroyed, added to that knowledge, and handed it on a silver platter to Western Christendom" (p.63). Further, "The years 750–900 may be called the age of translation during which time all Greek knowledge available was translated from Greek to Arabic. This treasure enriched and added to was to be returned to Latindom West during the eleventh and twelfth centuries" (p.63). Also, the author argues, "The immense cultural significance of Islam is that it finally brought together the two great intellectual streams which had flowed independently for a long time—Greek science and Semitic monotheism and morality of Islamic variety" (p.63).

The author concludes: "The march of mankind has been rhythm-like between East and West—from Mesopotamia and the Egyptian East to the Greek West; from the Greek West to the Arab East; from the Arab East to Latindom West, England and the Modern West" (p.64).

A-152. Naqvi, Syed Ali Raza. "Prophet Muhammad's Image in Western Enlightened Scholarship." *Islamic Studies* 20, no.2 (Summer 1981): 136–151.

The article begins with pointing out that "it was during the Middle Ages when an open war had ensued between Islam and Christendom that all sorts of blasphemies were invented against the Holy Prophet and a horribly distorted picture of Islam was painted by the venomous writers of the West" (p.138). "Even now with the lapse of half a millennium the distrust and disgust created in the Western mind has not been entirely removed." However, "With the birth of the modern age, of religious tolerance and freedom of thought, a new era of research and insight has dawned upon the world, engendering a keen desire to appreciate all that is right and good in whatever quarter of the human experience and conscience" (p.138).

The author then documents evidence of this enlightened perspective by citing numerous Western scholars, including the Vatican Declaration of 1966, which looks upon Muslims "with esteem. They adore one God, living and enduring, merciful and all-powerful, Maker of heaven and earth, and Speaker to men. They strive to submit wholeheartedly even to His inscrutable decrees, just as did Abraham, with whom the Islamic faith is pleased to associate itself" (p.138).

Several of the scholars quoted are: (1) Tor Andrae, (2) Joseph Schacht, (3) William Muir, (4) H.A.R. Gibb, (5) Reverend Bosworth Smith, (6) G.E. Von Grunebaum, (7) Reverend V.C. Badley, (8) Edward Gibbon, (9) W. Montgomery Watt, (10) Laura Veccia Vaglieri. The article concludes with a quote from Vaglieri: "Blinded by hate, the most powerful enemies of Islam have sought to smear the Prophet of God with calumnious charges. They forget that Muhammad before he began his mission was highly esteemed by his own countrymen for integrity of conscience and purity of life" (p.149).

A-153. O'Brien, Peter. "Islamic Civilization's Role in the Waning of the European Middle Ages." *The Medieval History Journal* 2, no.2 (July–December 1999): 387–404.

This essay explores "the effects, on Christians, of that protracted encounter between unevenly matched foes" (p.389). Thus, "From roughly 1000–1500, not only did the contacts between Christians and Muslims increase, but also they repeatedly and increasingly exposed the superiority of various Islamic ideas, institutions, technologies and personalities" (p.389). The paper is divided into two key sections: Islamic superiority; and the predominance and power of untruth. There is detailed discussion of both themes.

As for "Islamic superiority," the author draws parallels between contemporary Europe and the Third-World countries; and "the new knowledge, transferred in this 'one-way traffic in ideas,' from Islam to Christendom at the end of the Middle Ages was nothing short of staggering" (p.394). Further, "The discovery of Islam's intellectual treasures was a self-discovery," and to preserve "the inaccuracy and immaturity of their own ideas," medieval European scholars engaged in many "experiences with untruth" concerning "depictions and understandings of Islam itself" (p.399). And, "The encounter with Islam also led European scholars to expect multiple and competing truths" (p.401).

The author concludes, that while he has ventured a plausible story of the impact of Islamic civilization on medieval Europe, "conclusive evidence, however, will likely forever elude us for the simple reason that most Latin Christian leaders would, could, and/or did not disclose their actual opinions about Islamic civilization" (p.404).

A-154. O'Brien, Peter. "Platonism and Plagiarism at the End of the Middle Ages." Pages 304–318 in *Christianizing People and Converting Individuals*, edited by Guyda Armstrong and Ian N. Wood. Turnhot, Belgium: Brepols Publishers n.v., 2000.

The paper begins with a quote from Richard Southern: "The existence of Islam was the most far-reaching problem in medieval Christianity. It made the West profoundly uneasy" (p.303). Then, the author questions the premises of Straussian philosophy, in that "the most powerful and influential thinkers conceal their genuine message inside an esoteric shell designed to mislead and manipulate the vast majority of readers away from the esoteric core," according to the Straussians (p.303).

The purpose of this paper is to "probe the medieval origins of European esotericism that Strauss leaves largely uninvestigated" (p.304). The author argues that "a centuries-long encounter at the end of the Middle-Ages with undeniably superior non-Christian neighbors, especially Muslims, fostered esotericism" (p.304). Thus, "Western medieval thinkers cloaked the truth they knew about Islamic civilization" and "their encounter with and treatment of Islamic culture led medieval intellectuals to cast doubt on, rather than merely disguise, their notion of universal truth. By the close of the Middle Ages they had little hope of even discovering a universal truth to hide" (p.304).

The paper further argues that Western medieval intellectuals, in order to avoid persecution, not only distorted the truth ("employed untruth and half-truth" [p.313]) about their knowledge of Islam and borrowed without explicit admission of reliance on the "alien source," but their encounter with the Islamic culture led them to cast doubt about—not merely disguise—their notion of universal truth.

A-155. Paret, Rudi. "Islam and Christianity." *Islamic Studies* 3, no.1 (March 1964): 86–95.

The author notes that while Judaism, Christianity, and Islam are characterized by "lines of junction," they do not extend to Hinduism or Buddhism. The three monotheistic sister religions are part of the same family, though, as with members of a family, there are also differences. The article focuses on some considerations about the mutual relationship between Christianity and Islam. Differences are highlighted "precisely because these differences alone permit us to know the individuality of the one or the other side" (p.84).

A key ideological difference pointed out relates to the Christian notion of Jesus as the Son of God, though Islam recognizes Jesus (Issa) as highly ranked in its sacred history. Also, while the Christian Jesus died on the cross, in Islam God received him alive—and "not until the Day of Judgment will he suffer death" (p.86). However, as "People of the Book," Christians and Jews were treated with forbearance in the sense that no one forced them to accept Islam. This practice was "more tolerable than the Byzantine rule, or for that matter Persian authority (in Iraq)" (p.87). "The Christian-Occident, however," the author notes, "is not indebted to Islam for its own fanaticism" (p.90). Further, "It is shocking to see how medieval scholarship was obsessed with its pro-Christian and hence anti-Islamic biases" (p.90).

The article concludes: "One who deals with Islam must, we might say, possess a theological vein, an organ for transcendent terms and values. Only on the basis of humanity can Christianity and Islam, Occident and Orient, truly come closer to each other" (p.95).

A-156. Pingree, David. "The Greek Influence on Early Islamic Mathematical Astronomy." *Journal of the American Oriental Society* 93, no.1 (January–March 1973): 32–43.

The article explores "the problem of the influence of Greek mathematical astronomy upon the Arabs" (p.32). The problem, the author argues, is "complicated by the fact that the Hellenistic astronomical tradition had, together with Mesopotamian linear astronomy of the Achaemenid and Seleucid periods and its Greek adaptations, already influenced the other cultural traditions that contributed to the development of the science of astronomy within the area in which the

Arabic language became the dominant means of scientific communication in and
after the seventh century A.D." (p.32).

Further, the author suggests, with the mingling of various traditions (Graeco-
Indian, Graeco-Iranian, Ptolemaic Greco-Syrian, and the Ptolemaic Byzantine),
"Islamic astronomers turned to those areas where these several astronomical systems were in conflict. This led to the development in Islam of a mathematical
astronomy that was essentially Ptolemaic, but in which new parameters were
introduced and new solutions to problems in spherical trigonometry derived from
India tended to replace those of the *Almagest*" (p.32).

The author concludes, after detailed analysis, that these developments "were
not without influence on the Western astronomers who faced the same problems
in the Renaissance" (p.43).

A-157. Ragep, F. Jamil. "Duhem, the Arabs, and the History of Cosmology."
Synthese 83 (1990): 201–214.

The paper is a critique of some of the scholarship of an early 20th-century
French scholar, Pierre Duhem. The author suggests that Duhem was "rather
extreme in his notions of Arabic science," and he felt that "Islamic science is in
large part the plundered spoils of decadent Greek science" (p.212). Thus, the
paper is motivated by two considerations: (1) to evaluate Duhem's attitude
toward Arabic science, a task that is said to be "even more imperative than it
would otherwise be," given the "continuing influence of Duhem's historical
works," and (2) to examine Duhem's understanding of Arabic astronomy, which
he viewed as a "foil to put in bolder relief the genius of Greek science" (p.201).

The author explores these concerns in some detail, with special focus on Greek
and Arabic contributions to the science of astronomy. It is noted that while, over
the years, Duhem realized some of the shortcomings of the Greeks relative to the
contributions of some Arab scholars, he was "unable, or perhaps unwilling" to
diminish his "hostility toward the Arabs" (203). It is suggested that Duhem was
rather like his French predecessor, Ernest Renan, who "had denied both the
Arabs and Islam a role in the history of science" (p.209).

The author concludes that such hostility is a "tragedy not only for Duhem but
for the history of science since he was a man of great insights and intuitions. But
blinded by prejudice, he did not care to delve into the problems of those who
were 'slaves to the imagination'" (p.211).

A-158. Rashed, Roshdi. "Problems of the Transmission of Greek Scientific
Thought into Arabic: Examples from Mathematics and Optics." *History of Science* 27 (1989): 199–209.

The article argues that "the emergence of Arabic science is incomprehensible
unless one refers to the reception of its Greek heritage." And, "The same holds
for the history of the relationship between Greek and Latin Science whose understanding requires the examination of Greek texts translated into Arabic and then

into Latin" (p.199). However, the author rejects "the image of transmission as passive reception with one of conversion, reactivation, and even occasionally the renewal of one or more disciplines" (p.199).

The author then explores "the institutionalization of the Hellenistic scientific legacy" in early ninth-century Baghdad. Two reasons examined are the existence of social need, and research. For, "The aim of the translation of scientific texts at that time was not to write the history of science but make available in Arabic, texts necessary for the training of researchers or even the advance of research" (p.202). Based on further analysis of the paper's theme, using examples from mathematics and optics, the author concludes: "The dialectic between translation and research appears in multitude forms that only a differential approach can exhaust" (p.208).

A-159. Runciman, Steven. "Islam and Christendom in the Middle Ages: The Need for Restatement." *Islamic Studies* 3, no.2 (June 1964): 193–198.

The article is critical of a "specialized" view of human experience. Historians such as Edward Gibbon, who wrote sympathetically about Islam, was unaware of Oriental sources, and, says the author, "the orientalists and the medievalists would pounce on him, denouncing him for meddling in subjects of which he was insufficiently informed" (p.193). However, such specialization is "especially unhelpful over such subjects as Muslim–Christian relations in the past. History in our ancient seats of learning tends to mean occidental history only. Islamic history belongs to the realm of the Orientalists" (p.194).

Thus, since "history is not the history of one country or one civilization," but "the story of mankind," we must engage in a "freeing process" (p.194). The author explains four avenues. First, we must learn the language of each other— Arabic for Western scholars and Latin/Greek for Muslims. Second, we must always be mindful of the past; we "shall understand neither Christianity nor Islam unless we know something of the world into which each was born" (p.195). Third, since both civilizations share the legacy of a unified moral outlook, "we should be prepared to discard partisanship and prejudice" (p.196). "The ideal scholar," says the author, "is one who is religious himself but who is prepared to admit that other religions are not necessarily ungodly and who is prepared to overlook differences in creed in his search for the common spirit" (p.196). And, finally, the author advocates "a closer study of actual personal contacts between individual Muslims and Christians in the Middle Ages" (p.196). If such avenues are pursued, then "a study of the past may help to bring a better understanding that, in spite of differences that have arisen, the basic standards, ideals and moral code of the two great Faiths are closely akin" (p.198).

A-160. Russell, Josiah C. "Hereford and Arabic Science in England about 1175–1200." *ISIS: Journal of the History of Science in Society* 18, no.1 (July 1932): 14–25.

"For a country located so far from the Mediterranean the share of England in the spread of Arabic science was rather astonishing," begins the article. However, from his biographical explorations, the author discovered that "Hereford, possibly through a cathedral school, was a center of this learning in the second half of the twelfth century" (p.14). The article documents historical evidence pertaining to various translators and scholars who engaged in the transmission of Arabic science—Roger of Hereford, Daniel of Merlai, Alexander Neckam, Alfredus Anglicus, and others. Some of these scholars traveled to Spain and brought back Arabic learning. The article identifies several areas of knowledge so transmitted.

The author concludes, "The presence of these men together with other evidence points to a cathedral school at Hereford at which the liberal arts, theology, and Arabic science were taught" (p.25).

A-161. Sabra, A.I. "Situating Arabic Science: Locality versus Essence." *ISIS: Journal of the History of Science in Society* 87, no.4 (December 1996): 654–670.

The author, after noting that "contextualization is but an obvious consequence of the simple, undeniable fact of the local character of all events, including historical events," argues that "all *history* of science must be contextual, because all historical events are local" (p.655). Thus, the purpose of the article (an invited lecture at the 1995 History of Science Society) "is to try to illustrate the advantages of a strict adherence to the axiom of locality in situating the tradition of Arabic science with reference both to the place that this tradition occupies in the general history of science and to its place in the civilization where it emerged and developed" (p.655). The author notes that "all history of science is local, and no history of science can ever be neutral" (p.656).

The article explores, among other things, the context of "the translation movement [chiefly in Baghdad] that quickly acquired unprecedented proportions—unprecedented not only in the Middle East but in the world at large" (p.658). The discussion is divided into three detailed sections: (1) locality as a focus of historiography, (2) the intersection of Islamism, Arabism, and Hellenism in ninth-century Baghdad, (3) three loci of scientific activity in Islam: the court, the college, and the mosque.

The author concludes that the single, unitary *tradition* of the Arabic science was stimulated by "for the most part one language (Arabic) and Islamic religion as an everpresent point of reference though not always a point of departure" (p.669).

A-162. Salman, D. "Algazel et les Latins" ("Algazel and the Latins"). *Archives d'Histoire Doctrinale et Literaire du Moyen Age* (1935–1936): 103–127.

The author begins with the controversies surrounding Al-Ghazali's two philosophical works, *Maqasid al-Falasifa* (The Aims of Philosophers) and *Tafahut al-Falasifa* (The Incoherrence of Philosophers). The first discusses the philosophy of Ibn Sina and Al-Farabi and the second refutes some of their arguments. Similarly, the author discusses the problems encountered with these works by some Latin-European scholars.

Thus, the author discusses the linkages of Al-Ghazali's scholarship with Latin-Christian thinking at the time, the focus being on three issues: (1) the significance of the *Maqasid* and controversies surrounding its reception (available in translation in early 12th century), (2) the Latin prologue (controversies relating to the Latin prologue of Al-Ghazali's *Maqasid*), (3) the Latin text. The article abounds in controversies not only as to the authenticity of the translations of Al-Ghazali's works but also their interpretations in Latin scholarship.

A-163. Samarrai, Alauddin. "The Term 'Fief': A Possible Arabic Origin." *Studies in Medieval Culture* 4, no.1 (1973): 78–82.

The purpose of the paper is to consider the Arabic language as a possible source from which Europe might have acquired the term *fief*. The widely accepted view relates the term *feodum* (*feudum*) to the Frankish combination *fehu-od*, meaning "cattle goods," thus, interpreted as "movable objects" (p.78). Other Gothic and German roots are also suggested by some.

The relevant Arab term mentioned is *fay*, which "is that part of the war spoils" and "obtained under a peace treaty" (p.80). It also referred to "whatever was abandoned by fleeing owners without a fight" (p.80). Islamic scholars wrote about the category of *fay*, as "abandoned lands as well as lands whose owners are unknown," although it did not consist of land alone (p.80–81). Further, it is suggested, "The Arabic *fuyu* (the plural of *fay*) is phonetically similar to the term '*fief*,' particularly in its early forms (*feo, feu, feuum, feuo,* etc.), which made its first appearance when large areas of Europe were under Muslim occupation" (p.81). And the fact remains that both *fay* and *fief* consisted of land and income from land. Further, the author argues, "The acquisition of Arabic words by the West is a matter of commonplace knowledge" (p.81). Since the early scribes "made more than normal use of the spoken vocabulary," they were "simply attempting to transliterate the Arabic word *fuyu*" into *fief* (p.82).

A-164. Shanab, R.E.A. "Ghazali and Aquinas on Causation." *The Monist* 58 (1974): 140–150.

The article argues that while Ghazali's predecessor, Ibn Sina (Avicenna, 980–1037) and successor, Ibn Rushd (Averroes, 1126–1198) are better known for their influence on medieval philosophic thought, Ghazali's is known more for "being responsible for the decline of medieval philosophy, especially Islamic philosophy, a claim that is extremely difficult to prove" (p.140). Yet, the author argues, a careful study of Ghazali's works reveals his profound and widespread influence on Western medieval scholars, particularly St. Thomas Aquinas. The paper specifically focuses on these two scholars' discussion of the principle of causality and demonstrates "how the works of Ghazali have played an important role in the shaping of the philosophic ideas of Aquinas" (p.141). Further, it is stated that "as early as the twelfth century, Ghazali's books were translated chiefly in Toledo into Latin and from the outset exercised an influence on the Christian and Jewish thinkers of the medieval period" (p.148).

The author quotes several paragraphs on various topics from each scholar's works and demonstrates parallels in terms of words and thought; and it is concluded that when comparing the two, "one cannot help but detect the influential aspect of Ghazali's works on Aquinas" (p.150).

A-165. Siddiqi, Mazheruddin. "The Holy Prophet and the Orientalists." *Islamic Studies* 19, no.3 (Autumn 1980): 143–165.

The article is about the false accusations and misrepresentations on the part of Orientalists against the Holy Prophet of Islam. It responds to them and attempts to present an objective interpretation of facts.

Several such accusations and misrepresentations are evaluated. Some of these may be identified here: (1) his low birth and thus not worthy of prophethood, (2) suffered from epileptic fits, (3) learned his knowledge from the Christian monk, Bahirah, (4) doubtful divine mission, (5) Satanic verses issue, (6) happiness of Quraish at the Prophet's emigration to Medina, (7) Prophet's place in Medina Constitution insignificant, (8) he denied his own prophethood, (9) he tried to mould Islam on Judaism, (10) Muslims worshiped the Prophet, (11) questions raised about marriages, etc.

The author critically evaluates each of these accusations and charges.

A-166. Siddiqui, Razi-ud-Din. "The Contribution of Muslims to Scientific Thought." *Islamic Culture* (Hyderabad, India) 14 (January 1940): 34–44.

The article begins with a note that "it is fully recognized now that science in the modern sense owes its origin to the Islamic spirit of enquiry, and that the scientific method is one of the most fruitful contributions of Muslim culture" (p.34). The main focus of the article, however, is to provide "a broad outline of their contribution to Mathematics and Astronomy" (p.34). Before doing so, however, the author notes two illustrations that suggest anticipation of Newton's law of gravitation with a pre-12th-century Muslim scholar and that of the Darwinian theory of evolution with the 12th-century Persian, Jalaluddin Rumi.

As for mathematics, the author notes, "the Greeks and Hindus considered number as pure magnitude, and it was only when Khwarizmi conceived of number as a pure relation in the modern sense that the science of Algebra could originate" (p.36). Contributions in arithmetic, algebra, and trigonometry are discussed, and "by the end of the eleventh century, the Arabs had found, developed and perfected geometrical algebra, and could solve equations of the third and fourth degrees" (p.37).

With respect to astronomy, the author notes, while there was only one observatory (Alexandria) in the pre-Islamic world, Muslims erected numerous observatories in many regions and developed numerous instruments for investigations.

Reference is made to several Islamic scholars who contributed to the field of astronomy. "The Arabs had discovered the true mechanism of the solar system, i.e., the heliocentric doctrine, about 300 years before Copernicus" (p.41).

A-167. Sirry, Mun'im A. "Early Muslim–Christian Dialogue: A Closer Look at Major Themes of the Theological Encounter." *Islam and Christian–Muslim Relations* 16, no.4 (October 2005): 361–376.

This article documents the instances of constructive dialogue during the first four centuries of Islam when Muslims and Christians engaged in serious theological discussions. While Muslim–Christian relations are as old as Islam, over the centuries the relationship between the two communities has sometimes been one of antagonism, sometimes one of rivalry and competition. Yet, there have been periods of open and fruitful dialogue and collaboration and even moments of sincere friendship. Several factors in the early Abbasid era (749–1258) favored such interactions, such as the cosmopolitan nature of Baghdad and its provinces (often Christian clergy from Europe would visit there for the sake of learning as well as missionary work), the Caliph's patronage of scholarship, the emergence of Arabic as a *lingua franca*, and the deployment of dialectical reasoning (*kalam*).

The author selects such themes of the theological encounter with the purpose of demonstrating how religious ideas were developed over the centuries. There is a bibliography of numerous relevant references.

A-168. Thompson, Diane P. "Paradigms Lost: Western Civilization and the Orient Unexpressed." *Northern Virginia Review*, no.10 (Fall 1995): 5–8.

The author laments the "false" history that nurtured her early intellectual life: Greek genius created the essence of Western civilization, transmitted it to Rome, then Europeans rediscovered classical Greek knowledge, "which had been miraculously preserved (as in a corked bottle) by the Arabs during the Dark Ages" (p.6). Thus, she had understood, happened the European Renaissance, giving birth to the modern world. Later, working on a project with other scholars, her curiosity rekindled and she discovered "the amount of active interchange between the Islamic world and Europe in the Mediterranean basin, especially in Spain, southern Italy, and Sicily. No more Aristotle in bottle" (p.7).

These Islamic scholars "had understood the Greek texts deeply, built their own systems and philosophies upon them, and added profound commentaries of their own, which were often included in the translations that reached Western Europe" (p.7). And, thus, the author "began to understand that my paradigm had been created by Western Europeans, writing history teleologically as a progress leading only to themselves" (p.8).

A-169. Thompson, James W. "The Introduction of Arabic Science into Lorraine in the Tenth Century." *ISIS: Journal of the History of Science in Society* 12 (May 1929): 184–194.

The purpose of this paper is twofold: (1) to show the intellectual linkages between Spain and Europe beyond the Pyrenees, "which was as old as the Roman Empire, was never wholly closed," and (2) to provide evidence that "Arabic science was introduced into the schools of Lorraine and was cultivated before Gerbert" (p.184).

The author identifies several scholars through whom "Arabic learning across the Channel into England" became transmitted—Robert de Losinga, Walcher of Malvern, Walcher of Durham, Thomas of York, Samson of Worcester, and others. He concludes: "I am convinced that the schools of Lorraine in the last half of the tenth century were the seed-plot in which the seeds of Arabic science first germinated in Latin Europe, from which the knowledge radiated to other parts of Germany—witness Hermann Contractus in Reichenau—to France, and especially, owing to the preference of Knut the Great for Lotharingian churchmen, into England" (p.191).

A-170. Thomson, Rodney M. "England and the Twelfth Century Renaissance." *Past and Present* 101 (1983): 3–21.

For this article, the point of departure is a 1970 essay by Richard Southern in which he talked about the 12th-century intellectual activities in England as a "colony of the French intellectual empire" (p.4). This paper argues for a more positive interpretation of England's place in the 12th-century renaissance.

References are made to several native-born English "scientists," who might have initially attended French schools, "but all of whom ended up in Spain or Italy, in search of Arabic knowledge of the natural sciences" (p.5). Then, the author identifies manuscripts of "English origin" that included Khwarizmi's treatise on Hindu arithmetic and another contained "a collection of rare translations of Greek and Arabic works on chemistry, and some highly original western works on the composition of matter not found elsewhere" (p.7). Additionally, the author documents the "English character" of numerous scholars who were "culturally" English.

A-171. Tschanz, David W. "The Arab Roots of European Medicine." *Aramco World* 48, no.3 (May–June 1997): 20–32.

The article traces the Arab-Islamic heritage in the evolution of the medical sciences in medieval Europe. During the Dark Ages of Europe, "because the Christian church viewed care of the soul as far more important than care of the body, medical treatment and even physical cleanliness were little valued" (p.23). Further, sicknesses were viewed as due to "supernatural forces" and "diabolical possessions," and "cures could only be effected by religious means" (p.23).

As the Greek heritage was rediscovered in the eighth century, "the Islamic physicians first familiarized themselves with the works of Hippocrates, Galen and other Greek physicians. At the same time, they were also exposed to the medical knowledge of Byzantium, Persia, India, and China" (p.23). According to the author, "Islam teaches that 'God has provided a remedy for every illness,' and that Muslims should search for those remedies" (p.24). Further, "Like the hospital, the institution of pharmacy, too, was an Islamic development" (p.24). The author narrates the contributions of various Arab-Islamic scholars (Al-Razi, Ibn Sina, and others). Referring to Ibn Sina's *The Canon*, it is noted that "from the twelfth to the seventeenth century, its *materia medica* was the pharmacopoeia of Europe" (p.31).

The author concludes: "The Islamic world not only provided a slender but ultimately successful line of transmission for the medical knowledge of ancient Greece and the Hellenic world, it also corrected and enormously expanded that knowledge before passing it on to a Europe that had abandoned observation, experimentation and the very concept of earthly progress centuries before" (p.31). The article includes several sketches and pictures of some relevant historic Arabic-language documents.

A-172. Van Koningsveld, P.S. "Muslim Slaves and Captives in Western Europe during the Late Middle Ages." *Islam and Christian–Muslim Relations* 6, no.1 (1995): 5–23.

This article, based mainly on Islamic sources, deals with the vicissitudes of the lives of Muslim slaves and captives during the late medieval period, a topic not much studied so far. The author notes, "The earliest Muslims of medieval Western Europe consisted mainly of captives and slaves" (p.5). The discussion is divided into three parts. First, there is a discussion of the Islamic view of the juridical status of the Muslim captives in Christian territories and of the Islamic institutions of redemption and redeemer. Secondly, the threefold role of learned Muslim captives in Christian territories is explained, viz. as (1) transmitters of Arabic secular sciences, (2) as scribes of Arabic scientific manuscripts, mainly in the serve of Jewish scholars, and (3) as teachers of Arabic and Islam to Christians, especially missionary articles, who were employed, among others as participants in Christian–Islamic theological dialogue. The last part of the paper discusses the socio-juridical aspects of Muslim captives and salves, mainly from Christian sources and modern historical studies.

The geographic region covered is beyond Al-Andalus or Muslim Spain and extends to several islands in the Mediterranean and small Muslim enclaves in the south of France and south of Italy, as well as Sicily and Balearic Islands. It is noted that Muslims were "present in these areas even to the nineteenth century, when slavery was abolished" (p.5).

The author concludes that the history of these Muslims was one of christianization and assimilation, under the combined pressure of Western societies and the Church. This phenomenon is "one of the most important factors that could explain the present success of the revival-movements in the West" (p.18).

A-173. Walzer, Richard. "Arabic Transmission of Greek Thought to Medieval Europe." *Bulletin of the John Rylands Library* 29, no.1 (July 1945): 3–26.

The study of Islamic philosophy and science, the author says, "deserves to be considered as an important item in the history of European civilization" (p.3). Thus, given the title of this paper, he explores questions such as how the Greek legacy came to the medieval Latin world in Arabic guise and why the "Muhammadans took so keenly" to this legacy and not the Western Latin world.

The article provides some of the reasons. The Latin-speaking people within the Roman Empire had abandoned links with the Greek world, and subsequently the Platonic Academy was "closed forcibly by Justinian in 529, the professors still being pagans. But philosophical and medical teaching was still alive in Alexandria when it was conquered by the Arabs in 639 (p.9). And, the Arabs "not only showed a remarkable tolerance towards the conquered inhabitants," but "also an eager willingness to take what the other had to give" (p.10). And once translated, assimilated, and further developed, "the Arab achievements in philosophy, medicine, science, etc. could surpass those of the genuine heirs of Greek civilization" (p.14). After this foreign legacy served their own needs and transmitted to later generations, it "eventually could be made available to the Western Latin world" (p.15). And, as evidence of their "unconditional tolerance and open-mindedness," Arabs acknowledged their debt to the Greeks (p.16).

Numerous Arab scholars (including several Jewish and Christian translators–scholars) and Greek works are mentioned in this context. Further, the author notes, "The Muhammadan philosophical tradition represented by al-Farabi and Averroes achieved still more for the continuity of European thought" (p.24). And, "For more than three centuries the Western world studied Aristotle mainly with the help of Averroes' commentaries" (p.24).

A-174. Watt, W. Montgomery. "Muhammad in the Eyes of the West." *Boston University Journal* 22, no.3 (1974): 61–69.

The author begins with the suggestions that "some of the world's urgent political problems might be easier to solve if these two religious communities had a deeper respect for each other's religion. Yet for Westerners none of the world's religious leaders is so difficult to appreciate as Muhammad, since the West has a deep-seated prejudice against him" (p.61).

The article notes that it was during the years 1100 to 1300 when European scholars created a distorted image of Muhammad and Islam, something that has persisted to the present time. Several reasons are mentioned: the early military successes of Islam, some biblical justifications, and "in the intellectual field, there were even weightier reasons for the Europeans to feel inferior to Muslims" (p.62). In the 12th and 13th centuries, "European students of science and philosophy were busy learning all they could from the Arabs" (p.62). Further, as Europe gradually moved into a position of leadership, with increasing identification with Christianity, "it needed a negative image of what it was fighting against" (p.62). And, "It is because this distorted image had a function in the very making of Europe that it is so difficult to correct" (p.63). Additionally, uncritical acceptance of distortions suited the need to defend Christianity and enhance European identity. The main reason for the persistence of distortions, however, is the "negative aspect of the conception of Western self-identity" (p.63). And, such distortions have "persisted longest among Christian writers, especially those with missionary interests" (p.66). There were some, however, who saw Islam "as a natural religion, simple and reasonable, to be contrasted with the artificiality and irrationality of Christianity" (p.66).

In conclusion, the author asks for objectivity and a perspective that adopts "the standpoint of the whole," and, further, "it is necessary for each religion to see itself as somehow part of the total religious experience of mankind" (p.69).

A-175. Welborn, Mary C. "Lotharingia as a Center of Arabic and Scientific Influence in the Eleventh Century." *ISIS: Journal of the History of Science in Society* 16 (1931): 188–199.

The article begins by noting that before the end of the tenth century, European astronomers "were greatly handicapped" in their calculations due to lack of proper instruments, and "they were unable to improve upon them because they had not yet received from the Arabs better astronomical theories and instruments" (p.188). Then, "towards the end of the tenth century knowledge of the Arabic astrolabe began to penetrate into the Latin West," and "this astrolabe must have been used first by Lotharingian geometers and astronomers" (p.188).

The author then develops evidence to demonstrate "that the schools of Lotharingia should have been the earliest centers in Western Europe north of the Pyrenees in which Arabic learning was fostered, because in comparison with the famous schools of the tenth century, such as Reichenau, St. Gall, Reims, Paris, Chartres, and Cluny, those of Liege were especially outstanding for their real love of scientific subjects" (p.189). Names of numerous scholars are identified. Further, "The influence of Lotharingian mathematicians and astronomers not only extended southward to Reichenau but also westward to England" (p.197).

A-176. Wolf, C. Umhau. "Luther and Mohammedanism." *The Moslem World* (Hartford, CT) 31, no.3 (July 1941): 161–177.

The paper discusses Martin Luther's views about the Turks, "Mohammedans," and "Mohammedanism" (i.e., Muslims and Islam). The discussion is based on Luther's own works. The paper is divided into two sections: (1) Luther's Attitude toward the Turks and Mohammedanism, (2) Luther's Knowledge of Mohammedan Doctrines and Practices.

Luther decried the ignorance "regarding the Turks and the religion of Mohammed," but he thought "Turks constituted a punishment from God" and "both the Pope and the Turk were signs of the Last Days." Further, he linked Turks "with the Devil and the Antichrist," and leveled "similar charges against the papal hierarchy," that hierarchy being "a greater enemy and worse abomination than the

Turk" (p.163–164). And, Luther's "polemics against the Turks were less harsh and severe than those against the Papacy" (p.164).

Luther's knowledge of Islam, the author notes, "was usually accurate," but "occasionally he misinterprets the Koran, and this, unfortunately is still being done" (p.165). Luther believed that this faith was "patched together out of the faith of Jews, Christians, and heathen" (p.166). His main objection, however, was "the rejection of Trinity by Turkish rationalism" (p.168). And both Jews and Mohammedans, "show and prove that there is no more than one single God" (p.168). Further, whereas "Protestant Reforms took as their key 'justification by Faith' alone," the Mohammedans believe that they "will become holy and be saved by works" (p.172). Luther speaks contemptuously of "Mohammad with his doctrine of works" (p.172).

The author concludes: "We must state that Luther's attitude toward Islam was partly characteristic of the unfair polemic atmosphere of the age, but partly in advance of his age with respect to self-judgment and the urging of tolerance" (p.176).

A-177. Young, T. Cuyler. "The Cultural Contributions of Islam to Christendom." *The Moslem World* (Hartford, CT) 35, no.2 (April 1945): 89–110.

The article is a brief "evaluation of the chief cultural contributions of Islam to Europe and the west" (p.89). While "Islam owes a great debt to the areas of Christendom which it conquered," the author discusses the "later repayment of that debt to Christendom by the new culture created by Islam" (p.90). During the ninth and tenth centuries, there was the Islamic revival of classical learning, and then these "cultural creations" were transmitted "to the Latin world during the twelfth and thirteenth centuries," eventually becoming "the basis of the Western Renaissance of the fifteenth and sixteenth centuries" (p.90–91).

The author notes that Christendom's "greatest debt to Islam" pertains to the transmission of philosophy and sciences, especially medicine and mathematics. But, there is also the Islamic legacy in other fields—art and architecture, literature, music, law, and mysticism. Various Islamic scholars and their contributions, as well as their Latin-Christian successors, are discussed. The "geographical bridges" for transmission are also noted—"Spain, Sicily, and Syria, in that order of importance" (p.91).

The author discusses Islam's "real spirit of democracy" and the "personality and character traits" of Muslims. He concludes with this note: "All this should temper the spirit with which we of Christendom, and especially of the Christian Church, turn to Islam bearing our cultural and spiritual gifts. Verily we go as equals paying an ancient debt; it will be no more than justice if we return in kind with interest, and truly Christian if we forget the terms of the bond and pay with love and gratitude" (p.110).

(C) General

(I) SPAIN/AL-ANDALUS

A-178. Abercrombie, Thomas J. "When the Moors Ruled Spain." *National Geographic* 74, no.1 (July 1988): 86–119.

This long essay is like a travelogue that covers various aspects of the history of Moorish Spain—"the marks of the Moors on the face and heart of Spain." "Only recently have the Spanish begun to approach their Islamic past," notes one of the commentators, but "we are finding that much of what we think of as 'pure Spanish,' our architecture, our temperament, our poetry and music—even our language—is a blend from a long Arabic heritage" (p.92). And, "For several centuries after Toledo's recapture, the city remained bilingual, tolerant. Alfonso X patronized a major thirteenth-century translation school where Christian, Muslim, and Jewish scholars collaborated to render Arabic manuscripts into Latin—masterpieces like the commentaries on Aristotle by Ibn Rushd (Averroes), works on algebra and mathematics by al-Khwarizmi (from whose name comes our term "logarithm"), and the Canon of Ibn Sina (Avicenna), which remained Europe's standard medical textbook for 500 years" (p.93). The article provides numerous pictures of art and architecture in Al-Andalus, including pictures of contemporary life and of annual festivities in various Spanish cities that replicate aspects of the "Moorish" surrender. As for the Inquisition, established in 1480, "before it was over, three centuries later, thousands of Muslims and Jews had died; an estimated three million people were driven into exile" (p.96).

Referring to the Cordoba mosque, the author concludes, "No other artifact more richly evokes the golden age of the Moors, a stormy millennium that dovetailed two faiths, two cultures, two continents. Throughout, while king and sultan fought bitterly for the hand of Spain, ordinary life prospered as Arab, Visigoth, Castilian, and Berber worked together to forge the brilliant civilization that helped lead Europe out of the Dark Ages. Ultimately the cross replaced the crescent. The Moors themselves faded into history, leaving behind their scattered dreams. But Spain and the West stand forever in their debt" (p.119).

A-179. Aramco World Services. "The Art of Islamic Spain." *Aramco World* 43, no.5 (September–October 1992): 2–64.

This issue of the magazine is devoted to the art history of Islamic Spain, and there are five essays. Each essay, with author's name, article title, and a brief description as given in the magazine's table of contents is appended below:

(1) Zayn Bilkadi, "Heaven's Gate"—" 'There is the truth of legends and there is the legend of truths,' great-grandmother Mammati Fatma said, and Sidi Bou Said—simultaneously fishing village, tourist center and historical monument—is home to both." (2) Charles O. Cecil, "A Study in Blue and White"—"Blue doors, whitewashed houses and beautiful views of the sea—and of history— attract tourists and Tunisians alike to the cobbled streets and contemplative charms of Sidi Bou Said, still today 'the sea of reconciliation.' " (3) Caroline Stone, "Berber Silver, Arab Gold"—"In the rich variety of North African jewelry all the layers and distinctions of society are reflected in metal and stone. Men and women, married and unmarried, Berber and Arab—for each, there is an appropriate treasure." (4) Piney Kesting, "Recalling the Tales"—"Many Arab folk tales recorded even 130 years ago, from Morocco to Iraq, are still current in homes and teahouses, a Palestinian-American folklorist found—as well as in her own warm memories of home and family." (5) Patricia Countess Jellicoe, "The Art of Islamic Spain"—"Muslim Spain, for 700 years the occidental frontier of Islam, gave birth to a complex and original mixed culture whose exquisite art and architecture bear witness to power and opulence, but also to restraint and faith."

Each essay contains several pictures and sketches. Also, some references are cited in each.

A-180. Avila, Maria Luisa. "The Search for Knowledge: Andalusi Scholars and Their Travels to the Islamic East." *Medieval Prosopography* (Special Issue: Arab-Islamic Culture) 23 (2002): 125–139.

The author notes that for Andalusian scholars, among other things, "traveling to the Islamic East was an essential step in their period of formation, at least during the first centuries of the history of al-Andalus" (p.125). Based on an analysis of "prosopographical material" from "the oldest of Andalusi biographical dictionaries," the article explores three queries: "first, the age at which scholars began their period of scholarly preparation; second, when the travel to the East (the *rihla*) was usually undertaken; and, finally, how long these scholars stayed in the East. This will help us to arrive at a better understanding of how academic careers in al-Andalus were constructed" (p.125).

The exploration concludes that (1) "youth is an outstanding characteristic of these scholars, many of whom began their training before the age of twenty"; (2) travel to the East (typically "accompanied by parents, relatives, or friends") usually began at a maturer age, "after reaching the age of thirty"; (3) the period of study "normally ran from four to seven years" and "along the way, Andalusi scholars frequently spent time in Ifriqya and Egypt, where they attended famous masters' classes" (p.136–137).

A-181. Beech, George T. "Troubadour Contacts with Muslim Spain and Knowledge of Arabic: New Evidence Concerning William IX of Aquitaine." *Romania: Revue Trimestrielle* 113 (1992–1995): 14–42.

This article further explores the problem of the origin of the troubadour poetry in the 12th century, one of the most controversial issues in the study of medieval literature. There is the Arabist thesis that maintains the troubadours' origins lie with Muslim Spain's Arabic poets, encountered during the Spanish Reconquest. The Romancists, on other hand, argue that Arabic love poetry and French courtly love lyric are coincidental and have independent origins. More recently, however, some have argued that the first known troubadour, William IX of Aquitaine (1086–1126) did in fact have contacts with Muslims and Jewish Spain and knew Arabic.

The author explores this possibility further. While no direct evidence is found whether William knew Arabic, the author's historical approach demonstrates that first, he "knew much more about Islamic Spain than previously thought; second, that Arabic speaking people formed part of the circle of relatives, friends, and acquaintances in contact with him, and finally that he had friendly personal relations with the contemporary Muslim king of Zaragoza," who was a patron of "Jewish and Arabic scientists, philosophers, and poets" (p.18).

The author concludes that the evidence "places William IX much closer to direct personal contact with twelfth century Arab poets than previously thought. Consequently, the suggestions made by Arabists in the past that he may have known and borrowed from their poetry can no longer be dismissed as absurd, nor can the notion that he may have known some Arabic" (p.42).

A-182. Burshatin, Israel. "The Moor in the Text: Metaphor, Emblem, and Silence." *Critical Inquiry* 12, no.1 (Autumn 1985): 98–118.

The paper discusses the paradoxical image of the Moor (Muslim) in Spanish literature during the period between 1492 and the eventual expulsion of the Moriscos (baptized Moors) in 1609. The author notes the oppositional perspectives of the time: "On the 'vilifying' side, Morros are hateful dogs, miserly, treacherous, lazy *and* overreaching. On the 'idealizing' side, the men are noble, loyal, heroic, courtly—they even mirror the virtues that Christian knights aspire to—while the women are endowed with singular beauty and discretion" (p.98).

The discussion is approached in terms of textual (1) metaphors (the El Cid literature, specifically the *Poema de mio Cid*), which among other things, identified "the Moor as chattel *and* as romantic Other" (p.102); (2) emblem (focus is on the *Cronica Sarracina*)—"plays, ballads, histories, and novels from the fifteenth to the twentieth centuries stem from this seminal work" (p.103); and (3) silence, interpreted as "The end of debates over assimilation and conversion," which "point to the radical surgery, however, imperfectly accomplished, performed on the body politic, as historians now suggest. But the meaning of this official silence seems more properly as a discursive matter, namely, the culmination of the allegorical interpretation that apologists for the expulsion devised" (p.113). The author provides an extensive bibliography at the end.

A-183. Edwards, John. "Mission and Inquisition among *Conversos* and *Moriscos* in Spain, 1250–1550." *Studies in Church History* 21 (1984): 139–151.

Beginning with the observation that the coexistence between the three monotheistic faiths in medieval times should be an inspiration for multifaith societies, the article explores interfaith relations from the Christian perspective concerning the other two "religions of the book." Further, the paper examines the feasibility of long-term existence of Jewish and Muslim communities in Spain and the problems faced by converts to Christianity.

The paper first deals with the "Jewish problem." As the "ammunition" of missionaries to spread the faith among Jews and Muslims failed, pressures emerged to convert "the Christ-killers" by force. Thus, "Conversos" were Jews subjected to forced baptism. Eventually, however, the Inquisition took place, leading to persecutions of various forms, including expulsion, but many targeted people assimilated. Then, as for Muslims, "the policies which have been outlined with regard to relations between Christianity and Judaism also applied, *mutatis mutandis*, to Islam" (p.146). Muslims were viewed as "on the brink of conversion," but says the author, "It is hard to avoid seeing such enterprises as at best bravely outrageous and at worst comically foolish" (p.146). *Moriscos* were Muslims forced to baptize, or risk consequences (execution, expulsion, etc.); Cardinal Jimenez de Cisneros was the Inquisitor-General.

The author concludes that "there was no reason in principle why the *moriscos* could not have assimilated too. Politics, and excess of doctrinal purity, prevented this happy but confused state from being reached" (p.151).

A-184. Eigeland, Tor. "Escape from a Troubled World." *Aramco World* 41, no.5 (September–October 1990): 2–10.

This is short article, with breath-taking pictures, about the Andalusian Spain's Muslim heritage, "from the Alhambra to the humblest home, the lovely patios," where the "sun, shade, flowers and running water" create what the Andalusians call "antechambers of heaven" (p.5). The predecessors of these patios, the author notes, date back thousands of years; they were simply part of the natural way of constructing a home. The Muslim Andalusians "had a great love of beauty, nature, and growing things, and a positive passion for running water—qualities evident in their art, architecture, and above all in their patios" (p.5).

The author is most impressed by the "spiritual influence of these outdoor living rooms," whose ultimate refinement "was indeed achieved by the Muslims in Andalusia during their six centuries of rule" (p.5).

The article briefly traces the history of three Andalusian cities: Granada, Cordoba, and Seville.

A-185. Eigeland, Tor. "Islam in Al-Andalus." *Aramco World Magazine* 27, no.5 (September–October 1976): 1–32.

This entire issue of the magazine is devoted to a nostalgic history of the Islamic presence in Al-Andalus, from 711 AD to 1492 AD. There are seven short essays, each decorated with some color pictures, and each written by the author, who observes that the traces of Arab past "are to be found almost everywhere" (p.1).

The seven essays are: (1) Islam Comes to Europe, (2) Notes on Al-Andalus, (3) The Golden Caliphate, (4) The City of Al-Zahra, (5) The Ripening Years, (6) The Face of Al-Andalus, (7) The Final Flowering. The author notes, "The history of Islamic Spain is centered around three Andalusian cities: Cordoba, Seville, and Granada" (p.3).

A-186. Eigeland, Tor. "Touring Al-Andalus." *Aramco World* 50, no.2 (March–April 1999): 22–32.

The article is about the legacy of Islamic Spain, from the perspective of a tourist. "For 700 years, Cordoba and Granada were the cultural capitals of al-Andalus, the centers of the Muslim-ruled *convivencia*" (p.22). The Spanish Government has preserved this legacy, and by developing 11 historic routes across al-Andalus the area has become attractive for travelers. The article covers some key towns and cities in the region: Baena, Alcaudete, Valor, Sorvilan, Granada, Cordoba, Tabernas, Moclin, and Almeria.

The article is decorated with excellent color pictures from various parts of the region covered.

A-187. Fernandez, Maria Luisa. "Art of the Mudejars." *Aramco World* 44, no.1 (January–February 1993): 36–41.

Within varying territorial limits, Islamic rule prevailed in the Iberian Peninsula from 711 to 1492. In the post-Islamic era, Muslims who lived in Christian-held territories were called *Mudejars*, derived from the Arabic *al-mudajjamun*— "those permitted to remain, with a suggestion of 'tamed, domesticated'" (p.36). The article notes that the "Mudejar art and architecture derive from the Islam art traditions of the Iberian Peninsula, but must be viewed through the prism of the *reconquest*. By comparing an important Islamic monument, such as the Alhambra Palace in Granada, with a Mudejar structure of similar scale and purpose, like the Alcazar of Seville, we can identify Mudejar elements that are most likely to appear in Hispanic-American colonial art" (p.37).

But, the author asks, why would Christian rulers, dedicated to driving the Muslims from Spain, choose Islamic art and architectural forms? The explanation lies, according to the author, "in the application of temporal power: Mudejar style was deliberately used to express the authority of Christian kings over subject minorities in terms the subjects could understand. By appropriating the Islamic artistic tradition, Pedro the Cruel was able to express notions of power, luxury and wealth similar to his Muslim subjects. Islamic palaces and gardens, from Madinat al-Zahra to the Alhambra, had a long, well-established tradition in the peninsula, providing a large and lavish repertoire of royal symbols. By contrast, Gothic architecture's symbolism had been developed solely for religious purposes" (p.37). However, while "Mudejar influences contributed to the formation of Hispanic-American colonial art, the original Islamic meaning underlying the art was essentially lost. The Mudejar style in the New World developed not in an Islamic but in a Christian-baroque and neo-Hispanic context" (p.41).

The article is decorated with some elegant pictures from Spain and Ecuador. It may be noted that this entire issue of the magazine is devoted to "The Legacy of Al-Andalus."

A-188. Harvey, L.P. "The Moriscos and the *Hajj*." *Bulletin of the British Society for Middle Eastern Studies* 14, no.1 (1987): 11–24.

The author notes that "among all the lands of the Islamic world, the experience of Spain, al-Andalus, has been unique. It has been the only large and important area of initial Islamic implantation which has passed permanently out of Islamic lands" (p.11). Further, with the fall of Granada in 1492, the *reconquesta* was complete.

This article discusses the "*hajj* as it was known to Spanish Moriscos of the sixteenth century and as they sought to perform it" (p.12). The period under review is 1492 until the expulsion of 1609–1610. Moriscos were Muslims who were forcibly baptized; but they "continued to be Muslims under conditions of clandestinity while putting on some show of being Catholic Christians" (p.12). During this period, while there was strict surveillance of their "Islamic" habits and practices, the Inquisition never accused the "crypto-Muslims" if they had gone to Mecca. One reason, the author suggests, was that it was difficult to prove the intention of those who performed the *hajj*. Thus until 1609–1610, many Moriscos did perform *hajj*, some under the leadership of women. Then, after the expulsion orders of 1609, "Muslims of Spain were free to travel abroad and to make their hajj if they so wished. The freedom which was denied them after 1611 was that of returning home again after their *hajj* was completed" (p.23).

A-189. Hourani, George. "The Early Growth of the Secular Sciences in Andalusia." *Studia Islamic* 32 (1970): 143–156.

The purpose of the paper is to briefly "present the process by which Andalusia became the leading western base of Arabic science and philosophy" (p.143). After identifying the "two dramatic events" (the translations from Greek into Arabic during the ninth–tenth centuries and the translations from Arabic to Latin during the 12th–13th centuries), the author discusses the "intermediate transmission, from East to West, within the Arabic lands." Greek science and philosophy first traveled to eastern Islam (Iran, Syria, Iraq, etc.) and from this emerged new developments in eastern Arabic secular culture during the Abbasid period (850–1050 AD).

In the Islamic West (Andalusia), the author argues, there was little inherited scientific tradition from the Christian Spain. Thus the immigrant Arabs and Berbers looked to the East for secular learning. This was true concerning various fields—philosophy, medicine, pharmacy, botany, astronomy, mathematics, etc. Subsequently, secular learning flourished in Andalusia. And so, "Andalusia became the leading western base of Arabic science and philosophy" (p.143).

A-190. Irving, Thomas B. "The Process of Arab Thought in Spain." *Studies in Islam* 4, no.2 (April 1967): 65–96.

The article documents the contributions of Islamic Spain, over almost nine centuries, and the process through which this phenomena helped both Spain and Western Europe. "The greatest contribution of the Spanish Arabs to world thought was in conveying philosophic tradition from ancient civilization, especially the Hellenistic, to Western Christendom" (p.65). And, "Their labors came into Western consciousness in the late middle ages and held almost undisputed sway through the two Bacons, Hobbes and Locke until they were modified by Descartes and Kant." However, "The Spanish Arabs were not mere transmitters; some were very original thinkers" (p.66).

The paper then focuses on what the author calls "five great gestation periods in Spanish Arab thought." Covering the period from the ninth to 14th centuries, Spanish Arab scholars and their contributions (including what they acquired from Islamic East) in various areas are discussed, along with Latin-European scholars who utilized their knowledge. Among other things, it is suggested that Ibn Rushd's "double-truth" doctrine eventually "led to the idea of the separation of the church and state, a theory which developed further over Europe in later centuries and particularly in the United States and some Latin American republics. Ibn Rushd sought to harmonize religion and philosophy, not by synthesizing them but by their complete separation" (p.81).

The author concludes: "The products of this period were to shove the rest of Europe forward to the Renaissance just as the Arab world, under the impact of its own barbarian invasions, slipped off into its private medieval world, where it lasted until awakened by Napoleon in his transcendental invasion of Egypt. All this was due to the genius of Arab Spain. Spain and the West too often ignore both this debt and this glory" (p.93).

A-191. Jellicoe, Patricia Countess. "The Art of Islamic Spain." *Aramco World* 43, no.5 (September–October 1992): 24–31.

The article describes some of the art treasures of Islamic Spain. Referring to Granada's Alhambra, the author says, this "thirteenth-century citadel and palace complex set on a hilltop overlooking Granada is not only the best known monument of the Muslim era in Spain, but itself one of that period's greatest treasures" (p.26). With joint efforts of New York's Metropolitan Museum of Art and the Administration of Alhambra and Generalife, an art exhibition of 800 years of Islamic Spain was held in 1992. The exhibition included "some 120 pieces of the finest Hispano-Islamic art from collections in America, Britain, Russia, Sicily, Egypt, Morocco, Spain and other countries: ivory and marble carvings, bronze lamps and animals, coins, jewels and ceremonial swords, textiles, ceramics, astrolabes and the flowing calligraphy of Qur'ans, all restoring a vivid life to the rich, exotic beauty of the Alhambra's interiors" (p.26).

Further, the exhibition reflected the various dynasties of Islamic Spain, from 711 to 1492, and from the displays one absorbs "something of the origins of al-Andalus, of the powers and interests at play, of the widespread trade and travel of Spain's Muslims and the resulting influences on their arts and of the ebb and flow of hegemony in the peninsula, from the early days of Muslims-Christian-Jewish harmony and mutual tolerance to the final victory of the *reconquesta* in Granada" (p.26). The exhibition also included pieces from Cordoba and other cities.

With the aid of several colorful pictures, the author provides an excellent glimpse of the sociocultural history of Al-Andalus, including its significance as being "at the forefront of European sciences" by the end of the 11th century (p.28).

A-192. Latham, J.D. "Towns and Cities of Barbary: The Andalusian Influence." *Islamic Quarterly* 16 (1972): 189–204.

The article traces the "foundation, growth, and development"of various towns and cities of northwest Africa (known as the Barbary area, encompassing Morocco, Algeria, and Tunisia). For almost 900 years after the advent of Islam, "no single influence was more decisive, extensive, and pervasive than that exerted by the Andalusians" (p.189). By Andalusians, the author refers to (a) Muslim Spain, (b) Muslims inhabiting in "reconquered" Christian regions, (c) Moriscos, that is, Muslims who were forcibly baptized.

The Andalusian influence reached the Barbary region through various sources, including migration. The author presents a "panoramic view of these nine hundred years," and in doing so, he argues that "the phenomenon that is most interesting is the part played by Andalusian elements in the building, development, restoration, or revitalization of the towns and cities of Barbary" (p.189). The author concludes with a quote from a 13th-century Andalusian: "Were it not for al-Andalus, the Maghrib would never have been heard of, nor would anything of value ever have emerged from it" (p.204).

A-193. Lunde, Paul. "The Giralda." *Aramco World* 44, no.1 (January–February 1993): 32–35.

"Once the minaret of a huge congregational mosque, now the bell tower of Europe's third largest cathedral," the Giralda is "the symbol of Seville, endlessly reproduced on everything from key chains to cookie boxes" (p.33). Further, "When Seville fell to Christian armies in 1248, after a long siege, its Muslim inhabitants were forced to leave, and the mosque was transformed into a cathedral" (p.35). It was not until 1401, however, when the "decision was taken to build a 'modern'—in this case, Gothic—cathedral on the site of the mosque. In the course of building the third largest cathedral in Christendom, most of the old Almohad structure was demolished. A section of the wall, the beautiful Patio of the Orange Trees, the Gate of Pardon, with its magnificent bronze-plated door, and the minaret were spared" (p.35).

The author notes: "In a very real sense, the Giralda presents a paradigm of the complex history of the city it adorns. Its foundations are Roman or possibility Carthaginian; the main body of the tower is Islamic, which in turn supports a renaissance structure built according to the norms of classical architecture. The complexity of the image makes it a fitting symbol of a city where classical, Christian and Muslim cultures met and merged" (p.35).

The article includes some elegant pictures of this historic structure. It may be noted that this entire issue of the magazine is devoted to "The Legacy of Al-Andalus."

A-194. Lunde, Paul. "Ishbiliyah: Islamic Seville." *Aramco World* 44, no.1 (January–February 1993): 20–31.

The article is a narrative of the history of Spain's Seville, a city that was "a shining jewel of al-Andalus" during its glory days of more than 500 years of Islamic rule" (p.20). Called Hispalis during the Roman Empire, it came to be called Spalis, or Ishbiliyah, during the Islamic rule. At the time, "The Jewish community in Ishbiliyah was very large. It possessed at least four synagogues. The Jews had suffered severely under the Visigoths and welcomed the Muslim conquerors" (p.27). Further, "The presence of two significant non-Muslim communities in early Ishbiliyah contributed to the complexity of the urban texture" (p.27).

The author notes that "when Fernando III entered Ishbiliyah in 1248, it had been transformed. Hardly a trace remained of Roman times: He found himself in an enchanted world of palaces, gardens, fountains and mosques, the Torre del Oro still clad in the gold-luster tiles that gave its name. The Christians, even as they transformed the city in future centuries, would live under its spell. They still do today" (p.31). The article is decorated with some beautiful pictures of the city.

The entire issue of the magazine is devoted to "The Legacy of Al-Andalus."

A-195. Meadows, Ian. "Historical Markers." *Aramco World* 44, no.1 (January–February 1993): 10–11.

The article identifies scores of Arabic place names across the Iberian peninsula, and this list tells "a lot about the ebb and flow of Arab conquest and settlement in what is today Spain and Portugal, and provides a tantalizing insight into the minds of the soldiers, geographers, poets and simple folk who came, made Spain their home and—in creating a unique culture—gave the land so much in return" (p.10). The article provides a map in which numerous historic Arabic place names are identified. Numerous current names are etymologically Arabic in origins, such as names beginning with *guad* (means Wadi)—Guadalquivir (Arabic *al-Wadi al-Kabir*, great river), Guadalamir (*al-Wadi al-Ahmar*, red river), and others such as Alqueria (*al-Qariyah*, the village), Trafalgar, derived from the name of the cape, *Tara al-Ghar*, meaning Cave Point. The Arabic word *madinah*, or city, is found in some Spanish place names—for example, Medinaceli (*Madinat Salim*, the city of Salim), etc.

The author notes that while there have been some studies, "an exhaustive study of Arabic-origin names in Spain has yet to be done. The same is true of lands beyond Spain's borders" (p.11). The author refers to areas in France, Italy, and even Switzerland. "There, as well as across southern Spain, the names on the land record history" (p.11).

The entire issue of the magazine is devoted to "The Legacy of Al-Andalus."

A-196. Noakes, Greg. "Exploring Flamenco's Arab Roots." *Saudi Aramco World* 45, no.6 (November–December 1994): 32–35.

While there has been some controversy as to the roots of flamenco music, recent explorations have provided evidence of its Arabic roots, the author argues. Some scholars believed the word *flamenco* means "Flemish"; others viewed it as a corruption of the colloquial Arabic *felag mangu*, meaning "fugitive peasant." This Arabic ancestry was further reinforced through evidence from research as part of Spain's "new appreciation of al-Andalus and of Arab and Islamic culture."

Such explorations, as well as the collaboration of flamenco performers and Andalusi musicians, have "broken down long-standing cultural and historical barriers and demonstrated—in an era where some see only a 'clash of civilizations' between Islam and the West—that there is room for cooperation and creativity" (p.3).

A-197. Noakes, Greg. "The Other 1492." *Aramco World* 44, no.1 (January–February 1993): 2–9.

The year 1992 marks the 500th anniversary of Christopher Columbus' "discovery" of the New World. However, there was another 500th anniversary and the event was the fall of Granada (Gharnata in Arabic) on January 2, 1492, to the Castilian forces, thus ending the Arab-Islamic presence in Spain. The article highlights some aspects of 800 years of this presence.

According to the article, "The Arabs developed a society that was uniquely tolerant and heterogeneous, with Arab and Berber immigrants living side-by-side with Spanish Muslims, Christians, and Jews" (p.4). Further, "While Muslim rule in Spain had ended, the rich cultural and intellectual legacy of al-Andalus survived, both in the Iberian peninsula and throughout the world" (p.7). And, "The works of many of the most prominent thinkers and practitioners of al-Andalus, along with writings from the eastern Muslim world, were translated into Latin by Spaniards. Through these translations, philosophical and scientific thought from the Greek and Roman worlds, preserved and expanded upon by Muslims scholars, passed into European consciousness to fuel both the Renaissance and the Age of Enlightenment" (p.7–8).

A-198. Salloum, Habeeb. "Arabian Memories in Portugal." *Saudi Aramco World* 52, no.2 (March–April 2001): 1–5.

The author traces the Arab-Islamic legacy in Portugal, part of the Islamic Spain (Al-Andalus) for about 500 years, until about mid-13th century. The legacy is documented with respect to the Portuguese folkloric music tradition (in particular *fado* and *fadistas*, and the singers), the language, architecture, and knowledge of navigation. "The lateen sail and the astrolabe, introduced by the Arabs, were instrumental in launching our nation into its Age of Discovery," a Portuguese official is quoted. Also noted are contributions to farming techniques and introduction of various farm products, and further, "the colors, aromas and flavors of the Portuguese kitchen" have Arabic heritage.

The author also provides a list of numerous Portuguese words, with English equivalents, whose roots are Arabic.

A-199. Wolf, Kenneth B. "The Earliest Spanish Christian Views of Islam." *Church History* 55 (1986): 281–293.

The article "explores the pertinent documentation from post-conquest Spain in an attempt to construct a more meaningful historical context for Spanish Christian perceptions of Islam" (p.282). The author mentions two reasons for "extremely slow penetration of Islam as an intellectually identifiable fact in Western minds": geographical distance for Latin Christians and psychological barriers for the Christians of Spain.

The author notes, however, that as "Peoples of the Book," Muslims' absorption of the Iberian peninsula was not "principally a function of their military prowess; rather, it was a product of their willingness to offer remarkably favorable terms of surrender" (p.284). He differs with some other scholars who "assumed that the very presence of Islam forced Spanish Christians to come to terms with it as a potential threat and that their perceptions of Islam were necessarily warped by their fears of cultural absorption. But the evidence does not support this assumption" (p.293). The threat was not recognized by Christians, the author argues, until, during the ninth century, ecclesiastics such as "Eulogius wrote precisely to convince his fellow Christians that Islam was antithetical to

Christianity, when many, perhaps even most, of them were content to see Islam as a separate revelation and law that could coexist with their own" (p.293).

A-200. Zuwiyya, Z. David. "Arab Culture and Morisco Heritage in an Aljamiado Legend: 'Al-hadit del bano de Zaryeb.'" *Romance Quarterly* 48, no.1 (Winter 2001): 32–47.

The author begins with the observation that "in the absence of Aljamiado-Morisco historical works from Spain, like those present in romance and Hispano-Arabic literatures of the peninsula, one can only conjecture the knowledge that Spanish Muslims retained of Andalusian history after Christian conquest: Mudejars would have remembered for several generations the times preceding the conquest, in which their ancestors lived in an Islamic kingdom" (p.32). Further, the author says, Muslim adolescents and adults, during their conversions to Christianity between 1502 and 1526, must have lived with vivid memories of Mudejar Spain, but it is not clear what Moriscos knew of Andalusian history and culture.

This article explores "the concrete knowledge that Aragonese Moriscos possessed of al-Andalus and transmitted in a single Aljamiado tale set in tenth-century Cordoba" (p.32). The author observes that "if Aljamiado-Morisco authors had any knowledge of Arab Spain between the ninth and fifteenth centuries, it does not appear in their literary production, with the exception of the work that is the object of my study, 'Al-hadit del bano de Zaryeb'" (p.33). This scholarship is "unique in Aljamiado literature for its depiction of Cordoba during the pinnacle of Andalusian culture," the author says (p.33). He concludes: "Although familiarity with the content of a brief, legendary tale hardly constitutes significant knowledge of Andalusian history, perhaps Morisco intellectuals possessed a broader knowledge than surviving manuscripts reveal. It is to be hoped that the future will bring discovery of new Aljamiado manuscripts containing chronicles of Islamic Spain" (p.47).

(II) CRUSADES

A-201. Atiya, Aziz S. "The Crusades: Old Ideas and New Conceptions." *Journal of World History* 2 (1954): 470–475.

The article is based on a summary of two lectures by the author at the University of Chicago in January 1951. The author's purpose is to examine the history of the Crusades from a new perspective, focusing on the following key points: definition of the Crusade, limitations of the Age of Crusades, the Counter-Crusade, Results of the Crusades in world history. Each topic is discussed in some detail.

The reasons for the Crusades are more than what is usually argued (holy war, medieval fanaticism, migratory movements, economic colonization); they also represented a universal movement, "a joint action of the 'League of Nations' of

Western Christendom against the whole 'Pan-Islamic' Empire of the East. It was a war of faith, and of ideas and ideals—in Gibbon's words—'a world controversy'" (p.470). As for limitations, it is suggested the Crusades started earlier than 1095 and ended not in 1292, but 1396. The Counter-Crusade refers to the "vehement and continued reaction of the Islamic polity to action from the West" (p.472).

As for results, "the discovery of America may be regarded as an indirect result of the movement of the Crusades" (p.475). Others pertained to "the westward flow of wealth and new ideas in art, architecture and even literature, [which] helped in remodeling the Europe where the old order was giving way to the new. The Crusades, too, contributed no mean share to the shaping of the political, economic, social and intellectual structure of Europe in the later Medieval Age" (p.475).

A-202. Mateo, Matilde. "The Making of the *Saracen Style*: The Crusades and Medieval Architecture in the British Imagination in the 18th and 19th Centuries." Pages 115–141 in *The Crusades: Other Experiences, Alternative Perspectives, Selected Proceedings from the 32nd Conference of the Center for Medieval and Early Renaissance Studies*, edited by Khalil E. Semaan. Binghamton, NY: State University of New York Press, 2003.

At first sight, the author argues, the *Saracen Style* (also known as *Arabesque* and *Moresque*) seems no more than a label applied to what we call Gothic architecture, which was developed, after all, by *Christians in Western Europe*; thus one hardly finds any reference to the *Saracen Style* in the current art terminology. This style was at one time popular all over Europe, and especially admired in England—and it was also viewed with suspicion, the author suggests. It was also in Britain where it was first argued that the Crusades were the spreading agent for the *Saracen Style*. The author explores this role of the Crusades in the birth of the *Saracen Style* in Europe.

While there were some who argued that the Gothic style was something invented by the Goths, others referred to the style of buildings in the Holy Land and connected the style to the Crusades. These writers deduced, it is suggested, that "the Saracen Architecture as the model for the Gothic" was due to the fact that "the Saracens were the only people with architectural skills at the time of its invention. The Goths lacked constructive skills and were destroyers rather than builders, whereas the Saracens had preserved the knowledge of the building skills of the Greeks, especially geometry" (p.117–118). Further, "Crusades had not been a waste, but one of the most powerful agents of progress during the Middle Ages. And the building on the top—the church of the Holy Sepulcher—was one of the proofs" (p.123). However, with this structure as the model for the medieval architecture of the West, the term Gothic style was "erroneously" restored in Europe's architectural science, and "of course, that was nonsense" (p.124). However, "That meant the death of the *Saracen Style* in scholarly circles around the central years of the nineteenth century" (p.124).

The author corroborates her arguments with the aid of several diagrams and figures.

A-203. Moosa, Matti. "The Crusades: An Eastern Perspective, with Emphasis on Syriac Sources." *Muslim World* 93, no.2 (April 2003): 249–290.

This study explores the events of the Crusades, as recorded by Syriac and other Eastern writers, with special emphasis on the relations of Syrians (and to some degree, the Armenians, who were the majority population in cities like Edessa and the Cilicia province), their churches and communities, with the Greeks, Franks (Latins, Crusaders), and Turks.

The study reveals that the Syrians and Armenians were ill-treated by the Byzantine church and state and by the Church of Rome, to which the Crusaders belonged. Further, the author states, "Most Western writers on the Crusades make little mention of the Syrians and Armenians or the Maronites (a part of the Syrian Church of Antioch), except for a few comments by the twelfth-century historian, William of Tyre" (p.249). The sources consulted in this study not only discuss "the Syrians but also several other ethnic groups. Before the Franks' arrival, the Middle East was plagued by constant warfare among the Byzantines (Greeks), Arabs, Seljuk Turks, and Armenians" (p.251). Furthermore, one source (Bar Hebraeus, d. 1286) reports, "The Franks were filled with rage and, collecting troops, they went first to Spain and took possession of the cities there, shedding much blood. They cut off the ears, lips, and noses of many Arabs and blinded their eyes. Then they marched against Constantinople" (p.253).

This detailed study, extremely well-documented, provides an alternative perspective on the history of the Crusades.

A-204. Munro, Dana Carleton. "The Western Attitude Toward Islam During the Period of the Crusades." *Speculum: A Journal of Medieval Studies* 6 (1931): 329–343.

Despite the Crusades and "little if any information about the character of the Prophet or the beliefs of Islam and very little about the character and customs of the Saracens," the article begins, "what little is said in the earlier accounts is favorable" (p.329). Bernard the Wise often talked about experiencing "such peace" between "the Christians and pagans" during his journeys and that "pilgrims were not persecuted by the Muslims and were allowed freely to visit the Holy Sepulchre and other spots hallowed by the events of the Old and New Testaments" (p.329).

Then, "The inception of the Crusading movement was accompanied by propaganda to excite the passions of the Christians against the Muslims" (p.330). Numerous accounts of this phenomena are cited. An "inaccurate and error-filled" translation of the Qur'an "did much to perpetuate the false beliefs about Mohammed and Islam which are so common in the literature of the thirteenth and the following centuries" (p.337). There were some, however, who presented Islam somewhat accurately; writing in 1175 some emissaries "gave a good statement of the beliefs of Islam, and lauded their tolerance. In Alexandria he reported that there were several Christian churches. Every man was free to follow his own religion" (p.338).

The 13th century "saw the beginning of a period of great missionary activity. Later in the century, there was also a suggestion that Christian girls should be sent out as missionaries to marry Muslims and then convert their husbands" (p.339). Subsequently, however, "they felt that it was impossible to convert the Muslims. They were alarmed at the number of Christians who had gone over to Islam." Yet, the article ends, "the Popes were working for a new Crusade and encouraged the propaganda against Islam" (p.343).

(III) MISCELLANEOUS

A-205. Alam, Manzoor. "Ibn Khaldun's Concept of the Origin, Growth and Decay of Cities." *Islamic Culture* (Lahore, Pakistan) 34 (1960): 90–106.

The paper presents an analysis and a comparative study of Ibn Khaldun's (1332–1406) exposition of the evolution of urbanization as a historical process. The author notes that while Ibn Khaldun's *Muqaddimah* has been examined by others, none of these scholars "has critically appraised, evaluated and compared Ibn Khaldun's concept of urbanization" (p.90).

After a brief biographical sketch, the discussion is divided into six sections: (1) Ibn Khaldun's approach to the study of human activity, noting the "unity of all branches of knowledge" in his writings; (2) discussion and application of some ecological principles, explaining the genesis, growth and decay of human civilization as a natural process in the evolutionary cycle of civilization; (3) origin of cities, including identification of several factors (defense needs, proximity to rivers and oceans, agricultural, pastures, and forest lands); (4) age and stages of a city's development (various features of a "city cycle"—youthful, maturity, senility—are described); (5) size, classification, and characteristics of cities (including various crafts and occupations); (6) the decay of cities (reflected in the deteriorating economic conditions, with reduced purchasing power, followed by a slump in business).

In conclusion, the author notes, Ibn Khaldun "was indeed a man with a great mind who combined action with thought, a man of vision and penetrating intellect who always looked ahead of his age" (p.106).

A-206. Bloom, Jonathan M. "Revolution by the Ream: A History of Paper." *Aramco World* 50, no.3 (May–June 1999): 26–39.

The article traces the origin of papermaking techniques "invented in China more than 2000 years ago. Nearly a millennium passed, however, before Europeans first used it, and they only began to manufacture it in the eleventh and twelfth centuries, after Muslims had established the first paper mills in Spain" (p.28). How did paper (the word derives from *papyrus*, the original raw material) get from China to Europe?

"Soon after its invention," the author narrates, "Chinese merchants and missionaries transmitted paper, and knowledge of papermaking, to neighboring lands. It was there that Muslims first encountered it in the eighth century" (p. 29). Then, "The Islamic civilization spread this knowledge to Iraq, Syria, Egypt, North Africa, and, finally, Spain" (p.29). It is pointed out that "most accounts of the history of paper focus either on its origins in China or its development in Europe, and simply ignore the centuries when knowledge of paper and papermaking spread throughout the Islamic lands" (p.29). Via the Iberian Peninsula, "paper began to be used in Italy at the very end of the eleventh century, first in Sicily" (p.35). Further, "In both China and Europe, the start of paper manufacture was quickly followed by the development of printing, first with wooden blocks and then with moveable type. Block printing was also known in the Islam lands, as early as tenth-century Egypt" (p.39).

Knowledge of printing, however, died out during the 14th-century Islam, but then it came full circle, the author concludes.

A-207. Bosch, Gular Kheirallah. "Ibn Khaldun on Evolution." *The Islamic Review* 38, no.5 (1950): 26–34.

The paper begins with a long quotation from Ibn Khaldun's (1332–1406) *Muqaddima* and suggests that this 14th-century Spanish Muslim was a precursor of Charles Darwin's 19th-century theory of evolution. The quotation refers to various God's creations, "arranged in an orderly and exact manner, with effects linked to causes, and forms connected to forms, and the evolution of some existent beings into others. The significance of the connections in these states of existence is that the last plane is ready by close adaptability to become the first plane following it. So the animal world broadened, its varieties multiplied, and it terminated in the gradual formation of man, the master of thought and reflection" (p.26).

The author concludes, Ibn Khaldun's "careful observations led him to the keen observations of causes and effects we have quoted above, which offer us a world picture of the evolution of species in a modern sense" (p.26).

A-208. Bulliet, Richard W. "Medieval Arabic *Tarsh*: A Forgotten Chapter in the History of Printing." *Journal of American Oriental Society* 107, no.3 (1987): 427–438.

"Judging from paleography and the eight-century date of introduction of paper to the Islamic world, Arabic block printing must have begun in the ninth or tenth century," the paper states at the outset (p.427). And, the "thesis proposed here, that the word *tarsh* meant 'printblock' in the dialect of the medieval Muslim underworld, makes possible for the first time a history of medieval Arabic printing" (p.427). The author explores whether it came from China, or was it independently invented, and, more importantly, whether it was the source from which the Europeans adopted woodblock printing in the 14th century.

The author finds that the *tarsh* "printblocks were made of cast or molded metal rather than wood" (p.430). Further, "It seems more likely that Arabic blockprinting was an independent invention" (p.435). Later, *tarsh* printing disappeared in the 14th century, probably because of Muslim prohibitions against publishing sacred texts or because of the Sufi influence, or both. As for the *tarsh* blockprinting being linked to the origins of European printing, "no one has given serious consideration to this possibility of technological borrowing from the Arab world"; further explorations are warranted.

A-209. Foster, Benjamin R. "Agoranomics and Muhtasib." *Journal of Economic and Social History of the Orient* 13 (April 1970): 128–144.

The paper explores and clarifies the relationship between the agoranomics of Roman times and the *muhtasib* of the Islamic civilization, for some have argued the latter is derived from the former. The Greek "agoranomics" refers to "market inspector," with functions such as collecting fines and taxes, policing the markets, flogging offenders, ensuring cleanliness of roads and streets, checking market prices, etc. The word later transformed into Latin "aedile" (derived from the Arabic *aadel*, one who enforces *adel*, or justice), whose functions were broader, including some municipal functions.

The Arabic *muhtasib* derives from the Arabic *hisbah*, meaning "accountability"; *muhtasib* is one who may be defined as the "account-keeper," the contemporary equivalent being the "ombudsman." The paper explores the possible evolution of the word agoranomics, or its equivalents, into *hisbah* and *muhtasib* through the Byzantium or other sources. The functions of a Muslim *muhtasib* were much broader—from a market inspector to a "grand dignitary responsible for all the municipal functions" (p.139). This was a religious office, and thus *muhtasib*'s responsibilities included the enforcement of "what is good" and forbidding "what is bad." After noting that the *muhtasib*'s duties were "uniquely Islamic," the author concludes that "the connection of any functionary called 'agoranomics' and the Islamic *muhtasib* seems impossible" (p.139).

A-210. Gates, Warren E. "The Spread of Ibn Khaldun's Ideas on Climate and Culture." *Journal of History of Ideas* 28, no.3 (July–September 1967): 415–421.

This article attempts to demonstrate that the French scholar, Baron Charles Montesquieu (1689–1755), borrowed from Ibn Khaldun's (1332–1406) discussion on the theory of climate in his *Muqaddimah*; the latter scholar's work was well known in Europe before Montesquieu. The theory of climate is viewed by some as central in Montesquieu's thought. Some refer to Ibn Khaldun as "einen arabischen Montesquieu," and, further, it is noted that "many ideas discussed in

the European West long after Ibn Khaldun's time were found, amazingly enough, not to be as new as had been thought" (p.415).

Some, however, have argued that "parts of Montesquieu's theory of climate are already present in the work of Chardin" (p.416); so he perhaps borrowed from Chardin. But, it is argued, that Sir John Chardin (b. 1643) had traveled extensively in Persia and India, where he "became familiar with the ideas of Ibn Khaldun" (p.419). Thus, "Just as Ibn Khaldun's theory of climate resembles that of Montesquieu, so is Chardin's theory of climate identical with that of Montesquieu" (p.420). However, Chardin chose not to acknowledge his debt to Ibn Khaldun, for "he may have believed that his book would be less attractive with the names of Arabic writers strewn through it" (p.421). Therefore, "It would not be strange if Sir John should offer us a theory of climate which he had taken from the work of a fourteenth-century Arab writer without mention of its source" (p.421).

A-211. Gibb, H.A.R. "The Islamic Background of Ibn Khaldun's Political Theory." *Bulletin of the School of Oriental Studies* 7 (1933–1935): 23–31.

This paper draws attention to a shortcoming observed in other studies of Ibn Khaldun's (1332–1406) thought, in that there is "a certain tendency to exaggerate the independence and originality of Ibn Khaldun's thought, which in turn arises from a misrepresentation of his outlook, especially in its relation to religious questions" (p.25). The author points out that some writers have credited Ibn Khaldun "with freedom from religious bias or preoccupations." Further, they have argued that Ibn Khaldun's "principles are not theocentric," and that, for him, religion is "no more than one factor, however important it may be; and it does not alone give its content to the State, not even to the Islamic State" (p.27).

The author disagrees, in that "the ethical and Islamic basis of Ibn Khaldun's thought is, however, implicit throughout his exposition, quite apart from his constant appeal to texts from Qur'an and Tradition" (p.29). Nonetheless, it may be allowed, according to the author, that Ibn Khaldun stressed the cause-and-effect phenomenon as "natural law" much more than most other Muslim writers.

A-212. Glick, Thomas F. "Muhtasib and Mustasaf: A Case Study of Institutional Diffusion." *Viator: Medieval and Renaissance Studies* 2 (1971): 59–81.

This article represents a case study of cultural borrowing in the area of municipal institutions, specifically the administrative tradition called *Muhtasib* (derived from the Arabic *Hisba*, meaning "accountability"), whose chief characteristic was the unification of various civic functions (economic, civil, moral) under a single functionary. The author mentions the "selective bias of traditional Spanish ethnocentricity" among some scholars concerning such diffusion.

While the classical Greek *agoranomos* and Islamic *muhtasib*, the author suggests, are similar, the gap of several centuries "is too wide to permit proof of institutional continuity" (p.63). Further, there is no record of a similar office in the Byzantine municipal administration. However, the author argues, "The clue to the transitional office lies among the Semitic communities of Syria and Meso-potamia" (p.63). There was also an official called *sahib al-suq* ("master of the market") as a predecessor of *Muhtasib*, which later became *sahib al-madina* ("city prefect").

Subsequently, in the tenth-century Christian Spain, there were similar func-tionaries; for example, *zabazoque* derived from the Arabic *sahib al-suq*. In the 12th century, this became *almotacen* (the Arabic equivalent is "al-Mutaqeen," meaning God-fearing, God-trusting) in Castile, and later the term *mustasaf* emerged in various Mediterranean towns, also common in Valencia. "The *musta-saf* literature was most explicit in regard to duties of a religious or moral nature," the author notes.

The author concludes, "The diffusion of *hisba* was not limited to the Islamic West. Two other medieval Christian states, in close contact with the Islamic world—Tyre and Cyprus—also developed Latinized *muhtasibs*" (p.79).

A-213. Hannoum, Abdelmajid. "Translation and the Colonial Imaginary: Ibn Khaldun Orientalist." *History and Theory* 42 (February 2003): 61–81.

This article takes as a case study the translation into French of Ibn Khaldun (1332–1406), the 14th-century North African historian. The author says, "In order to know the natives, one had not only to observe them, study them, and understand their culture and their society, but also to know their past. The present was believed to be 'out there,' to be apprehended by observation; the past was assumed to be recorded in documents, to be grasped only by a work of transla-tion, either direct or indirect" (p.61). William de Slane's *Histoire des Berbers*, the French translation of Ibn Khaldun that relates to the history of Arabs and Berbers in the Maghreb, "the greatest textual event in the history of French Ori-entalism," has been the source of French knowledge of the Maghrib, as well as the basis upon which the colonial and post-colonial historians have constructed that knowledge.

The author shows how a portion of the writing of Ibn Khaldun was translated and transformed in the process in such a way as to become a French narrative with colonial categories specific to the 19th century. In showing this, the essay reveals that not only is translation not the transmission of a message from one language to another, it is indeed the production of a new text. It shows "not only how knowledge is regulated by power, but also how colonialism introduced and established a specific *imaginary* by transforming local knowledge and converting it into colonial knowledge" (p.62).

The article concludes with questioning "the whole colonial discourse that was built on the division of Arab versus Berber" from Slane's translation. Ibn Khal-dun viewed both groups as "Arabs, and therefore, not only is the French presence illegitimate, but so also was the Roman presence" (p.80–81). Yet, "Ibn Khal-dun's history became the *Histoire des Berbers*, a colonial text that employed colonialist categories to perceive, to think, and to re-present North African history" (p.81).

A-214. Khalid, Detlev H. "The Problem of Defining Islam and Modern Accentuations." *Islamic Studies* 16, no.3 (Autumn 1977): 217–281.

The author of this long article defines his thesis toward the end, his contention being "that a religious reformation does not seem feasible after Westernization. Various nationalisms may be able to profit from the cultural enrichment of their legacy as a result of the many centuries when their identity was derived from the universal religious community of Islam. However, a specific Muslim identity transcending national boundaries seems no longer intellectually tenable. Efforts to intellectualize the religious heritage lead, sooner or later, to a merger and identification with the achievements of humanity at large. In the course of this process, the margin of a separate Muslim identity narrows continuously. The craving for such Muslim individuality within a world community is in any case conditioned by a given historical situation and by the fact that colonialism invaded Muslim territories at a time when the old religious identity was still intact" (p.250).

The author concludes that "the diminishing margin of Islamic specificity makes it appear more likely that ultimately one of the liberal or socialist models developed outside the Muslim realm be transplanted to it more less in its entirety. This might further speed up cultural planification and the disintegration of religion, however, with the prospect of a greater degree of success in economic development and political competitiveness" (p.252).

The article's discussion is divided into seven sections: (1) Identify Crisis and the Prevalence of Islam, (2) Historical Synthesis and the Requirements of Modernity, (3) Theological Inadequacy and the Reduction of Islam, (4) Detheologization and the Primacy of Politics, (5) Recompensating Interiorization and the Question of Authenticity, (6) Moral Philosophy and the Impact of Humanism, (7) Religious Impasse and the New Frame of Reference.

This article includes about 30 pages (p.252–281) of detailed notes and references.

A-215. Khan, M. Saber. "A Classified Bibliography of Recent Publications on al-Biruni." *Muslim World Book Review* 10, no.3 (Autumn 1990): 65–77.

There have been several other bibliographic publications on the scholarship of Abu Rayhan Muhammad Ibn Ahmad al-Biruni (d. 1050); some of these are quite dated, however. In 1975, the author produced a select bibliography of Soviet (Russian) publications, but numerous books and articles on this scholar have been published in recent years. This article provides a bibliography of books and articles published in all major non-Russian languages, especially Western and Asian, in the last 20 years, from about 1970 to 1990. Also included are several pre-1970 items which appeared in less-known books and journals.

The author has organized the compilation according to various topics and disciplines (e.g., life and times, philosophy, astronomy, mathematics, geography, history, Indology, social and natural sciences).

A-216. Krek, Miroslav. "Arabic Block Printing as the Precursor of Printing in Europe: Preliminary Report." *Newsletter of the American Research Center in Egypt* (Princeton University, Princeton, NJ), no.129 (Spring 1985): 12–16.

Since the late 19th-century discovery of about two dozen Arabic xylographic prints (prints produced from wooden block), believed to be from the tenth–12th century Fatimid rule in Egypt, there has been some scholarly discussion as to linkages with the development of printing in Europe, although, the author says, the majority of relevant scholarship seems to ignore the evidence.

From visits to various Islamic museums, the author has gathered additional evidence and reports his analysis in order to authenticate the tenth–11th century origins of these prints, "in which case they may have preceded this type of printing in Europe" (p.15). It is reported that such printing also existed in China and "from Chinese sources we know that there were Muslim traders in Canton as early as 756 AD" (p.15). The various criteria employed, however, are not "as convincing as would be a dated specimen" (p.15). So additional evidence is needed, although "what was found so far, especially in Egypt, is merely the tip of the iceberg" (p.16).

A-217. Lunde, Paul. "The Missing Link." *Aramco World* 32, no.2 (March–April 1981): 26–27.

Based on the late 19th-century discovery in Egypt of block-printed Arabic texts, dating back to the tenth century, this article traces the history of "movable-type" printing to an era prior to the 1455 invention of Germany's Gutenberg. Prior to the tenth century, block-printed books were known in China. This discovery of block-printing is argued to be "the antecedent of movable type, linotype and the word processor" and the "precursor of both the Chinese and German systems of movable type, [that] entered Europe only shortly before the time of Gutenberg" (p.26).

Given that a block-printed book existed in 13th-century Italy, "following a process imported from Egypt," the author argues that "Muslims may have provided the route by which block printing did get to Europe" (p.27). While the inference may be hard to accept, he goes on, "the block prints from Egypt provide irrefutable evidence that the Islamic world possessed the technique of block printing before Europe. These block prints are, in effect, the missing link in the evolution of printing" (p.27).

A-218. Muhammad, Mi'raj. "Ibn Khaldun and Vico: A Comparative Study." *Islamic Studies* 19, no.3 (1980): 195–211.

Ibn Khaldun has been compared with several Western thinkers, such as Machiavelli, Bodin, Vico, Montesquieu, Adam Smith, Condorecet, Hegel, August

Comte, Herbert Spencer, and others. This article compares some aspects of Giambattista Vico's (1668–1744) thought with the corresponding views of Ibn Khaldun (1332–1406), "especially in the domain of the nature and development of human society" (p.195). Some consider Vico as the first European philosopher of history and Ibn Khaldun's equal in this field.

The article discusses several elements of the basic theory of civilization of both scholars. There is considerable resemblance as regards their cyclic theories, in that both, "anticipating the modern biological school of sociology, compare human society to an individual organism, having cycles of life, from birth, childhood and maturity to old age and death" (p.205). There are differences; whereas Vico views the role of religion as critical, Ibn Khaldun contends, according to the author, a society could well be organized on the basis of human reason, though religion is important. Further, whereas Ibn Khaldun views the process of history as slowly moving forward, Vico considers "regular alternation between progress and regression in an upward spiral movement" (p.206). Further, Ibn Khaldun deals with human society in its entirety and discusses all its aspects, but Vico "discusses human society within a limited field," with emphasis on "the role of Providence in history" (p.208). Both scholars, however, shared one merit: each established a new branch of knowledge—the philosophy of history. Both were original thinkers, although priority must be attributed to Ibn Khaldun, says the author.

A-219. Newby, Gordon D. "Ibn Khaldun and Frederick Jackson Turner: Islam and the Frontier Experience." *Journal of Asian and African Studies* 18, nos.3–4 (1983): 274–285.

The paper is about the "similarities between Ibn Khaldun's (1332–1406) conception of the frontier and that conception expressed in the ever-increasing body of frontier literature," beginning with Frederick Jackson Turner who, in an 1893 paper, proposed "that the frontier could explain the development of America" (p.274). While Turner does not seem familiar with Ibn Khaldun's works, the two scholars are "kindred spirits in the craft of historical analysis" (p.275).

It is noted that "the disparity between the fortitude of the Bedouin and the corruption of sedentary populations is the underlying cause of the historical process which Ibn Khaldun viewed as cyclical" (p.276). And, *asabiya* (group feeling) is a critical determinant of the rise and fall of civilizations. Further, the traits that both Ibn Khaldun and Turner "find in the frontiersman, the American pioneer and cowboy, and the Middle Eastern Bedouin are strikingly similar" (p.276). Both, whether "Indian Fighter or Camel Herder," are coarse, inquisitive, restless, individualistic, working for good and for evil (p.279).

The author concludes: "For Ibn Khaldun, frontier values are interconnected with the holy obligation to expand the boundaries of Islam just as in American culture, our participation in the world beyond our borders has often been justified by reference to comparable expansionist notions derived from our frontier heritage of 'Manifest Destiny'" (p.284).

A-220. Pasha, Mustapha Kamal. "Ibn Khaldun and World Order." Pages 56–70 in *Innovation and Transformation in International Studies*, edited by Stephen Gill and James E. Mittleman. Cambridge and New York: Cambridge University Press, 1997.

Given "the promise and challenge of globalization, with radical shifts in global economic activity, rearticulations in political space, and the emergence of new forms of cultural identity," this essay focuses on Ibn Khaldun as a step toward broadening the international relations theory to account for "alternative conceptions" of the emerging world order (p.56). It is argued that "Ibn Khaldun's ideas reclaim the humanistic tradition in International Studies" at a time when "a globalized market-based order appears to unleash new forces with far-reaching implications" (p.57).

The paper discusses Ibn Khaldun's views on history, politics, culture, and civilizations. "Acknowledging unity in human diversity, Ibn Khaldun held that history is a universal science," and he emphasized "the rationality of historical processes" (p.60). Society is the product of three elements—reason, social reproduction, and social cohesion; nature and nurture must coalesce to ensure the evolution of society.

As to guidance for the emerging world order, given Ibn Khaldun's consciousness of the Islamic world, he provides insights into the Muslim world in the context of world history. Further, he suggests "social orders are neither eternal nor natural, but historical, imbued with human intentionality" (p.62). And, "An acceptance of other civilizational principles, especially those that combine reason and faith, may temper economic development with spiritual concerns" (p.63). Since social solidarity, for Ibn Khaldun, is historically embedded, his realism makes "ethics contingent upon social forces" (p.63). As for upheavals in the Islamic world, "he would acknowledge that the roots of the crisis are primarily *internal* to Islamic civilization, only reinforced by outside forces" (p.63). The author concludes, "A discovery of the past and the recognition of its repressed consciousness may yield openings to rethink how we envision and make our world" (p.69).

A-221. Rosenthal, Erwin J. "Ibn Khaldun: A North African Muslim Thinker of the Fourteenth Century." *Bulletin of the John Rylands Library* 24 (1940): 307–320.

Referring to Ibn Khaldun (1332–1406) as "an exceptional man," who "cannot easily be fitted into the Medieval order of things," the author points to several recent studies, including those which "have focused attention upon a particular aspect of his teaching according to the particular approach and interests of various writers" (p.307). Some have suggested that Ibn Khaldun's works was dominated by his Islamic ethos and thus it is suited chiefly to an Islamic setting; the author disputes such suggestions.

The author begins by asserting "that Ibn Khaldun was a Muslim, and must be seen against the background of Medieval Islam if we are to understand his teaching" (p.307). In terms of his scholarship, he was a precursor of several 18th-century European thinkers (Comte, Hegel, Marx, Spengler, Machiavelli, and others).

The author says, however, that "he was not only a Muslim judge, he was also a statesman and a scholar" (p.308). His objective was to "find out empirically the laws underlying that process which is called history. There is no reason to style him a fatalist *qua* Muslim" (p.310). Further, reminiscent of Machiavelli, Ibn Khaldun insists on the absolute necessity of religion for the sake of generating *asabiyya* (group feeling), "for a united and effective State. But it is the State he has in mind, not the revealed truth of Islam" (p.311). Thus, Ibn Khaldun repeats from other Muslim and Jewish thinkers, "that the state based on human law cares for the citizen's earthly welfare only, whereas the State based on the revealed (superior) law, the *Shari'a* (or *Torah*) ensures earthly and other-worldly bliss" (p.319).

A-222. Schaefer, Karl R. "Eleven Medieval Arabic Block Prints in the Cambridge University Library." *Arabica* 48 (2001): 210–239.

Based on an examination of 11 medieval Arabic block prints held in the Cambridge University Library, the paper attempts to shed some light on the nature and character of medieval Arabic printing craft. Each piece is reported in terms of its particulars, including technical information and religious content. Further, each is analyzed for textual and physical attributes.

The author notes that "the Indian block-printed cloth is known to have been traded as far as China and the eastern Mediterranean. In China, Japan, and Korea, block-printing on paper was a well-established art form by the middle of the eighth century" (p.211–212). However, the time of its appearance in Europe is not known for certain, "although printed playing cards from late fourteenth century Italy are considered very early examples. The discovery of Arabic block printing is an unexpected addition to block printing history" (p.213).

The author concludes, "The medieval Arabic block print, while often crudely realized, was relatively well developed, showing a certain inventiveness in composition and a remarkable degree of sophistication in overall design." Further, the scripts "are not—at least not universally—the crude experimental trials of a would-be inventor but attest, rather, to a certain level of skilled endeavor" (p.228).

A-223. Schaefer, Karl R. "The Scheide *Tarsh*." *The Princeton University Library Chronicle* 56, no.3 (1995): 401–419.

The paper discusses one example of block printing and sheds some light on what can be discovered in the Arab world about the origins of printing. The paper begins: "About five centuries before block printing was introduced in Europe, Arabs were using the technique to produce miniature texts consisting of prayers, incantations, and verses from the Qur'an" (p.401). These medieval Arabic texts, called *tarshes*, available in the Scheide Library of Princeton University, have been further analyzed for their authenticity, typology, and various uses. Similar prints exist in some European libraries, the author reports. Reference is also made to the "popular misconception that printing with movable type was a European invention," ignoring "a system of printing with characters on individual blocks" that was being perfected in 11th-century China (p.401).

It is widely acknowledged, the author argues, that the Arabs introduced paper to Europe, having developed it themselves with knowledge from Chinese captives; evidence from the Arabic-language documents dating back to the eighth century is provided. Further, the early Arab–Chinese trading links also "bear witness to the transfer of printing technology" (p.404).

This early innovation did not survive in the Islamic world, one likely reason being "the prohibition against creating the sacred text of the Qur'an by any manner other than by hand" (p.419). However, the existence of the *tarshes* "suggests that some thought had been given to mass producing written materials in a more efficient manner" (p.419).

A-224. Schmidt, Nathaniel. "The Manuscripts of Ibn Khaldun." *Journal of the American Oriental Society* 46 (1926): 171–176.

The author suggests that whatever is available of Ibn Khaldun's (1332–1406) *Muqaddimah* is not altogether reliable, except for some parts; and "in no instance there has been an extensive collation. It is possible that some treatises are extant that have not yet been published" (p.171). The need for a survey of all extant manuscripts of Ibn Khaldun is emphasized, and to serve that purpose, the author has researched what is available.

This paper provides an alphabetical list of places (Berlin, Cairo, Fez, and others) where such manuscripts are available, along with names of libraries, museums, and individual collections where those manuscripts could be found. At the end, there is a listing of places (Algiers, Beirut, Cambridge, and others) where some manuscripts are known to exist but they are "still unverified" (p.176).

A-225. Stowasser, Barbara Freyer. "Religion and Political Development: Some Comparative Ideas of Ibn Khaldun and Machiavelli." *Occasional Paper Series*, Center for Contemporary Arab Studies, Washington, DC: Georgetown University Press, January 1983.

The paper begins with two long citations from Ibn Khaldun (1332–1406) and Machiavelli (d. 1527), which enables the author to observe that both scholars saw "religion as the strongest guarantee, as well as one of the sources, of civil obedience, collective morality, and virtue" (p.3). The work is thus prompted by the similarities of views of these scholars as to the role of religion and its effect on groups and nations. For this purpose, the author first describes several additional political forces visualized by the two thinkers: *asabiyya* (or group feeling) in the case of Ibn Khaldun; collective and individual *virtu* (virtue) for Machiavelli. Then the manner in which these notions relate specifically to religion and how religion relates to the foundations of each scholar's political thought are discussed.

After a detailed discussion, the author offers some concluding observations. While the pragmatic "Machiavelli saw religion as political useful," and "he denied the truth of Christianity and of religion as such" (p.22), Ibn Khaldun, on the other hand, "believed that religious and secular authority do not merely coexist, but are identical," and thus, "we find here the same conceptual difference that has continued to distinguish Islamic from Western political philosophy and social science" (p.23). Ibn Khaldun remained within the "orthodox Islamic political philosophy," an "all-inclusive political ideology and thereby the prime source of political legitimacy in the Islamic *umma*. Machiavelli, on the other hand, recognized the idea of government as an autonomous secular activity, independent of religion (but using religion if and when it wishes)" (p.23).

Bibliography

BOOKS

Abu-Lughod, Janet L. *Before European Hegemony: The World System A.D. 1250–1350.* New York and Oxford: Oxford University Press, 1989.

Abu-Nasir, Jamil M. *A History of the Maghrib in the Islamic Period.* Cambridge and New York: Cambridge University Press, 1987.

Adas, Michael, ed. *Islamic and European Expansion: The Forging of a Global Order.* Philadelphia, PA: Temple University Press, 1993.

Afsaruddin, Asma and A.H. Mathias Zahniser, eds. *Humanism, Culture, and Language in the Near East: Studies in Honor of Georg Krotkoff.* Winona Lake, IN: Eisenbrauns Inc., 1997.

Agius, Dionisius and Richard Hitchcock, eds. *The Arab Influence in Medieval Europe: Folia Scholastica Mediterranea.* Reading, UK: Ithaca Press, 1994.

Ahmad, Aziz. *A History of Islamic Sicily.* Edinburgh: Edinburgh University Press, 1975.

Ahmad, Ziauddin. *Influence of Islam on World Civilization.* Delhi, India: Adam Publishers and Distributors, 1996.

Ahmed, Leila. *Women and Gender in Islam: Historical Roots of a Modern Debate.* New Haven, CT: Yale University Press, 1992.

Ali, Basharat. *Muslim Social Philosophy.* Karachi, Pakistan: Jamiyatul Falah Publications, 1967.

Ali, Syed Ameer. *A Short History of the Saracens: Being a Concise Account of the Rise and Decline of the Saracenic Power and of the Economic, Social and Intellectual Development of the Arab Nation.* London and New York: Macmillan and Company, 1900.

Allison, Robert J. *The Crescent Obscured: The United States and the Muslim World, 1776–1815.* New York: Oxford University Press, 1995.

Allouche, Adel. *Mamluk Economics: A Study and Translation of Al-Maqrizi's* Ighathah (translated from Arabic). Salt Lake City, UT: University of Utah Press, 1994.

Altamira, Rafael. *A History of Spanish Civilization* (translated from Spanish by P. Volkov). London: Constable and Company, 1930.

Amin, Samir. *Eurocentrism* (translated from French by Russell Moore). New York: Monthly Review Press, 1989.

457

Arberry, A.J. *Aspects of Islamic Civilization: As Depicted in the Original Texts.* Westport, CT: Greenwood Press, 1964.

Ariew, Roger and Peter Barker, eds. (translated from French). *Pierre Duhem: Essays in the History and Philosophy of Science.* Indianapolis, IN, and Cambridge: Hackett Publishing Company, 1996.

Armstrong, Guyda and Ian N. Wood, eds. *Christianizing Peoples and Converting Individuals.* Turnhout, Belgium: Brepols Publishers, 2000.

Armstrong, Karen. *Islam: A Short History.* New York: Modern Library Edition, Random House, 2000.

Armstrong, Karen. *Muhammad: A Biography of the Prophet.* New York: HarperCollins, 1992.

Arnold, Thomas. *The Spread of Islam in the World: A History of Peaceful Preaching.* Delhi, India: Goodword Books, 2001; original 1896.

Arnold, Sir Thomas and Alfred Guillaume, eds. *The Legacy of Islam.* Oxford: Clarendon Press, 1931.

Artz, Frederick B. *The Mind of the Middle Ages, A.D. 200–1500: An Historical Survey.* Chicago and London: University of Chicago Press, 1980; original 1953.

Ascher, Abraham, Tibor Halasi-Kun, and Bela K. Kiraly, eds. *The Mutual Effects of the Islamic and Judeo-Christian Worlds: The East European Pattern.* Brooklyn, NY: Brooklyn College Press, 1979.

Asin-Palacios, Miguel. *Islam and the Divine Comedy* (translated and abridged from Spanish by Harold Sunderland). London: John Murray, 1926.

Asin-Palacios, Miguel. *The Mystical Philosophy of Ibn Masarra and His Followers* (translated from Spanish by Elmer H. Douglas and Howard W. Yoder). Leiden, Netherlands: E.J. Brill, 1978; original 1914.

Atiya, Aziz S. *Crusade, Commerce, and Culture.* Bloomington, IN: Indiana University Press, 1962.

Atiya, Aziz S. *The Crusade in the Later Middle Ages,* second edition. New York: Kraus Reprint Company, 1970.

Atiyeh, George N. and Ibrahim M. Oweiss, eds. *Arab Civilization: Challenges and Responses: Studies in Honor of Constantine K. Zurayk.* Albany, NY: State University of New York Press, 1988.

Atkinson, William C. *A History of Spain and Portugal.* Baltimore, MD: Penguin Books, Inc., 1960; reprinted 1961 and 1965.

Bammate, Haidar. *Muslim Contribution to Civilization.* Takoma Park, MD: Crescent Publications, 1962.

Banani, Amin and Speros Vryonis, Jr., eds. *Individualism and Conformity in Classical Islam.* Wiesbaden, Germany: Otto Harrassowitz, 1977.

Beckingham, C.F. *Between Islam and Christendom: Travellers, Facts and Legends in the Middle Ages and the Renaissance.* London: Variorum Reprints, 1983.

Benson, Robert L. and Giles Constable, eds. *Renaissance and Renewal in the Twelfth Century.* Cambridge, MA: Harvard University Press, 1982.

Berggren, J.L. *Episodes in the Mathematics of Medieval Islam.* New York, Berlin, and Tokyo: Springer-Verlag, 1986.

Berkey, Jonathan P. *The Formation of Islam: Religion and Society in the Near East, 600–1800.* Cambridge and New York: Cambridge University Press, 2003.

Blanks, David, ed. *Images of the Other: Europe and the Muslim World Before 1700.* Cairo Papers in Social Sciences, Volume 19, Monograph 2, Summer 1996. Cairo, Egypt: University of Cairo Press, 1997.

Bloom, Jonathan M., ed. *Early Islamic Art and Architecture.* Burlington, VT, and Hampshire, UK: Ashgate Publishing Ltd., 2002.

Bloom, Jonathan and Sheila Blair. *Islam: A Thousand Years of Faith and Power.* New York: TV Books, L.L.C., 2000.

Bosworth, C. Edmund, ed. *A Century of British Orientalists 1902–2001.* Published for The British Academy. Oxford: Oxford University Press, 2001.

Brann, Ross, ed. *Languages of Power in Islamic Spain.* Bethesda, MD: CXDL Press, 1997.

Brice, William M., ed. *An Historical Atlas of Islam.* Leiden, Belgium: E.J. Brill, 1981.

Briffault, Robert. *Rational Revolution: The Making of Humanity.* New York: The Macmillan Company, 1930.

Bulliet, Richard W. *The Case for Islamo–Christian Civilization.* New York: Columbia University Press, 2004.

Bulliet, Richard W. *Conversion to Islam in the Medieval Period.* Cambridge, MA: Harvard University Press, 1979.

Bulliet, Richard W. *The Patricians of Nishapur: A Study in Medieval Islamic Social History.* Cambridge, MA: Harvard University Press, 1972.

Burckhardt, Titus. *Moorish Culture in Spain* (translated by Alisa Jaffa). New York: McGraw-Hill Book Company, 1975.

Burke, Edmund, III, ed. *Rethinking World History: Essays on Europe, Islam, and World History (by Marshall G.S. Hodgson).* Cambridge and New York: Cambridge University Press, 1993.

Burke, James. *Connections.* Toronto, Boston, and London: Little, Brown and Company, 1978.

Burke, James. *The Day the Universe Changed.* Toronto, Boston, and London: Little, Brown and Company, 1985.

Burman, Edward. *Emperor to Emperor: Italy before the Renaissance.* London: Constable and Company Ltd., 1991.

Burnett, Charles. *The Introduction of Arabic Learning into England: The Panizzi Lectures 1996.* London: The British Library, 1997.

Burns, Robert Ignatius, S.J. *Islam under the Crusaders: Colonial Survival in the Thirteenth Century Kingdom of Valencia.* Princeton, NJ: Princeton University Press, 1973.

Burns, Robert Ignatius, S.J. *Medieval Colonialism: Postcrusade Exploitation of Islamic Valencia.* Princeton, NJ: Princeton University Press, 1975.

Butterfield, H. *The Origins of Modern Science, 1300–1800.* New York: The Macmillan Company, 1961.

Butterworth, Charles E. and Blake Andree Kessel, eds. *The Introduction of Arabic Philosophy into Europe.* Leiden, New York, and Cologne: E.J. Brill, 1994.

Calder, Norman, Jawid Mojaddedi, and Andrew Rippin, eds. and trans. *Classical Islam: A Sourcebook of Religious Literature.* London and New York: Routledge, 2003.

Calvert, Albert F. and Walter M. Gallichan. *Cordova: A City of the Moors.* London and New York: John Lane Company, 1907.

Campbell, Donald. *Arabian Medicine and Its Influence on the Middle Ages*, Volumes I and II. London: Kegan Paul, Trench, Trubner and Company, 1926.

Cantor, Norman F. *Western Civilization: Its Genesis and Destiny—From the Prehistoric Era to 1500.* Glenview, IL: Scott, Foresman and Company, 1969.

Cardini, Franco. *Europe and Islam* (translated from Italian by Caroline Beamish). Oxford: Blackwell Publishers, 2001.

Carlyle, Thomas. *Heroes, Hero Worship and the Heroic in History.* New York: A.L. Burt Company, n.d.

Casulleras, Josep and Julio Samso, eds. *From Baghdad to Barcelona: Studies in the Islamic Exact Sciences in Honor of Professor Juan Vernet,* Volumes I and II. Barcelona, Spain: Anuari de Filogia (Universitat de Barcelona) XIX, B-2, Instituto Millas Vallicrosa de Historia de la Ciencia Arabe, 1996.

El-Cheikh, Nadia Maria. *Byzantium Viewed by the Arabs.* Cambridge and London: Harvard University Press, 2004.

Chejne, Anwar. *Islam and the West: The Moriscos—A Cultural and Social History.* Albany, NY: State University of New York Press, 1983.

Chejne, Anwar G. *Muslim Spain: Its History and Culture.* Minneapolis, MN: The University of Minnesota Press, 1974.

Chew, Samuel C. *The Crescent and the Rose: Islam and England during the Renaissance.* New York: Octagon Books, Inc., 1965; original 1937.

Chiat, Marilyn J. and Kathryn L. Reyerson, eds. *The Medieval Mediterranean: Cross Cultural Studies.* St. Cloud, MN: North Star Press of St. Cloud, Inc., 1988.

Clagett, Marshall, Gaines Post, and Robert Reynolds, eds. *Twelfth Century Europe and the Foundations of Modern Society,* Proceedings of a Symposium. Madison, WI: University of Wisconsin Press, 1961.

Cobb, Stanwood. *Islamic Contributions to Civilization.* Washington, DC: Avalon Press, 1963.

Colish, Marcia L. *Medieval Foundations of the Western Intellectual Tradition, 400–1400.* New Haven, CT: Yale University Press, 1997.

Collins, Roger. *Early Medieval Spain: Unity in Diversity, 400–1000.* London: Macmillan Press, 1983.

Constable, Olivia Remie. *Trade and Traders in Muslim Spain: The Commercial Realignment of the Iberian Peninsula, 900–1500.* Cambridge and New York: Cambridge University Press, 1994.

Constable, Olivia Remie, ed. *Medieval Iberia: Readings from Christian, Muslim, and Jewish Sources.* Philadelphia, PA: University of Pennsylvania Press, 1997.

Corbin, Henry. *History of Islamic Philosophy* (translated from French by Liadain Sherrard). London: Kegan Paul International, in association with Islamic Publications for the Institute of Ismaili Studies, 1993.

Coulton, G.G. *Studies in Medieval Thought.* New York: Russell and Russell, 1965.

Courbage, Youssef and Philippe Fargues. *Christians and Jews under Islam* (translated from French by Judy Mabro). London and New York: I.B. Tauris Publishers, 1998.

Crombie, A.C. *Medieval and Early Modern Science: Vol. I, Science in the Middle Ages, V–XIII Centuries; Vol. II, Science in the Later Middle Ages and Early Modern Times, XIII–XVII Centuries.* New York: Doubleday and Company, revised second edition, 1959.

Crow, John A. *Spain: The Root and the Flower: An Interpretation of Spain and the Spanish People.* Berkeley, CA: University of California Press, 1985.

Dalafi, H.R. and M.H.A. Hassan, eds. *Renaissance of Sciences in Islamic Countries.* Singapore, London, and River Edge, NJ: World Scientific, 1994.

Dales, Richard C. *The Scientific Achievement of the Middle Ages.* Philadelphia, PA: University of Pennsylvania Press, 1973.

Daniel, Norman. *The Arabs and Medieval Europe.* London: Longman Group Ltd., 1975.

Daniel, Norman. *The Cultural Barrier: Problems in the Exchange of Ideas.* Edinburgh: Edinburgh University Press, 1975.

Daniel, Norman. *Heroes and Saracens: An Interpretation of the Chansons de Geste.* Edinburgh: Edinburgh University Press, 1984.

Daniel, Norman. *Islam and the West: The Making of an Image.* Boston: Oneworld Press, 1960; reprint 2000.

Daniel, Norman. *Islam, Europe and Empire.* Edinburgh: Edinburgh University Press, 1966.

Davies, Norman. *Europe: A History.* New York: Oxford University Press, 1996.

Dawson, Christopher. *The Formation of Christendom.* New York: Sheed & Ward, 1967.

Dawson, Christopher. *The Making of Europe: An Introduction to the History of European Unity.* New York: Sheed & Ward, 1952.

Dawson, Christopher. *Religion and the Rise of Western Culture.* Garden City, NY: Image Books, A Division of Doubleday and Company, Inc., 1958.

Djait, Hichem. *Europe and Islam* (translated from French by Peter Heinegg). Berkeley, CA: University of California Press, 1985.

Donner, Fred M. *The Early Islamic Conquests.* Princeton, NJ: Princeton University Press, 1981.

Douglas, David C. *The Norman Fate, 1100–1154.* Berkeley and Los Angeles: University of California Press, 1976.

Dozy, Reinhart. *Spanish Islam: A History of the Moslems in Spain* (translated from German, with a biographical introduction and additional notes, by Francis Griffin Stokes). London: Chatto & Windus, 1913.

Draper, John W. *History of the Conflict between Religion and Science.* New York and London: D. Appleton and Company, 1902; original 1874.

Draper, John W. *History of the Intellectual Development of Europe* (revised edition in two volumes). New York and London: Harper and Brothers Publishers, 1876 and 1904.

Dunlop, D.M. *Arab Civilization to A.D. 1500.* New York and Washington, DC: Praeger Publishers, 1971.

Durant, Will. *The Story of Civilization: The Age of Faith—A History of Medieval Civilization, Christian, Islamic, and Judaic, from Constantine to Dante, AD325–1300.* Volume 4. New York: Simon & Schuster, 1950.

Duri, A.A. *The Rise of Historical Writing Among the Arabs* (edited and translated from Arabic by Lawrence I. Conrad; introduction by Fred M. Donner). Princeton, NJ: Princeton University Press, Princeton, 1983; original 1960.

Eaton, Richard M. *Islamic History as Global History.* Washington, DC: American Historical Association, 1990.

Echevarria, Ana. *The Fortress of Faith: The Attitude towards Muslims in Fifteenth Century Spain.* Leiden, Netherlands: E.J. Brill, 1999.

Ernst, Carl W. *Following Muhammad: Rethinking Islam in the Contemporary World.* Chapel Hill, NC: University of North Carolina Press, 2003.

Esfandiari, Haleh and A.L. Udovitch, eds. *The Economic Dimensions of Middle Eastern History: Essays in Honor of Charles Issawi*. Princeton, NJ: The Darwin Press, Inc., 1990.

Esposito, John L., ed. *The Oxford History of Islam*. New York: Oxford University Press, 1999.

Ezzati, Abul-Fazl. *An Introduction to the History of the Spread of Islam*. London: News and Media Ltd., 1978.

Fakhry, Majid. *Averroes (Ibn Rushd): His Life, Works and Influence*. Oxford, UK: Oneworld Publications, 2001.

Fakhry, Majid. *A History of Islamic Philosophy*. New York: Columbia University Press, 1983.

Fakhry, Majid. *Islamic Occasionalism and Its Critique by Averroes and Aquinas*. London: George Allen and Unwin Ltd., 1958.

Faris, Nabih Amin, ed. *The Arab Heritage*. New York: Russell and Russell, Inc., 1963; original 1944.

Farmer, Henry G. *Historical Facts for the Arabic Musical Influence*. New York: Benjamin Bloom, Inc., 1971; original 1930.

Farrukh, Omar A. *The Arab Genius in Science and Philosophy* (translated from Arabic by John B. Hardie). Washington, DC: American Council of Learned Societies, 1954.

al-Faruqi, Ismail R. and Lois Lamya al-Faruqi. *The Cultural Atlas of Islam*. New York: The Macmillan Company, 1986.

Ferber, Stanley, ed. and comp. *Islam and the Medieval West*. Binghamton, NY: State University of New York Press, 1975.

Fierro, Maribel and Julio Samso, eds. *The Formation of al-Andalus, Part II (Language, Religion, Culture and the Sciences)*. Brookfield, VT: Ashgate Publishing Company, 1998.

Fletcher, Richard. *Moorish Spain*. Berkeley, CA: University of California Press, 1993.

Flint, Robert. *History of the Philosophy of History*. New York: Charles Scribner's Sons, 1894.

Frassetto, Michael and David R. Blanks, eds. *Western Views of Islam in the Medieval and Early Modern Europe: Perception of Other*. New York: St. Martin's Press, 1999.

Gabrieli, Francesco, ed. *Arab Historians of the Crusades: Selected and Translated from the Arabic Sources* (translated from Italian by E.J. Costello). Berkeley and Los Angeles: University of California Press, 1969.

George, Linda. *The Golden Age of Islam*. Tarrytown, NY: Benchmark Books, 1998.

Ghazanfar, S.M., ed. *Medieval Islamic Economic Thought: Filling the "Great Gap" in European Economics*. London and New York: RoutledgeCurzon, 2003.

Gilson, Etienne. *History of Christian Philosophy in the Middle Ages*. New York: Random House, 1955.

Gilson, Etienne. *Reason and Revelation in the Middle Ages*. New York and London: Charles Scribner's Sons, 1948.

Gimpel, Jean. *The Medieval Machine: The Industrial Revolution of the Middle Ages*. New York: Holt, Rinehart and Winston, 1976.

Glick, Thomas F. *Islamic and Christian Spain in the Early Middle Ages*. Princeton, NJ: Princeton University Press, 1979.

Goitein, S.D. *Studies in Islamic History and Its Institutions*. Leiden, Netherlands: E.J. Brill, 1966; reprinted 1968.

Goldstein, Thomas. *Dawn of Modern Science*. Boston: Houghton Mifflin, 1988.

Goodman, Lenn E. *Islamic Humanism*. New York: Oxford University Press, 2003.

Goss, Vladimir P. and Christine V. Bornstein, eds. *The Meeting of Two Worlds: Cultural Exchange between East and West during the Period of the Crusades*. Kalamazoo, MI: Medieval Institute Publications, Western Michigan University, 1986.

Gran, Peter. *Islamic Roots of Capitalism, Egypt, 1760–1840*. Syracuse, NY: Syracuse University Press, 1998.

Grant, Edward. *The Foundations of Modern Science in the Middle Ages: Their Religious, Institutional, and Intellectual Contexts*. Cambridge and New York: Cambridge University Press, 1996.

Grant, Edward. *God and Reason in the Middle Ages*. Cambridge and New York: Cambridge University Press, 2001.

Grant, Edward. *Studies in Medieval Science and Natural Philosophy*. London: Variorum Reprints, 1981.

Guizat, Pierre Guillaume. *General History of Civilization in Europe* (edited, with critical and supplementary notes, by George W. Knight). New York: D. Appleton and Company, 1899.

Gutas, Dimitri. *Greek Thought, Arabic Culture: The Graeco–Arabic Translation Movement in Baghdad and Early Abbasid Society (2nd–4th / 8th–10th Centuries)*. London and New York: Routledge, 1998.

Gwatkin, H.M. and J.P. Whitney, eds. *The Rise of the Saracens and the Foundation of the Western Empire*. Cambridge: Cambridge University Press, 1967; original 1913.

Hall, A. Ruper and Marie Boas Hall. *A Brief History of Science*. Ames, IA: Iowa State University Press, 1988.

Hallaq, Wael B., ed. *The Formation of Islamic Law*. Burlington, VT, and Hants, UK: Ashgate Publishing Company, 2004.

Hambly, Gavin R.G., ed. *Women in the Medieval Islamic World*. New York: St. Martin's Press, 1999.

Hamilton, Alastair. *Europe and the Arab World: Five Centuries of Books by European Scholars and Travellers from the Libraries of the Arcadian Group*. Oxford: Oxford University Press, 1994.

Hammond, Reverend Robert. *The Philosophy of Alfarabi and Its Influence on Medieval Thought*. New York: The Hobson Book Press, 1947.

Haq, Mahmudul. *Reason and Tradition in Islamic Thought*. Aligarh, India: Institute of Islamic Studies, Aligarh Muslim University, 1992.

Haren, Michael. *Medieval Thought: The Western Intellectual Tradition from Antiquity to the Thirteenth Century*. Toronto: University of Toronto Press, 1992.

Harvey, L.P. *Islamic Spain, 1250–1500*. Chicago: University of Chicago Press, 1990.

Haskins, Charles Homer. *The Renaissance of the Twelfth Century*. Cambridge, MA: Harvard University Press, 1927.

Haskins, Charles Homer. *The Rise of Universities*. New York: Henry Holt and Company, 1923.

Haskins, Charles Homer. *Studies in the History of Medieval Science*. Cambridge, MA: Harvard University Press, 1927.

Haskins, Charles Homer. *Studies in Mediaeval Culture*. Oxford: Clarendon Press, 1929.

al-Hassan, Ahmad Y. and Donald R. Hill. *Islamic Technology: An Illustrated History*. Cambridge and New York: Cambridge University Press, 1986.

Hattstein, Markus and Peter Delius, eds. *Islam: Art and Architecture* (translated from German). Cologne: Konemann Verlagsgesellschaft mbH, 2000.

Havighurst, Alfred F., ed. *The Pirenne Thesis: Analysis, Criticism, and Revision.* Lexington, MA: D.C. Heath and Company, revised edition, 1969.

Hawting, G.R. *The First Dynasty of Islam: The Umayyad Caliphate AD 661–750.* Carbondale, IL: Southern Illinois University Press, 1987.

Hayes, John R., ed. *The Genius of Arab Civilization: Source of Renaissance.* Cambridge, MA: The MIT Press, second edition, 1983.

Hearnshaw, F.J.C., ed. *Medieval Contributions to Modern Civilization: A Series of Lectures Delivered at King's College University of London.* New York: Henry Holt and Company, 1922.

Heer, Nicholas, ed. *Islamic Law and Jurisprudence: Studies in Honor of Farhat Ziadeh.* Seattle and London: University of Washington Press, 1990.

Hell, Joseph. *The Arab Civilization* (translated from German by S. Khuda Bukhsh). Cambridge: W. Heffer & Sons, 1926.

Hentsch, Thierry. *Imagining the Middle East* (translated from French by Fred A. Reed). Montreal and Cheektowaga, NY: Black Rose Books Ltd., 1992.

Hess, Andrew C. *The Forgotten Frontier: A History of the Sixteenth-Century Ibero-African Frontier.* Chicago and London: University of Chicago Press, 1978.

Hess, David J. *Science and Technology in a Multicultural World: The Cultural Politics of Facts and Artifacts.* New York: Columbia University Press, 1995.

El-Hibri, Tayeb. *Reinterpreting Islamic Historiography: Harun al-Rashid and the Narrative of the Abbasid Caliphate.* Cambridge and New York: Cambridge University Press, 1999.

Hill, Donald R. *A History of Engineering in Classical and Medieval Times.* La Salle, IL: Open Court Publishing Company, 1984.

Hill, Donald R. *Islamic Science and Engineering.* Edinburgh: Edinburgh University Press, 1993.

Hill, Donald R. (edited by David A. King). *Studies in Medieval Islamic Technology: From Philo to al-Jazari—From Alexandria to Diyar Bakr.* Variorum Collected Studies Series. Brookfield, VT, and Hampshire, UK: Ashgate Publishing Ltd., 1998.

Hill, Fred James and Nicholas Awde. *A History of the Islamic World.* New York: Hippocrene Books, Inc., 2003.

Hillenbrand, Carole. *The Crusades: Islamic Perspectives.* Chicago and London: Fitzroy Dearborn Publishers, 1999.

Hintzen-Bohlen, Brigitte. *Andalusia: Art and Architecture.* Cologne, Germany: Konemann Verlagsgesellschaft, 2000.

Hitti, Philip K. *The Arabs: A Short History.* Princeton, NJ: Princeton University Press, 1943.

Hitti, Philip K. *History of the Arabs.* London: Macmillan and Company, 1943.

Hitti, Philip K. *Makers of Arab History.* New York: St. Martin's Press, 1968.

Hodges, Richard and David Whitehouse. *Mohammed, Charlemagne and the Origins of Europe: Archeology and the Pirenne Thesis.* London: Gerald Duckworth and Company, 1983.

Hodgson, Marshall G.S. *The Venture of Islam: Conscience and History in a World Civilization—Volume One: The Classical Age of Islam; Volume Two: The Expansion of Islam in the Middle Periods; Volume Three: The Gunpowder Empires and Modern Times.* Chicago and London: University of Chicago Press, 1974; original 1961.

Hole, Edwyn. *Andalus: Spain under the Muslims.* London: Robert Hale Ltd., 1958.

Holt, P.M., Ann K.S. Lambton, and Bernard Lewis, eds. *The Cambridge History of Islam, Volume I, The Central Islamic Lands; Volume II, The Further Islamic Lands, Islamic Society and Civilization.* Cambridge and New York: Cambridge University Press, 1970.

Holmyard, Eric J. *Makers of Chemistry.* London: Oxford University Press, first published 1931; reprinted 1937, 1945, 1946, 1953, and 1962.

Hook, David and Barry Taylor, eds. *Cultures in Contact in Medieval Spain: Historical and Literary Essays Presented to L.P. Harvey.* Exeter, UK: King's College London Medieval Studies; Short-Run Press, 1999.

Hopwood, Derek, ed. *Studies in Arab History: The Antonius Lectures, 1978–87.* New York: St. Martin's Press, 1990.

Hourani, Albert. *Europe and the Middle East.* Berkeley and Los Angeles: University of California Press, 1980.

Hourani, Albert. *A History of the Arab Peoples.* Cambridge, MA: Harvard University Press, 2002; original 1991.

Hourani, Albert. *Islam in European Thought.* Cambridge and New York: Cambridge University Press, 1991.

Hourani, George F., ed. *Essays on Islamic Philosophy and Science.* Albany, NY: State University of New York Press, 1975.

Hovannisian, Richard G. and Georges Sabagh, eds. *Religion and Culture in Medieval Islam.* Cambridge and New York: Cambridge University Press, 1999.

Hoyt, Edwin P. *Arab Science: Discoveries and Contributions.* Nashville, TN, and New York: Thomas Nelson Inc., Publishers, 1975.

Huff, Toby E. *The Rise of Early Modern Science: Islam, China, and the West.* Cambridge and New York: Cambridge University Press, 1993.

Hull, L.W.H. *History and Philosophy of Science: An Introduction.* London and New York: Longmans, Green and Company, 1959.

Hussain, Iqbal S. *Islam and Western Civilization: Creating a World of Excellence.* Lahore, Pakistan: Humanity International, 1997.

Hyman, Arthur and James J. Walsh, eds. *Philosophy in the Middle Ages: The Christian, Islamic, and Jewish Traditions.* Indianapolis, IN: Hackett Publishing Company, 1973.

Ibrahim, Mahmood. *Merchant Capital and Islam.* Austin, TX: University of Texas Press, 1990.

Ihsanoglu, Ekmeleddin and Feza Gunergun, eds. *Science in Islamic Civilization.* Istanbul, Turkey: Research Center for Islamic History and Culture, 2000.

Imamuddin, S.M. *Some Aspects of the Socio-Economic and Cultural History of Muslim Spain, 711–1492.* Leiden, Netherlands: E.J. Brill, 1965.

Irving, Thomas B. *Falcon of Spain: A Study of Eighth-Century Spain.* Lahore, Pakistan: Sh. Muhammad Ashraf Publishers, 1991.

Issawi, Charles. *An Arab Philosophy of History: Selections from the* Prolegomena *of Ibn Khaldun of Tunis (1332–1406)* (translated and arranged by Charles Issawi). Princeton, NJ: The Darwin Press, Inc., 1987.

Issawi, Charles. *The Arab World's Legacy: Essays by Charles Issawi.* Princeton, NJ: The Darwin Press, Inc., 1981.

Ito, Shuntaro. *The Twelfth-Century Renaissance: Arabic Influences on the West* (original in Japanese language only). Iwanami Seminar Books, No. 42. Tokyo, Japan: Iwanami Shoten Publishers, 1993.

Izzeddin, Nejla. *The Arab World: Past, Present, and Future*. Chicago: Henry Regnery Company, 1953.

Japan Foundation. *The Islamic World and Japan: In Pursuit of Mutual Understanding*. Tokyo, Japan: Park Building, 3-6 Kioi-cho, Chiyoda-ku, 1981.

Jayyusi, Salma Khadra, ed. *The Legacy of Muslim Spain* (two volumes). Leiden, Netherlands, New York, and Cologne: E.J. Brill, 1994.

Jones, Catherine E. *Islamic Spain and Our Heritage: Al-Andalus, 711–1492 A.D.* Austin, TX: Middle East Outreach Council, University of Texas, 1996; second edition 1997.

Jones, Terry and Alan Ereira. *Crusades*. New York: Facts On File, published by arrangement with BBC Books, 1995.

Kamen, Henry. *The Spanish Inquisition*. London: Weidenfeld and Nicolson, 1965.

Kapoor, Subodh, ed. *The Muslims: Encyclopedia of Islam* (11 volumes). New Delhi, India: Cosmo Publications, 2004.

Kedar, Benjamin Z. *Crusade and Mission: European Approaches toward Muslims*. Princeton, NJ: Princeton University Press, 1984.

Kennedy, E.S. (and colleagues, former students; David A. King and Mary Helen Kennedy, editors). *Studies in the Islamic Exact Sciences*. Beirut, Lebanon: American University of Beirut, 1983.

Kennedy, Hugh. *The Early Abbasid Caliphate: A Political History*. London: Croom Helm, 1981.

Kennedy, Hugh. *The Prophet and the Age of the Caliphates: The Islamic Near East from the Sixth to Eleventh Century*. London and New York: Longman Group Ltd., 1986.

Kennedy, Hugh. *When Baghdad Ruled the Muslim World: The Rise and Fall of Islam's Greatest Dynasty*. Cambridge, MA: DaCapo Press (Perseus Books Group), 2005.

Kennedy, Hugh N. *Muslim Spain and Portugal: A Political History of al-Andalus*. London: Addison Wesley Longman Ltd., 1996.

Khalidi, Tarif. *Classical Arab Islam: The Culture and Heritage of the Golden Age*. Princeton, NJ: The Darwin Press, Inc., 1985.

Khan, M. Abdur Rahman. *Muslim Contribution to Science and Culture*. Lahore, Pakistan: Sh. Muhammad Ashraf Publishers, 1973; original 1946.

Kincheloe, Joe L. and Shirley R. Steinberg, eds. *The Miseducation of the West: How Schools and the Media Distort Our Understanding of the Islamic World*. Westport, CT: Praeger Publishers, 2004.

King, David A. and George Saliba, eds. *From Deferent to Equant: A Volume of Studies in the History of Science in the Ancient and Medieval Near East in Honor of E.S. Kennedy*. Volume 500. New York: Annals of the New York Academy of Sciences, New York Academy of Sciences, 1987.

Knowles, David. *The Evolution of Medieval Thought*. Baltimore, MD: Helicon Press, Inc., 1962.

Kraemer, Joel L. *Humanism in the Renaissance of Islam: The Cultural Revival during the Buyid Age*, second revised edition. Leiden, New York, and Koln: E.J. Brill, 1992.

Kristeller, Paul Oskar. *Renaissance Thought: The Classic, Scholastic, and Humanist Strains*. New York: Harper Torchbooks, Harper & Row Publishers, 1961.

Kritzeck, James. *Modern Islamic Literature from 1800 to the Present.* New York: A Mentor Book from New American Library, 1970.

Kritzeck, James, ed. *Anthology of Islamic Literature: From the Rise of Islam to Modern Times.* Toronto and New York: Mentor Books, Holt, Rinehart and Winston, Inc., 1966.

Lacoste, Yves. *Ibn Khaldun: The Birth of History and the Past of the Third World* (translated from French by David Macey). London: Verso Publishers, 1984.

Lacroix, Paul. *Science and Literature in the Middle Ages and the Renaissance.* New York: Frederick Ungar Publishing Company, 1964; original 1878.

Landau, Rom. *Arab Contribution to Civilization.* San Francisco: The American Academy of Asian Studies, 1958.

Landau, Rom. *The Arab Heritage of Western Civilization.* New York: Arab Information Center, 1962 and 1972.

Landau, Rom. *Islam and the Arabs.* New York: Macmillan Company, 1959.

Lane, Rose Wilder. *The Discovery of Freedom: Man's Struggle Against Authority.* New York: John Day Company, 1943; third edition 1993.

Lane-Poole, Stanley. *The Story of the Moors in Spain* (introduction by John G. Jackson). Baltimore, MD: Black Classic Press, 1990; original 1886.

Lapidus, Ira M. *A History of Islamic Societies,* second edition. Cambridge: Cambridge University Press, 2002.

Lapidus, Ira M. *Muslim Cities in the Later Middle Ages.* Cambridge, MA: Harvard University Press, 1967.

Laroui, Abdallah. *The History of the Maghrib: An Interpretative Essay* (translated from French by Ralph Manheim). Princeton, NJ: Princeton University Press, 1977.

Lea, Henry Charles. *The Moriscos of Spain: Their Conversion and Expulsion.* New York: Haskel House Publishers Ltd. (Publishers of Scarce Scholarly Books), 1968; original 1901.

Leaman, Oliver. *Averroes and His Philosophy.* Oxford: Clarendon Press, 1988.

Levy, Reuben. *The Social Structure of Islam.* Cambridge, London, and New York: Cambridge University Press, 1962.

Lewis, Archibald R. *Nomads and Crusaders, A.D. 1000–1368.* Bloomington and Indianapolis: Indiana University Press, 1988.

Lewis, Archibald R., ed. *The Islamic World and the West, A.D. 622–1492.* New York: John Wiley and Sons, Inc., 1970.

Lewis, Bernard, ed. and trans. *Islam: From the Prophet Muhammad to the Capture of Constantinople (Religion and Society).* New York: Walker and Company, 1974.

Lewis, Bernard, ed. *The World of Islam: Faith, People, and Culture.* London and New York: Thames and Hudson, Ltd., 1992.

Libby, Walter. *An Introduction to the History of Science.* New York: Houghton Mifflin Company, 1917.

Lindberg, David C. *The Beginnings of Western Science: The European Scientific Tradition in Philosophical, Religious, and Institutional Context, 600 B.C. to A.D. 1450.* Chicago and London: University of Chicago Press, 1992.

Lindberg, David C., ed. *Science in the Middle Ages.* Chicago: University of Chicago Press, 1978.

Lokkegaard, Frede. *Islamic Taxation in the Classic Period, with Special Reference to Circumstances in Iraq.* Philadelphia, PA: Porcupine Press, 1978; original 1950.

Lombard, Maurice. *The Golden Age of Islam* (translated from French by Joan Spencer). Amsterdam and New York: North-Holland Publishing Company/American Elsevier Publishing Company, 1975.

Lopez-Baralt, Luce. *Islam in Spanish Literature: From the Middle Ages to the Present* (translated from Spanish by Andrew Hurley). Leiden, Netherlands: E.J. Brill, 1992.

Lowick, Nicholas (edited by Joe Cribb). *Coinage and History of the Islamic World.* Aldershot, UK: Variorum-Grower Publishing Group, 1990.

Lowick, Nicholas M. (edited by Joe Cribb). *Islamic Coins and Trade in the Medieval World.* Aldershot, UK: Variorum-Grower Publishing Group, 1990.

Lowney, Chris. *A Vanished World: Medieval Spain's Golden Age of Enlightenment.* New York: Free Press, 2005.

Lowry, Joseph E., Devin J. Stewart, and Shawkat M. Toorawa, eds. *Law and Education in Medieval Islam: Studies in Honor of Professor George Makdisi.* Oakville, CT: David Brown Book Company, 2005.

Lunde, Paul. *Islam: Faith, Culture, History.* London and New York: DK Publishing Company, 2002.

Maalouf, Amin. *The Crusades through Arab Eyes* (translated from French by Jon Rothschild). New York: Schocken Books, 1985.

Macdonald, Duncan B. *Development of Muslim Theology, Jurisprudence and Constitutional Theory.* New York: Charles Scribner's Sons, 1903.

Magoffin, Ralph V.D. and Frederick Duncalf. *Ancient and Medieval History: The Rise of Classical Culture and the Development of Medieval Civilization.* New York and Chicago: Silver, Burdett and Company, 1934.

Makdisi, George. *The Rise of Colleges: Institutions of Learning in Islam and the West.* Edinburgh: Edinburgh University Press, 1981.

Makdisi, George. *The Rise of Humanism in Classical Islam and the Christian West: With Special Reference to Scholasticism.* Edinburgh: Edinburgh University Press, 1990.

Mann, Vivian B., Thomas F. Glick, and Jerrilynn D. Dodds, eds. *Convivencia: Jews, Muslims, and Christians in Medieval Spain.* New York: George Braziller, Inc., in association with The Jewish Museum, 1992.

Marin, Manuela, ed. *The Formation of al-Andalus, Part I (History and Society).* Brookfield, VT: Ashgate Publishing Company, 1998.

Marmura, Michael E. *Al-Ghazali's The Incoherence of the Philosophers* (*Tahafut al-Falasifa*; a parallel English–Arabic text translated, introduced, and annotated). Provo, UT: Brigham Young University, 1997.

Mason, Stephen F. *A History of the Sciences*, revised edition. New York: Collier Books, 1962.

Masters, Bruce. *The Origins of Western Economic Dominance in the Middle East: Mercantilism and the Islamic Economy in Aleppo, 1600–1750.* New York and London: New York University Press, 1988.

Matar, Nabil. *Islam in Britain, 1558–1685.* Cambridge: Cambridge University Press, 1998.

Matar, Nabil. *Turks, Moors and Englishmen in the Age of Discovery.* New York: Columbia University Press, 1999.

Matar, Nabil, ed. and trans. *In the Lands of the Christians: Arabic Travel Writing in the Seventeenth Century.* New York and London: Routledge, 2003.

Mazzaoui, Michel M. and Vera B. Moreen, eds. *Intellectual Studies in Islam: Essays Written in Honor of Martin B. Dickson.* Salt Lake City, UT: University of Utah Press, 1990.

McCabe, Joseph. *The Splendour of Moorish Spain.* London: Watts and Company, 1935.

Menocal, Maria Rosa. *The Arabic Role in Medieval Literary History: A Forgotten Heritage.* Philadelphia, PA: University of Pennsylvania Press, 1987.

Menocal, Maria Rosa. *The Ornament of the World: How Muslims, Jews, and Christians Created a Culture of Tolerance in Medieval Spain.* Boston, New York, and London: Little, Brown and Company, 2002.

Menocal, Maria Rosa, Raymond P. Scheindlin, and Michael Sells, eds. *The Literature of Al-Andalus.* Cambridge: Cambridge University Press, 2000.

Metlitzki, Dorothee. *The Matter of Araby in Medieval England.* New Haven, CT, and London: Yale University Press, 1977.

Meyerson, Mark D. *The Muslims of Valencia in the Age of Fernando and Isabel: Between Co-Existence and Crusade.* Berkeley and Los Angeles: University of California Press, 1991.

Meyerson, Mark D. and Edward D. English. *Christians, Muslims, and Jews in Medieval and Early Modern Spain: Interaction and Cultural Change.* Notre Dame, IN: University of Notre Dame Press, 1999.

Monroe, James T. *Islam and the Arabs in Spanish Scholarship (Sixteenth Century to the Present).* Leiden, Netherlands: E.J. Brill, 1970.

Murdoch, John Emery and Edith Dudley Sylla, eds. *The Cultural Context of Medieval Learning.* Dordrecht, Netherlands, and Boston: Reidel Publishing Company, 1975.

Murray, Alexander. *Reason and Society in the Middle Ages.* Oxford: Clarendon Press, 1978.

Myers, Eugene A. *Arabic Thought and the Western World in the Golden Age of Islam.* New York: Frederick Ungar Publishing Company, 1964.

An-Na'im, Abdullahi Ahmed (foreword by John Voll). *Toward an Islamic Reformation: Civil Liberties, Human Rights, and International Law.* Syracuse, NY: Syracuse University Press, 1990.

Naskosteen, Mehdi. *History of Islamic Origins of Western Education.* Boulder, CO: University of Colorado Press, 1964.

Nasr, Seyyed Hossein. *An Introduction to Islamic Cosmological Doctrines: Conceptions of Nature and Methods Used for Its Study by the Ikhwan al-Safa, al-Biruni, and Ibn Sina.* Albany, NY: State University of New York Press, revised edition, 1993.

Nasr, Seyyed Hossein. *Islamic Science: An Illustrated Study* (photographs by Roland Michaud). Kent, UK: World of Islam Festival Publishing Company, Westerham Press Ltd., 1976.

Nasr, Seyyed Hossein. *Science and Civilization in Islam.* Cambridge, MA: Harvard University Press, 1968.

Nasr, Seyyed Hossein and Oliver Leaman, eds. *History of Islamic Philosophy (Parts I and II).* London: Routledge, 1996.

Nawwab, Ismail I., Peter C. Speers, and Paul F. Hoye, eds. *Aramco and Its World: Arabia and the Middle East.* Washington, DC: Arabian American Oil Company, 1981.

Nebelsick, Harold P. *The Renaissance, the Reformation and the Rise of Science.* Edinburgh: T&T Clark, 1992.

Netton, Ian Richard. *Seek Knowledge: Thought and Travel in the House of Islam.* Surrey, UK: Curzon Press, 1996.

O'Callaghan, Joseph F. *A History of Medieval Spain*. Ithaca, NY, and London: Cornell University Press, 1975.

O'Leary, De Lacy. *Arabic Thought and Its Place in History*. London: Kegan Paul, Trench, Trubner and Company Ltd.; New York: E.P. Dutton and Company, 1922.

O'Leary, De Lacy. *How Greek Science Passed to the Arabs*, second edition. London: Routledge and Kegan Paul Ltd., 1951.

Packard, Sidney R. *Twelfth Century Europe: An Interpretive Essay*. Amherst, MA: University of Massachusetts Press, 1973.

Penrose, Boies. *Travel and Discovery in the Renaissance, 1420–1620*. Cambridge, MA: Harvard University Press, 1955.

Pereira, Jose. *The Sacred Architecture of Islam*. New Delhi, India: Aryan Books International, 2004.

Peretz, Don, Richard U. Moench, and Safia K. Mohsen. *Islam: Legacy of the Past, Challenge of the Future*. New York: North River Press/New Horizon Press Publishers, 1984.

Peters, Edward. *Europe: The World of Middle Ages*. Englewood Cliffs, NJ: Prentice-Hall, 1977.

Peters, F.E. *Aristotle and the Arabs: The Aristotelian Tradition in Islam*. New York and London: New York University Press/University of London Press, 1968.

Peters, F.E., ed. *The Arabs and Arabia on the Eve of Islam*. Brookfield, VT, and Hampshire, UK: Ashgate Publishing Company, 1999.

Pick, Lucy K. *Conflict and Coexistence: Archbishop Rodrigo and the Muslims and Jews of Medieval Spain*. Ann Arbor, MI: University of Michigan Press, 2004.

Pirenne, Henri. *Economic and Social History of Medieval Europe* (translated from French by I.E. Clegg). New York: Harcourt, Brace and Company, 1937.

Pirenne, Henri. *Mohammed and Charlemagne*. New York: Barnes & Noble, first published, 1939.

Powell, James M., ed. *Muslims under Latin Rule, 1100–1300*. Princeton, NJ: Princeton University Press, 1990.

Price, B.B. *Medieval Thought: An Introduction*. Cambridge, MA: Blackwell Publishers, 1992.

Qadir, C.A. *Philosophy and Science in the Islamic World*. Kent, UK: Croom Helm Ltd., 1988.

Ragep, F. Jamil and Sally P. Ragep, with Steven Livesey, ed. *Tradition, Transmission, Transformation: Proceedings of Two Conferences on Pre-Modern Science Held at the University of Oklahoma*. Leiden, New York, and Cologne: E.J. Brill, 1996.

Rashed, Roshdi, ed. (in collaboration with Regis Morelon). *Encyclopedia of the History of Arabic Science, Vol. 1, Astronomy: Theoretical and Applied; Vol. 2, Mathematics and the Physical Sciences; Vol. 3, Technology, Alchemy and Life Sciences*. London and New York: Routledge, 1996.

Read, Jan. *The Moors in Spain and Portugal*. London: Faber & Faber, London, 1974.

Reeves, Minou. *Muhammad in Europe: A Thousand Years of Western Myth-Making*. New York: New York University Press, 2000.

Rescher, Nicholas. *Studies in Arabic Philosophy*. Pittsburgh, PA: University of Pittsburgh Press, 1967.

Reynolds, Robert L. *Europe Emerges: Transition Toward an Industrial World-Wide Society 600–1750*. Madison, WI: University of Wisconsin Press, 1961.

Richards, D.S., ed. *Papers on Islamic History: Islam and the Trade of Asia—A Colloquium*. Published under the auspices of the Near Eastern History Group, Oxford, and the Near East Center, University of Pennsylvania; Bruno Cassirer, Oxford, and University of Pennsylvania Press, 1970.

Richards, D.S., ed. *Papers on Islamic History: Islamic Civilization, 950–1150; A Colloquium*. Published under the auspices of the Near Eastern History Group, Oxford, and the Near East Center, University of Pennsylvania; Bruno Cassirer (Publishers) Ltd., Oxford, 1973.

Robinson, Chase F., ed. *Texts, Documents and Artefacts: Islamic Studies in Honor of D.S. Richards*. Leiden, Netherlands, and Boston: E.J. Brill, 2003.

Robinson, David. *Muslim Societies in African History*. Cambridge: Cambridge University Press, 2004.

Robinson, Francis. *Islam and Muslim History in South Asia*. New Delhi, India: Oxford University Press, 2001.

Robinson, Francis, ed. *The Cambridge Illustrated History of the Islamic World*. London: Cambridge University Press, 1996.

Rodinson, Maxime. *Europe and the Mystique of Islam* (translated from French by Roger Veinus). Seattle, WA: University of Washington Press, 1987.

Rodinson, Maxime. *Islam and Capitalism* (translated from French, originally published in 1966, by Brian Pearce). Austin, TX: University of Texas Press, 1978.

Rogers, Michael. *The Spread of Islam*. Oxford: Elsevier-Phaidon, 1976.

Ronan, Colin A. *Science: Its History and Development among the World's Cultures*. New York: Facts On File Publications, 1982.

Rosenthal, Franz. *The Classical Heritage in Islam* (translated from German by Emile and Jenny Marmorstein). Berkeley and Los Angeles: University of California Press, 1965.

Rosenthal, Franz. *Knowledge Triumphant: The Concept of Knowledge in Medieval Islam*. Leiden, Netherlands: E.J. Brill, 1970.

Ross, Frank, Jr. *Arabs and the Islamic World*. New York: S.G. Phillips, Inc., 1979.

Ross, James F., ed. *Inquiries into Medieval Philosophy: A Collection in Honor of Francis P. Clarke*. Westport, CT: Greenwood Publishing Company, 1971.

Rubin, Uru, ed. *The Life of Muhammad*. Brookfield, VT, and Hampshire, UK: Ashgate Publishing Company, 1998.

Russell, G.A., ed. *The "Arabick" Interest of the Natural Philosophers in Seventeenth-Century England*. Leiden, Netherlands: E.J. Brill, 1994.

Sachedina, Abdulaziz. *The Islamic Roots of Democratic Pluralism*. New York: Oxford University Press, 2001.

Sahai, Surendra. *Indian Architecture: Islamic Period, 1192–1857*. New Delhi, India: Prakash Books (India) Ltd., 2004.

Said, Edward. *Orientalism*. New York: Vintage Books Edition, Random House, 1979.

Saliba, George. *A History of Arabic Astronomy: Planetary Theories during the Golden Age of Islam*. New York and London: New York University Press, 1994.

Salloum, Habeeb and James Peters. *Arabic Contributions to the English Vocabulary—English Words of Arabic Origin: Etymology and History*. Beirut, Lebanon: Librairie du Liban Publishers, 1996.

Samso, Julio. *Islamic Astronomy and Medieval Spain*. Brookfield, VT: Ashgate Publishing Company, 1994.

Sardar, Ziauddin, ed. *The Revenge of Athena: Science, Exploitation and the Third World.* New York and London: Mansell Publishing Ltd., 1988.

Sarton, George. *A Guide to the History of Science: A First Guide for the Study of the History of Science, with Introductory Essays on Science and Tradition.* Waltham, MA: Chronica Botanica Company, 1952.

Sarton, George. *The History of Science and the New Humanism.* New York: George Braziller, Inc., 1956.

Sarton, George. *The Incubation of Western Culture in the Middle East.* George C. Keiser Foundation Lecture, Library of Congress. Washington, DC: U.S. Government Printing Office, 1951.

Sarton, George. *Introduction to the History of Science: Volume I—From Homer to Omar Khayam.* Baltimore, MD: Published for the Carnegie Institution of Washington by William & Wilkins Company, 1927.

Sarton, George. *Introduction to the History of Science: Volume II—Part I, from Rabbi Ben Ezra to Ibn Rushd.* Baltimore, MD: Published for the Carnegie Institution of Washington by Williams & Wilkins Company, 1931.

Sarton, George. *Introduction to the History of Science: Volume III—Science and Learning in the Fourteenth Century, Part I: First Half of the Fourteenth Century; Part II: Second Half of the Fourteenth Century.* Baltimore, MD: Published for the Carnegie Institution of Washington by Williams & Wilkins Company, 1947.

Sarton, George. *The Life of Science: Essays in the History of Civilization.* New York: Henry Schuman, 1948.

Sarton, George. *The Normans in European History.* Boston and New York: Houghton Mifflin Company, 1915.

Saunders, J.J. *A History of Medieval Islam.* London: Routledge and Kegan Paul, 1965; reprinted 1972.

Sauvaget, Jean. *Introduction to the History of the Muslim East: A Bibliographical Guide.* Berkeley, CA: University of California Press, 1965.

Savory, R.M. *Introduction to Islamic Civilization.* Cambridge and New Delhi, India: Cambridge University Press/Vikas Publishing House, 1976.

Schacht, Joseph, ed. (assisted by C.E. Bosworth). *The Legacy of Islam*, second edition. Oxford: Clarendon Press, 1974.

Scott, S.P. *History of the Moorish Empire in Europe* (three volumes). Philadelphia, PA, and London: J.B. Lippincott Company, 1904.

Seherr-Thoss, Sonia P. and Hans C. Seherr-Thoss, eds. *Design and Color in Islamic Architecture: Afghanistan, Iran, Turkey.* Washington, DC: Smithsonian Institution Press, 1968.

Semaan, Khalil I., ed. *Islam and the Medieval West: Aspects of Intercultural Relations.* Albany, NY: State University of New York Press, 1980.

Sertima, Ivan Van, ed. *Golden Age of the Moor.* New Brunswick, NJ, and London: Transactions Publishers, 1993.

Sha'ban, Fuad. *Islam and Arabs in Early American Thought: The Roots of Orientalism in America.* Durham, NC: Published in Association with Duke University Islamic and Arabian Development Studies, The Acorn Press, 1991.

Sha'ban, M.A. *Islamic History, A.D. 600–750 (A.H. 132): A New Interpretation.* Cambridge: Cambridge University Press, 1971.

Sharif, M.M., ed. *A History of Muslim Philosophy, with Short Accounts of Other Disciplines and the Modern Renaissance in Muslim Lands* (two volumes). Wiesbaden, Germany: Otto Harrassowitz, 1963 and 1966.

Singer, Charles. *A Short History of Science to the Nineteenth Century.* Oxford, London, and New York: Clarendon Press, 1943.

Sinor, Denis, ed. *Orientalism and History,* second edition. Bloomington, IN, and London: Indiana University Press, 1970.

Siraisi, Nancy G. *Avicenna in Renaissance Italy: The* Canon *and Medical Teaching in Italian Universities after 1500.* Princeton, NJ: Princeton University Press, 1987.

Smith, Margaret. *Al-Ghazali: The Mystic.* London: Luzac and Company, 1944.

Sonn, Tamara. *A Brief History of Islam.* Oxford: Blackwell Publishing Ltd., 2004.

Sordo, Enrique. *Moorish Spain: Cordoba, Seville, Granada.* New York: Crown Publishers, 1963.

Southern, Richard W. *The Making of Middle Ages.* New Haven, CT: Yale University Press, 1959.

Southern, Richard W. *Western Views of Islam in the Middle Ages.* Cambridge, MA: Harvard University Press, 1962.

Stanton, Charles M. *Higher Learning in Islam: The Classical Period, A.D. 700–1300.* Savage, MD: Rowman & Littlefield Publishers, 1990.

Steiger, Arnald. *Origin and Spread of Oriental Words in European Languages.* New York: S.F. Vanni Publishers, 1963.

Stiefel, Tina. *The Intellectual Revolution in Twelfth-Century Europe.* New York: St. Martin's Press, 1985.

Stern, S.M., Albert Hourani, and Vivian Brown, eds. *Islamic Philosophy and the Classical Tradition: Essays Presented by His Friends and Pupils to Richard Walzer.* Columbia, SC: University of South Carolina Press, 1972.

Stewart, Desmond. *Early Islam.* New York: Time Inc., 1967.

Strayer, Joseph R., Hans W. Gatzke, and E. Harris Harbison. *The Mainstream of Civilization,* second edition. New York: Harcourt Brace Jovanovich, 1974.

Sweetman, John. *The Oriental Obsession: Islamic Inspiration in British and American Architecture, 1500–1920.* Cambridge and New York: Cambridge University Press, 1988.

Teresi, Dick. *Lost Discoveries: The Ancient Roots of Modern Science—From the Babylonians to the Maya.* New York and London: Simon & Schuster, 2002.

Thatcher, Oliver J. and Edgar Holmes McNeal. *Europe in the Middle Ages.* New York: Charles Scribner's Sons, 1896; reprint 1920.

Thomas, Bertram. *The Arabs: The Life of a People Who Have Left Their Deep Impress on the World.* New York: Doubleday, Doran and Company, 1937.

Tolan, John V. *Saracens: Islam in the Medieval European Imagination.* New York: Columbia University Press, 2002.

Toomer, G.J. *Eastern Wisedome and Learning: The Study of Arabic in Seventeenth-Century England.* Oxford: Clarendon Press, 1996.

Totah, Khalil A. *The Contribution of the Arabs to Education.* New York: Teachers College Press, Columbia University, 1926; AMS Press, 1972.

Treadgold, Warren, ed. *Renaissances Before the Renaissance: Cultural Revivals of Late Antiquity and the Middle Ages.* Stanford, CA: Stanford University Press, 1984.

Turner, Bryan S. *Weber and Islam*. London and Boston: Routledge and Kegan Paul, 1978; original 1973.

Turner, Howard R. *Science in Medieval Islam: An Illustrated Introduction*. Austin, TX: University of Texas Press, 1995.

Umaruddin, M. *The Ethical Philosophy of Al-Ghazzali*. Lahore, Pakistan: Institute of Islamic Culture, Combine Printers, 1988; original 1962.

United Nations Educational, Scientific and Cultural Organization. *Islam, Philosophy and Science*. New York: UNESCO Press, 1981.

Urvoy, Dominique. *Ibn Rushd (Averroes)* (translated from French by Olivia Steward). London and New York: Routledge, 1991.

Vryonis, Speros, Jr., ed. *Islam and Cultural Change in the Middle Ages*. Wiesbaden, Germany: Otto Harrassowitz, 1975.

Wahba, Mourad and Mona Abousenna, eds. *Averroes and the Enlightenment*. Amherst, MA, and New York: Prometheus Books, 1996.

Waines, David, ed. *Patterns of Everyday Life*. Burlington, VT, and Hampshire, UK: Ashgate Publishing Company, 2002.

Walzer, Richard. *Greek into Arabic: Essays in Islamic Philosophy*. Cambridge, MA: Harvard University Press, 1962.

Watt, W. Montgomery. *A History of Islamic Spain*. Edinburgh: Edinburgh University Press, 1965.

Watt, W. Montgomery. *The Influence of Islam on Medieval Europe*. Edinburgh: Edinburgh University Press, 1972.

Watt, W. Montgomery. *The Majesty That Was Islam: The Islamic World, 661–1100*. London: Sidgwick & Jackson Ltd., 1974.

Watt, W. Montgomery. *Muslim–Christian Encounters: Perceptions and Misperceptions*. London: Routledge, 1991.

Weaver, Henry Grady. *The Mainspring of Human Progress*. Irvington on Hudson, NY: The Foundation for Economic Education, Inc., 1953; original 1947.

Weinberg, Julius R. *A Short History of Medieval Philosophy*. Princeton, NJ: Princeton University Press, 1964.

Welch, Alford T. and Pierre Cachia, eds. *Islam: Past Influence and Present Challenge*. New York: State University of New York Press, 1979.

White, Lynn, Jr. *Medieval Technology and Social Change*. London: Oxford University Press, 1962.

Wiener, Leo. *Contributions Toward a History of Arabico-Gothic Culture* (four volumes). New York: Neale Publishing Company, 1917, 1919, 1920, and 1921.

Wiet, Gaston, Vadime Elisseeff, Philippe Wolff, and Jean Naudou. *History of Mankind: Cultural and Scientific Development—The Great Medieval Civilizations* (translated from French). New York and London: Sponsored by UNESCO, Harper & Row, 1975.

Williams, John Alden, ed. *Themes of Islamic Civilization*. Berkeley, Los Angeles, and London: University of California Press, 1971.

Wolff, Philippe. *The Cultural Awakening* (translated from French by Anne Carter). New York: Pantheon Books, 1968.

Wright, Thomas E. *Into the Moorish World*. London: Robert Hale, 1972.

Wulf, Maurice de. *History of Medieval Philosophy* (translated from French by P. Coffey). New York, Bombay, and Calcutta: Longmans, Green, and Company, 1909.

Young, M.J.L., J.D. Latham, and R.B. Serjeant. *Religion, Learning and Science in the Abbasid Period.* Cambridge and New York: Cambridge University Press, 1990.
Zacour, Norman P. and Harry W. Hazard. *A History of the Crusades: The Impact of the Crusades on the Near East.* Madison, WI: University of Wisconsin Press, 1985.
Ziad, Zeenut, ed. *The Magnificent Mughals.* Oxford and New York: Oxford University Press, 2002.

ARTICLES

Abercrombie, Thomas J. "When the Moors Ruled Spain." *National Geographic* 74, no.1 (July 1988): 86–119.
Ahmad, Imad-ad-Dean. "Economy, Technology, and the Environment: The Islamic Middle Way." *Journal of Faith and Science Exchange* 3 (1999): 55–61.
Ahmad, Imad-ad-Dean. "Islam and Markets." *Religion and Liberty* 6, no.3 (May–June 1996): 1–3.
Ahmad, Imad-ad-Dean. "Islam and the Progenitors of Austrian Economics." Pages 77–82 in *The Contributions of Murray Rothbard to Monetary Economics*, edited by C. Thies. Winchester, VA: Durrell Institute, Shenandoah University, 1996.
Ahmad, Imad-ad-Dean. "An Islamic Perspective on the Wealth of Nations." Pages 55–67 in *The Economics of Property Rights: Cultural, Historical, Legal, and Philosophical Issues*, edited by S. Pejovich. Cheltenham, UK: Edward Elgar Publishers, 2001.
Ahmad, Rafiq. "Ibn Khaldun: A Great Pioneer Economist." *University Economist: Journal of the Punjab University* 2, no.1 (March 1953): 52–61.
Ahmad, Rafiq. "The Origin of Economics and the Muslims: A Preliminary Survey." *Punjab University Economics* 7, no.1 (June 1969): 17–49.
Alam, Manzoor. "Ibn Khaldun's Concept of the Origin, Growth and Decay of Cities." *Islamic Culture* (Lahore, Pakistan) 34 (1960): 90–106.
Ali, Syed Ahmad. "Economics of Ibn Khaldun: A Selection." *Africa Quarterly* 10, no.3 (October–December 1970): 251–259.
Alonso, Manuel Alonso. "Influencia de Algazel en el Mundo Latino" ("The Influence of Algazel in the Latin World"). *Al-Andalus* 23 (1958): 371–380.
Alrefai, Ahmed and Michael Brun. "Ibn Khaldun: Dynastic Change and Its Economic Consequences." *Arab Studies Quarterly* 16, no.2 (Spring 1994): 73–86.
Andic, Suphan. "A Fourteenth Century Sociology of Public Finance." *Public Finance/Finances Publiques* 20, nos.1–2 (1965): 22–44.
Aramco Services Company. "Science: The Islamic Legacy." *Aramco World Magazine* 33, no.3 (May–June 1982): 2–64.
Aramco World Services. "The Art of Islamic Spain." *Aramco World* 43, no.5 (September–October 1992): 2–64.
Archer, John C. "Our Debt to the Moslem Arab." *The Moslem World* 24, no.3 (July 1939): 248–254.
Atiya, Aziz S. "The Crusades: Old Ideas and New Conceptions." *Journal of World History* 2 (1954): 470–475.
Avila, Maria Luisa. "The Search for Knowledge: Andalusi Scholars and Their Travels to the Islamic East." *Medieval Prosopography* (Special Issue: Arab-Islamic Culture) 23 (2002): 125–139.

Baeck, Louis. "Ibn Khaldun's Political and Economic Realism." Pages 83–99 in *Joseph A. Schumpeter, Historian of Economics: Perspectives on the History of Economic Thought, Selected Papers from the History of Economics Society Conference 1994*, edited by Laurence S. Moss. London: Routledge, 1996.

Baldwin, Marshall W. "Western Attitudes Toward Islam." *The Catholic Historical Review* 27, no.4 (January 1942): 403–411.

Bass, George F. "A Medieval Islamic Merchant Venture." *Archeological News* 7, nos.2–3 (Fall 1979): 85–94.

Beckingham, C.F. "Misconceptions of Islam: Medieval and Modern." *Journal of Royal Society of Arts* 126 (September 1976): 606–611.

Beech, George T. "Troubadour Contacts with Muslim Spain and Knowledge of Arabic: New Evidence Concerning William IX of Aquitaine." *Romania: Revue Trimestrielle* 113 (1992–1995): 14–42.

Benz, Ernst. "The Islamic Culture as Mediator of the Greek Philosophy to Europe." *Islamic Culture* (Lahore, Pakistan) 35 (1961): 147–165.

Berggren, J.L. "Islamic Acquisition of the Foreign Sciences: A Cultural Perspective." *American Journal of Islamic Social Sciences* 9 (1992): 310–324.

Bloom, Jonathan M. "Revolution by the Ream: A History of Paper." *Aramco World* 50, no.3 (May–June 1999): 26–39.

Bosch, Gular Kheirallah. "Ibn Khaldun on Evolution." *The Islamic Review* 38, no.5 (1950): 26–34.

Boulakia, Jean David C. "Ibn Khaldun: A Fourteenth-Century Economist." *Journal of Political Economy* 79, no.5 (September–October 1971): 1105–1118.

Bulliet, Richard W. "Medieval Arabic *Tarsh*: A Forgotten Chapter in the History of Printing." *Journal of American Oriental Society* 107, no.3 (1987): 427–438.

Bullis, Douglas. "The Longest Hajj: The Journeys of Ibn Battuta." *Saudi Aramco World* 51, no.4 (July–August 2000): 2–39.

Burns, Robert I. "Christian–Islamic Confrontation in the West: The Thirteenth Century Dream of Conversion." *American Historical Review* 76 (1971): 1386–1412; 1432–1434.

Burshatin, Israel. "The Moor in the Text: Metaphor, Emblem, and Silence." *Critical Inquiry* 12, no.1 (Autumn 1985): 98–118.

Butler, Pierce. "Fifteenth Century Editions of Arabic Authors in Latin Translation." Pages 63–71 in *Macdonald Presentation Volume: A Tribute to Duncan Black Macdonald*. Bridgeport, NY: Books for Libraries Press, 1933.

Chapra, M. Umar. "Socioeconomic and Political Dynamics of Ibn Khaldun's Thought." *American Journal of Islamic Social Sciences* 16, no.4 (Winter 1999): 17–38.

Chejne, Anwar G. "Intellectual Revival in the Arab World: An Introduction." *Islamic Studies* 11, no.4 (December 1973): 410–437.

Coulson, Noel J. "The Concept of Progress and Islam Law." Pages 74–92 in *Religion and Progress in Modern Asia*, edited by Robert N. Bellah. New York: The Free Press, 1965.

Cox, Robert W. "Toward a Post-Hegemonic Conceptualization of World Order: Reflections on the Relevancy of Ibn Khaldun." Pages 144–173 in *Approaches to World Order*, edited by Robert W. Cox and Timothy J. Sinclair. Cambridge and New York: Cambridge University Press, 1996.

Dannenfeldt, K. "The Renaissance Humanists and the Knowledge of Arabic." *Studies in the Renaissance* 2 (1955): 96–117.

Darling, Linda T. "Rethinking Europe and the Islamic World in the Age of Exploration." *Journal of Early Modern History* 2, no.3 (1998): 2230–2246.

Dawson, Christopher. "The Origins of the European Scientific Tradition: St. Thomas and Roger Bacon." *The Clergy Review* 2 (September 1930): 193–205.

Dennett, Daniel C., Jr. "Pirenne and Muhammad." *Speculum: A Journal of Medieval Studies* 23, no.2 (April 1948): 165–190.

Desomogyi, Joseph. "Economic Theory in Classical Arabic Literature." Pages 1–10 in *Studies in Islamic Economics, Series 8, Encyclopedic Survey of Islamic Culture*, edited by Mohamed Taher. New Delhi, India: Anmol Publications (Private) Ltd., 1997.

Druart, Therese-Anne. "Medieval Islamic Thought and the 'What Is X?' Question." *American Catholic Philosophical Quarterly* 73, no.1 (Winter 1999): 1–8.

Edwards, John. "Mission and Inquisition among *Conversos* and *Moriscos* in Spain, 1250–1550." *Studies in Church History* 21 (1984): 139–151.

Eigeland, Tor. "Escape from a Troubled World." *Aramco World* 41, no.5 (September–October 1990): 2–10.

Eigeland, Tor. "Islam in Al-Andalus." *Aramco World Magazine* 27, no.5 (September–October 1976): 1–32.

Eigeland, Tor. "Touring Al-Andalus." *Aramco World* 50, no.2 (March–April 1999): 22–32.

Essid, M. Yassine. "Islamic Economic Thought." Pages 77–102 in *Pre-Classical Economic Thought*, edited by S. Todd Lowry. Boston: Kluwer Academic Publishers, 1986.

Fakahani, Suzan J. "Islamic Influences on Emerson's Thought: The Fascination of a Nineteenth Century American Writer." *Journal of Muslim Minority Affairs* 18, no.2 (1998): 291–303.

Fakhry, Majid. "Philosophy and Scripture in the Theology of Averroes." *Medieval Studies* 30 (1968): 78–87.

Fernandez, Maria Luisa. "Art of the Mudejars." *Aramco World* 44, no.1 (January–February 1993): 36–41.

Forget, J. "De l'influence de la philosophie arabe sur la philosophie scholastique." *Revue Neo-Scholastique* 4, no.3665 (October 1894): 385–410.

Foster, Benjamin R. "Agoranomics and Muhtasib." *Journal of Economic and Social History of the Orient* 13 (April 1970): 128–144.

Gabriel, Judith. "Among the Norse Tribes: The Remarkable Account of Ibn Fadlan." *Aramco World* 50, no.6 (November–December 1999): 36–42.

Gabrieli, Francisco. "Frederick II and Moslem Culture." *East and West* 9 (1958): 53–61.

Gates, Warren E. "The Spread of Ibn Khaldun's Ideas on Climate and Culture." *Journal of History of Ideas* 28, no.3 (July–September 1967): 415–421.

Gaudiosi, Monica. "Comment: The Influence of the Islamic Law of *Waqf* on the Development of the Trust in England—The Case of Merton College." *University of Pennsylvania Law Review* 136 (April 1988): 1231–1261.

Ghazanfar, S.M. "Civilizational Dialogue: Medieval Social Thought, Latin-European Renaissance, and Islamic Influences." *Encounters: Journal of Intercultural Perspectives* 9, no.1 (2003): 21–36.

Ghazanfar, S.M. "The Economic Thought of Abu Hamid Al-Ghazali and St. Thomas Aquinas: Some Comparative Parallels and Links." *History of Political Economy* 32, no.4 (2000): 858–888.

Ghazanfar, S.M. "Medieval Islamic Socio-Economic Thought: Links with Greek and Latin-European Scholarship." *Humanomics* (Special Volume: Comparative Political Economy) 13, nos.3–4 (1997): 33–60.

Ghazanfar, S.M. "Post-Greek/Pre-Renaissance Economic Thought: Contributions of Arab-Islamic Scholastics during the 'Great Gap' Centuries." *Research in the History of Economic Thought and Methodology* 16 (1998): 65–89.

Ghazanfar, S.M. "Public Sector Economics in Medieval Economic Thought: Contributions of Selected Arab-Islamic Scholars." *Public Finance/Finances Publiques* 53, no.1 (1998): 19–36.

Ghazanfar, S.M. "Scholastic Economics and Arab Scholars: The 'Great Gap' Thesis Reconsidered." *Diogenes: International Review of Humane Sciences* (Paris) no.154 (April–June 1991): 117–139.

Ghazanfar, S.M. and A. Azim Islahi. "Economic Thought of an Arab Scholastic: Abu Hamid Al-Ghazali (AH450–505/AD1058–1111)." *History of Political Economy* 22, no.2 (1990): 381–403.

Ghazanfar, S.M. and A. Azim Islahi. "Explorations in Medieval Arab-Islamic Economic Thought: Some Aspects of Ibn Qayyim's Economics (691–751 AH/1292–1350 AD)." *History of Economic Ideas* (Italy) 5, no.1 (1997): 7–25.

Ghazanfar, S.M. and A. Azim Islahi. "Explorations in Medieval Arab-Islamic Economic Thought: Some Aspects of Ibn Taimiyah's Economics." Pages 45–63 in *Perspectives on the History of Economic Thought: Selected Papers from the History of Economics Conference 1990*, edited by S. Todd Lowry. Brookfield, VT: Edward Elgar Publishing Company, 1992.

Gibb, H.A.R. "The Influence of Islamic Culture on Medieval Europe." *Bulletin of the John Rylands Library* 95 (1955): 82–98.

Gibb, H.A.R. "The Islamic Background of Ibn Khaldun's Political Theory." *Bulletin of the School of Oriental Studies* 7 (1933–1935): 23–31.

Glick, Thomas F. "Muhtasib and Mustasaf: A Case Study of Institutional Diffusion." *Viator: Medieval and Renaissance Studies* 2 (1971): 59–81.

Goitein, S.D. "Between Hellenism and Renaissance: Islam, the Intermediate Civilization." *Islamic Studies* 2, no.2 (June 1963): 216–233.

Goitein, S.D. "The Rise of the Near-Eastern Bourgeoisie in Early Islamic Times." *Journal of World History* 3 (1957): 583–604.

Gomez, Reverend Eusebio. "Muslim Theology in Its Bearing on Scholasticism." *Clergy Review* 6 (1933): 99–109.

Gomez, Michael A. "Muslims in Early America." *Journal of Southern History* 60, no.4 (November 1994): 671–710.

Government of Saudi Arabia. "Islamic Science and Learning." Washington, DC: High Commission for the Development of Arriyadh, Culture Center (July 1989): 2–20.

Gran, Peter. "The Middle East in the Historiography of Advanced Capitalism." *Review of Middle East Studies* no.1 (1975): 135–154.

Gran, Peter. "Political Economy as a Paradigm for the Study of Islamic History." *International Journal of Middle East Studies* 11, no.4 (1980): 511–526.

Granara, William. "*Jihad* and Cross-Cultural Encounter in Muslim Sicily." *Harvard Middle Eastern and Islamic Review* 3, no.2 (1996): 42–61.

Gross, Charles G. "Ibn al-Haytham on Eye and Brain, Vision and Perception." *Bulletin of Islamic Medicine* 1 (1981): 309–312.

Gusau, Sule Ahmed. "Economic Views of Ibn Khaldun." *Journal of Objective Studies* (Aligarh, India) 3 (1990): 48–60.

Hamilton, Bernard. "Knowing the Enemy: Western Understanding of Islam at the Time of the Crusades." *Journal of Royal Asiatic Studies* 7, no.3 (1997): 373–387.

Hannoum, Abdelmajid. "Translation and the Colonial Imaginary: Ibn Khaldun Orientalist." *History and Theory* 42 (February 2003): 61–81.

Harvey, L.P. "The Moriscos and the *Hajj*." *Bulletin of the British Society for Middle Eastern Studies* 14, no.1 (1987): 11–24.

Haskins, Charles H. "Arabic Science in Western Europe." *ISIS: Journal of the History of Science in Society* 7 (1925): 478–485.

Haskins, Charles H. "The Reception of Arabic Science in England." *English Historical Review* 30 (January 1915): 56–69.

Haskins, Charles H. "The Spread of Ideas in the Middle Ages." *Speculum: A Journal of Medieval Studies* 1 (1926): 19–30.

al-Hibri, Azzizah Y. "Islamic and American Constitutional Law: Borrowing Possibilities or a History of Borrowing." *University of Pennsylvania Journal of Constitutional Law* (Symposium Issue: Contextuality and Universality—Constitutional Borrowing on the Global Stage) 1, no.3 (Spring 1999): 492–527.

al-Hibri, Azzizah Y. "Islamic Constitutionalism and the Concept of Democracy." *Case Western Reserve Journal of International Law* 24, no.1 (Winter 1992): 1–27.

Hill, Donald R. "Mechanical Engineering in the Medieval Near East." *Scientific American* 264, no.5 (May 1991): 100–105.

Hodgson, Marshall G.S. "Modernity and the Islamic Heritage." *Islamic Studies* 1, no.2 (June 1962): 89–129.

Hosseini, Hamid. "Contributions of Medieval Muslim Scholars to the History of Economics and Their Impact: A Refutation of the Schumpeterian Great Gap." Pages 28–45 in *A Companion to the History of Economic Thought*, edited by Warren J. Samuels, Jeff E. Biddle, and John B. Davis. New York: Blackwell Publishing Company, 2003.

Hosseini, Hamid. "The Inaccuracy of the Schumpeterian Great Gap Thesis: Economic Thought in Medieval Iran (Persia)." Pages 63–82 in *Joseph M. Schumpeter, Historian of Economics: Perspectives on the History of Economic Thought—Selected Papers from the History of Economics Society Conference 1994*, edited by Laurence S. Moss. London and New York: Routledge Publishers, 1996.

Hosseini, Hamid. "Medieval Islamic (Persian) Mirrors for Princes Literature and the History of Economics." *Journal of South Asian and Middle Eastern Studies* 24, no.4 (2001): 13–36.

Hosseini, Hamid. "Seeking the Roots of Adam Smith's Division of Labor in Medieval Persia (Iran)." *History of Political Economy* 30, no.3 (Winter 1998): 653–681.

Hosseini, Hamid. "Understanding the Market Mechanism before Adam Smith: Economic Thought in Medieval Islam." *History of Political Economy* 27, no.3 (1995): 539–561.

Hourani, George. "The Early Growth of the Secular Sciences in Andalusia." *Studia Islamica* 32 (1970): 143–156.

Huff, Toby E. "Science and the Public Sphere: Comparative Institutional Development in Islam and the West." *Social Epistemology* 11, no.1 (1997): 25–37.

Hunt, R.W. "English Learning in the Late Twelfth Century." *Transactions of the Royal Historical Society* 19 (1936): 19–42.

Irving, Thomas B. "The Process of Arab Thought in Spain." *Studies in Islam* 4, no.2 (April 1967): 65–96.

Isani, Mukhtar Ali. "Cotton Mather and the Orient." *New England Quarterly* 43, no.1 (March 1970): 46–58.

Ito, Shuntaro. "Islamic Civilization as Seen from Japan: A Non-Western View." Pages 131–138 in *The Islamic World and Japan: In Pursuit of Mutual Understanding*, Proceedings of the 1980 International Symposium, the Japan Foundation. Tokyo, Japan, 1981.

Jellicoe, Patricia Countess. "The Art of Islamic Spain." *Aramco World* 43, no.5 (September–October 1992): 24–31.

Joubin, Rebecca. "Islam and Arabs through the Eyes of the *Encyclopedie*: The 'Other' as a Case of French Cultural Self-Criticism." *International Journal of Middle East Studies* 32 (2000): 197–217.

Kagaya, Kan. "Changing Muslim Views of Islamic History and Modernization: An Interpretation of Religion and Politics in Pakistan." *The Developing Economies* 4 (June 1968): 193–202.

Khalid, Detlev H. "The Problem of Defining Islam and Modern Accentuations." *Islamic Studies* 16, no.3 (Autumn 1977): 217–281.

Khalidi, Tarif. "Islamic Views of the West in the Middle Ages." *Studies in Interreligious Dialogue* 5 (1995): 31–42.

Khan, M. Abdur Rehman. "A Survey of Muslim Contribution to Science and Culture, Part I." *Islamic Culture* 14 (January 1942): 1–20.

Khan, M. Abdur Rehman. "A Survey of Muslim Contribution to Science and Culture, Part II." *Islamic Culture* 14 (April 1942): 136–152.

Khan, M. Saber. "A Classified Bibliography of Recent Publications on al-Biruni." *Muslim World Book Review* 10, no.3 (Autumn 1990): 65–77.

Kidd, Thomas S. "'Is It Worse to Follow Mahomet Than the Devil?' Early American Uses of Islam." *Church History* 72, no.4 (December 2003): 766–790.

Kraemer, Joel L. "Humanism in the Renaissance of Islam: A Preliminary Study." *Journal of the American Oriental Society* 104, no.1 (January–March 1984): 135–164.

Krek, Miroslav. "Arabic Block Printing as the Precursor of Printing in Europe: Preliminary Report." *Newsletter of the American Research Center in Egypt* (Princeton University, Princeton, NJ), no.129 (Spring 1985): 12–16.

Labib, Subhi Y. "Capitalism in Medieval Islam." *Journal of Economic History* 29 (1969): 79–96.

Lapidus, Ira M. "The Separation of State and Religion in the Development of Early Islamic Society." *International Journal of Middle East Studies* 6, no.4 (October 1975): 363–385.

Latham, J.D. "Towns and Cities of Barbary: The Andalusian Influence." *Islamic Quarterly* 16 (1972): 189–204.

Lewis, Archibald R. "The Islamic World and the Latin West, 1350–1500." *Speculum: A Journal of Medieval Studies* 65, no.4 (October 1990): 833–844.

Lindberg, David C. "Medieval Science and Its Religious Context." *OSIRIS* 10 (1995): 61–79.

Lunde, Paul. "The Giralda." *Aramco World* 44, no.1 (January–February 1993): 32–35.

Lunde, Paul. "Ishbiliyah: Islamic Seville." *Aramco World* 44, no.1 (January–February 1993): 20–31.

Lunde, Paul. "The Middle East and the Age of Discovery." *Aramco World* 43, no.3 (May–June 1992): 2–64.

Lunde, Paul. "The Missing Link." *Aramco World* 32, no.2 (March–April 1981): 26–27.

Makdisi, George. "Interaction between Islam and the West." *Revue des etudes Islamiques* 44 (1976): 287–309.

Makdisi, George. "Muslim Institutes of Learning in Eleventh-Century Baghdad." *Bulletin of the School of Oriental and African Studies* 24, no.1 (1961): 1–56.

Makdisi, George. "The Scholastic Method in Medieval Education: An Inquiry into Its Origins in Law and Theology." *Speculum: A Journal of Medieval Studies* 49 (1974): 640–661.

Makdisi, John A. "The Islamic Origins of the Common Law." *North Carolina Law Review* 77 (June 1999): 1635–1739.

Matar, Nabil. "Muslims in Seventeenth-Century England." *Journal of Islamic Studies* 8, no.1 (1997): 63–82.

Matar, Nabil. "The Traveler as Captive: Renaissance England and the Allure of Islam." *Literature Interpretation Theory* 7 (1996): 187–196.

Mateo, Matilde. "The Making of the *Saracen Style*: The Crusades and Medieval Architecture in the British Imagination in the 18th and 19th Centuries." Pages 115–141 in *The Crusades: Other Experiences, Alternative Perspectives, Selected Proceedings from the 32nd Conference of the Center for Medieval and Early Renaissance Studies*, edited by Khalil E. Semaan. Binghamton, NY: State University of New York Press, 2003.

Meadows, Ian. "Historical Markers." *Aramco World* 44, no.1 (January–February 1993): 10–11.

Menocal, Maria Rosa. "Pride and Prejudice in Medieval Studies: European and Oriental." *Hispanic Review* 53 (1985): 61–78.

Meyerhof, Max. "The 'Book of Treasure,' an Early Arabic Treatise on Medicine." *ISIS: Journal of the History of Science in Society* 14, no.43 (May 1930): 55–76.

Meyerhof, Max. "On the Transmission of Greek and Indian Science to the Arabs." *Islamic Culture* 11, no.20 (January 1937): 17–29.

Millas-Vallicrosa, J.M. "Translations of Oriental Scientific Works (to the End of the Thirteenth Century)" (translated from Spanish by Daphne Woodword). *Journal of World History* 2, no.2 (1954): 395–428.

Mirakhor, Abbas. "The Muslim Scholars and the History of Economics: A Need for Consideration." *The American Journal of Islamic Social Sciences* 4, no.2 (1987): 245–275.

Moody, Ernest A. "Galileo and Avempace: The Dynamics of the Learning Tower Experiment." Part I, *Journal of the History of Ideas* 12, no.2 (April 1951): 163–193; Part II, *Journal of the History of Ideas* 12, no.3 (August 1951): 375–422.

Moorhead, John. "The Earliest Christian Theological Response to Islam." *Religion* 11 (1981): 265–274.

Moosa, Matti. "The Crusades: An Eastern Perspective, with Emphasis on Syriac Sources." *Muslim World* 93, no.2 (April 2003): 249–290.

Moosa, Matti I. "Al-Kindi's Role in the Transmission of Greek Knowledge to the Arabs." *Journal of the Pakistan Historical Society* 15 (January 1967): 1–18.

Mottahedeh, Roy. "Some Islamic Views of the Pre-Islamic Past." *Harvard Middle Eastern and Islamic Review* 1 (1994): 17–26.

Muhammad, Mi'raj. "Ibn Khaldun and Vico: A Comparative Study." *Islamic Studies* 19, no.3 (1980): 195–211.

Munro, Dana Carleton. "The Renaissance of the Twelfth Century." *Annual Report of the American Historical Association* (1906): 43–50.

Munro, Dana Carleton. "The Western Attitude Toward Islam During the Period of the Crusades." *Speculum: A Journal of Medieval Studies* 6 (1931): 329–343.

Myers, Eugene A. "Legacy of Arab Culture to the Western World." *The Muslim Digest* 19, no.5 (December 1968): 61–65.

Nadvi, S. Sulaiman. "Arab Navigation, Part I" (three-part essay). *Islamic Culture* (Hyderabad, India) 15 (October 1941): 435–448.

Nadvi, S. Sulaiman. "Arab Navitation, Part II." *Islamic Culture* (Hyderabad, India) 16 (April 1942): 181–198.

Nadvi, S. Sulaiman. "Arab Navigation, Part III." *Islamic Culture* (Hyderabad, India) 17 (January 1943): 72–86.

Naqvi, Syed Ali Raza. "Prophet Muhammad's Image in Western Enlightened Scholarship." *Islamic Studies* 20, no.2 (Summer 1981): 136–151.

Newby, Gordon D. "The Foundation of the University of Naples: Typological Parallels with Arab Institutions of Higher Learning." *Medieval Encounters* 3, no.2 (1997): 173–184.

Newby, Gordon D. "Ibn Khaldun and Frederick Jackson Turner: Islam and the Frontier Experience." *Journal of Asian and African Studies* 18, nos.3–4 (1983): 274–285.

Newby, Gordon D. "Trade in the Levant and the East Mediterranean in the Early Islamic Period: A Search for the Early Muslim Merchant." *Archeological News* 7, nos.2–3 (Fall 1979): 78–83.

Noakes, Greg. "Exploring Flamenco's Arab Roots." *Saudi Aramco World* 45, no.6 (November–December 1994): 32–35.

Noakes, Greg. "The Other 1492." *Aramco World* 44, no.1 (January–February 1993): 2–9.

O'Brien, Peter. "Islamic Civilization's Role in the Waning of the European Middle Ages." *The Medieval History Journal* 2, no.2 (July–December 1999): 387–404.

O'Brien, Peter. "Platonism and Plagiarism at the End of the Middle Ages." Pages 304–318 in *Christianizing People and Converting Individuals*, edited by Guyda Armstrong and Ian N. Wood. Turnhot, Belgium: Brepols Publishers n.v., 2000.

Omar, Saleh. "Ibn Al-Haytham's Theory of Knowledge and Its Significance for Later Science." *Arab Studies Quarterly* 1, no.1 (1979): 67–82.

Oran, Ahmad and Salim Rashid. "Fiscal Policy in Early Islam." *Public Finance/Finances Publiques* 44, no.1 (1989): 75–101.

Oweiss, Ibrahim M. "Ibn Khaldun, the Father of Economics." Pages 112–127 in *Arab Civilization: Challenges and Responses—Studies in Honor of Constantine K. Zurayk*, edited by George N. Atiyeh and Ibrahim M. Oweiss. Albany, NY: State University of New York Press, 1988.

Oweiss, Ibrahim M. "A View on Islamic Economic Thought." *Occasional Paper Series*, Center for Contemporary Arab Studies. Washington, DC: Georgetown University, 2000.

Paret, Rudi. "Islam and Christianity." *Islamic Studies* 3, no.1 (March 1964): 86–95.

Pasha, Mustapha Kamal. "Ibn Khaldun and World Order." Pages 56–70 in *Innovation and Transformation in International Studies*, edited by Stephen Gill and James E. Mittleman. Cambridge and New York: Cambridge University Press, 1997.

Pingree, David. "The Greek Influence on Early Islamic Mathematical Astronomy." *Journal of the American Oriental Society* 93, no.1 (January–March 1973): 32–43.

Ragep, F. Jamil. "Duhem, the Arabs, and the History of Cosmology." *Synthese* 83 (1990): 201–214.

Rahman, Fazlur. "Islam: Legacy and Contemporary Challenge." *Islamic Studies* 19, no.4 (Winter 1980): 235–246.

Rahman, Fazlur. "The Religious Situation of Mecca from the Eve of Islam up to the Hijra." *Islamic Studies* 16, no.4 (Winter 1977): 289–301.

Rahman, Fazlur. "The Status of the Individual in Islam." Pages 217–225 in *The Status of the Individual in East and West*, edited by Charles A. Moor (with assistance from Aldyth V. Morris). Honolulu, HI: University of Hawaii Press, 1968.

Rashed, Roshdi. "Problems of the Transmission of Greek Scientific Thought into Arabic: Examples from Mathematics and Optics." *History of Science* 27 (1989): 199–209.

Rashed, Roshdi. "Science as a Western Phenomenon." *Fundamenta Scientiae* (Paris) 1 (1980): 7–21.

Rosenthal, Erwin J. "Ibn Khaldun: A North African Muslim Thinker of the Fourteenth Century." *Bulletin of the John Rylands Library* 24 (1940): 307–320.

Rosenthal, Erwin J. "Some Reflections on the Separation of Religion and Politics in Modern Islam." *Islamic Studies* 3, no.3 (September 1964): 249–284.

Rozina, Parveen. "Ibn Khaldun as an Economist: A Comparative Study with Modern Economists." *Pakistan Journal of History and Culture* 15, no.1 (1994): 111–130.

Rubenstein, Rheta and Randy Schwartz. "Arabic from A (Algebra) to Z (Zero)." *Math Horizons* (September 1999): 16–18.

Runciman, Steven. "Islam and Christendom in the Middle Ages: The Need for Restatement." *Islamic Studies* 3, no.2 (June 1964): 193–198.

Russell, Josiah C. "Hereford and Arabic Science in England about 1175–1200." *ISIS: Journal of the History of Science in Society* 18, no.1 (July 1932): 14–25.

Sabra, A.I. "The Appropriation and Subsequent Naturalization of Greek Science in Medieval Islam: A Preliminary Statement." *History of Science* 25 (1987): 223–243.

Sabra, A.I. "Situating Arabic Science: Locality versus Essence." *ISIS: Journal of the History of Science in Society* 87, no.4 (December 1996): 654–670.

Salloum, Habeeb. "Arabian Memories in Portugal." *Saudi Aramco World* 52, no.2 (March–April 2001): 1–5.

Salman, D. "Algazel et les Latins" ("Algazel and the Latins"). *Archives d'Histoire Doctrinale et Literaire du Moyen Age* (1935–1936): 103–127.

Samarrai, Alauddin. "The Idea of Fame in Medieval Arabic Literature and Its Renaissance Parallels." *Comparative Literature Studies* 16, no.4 (December 1979): 279–293.

Samarrai, Alauddin. "Medieval Commerce and Diplomacy: Islam and Europe, A.D. 850–1300." *Canadian Journal of History* 15, no.1 (April 1980): 1–21.

Samarrai, Alauddin. "The Term 'Fief': A Possible Arabic Origin." *Studies in Medieval Culture* 4, no.1 (1973): 78–82.

Sattar, M. Abdus. "Ibn Khaldun's Contribution to Economic Thought." Pages 121–129 in *Contemporary Aspects of Economic Thinking in Islam*, Proceedings of the Third East Coast Regional Conference of the Muslim Students Association of the USA and Canada, 1968. Baltimore, MD: American Trust Publications, 1976.

Schaefer, Karl R. "Eleven Medieval Arabic Block Prints in the Cambridge University Library." *Arabica* 48 (2001): 210–239.

Schaefer, Karl R. "The Scheide *Tarsh.*" *The Princeton University Library Chronicle* 56, no.3 (1995): 401–419.

Schleifer, Aliah. "Ibn Khaldun's Theories of Perception, Logic, and Knowledge: An Islamic Phenomenology." *American Journal of Islamic Social Sciences* 2, no.2 (December 1985): 225–231.

Schmidt, Nathaniel. "The Manuscripts of Ibn Khaldun." *Journal of the American Oriental Society* 46 (1926): 171–176.

Shah, Shafqat A. "Aristotle, Al-Farabi, Averroes, and Aquinas: Four Views on Philosophy and Religion." *Sind University Research Journal* (Hyderabad, Pakistan) 19 (1980): 1–20.

Shah, Tahir. "The Islamic Legacy of Timbuktu." *Saudi Aramco World* 46, no.6 (November–December 1995): 1–5.

Shanab, R.E.A. "Ghazali and Aquinas on Causation." *The Monist* 58 (1974): 140–150.

Sharif, M.M. "Muslim Philosophy and Western Thought." *Iqbal: A Journal of the Bazm-I-Iqbal* (Lahore, Pakistan) 8, no.1 (July 1959): 1–14.

Sharif, M. Raihan. "Ibn-i-Khaldun, the Pioneer Economist" *Islamic Literature* (Lahore, Pakistan) 6, no.5 (May 1955): 33–40.

Sherwani, H. "Ibn-i-Taimiyah's Economic Thought." *Islamic Quarterly* (Lahore, Pakistan) 8 (1956): 9–21.

Siddiqi, M. Nejatullah and S.M. Ghazanfar. "Early Medieval Islamic Economic Thought: Abu Yusuf's (731–798 AD) Economics of Public Finance." *History of Economic Ideas* (Italy) 9, no.1 (2001): 13–38.

Siddiqi, Mazheruddin. "The Holy Prophet and the Orientalists." *Islamic Studies* 19, no.3 (Autumn 1980): 143–165.

Siddiqui, Razi-ud-Din. "The Contribution of Muslims to Scientific Thought." *Islamic Culture* (Hyderabad, India) 14 (January 1940): 34–44.

Sirry, Mun'im A. "Early Muslim–Christian Dialogue: A Closer Look at Major Themes of the Theological Encounter." *Islam and Christian–Muslim Relations* 16, no.4 (October 2005): 361–376.

Smith, Wilfred Cantwell. "The True Meaning of Scripture: An Empirical Historian's Non-reductionist Interpretation of the Qur'an." *International Journal of Middle East Studies* 11 (1980): 487–505.

Soofi, Abdol. "Economics of Ibn Khaldun Revisited." *History of Political Economy* 27, no.2 (1995): 387–404.

Spengler, Joseph J. "Alberuni: Eleventh Century Iranian Malthusian?" *History of Political Economy* 3, no.1 (Spring 1971): 93–104.

Spengler, Joseph J. "Economic Thought of Islam: Ibn Khaldun." *Comparative Studies in Society and History* 6, no.3 (April 1964): 268–306.

Stone, Caroline. "Doctor, Philosopher, Renaissance Man." *Saudi Aramco World* 54, no.3 (May–June 2003): 8–15.

Stowasser, Barbara Freyer. "Religion and Political Development: Some Comparative Ideas of Ibn Khaldun and Machiavelli." *Occasional Paper Series*, Center for Contemporary Arab Studies, Washington, DC: Georgetown University Press, January 1983.

Thompson, Diane P. "Paradigms Lost: Western Civilization and the Orient Unexpressed." *Northern Virginia Review*, no.10 (Fall 1995): 5–8.

Thompson, James W. "The Introduction of Arabic Science into Lorraine in the Tenth Century." *ISIS: Journal of the History of Science in Society* 12 (May 1929): 184–194.

Thomson, Rodney M. "England and the Twelfth Century Renaissance." *Past and Present* 101 (1983): 3–21.

Tolan, John. "'Saracen Philosophers Secretly Deride Islam.'" *Medieval Encounters* 8, nos.2–3 (2003): 184–208.

Tolmacheva, Marina. "Bertius and al-Idrisi: An Experiment in Orientalist Cartography." *Terrae Incognitae* 28 (1996): 36–45.

Tolmacheva, Marina. "Ibn Battuta on Women's Travel in the Dar al-Islam." Pages 119–140 in *Women and the Journey: The Female Travel Experience*, edited by Bonnie Frederick and Susan H. McLeod. Pullman, WA: Washington State University, 1993.

Tolmacheva, Marina. "The Medieval Arabic Geographers and the Beginning of Modern Orientalism." *International Journal of Middle East Studies* 27, no.2 (1995): 141–156.

Tolmacheva, Marina. "On the Arab System of Nautical Orientation." *Arabica* 27, no.2 (1980): 180–192.

Tolmacheva, Marina. "Ptolemaic Influence on Medieval Arab Geography: The Case Study of East Africa." Pages 125–141 in *Discovering New Worlds: Essays on Medieval Exploration and Imagination*, edited by Scott D. Westrem. New York and London: Garland Publishing, 1991.

Tschanz, David W. "The Arab Roots of European Medicine." *Aramco World* 48, no.3 (May–June 1997): 20–32.

Udovitch, Abraham L. "Bankers without Banks: Commerce, Banking, and Society in the Islamic World of the Middle Ages." Pages 255–273 in *The Dawn of Modern Banking*, Center for Medieval and Renaissance Studies, University of California, Los Angeles. New Haven, CT: Yale University Press, 1979.

Udovitch, Abraham L. "Labor Partnership in Early Islam." *Journal of Economic and Social History of the Orient* 10 (1967): 64–80.

Udovitch, Abraham L. "Reflections on the Institutions of Credit and Banking in the Medieval Islamic Near East." *Studia Islamica* 41 (1975): 5–21.

Van Koningsveld, P.S. "Muslim Slaves and Captives in Western Europe during the Late Middle Ages." *Islam and Christian–Muslim Relations* 6, no.1 (1995): 5–23.

Walzer, Richard. "Arabic Transmission of Greek Thought to Medieval Europe." *Bulletin of the John Rylands Library* 29, no.1 (July 1945): 3–26.

Wasserstein, David J. "Greek Science in Islam: Islamic Scholars as Successors to the Greeks." *Hermathena* 147 (1998): 57–72.

Watt, W. Montgomery. "Muhammad in the Eyes of the West." *Boston University Journal* 22, no.3 (1974): 61–69.

Watt, W. Montgomery. "Pre-Islamic Arabian Religion in the Qur'an." *Islamic Studies* 15, no.2 (Summer 1976): 73–79.

Weiss, Dieter. "Ibn Khaldun on Economic Transformation." *International Journal of Middle East Studies* 27 (1995): 29–37.

Welborn, Mary C. "Lotharingia as a Center of Arabic and Scientific Influence in the Eleventh Century." *ISIS: Journal of the History of Science in Society* 16 (1931): 188–199.

Wippel, John F. "The Condemnations of 1270 and 1277 at Paris." *Journal of Medieval and Renaissance Studies* 7 (Spring 1977): 169–201.

Wolf, C. Umhau. "Luther and Mohammedanism." *The Moslem World* (Hartford, CT) 31, no.3 (July 1941): 161–177.

Wolf, Kenneth B. "The Earliest Spanish Christian Views of Islam." *Church History* 55 (1986): 281–293.

Young, T. Cuyler. "The Cultural Contributions of Islam to Christendom." *The Moslem World* (Hartford, CT) 35, no.2 (April 1945): 89–110.

Zaid, Omar Abdullah. "Were Islamic Records Precursors to Accounting Books Based on the Italian Method?" *Accounting Historians Journal* 27, no.1 (June 2000): 73–90.

Zuwiyya, Z. David. "Arab Culture and Morisco Heritage in an Aljamiado Legend: 'Al-hadit del bano de Zaryeb.'" *Romance Quarterly* 48, no.1 (Winter 2001): 32–47.

Topical Bibliography

BOOKS

(A) Sciences/Humanities

(i) Social Sciences/Humanities

a. History

B-1. Abu-Nasir, Jamil M. *A History of the Maghrib in the Islamic Period.* Cambridge and New York: Cambridge University Press, 1987.

B-2. Ahmad, Aziz. *A History of Islamic Sicily.* Edinburgh: Edinburgh University Press, 1975.

B-3. Ali, Syed Ameer. *A Short History of the Saracens: Being a Concise Account of the Rise and Decline of the Saracenic Power and of the Economic, Social and Intellectual Development of the Arab Nation.* London and New York: Macmillan and Company, 1900.

B-4. Arberry, A.J. *Aspects of Islamic Civilization: As Depicted in the Original Texts.* Westport, CT: Greenwood Press, 1964.

B-5. Armstrong, Karen. *Islam: A Short History.* New York: Modern Library Edition, Random House, 2000.

B-6. Armstrong, Karen. *Muhammad: A Biography of the Prophet.* New York: HarperCollins, 1992.

B-7. Arnold, Thomas. *The Spread of Islam in the World: A History of Peaceful Preaching.* Delhi, India: Goodword Books, 2001; original 1896.

B-8. Artz, Frederick B. *The Mind of the Middle Ages, A.D. 200–1500: An Historical Survey.* Chicago and London: University of Chicago Press, 1980; original 1953.

B-9. Benson, Robert L. and Giles Constable, eds. *Renaissance and Renewal in the Twelfth Century.* Cambridge, MA: Harvard University Press, 1982.

B-10. Berkey, Jonathan P. *The Formation of Islam: Religion and Society in the Near East, 600–1800.* Cambridge and New York: Cambridge University Press, 2003.

B-11. Bloom, Jonathan and Sheila Blair. *Islam: A Thousand Years of Faith and Power.* New York: TV Books, L.L.C., 2000.

B-12. Brice, William M., ed. *An Historical Atlas of Islam.* Leiden, Belgium: E.J. Brill, 1981.

B-13. Bulliet, Richard W. *Conversion to Islam in the Medieval Period*. Cambridge, MA: Harvard University Press, 1979.

B-14. Bulliet, Richard W. *The Patricians of Nishapur: A Study in Medieval Islamic Social History*. Cambridge, MA: Harvard University Press, 1972.

B-15. Burke, Edmund, III, ed. *Rethinking World History: Essays on Europe, Islam, and World History (by Marshall G.S. Hodgson)*. Cambridge and New York: Cambridge University Press, 1993.

B-16. Burman, Edward. *Emperor to Emperor: Italy before the Renaissance*. London: Constable and Company Ltd., 1991.

B-17. Cantor, Norman F. *Western Civilization: Its Genesis and Destiny—From the Prehistoric Era to 1500*. Glenview, IL: Scott, Foresman and Company, 1969.

B-18. Carlyle, Thomas. *Heroes, Hero Worship and the Heroic in History*. New York: A.L. Burt Company, n.d.

B-19. El-Cheikh, Nadia Maria. *Byzantium Viewed by the Arabs*. Cambridge and London: Harvard University Press, 2004.

B-20. Clagett, Marshall, Gaines Post, and Robert Reynolds, eds. *Twelfth Century Europe and the Foundations of Modern Society*, Proceedings of a Symposium. Madison, WI: University of Wisconsin Press, 1961.

B-21. Courbage, Youssef and Philippe Fargues. *Christians and Jews under Islam* (translated from French by Judy Mabro). London and New York: I.B. Tauris Publishers, 1998.

B-22. Davies, Norman. *Europe: A History*. New York: Oxford University Press, 1996.

B-23. Dawson, Christopher. *The Formation of Christendom*. New York: Sheed & Ward, 1967.

B-24. Dawson, Christopher. *The Making of Europe: An Introduction to the History of European Unity*. New York: Sheed & Ward, 1952.

B-25. Dawson, Christopher. *Religion and the Rise of Western Culture*. Garden City, NY: Image Books, A Division of Doubleday and Company, Inc., 1958.

B-26. Donner, Fred M. *The Early Islamic Conquests*. Princeton, NJ: Princeton University Press, 1981.

B-27. Douglas, David C. *The Norman Fate, 1100–1154*. Berkeley and Los Angeles: University of California Press, 1976.

B-28. Draper, John W. *History of the Conflict between Religion and Science*. New York and London: D. Appleton and Company, 1902; original 1874.

B-29. Draper, John W. *History of the Intellectual Development of Europe*, revised edition in two volumes. New York and London: Harper and Brothers Publishers, 1876 and 1904.

B-30. Dunlop, D.M. *Arab Civilization to A.D. 1500*. New York and Washington, DC: Praeger Publishers, 1971.

B-31. Eaton, Richard M. *Islamic History as Global History*. Washington, DC: American Historical Association, 1990.

B-32. Esposito, John L., ed. *The Oxford History of Islam*. New York: Oxford University Press, 1999.

B-33. Ezzati, Abul-Fazl. *An Introduction to the History of the Spread of Islam*. London: News and Media Ltd., 1978.

B-34. George, Linda. *The Golden Age of Islam*. Tarrytown, NY: Benchmark Books, 1998.

B-35. Gimpel, Jean. *The Medieval Machine: The Industrial Revolution of the Middle Ages*. New York: Holt, Rinehart and Winston, 1976.

B-36. Goitein, S.D. *Studies in Islamic History and Its Institutions.* Leiden, Netherlands: E.J. Brill, Leiden, 1966; reprinted 1968.

B-37. Goldstein, Thomas. *Dawn of Modern Science.* Boston: Houghton Mifflin Company, 1988.

B-38. Guizat, Pierre Guillaume. *General History of Civilization in Europe* (edited, with critical and supplementary notes, by George W. Knight). New York: D. Appleton and Company, 1899.

B-39. Hambly, Gavin R.G., ed. *Women in the Medieval Islamic World.* New York: St. Martin's Press, 1999.

B-40. Haskins, Charles Homer. *The Renaissance of the Twelfth Century.* Cambridge, MA: Harvard University Press, 1927.

B-41. Haskins, Charles Homer. *Studies in Mediaeval Culture.* Oxford: Clarendon Press, 1929.

B-42. Havighurst, Alfred F., ed. *The Pirenne Thesis: Analysis, Criticism, and Revision.* Lexington, MA: D.C. Heath and Company, revised edition, 1969.

B-43. Hawting, G.R. *The First Dynasty of Islam: The Umayyad Caliphate AD 661–750.* Carbondale, IL: Southern Illinois University Press, 1987.

B-44. Hearnshaw, F.J.C., ed. *Medieval Contributions to Modern Civilization: A Series of Lectures Delivered at King's College University of London.* New York: Henry Holt and Company, 1922.

B-45. Hell, Joseph. *The Arab Civilization* (translated from German by S. Khuda Bukhsh). Cambridge: W. Heffer & Sons, 1926.

B-46. El-Hibri, Tayeb. *Reinterpreting Islamic Historiography: Harun al-Rashid and the Narrative of the Abbasid Caliphate.* Cambridge and New York: Cambridge University Press, 1999.

B-47. Hill, Fred James and Nicholas Awde. *A History of the Islamic World.* New York: Hippocrene Books, Inc., 2003.

B-48. Hitti, Philip K. *The Arabs: A Short History.* Princeton, NJ: Princeton University Press, 1943.

B-49. Hitti, Philip K. *History of the Arabs.* London: Macmillan and Company, 1943.

B-50. Hitti, Philip K. *Makers of Arab History.* New York: St. Martin's Press, 1968.

B-51. Holt, P.M., Ann K.S. Lambton, and Bernard Lewis, eds. *The Cambridge History of Islam, Volume I, The Central Islamic Lands; Volume II, The Further Islamic Lands, Islamic Society and Civilization.* Cambridge and New York: Cambridge University Press, 1970.

B-52. Hopwood, Derek, ed. *Studies in Arab History: The Antonius Lectures, 1978–87.* New York: St. Martin's Press, 1990.

B-53. Hourani, Albert. *A History of the Arab Peoples.* Cambridge, MA: Harvard University Press, 2002; original 1991.

B-54. Issawi, Charles. *An Arab Philosophy of History: Selections from the* Prolegomena *of Ibn Khaldun of Tunis (1332–1406)* (translated and arranged by Charles Issawi). Princeton, NJ: The Darwin Press, Inc., 1987.

B-55. Issawi, Charles. *The Arab World's Legacy: Essays by Charles Issawi.* Princeton, NJ: The Darwin Press, Inc., 1981.

B-56. Izzeddin, Nejla. *The Arab World: Past, Present, and Future.* Chicago: Henry Regnery Company, 1953.

B-57. Japan Foundation. *The Islamic World and Japan: In Pursuit of Mutual Understanding*. Tokyo, Japan: Park Building, 3-6 Kioi-cho, Chiyoda-ku, 1981.

B-58. Kapoor, Subodh, ed. *The Muslims: Encyclopedia of Islam* (11 volumes). New Delhi, India: Cosmo Publications, 2004.

B-59. Kennedy, Hugh. *The Early Abbasid Caliphates: A Political History*. London: Croom Helm, 1981.

B-60. Kennedy, Hugh. *The Prophet and the Age of the Caliphates: The Islamic Near East from the Sixth to Eleventh Century*. London and New York: Longman Group Ltd., 1986.

B-61. Kennedy, Hugh. *When Baghdad Ruled the Muslim World: The Rise and Fall of Islam's Greatest Dynasty*. Cambridge, MA: DaCapo Press (Perseus Books Group), 2005.

B-62. Khalidi, Tarif. *Classical Arab Islam: The Culture and Heritage of the Golden Age*. Princeton, NJ: The Darwin Press, Inc., 1985.

B-63. Knowles, David. *The Evolution of Medieval Thought*. Baltimore, MD: Helicon Press, Inc., 1962.

B-64. Lacroix, Paul. *Science and Literature in the Middle Ages and the Renaissance*. New York: Frederick Ungar Publishing Company, 1964; original 1878.

B-65. Landau, Rom. *Islam and the Arabs*. New York: Macmillan Company, 1959.

B-66. Lane, Rose Wilder. *The Discovery of Freedom: Man's Struggle Against Authority*. New York: John Day Company, 1943; third edition 1993.

B-67. Lapidus, Ira M. *A History of Islamic Societies*, second edition. Cambridge: Cambridge University Press, 2002.

B-68. Lapidus, Ira M. *Muslim Cities in the Later Middle Ages*. Cambridge, MA: Harvard University Press, 1967.

B-69. Laroui, Abdallah. *The History of the Maghrib: An Interpretative Essay* (translated from French by Ralph Manheim). Princeton, NJ: Princeton University Press, 1977.

B-70. Lewis, Bernard, ed. and trans. *Islam: From the Prophet Muhammad to the Capture of Constantinople (Religion and Society)*. New York: Walker and Company, 1974.

B-71. Lewis, Bernard, ed. *The World of Islam: Faith, People, and Culture*. London and New York: Thames and Hudson, Ltd., 1992.

B-72. Libby, Walter. *An Introduction to the History of Science*. New York: Houghton Mifflin Company, 1917.

B-73. Lombard, Maurice. *The Golden Age of Islam* (translated from French by Joan Spencer). Amsterdam and New York: North-Holland Publishing Company/American Elsevier Publishing Company, 1975.

B-74. Lunde, Paul. *Islam: Faith, Culture, History*. London and New York: DK Publishing Company, 2002.

B-75. Macdonald, Duncan B. *Development of Muslim Theology, Jurisprudence and Constitutional Theory*. New York: Charles Scribner's Sons, 1903.

B-76. Magoffin, Ralph V.D. and Frederick Duncalf. *Ancient and Medieval History: The Rise of Classical Culture and the Development of Medieval Civilization*. New York and Chicago: Silver, Burdett and Company, 1934.

B-77. Nawwab, Ismail I., Peter C. Speers, and Paul F. Hoye, eds. *Aramco and Its World: Arabia and the Middle East*. Washington, DC: Arabian American Oil Company, 1981.

B-78. Nebelsick, Harold P. *The Renaissance, the Reformation and the Rise of Science*. Edinburgh: T&T Clark, 1992.

B-79. O'Leary, De Lacy. *Arabic Thought and Its Place in History*. London: Kegan Paul, Trench, Trubner and Company Ltd.; New York: E.P. Dutton and Company, 1922.

B-80. O'Leary, De Lacy. *How Greek Science Passed to the Arabs*, second edition. London: Routledge and Kegan Paul Ltd., 1951.

B-81. Packard, Sidney R. *Twelfth Century Europe: An Interpretive Essay*. Amherst, MA: University of Massachusetts Press, 1973.

B-82. Peretz, Don, Richard U. Moench, and Safia K. Mohsen. *Islam: Legacy of the Past, Challenge of the Future*. New York: North River Press/New Horizon Press Publishers, 1984.

B-83. Peters, Edward. *Europe: The World of Middle Ages*. Englewood Cliffs, NJ: Prentice-Hall, 1977.

B-84. Peters, F.E., ed. *The Arabs and Arabia on the Eve of Islam*. Brookfield, VT, and Hampshire, UK: Ashgate Publishing Company, 1999.

B-85. Pirenne, Henri. *Economic and Social History of Medieval Europe* (translated from French by I.E. Clegg). New York: Harcourt, Brace and Company, 1937.

B-86. Powell, James M., ed. *Muslims under Latin Rule, 1100–1300*. Princeton, NJ: Princeton University Press, 1990.

B-87. Price, B.B. *Medieval Thought: An Introduction*. Cambridge, MA: Blackwell Publishers, 1992.

B-88. Reynolds, Robert L. *Europe Emerges: Transition Toward an Industrial World-Wide Society 600–1750*. Madison, WI: University of Wisconsin Press, 1961.

B-89. Richards, D.S., ed. *Papers on Islamic History: Islamic Civilization, 950–1150; A Colloquium*; Published under the auspices of the Near Eastern History Group, Oxford, and the Near East Center, University of Pennsylvania; Bruno Cassirer (Publishers) Ltd., Oxford, 1973.

B-90. Richards, D.S., ed. *Papers on Islamic History: Islam and the Trade of Asia—A Colloquium*. Published under the auspices of the Near Eastern History Group, Oxford, and the Near East Center, University of Pennsylvania; Bruno Cassirer, Oxford, and University of Pennsylvania Press, 1970.

B-91. Robinson, Chase F., ed. *Texts, Documents and Artefacts: Islamic Studies in Honor of D.S. Richards*. Leiden, Netherlands, and Boston: E.J. Brill, 2003.

B-92. Robinson, David. *Muslim Societies in African History*. Cambridge: Cambridge University Press, 2004.

B-93. Robinson, Francis. *Islam and Muslim History in South Asia*. New Delhi, India: Oxford University Press, 2001.

B-94. Robinson, Francis, ed. *The Cambridge Illustrated History of the Islamic World*. London: Cambridge University Press, 1996.

B-95. Rogers, Michael. *The Spread of Islam*. Oxford: Elsevier-Phaidon, 1976.

B-96. Rosenthal, Franz. *The Classical Heritage in Islam* (translated from German by Emile and Jenny Marmorstein). Berkeley and Los Angeles: University of California Press, 1965.

B-97. Ross, Frank, Jr. *Arabs and the Islamic World*. New York: S.G. Phillips, Inc., 1979.

B-98. Rubin, Uru, ed. *The Life of Muhammad*. Brookfield, VT, and Hampshire, UK: Ashgate Publishing Company, 1998.

B-99. Sarton, George. *The Normans in European History*. Boston and New York: Houghton Mifflin Company, 1915.

B-100. Saunders, J.J. *A History of Medieval Islam*. London: Routledge and Kegan Paul, 1965; reprinted 1972.

B-101. Sauvaget, Jean. *Introduction to the History of the Muslim East: A Bibliographical Guide*. Berkeley, CA: University of California Press, 1965.

B-102. Savory, R.M. *Introduction to Islamic Civilization*. Cambridge and New Delhi, India: Cambridge University Press/Vikas Publishing House, 1976.

B-103. Sha'ban, M.A. *Islamic History, A.D. 600–750 (A.H. 132): A New Interpretation*. Cambridge: Cambridge University Press, 1971.

B-104. Sonn, Tamara. *A Brief History of Islam*. Oxford: Blackwell Publishing Ltd., 2004.

B-105. Southern, Richard W. *The Making of Middle Ages*. New Haven, CT: Yale University Press, 1959.

B-106. Stiefel, Tina. *The Intellectual Revolution in Twelfth-Century Europe*. New York: St. Martin's Press, 1985.

B-107. Stewart, Desmond. *Early Islam*. New York: Time Inc., 1967.

B-108. Strayer, Joseph R., Hans W. Gatzke, and E. Harris Harbison. *The Mainstream of Civilization*, second edition. New York: Harcourt Brace Jovanovich, 1974.

B-109. Thatcher, Oliver J. and Edgar Holmes McNeal. *Europe in the Middle Ages*. New York: Charles Scribner's Sons, 1896; reprint 1920.

B-110. Thomas, Bertram. *The Arabs: The Life of a People Who Have Left Their Deep Impress on the World*. New York: Doubleday, Doran and Company, 1937.

B-111. Treadgold, Warren, ed. *Renaissances Before the Renaissance: Cultural Revivals of Late Antiquity and the Middle Ages*. Stanford, CA: Stanford University Press, 1984.

B-112. Watt, W. Montgomery. *The Majesty That Was Islam: The Islamic World, 661–1100*. London: Sidgwick & Jackson Ltd., 1974.

B-113. Weaver, Henry Grady. *The Mainspring of Human Progress*. Irvington on Hudson, NY: The Foundation for Economic Education, Inc., 1953; original 1947.

B-114. Welch, Alford T. and Pierre Cachia, eds. *Islam: Past Influence and Present Challenge*. New York: State University of New York Press, 1979.

B-115. Wiener, Leo. *Contributions Toward a History of Arabico-Gothic Culture* (four volumes). New York: Neale Publishing Company, 1917, 1919, 1920, and 1921.

B-116. Wiet, Gaston, Vadime Elisseeff, Philippe Wolff, and Jean Naudou. *History of Mankind: Cultural and Scientific Development—The Great Medieval Civilizations* (translated from French). New York and London: Sponsored by UNESCO, Harper & Row, 1975.

B-117. Williams, John Alden, ed. *Themes of Islamic Civilization*. Berkeley, Los Angeles, and London: University of California Press, 1971.

B-118. Wolff, Philippe. *The Cultural Awakening* (translated from French by Anne Carter). New York: Pantheon Books, 1968.

B-119. Ziad, Zeenut, ed. *The Magnificent Mughals*. Oxford and New York: Oxford University Press, 2002.

b. Economics/Commerce

B-120. Allouche, Adel. *Mamluk Economics: A Study and Translation of Al-Maqrizi's* Ighathah (translated from Arabic). Salt Lake City, UT: University of Utah Press, 1994.

B-121. Esfandiari, Haleh and A.L. Udovitch, eds. *The Economic Dimensions of Middle*

Eastern History: Essays in Honor of Charles Issawi. Princeton, NJ: The Darwin Press, Inc., 1990.

B-122. Ghazanfar, S.M., ed. *Medieval Islamic Economic Thought: Filling the "Great Gap" in European Economics*. London and New York: RoutledgeCurzon, 2003.

B-123. Gran, Peter. *Islamic Roots of Capitalism, Egypt, 1760–1840*. Syracuse, NY: Syracuse University Press, 1998.

B-124. Ibrahim, Mahmood. *Merchant Capital and Islam*. Austin, TX: University of Texas Press, 1990.

B-125. Lokkegaard, Frede. *Islamic Taxation in the Classic Period, with Special Reference to Circumstances in Iraq*. Philadelphia, PA: Porcupine Press, 1978; original 1950.

B-126. Masters, Bruce. *The Origins of Western Economic Dominance in the Middle East: Mercantilism and the Islamic Economy in Aleppo, 1600–1750*. New York and London: New York University Press, 1988.

B-127. Rodinson, Maxime. *Islam and Capitalism* (translated from French, originally published in 1996, by Brian Pearce). Austin, TX: University of Texas Press, 1978.

c. Philosophy

B-128. Asin-Palacios, Miguel. *The Mystical Philosophy of Ibn Masarra and His Followers* (translated from Spanish by Elmer H. Douglas and Howard W. Yoder). Leiden, Netherlands: E.J. Brill, 1978; original 1914.

B-129. Butterworth, Charles E. and Blake Andree Kessel, eds. *The Introduction of Arabic Philosophy into Europe*. Leiden, New York, and Cologne: E.J. Brill, 1994.

B-130. Corbin, Henry. *History of Islamic Philosophy* (translated from French by Liadain Sherrard). London: Kegan Paul International, in association with Islamic Publications for the Institute of Ismaili Studies, 1993.

B-131. Fakhry, Majid. *Averroes (Ibn Rushd): His Life, Works and Influence*. Oxford, UK: Oneworld Publications, 2001.

B-132. Fakhry, Majid. *A History of Islamic Philosophy*. New York: Columbia University Press, 1983.

B-133. Fakhry, Majid. *Islamic Occasionalism and Its Critique by Averroes and Aquinas*. London: George Allen and Unwin Ltd., 1958.

B-134. Flint, Robert. *History of the Philosophy of History*. New York: Charles Scribner's Sons, 1894.

B-135. Gilson, Etienne. *History of Christian Philosophy in the Middle Ages*. New York: Random House, 1955.

B-136. Gilson, Etienne. *Reason and Revelation in the Middle Ages*. New York and London: Charles Scribner's Sons, 1948.

B-137. Grant, Edward. *God and Reason in the Middle Ages*. Cambridge and New York: Cambridge University Press, 2001.

B-138. Grant, Edward. *Studies in Medieval Science and Natural Philosophy*. London: Variorum Reprints, 1981.

B-139. Haq, Mahmudul. *Reason and Tradition in Islamic Thought*. Aligarh, India: Institute of Islamic Studies, Aligarh Muslim University, 1992.

B-140. Haren, Michael. *Medieval Thought: The Western Intellectual Tradition from Antiquity to the Thirteenth Century*. Toronto: University of Toronto Press, 1992.

B-141. Hourani, George F., ed. *Essays on Islamic Philosophy and Science*. Albany, NY: State University of New York Press, 1975.

B-142. Hyman, Arthur and James J. Walsh, eds. *Philosophy in the Middle Ages: The Christian, Islamic, and Jewish Traditions*. Indianapolis, IN: Hackett Publishing Company, 1973.

B-143. Leaman, Oliver. *Averroes and His Philosophy*. Oxford: Clarendon Press, 1988.

B-144. Marmura, Michael E. *Al-Ghazali's The Incoherence of the Philosophers (Tahafut al-Falasifa*; a parallel English–Arabic text translated, introduced, and annotated). Provo, UT: Brigham Young University, 1997.

B-145. Mazzaoui, Michel M. and Vera B. Moreen, eds. *Intellectual Studies in Islam: Essays Written in Honor of Martin B. Dickson*. Salt Lake City, UT: University of Utah Press, 1990.

B-146. Murray, Alexander. *Reason and Society in the Middle Ages*. Oxford: Clarendon Press, 1978.

B-147. Nasr, Seyyed Hossein. *An Introduction to Islamic Cosmological Doctrines: Conceptions of Nature and Methods Used for Its Study by the Ikhwan al-Safa, al-Biruni, and Ibn Sina*. Albany, NY: State University of New York Press, revised edition, 1993.

B-148. Nasr, Seyyed Hossein and Oliver Leaman, eds. *History of Islamic Philosophy (Parts I and II)*. London: Routledge, 1996.

B-149. Peters, F.E. *Aristotle and the Arabs: The Aristotelian Tradition in Islam*. New York and London: New York University Press/University of London Press, 1968.

B-150. Qadir, C.A. *Philosophy and Science in the Islamic World*. Kent, UK: Croom Helm Ltd., 1988.

B-151. Rescher, Nicholas. *Studies in Arabic Philosophy*. Pittsburgh, PA: University of Pittsburgh Press, 1967.

B-152. Ross, James F., ed. *Inquiries into Medieval Philosophy: A Collection in Honor of Francis P. Clarke*. Westport, CT: Greenwood Publishing Company, 1971.

B-153. Sharif, M.M., ed. *A History of Muslim Philosophy, with Short Accounts of Other Disciplines and the Modern Renaissance in Muslim Lands*, two volumes. Wiesbaden, Germany: Otto Harrassowitz, 1963 and 1966.

B-154. Siraisi, Nancy G. *Avicenna in Renaissance Italy: The* Canon *and Medical Teaching in Italian Universities after 1500*. Princeton, NJ: Princeton University Press, 1987.

B-155. Smith, Margaret. *Al-Ghazali: The Mystic*. London: Luzac and Company, 1944.

B-156. Stern, S.M., Albert Hourani, and Vivian Brown, eds. *Islamic Philosophy and the Classical Tradition: Essays Presented by His Friends and Pupils to Richard Walzer*. Columbia, SC: University of South Carolina Press, 1972.

B-157. Umaruddin, M. *The Ethical Philosophy of Al-Ghazzali*. Lahore, Pakistan: Institute of Islamic Culture, Combine Printers, 1988; original 1962.

B-158. Urvoy, Dominique. *Ibn Rushd (Averroes)* (translated from French by Olivia Steward). London and New York: Routledge, 1991.

B-159. Wahba, Mourad and Mona Abousenna, eds. *Averroes and the Enlightenment*. Amherst, MA, and New York: Prometheus Books, 1996.

B-160. Walzer, Richard. *Greek into Arabic: Essays in Islamic Philosophy*. Cambridge, MA: Harvard University Press, 1962.

B-161. Weinberg, Julius R. *A Short History of Medieval Philosophy*. Princeton, NJ: Princeton University Press, 1964.

B-162. Wulf, Maurice de. *History of Medieval Philosophy* (translated from French by P. Coffey). New York, Bombay, and Calcutta: Longmans, Green, and Company, 1909.

d. Education/Learning

B-163. Duri, A.A. *The Rise of Historical Writing Among the Arabs* (edited and translated from Arabic by Lawrence I. Conrad; introduction by Fred M. Donner). Princeton, NJ: Princeton University Press, 1983; original 1960.

B-164. Haskins, Charles Homer. *The Rise of Universities*. New York: Henry Holt and Company, 1923.

B-165. Lowry, Joseph, Devin J. Stewart, and Shawkat M. Toorawa, eds. *Law and Education in Medieval Islam: Studies in Honor of Professor George Makdisi*. New York: David Brown Book Company, 2005.

B-166. Makdisi, George. *The Rise of Colleges: Institutions of Learning in Islam and the West*. Edinburgh: Edinburgh University Press, 1981.

B-167. Murdoch, John Emery and Edith Dudley Sylla, eds. *The Cultural Context of Medieval Learning*. Dordrecht, Netherlands, and Boston: Reidel Publishing Company, 1975.

B-168. Netton, Ian Richard. *Seek Knowledge: Thought and Travel in the House of Islam*. Surrey, UK: Curzon Press, 1996.

B-169. Rosenthal, Franz. *Knowledge Triumphant: The Concept of Knowledge in Medieval Islam*. Leiden, Netherlands: E.J. Brill, 1970.

B-170. Stanton, Charles M. *Higher Learning in Islam: The Classical Period, A.D. 700–1300*. Savage, MD: Rowman & Littlefield Publishers, 1990.

B-171. Totah, Khalil A. *The Contribution of the Arabs to Education*. New York: Teachers College Press, Columbia University, 1926; AMS Press, Inc., 1972.

B-172. United Nations Educational, Scientific and Cultural Organization. *Islam, Philosophy and Science*. New York: UNESCO Press, 1981.

B-173. Young, M.J.L., J.D. Latham, and R.B. Serjeant. *Religion, Learning and Science in the Abbasid Period*. Cambridge and New York: Cambridge University Press, 1990.

e. Geography

B-174. Penrose, Boies. *Travel and Discovery in the Renaissance, 1420–1620*. Cambridge, MA: Harvard University Press, 1955.

f. Humanities

B-175. Afsaruddin, Asma and A.H. Mathias Zahniser, eds. *Humanism, Culture, and Language in the Near East: Studies in Honor of Georg Krotkoff*. Winona Lake, IN: Eisenbrauns Inc., 1997.

B-176. Ahmed, Leila. *Women and Gender in Islam: Historical Roots of a Modern Debate*. New Haven, CT: Yale University Press, 1992.

B-177. Briffault, Robert. *Rational Revolution: The Making of Humanity*. New York: The Macmillan Company, 1930.

B-178. Calder, Norman, Jawid Mojaddedi and Andrew Rippin, eds. and trans. *Classical Islam: A Sourcebook of Religious Literature*. London and New York: Routledge, 2003.

B-179. Ernst, Carl. *Following Muhammad: Rethinking Islam in the Contemporary World.* Chapel Hill, NC: University of North Carolina Press, 2003.

B-180. Farmer, Henry G. *Historical Facts for the Arabic Musical Influence.* New York: Benjamin Bloom, Inc., 1971; original 1930.

B-181. Goodman, Lenn E. *Islamic Humanism.* New York: Oxford University Press, 2003.

B-182. Kraemer, Joel L. *Humanism in the Renaissance of Islam: The Cultural Revival during the Buyid Age,* second revised edition. Leiden, New York, and Koln: E.J. Brill, 1992.

B-183. Kristeller, Paul Oskar. *Renaissance Thought: The Classic, Scholastic, and Humanist Strains.* New York: Harper Torchbooks, Harper & Row Publishers, 1961.

B-184. Kritzeck, James. *Modern Islamic Literature from 1800 to the Present.* New York: A Mentor Book from New American Library, 1970.

B-185. Kritzeck, James, ed. *Anthology of Islamic Literature: From the Rise of Islam to Modern Times.* Toronto and New York: Mentor Books, Holt, Rinehart and Winston, Inc., 1966.

B-186. Makdisi, George. *The Rise of Humanism in Classical Islam and the Christian West: With Special Reference to Scholasticism.* Edinburgh: Edinburgh University Press, 1990.

B-187. An-Na'im, Abdullah Ahmed (foreword by John Voll). *Toward an Islamic Reformation: Civil Liberties, Human Rights, and International Law.* Syracuse, NY: Syracuse University Press, 1990.

B-188. Salloum, Habeeb and James Peters. *Arabic Contributions to the English Vocabulary—English Words of Arabic Origin: Etymology and History.* Beirut, Lebanon: Librairie du Liban Publishers, 1996.

B-189. Sarton, George. *The History of Science and the New Humanism.* New York: George Braziller, Inc., 1956.

B-190. Steiger, Arnald. *Origin and Spread of Oriental Words in European Languages.* New York: S.F. Vanni Publishers, 1963.

g. Social Sciences, General

B-191. Ali, Basharat. *Muslim Social Philosophy.* Karachi, Pakistan: Jamiyatul Falah Publications, 1967.

B-192. Atiyeh, George N. and Ibrahim M. Oweiss, eds. *Arab Civilization: Challenges and Responses: Studies in Honor of Constantine K. Zurayk.* Albany, NY: State University of New York Press, 1988.

B-193. Banani, Amin and Speros Vryonis, Jr., eds. *Individualism and Conformity in Classical Islam.* Wiesbaden, Germany: Otto Harrassowitz, 1977.

B-194. Coulton, G.G. *Studies in Medieval Thought.* New York: Russell and Russell, 1965.

B-195. Daniel, Norman. *The Cultural Barrier: Problems in the Exchange of Ideas.* Edinburgh: Edinburgh University Press, 1975.

B-196. Daniel, Norman. *Heroes and Saracens: An Interpretation of the Chansons de Geste.* Edinburgh: Edinburgh University Press, 1984.

B-197. al-Faruqi, Ismail R. and Lois Lamya al-Faruqi. *The Cultural Atlas of Islam.* New York: The Macmillan Company, 1986.

B-198. Hallaq, Wael B., ed. *The Formation of Islamic Law.* Burlington, VT, and Hants, UK: Ashgate Publishing Company, 2004.

B-199. Heer, Nicholas, ed. *Islamic Law and Jurisprudence: Studies in Honor of Farhat Ziadeh*. Seattle and London: University of Washington Press, 1990.

B-200. Hovannisian, Richard G. and Georges Sabagh, eds. *Religion and Culture in Medieval Islam*. Cambridge and New York: Cambridge University Press, 1999.

B-201. Kincheloe, Joe L. and Shirley R. Steinberg, eds. *The Miseducation of the West: How Schools and the Media Distort Our Understanding of the Islamic World*. Westport, CT: Praeger Publishers, 2004.

B-202. Lacoste, Yves. *Ibn Khaldun: The Birth of History and the Past of the Third World* (translated from French by David Macey). London: Verso Publishers, 1984.

B-203. Levy, Reuben. *The Social Structure of Islam*. Cambridge, London, and New York: Cambridge University Press, 1962.

B-204. Sachedina, Abdulaziz. *The Islamic Roots of Democratic Pluralism*. New York: Oxford University Press, 2001.

B-205. Vryonis, Jr., Speros, ed. *Islam and Cultural Change in the Middle Ages*. Wiesbaden, Germany: Otto Harrassowitz, 1975.

B-206. Waines, David, ed. *Patterns of Everyday Life*. Burlington, VT, and Hampshire, UK: Ashgate Publishing Company, 2002.

B-207. White, Lynn, Jr. *Medieval Technology and Social Change*. London: Oxford University Press, 1962.

(ii) Sciences

B-208. Ariew, Roger and Peter Barker, eds. (translated from French). *Pierre Duhem: Essays in the History and Philosophy of Science*. Indianapolis, IN, and Cambridge: Hackett Publishing Company, 1996.

B-209. Berggren, J.L. *Episodes in the Mathematics of Medieval Islam*. New York, Berlin, and Tokyo: Springer-Verlag, 1986.

B-210. Butterfield, H. *The Origins of Modern Science, 1300–1800*. New York: The Macmillan Company, 1961.

B-211. Casulleras, Josep and Julio Samso, eds. *From Baghdad to Barcelona: Studies in the Islamic Exact Sciences in Honor of Professor Juan Vernet*, Volumes I and II. Barcelona, Spain: Anuari de Filogia (Universitat de Barcelona) XIX, B-2, Instituto Millas Vallicrosa de Historia de la Ciencia Arabe, 1996.

B-212. Crombie, A.C. *Medieval and Early Modern Science: Vol. I, Science in the Middle Ages, V–XIII Centuries; Vol. II, Science in the Later Middle Ages and Early Modern Times, XIII–XVII Centuries*. New York: Doubleday and Company, revised second edition, 1959.

B-213. Dalafi, H.R. and M.H.A. Hassan, eds. *Renaissance of Sciences in Islamic Countries*. Singapore, London, and River Edge, NJ: World Scientific, 1994.

B-214. Dales, Richard C. *The Scientific Achievement of the Middle Ages*. Philadelphia, PA: University of Pennsylvania Press, 1973.

B-215. Grant, Edward. *The Foundations of Modern Science in the Middle Ages: Their Religious, Institutional, and Intellectual Contexts*. Cambridge and New York: Cambridge University Press, 1996.

B-216. Hall, A. Ruper and Marie Boas Hall. *A Brief History of Science*. Ames, IA: Iowa State University Press, 1988.

B-217. Haskins, Charles Homer. *Studies in the History of Medieval Science*. Cambridge, MA: Harvard University Press, 1927.

B-218. al-Hassan, Ahmad Y. and Donald R. Hill. *Islamic Technology: An Illustrated History*. Cambridge and New York: Cambridge University Press, 1986.

B-219. Hess, David J. *Science and Technology in a Multicultural World: The Cultural Politics of Facts and Artifacts*. New York: Columbia University Press, 1995.

B-220. Hill, Donald R. *A History of Engineering in Classical and Medieval Times*. La Salle, IL: Open Court Publishing Company, 1984.

B-221. Hill, Donald R. *Islamic Science and Engineering*. Edinburgh: Edinburgh University Press, 1993.

B-222. Hill, Donald R. (edited by David A. King). *Studies in Medieval Islamic Technology: From Philo to al-Jazari—From Alexandria to Diyar Bakr*. Variorum Collected Studies Series. Brookfield, VT, and Hampshire, UK: Ashgate Publishing Ltd., 1998.

B-223. Holmyard, Eric J. *Makers of Chemistry*. London: Oxford University Press, first published 1931; reprinted 1937, 1945, 1946, 1953, and 1962.

B-224. Huff, Toby E. *The Rise of Early Modern Science: Islam, China, and the West*. Cambridge and New York: Cambridge University Press, 1993.

B-225. Hull, L.W.H. *History and Philosophy of Science: An Introduction*. London and New York: Longmans, Green and Company, 1959.

B-226. Ihsanoglu, Ekmeleddin and Feza Gunergun, eds. *Science in Islamic Civilization*. Istanbul, Turkey: Research Center for Islamic History and Culture, 2000.

B-227. Kennedy, E.S. (and colleagues, former students; David A. King and Mary Helen Kennedy, editors). *Studies in the Islamic Exact Sciences*. Beirut, Lebanon: American University of Beirut, 1983.

B-228. King, David A. and George Saliba, eds. *From Deferent to Equant: A Volume of Studies in the History of Science in the Ancient and Medieval Near East in Honor of E.S. Kennedy*. Volume 500. New York: Annals of the New York Academy of Sciences, New York Academy of Sciences, 1987.

B-229. Lindberg, David C. *The Beginnings of Western Science: The European Scientific Tradition in Philosophical, Religious, and Institutional Context, 600 B.C. to A.D. 1450*. Chicago and London: University of Chicago Press, 1992.

B-230. Lindberg, David C., ed. *Science in the Middle Ages*. Chicago: University of Chicago Press, 1978.

B-231. Mason, Stephen F. *A History of the Sciences*, revised edition. New York: Collier Books, 1962.

B-232. Nasr, Seyyed Hossein. *Islamic Science: An Illustrated Study* (photographs by Roland Michaud). Kent, UK: World of Islam Festival Publishing Company, Westerham Press Ltd., 1976.

B-233. Nasr, Seyyed Hossein. *Science and Civilization in Islam*. Cambridge, MA: Harvard University Press, 1968.

B-234. Rashed, Roshdi, ed. (in collaboration with Regis Morelon). *Encyclopedia of the History of Arabic Science, Vol. 1, Astronomy*. London and New York: Routledge, 1996.

B-235. Rashed, Roshdi, ed. (in collaboration with Regis Morelon). *Encyclopedia of the History of Arabic Science, Vol. 2, Mathematics and the Physical Sciences*. London and New York: Routledge, 1996.

B-236. Rashed, Roshdi, ed. (in collaboration with Regis Morelon). *Encyclopedia of the*

History of Arabic Science, Vol. 3, Technology, Alchemy and Life Sciences. London and New York: Routledge, 1996.

B-237. Ronan, Colin A. *Science: Its History and Development among the World's Cultures.* New York: Facts On File Publications, 1982.

B-238. Saliba, George. *A History of Arabic Astronomy: Planetary Theories during the Golden Age of Islam.* New York and London: New York University Press, 1994.

B-239. Sarton, George. *A Guide to the History of Science: A First Guide for the Study of the History of Science, with Introductory Essays on Science and Tradition.* Waltham, MA: Chronica Botanica Company, 1952.

B-240. Sarton, George. *Introduction to the History of Science; Volume I—From Homer to Omar Khayam.* Baltimore, MD: Published for the Carnegie Institution of Washington by William & Wilkins Company, 1927.

B-241. Sarton, George. *Introduction to the History of Science: Volume II, Part I—From Rabbi Ben Ezra to Ibn Rushd.* Baltimore, MD: Published for the Carnegie Institution of Washington by Williams & Wilkins Company, 1931.

B-242. Sarton, George. *Introduction to the History of Science: Volume III, Science and Learning in the Fourteenth Century, Part I—First Half of the Fourteenth Century; Part II—Second Half of the Fourteenth Century.* Baltimore, MD: Published for the Carnegie Institution of Washington by Williams & Wilkins Company, 1947.

B-243. Sarton, George. *The Life of Science: Essays in the History of Civilization.* New York: Henry Schuman, 1948.

B-244. Singer, Charles. *A Short History of Science to the Nineteenth Century.* Oxford, London, and New York: Clarendon Press, 1943.

B-245. Teresi, Dick. *Lost Discoveries: The Ancient Roots of Modern Science—From the Babylonians to the Maya.* New York and London: Simon & Schuster, 2002.

B-246. Turner, Howard R. *Science in Medieval Islam: An Illustrated Introduction.* Austin, TX: University of Texas Press, 1995.

(B) Islam–West Linkages

B-247. Abu-Lughod, Janet L. *Before European Hegemony: The World System A.D. 1250–1350.* New York and Oxford: Oxford University Press, 1989.

B-248. Adas, Michael, ed. *Islamic and European Expansion: The Forging of a Global Order.* Philadelphia, PA: Temple University Press, 1993.

B-249. Agius, Dionisius and Richard Hitchcock, eds. *The Arab Influence in Medieval Europe: Folia Scholastica Mediterranea.* Reading, UK: Ithaca Press, 1994.

B-250. Ahmad, Ziauddin. *Influence of Islam on World Civilization.* Delhi, India: Adam Publishers and Distributors, 1996.

B-251. Allison, Robert J. *The Crescent Obscured: The United States and the Muslim World, 1776–1815.* New York: Oxford University Press, 1995.

B-252. Amin, Samir. *Eurocentrism* (translated from French by Russell Moore). New York: Monthly Review Press, 1989.

B-253. Arnold, Sir Thomas and Alfred Guillaume, eds. *The Legacy of Islam.* Oxford: Clarendon Press, 1931.

B-254. Ascher, Abraham, Tibor Halasi-Kun, and Bela K. Kiraly, eds. *The Mutual Effects of the Islamic and Judeo-Christian Worlds: The East European Pattern*. Brooklyn, NY: Brooklyn College Press, 1979.

B-255. Asin-Palacios, Miguel. *Islam and the Divine Comedy* (translated and abridged from Spanish by Harold Sunderland). London: John Murray, 1926.

B-256. Bammate, Haidar. *Muslim Contribution to Civilization*. Takoma Park, MD: Crescent Publications, 1962.

B-257. Beckingham, C.F. *Between Islam and Christendom: Travellers, Facts and Legends in the Middle Ages and the Renaissance*. London: Variorum Reprints, 1983.

B-258. Blanks, David, ed. *Images of the Other: Europe and the Muslim World Before 1700*. Cairo Papers in Social Sciences, Volume 19, Monograph 2, Summer 1996. Cairo, Egypt: University of Cairo Press, 1997.

B-259. Bosworth, C. Edmund, ed. *A Century of British Orientalists 1902–2001*. Published for The British Academy. Oxford: Oxford University Press, 2001.

B-260. Bulliet, Richard W. *The Case for Islamo–Christian Civilization*. New York: Columbia University Press, 2004.

B-261. Burke, James. *Connections*. Toronto, Boston, and London: Little, Brown and Company, 1978.

B-262. Burke, James. *The Day the Universe Changed*. Toronto, Boston, and London: Little, Brown and Company, 1985.

B-263. Burnett, Charles. *The Introduction of Arabic Learning into England: The Panizzi Lectures 1996*. London: The British Library, 1997.

B-264. Campbell, Donald. *Arabian Medicine and Its Influence on the Middle Ages,* Volumes I and II. London: Kegan Paul, Trench, Trubner and Company, 1926.

B-265. Cardini, Franco. *Europe and Islam* (translated from Italian by Caroline Beamish). Oxford: Blackwell Publishers, 2001.

B-266. Chew, Samuel C. *The Crescent and the Rose: Islam and England during the Renaissance*. New York: Octagon Books, Inc., 1965; original 1937.

B-267. Cobb, Stanwood. *Islamic Contributions to Civilization*. Washington, DC: Avalon Press, 1963.

B-268. Colish, Marcia L. *Medieval Foundations of the Western Intellectual Tradition, 400–1400*. New Haven, CT: Yale University Press, 1997.

B-269. Daniel, Norman. *The Arabs and Medieval Europe*. London: Longman Group Ltd., 1975.

B-270. Daniel, Norman. *Islam and the West: The Making of an Image*. Boston: Oneworld Press, 1960; reprint 2000.

B-271. Daniel, Norman. *Islam, Europe and Empire*. Edinburgh: Edinburgh University Press, 1966.

B-272. Djait, Hichem. *Europe and Islam* (translated from French by Peter Heinegg). Berkeley, CA: University of California Press, 1985.

B-273. Durant, Will. *The Story of Civilization: The Age of Faith—A History of Medieval Civilization, Christian, Islamic, and Judaic, from Constantine to Dante, AD325–1300*. Volume 4. New York: Simon & Schuster, 1950.

B-274. Faris, Nabih Amin, ed. *The Arab Heritage*. New York: Russell and Russell, Inc., 1963; original 1944.

B-275. Farrukh, Omar A. *The Arab Genius in Science and Philosophy* (translated from Arabic by John B. Hardie). Washington, DC: American Council of Learned Societies, 1954.

B-276. Ferber, Stanley, ed. and comp. *Islam and the Medieval West*. Binghamton, NY: State University of New York Press, 1975.

B-277. Frassetto, Michael and David R. Blanks, eds. *Western Views of Islam in the Medieval and Early Modern Europe: Perception of Other*. New York: St. Martin's Press, 1999.

B-278. Gutas, Dimitri. *Greek Thought, Arabic Culture: The Graeco–Arabic Translation Movement in Baghdad and Early Abbasid Society (2nd–4th / 8th–10th Centuries)*. London and New York: Routledge, 1998.

B-279. Gwatkin, H.M. and J.P. Whitney, eds. *The Rise of the Saracens and the Foundation of the Western Empire*. Cambridge: Cambridge University Press, 1967; original 1913.

B-280. Hamilton, Alastair. *Europe and the Arab World: Five Centuries of Books by European Scholars and Travellers from the Libraries of the Arcadian Group*. Oxford: Oxford University Press, 1994.

B-281. Hammond, Reverend Robert. *The Philosophy of Alfarabi and Its Influence on Medieval Thought*. New York: The Hobson Book Press, 1947.

B-282. Hayes, John R., ed. *The Genius of Arab Civilization: Source of Renaissance*. Cambridge, MA: The MIT Press, second edition, 1983.

B-283. Hentsch, Thierry. *Imagining the Middle East* (translated from French by Fred A. Reed). Montreal and Cheektowaga, NY: Black Rose Books Ltd., 1992.

B-284. Hodges, Richard and David Whitehouse. *Mohammed, Charlemagne and The Origins of Europe: Archeology and the Pirenne Thesis*. London: Gerald Duckworth and Company, 1983.

B-285. Hodgson, Marshall G.S. *The Venture of Islam: Conscience and History in a World Civilization–Volume One: The Classical Age of Islam; Volume Two: The Expansion of Islam in the Middle Periods; Volume Three: The Gunpowder Empires and Modern Times*. Chicago and London: University of Chicago Press, 1974; original 1961.

B-286. Hourani, Albert. *Europe and the Middle East*. Berkeley and Los Angeles: University of California Press, 1980.

B-287. Hourani, Albert. *Islam in European Thought*. Cambridge and New York: Cambridge University Press, 1991.

B-288. Hoyt, Edwin P. *Arab Science: Discoveries and Contributions*. Nashville, TN, and New York: Thomas Nelson Inc., Publishers, 1975.

B-289. Hussain, Iqbal S. *Islam and Western Civilization: Creating a World of Excellence*. Lahore, Pakistan: Humanity International, 1997.

B-290. Ito, Shuntaro. *The Twelfth-Century Renaissance: Arabic Influences on the West* (original in Japanese language only). Iwanami Seminar Books, No. 42. Tokyo, Japan: Iwanami Shoten Publishers, 1993.

B-291. Khan, M. Abdur Rahman. *Muslim Contribution to Science and Culture*. Lahore, Pakistan: Sh. Muhammad Ashraf Publishers, 1973; original 1946.

B-292. Landau, Rom. *Arab Contribution to Civilization*. San Francisco: The American Academy of Asian Studies, 1958.

B-293. Landau, Rom. *The Arab Heritage of Western Civilization*. New York: Arab Information Center, 1962 and 1972.

B-294. Lane, Rose Wilder. *The Discovery of Freedom: Man's Struggle Against Authority*. New York: John Day Company, 1943; third edition 1993.

B-295. Lewis, Archibald R., ed. *The Islamic World and the West, A.D. 622–1492*. New York: John Wiley and Sons, Inc., 1970.

B-296. Matar, Nabil. *Islam in Britain, 1558–1685.* Cambridge: Cambridge University Press, 1998.

B-297. Matar, Nabil. *Turks, Moors and Englishmen in the Age of Discovery.* New York: Columbia University Press, 1999.

B-298. Matar, Nabil, ed. and trans. *In the Lands of the Christians: Arabic Travel Writing in the Seventeenth Century.* New York and London: Routledge, 2003.

B-299. Menocal, Maria Rosa. *The Arabic Role in Medieval Literary History: A Forgotten Heritage.* Philadelphia, PA: University of Pennsylvania Press, 1987.

B-300. Metlitzki, Dorothee. *The Matter of Araby in Medieval England.* New Haven, CT, and London: Yale University Press, 1977.

B-301. Myers, Eugene A. *Arabic Thought and the Western World in the Golden Age of Islam.* New York: Frederick Ungar Publishing Company, 1964.

B-302. Naskosteen, Mehdi. *History of Islamic Origins of Western Education.* Boulder, CO: University of Colorado Press, 1964.

B-303. Pirenne, Henri. *Mohammed and Charlemagne.* New York: Barnes & Noble, first published, 1939.

B-304. Ragep, F. Jamil and Sally P. Ragep, with Steven Livesey, ed. *Tradition, Transmission, Transformation: Proceedings of Two Conferences on Pre-Modern Science Held at the University of Oklahoma.* Leiden, New York, and Cologne: E.J. Brill, 1996.

B-305. Reeves, Minou. *Muhammad in Europe: A Thousand Years of Western Myth-Making.* New York: New York University Press, 2000.

B-306. Rodinson, Maxime. *Europe and the Mystique of Islam* (translated from French by Roger Veinus). Seattle, WA: University of Washington Press, Seattle, 1987.

B-307. Russell, G.A., ed. *The "Arabick" Interest of the Natural Philosophers in Seventeenth-Century England.* Leiden, Netherlands: E.J. Brill, 1994.

B-308. Said, Edward. *Orientalism.* New York: Vintage Books Edition, Random House, 1979.

B-309. Sardar, Ziauddin, ed. *The Revenge of Athena: Science, Exploitation and the Third World.* New York and London: Mansell Publishing Ltd., 1988.

B-310. Sarton, George. *The Incubation of Western Culture in the Middle East.* George C. Keiser Foundation Lecture, Library of Congress. Washington, DC: U.S. Government Printing Office, 1951.

B-311. Schacht, Joseph, ed. (assisted by C.E. Bosworth). *The Legacy of Islam,* second edition. Oxford: Clarendon Press, 1974.

B-312. Semaan, Khalil I., ed. *Islam and the Medieval West: Aspects of Intercultural Relations.* Albany, NY: State University of New York Press, 1980.

B-313. Sha'ban, Fuad. *Islam and Arabs in Early American Thought: The Roots of Orientalism in America.* Durham, NC: Published in Association with Duke University Islamic and Arabian Development Studies, The Acorn Press, 1991.

B-314. Sinor, Denis, ed. *Orientalism and History,* second edition. Bloomington, IN, and London: Indiana University Press, 1970.

B-315. Southern, Richard W. *Western Views of Islam in the Middle Ages.* Cambridge, MA: Harvard University Press, 1962.

B-316. Tolan, John V. *Saracens: Islam in the Medieval European Imagination.* New York: Columbia University Press, 2002.

B-317. Toomer, G.J. *Eastern Wisedome and Learning: The Study of Arabic in Seventeenth-Century England.* Oxford: Clarendon Press, 1996.

B-318. Turner, Bryan S. *Weber and Islam*. London and Boston: Routledge and Kegan Paul, 1978; original 1973.

B-319. Watt, W. Montgomery. *The Influence of Islam on Medieval Europe*. Edinburgh: Edinburgh University Press, 1972.

B-320. Watt, W. Montgomery. *Muslim–Christian Encounters: Perceptions and Misperceptions*. London: Routledge, 1991.

(C) General

(i) Spain/Al-Andalus

B-321. Altamira, Rafael. *A History of Spanish Civilization* (translated from Spanish by P. Volkov). London: Constable and Company, 1930.

B-322. Atkinson, William C. *A History of Spain and Portugal*. Baltimore, MD: Penguin Books, Inc., 1960; reprinted 1961 and 1965.

B-323. Brann, Ross, ed. *Languages of Power in Islamic Spain*. Bethesda, MD: CXDL Press, 1997.

B-324. Burckhardt, Titus. *Moorish Culture in Spain* (translated by Alisa Jaffa). New York: McGraw-Hill Book Company, 1975.

B-325. Burns, Robert Ignatius, S.J. *Medieval Colonialism: Postcrusade Exploitation of Islamic Valencia*. Princeton, NJ: Princeton University Press, 1975.

B-326. Calvert, Albert F. and Walter M. Gallichan. *Cordova: A City of the Moors*. London and New York: John Lane Company, 1907.

B-327. Chejne, Anwar. *Islam and the West: The Moriscos—A Cultural and Social History*. Albany, NY: State University of New York Press, 1983.

B-328. Chejne, Anwar G. *Muslim Spain: Its History and Culture*. Minneapolis, MN: The University of Minnesota Press, 1974.

B-329. Chiat, Marilyn J. and Kathryn L. Reyerson, eds. *The Medieval Mediterranean: Cross Cultural Studies*. St. Cloud, MN: North Star Press of St. Cloud, Inc., 1988.

B-330. Collins, Roger. *Early Medieval Spain: Unity in Diversity, 400–1000*. London: Macmillan Press, 1983.

B-331. Constable, Olivia Remie. *Trade and Traders in Muslim Spain: The Commercial Realignment of the Iberian Peninsula, 900–1500*. Cambridge and New York: Cambridge University Press, 1994.

B-332. Constable, Olivia Remie, ed. *Medieval Iberia: Readings from Christian, Muslim, and Jewish Sources*. Philadelphia, PA: University of Pennsylvania Press, 1997.

B-333. Crow, John A. *Spain: The Root and the Flower: An Interpretation of Spain and the Spanish People*. Berkeley, CA: University of California Press, 1985.

B-334. Dozy, Reinhart. *Spanish Islam: A History of the Moslems in Spain* (translated from German, with a biographical introduction and additional notes, by Francis Griffin Stokes). London: Chatto & Windus, 1913.

B-335. Echevarria, Ana. *The Fortress of Faith: The Attitude towards Muslims in Fifteenth Century Spain*. Leiden, Netherlands: E.J. Brill, 1999.

B-336. Fierro, Maribel and Julio Samso, eds. *The Formation of al-Andalus, Part II (Language, Religion, Culture and the Sciences)*. Brookfield, VT: Ashgate Publishing Company, 1998.

B-337. Fletcher, Richard. *Moorish Spain*. Berkeley, CA: University of California Press, 1993.

B-338. Glick, Thomas F. *Islamic and Christian Spain in the Early Middle Ages*. Princeton, NJ: Princeton University Press, 1979.

B-339. Harvey, L.P. *Islamic Spain, 1250–1500*. Chicago: University of Chicago Press, 1990.

B-340. Hess, Andrew C. *The Forgotten Frontier: A History of the Sixteenth-Century Ibero-African Frontier*. Chicago and London: University of Chicago Press, 1978.

B-341. Hintzen-Bohlen, Brigitte. *Andalusia: Art and Architecture*. Cologne, Germany: Konemann Verlagsgesellschaft, 2000.

B-342. Hole, Edwyn. *Andalus: Spain under the Muslims*. London: Robert Hale Ltd., 1958.

B-343. Hook, David and Barry Taylor, eds. *Cultures in Contact in Medieval Spain: Historical and Literary Essays Presented to L.P. Harvey*. Exeter, UK: King's College London Medieval Studies; Short-Run Press, 1999.

B-344. Imamuddin, S.M. *Some Aspects of the Socio-Economic and Cultural History of Muslim Spain, 711–1492*. Leiden, Netherlands: E.J. Brill, 1965.

B-345. Irving, Thomas B. *Falcon of Spain: A Study of Eighth-Century Spain*. Lahore, Pakistan: Sh. Muhammad Ashraf Publishers, 1991.

B-346. Jayyusi, Salma Khadra, ed. *The Legacy of Muslim Spain* (two volumes). Leiden, Netherlands, New York, and Cologne: E.J. Brill, 1994.

B-347. Jones, Catherine E. *Islamic Spain and Our Heritage: Al-Andalus, 711–1492 A.D.* Austin, TX: Middle East Outreach Council, University of Texas, 1996, second edition 1997.

B-348. Kamen, Henry. *The Spanish Inquisition*. London: Weidenfeld and Nicolson, 1965.

B-349. Kennedy, Hugh N. *Muslim Spain and Portugal: A Political History of al-Andalus*. London: Addison Wesley Longman Ltd., 1996.

B-350. Lane-Poole, Stanley. *The Story of the Moors in Spain* (introduction by John G. Jackson). Baltimore, MD: Black Classic Press, 1990; original 1886.

B-351. Lea, Henry Charles. *The Moriscos of Spain: Their Conversion and Expulsion*. New York: Haskel House Publishers Ltd. (Publishers of Scarce Scholarly Books), 1968; original 1901.

B-352. Lopez-Baralt, Luce. *Islam in Spanish Literature: From the Middle Ages to the Present* (translated from Spanish by Andrew Hurley). Leiden, Netherlands: E.J. Brill, 1992.

B-353. Lowney, Chris. *A Vanished World: Medieval Spain's Golden Age of Enlightenment*. New York: Free Press, 2005.

B-354. Mann, Vivian B., Thomas F. Glick, and Jerrilynn D. Dodds, eds. *Convivencia: Jews, Muslims, and Christians in Medieval Spain*. New York: George Braziller, Inc., in association with The Jewish Museum, 1992.

B-355. Marin, Manuela, ed. *The Formation of al-Andalus, Part I (History and Society)*. Brookfield, VT: Ashgate Publishing Company, 1998.

B-356. McCabe, Joseph. *The Splendour of Moorish Spain*. London: Watts and Company, 1935.

B-357. Menocal, Maria Rosa. *The Ornament of the World: How Muslims, Jews, and Christians Created a Culture of Tolerance in Medieval Spain*. Boston, New York, and London: Little, Brown and Company, 2002.

B-358. Menocal, Maria Rosa and Raymond P. Scheindlin, and Michael Sells, eds. *The Literature of Al-Andalus*. Cambridge: Cambridge University Press, 2000.

B-359. Meyerson, Mark D. *The Muslims of Valencia in the Age of Fernando and Isabel: Between Co-Existence and Crusade*. Berkeley and Los Angeles: University of California Press, 1991.

B-360. Meyerson, Mark D. and Edward D. English, eds. *Christians, Muslims, and Jews in Medieval and Early Modern Spain: Interaction and Cultural Change*. Notre Dame, IN: University of Notre Dame Press, 1999.

B-361. Monroe, James T. *Islam and the Arabs in Spanish Scholarship (Sixteenth Century to the Present)*. Leiden, Netherlands: E.J. Brill, 1970.

B-362. O'Callaghan, Joseph F. *A History of Medieval Spain*. Ithaca, NY, and London: Cornell University Press, 1975.

B-363. Pick, Lucy K. *Conflict and Coexistence: Archbishop Rodrigo and the Muslims and Jews of Medieval Spain*. Ann Arbor, MI: University of Michigan Press, 2004.

B-364. Read, Jan. *The Moors in Spain and Portugal*. London: Faber & Faber, London, 1974.

B-365. Samso, Julio. *Islamic Astronomy and Medieval Spain*. Brookfield, VT: Ashgate Publishing Company, 1994.

B-366. Scott, S.P. *History of the Moorish Empire in Europe*, volume one. Philadelphia, PA, and London: J.B. Lippincott Company, 1904.

B-367. Scott, S.P. *History of the Moorish Empire in Europe*, volume two. Philadelphia, PA, and London: J.B. Lippincott Company, 1904.

B-368. Scott, S.P. *History of the Moorish Empire in Europe*, volume three. Philadelphia, PA, and London: J.B. Lippincott Company, 1904.

B-369. Sertima, Ivan Van, ed. *Golden Age of the Moor*. New Brunswick, NJ, and London: Transactions Publishers, 1993.

B-370. Sordo, Enrique. *Moorish Spain: Cordoba, Seville, Granada*. New York: Crown Publishers, 1963.

B-371. Watt, W. Montgomery. *A History of Islamic Spain*. Edinburgh: Edinburgh University Press, 1965.

B-372. Wright, Thomas E. *Into the Moorish World*. London: Robert Hale, 1972.

(ii) The Crusades

B-373. Atiya, Aziz S. *Crusade, Commerce, and Culture*. Bloomington, IN: Indiana University Press, 1962.

B-374. Atiya, Aziz S. *The Crusade in the Later Middle Ages*, second edition. New York: Kraus Reprint Company, 1970.

B-375. Burns, Robert Ignatius, S.J. *Islam under the Crusaders: Colonial Survival in the Thirteenth Century Kingdom of Valencia*. Princeton, NJ: Princeton University Press, 1973.

B-376. Gabrieli, Francesco, ed. *Arab Historians of the Crusades: Selected and Translated from the Arabic Sources* (translated from Italian by E.J. Costello). Berkeley and Los Angeles: University of California Press, 1969.

B-377. Goss, Vladimir P. and Christine V. Bornstein, eds. *The Meeting of Two Worlds:*

Cultural Exchange between East and West during the Period of the Crusades. Kalamazoo, MI: Medieval Institute Publications, Western Michigan University, 1986.

B-378. Hillenbrand, Carole. *The Crusades: Islamic Perspectives.* Chicago and London: Fitzroy Dearborn Publishers, 1999.

B-379. Jones, Terry and Alan Ereira. *Crusades.* New York: Facts On File, published by arrangement with BBC Books, 1995.

B-380. Kedar, Benjamin Z. *Crusade and Mission: European Approaches toward Muslims.* Princeton, NJ: Princeton University Press, 1984.

B-381. Lewis, Archibald R. *Nomads and Crusaders, A.D. 1000–1368.* Bloomington and Indianapolis: Indiana University Press, 1988.

B-382. Maalouf, Amin. *The Crusades through Arab Eyes* (translated from French by Jon Rothschild). New York: Schocken Books, 1985.

B-383. Zacour, Norman P. and Harry W. Hazard. *A History of the Crusades: The Impact of the Crusades on the Near East.* Madison, WI: University of Wisconsin Press, 1985.

(iii) Miscellaneous

B-384. Armstrong, Guyda and Ian N. Wood, eds. *Christianizing Peoples and Converting Individuals.* Turnhout, Belgium: Brepols Publishers, 2000.

B-385. Bloom, Jonathan M., ed. *Early Islamic Art and Architecture.* Burlington, VT, and Hampshire, UK: Ashgate Publishing Ltd., 2002.

B-386. Hattstein, Markus and Peter Delius, eds. *Islam: Art and Architecture* (translated from German). Cologne: Konemann Verlagsgesellschaft mbH, 2000.

B-387. Lowick, Nicholas (edited by Joe Cribb). *Coinage and History of the Islamic World.* Aldershot, UK: Variorum-Grower Publishing Group, 1990.

B-388. Lowick, Nicholas M. (edited by Joe Cribb). *Islamic Coins and Trade in the Medieval World.* Aldershot, UK: Variorum-Grower Publishing Group, 1990.

B-389. Pereira, Jose. *The Sacred Architecture of Islam.* New Delhi, India: Aryan Books International, 2004.

B-390. Sahai, Surendra. *Indian Architecture: Islamic Period, 1192–1857.* New Delhi, India: Prakash Books (India) Ltd., 2004.

B-391. Seherr-Thoss, Sonia P. and Hans C. Seherr-Thoss, eds. *Design and Color in Islamic Architecture: Afghanistan, Iran, Turkey.* Washington, DC: Smithsonian Institution Press, 1968.

B-392. Sweetman, John. *The Oriental Obsession: Islamic Inspiration in British and American Architecture, 1500–1920.* Cambridge and New York: Cambridge University Press, 1988.

ARTICLES

(A) Sciences/Humanities

(i) Social Sciences/Humanities

a. History

A-1. Gomez, Michael A. "Muslims in Early America." *Journal of Southern History* 60, no.4 (November 1994): 671–710.

A-2. Gran, Peter. "Political Economy as a Paradigm for the Study of Islamic History." *International Journal of Middle East Studies* 11, no.4 (1980): 511–526.

A-3. Granara, William. "*Jihad* and Cross-Cultural Encounter in Muslim Sicily." *Harvard Middle Eastern and Islamic Review* 3, no.2 (1996): 42–61.

A-4. Haskins, Charles H. "The Spread of Ideas in the Middle Ages." *Speculum: A Journal of Medieval Studies* 1 (1926): 19–30.

A-5. Hodgson, Marshall G.S. "Modernity and the Islamic Heritage." *Islamic Studies* 1, no.2 (June 1962): 89–129.

A-6. Kagaya, Kan. "Changing Muslim Views of Islamic History and Modernization: An Interpretation of Religion and Politics in Pakistan." *The Developing Economies* 4 (June 1968): 193–202.

A-7. Lapidus, Ira M. "The Separation of State and Religion in the Development of Early Islamic Society." *International Journal of Middle East Studies* 6, no.4 (October 1975): 363–385.

A-8. Mottahedeh, Roy. "Some Islamic Views of the Pre-Islamic Past." *Harvard Middle Eastern and Islamic Review* 1 (1994): 17–26.

A-9. Munro, Dana Carleton. "The Renaissance of the Twelfth Century." *Annual Report of the American Historical Association* (1906): 43–50.

A-10. Rahman, Fazlur. "The Religious Situation of Mecca from the Eve of Islam up to the Hijra." *Islamic Studies* 16, no.4 (Winter 1977): 289–301.

A-11. Rosenthal, Erwin J. "Some Reflections on the Separation of Religion and Politics in Modern Islam." *Islamic Studies* 3, no.3 (September 1964): 249–284.

A-12. Shah, Tahir. "The Islamic Legacy of Timbuktu." *Saudi Aramco World* 46, no.6 (November–December 1995): 1–5.

A-13. Watt, W. Montgomery. "Pre-Islamic Arabian Religion in the Qur'an." *Islamic Studies* 15, no.2 (Summer 1976): 73–79.

b. Economics/Commerce

A-14. Ahmad, Imad-ad-Dean. "Economy, Technology, and the Environment: The Islamic Middle Way." *Journal of Faith and Science Exchange* 3 (1999): 55–61.

A-15. Ahmad, Imad-ad-Dean. "Islam and Markets." *Religion and Liberty* 6, no.3 (May–June 1996): 1–3.

A-16. Ahmad, Imad-ad-Dean. "Islam and the Progenitors of Austrian Economics." Pages 77–82 in *The Contributions of Murray Rothbard to Monetary Economics*, edited by C. Thies. Winchester, VA: Durrell Institute, Shenandoah University, 1996.

A-17. Ahmad, Imad-ad-Dean. "An Islamic Perspective on the Wealth of Nations." Pages 55–67 in *The Economics of Property Rights: Cultural, Historical, Legal, and Philosophical Issues*, edited by S. Pejovich. Cheltenham, UK: Edward Elgar Publishers, 2001.

A-18. Ahmad, Rafiq. "Ibn Khaldun: A Great Pioneer Economist." *University Economist: Journal of the Punjab University* 2, no.1 (March 1953): 52–61.

A-19. Ahmad, Rafiq. "The Origin of Economics and the Muslims: A Preliminary Survey." *Punjab University Economics* 7, no.1 (June 1969): 17–49.

A-20. Ali, Syed Ahmad. "Economics of Ibn Khaldun: A Selection." *Africa Quarterly* 10, no.3 (October–December 1970): 251–259.

A-21. Alrefai, Ahmed and Michael Brun. "Ibn Khaldun: Dynastic Change and Its Economic Consequences." *Arab Studies Quarterly* 16, no.2 (Spring 1994): 73–86.

A-22. Andic, Suphan. "A Fourteenth Century Sociology of Public Finance." *Public Finance/Finances Publiques* 20, nos.1–2 (1965): 22–44.

A-23. Baeck, Louis. "Ibn Khaldun's Political and Economic Realism." Pages 83–99 in *Joseph A. Schumpeter, Historian of Economics: Perspectives on the History of Economic Thought, Selected Papers from the History of Economics Society Conference 1994*, edited by Laurence S. Moss. London: Routledge, 1996.

A-24. Bass, George F. "A Medieval Islamic Merchant Venture." *Archeological News* 7, nos.2–3 (Fall 1979): 85–94.

A-25. Boulakia, Jean David C. "Ibn Khaldun: A Fourteenth-Century Economist." *Journal of Political Economy* 79, no.5 (September–October 1971): 1105–1118.

A-26. Chapra, M. Umar. "Socioeconomic and Political Dynamics of Ibn Khaldun's Thought." *American Journal of Islamic Social Sciences* 16, no.4 (Winter 1999): 17–38.

A-27. Desomogyi, Joseph. "Economic Theory in Classical Arabic Literature." Pages 1–10 in *Studies in Islamic Economics, Series 8, Encyclopedic Survey of Islamic Culture*, edited by Mohamed Taher. New Delhi, India: Anmol Publications (Private) Ltd., 1997.

A-28. Essid, M. Yassine. "Islamic Economic Thought." Pages 77–102 in *Pre-Classical Economic Thought*, edited by S. Todd Lowry. Boston: Kluwer Academic Publishers, 1986.

A-29. Ghazanfar, S.M. "The Economic Thought of Abu Hamid Al-Ghazali and St. Thomas Aquinas: Some Comparative Parallels and Links." *History of Political Economy* 32, no.4 (2000): 858–888.

A-30. Ghazanfar, S.M. "Post-Greek/Pre-Renaissance Economic Thought: Contributions of Arab-Islamic Scholastics during the 'Great Gap' Centuries." *Research in the History of Economic Thought and Methodology* 16 (1998): 65–89.

A-31. Ghazanfar, S.M. "Public Sector Economics in Medieval Economic Thought: Contributions of Selected Arab-Islamic Scholars." *Public Finance/Finances Publiques* 53, no.1 (1998): 19–36.

A-32. Ghazanfar, S.M. "Scholastic Economics and Arab Scholars: The 'Great Gap' Thesis Reconsidered." *Diogenes: International Review of Humane Sciences* (Paris) no.154 (April–June 1991): 117–139.

A-33. Ghazanfar, S.M. and A. Azim Islahi. "Economic Thought of an Arab Scholastic: Abu Hamid Al-Ghazali (AH450–505 / AD1058–1111)." *History of Political Economy* 22, no.2 (1990): 381–403.

A-34. Ghazanfar, S.M. and A. Azim Islahi. "Explorations in Medieval Arab-Islamic Economic Thought: Some Aspects of Ibn Qayyim's Economics (691–751 AH / 1292–1350 AD)." *History of Economic Ideas* (Italy) 5, no.1 (1997): 7–25.

A-35. Ghazanfar, S.M. and A. Azim Islahi. "Explorations in Medieval Arab-Islamic Economic Thought: Some Aspects of Ibn Taimiyah's Economics." Pages 45–63 in *Perspectives on the History of Economic Thought: Selected Papers from the History of Economics Conference 1990*, edited by S. Todd Lowry. Brookfield, VT: Edward Elgar Publishing Company, 1992.

A-36. Goitein, S.D. "The Rise of the Near-Eastern Bourgeoisie in Early Islamic Times." *Journal of World History* 3 (1957): 583–604.

A-37. Gusau, Sule Ahmed. "Economic Views of Ibn Khaldun." *Journal of Objective Studies* (Aligarh, India) 3 (1990): 48–60.

A-38. Hosseini, Hamid. "Contributions of Medieval Muslim Scholars to the History of Economics and Their Impact: A Refutation of the Schumpeterian Great Gap." Pages 28–45 in *A Companion to the History of Economic Thought*, edited by Warren J. Samuels, Jeff E. Biddle, and John B. Davis. New York: Blackwell Publishing Company, 2003.

A-39. Hosseini, Hamid. "The Inaccuracy of the Schumpeterian Great Gap Thesis: Economic Thought in Medieval Iran (Persia)." Pages 63–82 in *Joseph M. Schumpeter, Historian of Economics: Perspectives on the History of Economic Thought—Selected Papers from the History of Economics Society Conference 1994*, edited by Laurence S. Moss. London and New York: Routledge Publishers, 1996.

A-40. Hosseini, Hamid. "Medieval Islamic (Persian) Mirrors for Princes Literature and the History of Economics." *Journal of South Asian and Middle Eastern Studies* 24, no.4 (2001): 13–36.

A-41. Hosseini, Hamid. "Seeking the Roots of Adam Smith's Division of Labor in Medieval Persia (Iran)." *History of Political Economy* 30, no.3 (Winter 1998): 653–681.

A-42. Hosseini, Hamid. "Understanding the Market Mechanism before Adam Smith: Economic Thought in Medieval Islam." *History of Political Economy* 27, no.3 (1995): 539–561.

A-43. Labib, Subhi Y. "Capitalism in Medieval Islam." *Journal of Economic History* 29 (1969): 79–96.

A-44. Mirakhor, Abbas. "The Muslim Scholars and the History of Economics: A Need for Consideration." *The American Journal of Islamic Social Sciences* 4, no.2 (1987): 245–275.

A-45. Newby, Gordon D. "Trade in the Levant and the East Mediterranean in the Early Islamic Period: A Search for the Early Muslim Merchant." *Archeological News* 7, nos.2–3 (Fall 1979): 78–83.

A-46. Oran, Ahmad and Salim Rashid. "Fiscal Policy in Early Islam." *Public Finance/ Finances Publiques* 44, no.1 (1989): 75–101.

A-47. Oweiss, Ibrahim M. "Ibn Khaldun, the Father of Economics." Pages 112–127 in *Arab Civilization: Challenges and Responses—Studies in Honor of Constantine K. Zurayk*, edited by George N. Atiyeh and Ibrahim M. Oweiss. Albany, NY: State University of New York Press, 1988.

A-48. Oweiss, Ibrahim M. "A View on Islamic Economic Thought." *Occasional Paper Series*, Center for Contemporary Arab Studies. Washington, DC: Georgetown University, 2000.

A-49. Rozina, Parveen. "Ibn Khaldun as an Economist: A Comparative Study with Modern Economists." *Pakistan Journal of History and Culture* 15, no.1 (1994): 111–130.

A-50. Samarrai, Alauddin. "Medieval Commerce and Diplomacy: Islam and Europe, A.D. 850–1300." *Canadian Journal of History* 15, no.1 (April 1980): 1–21.

A-51. Sattar, M. Abdus. "Ibn Khaldun's Contribution to Economic Thought." Pages 121–129 in *Contemporary Aspects of Economic Thinking in Islam*, Proceedings of the Third East Coast Regional Conference of the Muslim Students Association of the USA and Canada, 1968. Baltimore, MD: American Trust Publications, 1976.

A-52. Sharif, M. Raihan. "Ibn-i-Khaldun, the Pioneer Economist." *Islamic Literature* (Lahore, Pakistan) 6, no.5 (May 1955): 33–40.

A-53. Sherwani, H. "Ibn-i-Taimiyah's Economic Thought." *Islamic Quarterly* (Lahore, Pakistan) 8 (1956): 9–21.

A-54. Siddiqi, M. Nejatullah and S.M. Ghazanfar. "Early Medieval Islamic Economic Thought: Abu Yusuf's (731–798 AD) Economics of Public Finance." *History of Economic Ideas* (Italy) 9, no.1 (2001): 13–38.

A-55. Soofi, Abdol. "Economics of Ibn Khaldun Revisited." *History of Political Economy* 27, no.2 (1995): 387–404.

A-56. Spengler, Joseph J. "Alberuni: Eleventh Century Iranian Malthusian?" *History of Political Economy* 3, no.1 (Spring 1971): 93–104.

A-57. Spengler, Joseph J. "Economic Thought of Islam: Ibn Khaldun." *Comparative Studies in Society and History* 6, no.3 (April 1964): 268–306.

A-58. Udovitch, Abraham L. "Bankers without Banks: Commerce, Banking, and Society in the Islamic World of the Middle Ages." Pages 255–273 in *The Dawn of Modern Banking*, Center for Medieval and Renaissance Studies, University of California, Los Angeles. New Haven, CT: Yale University Press, 1979.

A-59. Udovitch, Abraham L. "Labor Partnership in Early Islam." *Journal of Economic and Social History of the Orient* 10 (1967): 64–80.

A-60. Udovitch, Abraham L. "Reflections on the Institutions of Credit and Banking in the Medieval Islamic Near East." *Studia Islamica* 41 (1975): 5–21.

A-61. Weiss, Dieter. "Ibn Khaldun on Economic Transformation." *International Journal of Middle East Studies* 27 (1995): 29–37.

A-62. Zaid, Omar Abdullah. "Were Islamic Records Precursors to Accounting Books Based on the Italian Method?" *Accounting Historians Journal* 27, no.1 (June 2000): 73–90.

c. Philosophy

A-63. Fakhry, Majid. "Philosophy and Scripture in the Theology of Averroes." *Medieval Studies* 30 (1968): 78–87.

A-64. Schleifer, Aliah. "Ibn Khaldun's Theories of Perception, Logic, and Knowledge: An Islamic Phenomenology." *American Journal of Islamic Social Sciences* 2, no.2 (December 1985): 225–231.

A-65. Shah, Shafqat A. "Aristotle, Al-Farabi, Averroes, and Aquinas: Four Views on Philosophy and Religion." *Sind University Research Journal* (Hyderabad, Pakistan) 19 (1980): 1–20.

A-66. Sharif, M.M. "Muslim Philosophy and Western Thought." *Iqbal: A Journal of the Bazm-I-Iqbal* (Lahore, Pakistan) 8, no.1 (July 1959): 1–14.

A-67. Stone, Caroline. "Doctor, Philosopher, Renaissance Man." *Saudi Aramco World* 54, no.3 (May–June 2003): 8–15.

A-68. Tolan, John. "'Saracen Philosophers Secretly Deride Islam.'" *Medieval Encounters* 8, nos.2–3 (2003): 184–208.

A-69. Wippel, John F. "The Condemnations of 1270 and 1277 at Paris." *Journal of Medieval and Renaissance Studies* 7 (Spring 1977): 169–201.

d. Education/Learning

A-70. Government of Saudi Arabia. *"Islamic Science and Learning."* Washington, DC: High Commission for the Development of Arriyadh, Culture Center (July 1989): 2–20.

A-71. Makdisi, George. "Muslim Institutes of Learning in Eleventh-Century Baghdad." *Bulletin of the School of Oriental and African Studies* 24, no.1 (1961): 1–56.

A-72. Makdisi, George. "The Scholastic Method in Medieval Education: An Inquiry into Its Origins in Law and Theology." *Speculum: A Journal of Medieval Studies* 49 (1974): 640–661.

A-73. Newby, Gordon D. "The Foundation of the University of Naples: Typological Parallels with Arab Institutions of Higher Learning." *Medieval Encounters* 3, no.2 (1997): 173–184.

e. Geography

A-74. Bullis, Douglas. "The Longest Hajj: The Journeys of Ibn Battuta." *Saudi Aramco World* 51, no.4 (July–August 2000): 2–39.

A-75. Gabriel, Judith. "Among the Norse Tribes: The Remarkable Account of Ibn Fadlan." *Aramco World* 50, no.6 (November–December 1999): 36–42.

A-76. Lunde, Paul. "The Middle East and the Age of Discovery." *Aramco World* 43, no.3 (May–June 1992): 2–64.

A-77. Nadvi, S. Sulaiman. "Arab Navigation, Part I" (three-part essay). *Islamic Culture* (Hyderabad, India) 15 (October 1941): 435–448.

A-78. Nadvi, S. Sulaiman. "Arab Navigation, Part II." *Islamic Culture* (Hyderabad, India) 16 (April 1942): 181–198.

A-79. Nadvi, S. Sulaiman. "Arab Navigation, Part III." *Islamic Culture* (Hyderabad, India) 17 (January 1943): 72–86.

A-80. Tolmacheva, Marina. "Bertius and al-Idrisi: An Experiment in Orientalist Cartography." *Terrae Incognitae* 28 (1996): 36–45.

A-81. Tolmacheva, Marina. "Ibn Battuta on Women's Travel in the Dar al-Islam." Pages 119–140 in *Women and the Journey: The Female Travel Experience*, edited by Bonnie Frederick and Susan H. McLeod. Pullman, WA: Washington State University, 1993.

A-82. Tolmacheva, Marina. "The Medieval Arabic Geographers and the Beginning of Modern Orientalism." *International Journal of Middle East Studies* 27, no.2 (1995): 141–156.

A-83. Tolmacheva, Marina. "On the Arab System of Nautical Orientation." *Arabica* 27, no.2 (1980): 180–192.

A-84. Tolmacheva, Marina. "Ptolemaic Influence on Medieval Arab Geography: The Case Study of East Africa." Pages 125–141 in *Discovering New Worlds: Essays on Medieval Exploration and Imagination*, edited by Scott D. Westrem. New York and London: Garland Publishing, 1991.

f. Humanities

A-85. Dannenfeldt, K. "The Renaissance Humanists and the Knowledge of Arabic." *Studies in the Renaissance* 2 (1955): 96–117.

A-86. Kraemer, Joel L. "Humanism in the Renaissance of Islam: A Preliminary Study." *Journal of the American Oriental Society* 104, no.1 (January–March 1984): 135–164.

A-87. Smith, Wilfred Cantwell. "The True Meaning of Scripture: An Empirical Historian's Nonreductionist Interpretation of the Qur'an." *International Journal of Middle East Studies* 11 (1980): 487–505.

g. Social Sciences, General

A-88. Chejne, Anwar G. "Intellectual Revival in the Arab World: An Introduction." *Islamic Studies* 11, no.4 (December 1973): 410–437.

A-89. Coulson, Noel J. "The Concept of Progress and Islam Law." Pages 74–92 in *Religion and Progress in Modern Asia*, edited by Robert N. Bellah. New York: The Free Press, 1965.

A-90. Cox, Robert W. "Toward a Post-Hegemonic Conceptualization of World Order: Reflections on the Relevancy of Ibn Khaldun." Pages 144–173 in *Approaches to World Order*, edited by Robert W. Cox and Timothy J. Sinclair. Cambridge and New York: Cambridge University Press, 1996.

A-91. al-Hibri, Azzizah Y. "Islamic Constitutionalism and the Concept of Democracy." *Case Western Reserve Journal of International Law* 24, no.1 (Winter 1992): 1–27.

A-92. Rahman, Fazlur. "Islam: Legacy and Contemporary Challenge." *Islamic Studies* 19, no.4 (Winter 1980): 235–246.

A-93. Rahman, Fazlur. "The Status of the Individual in Islam." Pages 217–225 in *The Status of the Individual in East and West*, edited by Charles A. Moor (with assistance from Aldyth V. Morris). Honolulu, HI: University of Hawaii Press, 1968.

A-94. Samarrai, Alauddin. "The Idea of Fame in Medieval Arabic Literature and Its Renaissance Parallels." *Comparative Literature Studies* 16, no.4 (December 1979): 279–293.

(ii) Sciences

A-95. Aramco Services Company. "Science: The Islamic Legacy." *Aramco World Magazine* 33, no.3 (May–June 1982): 2–64.

A-96. Dawson, Christopher. "The Origins of the European Scientific Tradition: St. Thomas and Roger Bacon." *The Clergy Review* 2 (September 1930): 193–205.

A-97. Gross, Charles G. "Ibn al-Haytham on Eye and Brain, Vision and Perception." *Bulletin of Islamic Medicine* 1 (1981): 309–312.

A-98. Hill, Donald R. "Mechanical Engineering in the Medieval Near East." *Scientific American* 264, no.5 (May 1991): 100–105.

A-99. Lindberg, David C. "Medieval Science and Its Religious Context." *OSIRIS* 10 (1995): 61–79.

A-100. Meyerhof, Max. "The 'Book of Treasure,' an Early Arabic Treatise on Medicine." *ISIS: Journal of the History of Science in Society* 14, no.43 (May 1930): 55–76.

A-101. Moody, Ernest A. "Galileo and Avempace: The Dynamics of the Learning Tower Experiment." Part I, *Journal of the History of Ideas* 12, no.2 (April 1951): 163–193; Part II, *Journal of the History of Ideas* 12, no.3 (August 1951): 375–422.

A-102. Omar, Saleh. "Ibn Al-Haytham's Theory of Knowledge and Its Significance for Later Science." *Arab Studies Quarterly* 1, no.1 (1979): 67–82.

A-103. Rashed, Roshdi. "Science as a Western Phenomenon." *Fundamenta Scientiae* (Paris) 1 (1980): 7–21.

A-104. Rubenstein, Rheta and Randy Schwartz. "Arabic from A (Algebra) to Z (Zero)." *Math Horizons* (September 1999): 16–18.

A-105. Sabra, A.I. "The Appropriation and Subsequent Naturalization of Greek Science in Medieval Islam: A Preliminary Statement." *History of Science* 25 (1987): 223–243.

A-106. Wasserstein, David J. "Greek Science in Islam: Islamic Scholars as Successors to the Greeks." *Hermathena* 147 (1998): 57–72.

(B) Islam–West Linkages

A-107. Alonso, Manuel Alonso. "Influencia de Algazel en el Mundo Latino" ("The Influence of Algazel in the Latin World"). *Al-Andalus* 23 (1958): 371–380.

A-108. Archer, John C. "Our Debt to the Moslem Arab." *The Moslem World* 24, no.3 (July 1939): 248–254.

A-109. Baldwin, Marshall W. "Western Attitudes Toward Islam." *The Catholic Historical Review* 27, no.4 (January 1942): 403–411.

A-110. Beckingham, C.F. "Misconceptions of Islam: Medieval and Modern." *Journal of Royal Society of Arts* 126 (September 1976): 606–611.

A-111. Benz, Ernst. "The Islamic Culture as Mediator of the Greek Philosophy to Europe." *Islamic Culture* (Lahore, Pakistan) 35 (1961): 147–165.

A-112. Berggren, J.L. "Islamic Acquisition of the Foreign Sciences: A Cultural Perspective." *American Journal of Islamic Social Sciences* 9 (1992): 310–324.

A-113. Burns, Robert I. "Christian–Islamic Confrontation in the West: The Thirteenth Century Dream of Conversion." *American Historical Review* 76 (1971): 1386–1412; 1432–1434.

A-114. Butler, Pierce. "Fifteenth Century Editions of Arabic Authors in Latin Translation." Pages 63–71 in *Macdonald Presentation Volume: A Tribute to Duncan Black Macdonald.* Bridgeport, NY: Books for Libraries Press, 1933.

A-115. Darling, Linda T. "Rethinking Europe and the Islamic World in the Age of Exploration." *Journal of Early Modern History* 2, no.3 (1998): 2230–2246.

A-116. Dennett, Daniel C., Jr. "Pirenne and Muhammad." *Speculum: A Journal of Medieval Studies* 23, no.2 (April 1948): 165–190.

A-117. Druart, Therese-Anne. "Medieval Islamic Thought and the 'What Is X?' Question." *American Catholic Philosophical Quarterly* 73, no.1 (Winter 1999): 1–8.

A-118. Fakahani, Suzan J. "Islamic Influences on Emerson's Thought: The Fascination of a Nineteenth Century American Writer." *Journal of Muslim Minority Affairs* 18, no.2 (1998): 291–303.

A-119. Forget, J. "De l'influence de la philosophie arabe sur la philosophie scholastique." *Revue Neo-Scholastique* 4, no.3665 (October 1894): 385–410.

A-120. Gabrieli, Francisco. "Frederick II and Moslem Culture." *East and West* 9 (1958): 53–61.

A-121. Gaudiosi, Monica. "Comment: The Influence of the Islamic Law of *Waqf* on the Development of the Trust in England—The Case of Merton College." *University of Pennsylvania Law Review* 136 (April 1988): 1231–1261.

A-122. Ghazanfar, S.M. "Civilizational Dialogue: Medieval Social Thought, Latin-European Renaissance, and Islamic Influences." *Encounters: Journal of Intercultural Perspectives* 9, no.1 (2003): 21–36.

A-123. Ghazanfar, S.M. "Medieval Islamic Socio-Economic Thought: Links with Greek and Latin-European Scholarship." *Humanomics* (Special Volume: Comparative Political Economy) 13, nos.3–4 (1997): 33–60.

A-124. Gibb, H.A.R. "The Influence of Islamic Culture on Medieval Europe." *Bulletin of the John Rylands Library* 95 (1955): 82–98.

A-125. Goitein, S.D. "Between Hellenism and Renaissance: Islam, the Intermediate Civilization." *Islamic Studies* 2, no.2 (June 1963): 216–233.

A-126. Gomez, Reverend Eusebio. "Muslim Theology in Its Bearing on Scholasticism." *Clergy Review* 6 (1933): 99–109.

A-127. Gran, Peter. "The Middle East in the Historiography of Advanced Capitalism." *Review of Middle East Studies*, no.1 (1975): 135–154.

A-128. Hamilton, Bernard. "Knowing the Enemy: Western Understanding of Islam at the Time of the Crusades." *Journal of Royal Asiatic Studies* 7, no.3 (1997): 373–387.

A-129. Haskins, Charles H. "Arabic Science in Western Europe." *ISIS: Journal of the History of Science in Society* 7 (1925): 478–485.

A-130. Haskins, Charles H. "The Reception of Arabic Science in England." *English Historical Review* 30 (January 1915): 56–69.

A-131. al-Hibri, Azzizah Y. "Islamic and American Constitutional Law: Borrowing Possibilities or a History of Borrowing." *University of Pennsylvania Journal of Constitutional Law* (Symposium Issue: Contextuality and Universality—Constitutional Borrowing on the Global Stage) 1, no.3 (Spring 1999): 492–527.

A-132. Huff, Toby E. "Science and the Public Sphere: Comparative Institutional Development in Islam and the West." *Social Epistemology* 11, no.1 (1997): 25–37.

A-133. Hunt, R.W. "English Learning in the Late Twelfth Century." *Transactions of the Royal Historical Society* 19 (1936): 19–42.

A-134. Isani, Mukhtar Ali. "Cotton Mather and the Orient." *New England Quarterly* 43, no.1 (March 1970): 46–58.

A-135. Ito, Shuntaro. "Islamic Civilization as Seen from Japan: A Non-Western View." Pages 131–138 in *The Islamic World and Japan: In Pursuit of Mutual Understanding*, Proceedings of the 1980 International Symposium, the Japan Foundation. Tokyo, Japan, 1981.

A-136. Joubin, Rebecca. "Islam and Arabs through the Eyes of the *Encyclopedie*: The 'Other' as a Case of French Cultural Self-Criticism." *International Journal of Middle East Studies* 32 (2000): 197–217.

A-137. Khalidi, Tarif. "Islamic Views of the West in the Middle Ages." *Studies in Interreligious Dialogue* 5 (1995): 31–42.

A-138. Khan, M. Abdur Rehman. "A Survey of Muslim Contribution to Science and Culture, Part I." *Islamic Culture* 14 (January 1942): 1–20.

A-139. Khan, M. Abdur Rehman. "A Survey of Muslim Contribution to Science and Culture, Part II." *Islamic Culture* 14 (April 1942): 136–152.

A-140. Kidd, Thomas S. "'Is It Worse to Follow Mahomet Than the Devil?' Early American Uses of Islam." *Church History* 72, no.4 (December 2003): 766–790.

A-141. Lewis, Archibald R. "The Islamic World and the Latin West, 1350–1500." *Speculum: A Journal of Medieval Studies* 65, no.4 (October 1990): 833–844.

A-142. Makdisi, George. "Interaction between Islam and the West." *Revue des etudes Islamiques* 44 (1976): 287–309.

A-143. Makdisi, John A. "The Islamic Origins of the Common Law." *North Carolina Law Review* 77 (June 1999): 1635–1739.

A-144. Matar, Nabil. "Muslims in Seventeenth-Century England." *Journal of Islamic Studies* 8, no.1 (1997): 63–82.

A-145. Matar, Nabil. "The Traveler as Captive: Renaissance England and the Allure of Islam." *Literature Interpretation Theory* 7 (1996): 187–196.

A-146. Menocal, Maria Rosa. "Pride and Prejudice in Medieval Studies: European and Oriental." *Hispanic Review* 53 (1985): 61–78.

A-147. Meyerhof, Max. "On the Transmission of Greek and Indian Science to the Arabs." *Islamic Culture* 11, no.20 (January 1937): 17–29.

A-148. Millas-Vallicrosa, J.M. "Translations of Oriental Scientific Works (to the End of the Thirteenth Century)" (translated from Spanish by Daphne Woodword). *Journal of World History* 2, no.2 (1954): 395–428.

A-149. Moorhead, John. "The Earliest Christian Theological Response to Islam." *Religion* 11 (1981): 265–274.

A-150. Moosa, Matti I. "Al-Kindi's Role in the Transmission of Greek Knowledge to the Arabs." *Journal of the Pakistan Historical Society* 15 (January 1967): 1–18.

A-151. Myers, Eugene A. "Legacy of Arab Culture to the Western World." *The Muslim Digest* 19, no.5 (December 1968): 61–65.

A-152. Naqvi, Syed Ali Raza. "Prophet Muhammad's Image in Western Enlightened Scholarship." *Islamic Studies* 20, no.2 (Summer 1981): 136–151.

A-153. O'Brien, Peter. "Islamic Civilization's Role in the Waning of the European Middle Ages." *The Medieval History Journal* 2, no.2 (July–December 1999): 387–404.

A-154. O'Brien, Peter. "Platonism and Plagiarism at the End of the Middle Ages." Pages 304–318 in *Christianizing People and Converting Individuals*, edited by Guyda Armstrong and Ian N. Wood. Turnhot, Belgium: Brepols Publishers n.v., 2000.

A-155. Paret, Rudi. "Islam and Christianity." *Islamic Studies* 3, no.1 (March 1964): 86–95.

A-156. Pingree, David. "The Greek Influence on Early Islamic Mathematical Astronomy." *Journal of the American Oriental Society* 93, no.1 (January–March 1973): 32–43.

A-157. Ragep, F. Jamil. "Duhem, the Arabs, and the History of Cosmology." *Synthese* 83 (1990): 201–214.

A-158. Rashed, Roshdi. "Problems of the Transmission of Greek Scientific Thought into Arabic: Examples from Mathematics and Optics." *History of Science* 27 (1989): 199–209.

A-159. Runciman, Steven. "Islam and Christendom in the Middle Ages: The Need for Restatement." *Islamic Studies* 3, no.2 (June 1964): 193–198.

A-160. Russell, Josiah C. "Hereford and Arabic Science in England about 1175–1200." *ISIS: Journal of the History of Science in Society* 18, no.1 (July 1932): 14–25.

A-161. Sabra, A.I. "Situating Arabic Science: Locality versus Essence." *ISIS: Journal of the History of Science in Society* 87, no.4 (December 1996): 654–670.

A-162. Salman, D. "Algazel et les Latins" ("Algazel and the Latins"). *Archives d'Histoire Doctrinale et Literaire du Moyen Age* (1935–1936): 103–127.

A-163. Samarrai, Alauddin. "The Term 'Fief': A Possible Arabic Origin." *Studies in Medieval Culture* 4, no.1 (1973): 78–82.

A-164. Shanab, R.E.A. "Ghazali and Aquinas on Causation." *The Monist* 58 (1974): 140–150.

A-165. Siddiqi, Mazheruddin. "The Holy Prophet and the Orientalists." *Islamic Studies* 19, no.3 (Autumn 1980): 143–165.

A-166. Siddiqui, Razi-ud-Din. "The Contribution of Muslims to Scientific Thought." *Islamic Culture* (Hyderabad, India) 14 (January 1940): 34–44.

A-167. Sirry, Mun'im A. "Early Muslim–Christian Dialogue: A Closer Look at Major Themes of the Theological Encounter." *Islam and Christian–Muslim Relations* 16, no.4 (October 2005): 361–376.

A-168. Thompson, Diane P. "Paradigms Lost: Western Civilization and the Orient Unexpressed." *Northern Virginia Review*, no.10 (Fall 1995): 5–8.

A-169. Thompson, James W. "The Introduction of Arabic Science into Lorraine in the Tenth Century." *ISIS: Journal of the History of Science in Society* 12 (May 1929): 184–194.

A-170. Thomson, Rodney M. "England and the Twelfth Century Renaissance." *Past and Present* 101 (1983): 3–21.

A-171. Tschanz, David W. "The Arab Roots of European Medicine." *Aramco World* 48, no.3 (May–June 1997): 20–32.

A-172. Van Koningsveld, P.S. "Muslim Slaves and Captives in Western Europe during the Late Middle Ages." *Islam and Christian–Muslim Relations* 6, no.1 (1995): 5–23.

A-173. Walzer, Richard. "Arabic Transmission of Greek Thought to Medieval Europe." *Bulletin of the John Rylands Library* 29, no.1 (July 1945): 3–26.

A-174. Watt, W. Montgomery. "Muhammad in the Eyes of the West." *Boston University Journal* 22, no.3 (1974): 61–69.

A-175. Welborn, Mary C. "Lotharingia as a Center of Arabic and Scientific Influence in the Eleventh Century." *ISIS: Journal of the History of Science in Society* 16 (1931): 188–199.

A-176. Wolf, C. Umhau. "Luther and Mohammedanism." *The Moslem World* (Hartford, CT) 31, no.3 (July 1941): 161–177.

A-177. Young, T. Cuyler. "The Cultural Contributions of Islam to Christendom." *The Moslem World* (Hartford, CT) 35, no.2 (April 1945): 89–110.

(C) General

(i) Spain/Al-Andalus

A-178. Abercrombie, Thomas J. "When the Moors Ruled Spain." *National Geographic* 74, no.1 (July 1988): 86–119.

A-179. Aramco World Services. "The Art of Islamic Spain." *Aramco World* 43, no.5 (September–October 1992): 2–64.

A-180. Avila, Maria Luisa. "The Search for Knowledge: Andalusi Scholars and Their Travels to the Islamic East." *Medieval Prosopography* (Special Issue: Arab-Islamic Culture) 23 (2002): 125–139.

A-181. Beech, George T. "Troubadour Contacts with Muslim Spain and Knowledge of Arabic: New Evidence Concerning William IX of Aquitaine." *Romania: Revue Trimestrielle* 113 (1992–1995): 14–42.

A-182. Burshatin, Israel. "The Moor in the Text: Metaphor, Emblem, and Silence." *Critical Inquiry* 12, no.1 (Autumn 1985): 98–118.

A-183. Edwards, John. "Mission and Inquisition among *Conversos* and *Moriscos* in Spain, 1250–1550." *Studies in Church History* 21 (1984): 139–151.

A-184. Eigeland, Tor. "Escape from a Troubled World." *Aramco World* 41, no.5 (September–October 1990): 2–10.

A-185. Eigeland, Tor. "Islam in Al-Andalus." *Aramco World Magazine* 27, no.5 (September–October 1976): 1–32.

A-186. Eigeland, Tor. "Touring Al-Andalus." *Aramco World* 50, no.2 (March–April 1999): 22–32.

A-187. Fernandez, Maria Luisa. "Art of the Mudejars." *Aramco World* 44, no.1 (January–February 1993): 36–41.

A-188. Harvey, L.P. "The Moriscos and the *Hajj*." *Bulletin of the British Society for Middle Eastern Studies* 14, no.1 (1987): 11–24.

A-189. Hourani, George. "The Early Growth of the Secular Sciences in Andalusia." *Studia Islamic* 32 (1970): 143–156.

A-190. Irving, Thomas B. "The Process of Arab Thought in Spain." *Studies in Islam* 4, no.2 (April 1967): 65–96.

A-191. Jellicoe, Patricia Countess. "The Art of Islamic Spain." *Aramco World* 43, no.5 (September–October 1992): 24–31.

A-192. Latham, J.D. "Towns and Cities of Barbary: The Andalusian Influence." *Islamic Quarterly* 16 (1972): 189–204.

A-193. Lunde, Paul. "The Giralda." *Aramco World* 44, no.1 (January–February 1993): 32–35.

A-194. Lunde, Paul. "Ishbiliyah: Islamic Seville." *Aramco World* 44, no.1 (January–February 1993): 20–31.

A-195. Meadows, Ian. "Historical Markers." *Aramco World* 44, no.1 (January–February 1993): 10–11.

A-196. Noakes, Greg. "Exploring Flamenco's Arab Roots." *Saudi Aramco World* 45, no.6 (November–December 1994): 32–35.

A-197. Noakes, Greg. "The Other 1492." *Aramco World* 44, no.1 (January–February 1993): 2–9.

A-198. Salloum, Habeeb. "Arabian Memories in Portugal." *Saudi Aramco World* 52, no.2 (March–April 2001): 1–5.

A-199. Wolf, Kenneth B. "The Earliest Spanish Christian Views of Islam." *Church History* 55 (1986): 281–293.

A-200. Zuwiyya, Z. David. "Arab Culture and Morisco Heritage in an Aljamiado Legend: 'Al-hadit del bano de Zaryeb.'" *Romance Quarterly* 48, no.1 (Winter 2001): 32–47.

(ii) Crusades

A-201. Atiya, Aziz S. "The Crusades: Old Ideas and New Conceptions." *Journal of World History* 2 (1954): 470–475.

A-202. Mateo, Matilde. "The Making of the *Saracen Style*: The Crusades and Medieval Architecture in the British Imagination in the 18th and 19th Centuries." Pages 115–141 in *The Crusades: Other Experiences, Alternative Perspectives, Selected Proceedings from the 32nd Conference of the Center for Medieval and Early Renaissance Studies*, edited by Khalil E. Semaan. Binghamton, NY: State University of New York Press, 2003.

A-203. Moosa, Matti. "The Crusades: An Eastern Perspective, with Emphasis on Syriac Sources." *Muslim World* 93, no.2 (April 2003): 249–290.

A-204. Munro, Dana Carleton. "The Western Attitude Toward Islam During the Period of the Crusades." *Speculum: A Journal of Medieval Studies* 6 (1931): 329–343.

(iii) Miscellaneous

A-205. Alam, Manzoor. "Ibn Khaldun's Concept of the Origin, Growth and Decay of Cities." *Islamic Culture* (Lahore, Pakistan) 34 (1960): 90–106.

A-206. Bloom, Jonathan M. "Revolution by the Ream: A History of Paper." *Aramco World* 50, no.3 (May–June 1999): 26–39.

A-207. Bosch, Gular Kheirallah. "Ibn Khaldun on Evolution." *The Islamic Review* 38, no.5 (1950): 26–34.

A-208. Bulliet, Richard W. "Medieval Arabic *Tarsh*: A Forgotten Chapter in the History of Printing." *Journal of American Oriental Society* 107, no.3 (1987): 427–438.

A-209. Foster, Benjamin R. "Agoranomics and Muhtasib." *Journal of Economic and Social History of the Orient* 13 (April 1970): 128–144.

A-210. Gates, Warren E. "The Spread of Ibn Khaldun's Ideas on Climate and Culture." *Journal of History of Ideas* 28, no.3 (July–September 1967): 415–421.

A-211. Gibb, H.A.R. "The Islamic Background of Ibn Khaldun's Political Theory." *Bulletin of the School of Oriental Studies* 7 (1933–1935): 23–31.

A-212. Glick, Thomas F. "Muhtasib and Mustasaf: A Case Study of Institutional Diffusion." *Viator: Medieval and Renaissance Studies* 2 (1971): 59–81.

A-213. Hannoum, Abdelmajid. "Translation and the Colonial Imaginary: Ibn Khaldun Orientalist." *History and Theory* 42 (February 2003): 61–81.

A-214. Khalid, Detlev H. "The Problem of Defining Islam and Modern Accentuations." *Islamic Studies* 16, no.3 (Autumn 1977): 217–281.

A-215. Khan, M. Saber. "A Classified Bibliography of Recent Publications on al-Biruni." *Muslim World Book Review* 10, no.3 (Autumn 1990): 65–77.

A-216. Krek, Miroslav. "Arabic Block Printing as the Precursor of Printing in Europe: Preliminary Report." *Newsletter of the American Research Center in Egypt* (Princeton University, Princeton, NJ), no.129 (Spring 1985): 12–16.

A-217. Lunde, Paul. "The Missing Link." *Aramco World* 32, no.2 (March–April 1981): 26–27.

A-218. Muhammad, Mi'raj. "Ibn Khaldun and Vico: A Comparative Study." *Islamic Studies* 19, no.3 (1980): 195–211.

A-219. Newby, Gordon D. "Ibn Khaldun and Frederick Jackson Turner: Islam and the Frontier Experience." *Journal of Asian and African Studies* 18, nos.3–4 (1983): 274–285.

A-220. Pasha, Mustapha Kamal. "Ibn Khaldun and World Order." Pages 56–70 in *Innovation and Transformation in International Studies*, edited by Stephen Gill and James E. Mittleman. Cambridge and New York: Cambridge University Press, 1997.

A-221. Rosenthal, Erwin J. "Ibn Khaldun: A North African Muslim Thinker of the Fourteenth Century." *Bulletin of the John Rylands Library* 24 (1940): 307–320.

A-222. Schaefer, Karl R. "Eleven Medieval Arabic Block Prints in the Cambridge University Library." *Arabica* 48 (2001): 210–239.

A-223. Schaefer, Karl R. "The Scheide *Tarsh.*" *The Princeton University Library Chronicle* 56, no.3 (1995): 401–419.

A-224. Schmidt, Nathaniel. "The Manuscripts of Ibn Khaldun." *Journal of the American Oriental Society* 46 (1926): 171–176.

A-225. Stowasser, Barbara Freyer. "Religion and Political Development: Some Comparative Ideas of Ibn Khaldun and Machiavelli." *Occasional Paper Series*, Center for Contemporary Arab Studies, Washington, DC: Georgetown University Press, January 1983.

Author, Editor, Translator Index

Title Index

529

Islamic Law and Jurisprudence: Studies in Honor of Farhat Ziadeh, B-199
"The Islamic Legacy of Timbuktu," A-12
Islamic Occasionalism and Its Critique by Averroes and Aquinas, B-133
"The Islamic Origins of the Common Law," A-143
"An Islamic Perspective on the Wealth of Nations," A-17
Islamic Philosophy and the Classical Tradition: Essays Presented by His Friends and Pupils to Richard Walzer, B-156
Islamic Roots of Capitalism, Egypt, 1760–1840, B-123
The Islamic Roots of Democratic Pluralism, B-204
Islamic Science: An Illustrated Study, B-232
Islamic Science and Engineering, B-221
"Islamic Science and Learning," A-70
Islamic Spain, 1250–1500, B-339
Islamic Spain and Our Heritage: Al-Andalus, 711–1492 A.D., B-347
Islamic Taxation in the Classic Period, with Special Reference to Circumstances in Iraq, B-125
Islamic Technology: An Illustrated History, B-218
"Islamic Views of the West in the Middle Ages," A-137
The Islamic World and Japan: In Pursuit of Mutual Understanding, B-57
"The Islamic World and the Latin West, 1350–1500," A-141
The Islamic World and the West, A.D. 622–1492, B-295
"Islam in Al-Andalus," A-185
Islam in Britain, 1558–1685, B-296
Islam in European Thought, B-287
Islam in Spanish Literature: From the Middle Ages to the Present, B-352
Islam under the Crusaders: Colonial Survival in the Thirteenth Century Kingdom of Valencia, B-375

"*Jihad* and Cross-Cultural Encounter in Muslim Sicily," A-3

"Al-Kindi's Role in the Transmission of Greek Knowledge to the Arabs," A-150
"Knowing the Enemy: Western Understanding of Islam at the Time of the Crusades," A-128
Knowledge Triumphant: The Concept of Knowledge in Medieval Islam, B-169

"Labor Partnership in Early Islam," A-59
Languages of Power in Islamic Spain, B-323
Law and Education in Medieval Islam: Studies in Honor of Professor George Makdisi, B-165
"Legacy of Arab Culture to the Western World," A-151
The Legacy of Islam (Arnold and Guillaume), B-253
The Legacy of Islam (Schacht), B-311
The Legacy of Muslim Spain, B-346
The Life of Muhammad, B-98
The Life of Science: Essays in the History of Civilization, B-243
The Literature of Al-Andalus, B-358
"The Longest Hajj: The Journeys of Ibn Battuta," A-74

The Mutual Effects of the Islamic and Judeo-Christian Worlds: The East European Pattern, B-254
The Mystical Philosophy of Ibn Masarra and His Followers, B-128

Nomads and Crusaders, A.D. 1000–1368, B-381
The Norman Fate, 1100–1154, B-27
The Normans in European History, B-99

"On the Arab System of Nautical Orientation," A-83
"On the Transmission of Greek and Indian Science to the Arabs," A-147
Orientalism, B-308
Orientalism and History, B-314
The Oriental Obsession: Islamic Inspiration in British and American Architecture, 1500–1920, B-392
Origin and Spread of Oriental Words in European Languages, B-190
"The Origin of Economics and the Muslims: A Preliminary Survey," A-19
The Origins of Modern Science, 1300–1800, B-210
"The Origins of the European Scientific Tradition: St. Thomas and Roger Bacon," A-96
The Origins of Western Economic Dominance in the Middle East: Mercantilism and the Islamic Economy in Aleppo, 1600–1750, B-126
The Ornament of the World: How Muslims, Jews, and Christians Created a Culture of Tolerance in Medieval Spain, B-357
"The Other 1492," A-197
"Our Debt to the Moslem Arab," A-108
The Oxford History of Islam, B-32

Papers on Islamic History: Islam and the Trade of Asia, A Colloquium, B-90
Papers on Islamic History: Islamic Civilization, 950–1150, A Colloquium, B-89
"Paradigms Lost: Western Civilization and the Orient Unexpressed," A-168
The Patricians of Nishapur: A Study in Medieval Islamic Social History, B-14
Patterns of Everyday Life, B-206
Philosophy and Science in the Islamic World, B-150
"Philosophy and Scripture in the Theology of Averroes," A-63
Philosophy in the Middle Ages: The Christian, Islamic, and Jewish Traditions, B-142
The Philosophy of Alfarabi and Its Influence on Medieval Thought, B-281
Pierre Duhem: Essays in the History and Philosophy of Science, B-208
"Pirenne and Muhammad," A-116
The Pirenne Thesis: Analysis, Criticism, and Revision, B-42
"Platonism and Plagiarism at the End of the Middle Ages," A-154
"Political Economy as a Paradigm for the Study of Islamic History," A-2
"Post-Greek/Pre-Renaissance Economic Thought: Contributions of Arab-Islamic Scholastics during the 'Great Gap' Centuries," A-30
"Pre-Islamic Arabian Religion in the Qur'an," A-13
"Pride and Prejudice in Medieval Studies: European and Oriental," A-146
"The Problem of Defining Islam and Modern Accentuations," A-214
"Problems of the Transmission of Greek Scientific Thought into Arabic: Examples from Mathematics and Optics," A-158

About the Author

S.M. (Ghazi) Ghazanfar is professor of economics (1968–2002; emeritus, 2002), former chairman of the Department of Economics (1979–1981; 1993–2001), former director of International Studies Program (1989–1993), and served as adjunct professor (2002–2003; 2005–2006), University of Idaho, Moscow. He has published papers, books, and monographs in various areas of economics and contributed chapters in books and entries in encyclopedic works. Recent publications pertain to the origins of economic thought in medieval Islamic scholarship, including numerous journal articles; the book *Economic Thought of Al-Ghazali (450–505AH / 1058–1111AD)*, King Abdulaziz University Press, Jeddah, Saudi Arabia (1998); and the edited volume *Medieval Islamic Economic Thought: Filling the "Great Gap" in European Economics*, RoutledgeCurzon, London (2003). He also contributed to the 2001 PBS television documentary *Islam: Empire of Faith*.

Dr. Ghazanfar held visiting assignments at the University of the Punjab, Lahore, Pakistan, and the University of Maryland (College Park), both during 1974–1975, and King Abdulaziz University, Jeddah, Saudi Arabia (1983–1986). He was a consultant on budgetary issues for the Idaho Legislature (1974–1996) and is an occasional referee for professional journals. Listed in several Who's Who's, he has received honors and awards for teaching and other scholarly contributions, as well as recognitions for voluntary civic and human-rights activities.